15 Reasons for Falling in Love with Brooklyn

1. Forget Manhattan skyscrapers. In Brooklyn you can see sky.
2. You have keys to your neighbor's apartment.
3. The dry cleaner doesn't speak English, but his daughter goes to an Ivy League college.
4. On a spring morning, birds' songs wake you up.
5. There's every kind of skin color on a Brooklyn subway and nobody seems to notice.
6. The views of the water, Manhattan, the bridges never, ever get old.
7. You can see free movies and concerts in more than one park.
8. The beach is just a subway ride away.
9. You can get seltzer delivered (the kind in squirt bottles), and a knife sharpener comes by clanging his bell.
10. At a Cyclones game, you get baseball, sea breezes, and shtick.
11. You can cross-country ski in Prospect Park.
12. There's not one Brooklyn newspaper. There are more than a dozen.
13. First Saturdays at the Brooklyn Museum, the BARC costume parade for dogs, the West Indian American Labor Day Parade, and the Mermaid Parade—all free.
14. You might have a little back garden. With a frog.
15. And everything—food, clothes, rent—is cheaper than in Manhattan.

THIRD EDITION

Brooklyn!

THE ULTIMATE GUIDE TO NEW YORK'S
MOST HAPPENING BOROUGH

Ellen Freudenheim
with Anna Wiener

St. Martin's Griffin
New York

To the communities, large and small,
that make Brooklyn the surprising place it is.

www.stmartins.com

BOOK DESIGN BY AMANDA DEWEY

ISBN 0-312-32331-X
EAN 978-0312-32331-8

Third Edition: April 2004

2 4 6 8 10 9 7 5 3 1

CONTENTS

ACKNOWLEDGMENTS

It's hard to know where to start saying "thank you."

The following Brooklyn mavens were incredibly helpful in sharing information and contacts. Many thanks to all for your time and, most of all, for your contributions to the borough and its civic, educational, and cultural institutions. The first thanks go to Ken Adams of the Brooklyn Chamber of Commerce, a one-man whirlwind of activity. Information provided by Ella Weiss of the Brooklyn Arts Council about the range of cultural activities going on was eye-popping and invaluable. Thanks also for informative interviews and conversations to many others working to advance Brooklyn on various fronts, namely: Peggy Aguayo, Karen Auster, the staff at BRIC, M.B., Michael Crane, Richard Drucker, Joe Fodor, Sandi Franklin, Jennifer Gerend, Joy Glidden, Monique Greenwood, Jessie Kelly, Stuart Leffler, Jeanne Lufty, Erik Paulsen, Ellen Salpeter, Katie Schmid, David Sharps, Pat Singer, Judy Stanton, Phaedra Thomas, Daniel Wiener, David Wiener, Horace Williams, David Yasskey, and Dick Zigun. (We apologize for not giving their titles; space doesn't permit.) Andy Ross, the communications director for the Brooklyn Borough President's Office, was always extremely helpful. A hug of appreciation, too, goes to my friends Jean Halloran, Jeff and Sharon Golden, Linda Lamm, Pam and Billy Rohl, John Adam, and Michele Monteleone for their input.

Hats off to Borough President Marty Markowitz for his energetic commitment to Brooklyn.

Freelance writers Seth "the Barbinger" Kennedy, Nina Rubin, and Minju Pak provided fascinating material about Brooklyn's bar scene, music shops, and Asian shops and restaurants, respectively. They unearthed things I wouldn't have found (and drank me under the table, in the case of one Bostonian). Hugs to guitarist Rubens de La Corte for a fun musical tour through Sunset Park and to Chris Varmus and Jamal Greene for patiently answering my questions regarding hip-hop. I am very grateful to Mark Naison, Ph.D., whom I reached via George Haywood, and Dr. Dan Harris, for lending their expertise on the African Diaspora and steel drums, respectively. I am grateful for the generous time given me by total strangers: John Broderick, Michael Crane, Breuk Iversen, Jan Larsen, and Chris Ricciardi. Thanks, too, to Marty Stiglich, who knows more about food in Bay Ridge than possibly God herself does.

Thank you to the countless small businesspeople and entrepreneurs throughout the borough with whom we spoke, and the PR or communications directors of over four dozen cultural organizations, galleries, and nonprofits who reviewed their write-ups.

As this is the third edition of *Brooklyn!*, there are people from previous editions to whom I am still indebted: Greg Cohn, Hal Cohn, Andy Gersick, Joe Hagen, Howard Pitsch, Joan and James Rizzo, and Anne Savarese. (After she read the book, she moved to Brooklyn.)

This edition's editor, Esti Iturralde, another bright light, has also been a pleasure to work with; thank you, Esti, for all those weekend hours spent editing in Brookyn! To the staff at SMP, and Tom Mercer, too, thanks for your expertise. David Lindroth's maps are wonderful new additions to the book, and the design by Amanda Dewey has captured the spirit of the book. Elizabeth Dotson-Westphalen has created our new Web site.

Anna and I gleaned a great deal of information from references such as publications by the Brooklyn Historical Society. Noted throughout are references to a new guidebook to public schools in New York City by Clara Hemphill, which are invaluable.

"The Brooklyn book," as we call it, has almost become a member of our family, even a part of our little community on the block where we live. We've all lived with "the Brooklyn book" on and off since 1991. David, six when the first edition of the book was published and now away at his first year of college, gleefully missed the show on this third edition of *Brooklyn!*. Daniel, my husband and the original coauthor, has been, as always, a tower of support, a steady source of laughter and good banter, the best red-pencil editor of all, and, hyperbole notwithstanding, the most wonderful partner.

Acknowledgments are due to my young coauthor, our daughter Anna, who was three (and being schlepped all over Brooklyn in a stroller) when the first book was written; eleven (participating as a junior researcher, with a friend) when the second *Brooklyn* was underway; and fifteen when I signed the contract for this edition. She stepped up when I announced one night at dinner that, having written this book twice already, I was getting jaded and was looking for help and "new eyes" from someone younger. We drew up an agreement outlining her job: neighborhood research (bars and expensive restaurants omitted), a good portion of the writing and fact checking—in other words, the nuts and bolts of a guidebook. She delivered the goods on time and well done, despite a grueling school schedule. She saw, understood, and appreciated things I'd have never even noticed. Watching Anna knock off entry after entry, with a natural writer's aplomb, has been one of the pleasures of this edition. In places, she's captured what makes a tea lounge or youth's clothing store "tick," with the eyes of a new generation. More important, if you average our ages, you get about thirty-three—the average age of the person moving to Brooklyn for the first time! Thank you, Anna, for all your legwork and creativity.

Last but not least, it has to be said that all of New York was changed on September 11, 2001. Although things are great in Brooklyn, and so much that's wonderful is going on, the long shadow cast by that day remains with all of us. A moment's silence, in memory.

Thank you, all.

Ellen Freudenheim, July 2003
Brooklyn, New York

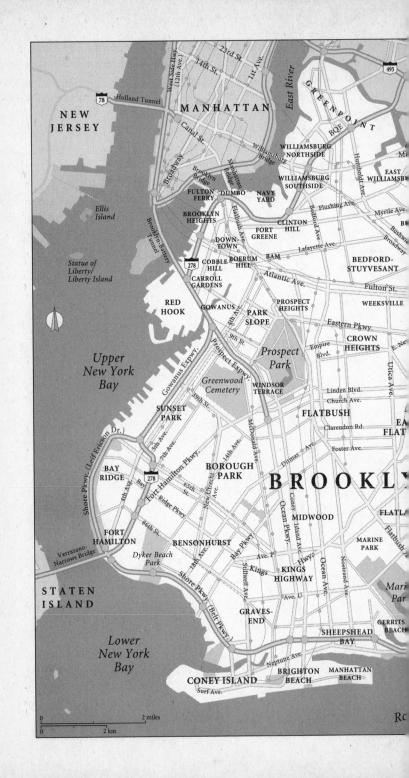

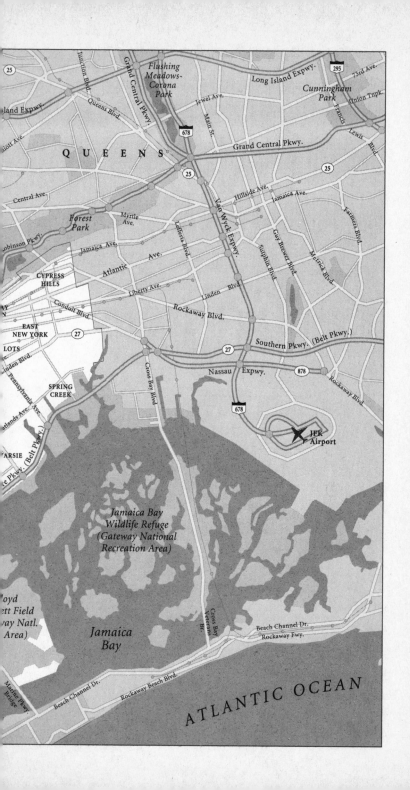

INTRODUCTION

Brooklyn is a *people's* place. According to the 2000 census, New York has about 8 million residents. About one-third of us live in Brooklyn. Long the most populous of the city's five boroughs, Brooklyn would be the fourth largest city in the nation, if we stood alone as a city.

But it doesn't feel overwhelming. Brooklyn divides naturally into dozens of distinct, walkable neighborhoods, each with its own history and style, sometimes with a distinct ethnic flavor. Many of Manhattan's wonderful quirky old neighborhoods have been gentrified out of existence. But they're going strong here, and, as a result, Brooklyn's bursting with diversity and personality. The neighborhoods make Brooklyn a spectacular place to grow up, to raise a family, to live a life. When you come *from* Brooklyn, and a specific neighborhood in Brooklyn, you are coming from *somewhere*.

Which maybe explains why, in the past few years, people are moving *to* Brooklyn in droves. Singles, young couples, new families, screenwriters, businesspeople, dreamers, UN employees, graduate students, artists of all stripes, restaurateurs, professionals. A decade ago, some Manhattanites wouldn't be caught dead here. Today, these same people are spending big bucks to buy a floor of a brownstone in Carroll Gardens or Prospect Heights. The simple arithmetic of real estate has been a driving force; you can get more space and a better location here than in Manhattan. Brooklyn's the place to be.

Brooklyn's incredibly accessible. If you're planning a trip to Brooklyn, or recently arrived, consider this: Within a mere hour, you can drive through lush Prospect Park, through elegant Park Slope, to bustling Sunset Park—home to a large immigrant Latino population (with a great Mexican cowboy boot store) and also to a Chinese community that's significantly more populous than London's famous Chinatown. With a half hour still left, you can gawk at the fabulous, colonial-style homes on a bluff overlooking the Verrazano Bridge in Bay

Ridge. Or nip into Italian Bensonhurst for some still-warm, soft, squishy, *fresh* mozzarella. Or head straight to Coney Island or Russian Brighton Beach. Why bother traveling, when you can stay at home and see the world?

Brooklyn's art scene is hot, hot, hot. Ask anyone involved in the arts—music, photography, visual and performance art, dance, writing of all sorts—where the action is in New York today, and they'll tell you without hesitation: *Brooklyn.* This is something quite new. It's because there's a critical mass of artists, musicians, writers, and audiences here now, attracting more like-minded people. Rents are affordable in Williamsburg, Greenpoint, DUMBO, Red Hook, and Fort Greene, and there are even subsidized office rents available for some in the BAM cultural district. Professionals in arts-administration organizations report with mild amazement that Manhattan-based creative groups are increasingly *choosing* to relocate to Brooklyn. Brooklyn is replete with live music—in restaurants, parks, concert halls, subway stations, dance clubs, bars.

What's in the air that makes Brooklyn breed creativity? The borough has a long history as a pass-through for immigrants who, today, come from countries as diverse as Poland and Senegal, Mexico and China, and yesteryear came from Italy, Ireland, Sweden, Germany, and elsewhere. It's a place where people from different worlds, with different religions, languages, beliefs, and skin colors, are forced, through proximity, to get along. There's room to grow, in Brooklyn.

You might be surprised at what you'll find in certain neighborhoods. You're likely to have a meal at little eateries seating only several dozen people, opened by chefs who've worked in Manhattan's fanciest restaurants and who decided to work closer to home. If you know where to look, in Brooklyn you can find fine craftsmen who build handmade furniture, makers of steel drums and African skin drums, a world-class violinmaker, and a high-end electric guitar–maker who supplies every rock-and-roll artist you've ever grooved to. You might also end up in a long, satisfying chew about the state of the world with your local greengrocer, who has no more than a high school diploma but a degree from the school of street smarts.

Diversity is Brooklyn's middle name. You don't have to be a rocket scientist to notice the difference between the Hasidim in Williamsburg or Borough Park, the religious Muslims on Coney Island Avenue, and the kids in hip-hop clothing.

Part of what makes the place so endearing is its small genius for improvisation. Green-Wood Cemetery, the burial place of many famous and colorful nineteenth- and early-twentieth-century New Yorkers, hosts an occasional series of plays based on the lives of their interred, through the Brooklyn Lyceum theater group. The "kids" moving into Williamsburg have turned crummy old industrial buildings into playful spaces where multimedia events are being held. Coney Island is a breeding ground for the weird, the outrageous, the creative, and the offbeat. Artists and individualists see beauty and potential in a fetid Gowanus Canal and figure out a way to clean it up, against serious odds. Not one, but two people have single-handedly made cultural institutions out of old barges and boats; one is BargeMusic, which hosts classical chamber music; the other is the Hudson Waterfront Museum and Showboat Barge. A high-powered magazine executive sees an old mansion in Bedford-Stuyvesant and, instead of recoiling from its dilapidation, envisions a luxury bed-and-breakfast. The list goes on and on.

If you're coming from out of town, think about staying in one of Brooklyn's bed-and-breakfasts. The fact that there are almost two dozen B&Bs in Brooklyn is little known, and, after twenty years of living here, we were astonished to uncover it. Staying in a neighborhood gives you the best chance to understand the wry combination of grit and glory that gives Brooklyn its character. Brooklyn is not a Disney set with neatly swept corners. You can't really predict—as you can in certain suburbs, a chain hotel, or corporate malls—what you are likely to see when you turn the next corner. Brooklyn is not a "designed environment." It's dynamic.

ABOUT THIS BOOK

This is the third edition of this guidebook. The first edition was a husband-wife team effort. Lost ex-Manhattanites, we drove around the borough and tried the pizza and cannoli, enjoyed amusement park rides, shopped for dishes, walked the streets of different neighborhoods, and researched and wrote after the kids went to sleep. When it was published in 1991, it made a splash as the first commercially published guidebook to Brooklyn in fifty years. The larger 1999 edition documented an upswing in the borough's restaurants, shops, and mood. Keeping things in the family, this 2004 edition is a mother-daughter collaboration, between an older-but-wiser mom and that three-year-old, now fifteen. Documenting the growth and changes in Brooklyn has been a pleasure and an honor.

ICON KEY

Free!	Free
☺	Child Friendly and Kidstuff
♨	Dog Friendly
●	Teen Pick
♪	Live Music
★	Artisanal/Made in Brooklyn
🎓	Educational Institution
☞	TIP
🎬	Movies

Brief User's Guide to Brooklyn

Eleven Quick Itineraries and Best Bets

Anonymity is one great reward of living in a big city: you can be anyone you want to be. Take your pick for touring Brooklyn:

THE SEE-IT-IN-ONE-DAY TRAVELER

Walk over the **Brooklyn Bridge** (but don't buy it!). Stoke up on pancakes at **Teresa's** in Brooklyn Heights and ogle the view on the **Promenade**. Take a ten-minute subway ride to the **Brooklyn Museum**. Visit either the **Botanic Garden** or **Prospect Park Zoo** or the **Brooklyn Children's Museum**. Hop the above-ground Q train to Coney Island, and watch the neighborhoods roll by. Check out the **Cyclone, the beach**, and the **New York Aquarium**. If you can get tickets, go to a **Cyclones** baseball game at KeySpan Park. Or stroll the **Boardwalk** to **Brighton Beach**, pretend you are Russian, stop by **M & I** for coffee—and a *pierogi*.

THE "GOING NATIVE IN BROOKLYN" TOURIST

Stay at a B&B. Get a haircut at the Sinatra-era **Park Slope Barbershop**. Ice skate at **Wollman Rink** or jog in **Prospect Park**. Argue loudly about who makes better pizza: **Grimaldi's** or **Totonno's**. Go shopping but don't pay full price: get ladies' lingerie at **UnderWorld Plaza**, kids' clothes at **Rachel's**, vintage at **Hooti's**. Bargain. Have a sunset picnic with your kids or lover at **Coffey Pier**. Or drive down to **Brennan & Carr** for some good, cheap roast beef. Relax to raucous humor at **Pips Comedy Club**, followed by fried clams at **Randazzo's**, where you'll schmooze with the other customers.

THE DOTING GRANDPARENT

Take your little angels to the **Brooklyn Children's Museum**, and then for pizza at **Two Boots**. Get them a haircut with toys for a bribe at **Lulu's Cuts and Toys**. Go to a performance at **Puppetworks**. Don't forget to top it off with one of **Luigi's Ices**.

Head down to the **New York Aquarium** for a full day of fun. Or have they ever walked across the **Brooklyn Bridge**?

THE DIVERSITY SEEKER (CAR REQUIRED)

Have mind-bending experience of ethnic variety. See how many neighborhoods you can touch base in: **Borough Park** (Hasidic), **Bensonhurst** (Italian), **Bedford-Stuyvesant** (African-American), **Fort Greene** (African-American), **Coney Island Avenue/East Flatbush** (Caribbean/West Indian), **Sunset Park** (Latino and Chinese), and **Smith Street in Carroll Gardens** (Yuppie; faux French). Stop everywhere to eat. It is OK to photograph the architecture but not necessarily the natives.

THE CULTURE VULTURE (WEEKENDS ONLY)

Sleep late; nothing opens before noon. Take the L train to Williamsburg, see some galleries (plan ahead). Hang with locals at **L Café** or **Fabiannes**. Browse used art books at **Spoonbill**. Spend freely at vintage boutiques. Cab to **DUMBO**, visit **d.a.c.** or **Smack Mellon** galleries, go off your diet at **Jacques Torres Chocolates**, and see edgy performance at **St. Ann's Warehouse** or **Brooklyn Academy of Music**. Or start at **Brooklyn Museum of Art** and go in reverse direction.

THE OUTDOORSY TOURIST

Fly a kite in **Prospect Park** or on **Shore Parkway**. Have a day at the ocean side: Visit the **New York Aquarium**, **Coney Island**, and **Manhattan Beach**. Advance-book a paddling tour of the **Gowanus Canal**. Bike down the **Ocean Parkway** bike path. Hit golf balls at **Gateway Recreation Center**, or play a round at **Dyker Park Golf Course**.

THE WALK-THE-NEIGHBORHOODS TOURIST

Walk through prosperous landmark districts in **Park Slope** and **Brooklyn Heights**. Stroll **Smith Street** with its slew of boutiques and eateries. Take a guided tour of historic **Green-Wood Cemetery** and **Clinton Hill**. Stroll the **Promenade**, eat at **Henry's End**, see **Plymouth Church**, a stop on the Underground Railroad, and walk down to see the Manhattan skyline from the tiny **Empire Fulton Ferry State Park** in DUMBO.

THE ARCHITECTURE BUFF

Feast your eyes in **Brooklyn Heights**, **Park Slope**, **Stuyvesant Heights**, and **Ditmas Park**. Take a house tour anywhere you can (see our listings). Obtain Brooklyn Historical Society self-guided-walking-tour info. Tour the historic free-black community of **Weeksville**.

THE REALLY HUNGRY TOURIST

In **Greenpoint**, get a kielbasa or babka to take home. Along **Atlantic Avenue**, go to **Sahadi's** for takeout taboulleh. Check out **Smith Street** and **DeKalb Avenue** for bistros, and **East Flatbush** for cheap, authentic Caribbean food. Choose between all-you-can-eat Sunday brunches at **Akwaaba Café** and **Lundy's**. For big Italian portions, go to **La Villa**; for Russian, anywhere in **Brighton Beach**. To play it safe and expensive, go to **Peter Luger** (reserve three weeks in advance), **Blue Ribbon**, or **River Café**.

THE NATURE LOVER

Go kayaking at the **Sebago Kayak Club** and horseback riding at **Jamaica Bay Riding Academy**. Enjoy the **Brooklyn Botanic Garden**, especially at tulip, lilac, or cherry blossom time, and **Prospect Park**. Check out the **Salt Marsh Center** in **Marine Park**.

THE "I LOVE A SPECTACLE" TOURIST

Put the following on your calendar: International African Arts Festival, Mermaid Parade, West Indian American Day Parade, BARC Dog Parade, Park Slope Halloween Parade, First Saturday at Brooklyn Museum, Christmas lights in Dyker Heights.

Getting There and Basics

Due to changes announced as this book went to press, subway service shown on the maps may be incorrect. Please consult on official map or the MTA Web site (*www.mta.info*) for updated information.

GOING *TO* BROOKLYN

One good reason to write a guidebook to the place you live in is to avoid getting lost so often. It hasn't really worked in the case of this author, who is directionally challenged. However, we have it on good authority that you can't go wrong if you actually look at a map.

Roughly:

FROM MANHATTAN You can get to a lot of places in Brooklyn by subway. Pick your neighborhood and then see our "How to Get There" in that chapter. If you hope to visit more than one neighborhood in a day, plot out your subway route. Or take a subway to the first stop and use a few car services, also listed, to hop from place to place within Brooklyn. Nothing is more than about a twenty-minute ride away. (If you come by subway, tuck your expensive camera in a grubby backpack.)

BAM patrons can take the BAMbus.

There are three bridges. The Manhattan and Brooklyn Bridges dump you more or less in the same place on the Brooklyn side, so it doesn't matter much if you take the wrong one. The Williamsburg Bridge dumps you (surprise!) in Williamsburg, near Peter Luger. Or you can take the Queensboro Bridge and get on the Brooklyn-Queens Expressway (BQE) to Brooklyn, which only makes sense if it is not rush hour.

FROM WESTCHESTER, THE BRONX, QUEENS, OR CONNECTICUT Triborough Bridge to BQE/Manhattan Bridge exit to Tillary Street.

FROM STATEN ISLAND AND SOUTHERN OR CENTRAL NEW JERSEY Verrazano-Narrows Bridge. Look at the map before you get off the bridge, because you have no more than two seconds to decide which way to go, depending on whether you want to go in the direction of Coney Island or Brooklyn Heights.

FROM NORTHERN OR NORTH-CENTRAL NEW JERSEY George Washington Bridge or Holland or Lincoln Tunnel to Manhattan; follow Manhattan directions, do not stop for bagels as there is better food in Brooklyn.

FROM LONG ISLAND Grand Central Parkway to Jackie Robinson Parkway; exit at Bushwick Avenue; left at third traffic light to Eastern Parkway; approximately three miles to Washington Avenue. You know for sure you are in Brooklyn when you see the Brooklyn Museum on the left.

FROM THE AIRPORTS TO DOWNTOWN BROOKLYN

Kennedy: Take the Belt Parkway west to BQE (I-278) east; exit Tillary Street.

LaGuardia: Take the Grand Central Parkway west to BQE (I-278); exit Tillary Street.

Newark: Take the New Jersey Turnpike to Holland Tunnel (Exit 14C). Exit onto Canal Street East to Manhattan Bridge. Exit onto Flatbush Avenue.

OTHER BASICS

Public Schools

We included only those schools considered among the best in neighborhoods we cover. For this information we are indebted to Clara Hemphill, whose school reference books are cited throughout the text.

Phone Numbers and Web Sites

All of the phone numbers listed in this book are in the 718 area code unless otherwise noted. You have to dial 1-718 before any local phone number, even when calling within Brooklyn.

We've listed as many URLs as we could find—several hundred.

Where to Stay
Bed-and-Breakfasts Galore

HOTELS

AVENUE PLAZA HOTEL.   *Borough Park.*

4624 13th Ave. at 47th St., 552-3200, www.theavenueplaza.com.

About $170 per night. New, full-service 52-room hotel with luxury accommodations, geared to Orthodox Jewish clientele. Rooms are spacious, clean, with minifridges and extra sinks. Full breakfast buffet, restaurant on premises.

COMFORT INN GREGORY.   *Bay Ridge.*

8315 4th Ave. off 83rd St., 238-3737, 800-447-3467, www.choicehotels.com.

About $160 double occupancy. Standard, deluxe, and Jacuzzi suites available. Near Bay Ridge shops, Verrazano Bridge, BQE.

COMFORT INN.   *Sheepshead Bay.*

Emmons Ave. corner of Coyle St., 800-447-3467.

Under construction as we go to press.

NEW YORK MARRIOTT AT THE BROOKLYN BRIDGE.   *Downtown Brooklyn.*

333 Adams St., 246-7000, 800-228-9900, www.marriott.com.

About $180–240 per night. Brooklyn's only full-service upscale hotel features hundreds of guest rooms, huge meeting and ballroom spaces, a health club. Located near Brooklyn Bridge, Brooklyn Heights.

PARK HOUSE HOTEL.   *Borough Park.*

1206 48th St. at 12th Ave., 871-8100.

About $90 per night. Caters to the kosher crowd.

HABITAT NEW YORK.

212-255-8018, www.nyhabitat.com/index.html.

This is a reservation service, not a hotel. Rates vary from $81 per night or $400 per week to $2,000 for a four-bedroom duplex. Usually a minimum stay of three days is required. Considered a good short-term sublet service. Check the Web site for photos, dates, and prices. No maid service or meals are provided.

 ## What's **NEW?**

Brooklyn's Bursting with Bed & Breakfasts

With over twenty bed-and-breakfasts in Brooklyn (listed below), the large upscale **New York Marriott at the Brooklyn Bridge**, a coming-soon **Comfort Inn**, there's no limit to the range of Brooklyn accommodations.

Staying in a B&B is a fun way to see New York and can give you ground-level insights into the sounds, sights, and feel of Brooklyn's neighborhoods. If you have four or five days to devote to Brooklyn, stay for two nights in two different B&Bs. Go native! See how the locals live!

☛ **TIP:** Important things to know about B&Bs

RESERVATIONS AND DEPOSITS Many B&Bs require a two-day minimum stay. Reservations and sometimes deposits are required. Please *don't* drop by without an appointment. Book early.

RATES Rates vary but are generally lower than better hotels in Manhattan—in most cases, in the $75–150 range per night, depending on the room, season, and number of guests.

TAKE THE B&B ADDRESS OR TELEPHONE NUMBER WITH YOU You won't find big signs or awnings on these establishments. In fact, most have no signage, because they are located on residential, not commercial streets.

INQUIRE IF YOU HAVE SPECIAL CONCERNS about children, pets, special food needs, or allergies.

ASK, ASK, ASK If you can't get into any of the B&Bs listed below, ask for a referral.

SERVICES VARY *Not all serve breakfast.* Most *but not all* take credit cards. Some may offer private baths, Internet access, private telephones, use of laundry, refrigerators, common space. Most rent only two or three rooms; others rent apartments on a short-term basis.

BED-AND-BREAKFASTS

AKWAABA MANSION.   *Bedford-Stuyvesant.*

347 MacDonough St., TEL. 455-5958, FAX 774-1744, www.akwaaba.com.

From $125 per night. An elegant B&B in an eighteen-room 1860s Italianate villa. Tastefully appointed African-themed rooms include Ashante Suite. This B&B has seen many marriage proposals, honeymoons, and celebrations. A good home-cooked breakfast, pampering afternoon tea, terrycloth robes, Jacuzzis. Old-fashioned backyard and a full porch. *Akwaaba* means "welcome" in a language spoken in Ghana. Hosts on premises.

ANGELIQUE BED & BREAKFAST.   *Carroll Gardens.*

405 Union St., TEL. 852-8406, FAX 923-0060, www.bedandbreakfast.com, E-MAIL sspoerri@citlink.net.

From $100–150 per night. Comfortably shabby chic with 1890 brownstone touches, such as clawfoot tubs. Close to **Smith St.** action. Popular with English-speaking visitors. Six guest rooms; one room accommodates a family of four. Self-served breakfast in dining room or garden. Host on premises.

AWESOME BED & BREAKFAST.   *Downtown Brooklyn, near Brooklyn Hts.*

136 Lawrence St., TEL. 888-LODGING (563-4464) U.S. only, 858-4859, CELL 917-783-1921 or 858-4859, FAX 858-4859, www.awesome-bed-and-breakfast.com.

Affordable rates. Urban and funky, close to the Brooklyn Bridge, Smith Street, Brooklyn Heights. Rooms are spare, with imaginative decor. Seven rooms share three modest bathrooms. Light continental breakfast is served to the room, if desired. Consider bringing earplugs. Online bookings available. Discounts for AARP and AAA members, and corporations. Host on premises.

BAISLEY HOUSE.   *Carroll Gardens.*

294 Hoyt St., TEL./FAX 935-1959, E-MAIL baisleyhousenyc@aol.com.

From $95 to $150. Authentic 1850s home featuring exquisite Victorian décor with 150 pieces of period furniture, rugs, paintings, and precious knickknacks. Three guest rooms share one bathroom. Breakfast served in elegant sitting and formal dining rooms. Two-minute walk to **Smith St.** Host Harry Paul on premises.

BED & BREAKFAST MARISSA'S.   *Prospect Heights.*

288 Park Pl., TEL./FAX 399-9535, www.brooklynbedandbreakfast.net, E-MAIL jupti@hotmail.com.

Affordable rates. Old-world décor, conservative in a homey style. Breakfast delivered on a tray in your room, if you wish; no access to parlor. Centrally located for Brooklyn Museum, Botanic Garden, Park Slope, and BAM. Two individual rooms with shared bath, one with a full kitchen. A garden apartment for longer-term stays is also available. Hosts Billy and Marissa Tashman on premises.

BED AND BREAKFAST ON THE PARK.   *Park Slope.*

113 Prospect Park West bet. 6th and 7th Sts., TEL. 499-6115, FAX 499-1385, www.bbnyc.com, E-MAIL liana@bbnyc.com.

From $125 per couple per night for a shared bath to $300 for the Grand Victorian bedroom suite. Sumptuous, ornate, and extraordinary, lavishly feminine Victoriana in 1890s landmark brownstone across from Prospect Park. Full breakfasts served in Victorian dining nook. Host on premises.

BROWNSTONE BROOKLYN BED & BREAKFAST.   *Prospect Heights.*

290 Park Pl. bet. Vanderbilt and Underhill Aves., TEL. 857-6066, FAX 857-4743, E-MAIL dawhit36@aol.com.

From $100 for a single with a full breakfast. A lovingly cared-for nineteenth-century brownstone featuring original stained-glass windows, large dining room with a fireplace, and a piano. Close to **Heart of Brooklyn, Park Slope, BAM.** Rents two rooms with shared bath. Full cooked breakfast on parlor floor. Host on premises.

DEKOVEN SUITES.   *Midwood (Brooklyn College area).*

30 DeKoven Ct., TEL. 421-1052, FAX 434-2478, www.virtualcities.com/ons/ny/n/nynb101.htm, E-MAIL suzieboo@aol.com.

From $125 for family of four. A lived-in, comfortable Victorian home well-suited to children. One spacious downstairs area with Ping-Pong table, access to back garden, private entrance. Breakfast available upstairs in family kitchen, or on the porch. Located one block from Q train, on a leafy residential street. Hosts Susan Lehrer and Chalo Smukler on premises.

DIANA'S B&B.   *Brooklyn Heights.*

131 Hicks St. near Clark St., 624-0386, E-MAIL prizeman@earthlink.net.

From $125 a night. 1850s Gothic building, vintage Brooklyn Heights. One large, very pleasant room with private entrance, foyer, and alcove half-kitchen. Two blocks from the 4 and 5 train, half a block from 2 and 3; close to **Promenade, Brooklyn Bridge, DUMBO,** and **Montague St.** Breakfast items left in the fridge; maid service is included. TV available but no phone. Children welcome. Host upstairs.

EVE'S BED & BREAKFAST.   *Midwood.*

751 Westminster Rd., TEL. 636-1492 or 347-256-4377, FAX 435-8510, E-MAIL evesplace_2001@yahoo.com.

Affordable. Rents several two-bedroom apartments with modern baths, fireplaces, living rooms, kitchens, and garden. Self-catered. Host sometimes on premises.

FOY HOUSE.   *Park Slope.*
819 Carroll St. bet. 8th Ave. and Prospect Park West, 636-1492.

From $125 up. Ample 1894 landmark Park Slope home, one block from Prospect Park. Living- and dining-room areas appointed with cozy antiques. Lovely rooms with original architectural detail, such as porcelain sinks. Self-served breakfast. Popular with grandparents of young Brooklynites. Three-room garden apartment sometimes available for longer stays.

GARDEN GREEN BED & BREAKFAST.   *Fort Greene/Clinton Hill.*
641 Carlton Ave. bet. Park and Prospect Places, TEL. 783-5717, FAX 638-7854,
www.virtualcities.com/ons/ny/n/nyn76010.htm, E-MAIL gardengren@aol.com.

Affordable rates. An 1865 four-story redbrick row house furnished with antiques. Two guest rooms and a one-bedroom apartment that sleeps four, with access to the rear garden. No breakfast; local cafés nearby.

HONEY'S HOME BED & BREAKFAST.   *Midwood.*
770 Westminster Rd. bet. Ave. H and Glenwood Rd., 434-7628, http://honeysbedandbreakfast.com,
E-MAIL lciberg@aol.com.

From $75 to $100 per night for room with semi-private bath. Private suite available. Peaceful Victorian house with three ample porches on shady residential street. Guests welcome to use family kitchen for breakfast, sitting room with TV, VCR, and lacy curtains. Breakfast features organic cereals and breads, fruits. Equidistant to the Heart of Brooklyn institutions and Coney Island. Host Laura Berger on premises.

MERZ HOUSE AT WILLOW PLACE.   *Brooklyn Hts./Atlantic Ave.*
48 Willow Pl., TEL. 855-8996, FAX 522-6550, E-MAIL willowfunk@aol.com.

Contact for rates. Brooklyn Heights area. Contemporary design; several types of accommodations, each with private bath. Short-term rental apartment includes three bedrooms, three baths, and access to a lovely garden, starting at $1,200 a week. Many eateries within walking distance. Breakfast is available. Book in advance. Hosts Mary and Joe Merz on premises.

MIDWOOD SUITES.   *Ave. J, Midwood.*
1078 E. 15th St., TEL. 253-9535 or 877-MIDWOOD (643-9663), www.midwoodsuites.com.

From $79 to $149 a night. Budget-motel style, floral décor. Eight two-room suites. Near many synagogues, kosher restaurants. No breakfast, but $3.50

voucher is included in rate for breakfast. Q train, thirty-five minutes from the first stop in Lower Manhattan.

MONSIGNOR DEL VECCHIO PL.   *Carroll Gardens.*
83 Summit St. off Columbia St., 875-4554.

Call for rates. One brightly lit, small modern apartment on side street. Minimum stay of three days. Can accommodate a couple or a family of four. Deck access. No maid service and no breakfast served.

PSC GREENPOINT YMCA BED & BREAKFAST.   *Greenpoint.*
99 Meserole Ave. bet. Manhattan Ave. and Lorimer St., TEL. 389-3700, FAX 349-2146.

From $58 (student rate $52). It's a Y, although they call it B&B. Institutional rooms with shared baths. Access to twenty-four-hour gym facilities, including pool. Some semipermanent residents rent rooms by the week. In the summer, European student tourists stay here. Reserve ahead for a deluxe room (similar to a private room at a hostel). Request a second-floor room; lower rooms seem cleaner. Traveling with a companion or group is recommended.

SADDLE DOWN BED & BREAKFAST.   *Fort Greene/Clinton Hill.*
266 Washington Ave., Ste. B9, near Myrtle Ave., 399-7913, www.saddledown.com.

Three rooms in a tiny B&B in an apartment building, all share one and a half baths. Close to **Pratt Institute**. Southwestern-cowboy-Native-American style. Rates are reasonable; based on number of people, not per room. Full hot breakfast. Reservations by phone only.

SAINTS AND SINNERS.   *Carroll Gardens.*
54 Strong Pl. bet. Kane, DeGraw, Henry, and Clinton Sts., 855-9614, www.saintsandsinnersbedandbreakfast.com.

From $100 for doubles and $75 for singles. Brownstone-style in Carroll Gardens, close to **Smith Street**. Three rooms on third floor share one bathroom. Breakfast is served on parlor floor.

STRANGE DOG INN.   *Midwood (Brooklyn College area).*
51 DeKoven Court off E. 17th St. bet. Foster Ave. and Glenwood Rd. TEL. 338-7051, FAX 434-0418, hometown.aol.com/dekoven51/myhomepage/business.html, E-MAIL Dekoven51@aol.com.

From $100 a night for doubles and $75 for singles. Midwood residential area, a sunny, spacious two-room suite. Breakfast, afternoon tea, and dinner available (optional): hostess is a professional chef. Two friendly cats. Guests can use the hosts' home office and kitchen, and the downstairs common area. No children under twelve allowed as guests. Hosts Paula and Gail Munroe on premises.

THE HOUSE ON 3RD ST.   *Park Slope.*

422 3rd St. bet. 5th and 6th Ave., 788-7171, www.houseon3st.com.

Rates from $130 per night. Favorite of grandparents and guests for special events. A classic brownstone building in central Park Slope. A bedroom with a double cast-iron bed, a twin in the adjacent "piano" room, and a pullout sofa in the front parlor; private bath, small private deck. No breakfast served. Host Jane White.

WESTMINSTER SUITES.   *Midwood.*

762 Westminster Rd. bet. Glenwood Rd. and Ave. H, 434-3119, www.bedandbreakfast.com/property/ppf/id/622158/ index.aspx, E-MAIL westminstersuite@aol.com.

From $65 to $150. Two nicely sized apartments. Takes the cake for spic-and-span cleanliness. Third floor is a big, brightly lit, cheerfully decorated apartment. Basement apartment has two rooms (which can be rented separately) and a shared bath. Self-catered breakfast. Hosts Stephanie and Harry.

Boutique Shopping
Made in Brooklyn!

This book lists sixty—count 'em, folks, *sixty*—designer boutiques featuring made-in-Brooklyn clothing, jewelry, and home furnishings. The boutiques are concentrated in just a half dozen neighborhoods, close enough to visit several in a day. You'll find them in little clusters: in Carroll Gardens along Smith Street and Atlantic Avenue; in Bedford-Stuyvesant and Fort Greene along Fulton Street (but don't miss that great body-products shop, and that fun hat store on nearby DeKalb Avenue); in Prospect Heights along Vanderbilt Avenue; and on Park Slope's 5th Avenue.

Woodstock, New York; Providence, Rhode Island; and Portland, Oregon, are often considered centers of "wearable art," jewelry, and crafts. Brooklyn recently has joined the ranks, a hotbed of creative artists and artisans who sell affordable work in local boutiques, from jewelry to cutting-edge women's clothing to hand-blown glassware to furniture to fabulous bath creams. Brooklyn also has a handful of artisanal shops that boast national stature in their field, including **Sadowsky Guitars** and **Clay Pot**. You'll even find artisanal chocolate here, for heaven's sake. Look for the icon ✪ for Made in Brooklyn.

Finding the Beat
Hip-Hop to Handel, Live Music
in Brooklyn

Brooklyn is rocking. You can find jazz jams, string quartets, and European avant-garde; bohemians, visitors, and New York natives all tapping their toes to the beats of calypso, reggae, classical, indie, rock and soul, hip-hop, Russian rock, gospel, Irish folk music, and more. In the summer, **Celebrate Brooklyn** is a fabulous showcase for a wide array of music, from the Lincoln Center Jazz Orchestra to salsa.

There's live music at Brooklyn venues every weekend, and it's generally much less expensive (and less pretentious) than in Manhattan. (And there are DJs spinning all over the borough, too.) Many musicians live here, of course; you can see them with their gig bags and instrument cases. Look for the icon ♫ for Live Music.

II

The Neighborhoods

Deciding Where to Go
in Brooklyn

We've organized this book by neighborhood. But most of the time, people find themselves traveling in certain circles. For instance, the Orthodox Jewish man who lives in Borough Park buys matzoh in Williamsburg, or the Trinidadian who lives in East Flatbush visits relatives in Crown Heights. There are invisible connections running all through the borough. So we've devised a little tool you can use.

If you're interested in one of the categories on the left, chances are that you'll be interested in the neighborhoods on the right.

African Diaspora	Bedford-Stuyvesant, East Flatbush, Fort Greene
Art	Williamsburg area, DUMBO, Brooklyn Museum of Art
Beach	Coney Island, Brighton Beach, Sheepshead Bay, Plum Beach
Big green spaces	Fort Greene Park, Prospect Park, Marine Park, Green-Wood Cemetery
Boutiques	Carroll Gardens, Park Slope, Fort Greene, Williamsburg, Atlantic Avenue, Prospect Heights
Brownstones	Brooklyn Heights, Bedford-Stuyvesant, Carroll Gardens, Fort Greene, Park Slope, Prospect Heights
Caribbean	East Flatbush, Flatbush, Bedford-Stuyvesant (Crown Heights)
Chinese	Sunset Park, Avenue U in Sheepshead Bay, Bensonhurst

Colleges	Downtown Brooklyn, Fort Greene/Clinton Hill, Flatbush, Sheepshead Bay (Crown Heights)
Food	Everywhere
Gentrified	Park Slope, Carroll Gardens, Brooklyn Heights, Fort Greene/Clinton Hill, Prospect Heights, Stuyvesant Heights
Gentrifying	Columbia Street area, Greenpoint, Williamsburg, Bedford-Stuyvesant, Fort Greene/Clinton Hill (Myrtle Avenue, Park Slope (4th Avenue), Red Hook, DUMBO, Prospect Heights
Irish	Bay Ridge, Windsor Terrace, Park Slope
Islamic	Atlantic Avenue, Midwood along Coney Island Avenue, Bay Ridge
Italian	Bensonhurst, Carroll Gardens, Red Hook
Jewish	Flatbush, Midwood
Jewish Orthodox	Borough Park, Williamsburg, Midwood (Crown Heights)
Latino	Sunset Park, Williamsburg, Red Hook
Music	Everywhere
New families	Prospect Heights, Carroll Gardens area, Flatbush, Park Slope/Windsor Terrace/Ditmas Park
Performance	Williamsburg/Greenpoint, DUMBO, Red Hook, Gowanus, Coney Island
Polish	Greenpoint
Postcollege, artistic	Williamsburg/Greenpoint, DUMBO, Red Hook, Gowanus, Coney Island
Postcollege trustafarians	Williamsburg/Greenpoint, DUMBO
Republican	Bay Ridge
Russian	Brighton Beach, Sheepshead Bay, Flatbush

Theater	BAM Cultural District, DUMBO, Williamsburg
Urban pioneering	Red Hook, Bushwick extension of Williamsburg, Coney Island
Waterfront	Brooklyn Bridge, Greenpoint, Williamsburg, DUMBO, Brooklyn Heights, Columbia Street area, Gowanus, Red Hook, Sunset Park, Bay Ridge, Coney Island, Brighton Beach, Sheepshead Bay, Canarsie, Jamaica Bay

NOTE: *We couldn't get to all the neighborhoods, so you'll find mention of places like Crown Heights and Canarsie, but not full chapters dedicated to them. We apologize for the space constraints, but, hey, Brooklyn is huge!*

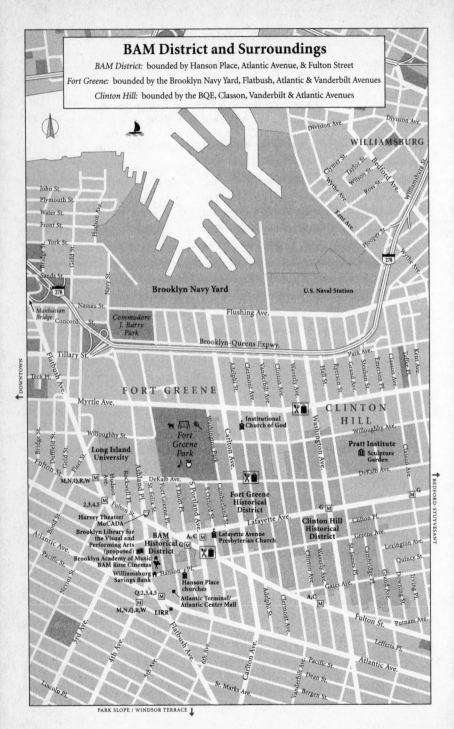

BAM District and Surroundings

BAM District: bounded by Hanson Place, Atlantic Avenue, & Fulton Street

Fort Greene: bounded by the Brooklyn Navy Yard, Flatbush, Atlantic & Vanderbilt Avenues

Clinton Hill: bounded by the BQE, Classon, Vanderbilt & Atlantic Avenues

WILLIAMSBURG

Division Ave.

Division Ave.

Clymer St.

Taylor St.

Wilson St.

Ross St.

Wythe Ave.

Bedford Ave.

Kent Ave.

Williamsburg St.

Hooper St.

278

Wythe Ave.

John St.

Plymouth St.

Water St.

Front St.

York St.

Hudson Ave.

Bridge St.

Gold St.

Sands St.

278

← Manhattan Bridge

Navy St.

Nassau St.

Concord

Brooklyn Navy Yard

U.S. Naval Station

Commodore J. Barry Park

Flushing Ave.

Tillary St.

Brooklyn-Queens Expwy.

Park Ave.

Emerson Pl.

Classon Ave.

Kent Ave.

Taaffe Pl.

← DOWNTOWN

Flatbush Ave.

Tech Pl.

FORT GREENE

Myrtle Ave.

Adelphi St.

Clermont Ave.

Vanderbilt Ave.

Clinton Ave.

Waverly Ave.

Hall St.

Ryerson St.

Grand Ave.

Steuben St.

CLINTON HILL

Willoughby Ave.

Institutional Church of God

Pratt Institute
Sculpture Garden

Willoughby St.

Long Island University

Fort Greene Park

Washington Park

Carlton Ave.

Washington Ave.

Bridge St.

Duffield St.

Gold St.

Fleet St.

Fulton St.

M,N,Q,R,W M

Hudson Ave.

Rockwell Pl.

Ashland Pl.

St. Felix St.

Fort Greene Pl.

S. Elliott Pl.

S. Portland Ave.

S. Oxford St.

Cumberland St.

Carlton Ave.

DeKalb Ave.

DeKalb Ave.

M

2,3,4,5

Harvey Theater/ MoCADA

Brooklyn Library for the Visual and Performing Arts (proposed)

Brooklyn Academy of Music BAM Rose Cinemas

Williamsburg Savings Bank

Q,2,3,4,5 M

M,N,Q,R,W

LIRR

BAM Historical District

A,C M

G M

Hanson Pl.

Hanson Place churches

Atlantic Terminal/ Atlantic Center Mall

Fort Greene Historical District

Lafayette Ave.

Lafayette Avenue Presbyterian Church

G M

Clinton Hill Historical District

Clifton Pl.

Greene Ave.

Waverly Ave.

Clinton Ave.

Adelphi St.

Clermont Ave.

Gates Ave.

A,C M

St. James Pl.

Cambridge Pl.

Grand Ave.

Downing St.

Lexington Ave.

Quincy St.

Irving Pl.

Fulton St.

Putnam Ave.

Lefferts Pl.

Atlantic Ave.

Atlantic Ave.

Pacific St.

Nevins St.

Bond St.

3rd Ave.

4th Ave.

5th Ave.

Flatbush Ave.

6th Ave.

Carlton Ave.

St. Marks Ave.

Pacific St.

Dean St.

Bergen St.

Vanderbilt Ave.

Lincoln Pl.

→ BEDFORD-STUYVESANT

PARK SLOPE / WINDSOR TERRACE ↓

1

BAM
Cultural District

ABOUT THE BAM CULTURAL DISTRICT

This brief section doesn't describe so much a neighborhood as a phenomenon: the coalescence of a new cultural center in the city of New York. For history, parks, shopping, restaurants, and general information on Fort Greene and Clinton Hill, the actual neighborhood where the new BAM cultural district is located, see p. 290. What follows is a peek at the BAM cultural district as it gathers momentum and reaches critical mass.

BY SUBWAY 2, 3, 4, 5, or B, Q train to Atlantic Avenue; D, M, N, or R train to Pacific Street; C train (A on weekends) to Lafayette Avenue.

For most events, a BAMbus leaves for BAM one hour before curtain time, from 120 East 42nd Street in Manhattan, across from Grand Central Terminal.

 ## What's **NEW?**

A BAM Cultural District Is Born

One of the fastest-changing areas in Brooklyn, the fourteen-block area around BAM will be unrecognizable to a visitor who hasn't been here since, say, 1990. The BAM area is rapidly becoming a Brooklyn-style Lincoln Center cultural district (albeit hipper and more integrated with its surrounding neighborhood), garnering a reputation internationally as a center for high-quality, sometimes offbeat contemporary performing arts.

Here are some high points: The Atlantic Terminal shopping area, the new **Atlantic Terminal Mall,** the arrival of **Mark Morris Dance Group** in a new building across from BAM, the fabulous new **Visual and Performing Arts Library** slated for construction starting in 2005, plus the conversion of nearby industrial sites, such as **NewsWalk,** into condominiums has caused a tsunami of change. To ease the space crisis for arts groups who can't afford Manhattan rents, new offices at below-market rents at the **South Oxford Space** and **80 Arts, The James E. Davis Arts Building,** have attracted dozens of arts and theater groups, bringing vitality to the area. The **Museum of African Diasporan Arts** is moving here. An incubator and catalyst for much of this activity, **BAM** itself continues to expand its programming and audiences. Even the Atlantic Avenue LIRR train and subway station is undergoing a complete renovation. And, of course, the Brooklyn Arena Stadium and arrival of the NJ Nets (to be renamed!) will change the face of the neighborhood.

The following lists important elements in the emerging BAM cultural district:

BROOKLYN ACADEMY OF MUSIC. 30 Lafayette Ave. at Ashland Pl., 636-4100, www.bam.org. Phone to be put on the mailing list.

BAM, the jaunty nickname for the **Brooklyn Academy of Music,** is one of New York City's premier cultural institutions. Less than one mile from either the Brooklyn or Manhattan Bridges, it is near to brownstone neighborhoods, fine eateries, and extensive public transportation. BAM is creating a minicultural space here, akin to London's National Theater complex, combining movies and live performances, bookshop and café—a cultural destination with amenities, a good place to meet friends. Venues include the **BAM Howard Gilman Opera House, BAM Harvey Theater, BAM Rose Cinemas**, and BAMcafé.

The **Next Wave Festival** is an internationally acclaimed showcase for leading avant-garde performance art. BAM's Spring Season features opera, music, theater, and dance, through June. **DanceAfrica,** the largest festival of African-American dance and culture in the United States, features companies from throughout the African Diaspora every spring, and the **Brooklyn Philharmonic** performs regularly in BAM's theaters.

Excellent children's shows are staged during the school year through the BAM Education & Humanities. There's also a **BAMfamily** series on weekend afternoons in the spring, and, in 1999, the **BAMkids International Children's Film Festival** was launched, featuring forty-five films from fourteen countries— almost all New York premieres.

BAM is home to several film festivals, including the **Brooklyn International Film Festival** (see p. 441 in chapter 17), the **Brooklyn Jewish Film Festival**, and an annual **Village Voice Critics' Choice** series.

Harvey Lichtenstein, BAM's president and executive producer from 1967 to 1999, was the powerhouse behind many of these innovative programs. Since stepping down, he has focused on the revitalization of the sixteen-block area surrounding the academy as chairman of the BAM Local Development Corporation. BAM currently is helmed by BAM veterans Karen Brooks Hopkins and Joseph Melillo.

The oldest performing arts center in America, BAM opened in 1859 in Brooklyn Heights and moved to its present quarters in 1908, after the original theater burned down.

BAM'S "THE HARVEY" (formally the Harvey Lichtenstein Theater, and previously BAM Majestic). 651 Fulton St. corner of Ashland Pl., 636-4100, www.bam.org. Call for a schedule.

Back in 1904, when the Majestic Theater opened, there were twenty large theaters in Brooklyn, with resonant names like the Star, Billy Watson's Pearl, the Novelty, the Gaiety, the Unique, and the Folly. (Very few of them are still standing; most have been razed, some are churches, and the Prospect Theater on 9th Street between 5th and 6th Avenues in Park Slope became a supermarket.) In its early years, the 1,800-seat Harvey was considered an important "tryout" house for Broadway-bound theatrical productions. Subsequently it hosted everything from Shakespearean plays to opera, vaudeville, and movies. Then it lay dormant for two decades. A cooperative effort by the city and the Brooklyn Academy of Music led to the theater's restoration in 1987. The façade has been preserved, but the interior, seating nine hundred people, has been remodeled after Peter Brook's Parisian theater, Les Bouffes du Nord (which means that the peeling paint and exposed ducts are intentional). The theater was renamed in 1999, to honor retiring BAM impresario Harvey Lichtenstein. Watch www.bam.org for a schedule of programs.

BAM OPERA HOUSE (AKA HOWARD GILMAN OPERA HOUSE). Brooklyn Academy of Music, 30 Lafayette Ave., 636-4111, www.bam.org.

BAM's main building is home to the 2,100-seat Opera House, as well as **BAM Rose Cinemas, BAMcafé,** and Shakespeare & Co.'s **BAMshop.** The neo-Renaissance building dates from 1908, and was designed by theater architects Herts & Tallent. In its early years, BAM hosted Enrico Caruso, Isadora Duncan, Mary Pickford, Gustav Mahler, Martha Graham, and even Gertrude Stein. The building was renamed in honor of philanthropist Howard Gilman in 2000.

BAM ROSE CINEMAS. Brooklyn Academy of Music, 30 Lafayette Ave., 623-2770, www.bam.org.

Comfortable, trendy, and, well, *exciting,* the Brooklyn Academy of Music's four movie theaters, opened in 1998, show first-run independent and foreign films, and often offer discussions with filmmakers as well. The theaters also screen films as part of BAM's music and dance programs. The cinemas have a combined seating of eight hundred, and are open seven days a week. They were built as part of an $18-million renovation project (also creating the BAMcafé and BAMshop, and sprucing up the lobby) and named in honor of a major donor. An excellent addition to moviegoing in Brooklyn.

♩ **BAMCAFÉ.** Brooklyn Academy of Music (2nd floor), 636-4100, F–Sa 5–10:30 p.m. During the week, the café is open only prior to shows, as follows: Su–Th 5–7:30 p.m. For weekend matinees, two hours prior to show. However, if there's a show *just* at the Opera House and *not* at The Harvey, theater patrons can go to the third-floor Diker Gallery Café for an open bar and hot à la carte appetizers from 5:30 to 7:30 p.m.

BAMcafé is a scene not to be missed: the international, eclectic crowd that gathers here before any BAM performance, both live theater and foreign flicks, makes for great people-watching. The oversized armchairs and potted trees are inviting, there's preconcert live jazz, and the architecture is notable, too; this used to be the Opera House's grand ballroom, the Lepercq Space.

Whether you are coming from Park Slope or Park Avenue, you'll enjoy a delicious meal here; a two-course dinner, without drinks but with tip, runs about $25 per person. For hungry movie buffs, a $31 package including dinner in BAMcafé and a movie ticket to BAM Rose Cinemas is available at the box office only. There are weekend live performances, too!

BAMSHOP. Brooklyn Academy of Music Opera House (2nd floor), 636-4100, www.bam.org.

Run by the premier New York City bookstore Shakespeare & Co., this little retail shop has a small but fabulous collection of performing- and visual-arts books. You can find coffee-table gift books, biographies, in-depth analyses of dance, theater, and art, as well as CDs, and, of course, BAM souvenirs.

BAMBUS. If you don't like subways and don't have a car, you can get to BAM from Manhattan (and home again) by **BAMbus**, a special bus that leaves from Park Avenue and 42nd Street an hour prior to performance time. Call 636-4100 to make a reservation at least twenty-four hours in advance. The 2003 fee was $5 each way.

DANCEAFRICA PERFORMANCES AND OUTDOOR BAZAAR. (See BAM, p. 28.)

Entering its 26th year, BAM's annual **DanceAfrica** festival at the BAM Howard Gilman Opera House continues to explore the dance, music, film, and culture of the African Diaspora. This Memorial Weekend event regularly features outstanding international dance troupes and, often, parallel movies and events at BAM. Don't miss the one-and-only **DanceAfrica Outdoor Bazaar.**

NEXT WAVE FESTIVAL. (See BAM, p. 28.)

One of the hottest tickets in New York City, BAM's famous Next Wave Festival is an international event. It presents leading performers from composers Philip Glass to Tan Dun, choreographers Pina Bausch to Mark Morris, as well as Britain's Peter Brook and Donmar Warehouse, other international troupes, and works by playwrights such as Charles L. Mee. The people-watching is invigorating, with a mixed crowd drawn from the hippest corners of New York.

BROOKLYN LIBRARY FOR THE VISUAL AND PERFORMING ARTS (planned). The triangle at the intersection of Ashland Pl. and Flatbush and Lafayette Aves., across from the BAM's main building (now a parking lot).

A contemporary arts library is on its way to Brooklyn. The highly acclaimed design—a shapely, aerodynamic-looking, V-shaped eight-story glass building—by Mexican architect Enríque Norten/TEN Arquitectos was selected in a juried competition under the auspices of the National Endowment for the Arts. Plans call for an internal courtyard with a Brooklyn mini-version of Rome's Spanish Steps—that is, a place for meeting, events, and performances. Inside, there will be an Information Age resource center for visual and performing arts. New York's fiscal troubles post 9-11 have forced a delay in plans to build this gem of a library, now slated to begin construction in 2005. When built, it will be a major component in the evolving cultural complex in the BAM area.

Free! **⊙ BROOKLYN COMMUNITY ACCESS TELEVISION (BCAT).** 57 Rockwell Pl. (2nd floor) off DeKalb Ave., 935-1122, www.brooklynx.org/bcat/aboutbcat.asp. Production studios open M–F 10 a.m.–10 p.m., Sa–Su 10 a.m.–4 p.m. Aired on Time Warner channels 34, 35, 56, and 57; Cablevision channels 67, 68, 69, and 70. See Web site or newspaper for schedule.

Think globally, act locally. In an age of media consolidation, when few towns have access to even one TV station's programming, Brooklyn Community Access Television operates *four* public-access cable TV channels. BCAT boasts the nation's eighth largest public-access audience.

For viewers Tune into Brooklyn. See your local elected officials. Learn about street fairs, community board meetings, and local art shows. Check the online bulletin board used by hundreds of community-based organizations (www. brooklynx.org/neighborhoods).

For doers If you are a Brooklyn resident over eighteen, BCAT classes teach how to run TV cameras, set lights, use video-editing equipment and graphics facilities, do desktop publishing, and more.

What does "public access TV" mean? Defined by the FCC as TV channels made available for use by the general public, it's part of that powerful First Amendment concept: freedom of expression. BCAT funding comes from New York City government fees on local cable TV operators.

♫ **BROOKLYN MUSIC SCHOOL & PLAYHOUSE.** 126 St. Felix St. bet. Hanson Pl. and Lafayette Ave., 638-5660, www.natguild.org/bms85.htm. Phone for a schedule.

A community school for the performing arts, BMS was founded in 1912. It provides training in music and dance without regard to income, age, previous experience, or professional aspirations. The four-story building has twenty classrooms, several dance studios, and a professional theater seating over two hundred people.

BRIC STUDIO. 647 Fulton St., enter on Rockwell Pl., 855-7882, www.brooklynx.org.

This publicly funded, seventy-four-seat black-box performing arts space enables local artists to produce theater, musical works, and multimedia presentations. It is part of a network of borough services that include **BCAT** and the **Rotunda Gallery** (see pp. 31 and 171, respectively). BRIC studio is located in the old **Strand Theater** (see p. 35).

♫ **BROOKLYN PHILHARMONIC.** 1 Hanson Pl. corner of Flatbush Ave., 622-5555 or 636-4100 for concert and ticket information, www.brooklynphilharmonic.org.

Like so much else about Brooklyn's art scene these days, the Brooklyn Philharmonic is surprisingly intimate, creative, and exciting. A freelance ensemble with a national reputation, the Brooklyn Philharmonic has flourished under the musical direction of the talented Robert Spano, gaining increasing recognition for adventuresome, inventive, emotionally gripping programming since his arrival in 1996. Some of their works are classics, some multicultural. You can often sit quite close to the musicians, and feel "in" the music—an experience that's hard to have in the big Manhattan venues unless you've paid for an orchestra seat in the first ten rows.

Mr. Spano, who has conducted nearly every major North American orchestra, is also music director of the Atlanta Symphony Orchestra, which has a fourteen-week season. Under his direction, the Brooklyn Philharmonic performs over two hundred concerts throughout Brooklyn and provides concert experiences for more than fifteen thousand of Brooklyn's school children every year. It has received twenty ASCAP Awards for "Adventurous Programming of Contemporary Music," including the 2002 award. Their 50th anniversary season included an eclectic menu of pieces, from the New York premiere of John Corigliano's *Mr. Tambourine Man*, an orchestrated work based on Bob Dylan songs, to a collaboration with the author of *The Hours*, Pulitzer Prize–winner Michael Cunningham (including the New York premiere of Philip Glass's suite from *The Hours*). The Brooklyn Philharmonic has a relationship with, but is not part of, BAM.

80 ARTS, THE JAMES E. DAVIS ARTS BUILDING.

It's not much to look at, but this eight-story building is part of the story of change being played out in the BAM area. It's being turned into below-market office space for several dozen arts and arts services groups. As a result, increasing numbers of art-related nonprofit organizations will be clustered around the downtown Brooklyn/Fort Greene area. (See also **South Oxford Space** and **Brooklyn Library for the Visual and Performing Arts**, pp. 34 and 31, respectively.)

♩ **MARK MORRIS DANCE GROUP.** 3 Lafayette Ave. off Flatbush Ave., 624-8400, www.mmdg.org. Check their Web site and local listings for information on classes, performances.

Mark Morris has been hailed as one of the creative geniuses of contemporary choreography, not far down the rungs of glory from such biggies as Martha Graham and Paul Taylor. His dancers are fast and athletic, the choreography is often wry and occasionally laugh-out-loud funny, and the costumes, especially when designed by Isaac Mizrahi, are *fabulous*. In 2001, the eighteen-person Mark Morris troupe moved into a room of their own across from BAM. This is unusual; most U.S. dance troupes don't even own their own studios, let alone an entire multimillion-dollar building. Yet they made the leap, and now enjoy thirty thousand square feet of new gorgeous offices and three rehearsal spaces with dance-perfect floors—in *Brooklyn*.

Although based in Brooklyn, the Mark Morris troupe tours about half the year in the United States and Europe. When in New York City, they often perform at BAM; don't miss it. Meanwhile, their presence in Fort Greene has given a boost to efforts to create a cultural and arts center here. Mark Morris Dance Center is a boon to the community, providing studios at subsidized rates and offering classes for hundreds of dancers of all ages and levels.

MOCADA. MUSEUM OF CONTEMPORARY AFRICAN DIASPORAN ARTS (planned). 80 Hanson Pl., 602-4041, W–Su 11 a.m.–6 p.m., closed M, Tu, www.mocada.org.

MoCADA (an acronym for Museum of Contemporary African Diasporan Arts) is Brooklyn's first museum for artists of African descent. It's committed to increasing public awareness of the art and culture of the African Diaspora as it relates to contemporary urban issues through innovative exhibitions, public programs, and interactive tours.

Since it opened in 1999, at a space made available by the Bridge Street AME Church in Bedford-Stuyvesant, there's been a buzz about this museum. It's the brainchild of Laurie Cumbo, a young woman with energy and a vision, who recognized that every large American city in the United States has a museum dedicated to African-Americans—except her hometown of Brooklyn, demographically the nation's fourth largest metropolitan area. MoCADA filled that gap. Leaving history to others, MoCADA mounts exhibitions that reflect on, and articulate, the *contemporary* experience of the African Diaspora, both in the United States and internationally. Educational programming, both formal and informal, and community outreach are part of their menu; MoCADA runs the **KidFlix** film festival in Bedford-Stuyvesant (see p. 66).

Moving into the BAM cultural district with a new 1,200-foot space in 2004, the museum plans to mount four exhibitions annually, featuring diaspora art that has both artistic merit and social significance. This is a museum that's bound to make its mark; stay tuned.

♫ **PAUL ROBESON THEATRE.** 40 Greene Ave. bet Carlton Ave. and Adelphi St., 783-9794.

The Paul Robeson Theatre, founded in 1979 and named after the famous African-American singer and actor, produces a range of entertainment, including ethnically oriented theater, dance, and movies. Classics such as the works of Athol Fugard and August Wilson are often part of the repertory. The building used to be a Polish Catholic church and is now a community cultural center. There's a three-thousand-foot space for performances on the lower level. Most tickets are $20.

♫ **651 ARTS.** 651 Fulton St. corner of Ashland Pl., 636-4181, www.651ARTS.org.

For almost two decades, 651 ARTS has been presenting African-American contemporary theater, dance, and music programs. It was born in 1988 under the auspices of a New York City financing arrangement for the renovation of BAM's Harvey Theater, where it is now housed.

This energetic organization has brought Betty Carter, Tito Puente, Abbey Lincoln, and Anna Deavere Smith to the Brooklyn stage. To get the sense of their mission, their 2003 Ronald K. Brown/Evidence piece, "Dirt Road," was described as "an evocative work using African and contemporary dance, along with poetry and music to create a collage about one family's journey through time and circumstances."

651 ARTS does important international work, too. Their Africa Exchange program, launched in the mid-1990s and funded by the Ford and Rockefeller Foundations, was perhaps the first to underwrite new collaborations between African and African-American artists. 651 ARTS has nurtured a network of about twenty performing arts institutions that now commission new work and host residencies by international artists.

SOUTH OXFORD SPACE (A.R.T./New York). 138 So. Oxford St., 398-3078, www.offbroadwayonline.com.

If you see theatrical types zooming off to work and back here, it's because, since 2001, the BAM area has become home to a creative crucible of twenty professional theater companies.

Old-timers may recall this 1930s–era building as the Visiting Nurses Association. A few years ago, the prestigious Alliance of Resident Theatres, a nonprofit umbrella organization for some of the city's best known theaters bought and renovated this office building. Their goal was to relieve young talent and small, experimental theater companies from oppressively expensive rents in Manhattan.

And so, Off Broadway has arrived in Brooklyn. The resident companies, all nonprofits, pay subsidized rents and have their own office space, but share office basics such as copy machines and kitchen facilities. There's a gallery, and rehearsal studios on the way. Many of these companies used to work out of apartments, or in small rented areas. With all that creative theater talent cooking away under one roof, who knows what great things might emerge? Reflecting the success of this venture, another similar building is being opened to nonprofit arts groups at **80 Arts, The James E. Davis Arts Building.**

STRAND THEATER. 57 Rockwell Pl. off Fulton St.

The Strand was built in 1918 as an enormous vaudeville theater seating as many as four thousand people. With the demise of vaudeville and rise of movies, the Strand was converted into a movie theater. After World War II, this part of town became run down, and the interior was demolished to make way for a bowling alley. Finally it was degraded to manufacturing space. In the 1990s, new creative projects found a home here, including **BCAT** and **Urban-Glass,** and, more recently, echoing the building's original purpose, **BRIC Studio**, a small theater space.

☺ ✷ ✪ **URBANGLASS—NEW YORK CENTER FOR CONTEMPORARY GLASS.** 647 Fulton St., enter on Rockwell Pl., 625-3685, M—W 10 a.m.—7 p.m., Th 10 a.m.—8 p.m., Sa 10 a.m.—6 p.m., Su 11 a.m.— 5 p.m., www.urbanglass.org.

UrbanGlass is a nationally recognized center for the creation of new art made from glass. It was founded in 1977 as the New York Experimental Glass Workshop, moved to Brooklyn in 1991, and is one of the largest artist-accessible glass-making centers in the world. Hundreds of trained artists (and well-heeled beginners, too) rent time at the glass-working facilities at this 17,000-square-foot studio. UrbanGlass is part of a long Brooklyn tradition of glassblowing.

Classes include a $350 weekend workshop and a $750 semester program. Other activities are the Urbanites program, cocktail parties for twenty-something art-glass connoisseurs (at one such event, guests were invited to make their own martini glasses), curated exhibits in the **Robert Lehman Gallery,** and bimonthly open houses (during which you can learn to make glass paper-weights, but register in advance for this: $50; over twelve years old only).

OTHER POINTS OF CULTURAL INTEREST

WILLIAMSBURGH SAVINGS BANK. 1 Hanson Pl. across from the Long Island Rail Road, 722-5300, M—F 9 a.m.—5 p.m., closed weekends and bank holidays.

Brooklyn's tallest building (so far) offers breathtaking views of Brooklyn and beyond. It's visible from as far away as Sutton Place.

This 1929 New York City landmarked building was designed as a "skyscraper" by the firm of Halsey, McCormack, and Helmer just a few years before the Great Depression, and it resembles the Bowery Savings Bank opposite Grand Central Terminal. It is 512 feet high, with setbacks at the thirteenth and twenty-sixth floors. Inside there's a wonderful mosaic mural on the ground floor, a gilded dome, arches, stained glass, and marble rails. The Williamsburgh Savings Bank building at **175 Broadway** is also a New York City landmark (see p. 445).

Taller than London's Big Ben, and visible from many parts of Brooklyn—as far away as twenty-five miles!—the four-faced Williamsburgh Savings Bank Clock sits more than four hundred feet above sidewalk level, and measures twenty-seven feet in diameter. The 1929 clock still has all its original mechanisms and equipment, except for the north-facing hour hand, replaced after damage incurred in a winter storm.

2

Bay Ridge

ABOUT BAY RIDGE

Bay Ridge is distinguished in Brooklyn by its historically strong Republican voting presence, great restaurants, fabulous views of the **Verrazano Bridge,** and the fact that Spectrum, the club where John Travolta danced in *Saturday Night Fever,* is still going strong. Its shops, restaurants, and community events reflect the solid middle-class family values of the residents. It's a neighborhood where many people still retain their extended family networks, with cousins, grandparents, and aunts and uncles nearby.

The shops, restaurants, and community events in Bay Ridge celebrate its ethnic diversity. The early Scandinavian settlers' presence is still felt in the neighborhood bakeries and food shops. The annual Norwegian Constitution Day Parade culminates with the crowning of Miss Norway in **Leif Ericson Park.** The sizable Italian population is reflected in the many excellent Italian restaurants and cafés serving cappuccino and espresso. The Irish, and more recently the Asian, Polish, Russian, Greek, Lebanese, and Syrian presence is seen in small specialty shops that sell international food, clothing, and gift items.

HOW IT GOT ITS NAME Although Bay Ridge was known first as Yellow Hook, for the yellow clay in its soil, the infelicitous name was changed in 1853, after New York City suffered a bout of yellow fever. The spectacular views from a ridge overlooking New York Bay gave Bay Ridge its current name.

BY SUBWAY R train to 86th Street (at 4th Avenue).

HISTORICAL NOTES

The area called Bay Ridge was purchased from the Nyack Indians by the Dutch West India Company in 1652. A rural farming area until the late 1890s, Bay Ridge, like Brooklyn Heights, was developed as a retreat for wealthy Manhattan-

SUNSET PARK

54th St.
55th St.
56th St.
57th St.
58th St.
59th St.
60th St.
61st St.
62nd St.

Gowanus Expwy.

2nd Ave.

(Leif Ericson Dr.)

Shore Pkwy.

Owls Head Park
(Millenium Skate Park)

67th St.

Senator St.

68th St.

Bay Ridge Ave.

69th St. Pier

9/11
Memorial

70th St.

MacKay Pl.

Narrows
Botanical
Gardens

72nd St.

73rd St.

74th St.

Colonial Rd.

Narrows Ave.

Ridge Blvd.

Bay Ridge Pkwy.

76th St.

77th St.

78th St.

79th St.

80th St.

81st St.

82nd St.

BAY
RIDGE

Fort Hamilton
Athletic Field

83rd St.

85th St.

86th St.

"Restaurant Row"

87th St.

88th St.

89th St.

Monastery
Square

91st St.

92nd St.

Oliver St.

FORT
HAMILTON

95th St.

96th St.

97th St.

Bennet-
Farrel-Feldman
House

Shore Rd.

Shore Road Park

Upper New York Bay

Shore Pkwy. (Leif Ericson Dr.)

Verrazano
Narrows Bridge

The Narrows

65th St.

3rd Ave.

Leif Ericson Park

66th St.

67th St.

Senator St.

68th St.

R M Bay Ridge
Alpine
Ave.

Ovington Ave.

72nd St.

73rd St.

74th St.

Bay Ridge
Branch Library

4th Ave.

3rd Ave.

76th St.

77th St.

78th St.

79th St.

80th St.

81st St.

82nd St.

83rd St.

84th St.

85th St.

R M

5th Ave.

90th St.

91st St.

92nd St.

93rd St.

94th St.

95th St.

96th St.

97th St.

99th St.

100th St.

101st St.

Marine Ave.

Fort Hamilton
Branch Library
M R

Harbor
Defense
Museum

278

Gowanus Expwy.

6th Ave.

Gatling Pl.

Gelston Ave.

Battery Ave.

Dyker Pl.

Parrott Pl.

Dahlgren Pl.

Fort Hamilton Pkwy.

278

U. S.
Government
Reservation

Fort Hamilton

Dyker Beach
Golf Club

Dyker Beach
Park

63rd St.

64th St.

8th Ave.

7th Ave.

6th Ave.

5th Ave.

4th Ave.

BOROUGH PARK

66th St.

67th St.

68th St.

Bay Ridge Ave.

70th St.

71st St.

72nd St.

Loews
Fortway

McKinley
Park Branch
Library

9th Ave.

10th Ave.

Bay Ridge Pkwy.

73rd St.

75th St.

76th St.

77th St.

78th St.

79th St.

80th St.

81st St.

82nd St.

83rd St.

84th St.

85th St.

86th St.

11th Ave.

12th Ave.

7th Ave.

Fort Hamilton Pkwy.

BENSONHURST

Bay Ridge

Bounded by 65th Street,
101st Street, Upper New
York Bay, & Fort Hamilton
Parkway

ites. The spectacular views from a ridge overlooking the entrance to New York Bay attracted industrialists, who built summer estates along the bluffs of Shore Road. But with the extension of the 4th Avenue Subway in 1915, the exclusivity of the area was destroyed. The neighborhood's population changed, as Manhattan workers seeking more suburban surroundings began to settle in the area.

The long history of Bay Ridge remains visible in its homes and churches. Elegant turn-of-the-century houses line Colonial Road and Shore Road between 80th and 83rd Streets. The land on which Fort Hamilton was built played a role in George Washington's failed Battle of Long Island against the British in 1776. Nearby Saint John's Episcopal Church at 99th Street and Fort Hamilton Parkway, known as the "church of the generals," was frequented by military leaders Stonewall Jackson and Robert E. Lee.

Kidstuff

☺ Bike, fly a kite, or fish at **Shore Road Park**, picnic or skateboard at **Owl's Head Park**, visit **Narrows Botanical Gardens**, check out the **Harbor Defense Museum**, shop for sports gear at **Panda**, get a new book to read at **Novel Idea Bookstore**.

POINTS OF CULTURAL INTEREST

SPECIAL EVENTS.

Norwegian Constitution Day Parade (first Sunday after May 17); Ragamuffin Parade and 3rd Avenue Festival (first weekend in October); call 836-6700 for information.

BENNET-FARREL-FELDMAN HOUSE. 119 95th St. near Shore Rd.

Long recognized as an outstanding mid-nineteenth-century house, this is a survivor from the era when fashionable villas lined Shore Road, overlooking the bluffs of the Narrows. Built in 1847 for Joseph Bennet, it is one of three houses near Shore Road erected in the 1840s by the Bennet family. Note its columned front and rear porches, corner pilasters, dentil cornices, and molded window surrounds. It was designated a New York City landmark in 2001.

FONTBONNE HALL ACADEMY. 9901 Shore Rd. corner of 99th St.

Life was tough for the industrial barons of the nineteenth century, as you can see from this extraordinary mansion. Lore has it that Diamond Jim Brady bought this home for Lillian Russell. Party guests arrived by boat. Today the halls of this Catholic school are filled with young female students. No tours are available, but it's worth a look from the outside just the same.

"GINGERBREAD HOUSE." 82nd St. near Narrows Ave.

Thatched cottages in England dating back to the 1600s were considered so quaint by the turn of the twentieth century that some whimsical, wealthy folks used the style as a theme for their second (or third) homes. This house dates from the era when Brooklyn was full of rolling green hills, meadows, and the sounds of nature. It is a private home; no tours are available.

☺ **HARBOR DEFENSE MUSEUM AT FORT HAMILTON.** Fort Hamilton Pkwy. at 101st St., almost under Verrazano-Narrows Bridge, 630-4349, open some afternoons M–F and some Saturdays, www.hamilton.army.mil. Call for hours. Take the B63 bus or B16 bus and ask the driver for the stop nearest the fort, which is some distance from commercial Bay Ridge.

It seems incongruous that you'd find a military institution smack in the middle of contemporary Brooklyn, but the sign at the entrance stating "YOU ARE ENTERING A MILITARY BASE" is no fake. The base houses about two thousand military personnel and their families.

A self-guided walking tour takes you past a block of cannons, Robert E. Lee's house (he was posted here as chief engineer from 1841 to 1846), the barracks, stable, and commissary, as well as the old Officers' Club, now a popular venue for wedding receptions. Note the small monument marking the site of a Native American longhouse, part of the former Nyack tribe's village there.

The Harbor Defense Museum is one of only four dozen Army base museums in the United States. Located in a 160-year-old, wedge-shaped stone structure called a caponier, the building was once used to protect Fort Hamilton from a rear-guard attack. Inside, the museum chronicles the defense of New York Harbor, with exhibits of guns, mines, cannons, and missiles, as well as weapons captured during the Gulf War. Kids may enjoy the exhibit of G.I. Joe action figures.

Both the museum building and Officers' Club are listed in the National Register of Historic Places.

🎓 **HIGH SCHOOL OF TELECOMMUNICATION ARTS AND TECHNOLOGY.** 350 67th St., 759-3400, www.hstat.org.

An ethnically diverse student body of 1,200 students go to classes in this public high school located in an old Gothic-style building, turrets and all; but once inside, they are firmly in the twenty-first century. Telecommunication HS has TV and computer labs, and Internet access in every classroom. Experts say that this school is building its reputation by attracting first-rate teachers. Graduation rate is about 65 percent. (Source: *New York City's Best Public High Schools: A Parents' Guide: Second Edition,* by C. Hemphill with P. Wheaton and J. Wayans.)

9-11 MEMORIAL. 69TH ST. PIER.

Located at the 69th Street Pier overlooking the Statue of Liberty, this is the spot to which local people raced the morning of September 11, 2001, to see the fires and then the horrific collapse of the World Trade Center towers. As we go to publication, a memorial is being designed.

POLY PREP COUNTRY DAY SCHOOL. 92nd St. corner of 7th Ave., 836-9800, www.polyprep.org.

Founded in Brooklyn Heights in 1854, Poly Prep is a highly regarded private school nestled in a vast, twenty-five-acre greenbelt of a campus, complete with duck ponds, swimming pools, and tennis courts. It is one of just a handful of New York City schools with onsite playing fields, and athletics play a large role in the lives of Poly students. The Middle and Upper School is located on the large main campus here in Bay Ridge. Pre-K through fourth graders attend the Lower School, now located in Park Slope directly across from Prospect Park.

The school offers a coed, college preparatory Pre-K–12 program for an ethnically and socioeconomically diverse student body from all five boroughs. Poly enjoys the support of enthusiastic alumni and parent associations. Admissions are highly selective, and college placements are excellent.

PUBLIC SCHOOLS.

Among those considered to be New York City's "best public elementary schools" are PS 102, which has a Delta gifted program (211 72nd Street), and PS 185 (8601 Ridge Boulevard). (Source: *New York City's Best Public Elementary Schools: A Parents' Guide,* 2002, by C. Hemphill with P. Wheaton.)

VERRAZANO-NARROWS BRIDGE. Shore Pkwy. and Fort Hamilton Pkwy.

Visible from many Brooklyn neighborhoods, the Verrazano-Narrows Bridge is a beautiful sight at night, a necklace of lights strung across the water. It is named after Giovanni da Verrazano, the first European to see Staten Island (in 1524). Opened in 1964, a project of New York builder Robert Moses, the steel bridge is 4,260 feet long, the longest suspension bridge in the United States, and the sixth longest in the world. The bridge connects Brooklyn with Staten Island and is a quick route to southern New Jersey and points south—and is the starting point for the New York City Marathon each fall. Its construction created great controversy, as many homes in the tight-knit German and Scandinavian immigrant community were torn down to accommodate the building of its infrastructure.

As of this writing, the crossing to Staten Island will cost you $7; the return trip is free.

ENTERTAINMENT

HALL OF FAME BILLIARDS. 505 Ovington Ave. at 5th Ave., 921-2694, open 24/7, $9.60 per hour.

☺ **LEE MARK LANES.** 423 88th St. bet. 4th and 5th Aves., 745-3200, daily 9 a.m.–6 p.m.

This two-floor, thirty-six-lane renovated bowling alley is popular for birthday parties and league play. Babysitting is available.

🎬 **LOEWS CINEPLEX ALPINE 7.** 6817 5th Ave. at 69th St., 748-4200.

This small seven-screen, first-run movie theater is located at the beginning of the 5th Avenue commercial strip in Bay Ridge. Walk two blocks to lots of great restaurants on 3rd Avenue. There's easy local parking and bargain matinees.

🎬 **LOEWS CINEPLEX FORTWAY 5.** 6720 Fort Hamilton Pkwy. bet. 67th and 68th Sts., 212-777-FILM #578.

This movie theater is not in the heart of Bay Ridge's restaurant and bar scene, but it's a Loews that shows first-run movies.

IRISH PUB-CRAWL AND DANCIN' IN BAY RIDGE

Everyone's heard about Brighton Beach Russian nightclubs. But one of New York's best-kept partying secrets is Bay Ridge's abundance of Irish bars—many with live bands on weekends. Sure, there are scores of great neighborhood bars, and other Irish bars, in Brooklyn. But Bay Ridge offers an unusual opportunity: an Old World pub crawl to almost a dozen drinking destinations, within a one-mile stretch, between 68th and 95th Streets. Typically open until 4 a.m., these pubs give you a chance to taste life in a high-spirited, "outer-borough-and-proud-of-it" neighborhood that takes its partying seriously. Call for information on bands. The following are organized by avenue, starting from the highest street number.

3rd Avenue
♫ **BALLY BUNION.** 9510 3rd Ave. off 95th St., 833-2801, M–Th 11 a.m.–11 p.m., F–Su 11 a.m.–4 a.m.
LILY'S PUBLIC HOUSE. 8814 3rd Ave. bet. 88th and 89th Sts., 833-6466, daily noon–4 a.m.
FITZPATRICK. 8622 3rd Ave. bet. 86th and 87th Sts., 680-7862, M–F 4 p.m.–4 a.m., Sa–Su noon–4 a.m.
♫ **KITTY KIEMAN'S.** 7915 3rd Ave. bet. 79th and 80th Sts., 491-0217, daily 10 a.m.–4 a.m.

♫ **JUDGE N JURY.** 7901 3rd Ave. corner 79th St., 491-2967, M–F 11 a.m.–4 a.m., Sa–Su noon–4 a.m.

4th Avenue

♫ **KELLY'S TAVERN.** 9259 4th Ave. bet. 92nd and 93rd Sts., 745-9546, daily 11 a.m.–4 a.m.
SNOOK INN. 8608 4th Ave. near 86th St., 745-8439, daily noon–4 a.m.
SCRUFFY MURPHY. 6816 4th Ave. bet. 86th and 87th Sts., 745-9164, daily noon–4 a.m.

And, to get the feel of these places, read on:

♫ **PEGGY O'NEILL'S.** 8121 5th Ave. bet. 81st and 82nd Sts., 748-1400, daily 11–4 a.m., www.peggyoneills.com.
   Stainte! ("Cheers!" in Irish). A favorite among New York's Finest, this pub is an "official stop" on the local St. Patrick's Day parade route. The restaurant is long gone, but the bands play on, every weekend evening, attracting a youngish crowd. There's a new branch at the Cyclones stadium in Coney Island.

♫ **WICKED MONK.** 8415 5th Ave. bet. 84th and 85th Sts., 921-0601, M–F 11 a.m.–4 a.m., Sa–Su noon–4 a.m., www.wickedmonk.com.
   Wicked Monk has a cheerfully sinful air. With its monastery pulpit (housing a DJ) offset by a pool table, a confessional (now a phone booth), and spooky gargoyles leering from the bar, this local favorite certainly gets high marks for unusual décor. The owners imported pieces of the bar, stained glass, and other religious accoutrements from the 1897 Chapel in Greenmount Monastery (Gallows Green), Cork, Ireland. The entertaining thirty-six-foot-long ceiling mural immortalizes everyone who helped get Wicked Monk started—along with some long-gone monks, of course. For band schedule, dates of ski and golf outings, and more stories, see the Web site.

❷ ☺ **NARROWS COMMUNITY THEATER.** 9728 3rd Ave. at 97th St., Fort Hamilton Army Base Theater, 482-3173, www.nctheater.com.
   For over three decades, this community theater has paired local talent with professional theater directors. The happy result is entertaining and affordable.

♫ **SPECTRUM.** 802 64th St. at 8th Ave., 745-8970, Th–Sa 9:30 p.m.–4:30 a.m., www.spectrum.com. Cash only. Call for cover price.
   John Travolta danced his famous *Saturday Night Fever* numbers on this very dance floor. Stuck in a time warp, Spectrum combines disco with a well-known gay dating scene on the back patio.

PARKS AND PLAYGROUNDS

☺ **5TH AVE. PLAYGROUND.** 84th St. on 5th Ave.

☺ **LEIF ERICSON PARK.** 4th Ave. bet. 66th and 67th Sts.

Reflecting the neighborhood's early Scandinavian roots, this sixteen-acre park is the site of the annual crowning of Miss Norway during Bay Ridge's Norwegian Constitution Day Parade in May.

◑ ☺ **MILLENNIUM SKATE PARK.** Owl's Head Park, daily 9 a.m.–8 p.m. Free.

Once rated "best skate park" by *New York* magazine, Millennium attracts skateboard fans from all over the city. It's free, of course, and there are two concrete bowls, one of which feels like an empty swimming pool. Helmets are a must. While the kids are skating, the rest of the family can picnic in **Owl's Head Park,** jog along **Shore Road Park,** or shop on 3rd or 5th Avenue.

☺ **NARROWS BOTANICAL GARDENS.** Shore Rd. bet. 69th and 72nd Sts., May to November.

This lovely 4.5-acre garden is known for its flowers, tranquility, and great views of the Narrows, the Statue of Liberty, and the Verrazano Bridge. Come in the spring to enjoy the rose gardens, the lady slipper orchids, and a miniature bog and pond. It's all tended and paid for by volunteers who transformed it from a grubby piece of untended land. To quote one, "The lily pond in an old sandbox is the best thing you've ever saw." Little kids will love it.

🐾☺ **OWL'S HEAD PARK.** Bounded by Shore Pkwy., Shore Rd., Colonial Rd., and 68th St.

With almost thirty acres on a bluff overlooking the harbor, **Owl's Head Park** is popular for family picnics. Get here early to watch the OPSAIL Parade of Tall Ships sailboat flotilla on Fourth of July weekends, or enjoy the summer concerts sponsored by the Brooklyn Arts Council, **BAC** (see p. 170).

☺ **RUSSELL PEDERSON PLAYGROUND.** Colonial Rd. at 84th St.

☺ **79TH AND 95TH STREET PLAYGROUNDS.** Along Shore Rd., 965-6528.

SHORE PARKWAY PROMENADE. From Owl's Head Park at 68th St. to Bensonhurst Park at Bay Pkwy.

Running along Brooklyn's westernmost edge, this long, narrow band of asphalt and benches between the Belt Parkway and the water connects Owl's Head Park at 68th Street to Bensonhurst Park and passes under the Verrazano Bridge. Bikers, joggers, and walkers love this stretch on warm days. You can cross over the Belt Parkway at the exits or stop in one of the parking areas just to the side of the Parkway. When you near the bridge, keep your eyes open for some of the peregrine falcons that nest in its superstructure.

♨☺ SHORE ROAD PARK. Shore Rd. bet. 68th St. and Colonial Rd., 965-6524.

This fifty-eight-acre park has a 2.5-mile path along the waterside. At 69th Street, a footbridge crosses the Belt Parkway to the waterside promenade, where the walking, jogging, and biking path starts. The 97th Street ball fields are popular for amateur baseball games. Nearby there are two playgrounds and tennis courts (call 965-8993 for permit information). Take a stroll along the sidewalk from 100th Street back down to 69th Street for fresh breezes, and views of the Verrazano Bridge and some lovely homes. At John Paul Jones Park, at 4th Avenue and 101st Street, adjacent to the entrance to Fort Hamilton, there are frequent summer concerts. There's a dog run at 68th Street and Shore Road.

BAY RIDGE RESTAURANTS

There are many good restaurants in Bay Ridge. For tips on where to find quick snacks and inexpensive meals, see the separate listings at the end of this section.

AREO RISTORANTE ITALIANO. 8424 3rd Ave. corner of 85th St., 238-0079, open for lunch and dinner, closed Su. Reservations are recommended.

When you see the limos and fancy cars double parked on weekends, you'll know you've found Areo. The antipasti are superb, as are specials, such as sliced filet mignon marsala, *zuppa di pesce,* and spinach with garlic. And they take special requests. All this doesn't come cheap, though; dinner for two with a couple of drinks comes to about $75.

☯☺ ARIRANG HIBACHI STEAK HOUSE AND SUSHI BAR. 8814 4th Ave. bet. 88th and 89th Sts., 238-9880, M–Th 5–10:30 p.m., F 5 p.m.–1 a.m., Sa 4:30 p.m.–1 a.m., Su 3–10 p.m., http://ariranghibachi.com.

The kids will love the showy, twirling tricks that the waiters perform while cooking your food over a tabletop hibachi. The Korean-Japanese seasonings are good; the steak is recommended.

BACI. 7107 3rd Ave. near 71st St., 836-5536, Tu–Th 5–11 p.m., F–Sa 5 p.m.–midnight, Su 4–10 p.m. Valet parking on weekends. Reservations are recommended.

Some locals rave about this sparse Italian restaurant with the French doors opening onto the sidewalk, while others find the food "sometimes great, sometimes fair." Baci runs about $30 per person.

♪ **BALLY BUNION, AN IRISH HOUSE.** 9510 3rd Ave. off 95th St., 833-2801, M–Th 11 a.m.–11 p.m., F–Su 11 a.m.–4 a.m.

This informal Irish restaurant/bar with a golf theme (named after a famous course in County Kerry) serves up a bit of Irish schmaltz with songs by the bar, a dreamy open fireplace, and lots of warm feelings. Skip the burgers and go for bangers and mash, and maybe an Irish whiskey cake. Live music on weekends.

CANEDO'S. 7316 3rd Ave. bet. 73rd and 74th Sts., 748-1908, M–F noon–3:30 p.m., Sa 4 p.m.–midnight, Su 1–10 p.m., www.canedos.com. Reservations are recommended.

Ssshhhh. This great Italian restaurant has somehow eluded the crowds. An elegant wooden façade and framed turn-of-the-century posters and mirrors are matched by excellent Northern Italian food. Try shrimp and artichoke in white sauce, stuffed mushrooms and artichokes, or veal Fiorentino. The service is good, and dress is casual. Dinner entrées hover around $18.

● ☺ **CANTEENA.** 8001 5th Ave. corner of 80th St., 745-9160, M–Th 11 a.m.–11 p.m., F–Sa 11 a.m.– 2 a.m., Su noon–midnight.

Beloved by locals, this Mexican restaurant serves healthy portions of fresh—and mild—Mexican cuisine in a relaxing and easygoing atmosphere. There's an extensive children's menu, and a very traditional American Sunday brunch.

CASA PEPE. 114 Bay Ridge Ave. off Colonial Rd., 833-8865, daily noon–11 p.m., www.casapepe.com.

A fireplace in the winter and garden in the summer make Casa Pepe a local favorite for fans of Spanish and Mexican cuisine. The seafood and tacos are reliably good. Come hungry; the food is a bit heavy.

CHADWICK'S. 8822 3rd Ave. bet. 88th and 89th Sts., 833-9855, daily 11:30 a.m.–10:30 p.m.

A Chicago-style meat lovers' restaurant, Chadwick's serves what our waitress described to us as a "meal for a man"–big portions of steak and potatoes. Expect a wide variety of beef dishes with few surprises except for the extremely good beef Wellington, a Saturday night special. Vegetarians will be satisfied with the pasta. Entrées cost about $18.

CHEF NATALE. 7803 3rd Ave. at 78th St., 921-0717, daily 5–10:30 p.m.

There's a small menu of well-prepared Sicilian peasant food in this tiny place, and it gets rave reviews for the seafood and osso buco (though not the décor). Chef Natale was Frank Sinatra's personal chef. So let's face the music and dance.

CHIANTI'S. 8530 3rd Ave. corner of 86th St., 921-6300, Tu–F 5–10 p.m., Sa 5–11 p.m., Su 2–10 p.m., http://nycwebz.com/chianti. Valet parking.

If you've just run a marathon or are feeding a crowd, come here for large portions of inexpensive Italian fare. Some people rave about the eggplant dishes, others about the veal. Pocketbook tips: You can eat two-for-the-price-of-one, because the "family-style" portions are so big; the antipasti can be a meal in themselves.

☺ **EMBERS.** 9519 3rd Ave. near 95th St., 745-3700, M–F 5–10:30 p.m., Sa 4:30–midnight, Su 2–9 p.m. Reservations accepted weekdays only.

Embers is a family restaurant and is run by the folks who own Vinnie's meat market next door. It's crowded and noisy, and the fresh steaks and chops arrive in big portions at great prices; locals like to say it's Bay Ridge's response to Peter Luger. Entrées start at $13.

ESTIATORIO ELIA. 8611 3rd Ave. bet. 86th and 87th Sts., 748-9891, Tu–Th 5–10 p.m., F–Sa 5–11 p.m., Su 4–9 p.m.

Nobody dances on the taverna tables here, but the austere white walls and arches behind the inviting bar are vaguely reminiscent of restaurants on the Greek islands. The seafood, while not exactly Aegean, is fresh and tasty—and don't forget to have a shot of ouzo after dinner. This is an intimate restaurant where you can actually hear what your date is saying. Entrées run about $20.

☺ **INDIA PASSAGE.** 7407 3rd Ave. bet. 74th and 75th Sts., 833-2160, daily noon–11 p.m.

Faruk, the owner of India Passage, one of the borough's better Indian restaurants, serves up traditional northern Indian favorites from the clay oven as well as Bengal shrimp and some southern Indian specialties. Kids will love the tandoori chicken, which falls off the bone into your mouth. The décor at India Passage is spare and contemporary, prices are reasonable, and the spices are tempered to meet local (OK, even Irish) palates.

☺ ♫ **LOLA BELL'S CAFÉ.** 7428 5th Ave. at Bay Ridge Pkwy., 921-6200, daily 11 a.m.–11 p.m.

Located in the old Brooklyn Trust Company building, Lola Bell's features eclectic 1890s décor, decorative lampshades, and long wooden bar. It's genteel, and a nice quiet place to come for an egg cream, panini sandwich, or ice cream. Kid-friendly, too. There's jazz on weekends.

◐ ☺ ♫ **MAMBO ITALIANO.** 8803 3rd Ave. near corner of 88th St., 833-3891, M 4–11 p.m., Tu–Th 11:30 a.m.–11 p.m., F–Sa 11:30 a.m.–midnight, Su 2–10 p.m., www.nycwebz.com/mambo.

With a hearty, something-for-everyone Italian menu, live entertainment, funny decorations, including huge murals, and a robust party atmosphere, Mambo remains one of the local favorites in Bay Ridge. It's very popular with families and starving teenagers—could it be those family-sized appetizer platters?

MEZZANOTTE. 8408 3rd Ave. bet. 84th and 85th Sts., 238-5000 or 745-4602, Tu–W 5–11 p.m., Th–Sa 5 p.m.–midnight, Su 2–10 p.m., www.nycwebz.com/mezz.

Mezzanotte makes hearty Italian food, with a larger-than-usual selection of seafood dishes. From baked clams oreganata to fried calamari to the linguine with seafood and the zesty grilled veal chop, this is a place to sit back, loosen your belt, and dig in. Call for information about wine tastings.

NEW CORNER RESTAURANT. 7201 8th Ave. near 72nd St., 833-0800, daily noon–11 p.m.

You won't find New Corner just around the corner; it's tucked away in a residential section. But it's worth finding, particularly if you are fond of traditional Italian food. The portions are beyond huge: one bowl of minestrone is a full meal. The menu is à la carte, and most entrées run $13 to $15. Weekend reservations are recommended.

101. 1003 4th Ave. near 101st St., at the foot of the Verrazano Bridge, 833-1313, Su–W noon–midnight, Th–Sa noon–1 a.m.

Young-at-heart customers love the hopping, noisy bar scene here. It's pure Bay Ridge, with a snazzy bar, several big blaring television screens, and so little distance between the bar and restaurant tables that you can wave hello to your pals from across the room. The 101 crowd is mostly well dressed, and comfortably middle class. Restaurant 101 serves Italian fare, such as simple pastas and meat or seafood entrées. In the winter, when the leaves have fallen, you can gaze at great views of New York Harbor. It costs about $45 for dinner for two, including a drink.

PEARL ROOM. 8203 3rd Ave. near 82nd St., 833-6666, M–Th 5–11 p.m., F–Sa 5 p.m.–12:30 a.m., Su 2–10 p.m. Valet parking on weekends.

It's crowded and noisy, but fans say the seafood preparation is excellent (and there are pasta and meat dishes as well). Entrées average about $15.

PHO HOAI. 8616 4th Ave. bet. 86th and 87th Sts., 745-1640, daily 10:30 a.m.–10:30 p.m.

Pho Hoai began on Avenue U and was hailed by an area newspaper as a place where one can have "some of the best, straightforward Vietnamese food in New York." The food is subtly spiced, fresh, and tasty. Try the Beef Balls Noodle Soup, Grilled Chicken with Rice, or Shrimp with Little Salt (gotta love those translations), or one of the excellent vegetable dishes.

PROVENCE EN BOÎTE. 8303 3rd Ave. bet. 83rd and 84th Sts., 759-1515, daily 8 a.m.–8 p.m.

Life's short—so start with dessert. The second you step inside Provence en Boîte, you're face-to-face with a truly mouthwatering display of pastries. Part café, part takeout bakery, and part restaurant, Provence en Boîte is attractively decorated and intimate, which makes it an appealing alternative to some of the larger, more boisterous local eateries. There's a standard bistro menu of such dishes as steak frites. Average entrées are $16. Check out brunch on the weekends.

ST. MICHEL. 7518 3rd Ave. bet. 75th and 76th Sts., 748-4411, Tu–Th 5–9:30 p.m., F–Sa 5:15–10:30 p.m. Reservations are recommended.

Something is right with this picture: romantic and French, but not stuffy. The owners—chef and maître d'—are two brothers from northeastern France, who've created a homey, relaxed atmosphere. Try the escargots, crab cakes, steak au poivre, or fish dishes, but save room for desserts, which shouldn't be missed. Service is casual, and classical music plays in the background. About $45 per person.

SALLY AND GEORGE. 7809 3rd Ave. near 78th St., 680-4615, Tu–Su 9:30 a.m.–10 p.m. Weekend reservations are recommended.

Sally's white-tableclothed ambience provides an alternative to the predominately Italian fare in the area. Try the tasty Middle Eastern dishes, or the mini-soufflé omelet.

SALTY DOG. 7509 3rd Ave. near 75th St., 238-0030, daily 11:30–4 a.m., www.SaltyDogBar.com.

The kids will love this sports bar started by a couple of New York's Bravest. Besides the gorgeous, bright red, antique fire truck in the middle of the restaurant, there's plenty of firefighter memorabilia on the walls, large-screen televisions and monitors—there's almost always a game to watch while you munch on enormous salads, burgers, barbecued chicken and ribs, and brick-oven pizzas. The cost is about $15 for the average meal. Parental advisory: There's a kids' menu, but be aware that serious drinking can go on at night.

T. J. BENTLEY. 7110 3rd Ave. near 71st St., 745-0748, Tu–Th 11:30 a.m.–10 p.m., W–Sa 11:30 a.m.–11 p.m. (dancing till midnight), Su noon–10 p.m. Call for a reservation.

Put on your dancing shoes. There's live music and lots of action nightly. The moderately priced American cuisine averages about $15 per entrée, and you can wait until the music starts, or have a drink at the bar, once part of the famous Luchow's restaurant in Manhattan. Casual attire is acceptable during weekdays, but dress up, please, for weekends. This is serious partying.

TUSCANY GRILL. 8620 3rd Ave. off 86th St., 921-5633, M–W 5–10 p.m., Th–Sa 5–11 p.m., Su 4–9 p.m. Reservations are recommended on weekends.

Since it opened in 1992, Tuscany Grill has garnered rave reviews for its satisfying, high-quality Tuscan cuisine, with entrées running about $18 on average. Try the bruschetta, grilled vegetables, shrimp, and garlic mashed potatoes. Traditional Brooklynites who are wed to red-saucy Italian food say this "ain't really Italian," perhaps a backhanded recommendation. Worth the trip from another neighborhood.

Inexpensive, at under $10 per person

CAFFÈ CAFÉ. 8401 3rd Ave. corner of 84th St., 748-8700, daily 7–2 a.m.

Besides espresso, Caffè Café serves lots of great desserts, flavored coffees, Japanese and Chinese green tea, smoothies, and Italian sodas.

CASABLANCA. 6744 5th Ave. off 67th St., 491-0105, daily 11 a.m.–9 p.m. Cash only.

Lawrence of Arabia would have enjoyed this simple, from-the-desert fare: *harira* (a Moroccan soup), shish kebabs, and flavorful couscous. Today it's the local Lebanese residents who come to this modest eatery. Try the Moroccan salad and *bastilla*, a sweet entrée that's a Moroccan specialty. If you call the day before, you can order *beghrir,* a kind of buttery crepe that's unusually delicious. For less than $8 per entrée, you also get a map of Morocco on the back of your menu, just in case you are feeling lost.

☺ **GOODFELLA'S BRICK OVEN PIZZA.** 9606 3rd Ave. corner of 96th St., 833-6200, M–Sa 11:30 a.m.–11 p.m., Su 2–11 p.m., www.goodfellas.com. Valet parking.

Award-winning, thin-crusted pizza rolls out of Goodfella's, and you have a choice of such toppings as fresh garlic, black olives, and other vegetables. If you like vodka sauce—well, it's the house special.

☺ **HINSCH'S.** 8518 5th Ave. bet. 85th and 86th Sts., 748-2854, M–Sa 7 a.m.–7 p.m., Su 10 a.m.–5 p.m.

For more than eighty-five years there has been an ice-cream parlor at this location, and Hinsch's keeps the tradition alive. Old-fashioned soda fountain and booths will remind you of your childhood—no matter where you grew up. Hinsch's makes their own ice cream and candies and sells a line of candy cigarettes and solid chocolate crayons. Kids will enjoy it.

KARAM. 8519 4th Ave. bet. 85th and 86th Sts., 745-5227, daily 6 p.m.–1 a.m. Cash only.

At this Lebanese restaurant, the lamb–lima bean stew happens to be delicious, but so is the chicken *schwarma* with garlic sauce, baba ghanoush, tabbouleh, hummus, and protein-perfect rice-and-lentil *moujadara*. The ambience is "hole in the wall," but surprisingly fresh, authentic food makes up for it.

LA MAISON DU COUSCOUS. 484 77th St. bet. 4th and 5th Aves., 921-2400, daily noon–midnight, www.lamaisonducouscous.com.

This modest café seats only fourteen or so, it's BYOB, and if there's ambience, it's accidental. But it dishes up decent home-style Moroccan dishes. Start with sautéed spinach, chicken-stuffed pastries, or eggplant-lemon salad. Couscous is the main attraction; you can choose from a variety of toppings. Or order a chicken, lamb, or veggie tagine, a Moroccan stew served in an earthenware pot.

⊘ ☺ **LENTO'S.** 7003 3rd Ave. near Ovington Ave., 745-9197, daily noon–11:30 p.m.

Food and history. Thin-crust lovers, this bar-cum-pizzeria is heaven! (Just make sure you eat on the premises, or the thin crust gets hard.) This restaurant was opened in the 1920s as a speakeasy, by the grandfather of the current owner; check out the old photos over the original booth seats here.

MAZZA PLAZA. 8002 5th Ave. corner of 89th St, 238-9576, daily 6 a.m.–midnight.

Spicy lamb-sausage sandwiches, chicken *schwarma,* and falafels get rave reviews at this plain-Jane Middle Eastern takeout/eat-in place. Also try the *moujadara,* a lentil, rice, and onion dish, and the *kibbe* balls. There's a huge selection of foods, which haven't been altered to please American tastes.

POLONICA. 7214 3rd Ave. bet. 72nd and 73rd Sts., 630-5805, M 3–11 p.m., Tu–Su 11 a.m.–11 p.m. Cash only.

Pretty, red tablecloths with pink lampshades and authentic Polish food give the feel of a country cottage here. Choose from among peach, strawberry, or cherry blinis, thick soulful barley soup, beef stuffed with pickles and carrots, kielbasa and pierogi, stuffed peppers, and more. No alcohol is served.

TANOREEN. 7704 3rd Ave. at 77th St., 748-5600, daily 11 a.m.–11 p.m.

Dress down, go garlic, and treat your taste buds to a flavor sensation. Tanoreen has sent more than one reviewer into rhapsody over 1) breakfasts of veggie fritters and hummus with meat; 2) uncommonly good appetizers, such as stuffed grape leaves, hummus, cauliflower, tabbouleh, and eggplant dishes; 3) everything and anything made of lamb.

SHOPPING

There are two main shopping areas: 86th Street (national chain stores) and 5th Avenue (specialty and ethnic shops).

Ethnic Food Shops

The Eastern European, Mexican, Greek, Turkish, Egyptian, and Italian delis in Bay Ridge give you a UN-worthy choice of authentic ethnic foods to sample. You could buy the same items in a fancy-schmancy specialty store, of course—at twice the price.

Greek

A&S GREEK-AMERICAN MEAT MARKET. 798 5th Ave. near 79th St., 833-1307, M–Sa 8 a.m.–9 p.m., Su 9 a.m.–6 p.m. Cash only.

Bay Ridge has a sizable Greek population, and alongside tuna and chicken salads, this Greek deli sells traditional large, crusty loaves of bread, imported feta cheese, olives, phyllo dough, squid salad, and packaged goods, including Greek incense and cake mixes.

BAY RIDGE BAKERY II CLASSIC PATISSERIE. 7805 5th Ave. near 78th St., 238-0014, daily 9 a.m.–9 p.m. Cash only.

John Nikolopaulos and his family started this spic-and-span bakery several years back. They turn out classic French pastries alongside Greek breads and snacks, such as savory, olive-stuffed, homemade "mama's bread." Choose among beautiful chocolate cakes and fruit pies, cheese Danish, mini pastries, baklava, and feta-cheese turnovers.

HELLAS AMERICAN FOOD MARKET. 8704 4th Ave. at 87th St., 748-2554, daily 8 a.m.–8 p.m. Cash only.

Greek-imported packaged goods, from soaps to cake mixes to sea salt to pastas and grains, are mixed in among the standard American products.

Italian

CANGIANO'S ITALIAN DELI. 6931 3rd Ave., 836-5521, M–Th 9 a.m.–7 p.m., F 8 a.m.–9 p.m., Sa 8 a.m.–7 p.m., Su 8 a.m.–5 p.m.

Cangiano's claims to be the largest Italian deli in Brooklyn and Staten Island. Their motto: "When you see Cangiano's on the label, you have quality on your table."

PANEANTICO. 9124 3rd Ave. off 91st St., 680-2347, Su–Th 6:30 a.m.–11 p.m., F–Sa 6:30 a.m.–midnight.

You can eat in at one of eight little tables, or take out. But don't miss this little store that uses the best bread in Brooklyn, **Royal Crown Bakery**'s light, crusty, brick-oven loaves. Select from sandwiches (try hot *capicollo*: mozzarella and roasted peppers), little artisanal pizzas, and excellent broccoli rabe. The menu is extensive—and the espresso is straight out of Italy. **Piazza Mercato, "The Mar-**

ketplace," down the street is owned by the same food experts. There's a branch in Carroll Gardens, **Brooklyn Bread Café.**

PIAZZA MERCATO. 9204 3rd Ave., 513-0071, M–Sa 9 a.m.–8 p.m., Su 9 a.m.–6 p.m.

Fresh fish, fresh meats, fabulous sausages and cheeses, plus upscale imported Italian food staples are sold here, plus the incomparable breads from the **Royal Crown Bakery** in Bensonhurst. Owned by the same folks who brought you **Paneantico,** this is an excellent resource for quick dinners, picnics, and generally great food.

Middle Eastern

AL-AMIR EASTERN AND AMERICAN GROCERY. 7813 5th Ave. near 78th St., 748-7896, daily 10 a.m.–10 p.m. Cash only.

The huge hookah in the window is a giveaway to the distant roots of this little shop, which greets you with the scent of spices, and signs in swirling Arabic. This is a good place to stock up on Middle Eastern cheeses, breads, olives, lentils, cracked wheat–and tons of atmosphere. The owners, Moroccan-born Fouizia and her Egyptian husband, Abdou Gawad, also sell other necessities of life, such as jellabas, embroidered floor-length dresses, and tinted glasses for mint tea and Turkish coffee.

A&T TURKISH HALAL MEAT MARKET. 7919 5th Ave. near 79th St., 680-5057, M–Sa 9 a.m.–9 p.m., Su 10 a.m.–9 p.m. Cash only.

It looks like a butcher shop from the outside, but venture in and you will find a small Middle Eastern oasis, with open bins of dried fruits and nuts, as well as inexpensive olive oil and Turkish delight candy. The meats, by the way, are "halal," which is to orthodox Muslims what "kosher" is to orthodox Jews.

FAMILY STORE. 6905 3rd Ave. corner of 69th St., 748-0207, M–Sa 8 a.m.–8 p.m.

One of the older Middle Eastern emporiums in this neighborhood, Family Store sells tasty hummus, cheeses, a variety of Middle Eastern breads, and unusual packaged sweets.

Nordic

LESKE'S BAKERY. 7612 5th Ave. bet. 76th and 77th Sts., 680-2323, T–F 6 a.m.–6:30 p.m., Sa 6 a.m.–6 p.m., Su 6 a.m.–3 p.m.

A vestige of Bay Ridge's Norwegian population, Leske's sells a mouthwatering array of authentic Danish pastries, breads, cakes, and cookies, also known as *kringlers yulekarger, vorkarger, limpia* bread, and *kransekagge.*

MEJLANDER AND MULGANNON. 7615 5th Ave. at 76th St., 238-6666, daily 8 a.m.–8 p.m.

Fill your pantry with hard-to-find Scandinavian staples, including delicious, not-too-sweet lingonberry jam, a variety of flatbreads, canned fish balls, and candies.

NORDIC DELICACIES. 6909 3rd Ave. near 69th St., 748-1874, M–Sa 9 a.m.–6 p.m., www.nordicdeli.com.

Nordic Delicacies makes meatballs on Monday, beef stew *lapskaus* on Tuesday, *komper* (potato dumplings) on Wednesday, and so on, throughout the week. Their potato cakes and traditional open-faced sandwiches are great. You can get imported cheeses, WASA breads, Joika reindeer meatballs, Husmor brand fishballs, mackerel fillets smoked in soybean oil, Skansen herring tidbits in wine, and of course healthful cod-liver oil and traditional *Grønnsåpe* (green soap). This and Leske's Bakery are vestiges of the area's original Norwegian presence.

Russian/Polish

ASTORIA EUROPEAN FOODS. 507 84th St. off 5th Ave., 745-5242, daily 8 a.m.–8 p.m.

If you had a Russian grandma, her pantry would probably have looked a lot like this stuffed-like-a-sausage shop. It's crammed with stuffed cabbage and peppers, army-sized loaves of thick-crusted breads, a wall of colorfully wrapped candies from Moscow and matzos from Israel, rows of jarred pickles, and a refrigerator case brimming with sausages and cold cuts. Ukrainian-born owners Alla and Irina recommend eating the soft cheeses with pumpernickel bread.

Other Interesting Neighborhood Shops

A&J POLICE EQUIPMENT. 7115 3rd Ave., 833-5535, M–F 10 a.m.–7 p.m., Sa 10 a.m.–6 p.m.

Here's where the NYPD (yes, the New York Police Department)—and you—can buy police gear. Of course, you need a badge to get the official stuff, but the sign on the window says the general public is welcome. Venture inside to find T-shirts, sweatshirts, and hats with NYPD logos and slogans.

🔘☺ **BROOKLYN GALLERY OF COINS AND STAMPS.** 8725 4th Ave. near 87th St., M–F 9 a.m.–5:30 p.m., Sa 9 a.m.–4 p.m., www.brooklyngallery.com.

This small thirty-year-old shop is a wonderful resource for beginner-to-experienced collectors of stamps, coins, antique toys, world's fair items, trains, and baseball cards. Plus, there are some seven hundred reference books for every level and interest. People come from all over the tristate area to buy and sell.

CHOC-OH-LOT-PLUS. 7911 5th Ave. near 79th St., 748-2100, M–W and F 10 a.m.–6 p.m., Th 10 a.m.–8 p.m., Sa 10 a.m.–5 p.m., Su noon–4 p.m.

This mom-and-pop specialty store sells more than five hundred plastic candy molds and several dozen Wilton cake molds in the form of Superman, Batman, Sesame Street characters, and other popular figures. There are bins of inexpensive cake toppings, and over 250 varieties of Mylar balloons.

DAN SACKS FABRICS. 8214 3rd Ave. near 82nd St., 748-0059, M–Sa 9 a.m.–4 p.m. Cash and checks only.

One of Brooklyn's best (and most colorful) fabric shops, Dan Sacks sells bolts of just about everything short of lightning. You can purchase cotton goods, upholstery fabric, velvet and velveteen, lace, and more, at prices that run about half of comparable goods elsewhere. The store is run by two elderly sisters who are very knowledgeable, very quirky, and very endearing.

GRASSROOTS. 8505 3rd Ave. corner of 85th St., 745-9679, daily 10 a.m.–9 p.m.

Stop and enjoy yummy panini sandwiches and a glass of healthy, fresh-squeezed juice (try the strawberry-banana-coconut) at this rustic little getaway health café and antique shop decorated with lovely, worn bits and folkloric pieces from a simpler era. Each piece speaks volumes—a rusty gate, antique tin canisters, an old red wooden bench; it feels more like SoHo or Vermont. Prices are moderate.

HARRY'S P & G FURNITURE. 241 Bay Ridge Ave. bet. 2nd and 3rd Aves., 745-0730, daily 8 a.m.–5:30 p.m., M and Th 8 a.m.–8:30 p.m.

Every ten days new merchandise arrives at this large warehouse that handles overstocks, including leather and contemporary styles. Most of the merchandise comes from large department stores or straight from the North Carolina manufacturers. Sofas, chairs, tables, and bedroom sets are 20 percent less than at retail outlets.

I. KLEINFELD AND SON. 8206 5th Ave. bet. 82nd and 83rd Sts., 833-1100, Tu and Th 11 a.m.–9 p.m., W and F 11 a.m.–6 p.m., Sa 10 a.m.–6 p.m., www.kleinfelds.com.

One of New York's most famous specialty stores, Kleinfeld's is a magnet for thousands of brides each year. They come from all over the United States, Europe, and China for the enormous selection of gowns, accessories, and evening and dress wear for the bridal party. The main store has evening dresses, clothes for the mother of the bride or groom, formal wear, and more than a thousand wedding sample gowns. The average gown costs between $1,500 and $5,000. An appointment is required. Allow six months for the gown to be measured, fitted, and sewn. **Zeller's Tuxedo** for the gents is across the street.

JET BEAUTY SUPPLIES. 8301 5th Ave. corner of 83rd St., 748-3678, M 10 a.m.–7 p.m., Tu–F 9 a.m.–7 p.m., Sa 10 a.m.–6 p.m., Su 11 a.m.–5 p.m. (Sister store **Zoe** is in Greenpoint at 111 Greenpoint Ave.)

JOHN T. JOHNSTON'S JUKEBOX CLASSICS AND VINTAGE SLOT MACHINES. 6742 5th Ave. near 67th St., 833-8455, by appointment only or Sa 1–5 p.m., www.jukeboxclassics.com.

You don't have to be a connoisseur to love John T. Johnston's colorful collection of antique gumball machines and jukeboxes. Rock stars, Fortune 500 CEOs, and other deep-pocket types have all come to Johnston's for Wurlitzer jukeboxes dating from the 1930s and 1940s ($20,000 for the vintage models; reproductions starting at about $2,000). For those of you on a tighter budget, there are over 150 Betty Boop items (John claims to have the largest Boop selection in the country), as well as antique slot, vending, and arcade machines, cash registers, syrup dispensers, and neon signs and clocks.

LA BARONESSA. 8418 3rd Ave. bet. 84th and 85th Sts., 921-4432, M–Sa 11 a.m.–6 p.m.

La Baronessa specializes in home and personal gifts. You will find hand-painted ceramics and pottery, découpage items, and silver platters, in addition to evening bags and scarves. Gift baskets are a specialty and can be ordered by phone.

☺ **LITTLE LORDS AND LITTLE LADIES.** 8217 5th Ave. corner of 82nd St., 748-4366, M–F 10 a.m.–6 p.m., Sa 10 a.m.–6:30 p.m.

Doting grandmothers, take note: Here you will find baby and children's clothes that will remind you of picture-perfect Victorian children—starched bibs, lacy white dresses, divine dress-up outfits, some imported, for boys and girls ages five to ten.

MATERNITY PROFILE. 7311 3rd Ave. near 73rd St., 680-8399, M–Sa 10:30 a.m.–6 p.m., Su noon–4 p.m., www.maternityprofile.com.

Pregnant or nursing women will find a good selection of career and casual clothes at moderate prices here. This is one of the few maternity stores in Brooklyn, outside of the Orthodox Jewish neighborhoods. The service is friendly. And check the Web site!

🌐☺ **NOVEL IDEA BOOKSTORE.** 8415 3rd Ave. bet. 84th and 85th Sts., 833-5115, daily 10 a.m.–8 p.m. Closed Su in summers.

This is a wonderful neighborhood asset. People get together here to exchange information about what they are reading, as well as neighborhood gossip. Novel is chockablock with great reading, too. Novels, children's books, Brooklyn history, poetry, cookbooks, and mysteries are on display at this welcoming bookstore. The carpet and comfortable chairs make you feel at home instantly, as do founders Mrs. Heaney and her beautiful daughters, who, together, seem like characters out of *Little Women*.

☺ **ONCE UPON A CHILD.** 7912 5th Ave. near 72nd St., 491-0300, M–W 10 a.m.–7 p.m., Th–F 10 a.m.–8 p.m., Sa 10 a.m.–6 p.m., Su 11 a.m.–5 p.m.

This secondhand children's clothing store carries a large selection of brand-name children's apparel up to size 6X. The price can't be beat: OshKosh jeans that cost $20 new can be had for as little as $6. Car seats, cribs, and playpens meet current safety standards and are priced at less than half retail.

☺ ☺ **PANDA SPORT.** 9213 5th Ave. near 92nd St., 238-4919, M–Sa 11 a.m.–7 p.m., Th 11 a.m.–9 p.m., Su 11 a.m.–4 p.m., www.gopandasport.com.

In winter you'll find top-of-the-line ski equipment (including rentals), trained staff who know how to tune skis, and a schedule of ski trips that you can sign up for, whether you are single or traveling with the family. For beach bums, Panda's got rafts, wet suits, kid-sized vests, goggles, and surfboards. In-line skaters can find lots of gear, including a range of high-end and highly specialized stunt skates.

☺ **SWEE' PEAS.** 8416 3rd Ave. corner of 84th St., 680-5766, Tu–Sa 11 a.m.–6 p.m.

Swee' Peas carries lovely, upscale, special-occasion clothing for children. Perfect for communions, bridal parties, and first birthday parties with the grand-parents.

THE HUTCH. 8211 5th Ave. near 82nd St., 748-4574 or 800-303-9702, Tu–Sa 10 a.m.–6 p.m.

The Hutch sells a large selection of fine gift items, including crystal, silver-ware, place settings, imported ceramic bowls, and silver picture frames. You'll find Herend hand-painted porcelain, Lalique, and Mdme. Alexander dolls here as well.

☺ ☺ **THE PAINTED POT.** 8009 3rd Ave. at 80th St., 491-6411, Su–M 11 a.m.–7 p.m., Tu–W 11 a.m.–9 p.m., Th–F 11 a.m.–10 p.m., Sa 11 a.m.–9 p.m.

A ceramics studio where you can paint and create personalized pottery. (Also in Carroll Gardens.)

☺ **THREADZ FOR WOMEN AND THREADZ FOR MEN.** 8503 and 8507 3rd Ave. near 85th St., 745-1500, M noon–7 p.m., Tu–W and Sa 11 a.m.–7 p.m., Th–F 1 p.m.–8 p.m., Su noon–5 p.m., www.Threadz Online.com.

Here's a trendsetting Bay Ridge clothing store that keeps pace with hot new fashions for slim, trendy young women and men. Designers include Miss Sixty, Biscote, Elita, and Free People. Reasonable prices, personable service.

VILLAGE IRISH IMPORTS. 8508 3rd Ave. near 85th St., 238-2582, M and Sa 10 a.m.–6 p.m., Tu–W 10 a.m.–6:30 p.m., Th–F 10 a.m.–7p.m., www.irishgiftstoyou.com.

This little shop proudly sells things for which an Irish expatriate might yearn, from Irish imported china and foodstuffs to dolls, crests, and clothing.

ACCOMMODATIONS

COMFORT INN GREGORY. (See p. 12.)

3

Bedford-Stuyvesant

ABOUT BEDFORD-STUYVESANT

Bedford-Stuyvesant is one of New York's best-known black neighborhoods, and the largest center of African-American life in Brooklyn.

In a sense, Bedford-Stuyvesant is two neighborhoods grafted together: smaller Stuyvesant Heights, a landmark district, and the grittier, generally poorer area that was once known simply as Bedford. Even "liberal" New Yorkers lump this huge area together in the sound bite "Bed-Stuy," as though there were one homogeneous lifestyle here. There's not, of course. There's as broad a range of education, income, attitude, religiousness, and so on in Bedford-Stuyvesant as you will find in other large neighborhoods—say, Williamsburg or Flatbush.

So, clear your mind of preconceptions and go take a look. The historic brownstones are an architectural feast. You can follow a long thread of American history at many of the area's churches; some founded before the Civil War. Churches give a palpable sense of the powerful community ties here. Certainly, when you visit Bedford-Stuyvesant, you also can't miss seeing the human cost of poverty and related urban ills. There are boarded-up storefronts on Fulton Street, and an unemployment rate that exceeds New York's average. In a city that usually sports a vegetable-and-fruit stand every few blocks, it's hard to find a fresh peach or apple here without making a special trip to the supermarket. There's a remarkable dearth of amenities that elsewhere are taken for granted.

As in Harlem, these days you see Dumpsters on the street. (Dumpsters are usually a sign, in brownstone Brooklyn, of renovations and urban renewal.) Who's moving in? All types. Some people are returning to their Brooklyn roots here; others hail from Manhattan, New Jersey, and the southern United States. Not a few are just moving a little further up Fulton Street, propelled by rising real estate prices in nearby Clinton Hill and Fort Greene. The housing stock is the big lure. It is lost on no one—not wary longtime residents, nor potential

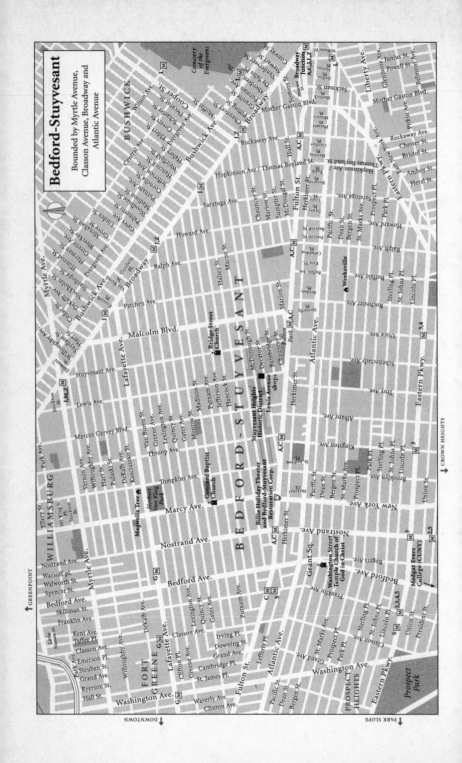

home buyers, and certainly not real estate agents—that there's a large inventory of brownstones here that are the same vintage and quality (some bigger and better) as those in Fort Greene and Park Slope. And they can be purchased at a fraction of the price.

Longtime homeowners express concern about having a "different" kind of person—not just white, but *richer*—moving in, and possibly outpricing their own next generation. That pattern has occurred repeatedly in other neighborhoods. Gentrification, if it ever reaches a tipping point in Bedford-Stuyvesant, will bring change. There goes the neighborhood.

HOW IT GOT ITS NAME Bedford and Stuyvesant were two separate communities until the middle of the twentieth century. While they still retain some of their original differences, the combined name has been in use since the 1930s. Some experts say it gained prominence in 1931, when the *Brooklyn Eagle* reported on racial conflict between blacks in Bedford and whites in Stuyvesant; others suggest that it was coined by the Brooklyn Con Edison Company.

BY SUBWAY A or C train to Nostrand Avenue for Restoration Plaza, or to the Utica Avenue–Fulton Street stop for Stuyvesant Heights; A, C, and G trains and the LIRR to Nostrand Avenue stop.

Stuyvesant Heights

This well-maintained twelve-block landmark district boasts perhaps the largest stock of Gothic, Victorian, French, and other classic brownstones in New York City. The homeowners include lawyers, judges, businesspeople, teachers, and civil servants; some families have lived here for several generations. The middle-class residential fabric of the area is strong. Central to the area is petite **Fulton Park,** site of an annual art show.

Only recently, however, have some amenities and retail shops opened to service this community. An independent bookstore, furniture restoration shop, informal café, and a good restaurant sprouted along Lewis Avenue, one little action-packed block that's fast becoming a new community hub in Stuyvesant Heights.

If you can, take the annual **Brownstoners of Bedford-Stuyvesant House Tour.** Otherwise, just take a walk through Stuyvesant Heights along such dignified streets as Chauncey, Macon, Decatur, Bainbridge, MacDonough, Hancock, Jefferson, and Stuyvesant, and stop at the **Lewis Avenue shops**.

Other Highlights

CHURCHES It would be hard to overestimate the importance of the churches in Bedford-Stuyvesant. They provide a historical memory and continuity for the community, create social service programs to fill the vacuums left by inadequate government programs, and help knit together the area's social fabric. Among several outstanding institutions, the **Bridge Street African Wesleyan Methodist Episcopal Church** is the oldest African-American church in Brooklyn, dating from 1818. The pre-Civil-War-era **Siloam Presbyterian Church** was one of several stops in Brooklyn for slaves fleeing north via the Underground Railroad. The activist **Concord Baptist Church** has one of the largest black congregations in the United States, estimated at about twelve thousand.

HISTORY AND ARCHITECTURE Visit the reconstructed nineteenth-century houses and museum at **Weeksville,** a free-black community well before emancipation. Take a trip down memory lane by visiting the **historical homes of celebrities,** such as musician Eubie Blake, politician Shirley Chisholm, writer June Jordan, athlete Jackie Robinson, and singer Lena Horne. The official New York City landmarks in this area are a varied lot: the incomparable remnants of a free-black community during the era of slavery, the Weeksville houses; vast elegant apartment buildings designed by Montrose Morris, with grandiose names such as the **Alhambra, Renaissance, and Imperial Apartments;** educational institutions that played a role in the earliest history of public schooling in New York City, such as **Boys' High School** and **Girls' High School;** churches such as **St. Bartholomew's** and **St. George's;** the ornate **23rd Regiment Armory**—and a tree, the **Magnolia Grandiflora.**

CONTEMPORARY CULTURE Highlights include the **Billie Holiday Theater,** which produces shows written and performed by African-American playwrights, **Skylight Gallery** art shows, and the magnificent **gospel choirs** at Sunday church services. The weeklong **International African Arts Festival** in July is famous for the three-hundred-plus vendors it attracts from around the world and the continuous entertainment by Africans and African-Americans.

AFRICAN DIASPORA ON NOSTRAND AVENUE AND FULTON STREET The range of the goods along Nostrand Avenue attests to the vibrancy and cultural richness of the neighborhood, frequented by Africans, West Indians, and African-Americans alike. If you are longing for, or curious about, the sounds, smells, style of African and Caribbean cultures, you can find a good sampling here, ranging from vegetarian Jamaican cuisine, fresh bottled juices, patties and Trinidadian roti, to cow's feet or Senegalese men's suits. At the intersection of Bedford and Fulton, there are several blocks of halal restaurants, bakeries, and Islamic religious shops.

☛ **TIP:** You can obtain an excellent tourist map of the area, "Bedford-Stuyvesant: A Cultural Heritage Guide," from the Brooklyn Chamber of Commerce and many local shops. Visit www.ibrooklyn.com/fultonfirst.

👁 What's **NEW?**

Fulton Street's Changing

As noted above, Stuyvesant Heights is slowly changing.

Fulton Street has been the subject of intense study and community planning (like Smith Street, Atlantic Avenue, Coney Island, and other rejuvenating areas). The Brooklyn Chamber of Commerce has launched a three-year planning economic revitalization booster shot, called "Fulton First." Community participants include several we've described in this book: **Akwaaba Enterprises, Bedford-Stuyvesant Restoration Corporation, Braggin' About Brooklyn, Brownstoners, International African Arts Festival, MoCADA, 651 Arts,** and **Society for the Preservation of Weeksville and Bedford-Stuyvesant History**. Changes in Fort Greene and even the development of the Atlantic Terminal Mall affect Bedford-Stuyvesant.

HISTORICAL NOTES

The two communities that comprise Bedford and Stuyvesant Heights today have very different histories. Bedford was originally a Dutch hamlet established in 1663. Even before the 1827 abolition of slavery in New York State, a free-black community thrived in the area. Bedford was also home to the Brooklyn Howard Colored Orphan Asylum (1866) and the Zion Home for the Colored Aged (1869).

To the east of Bedford, Stuyvesant was a fancier community built during the 1890s by the staunch upper middle class. F. W. Woolworth, the dime-store titan, lived here, at 209 Jefferson Avenue. The architecture is lavish, and many remaining structures recall Stuyvesant's high-rolling past: the Masonic Lodge, the fabulously ornate Boys' High School, the Renaissance and Alhambra Apartments, and Fulton Park, designed to be reminiscent of London's Bloomsbury Square.

Through the 1930s, Bedford, along with Harlem, was a major destination for rural southern blacks and West Indians. Many bought homes in the area. When the Brooklyn Navy Yard expanded during the 1940s, a huge influx of workers created intense housing pressure in both Bedford and Stuyvesant Heights. Many of the area's new residents were African-American or Caribbean islanders, and the now-familiar syndrome of "fright-and-flight" occurred. (Racist scare tactics used by unscrupulous real estate agents in a blockbusting campaign led to the diminishing white population who sold their homes, fearing that the neighborhood was "changing" and that their homes would lose value. Indeed, as building prices plummeted, slumlords purchased and then parceled residential buildings into small apartments, without attending to upkeep. Over time, services diminished and the area experienced a downward spiral.) In the wave of inner-city riots that occurred across the nation in the 1960s, Bedford-Stuyvesant "blew up" in riots twice, following the killing of a young boy by a policeman and following the assassination of the Reverend Martin Luther King Jr. After a tour of the area, Robert Kennedy helped establish the Bedford-Stuyvesant Restoration Corporation, the nation's first community-development corporation.

Kidstuff

☺ The **Brooklyn Children's Museum** in nearby Crown Heights is one of the best places in all of New York City for preschool and grade school–age children. The **Magnolia Tree Earth Center** and **Weeksville** are naturals for an educational family visit. There are also several parks and playgrounds in the neighborhood. The **International African Arts Festival** in July is a huge attraction, with contests, performances, crafts, and other special entertainment for children. If your kids appreciate architecture, history, and soul food, there is plenty here for them to enjoy.

POINTS OF CULTURAL INTEREST

SPECIAL EVENTS.

Fulton Art Fair, three consecutive weekends at Fulton Park (June and July); Juneteenth (June, see p. 296); International African Arts Festival at Boys' and Girls' High School, featuring one week of children's and evening entertainment and hundreds of vendors (July); Weeksville Family Festival (August); fall house tour organized by Brownstoners of Bedford-Stuyvesant (October).

Contemporary Bedford-Stuyvesant

AFRICAN STREET FESTIVAL. See International African Arts Festival, below.

BEDFORD-STUYVESANT RESTORATION CORPORATION. At Restoration Plaza, 1368 Fulton St. at New York Ave., 636-6900 or 636-6906, www.restorationarts.org.

The enclosed mall and office complex called Restoration Plaza, which is located in the renovated Sheffield Farms milk-bottling plant, is an important piece of recent Bedford-Stuyvesant history. The nation's first community-development corporation, the Bedford-Stuyvesant Restoration Corporation was founded in 1967 with the bipartisan support of senators Robert F. Kennedy and Jacob K. Javits. Constructed with private and public capital and community resources, it has been a visible force in improving the neighborhood's business and residential communities. Among its achievements: restoration of the exteriors of thousands of homes, underwriting of home mortgages, creation of jobs, assisting local entrepreneurship, improving health services, and a range of cultural and recreational programs. Restoration Plaza is the unofficial "downtown" of the neighborhood, with its concentration of such services as utilities and post office.

The **Billie Holiday Theater** and **Restoration Dance Theater** are located within the complex, as much a part of the **Center for Arts and Culture** at Bedford-Stuyvesant Restoration Corporation (636-6949) as is the **Skylight Art Gallery** on the third floor. Its mission is to help preserve and promote the artistic contributions of African people. Offerings include the **Youth Arts Academy** (employing professional artists for after-school and artist-in-residence programs) and the annual **Under One Sun** and **Phat Tuesday** programs.

BEDFORD-STUYVESANT YMCA. 1121 Bedford Ave. at Monroe St., 789-1497.

The "Bed-Stuy Y" has been a landmark and resource for thousands of neighborhood youth since its founding in 1889. Known once as the "White Y" (the "Black Y" was located on Carlton Avenue), the institution now serves a racially diverse clientele and is home to championship swimming and basketball teams as well as the "I Have a Dream" program sponsored by financier Paul Tudor Jones. Its pool, basketball courts, fitness center, and summer camps are extremely popular. Membership is a bit over $400 per year for a family, about the cost of a couple of months at a Manhattan "gym" without all the programs. The Y is now undergoing a $7 million rehabilitation and rebuilding.

BILLIE HOLIDAY THEATER. 1368 Fulton St. at New York Ave., Restoration Plaza, 636-0918, www.the billieholiday.org. Call for a schedule or to get on the mailing list.

Described as a "theater with a soul and a mission," the Billie Holiday Theater is home to one of New York's professional resident black theater companies. Its forty-week season of shows that are written by African-American playwrights and showcase Equity actors gets consistently good reviews from critics in the major New York dailies. Among the stars who've worked there are Samuel L. Jackson, Debbie Allen, producer Samm-Art Williams, actress Tichina Arnold, award-winning scenic designer Felix Cochren, and many others. About thirty thousand people a year attend performances here.

BROWNSTONERS OF BEDFORD-STUYVESANT ANNUAL HOUSE TOUR. 953-7328 or 574-1979. Reserve in advance; tickets cost about $15.

On the third weekend in October, the volunteers of Brownstoners of Bedford-Stuyvesant conduct a house tour of the interiors and gardens of several handsome restored nineteenth-century brownstones in the area. The activist

Brownstoners group has included prominent Bedford-Stuyvesant activists: a judge, an airline executive, a lawyer, and other professionals committed to the neighborhood. Their motto: "Come Home to Bedford-Stuyvesant."

Free! GOSPEL MUSIC.

You can attend Sunday gospel services in Bedford-Stuyvesant at: **Concord Baptist** and **Bethany Baptist** churches. Or try **New Life Tabernacle** at the corner of Bedford Avenue and Sterling Place. In other neighborhoods, at **Institutional Church of God in Christ** in Fort Greene and **Brooklyn Tabernacle** in Downtown Brooklyn; **International Revival Tabernacle** (346-8839) or **Washington Temple Church of God in Christ** (789-7545).

☺ KIDFLIX Film Festival. Fulton Park. Fridays in August. Free.

MoCADA sponsors an outdoor film festival geared to six- to twelve-year-olds and their families. Partnering with the African Film Festival, they show movies that have a focus on the youth of the African Diaspora. Bring a picnic and have a fun family night out.

FULTON ART FAIR. Fulton Park. Fulton St. bet. Stuyvesant and Lewis Aves., 707-1457.

Organized by the Fulton Art Consortium, this summer art fair has been happening for over forty years. It shows primarily art from the African Diaspora and includes occasional performances.

☺ INTERNATIONAL AFRICAN ARTS FESTIVAL. Boys' and Girls' High School, 1700 Fulton St. near Utica Ave., 467-1700, www.iaafestival.com. Admissions fee.

Started in 1971, this July celebration is a feast of African-American and African Diasporan cultures. A traditional African libation ceremony officially opens the festival each year. One of the main attractions is the "African Marketplace"—the largest Afrocentric market in the United States, with hundreds of international vendors selling art and artifacts, crafts, clothing and wearable art, jewelry, home furnishings, books, musical instruments, toys, and more. The program is huge. Live entertainment includes musicians from Africa and reggae, calypso, soca, Latin, jazz, gospel, hip-hop, and R&B artists—some with worldwide reputations. And you can see dance, comedy, fashion, and martial-arts shows, too. One year, a Harriet Tubman character in full costume walked around talking with children. There's an annual youth talent search, African dance workshops, "Living Legend" awards, and scholarship events. Political organizers gravitate toward the Kawaida Symposium, chaired by Maulana Karenga, the creator of the holiday Kwanzaa.

There's food galore: soul food, Caribbean, African, Latin, Asian, and vegetarian dishes. Weekend events attract up to fifty thousand people. See the Web site for a fascinating history of the event.

INTERNATIONAL REVIVAL TABERNACLE. 2260 Pacific St. bet. Eastern Pkwy. and Rockaway Ave., 346-8839.

If you want to experience gospel music in its home setting, come here on a Sunday morning. Reverend Timothy Wright, known for both his live concerts and recordings of gospel music, recently moved here from Washington Temple.

JACKIE ROBINSON SCHOOL. 46 McKeever Pl. bet. Sullivan Pl. and Montgomery St., 693-6655.

This school (in nearby Crown Heights) was the site of the home of barrier-breaking baseball player Jackie Roosevelt Robinson (1919–1972). Robinson was one of the most famous of the Brooklyn Dodgers who helped them win pennants in 1947, 1949, 1952, 1953, and a World Series Championship in 1955.

MEDGAR EVERS COLLEGE. 1650 Bedford Ave. near Montgomery St. (Crown Heights), 270-4900, www.mec.cuny.edu.

Medgar Evers College, a senior college of the City University of New York, was founded in 1970 and named after civil-rights hero Medgar Evers, who was slain while working for the NAACP in Mississippi. The college describes itself as more than an educational institution: "A family whose members strive to fulfill their namesake's legacy through a commitment to the educational empowerment of the African Diaspora community."

With a faculty list studded with PhDs and other advanced degrees from well-known institutions including Columbia, University of North Carolina, New School for Social Research, and NYU, Medgar Evers offers bachelor's degrees and certificate programs to about five thousand students enrolled in schools of business, liberal arts, science, health, and technology. It has nearly a dozen academic centers, including ones for Caribbean Research, Black Literature, Law and Social Justice, and the DuBois-Bunche Center for Public Policy. The college offers continuing education classes at Metro Tech Center and in Sunset Park.

For a decade, academic researchers based at Medgar Evers have been the recipients of NASA-related federal grants for climate and weather analysis and aerospace science research, generating opportunities for students of color.

Medgar Evers is expanding, with a new student building and a new academic complex.

Activities that are open to the community include workshops organized by the National Black Writers Conference with some well-known authors.

🎓 **MIDDLE COLLEGE HIGH SCHOOL** at Medgar Evers College. 1186 Carroll St., 703-5400.

Located on the campus of Medgar Evers College, Middle College High School offers about seven hundred students beautiful facilities and an accelerated program that gives them the chance to complete two years of college courses while they are still in high school. The majority of students are African-American; graduation rate is 60 percent. (Source: *New York City's Best Public High Schools: A Parents' Guide: Second Edition,* by C. Hemphill with P. Wheaton and J. Wayans.)

MOCADA. MUSEUM OF CONTEMPORARY AFRICAN DIASPORAN ARTS.

SIMMONS AFRICAN ARTS MUSEUM. 1063 Fulton St. bet. Classon and Grand Aves., 230-0933. Call to check hours.

An unusual collection of contemporary African art and masks from twelve West African nations forms the nucleus of this neighborhood art gallery. The pieces are part of the private, nonfunded collection of the owner, who has traveled and collected in Africa for more than thirty years. He presents educational exhibits designed primarily for community residents, but all visitors are welcome.

Historic Bedford-Stuyvesant

ALHAMBRA APARTMENTS. 500–518 Nostrand Ave. and 29–33 Macon St.

An example of upper-middle-class Brooklyn apartment living, this landmarked building is "notable for its six towers, steep roof slopes, gables, loggias, arcades and lively terra-cotta detail," according to the *Guide to New York City Landmarks.* It was the first of three in the area commissioned by prominent developer Louis F. Seitz around 1890 and designed by Montrose Morris.

🎓 **BOYS' AND GIRLS' HIGH SCHOOL.** 1700 Fulton St. near Utica Ave., 467-1700. The interior may be viewed by appointment.

This 1974 building, the largest school in the neighborhood and the site of many important community events, has a special significance. In 1990 this was Nelson Mandela's first stop during his three-day visit to New York. The exterior artwork includes a powerful mural done by Ernest Crichlow, depicting the struggles of African-Americans from slavery to present times. Inside, works by such African-American artists as Norman Lewis line the corridors.

Today, the school draws kids from some of the lowest-performing middle schools in the city; on the other hand, some graduates have been admitted to such schools as Columbia, Tufts, Dartmouth, Cornell, and Brown. The sometimes-controversial principal has been described by the media as a stern but effective disciplinarian.

BOYS' HIGH SCHOOL. 832 Marcy Ave. bet. Putnam Ave. and Madison St.

Boys' High School's ornate architecture reflects its importance in society as a highly recognized public educational institution of late nineteenth-century Brooklyn. This Romanesque Revival landmark building boasts a tower, a campanile, and other architectural flourishes.

GIRLS' HIGH SCHOOL. 475 Nostrand Ave. bet. Halsey and Macon Sts.

The oldest surviving high school building in New York City, this 1886 Victorian Gothic structure was built about ten years after the establishment of Brooklyn's first public high school, old Central Grammar School. Brooklyn's population was expanding rapidly, and this single-sex institution was their answer to school overcrowding. A perennial problem, it seems.

HISTORICAL HOMES OF CELEBRITIES.

Scattered throughout the large area covered by Bedford-Stuyvesant you can see the historical homes of celebrities. Musician Eubie Blake (1883–1993) lived at 284 Stuyvesant Avenue. Politician Shirley Chisholm, the nation's first black woman in the U.S. House of Representatives, lived at 420 Ralph Avenue. Business leader Earl Graves lived at 376 Macon Street. Activist and writer June Jordan (1936–2002) lived at 681 Hancock Street. Athlete Jackie Robinson (1919–1972), who broke the race barrier in baseball, lived at 526 MacDonough Street. Singer Lena Horne lived at 180 Chauncey Street. (Based in part on "Bedford-Stuyvesant: A Cultural Heritage Guide" tourist map; you can obtain one at www.ibrooklyn.com/fultonfirst.)

IMPERIAL APARTMENTS. 1198 Pacific St. and 1327 Bedford Ave. corner of Bedford Ave. and Pacific St.

An ornate, upscale 1892 apartment building erected by the architect-developer team of Montrose Morris and Louis F. Seitz, the Imperial was occupied by the affluent middle class at the turn of the nineteenth century. Many people were building brownstones in the late 1800s; apartments represented a different concept in urban living.

☺ **MAGNOLIA GRANDIFLORA AND MAGNOLIA TREE EARTH CENTER.** 677 Lafayette Ave. opposite Herbert Van King Park, 387-2116. Call for hours and appointment.

This environmental education center, established in 1972, is famous for its lovely magnolia tree transplanted from North Carolina and now an official New York City landmark. People come from all over to enjoy the various exhibits at the George Washington Carver Gallery. The Earth Center provides programs on recycling and conservation to more than two thousand schoolchildren a year, and has organized the planting of thousands of trees—including sycamores, ginkgos, and honey locusts—in the area. The staff also provides assistance to community groups on greening projects and care of street trees. Magnolia is intensely committed to improving the quality of life in African-American communities.

🎓 PUBLIC SCHOOLS.

Among those considered to be New York City's "best public elementary schools" are PS 21 (180 Chauncey Street) and PS 308 (616 Quincy Street). Call 636-3239 for information about districtwide programs for gifted children. (Source: *New York City's Best Public Elementary Schools: A Parents' Guide,* 2002, by C. Hemphill with P. Wheaton.)

RENAISSANCE APARTMENTS. 488 Nostrand Ave. bet. Hancock and Halsey Sts.

Renovated in 1995–96, the Renaissance was first built in 1892 by Louis F. Seitz, who commissioned architect Montrose Morris for this third large apartment building in the area. Seitz, a prominent developer of his time, built a number of important apartment buildings in Brooklyn.

SOCIETY FOR THE PRESERVATION OF WEEKSVILLE AND BEDFORD-STUYVESANT HISTORY. See **Weeksville**, below.

STUYVESANT HEIGHTS HISTORIC DISTRICT.

This historic district within the larger Bedford-Stuyvesant neighborhood is roughly bounded by Stuyvesant Avenue to the east and Tomkins Avenue to the west, along MacDonough Street. It also includes sections of Decatur and Bainbridge Streets, between Lewis and Stuyvesant Avenues. (See p. 63.)

THE 23RD REGIMENT ARMORY. 1322 Bedford Ave. at Atlantic Ave.

An 1890s architectural monument to the military, this vast, impressive armory was designed by local Brooklyn architects Fowler & Hough, with assistance from New York State architect Isaac Perry. It is considered the most outstanding of all Brooklyn armories. Today it serves as a social services center.

WEEKSVILLE (HUNTERFLY ROAD) HOUSES. 1698–1708 Bergen St. bet. Rochester and Buffalo Aves., 756-5250, www.weeksvillesociety.org. Call for hours.

Imagine a woodland area when you make the pilgrimage here. These four frame homes are remnants of nineteenth-century Weeksville, a prominent freeblack community in central Brooklyn. The houses date from the period following emancipation in New York State (1827) and after the Civil War. To learn about Weeksville is to learn about the proud and difficult odyssey that American blacks made from slavery to freedom. The figures associated with Weeksville include Moses R. Cobb, a black policeman born into slavery in North Carolina who is said to have walked from North Carolina to New York City after emancipation; Major Martin Delaney, grandson of an enslaved West African prince, who became active in the Underground Railroad and wrote for the Weeksville newspaper, *Freedman's Torchlight*; and Dr. Susan Smith McKinney-Steward, the third black female physician in the nation, born in Weeksville in 1847.

The Weeksville houses were discovered in 1968, when historian James Hurley set out on an aerial exploration over an area that nineteenth-century documents indicated had been a thriving black community. He and pilot Joseph Haynes noted an oddly situated lane that did not coincide with the modern block layout. What they found were four frame houses, circa 1840 to 1883, located on the old Hunterfly Road. Since that exciting moment, the houses have been restored and declared landmarks, a small museum has been created, and the Society for the Preservation of Weeksville and Bedford-Stuyvesant History has produced award-winning films, traveling exhibits, and educational materials dedicated to the rediscovery of black cultural roots in Brooklyn. Their excellent booklet on Weeksville is a must-read for people interested in historic Brooklyn. New research is being conducted, and new school and public programs developed for the opening of the Houses in 2004. Weeksville continues to be a "must-see" and a rarity among New York City's historical sites.

Free! ☺ **WEEKSVILLE ANNUAL FAMILY FESTIVAL.** Hunterfly Road Houses, 756-5250, first Sa in August, www.weeksvillesociety.org/programs.html.

A free all-day annual event with music and dance performances, arts and crafts workshops, face painting, storytelling, Black Cowboys Rodeo, pony rides, petting zoo, and the Rappin' Fireman, it celebrates the lives of ordinary black people by highlighting traditions that have been passed down from generation to generation. Hear African storytelling, early African-American spirituals and slave songs, and participate in community quilt-making, blacksmith activities, and other art workshops throughout the day.

Churches

There are many important historic churches in the neighborhood, some founded as early as the seventeenth and eighteenth centuries. The following lists several of architectural and historical significance. However, the brief survey below doesn't do full justice to the extraordinary histories of the oldest churches and their role in supporting the black community of Brooklyn through the centuries-long travails of slavery, racism, race riots, discrimination, and poverty. The histories of these institutions provide a window onto the black experience in New York. (For more on churches, see "Bedford-Stuyvesant: A Cultural Heritage Guide" tourist map; you can obtain one at www.ibrooklyn.com/fultonfirst. For in-depth information, we suggest taking a tour of the area. See p. 65.)

BEREAN MISSIONARY BAPTIST CHURCH. 29 Bergen St. bet. Rochester and Utica Aves., 778-6987, Su 7:45, 9:15, and 11 a.m.

Founded in 1635, Berean was originally located near Weeksville, a free-black community, but included both blacks and whites. It subsequently became an all-black congregation. It has been at this location for over a century, since 1898.

BETHANY BAPTIST CHURCH. 460 Marcus Garvey Blvd. bet. Decatur and MacDonough Sts., 455-8400, Su 8 a.m. and 11 a.m.

Founded in 1883, this was the first black church to move into Bedford-Stuyvesant during the great northward migration of rural blacks. It has a proud history of social activism.

BRIDGE STREET AFRICAN WESLEYAN METHODIST EPISCOPAL CHURCH. 273 Stuyvesant Ave. bet. Jefferson Ave. and Hancock St., 452-3936, Su 8 a.m. and 11 a.m.

This is Brooklyn's oldest African-American church, founded in 1818. In the 1820s, the church established an African Free School, and is known to have been a stop on the Underground Railroad.

CONCORD BAPTIST CHURCH OF CHRIST. 833 Marcy Ave. at Madison St., 622-1818, Su 10 a.m.

Founded in 1847, Concord Baptist Church boasts one of the nation's largest African-American congregations, numbering about twelve thousand and including many of Bedford-Stuyvesant's most prominent residents. A leader in community affairs today, the church has organized a credit union, scholarships, nursing home care, and other services.

OUR LADY OF VICTORY ROMAN CATHOLIC CHURCH. 583 Throop Ave. bet. Macon and MacDonough Sts., 574-5772.

The bright red fences and window trim, well-tended shrubbery, and black stones give this stunning 1895 Gothic Revival church a striking appearance. Almost a half block in size, it is within walking distance of attractive brownstone blocks. A church of architectural note.

ST. BARTHOLOMEW'S CHURCH. 1227 Pacific St. at Rogers Ave.

Set back from the street behind a garden, this irregularly shaped small church was built in the late 1880s by George Chappel, considered a "creative architect" of his time, who utilized some motifs of British Queen Anne–style architecture.

ST. GEORGE'S EPISCOPAL CHURCH. 800 Marcy Ave. bet. Monroe St. and Gates Ave.

Designed in the late 1880s by nationally acclaimed architect Richard M. Upjohn, who resided in Cobble Hill, this church displays striking, high Victorian Gothic architecture as well as Tiffany windows. Another church of architectural significance by Upjohn is **St. Mary's Church** at 230 Classon Avenue, built in 1887; also with original Tiffany windows.

SILOAM PRESBYTERIAN CHURCH. 260 Jefferson Ave. bet. Nostrand and Marcy Aves., 789-7050, Su 9:30 a.m. and 11 a.m.

Founded in 1849, this church was one of several stops in Brooklyn for slaves fleeing north via the Underground Railroad. It was started by Rev. James N. Gloucester, who introduced Presbyterianism to the black community in Philadelphia. Siloam has a proud history of community service and social activism.

WASHINGTON TEMPLE CHURCH OF GOD IN CHRIST. 1372 Bedford Ave. bet. Bergen and Dean Sts., 789-7545, Su 11:30 a.m.–1:30 p.m., music 11:30 a.m.–12:30 p.m.

Music lovers, take note! To hear a traditional gospel choir accompanied by keyboards and percussion instruments, come to Sunday services here. Washington Temple has not one, but several different choirs. According to the *Encyclopedia of the City of New York,* in the 1940s, when gospel first debuted at the Cotton Club in Harlem, Washington Temple was "the best known" venue in New York for gospel concerts.

ENTERTAINMENT

♫ **JAZZ SPOT. 179** DeKalb Ave. at Marcus Garvey Blvd., 453-7825, F–Sa and M, http://thejazz.8m.com. Call for schedule and for travel directions. Reservations recommended.

This is a simple café with brick walls, a fireplace, and healthful fare (organic food, and no alcohol), run by a mother-daughter team. Performances on Friday and Saturday are $15 at the door, Monday jam sessions $5 cover.

♫ **SISTA'S PLACE.** 456 Nostrand Ave. at Jefferson Ave., 398-1766. Call for information.

A hub for the black avante-garde performers, thinkers, and musicians, Sista's coffee shop is one of those important community institutions that make things happen. It's a café/coffee shop that also serves up live jazz on Saturday nights, and spoken-word performances on the weekends, including Jazzoetry on the first and third Sundays of the month. (They've booked well-known poets, such as Willie Perdomo, and musicians who are making the rounds of college campuses.) The brainchild of Viola Plummer, this forum operates as a collective, bringing issues, speakers, and ideas into the community.

PARKS AND PLAYGROUNDS

☺ **CRISPUS ATTUCKS PLAYGROUND.** Corner of Fulton St. and Classon Ave.

When the kids need a romp, you can stop at this nicely renovated playground that's equipped with all the usual brightly painted playground toys: slides, jungle gyms, and the like.

☺ **FULTON PARK.** Fulton St. bet. Stuyvesant and Lewis Aves.

Many cultural events are held in this renovated neighborhood park, including jazz concerts and the **Fulton Art Fair** during the summer. There is a play space for children here, too. While the kids are playing, take a long look at the lovely nineteenth-century houses along Chauncey Street. In the middle of this quiet park note the old statue of Robert Fulton holding a replica of his steamboat *Nassau*, the first to ferry between Brooklyn and Manhattan's Nassau Street.

BEDFORD-STUYVESANT RESTAURANTS

♫ **AKWAABA CAFÉ.** 393 Lewis Ave. bet. Decatur and MacDonough Sts. (in Stuyvesant Hts. area), 744-1444, Th–Sa 5:30–11 p.m., Su brunch 11 a.m.–4 p.m., www.akwaaba.com/restaurant.html.

Opened in 1998, this seventy-two-seat restaurant serves an eclectic ethnic cuisine with a strong nod toward Southern cooking and Caribbean and African influences. There's lots of fish, pasta, and interesting appetizers and desserts on the menu. "Diaspora Dishes" include Southern fried chicken with macaroni and cheese and collard greens, Caribbean jerk chicken with peas and rice and plantains, and West Indian curry chicken. The food's great, the atmosphere neighborly, and on Friday and Saturday nights, live jazz accompanies dinner. Entrées run from $8 to $15.

Don't miss the all-you-can-eat $13 Sunday brunch; however, as this is a popular after-church destination, you may have to wait. In fine weather, there are seats outdoors.

AMY RUTH. 327 Stuyvesant Ave. at Macon St. (in Stuyvesant Hts. area), 574-3728, www.amyruthsrestaurant. com. Opening soon; call for hours.

One of Harlem's most famous home-style Southern restaurants has arrived in Bedford-Stuyvesant. Known for a great breakfast and generally fabulous soul food, Amy Ruth gets down with collard greens, BBQ, and cornbread. Owner Carl Redding (who named the restaurant after his grandmother) pokes fun with his menus, naming some stellar dishes after famous public figures. Ready to order a Clarence Thomas, a William Augustus Jones, a Marty Markowitz?

Other Eateries, Cafés, and Bars

AUGGIE'S BROWNSTONE INN. 1550 Fulton St. bet. Albany and Kingston Aves., 773-8940, daily 4–11 p.m.

Auggie's Brownstone Inn is the oldest black-owned bar in Bedford-Stuyvesant. There's a garden area for eating, TV and music in the background.

GLENDA'S. 854 St. Johns Pl. near Nostrand Ave., 778-1997, M–Sa 10 a.m.–10 p.m. Cash only.

Glenda's specializes in Trinidadian food. You can get typical West Indian drinks here, like the healthful sorrel juice. The curried dishes are well spiced, and goat recipes from home are delicious. Try any of the stuffed pancakes.

JAMAICAN SOLDIERS. 1444 Fulton Street off Tompkins Ave., 773-9589, daily 10 a.m.–10 p.m. Cash only.

Reflecting the different Caribbean communities here, you can get "island food" as they make it back home. Jamaican specialties include anything with curry, goat, and the ever-present rice and peas. Eat in or take home—it's good with a cold beer on a hot day.

MIRRORS COFFEE HOUSE. 401 Lewis Ave. bet. Decatur and MacDonough Sts. (in Stuyvesant Hts. area), 771-0633, M–F 7 a.m.–7 p.m., Sa 8 a.m.–7 p.m., Su 10 a.m.–5 p.m.

Ooooh, red velvet cake. Or the old-fashioned Brooklyn sodas. Opened in 2000, this cozy shop specializes in gourmet coffee and teas, and homemade Southern desserts. Check the bulletin board where people post local activities and business cards.

SHALA'S ROTI SHOP AND BAKERY. 1285 Fulton St. bet. Nostrand and Bedford Aves., 783-2646, M–Sa noon–9 p.m., Su noon–7 p.m. Cash only.

West Indian roti with delicious goat, vegetable, and fish fillings are served at this popular little West Indian shop. If you are unfamiliar with the cuisine, the owners will help you out.

SOUL FOOD KITCHEN. 84 Kingston Ave. bet. Dean and Pacific Sts., 363-8844, M–Th 9 a.m.–11 p.m., F–Su 24 hours.

A simple local takeout joint also delivers to brownstone Brooklyn (or, they say, *anywhere* in Brooklyn if you're willing to be patient). If you can wiggle yourself into a place at the tiny counter, you can get soupy black-eyed peas (good luck for New Year) as well as North Carolina–style BBQ, pork chops and collard greens, and other regional specialties.

♫ **SUGARHILL RESTAURANT SUPPER CLUB.** 609 DeKalb Ave. at Nostrand Ave., 797-1727, M–Th 8 a.m.–11 p.m., F–Sa 24 hours. Valet parking. Call for information on entertainment.

A large, mainstream restaurant, Sugarhill serves soul food and American country-style cooking. There's an upstairs and a downstairs room; dance parties take place regularly downstairs. And with live jazz, blues, and entertainment on the weekends, it's a Bed-Stuy hot spot that has dancing and offers a good time for all.

YOLELE AFRICAN BISTRO. 1108 Fulton St. bet. Classon and Franklin Aves., 622-0101, M–Th noon–10 p.m., Sa–Su 9 a.m.–midnight, www.yolele.com.

Upscale comes to Bed-Stuy. A new restaurant, launched with Pierre Thiam, a well-known Senegalese chef who has brought his magic to a lot of New York City restaurants, has come to Fulton Street. It's a sit-down restaurant serving café food with a Senegalese twist. There'll be an art gallery showcasing local art. Plan to come to some cultural events in this space, too. It was opening as of this writing.

YOUNG APACHE. 1501 Fulton St. at Kingston Ave., 778-9341, M–Sa 8 a.m.–8 p.m. Cash only.

Just a few blocks from Restoration Plaza, this bakery sells a range of Caribbean and Jamaican specialties, including roti and hardo bread, and cow-foot soup.

SHOPPING

DESIGN SCHEMES AT HOME. Restoration Plaza at 1368 Fulton St. bet. Brooklyn and New York Aves., 399-2818, M 2–6 p.m., Tu–Sa 11 a.m.–6 p.m., Su by appointment.

Design Schemes offers something new to the discerning decorator: a source of artisanal and ethnic decorative elements. Owner Linda Lindsay has a talent for making upholstery, drapery, furniture, and decorative elements all work together. If you're tired of that mass-produced look, perk things up with unusual touches in a fusion blend of European and African styles, like big "men's chairs" for $1,200, or girlish lampshades and silk pillows for $40 and up.

DJEMA IMPORTS. 1793 Fulton St. near Utica Ave., 773-3334, daily 10 a.m.–7 p.m., www.djemaimports.com.

Founded in 1992, Djema imports West African mud cloth and textiles. If you like to sew, or do any kind of interior decoration or artwork involving fabric, check it out. They have a store on 125th Street in Harlem, and a vivid Web site.

GREENMARKET. Fulton St. bet. Stuyvesant and Utica Aves. Sa 8 a.m.–3 p.m., July–Oct.

A new Greenmarket has recently opened here, with lots of wonderful produce from local farms.

IBO LANDING. 402 Tompkins Ave. bet. Hancock St. and Jefferson Ave., 230-7900. Call for hours.

As of this writing, another new store has appeared in Bedford-Stuyvesant, geared to the affluent new homeowners in the area. It specializes in "ethno-modern living" and custom furniture.

• *Lewis Avenue Shops* •

It's not the formal name, but residents of the nearby brownstones often call the block between Decatur and MacDonough Streets "the shops of Lewis Avenue" or "Akwaaba Way" (because the block was developed by the owners of nearby Akwaaba Mansion). So far, there's **Akwaaba Café, Mirrors Coffee House,** and these two shops:

BROWNSTONE BOOKS. 409 Lewis Ave bet. Decatur and MacDonough Sts. (in Stuyvesant Hts. area), 953-7328, Tu–Sa 10 a.m.–7 p.m., Su noon–5 p.m., www.brownstonebooks.com.

Brownstone Books is run by a charming, born-and-bred Brooklynite, Crystal Bobb-Semple, along with her husband who runs the antique store next door. Part bookstore, part community hub, they carry current best sellers, gift books, and a selection of books written for, or by, African-Caribbean-Americans. You can find books with a place in African history here, "important books" that shed light on the diasporan experience.

Brownstone hosts monthly book clubs for adults and for teens, and holds almost weekly readings by new authors, poetry readings, and so on. Posters on the wall advertise a dozen newly released books for children, adults, and teens, with an African focus. Children's story time is Saturday noon–1 p.m.

PARLOR FLOOR. 411 Lewis Ave. (in Stuyvesant Hts. area), 363-3246, W–Sa 11 a.m.–7 p.m., Su noon–5 p.m.

The amiable owner, Walston Bobb-Semple, both sells refurbished furniture pieces from the late twentieth century and restores pieces, at reasonable prices. He's familiar with other furniture dealers in the tristate area, and can help you find, sell, and fix up that special table, chair, or armoire.

NORTH CAROLINA COUNTRY KITCHEN. 1991 Atlantic Ave. at Saratoga Ave., 498-8033, daily 7:30 a.m.–8 p.m. Cash only.

Toss together a truck stop, a neighborhood store, and a pinch of Deep South, and you've got the North Carolina Country Kitchen. From Flatbush Avenue, go three miles east—it seems like forever—on gritty Atlantic Avenue to a most unlikely country-style building. The thirty-five-year-old food store sells hard-to-find items that spell home to traditional Southern palates, including hams and sausages, fresh greens, and canned goods such as King Syrup.

RUTH'S ROBES. 1331 Fulton St. near Nostrand Ave., 230-0981, M–Sa 10 a.m.–6 p.m.

This large and centrally located store sells church supplies and religious objects, including the ankle-length robes used by members of gospel choirs.

STREET MARKET. Fulton St. corner of Albany Ave.

In 2003, organizers of the **African Street Festival** were rumored to be taking over the management of this weekend market. Look for big improvements and an interesting source of African-American and Diaspora crafts, clothes, and related items.

ACCOMMODATIONS

AKWAABA MANSION. (See p. 14.)

4

Bensonhurst

ABOUT BENSONHURST

Bensonhurst is like a little guy with a big personality. Stuck way the heck out in the *outer* parts of the *outer* borough of Brooklyn, tough-love, wisecracking little Bensonhurst has made a disproportionate impact on New York, and American, culture. Local-boys-made-*good* include Phil Silvers, Dom DeLuise, and Abe Burrows. Bensonhurst was also the home of television's most beloved bus driver of *Honeymooners* fame, Ralph Kramden. Local-boys-gone-*bad* include more than one fellow associated with the Mafia. (Along with Carroll Gardens, Red Hook, and Williamsburg, Bensonhurst has had its share of notoriety in that department.) And, of course, John Travolta in *Saturday Night Fever* played a young main striving to get out of . . . Bensonhurst.

For urbanites who love to see neighborhoods in transition, unlikely Bensonhurst—the last place in Brooklyn that you'd expect to change—should be at the top of your list. If you want to get a heavy dose of old Italian Bensonhurst, read our section, **Italian Bensonhurst**. To see what's new and unexpected here, read on.

HOW IT GOT ITS NAME Bensonhurst was named after the Benson family, resident cabbage-and-potato farmers in the mid-1800s.

BY SUBWAY D or M train to the 18th Avenue station.

Italian Bensonhurst

Bensonhurst's foods—crusty loaves of bread, homemade pastas and sauces, fresh Italian cheeses and sausages, outrageously calorific and beautifully decorated cakes and pastries—regularly appear on the fanciest shelves and restaurants in food-snobby Manhattan and beyond.

Start with food. You can find excellent, if predictable, Southern Italian food at **Tomasso's,** where you can also hear opera, or at a garden setting at **Villa Vivolo.**

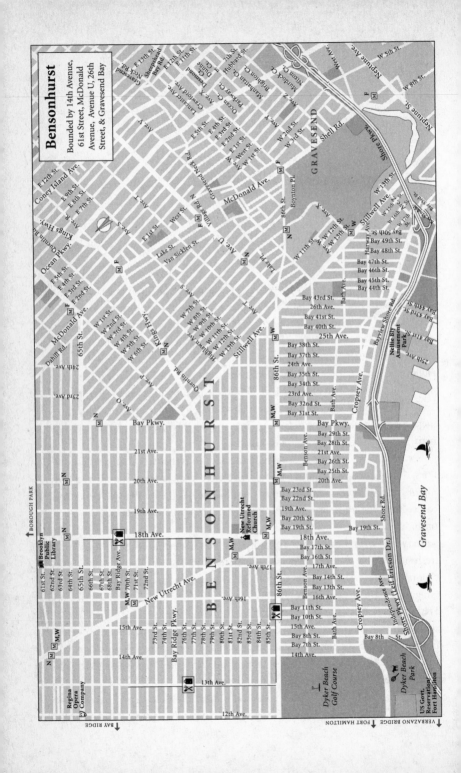

👁 What's **NEW?**

Mamma mia, There's Chinese Food in My Pasta!

Bensonhurst has long been considered Brooklyn's Little Italy.

But don't be fooled by the main shopping drag, 18th Avenue, having been officially renamed "Cristoforo Colombo Avenue." Because there are new kids on the block, and they're not Italian.

Suddenly, next door to the decades-old **18th Avenue Bakery**, a new vegetable-and-fruit stand bearing a big Chinese red awning, with writing in both Chinese and English, has sprouted up. Tucked among the bakeries and Sicilian-style cafés are the new, large, eat-in **Ocean Plaza Restaurant**, straight out of Chinatown, and **Tashkent Restaurant**, which serves Italo-Russian food. **Pho Nam Bo Vietnamese Restaurant**, heralded by the food critics of the *Village Voice*, is a stone's throw from the Santa Rosalia Society, a men's club that's by-invitation-only. **Healing Treasure**, a Chinese herbalist, sits across the street from the mozzarella maker **Aiello Brothers**. Within several blocks, there are fur-coat stores catering to a Russian clientele, a doctor's sign advertising "Psychiatry, Dr. Leonid Vorobeev," and a class full of young Chinese kids taking karate at a Tiger Schulmann's Karate school.

On nearby 86th Street, where commercial rents are cheaper, there's an explosion of Russian- and Asian-owned shops. Check out **St. Petersburg Publishers**, one of several Russian video, book, and music centers in the borough, and the fresh-produce cornucopia at **Russian Village Supermarket**.

Stroll further down 86th Street, a quarter of a mile to 22nd and 26th Avenues, to find a greater concentration of Asian stores. You'll pass Tokyo Café, which serves sushi, and the Golden Palace Chinese restaurant. It's worth the walk to visit the huge and highly recommended Asian specialty food store, the Zabar's of this neighborhood: **T & H Supermarket**.

There are pork stores selling homemade sausages; *focaccerias* (selling pizza, riceballs, and other Italian snack foods); *fornaios* (bread bakeries); *pasticcerias* (pastry bakeries); and *latticini* (dairy shops). Bensonhurst is hometown to both the national Sbarro pizza empire and the successful **Pastosa Ravioli** chain. If you like fresh mozzarella, go to the decades-old **Lioni Latticini** or **Aiello Brothers**. For caponata and Italian imported goods, there's **Trunzo Brothers**, a wonderful Italian grocery. See the coffee roasting the old-fashioned way at **J & A Espresso Plus**. You can indulge in gorgeous, rich Italian cakes and pastries at **Alba's, Temptations,** or **Villabate**. Decide for yourself if reputations are deserved at acclaimed pizzeria **L & B Spumoni Gardens** (try the spumoni, too) and **Cristardi's Pizzeria**.

Of course, there's always shopping. Italian imports are readily available here, from jewelry to clothing to baby bunting. And bargain hunters will revel in the display of everyday items, from cheap wristwatches to garbage pails, sold from outdoor stalls on two blocks along 86th Street.

And then there's tradition. Religious festivals are wonderful occasions to visit Bensonhurst. Most summer weekends you'll find a feast honoring a patron saint, culminating in the huge, ten-day **Santa Rosalia Festival** in September. And the extravagant, elaborate neighborhood Christmas lights in **Dyker Heights** are a labor of love that often gets a spot on tristate area news. (It's well worth a trip.) If you can come in the spring, try to attend the Good Friday candlelight procession, as thousands of people carry statues and banners through the streets to a late-night mass at Our Lady of Guadalupe Church.

Looking somewhat mysterious from the outside are a half dozen or so private social clubs whose unadorned signs bear the names of Italian towns; if you peek inside, you'll see just tables and chairs. Mostly located on 18th Avenue, they have names such as Societa Figli di Ragusa, Santa Rosalia Society, and the Sciacci Social Club. After a decade-long crackdown on the Mafia in the 1990s, carried out by Rudy Giuliani, it is hard to know if the locals are kidding or serious when they say things are quiet because "everyone's either locked up or dead."

HISTORICAL NOTES

Little remains of Bensonhurst's early years as a rural farming area. One remnant of the Revolutionary War is a "liberty pole" at the New Utrecht Reformed Church, which marks the site where colonial rebels taunted English soldiers by hoisting the American flag.

In the 1890s, when Coney Island was a world-famous seaside resort, a competitive complex called Bensonhurst-by-the-Sea was built. Although it tried to lure customers with new hotels, an amusement park, and racetracks, Bensonhurst-by-the-Sea never succeeded. Unfortunately, none of its grandeur remains.

The growth of Bensonhurst as a middle- and working-class community followed the extension of the subway lines in 1915. The 4th Avenue Subway (now the R and N trains) provided an escape for Italian and Jewish immigrants stuck in Manhattan's cramped and dirty Lower East Side. Many descendants of the neighborhood's original families still live here. Successive generations of immigrants settled here, seeking out members of their extended families to help them adjust to the new country. Some have made their fortunes in America and returned to Italy; others have homes in both Italy and America. These multigenerational, bicultural ties contribute to the neighborhood's conservative, slightly Old World flavor. A long-standing Jewish community remains here, along with Irish, Polish, and most recently, Asian and Russian residents.

Kidstuff

☺ Visit **Nellie Bly Amusement Park**, check out numerous pizza parlors, have fun at a weekend street festival, plan a picnic near the bike path and fly a kite in **Bensonhurst Park**.

POINTS OF CULTURAL INTEREST

SPECIAL EVENTS.

Good Friday procession to Our Lady of Guadalupe Church (April); Procession of Santa Fortunata (July); Santa Rosalia Festival, celebrated by immigrants from Palermo, Sicily (September).

BETH HATALMUD YESHIVA. 2127 82nd St. at 21st Ave., 259-2525.

This nationally known Orthodox boys' school is one of many local institutions, including nearly two dozen synagogues, that have been supported for decades by Bensonhurst's sizable Jewish community.

☺ ❂ *Free!* **CHRISTMAS LIGHTS IN DYKER HEIGHTS.** Christmas season only, evenings.

Around Christmas, an evening drive past the bright, elaborately decorated homes in this area, called Dyker Heights, would put a smile on any Scrooge's face. To see these extravaganzas, head toward 84th Street between 11th and 12th Avenues, and on 5th Avenue at 83rd Street.

MAGEN DAVID SYNAGOGUE. 2028 66th St., 236-6122. Closed F p.m. and Sa.

Magen David was the first synagogue built for the Syrian Jewish immigrants who came to the United States from Aleppo and Damascus at the turn of the twentieth century. This New York City landmark is a brick, neo-Romanesque revival style building, constructed in 1920. It has Egyptian motifs, designed by Maurice Courland, a native of Palestine and a graduate of the Ecole des Beaux-Arts. The center of the contemporary Syrian Jewish community has moved to the Ocean Parkway section of Flatbush.

NEW UTRECHT REFORMED CHURCH. 1828 83rd St. at 18th Ave., 236-0678.

The oldest church in the area, this lovely, well-kept landmark was constructed in 1828. The stones come from a church built in 1700 that once stood in what is now the New Utrecht Cemetery, also a landmark, located nearby at 16th Avenue and 84th Street.

The liberty pole in the front marks the site where the American flag was first raised at the end of the American Revolution.

🎓 PUBLIC SCHOOLS.

Among those considered to be New York City's "best public elementary schools" are PS 229 (1400 Benson Avenue), PS 247 (7000 21st Avenue), and PS 200 (1940 Benson Avenue). Call for information about the Sigma gifted program (714-2548/2549) at PS 177 (346 Avenue P). (Source: *New York City's Best Public Elementary Schools*, 2002, by C. Hemphill with P. Wheaton.)

REGINA PACIS. 65th St. and 12th Ave., 236-0909.

This is the largest church in Bensonhurst, with about four thousand congregants. During Easter, Christmas, and other festivals, there are huge turnouts. On Good Friday about seven thousand people participate in a candlelit procession carrying large statues as far as a mile and a half. The **Regina Opera Company** is affiliated with this church.

SANTA ROSALIA SOCIETY. 18th Ave. at 70th St., no phone.

Social clubs like this one dot 18th Avenue in Bensonhurst. Named after a hometown in Italy by new immigrants from that town, these modest storefront clubs provide friendship and an opportunity to engage in what Americans now call "networking." It's a guy thing; men gather in privacy to talk, gripe, reminisce, and to get help in finding jobs and housing contacts. The Santa Rosalia Festival, organized by the Santa Rosalia Society, is one of the city's largest.

ENTERTAINMENT

☺ MAPLE LANES. 570 60th St. near 15th Ave., 331-9000, daily 9–1 a.m.

For great people-watching, roll a ball or two down Maple Lanes. For outings with little kids call a day in advance, so they can set up bumpers in the gutters. These almost guarantee that your tot will get a strike.

☺ NELLIE BLY AMUSEMENT PARK. 1824 Shore Pkwy., near Toys "R" Us, 996-4002 or 373-0828, www.nellieblypark.com. Open Easter to Halloween (weather permitting), noon to dusk. Rides average $2–$3 each; no admission or parking fee.

This petite, relatively clean amusement park is just a couple minutes' drive from Toys "R" Us. Not only is it a little bit of heaven for toddlers and preteens, but it's also not too much of a headache for parents. The park features more than a dozen kiddie-sized rides, including a miniature roller coaster, Ferris wheel, carousel, and train, plus a petting farm, an eighteen-hole miniature golf course, puppet theater, and an arcade of games. This park is not nearly as hectic or as tacky as Coney Island, but note that aside from the small Ferris wheel, batting cages, and go-carts, Nellie Bly is strictly for young children.

♪ ✪ **THE PUNK TEMPLE.** Temple Beth Ahavath Sholom, 2166 Benson Ave., 372-0933.

Seeing a show at the Punk Temple is an experience like no other. Pay $8 to see local and rising punk, metal, ska, and rock bands play among showcases of menorahs and biblical artifacts. The concert space is intimate, with the stage only a foot above the ground floor. Shows are always on the weekends, and start early. (5:00 is the usual kickoff.) One of the focuses of the Punk Temple is to get kids off the streets and give them a safe haven . . . like a mosh pit, for example. But, parents, never fear; the teenagers who come to the temple are respectful and nonviolent.

♪ **REGINA OPERA COMPANY.** Regina Hall, corner of 12th Ave. and 65th St., 232-3555, www.regina opera.org. Performances are Sa 7 p.m. and Su 4 p.m.

For opera buffs on a budget, this is one of the better small opera bargains in New York City. Thrice yearly, operas with full orchestra are staged with elaborate scenery and costumes, including *La Traviata* and *Madama Butterfly*. At $15 for adults and no charge for kids twelve and under, the price is right. Performing for over thirty years, the company has helped launch the likes of Dolora Zajic, who sang with the Metropolitan Opera.

PARKS AND PLAYGROUNDS

☺ **BENSONHURST PARK.** Bay Pkwy. at Cropsey Ave.

The largest of Brooklyn's eighteen municipal neighborhood miniparks, this promenade and park stretches for over three miles along the Belt Parkway. It's a favorite for jogging, roller-skating, and biking. You'll get views here of Staten Island's wooded shore from one end of the promenade and of the Statue of Liberty from the other. Summer concerts are held at the Cropsey Avenue end. You can go kite flying and fishing at Bay 8th Street, just before Exit 5 on the Belt Parkway.

☺ **BENSONHURST PLAYGROUND.** 14th Ave. at 86th St.

This well-maintained, safe space is just a five-minute drive from the 86th Street shopping area. There is plenty of room for running around, plus modern wooden climbing equipment and swings.

☺ **DYKER BEACH PARK.** From 86th St. to Shore Pkwy. bet. 7th and 14th Aves., 836-9722.

Less than half the size of Prospect Park, Dyker nonetheless has 216 acres of grassy space that includes a soccer field, tennis courts, and the **Dyker Beach Golf Course** (see below).

DYKER BEACH GOLF COURSE. 86th St. and 7th Ave., 836-9722, www.golfinnyc.com/DykerBeachGC.htm (unofficial). Open seasonally.

One of the few public golf courses in New York City, this peaceful, eighteen-hole, seventy-one par golf course is open daily. You rent clubs and carts, and even get a lesson from the on-site pro. From some holes you can get great views of the Verrazano Bridge. It costs under $30 during the week, and under $35 on weekends, before 4 p.m. The first tee is near 86th Street and 7th Avenue.

☺ **GARIBALDI PLAYGROUND.** 18th Ave. at 84th St.

This small urban playground, across from the lovely **New Utrecht Reformed Church,** is a place for the little kids to let off some steam while you sneak a nibble of one of Bensonhurst's dreamy Italian pastries.

BENSONHURST RESTAURANTS

JOHN'S DELI. 2033 Stillwell Ave. at 86th St., 372-7481, daily 6 a.m.–6 p.m. Cash only.

Time Out New York flagged this little shop one year as one of their famous top picks for "cheap eats." An unpretentious, hungry crowd gathers here for John's special hot roast-beef sandwich, priced at an old-fashioned $6, available only three days a week: Saturday, Wednesday, and Thursday. So, if you want roast beef on Monday, *fuggedaboutit!*

PHO NAM BO VIETNAMESE RESTAURANT. 7524 18th Ave. bet. 75th and 76th Sts., 331-9259, daily 11 a.m.–11 p.m.

Pho Nam Bo serves up mama's specials (Southeast Asian, not Sicilian style): shredded pork rolls with vegetables delicately rolled in rice paper, grilled beef with lemongrass on a tiny rice stick, crab meat with asparagus soup, and other tasty specials. Wash it all down with salty plum soda, or a Vietnamese beer. The *Village Voice* gave this eatery a rave review a few years back.

PHO TAY HO. 2351 86th St. bet. 23rd and 24th Aves., 449-0199, Su–Th 10 a.m.–10:30 p.m., F–Sa 10 a.m.–11 p.m.

Just when you didn't expect to find much more than pizzerias and maybe a sushi joint, here's a good little café which, despite its Chinese restaurant décor, serves tasty Vietnamese dishes.

ROCCO'S. 6408 Fort Hamilton Pkwy. near 64th St., 833-2109, Tu–Sa 6:30 a.m.–8 p.m. Cash only.

Unpretentious, fresh, and lovingly made homestyle Italian food is the fare here. Try the clams, artichokes, and, of course, pasta dishes. It's a great place to bring the kids for lunch or an early dinner after an afternoon of sleuthing around Brooklyn. Entrées are inexpensive; a big plate of fried calamari is less than $8. Note the hours.

♩ **TOMASSO'S.** 1464 86th St. bet. 14th and 15th Aves., 236-9883, daily lunch 11:30 a.m.–4 p.m., dinner 4–11 p.m.

The food is good, but the *singing* is why people travel here. Loud, exuberant opera with piano accompaniment is performed Wednesday through Saturday.

| ☛ **TIP:** Come here before Lent for Carnevale.

TORRE'S RESTAURANT. 6808 Bay Pkwy. near 68th St., 256-1140, M–Sa 11:30 a.m.–11:00 p.m., Su 11:30 a.m.–10 p.m. Cash only.

Good Neapolitan cuisine at moderate prices make this a terrific local restaurant. The best dishes are the barbecued jumbo shrimps slathered with garlic, olive oil, and lemon juice for $13.50, lobster tail fra diavolo, and a heaping plateful of veal marsala for under $10.

VILLA FIORITA. 7720 18th Ave. bet. 77th and 78th Sts., 837-7950, M–Sa noon–11 p.m., Su 11:30 a.m.–10 p.m.

If ravioli is your thing, note that the daily homemade version here is worthy of Manhattan's best restaurants, but at very moderate prices. The restaurant's simple, intimate ambience and fresh Italian fare make this the kind of restaurant visitors wish they had in their own neighborhoods. A full meal comes to less than $22 a person.

VILLA RUGGIERO. 2274 86th St. bet. 23rd Ave. and Bay 32nd St., 373-2590, Tu–Su noon–10:30 p.m.

If you want a good but inexpensive Southern Italian meal, try this local favorite. Sample freshly prepared spaghetti, veal parmigiana, shrimp scampi, and other entrées for about $12.

VILLA VIVOLO. 8829 26th Ave. near 88th St., 372-9860, M–F noon–9 p.m., Sa–Su 12:30–10 p.m. Parking is available on the premises; call for directions. Weekend reservations are recommended.

This sixty-year-old restaurant may be off the beaten track, but it serves wonderful homemade pasta and veal dishes, stuffed artichokes, and other Italian specialties at about $20 per dinner. Located in an attractive old home on a pleasant residential street, the patio garden will appeal to claustrophobic New Yorkers. Rudolph Valentino (one of many Bensonhurst-born entertainers) is rumored to have worked here before he became a cinema heartthrob.

Cafés, Ice Cream Parlors

ALBA. See p. 90.

CRISTARDI'S PIZZA. 7001 13th Ave. off 70th St., 256-9000, daily 11:30 a.m.–10 p.m.

Cristardi's sticks with what it does best: pizza, calzone, and antipasti. The mozzarella—fresh, of course—is made by famous **Lioni Latticini,** nearby. Toppings include fresh arugula, artichokes, and sun-dried tomatoes. If you're a pizza snob, add this one to your list. *Pies,* no slices.

L&B SPUMONI GARDENS. 275 86th St. near W. 11th St., 372-8400, Su–Th 11:30 a.m.–11:30 p.m., F–Sa 11:30–2 a.m., www.spumonigardens.com.

People come here from midtown Manhattan just for a slice of Sicilian pizza. It's that good. L&B is an old pizzeria that serves a pie that is nothing less than splendid. The crust is light and crisp, and the toppings are fresh. A large outdoor seating area that's open in the summer makes the place as much fun as the food is tasty: you can eat in the sunshine, and the kids can run around. Homemade spumoni ice cream is sold next door, and you can get "real food" in the restaurant inside, where pasta or seafood entrées cost less than $11.

PANORAMA CAFÉ. 7109 13th Ave. near 71st St., 236-3342, daily 9:30 a.m.–10 p.m.

Your morning greeting at this mirror-and-chrome Milano-style café is *"buon giorno"* not "hey." As in European cafés, there are different prices for the freshly brewed cappuccino and espresso, depending on whether you stand, sit at a table, or take it to go. The debate at the wood-paneled coffee bar is likely to be about last night's soccer game. Italian ices are sold here in the summer, too.

UNCLE LOUIE G'S. 6517 18th Ave. bet. 65th and 66th Sts.

SHOPPING

Shopping Areas

Take a walk up **13th Avenue** from about 70th to 86th Street. This avenue is a shopping strip serving Dyker Heights, a 1920s-era residential area of well-kept houses with ample lots on nicely kept streets. Culturally, it is a stable Italian community, rooted in old Italian family relationships. Many new homes are sold to relatives of current residents.

The half-mile stretch on **18th Avenue** from about 65th to 78th Street has a handful of Chinese and Russian shops sprinkled among Italian stores selling traditional foods and imported Italian records, linens, and toiletries.

Underneath the elevated subway, a mile-long stretch of **86th Street** is jammed with stores and large outdoor market displays selling food and inexpensive merchandise alongside some chain clothing stores. You will hear English, Italian, Russian, Vietnamese, and Chinese spoken on this street.

Specialty Food Shops

13TH AVENUE AND VICINITY

AUNT BUTCHIE'S. 6901 13th Ave. corner of 69th St. (also on Ave. N), 256-2933, M–F 9 a.m.–6 p.m., Sa 9 a.m.–4 p.m., www.auntbutchies.com. Cash only.

If you're still dreaming about that chocolate mousse cake you enjoyed recently, it may well have come from Aunt Butchie's bakery. They sell this, as well as cheesecakes, to fancy Manhattan restaurants and retail customers like you.

GOLD STAR BAKERY. 7409 13th Ave. corner of 74th St., 236-8560, daily 7:30 a.m.–8 p.m.

The Sciandivasci family, originally from the Matera province of Italy, has a secret: they love breads. Try them stuffed with prosciutto and salami, topped with thinly sliced fried potato rounds, or filled with onion and rosemary.

J & A ESPRESSO PLUS. 6302 14th Ave. and 63rd St., 232-7736, M–F 5:30 a.m.–6 p.m. (entrance around the corner on 63rd St.).

Aaahhh . . . the smell of fresh, really fresh, roasting coffee! You can get regular, decaf, and decaf water-processed, and see coffee roasted the old-fashioned way.

LIONI LATTICINI MOZZARELLA. 7819 and 7803 15th Ave. off 78th St., 232-7852 and 232-1166, M–F 8 a.m.–4:30 p.m., Sa 8 a.m.–3 p.m., www.lionimozzarella.com.

Oooooh. Try the mozzarella while it is still a little warm; it's a primal experience that reminds you of the best of mama (even if yo' mama *wasn't* Italian). Lioni produces over a dozen different kinds of fresh mozzarella for both retail and wholesale customers. The owners, the Salzarulo family, come from a long line of Italian cheesemakers. Lioni Latticini has three storefronts, and now they offer an olive bar, take credit cards, and advertise that they deliver to Manhattan.

TEMPTATIONS. 476 86th St. bet. 14th and 15th Aves., 680-5959, Tu–Su 7:30 a.m.–8 p.m.

Temptations specializes in high-end, artistic, calories-be-damned Italian pastries. You've probably never seen anything like the window display, a look-alike Madame Alexander doll in a wedding dress made of frosting and cake. The blueberry tart sports a lush pile of fresh, unadorned blueberries! The opera cake is classy enough to debut at the Met! (They have a separate facility that makes special-occasion kosher cakes, serving nearby Borough Park, where the bakeries are more staid. 680-4004.)

18TH AVENUE AND VICINITY

AIELLO BROTHERS CHEESE COMPANY. 7609 18th Ave., 256-1151, M–F 5 a.m.–3 p.m., Sa 5–11 a.m.

Twelve generations in the cheese business, this forty-thousand-pound-per-week cheese manufacturer is famous for their incredibly satisfying mozzarella (salted, unsalted, smoked, part skim, rolled with fillings, such as prosciutto).

ALBA. 7001 18th Ave. corner of 70th St., 232-2122, daily 8:30 a.m.–8 p.m., www.albapastry.com.

"Internationally Famous for Four Generations" is what Alba's card says. With pastries this fabulous, it is easy to see why this bakery has been in business since 1932. The specialties are cream-filled confections. Everything is artfully done. One of the best products is a strawberry layer cake with whipped cream. There are ices and tartufo in the summer.

☉ ALEXANDRA AND NICOLAY. 6502 20th Ave., 331-4985, M–F noon–8 p.m., Sa 10 a.m.–6 p.m., www.alexandraandnicolay.com.

This husband-and-wife team of chocolatiers from Odessa, Ukraine, make premium chocolates with names like "Rasputin's Wafers," "Breakfast of the Czars" (little truffles, some shaped like peasant women wearing babushkas), "Anastasia's Delight" (stamped with imperial seals), and so on. Sold at fine department stores in Manhattan; about $22 a pound.

As the story goes, some of their products are based on the "lost chocolate recipes of the Romanov Dynasty" (see the Web site for an entertaining story).

ANGELO'S BAKERY. 2482 86th St. near 25th Ave., 372-3866, Tu–Su 8 a.m.–7 p.m.

Angelo's is a few minutes' drive away from the center of Bensonhurst, and customers have been taking the extra time to shop here for more than thirty-five years. The selection includes artful marzipan, cookies, and semolina bread, as well as Italian cheesecake. Along traditional lines, they make *pipatelle* (biscuits); tiramisù (made with mascarpone, Italian cream cheese); *sanguinaccio* (a folk dish associated with Carnevale); and *gelati di campagna* (which comes in the red, white, and green colors of the Italian flag).

BARI PORK STORE. 7119 18th Ave. near 71st St., 266-9300, M–Sa 8 a.m.–7 p.m., Su 8 a.m.–2 p.m.

In this era of lean cuisine, the words "pork store" (and there are many such stores in Brooklyn) can evoke flashing red lights for health-conscious consumers. However, this store also sells low-cholesterol, low-sodium meats and cold cuts. The traditional Southern Italian foods are fresh and truly tasty: fresh mozzarella and scamorza cheese, pizza rustica (which looks like apple pie but is filled with dried sausage and cheeses), homemade veal, pepper-onion, and broccoli-rabe sausages. Bari is the name of a province in the Apulia region of Italy, from which many of the local residents emigrated.

18TH AVENUE FRUIT AND VEGETABLE MARKET, corner 69th St., 331-0766, M–Sa 8 a.m.–8 p.m.

A cornucopia wouldn't be big enough to hold all the fresh fruits and vegetables you will want to buy at this overflowing fruit stand. You can find treasures here: baby artichokes; three different price levels of fresh apricots; several types of plump, purple eggplant; fistfuls of parsley; elephant garlic; and other fresh ingredients essential to the discerning Italian cook.

EUROPA BAKERY. 6423 20th Ave. near 64th St., 232-4845, M–Sa 7 a.m.–10 p.m., Su 7 a.m.–9 p.m., www.europapastries.com.

Still hungry? Europa has a broad variety of treats, including marzipan surprises, cakes, cookies, and pastries that look almost too good to eat.

INTERNATIONAL FOOD. 7108 18th Ave. near 71st St., 259-6576, M–Sa 8 a.m.–6:30 p.m., Su 8 a.m.–4 p.m.

As the first Russian deli on Italian 18th Avenue, International helped internationalize Bensonhurst. The foods are labeled in Russian only, which suggests that the local Italian residents are not yet sold on kasha varnishkes. The underwhelmingly friendly staff sells big brochettes of beef, barley, bags of poppyseed, and heavy rye breads.

PAPA PASQUALE RAVIOLE & PASTA CO. 7817 15th Ave. bet. 78th and 79th Sts., 232-1798, M–Sa 9 a.m.–6 p.m., Su 8 a.m.–3 p.m. Cash only.

Welcome to Bensonhurst, Kingdom of Homemade Pasta. This shop specializes in homemade ravioli, sauces, and other traditional specialties made using well-guarded family recipes.

PASTOSA RAVIOLI. 7425 New Utrecht Ave. near 75th St., 236-9615, M–Sa 8:30 a.m.–6 p.m., Su 8:30 a.m.–3 p.m., www.pastosa.com (under construction).

Headquarters of a small pasta empire, Pastosa has multiple stores in Brooklyn alone and about a dozen in the tristate area. Each store makes pasta daily. With thirty-five years of experience, they've got their recipes right for homemade ravioli, prosciutto balls, artichoke salad, stuffed mushrooms, meatballs, and sauces.

QUEEN ANN RAVIOLI. 7205 18th Ave. near 72nd St., 256-1061, Tu–Sa 9 a.m.–6 p.m., Su 8 a.m.–2 p.m., www.queenannravioliandmacaroni.com.

The pasta sold here is made in the huge modern facility visible at the back of the store. Pasta doesn't come any fresher, unless you make it yourself. Condiments and bottles of strained fresh tomatoes are also available.

ROYAL CROWN I AND II. 6308 14th Ave. near 63rd St., 234-3208, M–Sa 7 a.m.–8 p.m.; 6512 14th Ave. near 65th St., 234-1002, M–Sa 7 a.m.–4 p.m.

Even Dr. Atkins would have to believe carbs are good for you, body and soul, after diving into these loaves. You'd never think these two little storefronts, nestled across from churches and a few shops, are renowned for producing some of the best crusty breads in New York. Royal Crown I sells a variety of breads and pastries, Royal Crown II specializes in breads and sandwiches. (See **Paneantico** in Bay Ridge.)

SBARRO. 1705 65th St. corner of 17th Ave., 331-8808, M–F 8 a.m.–6:30 p.m., Sa–Su 8 a.m.–8 p.m., www.Sbarro.com.

Welcome to Sbarro's *original* store, still in the same location where it first opened in 1959. You can buy salads, pasta, gift packages, and a roster of prepared foods for catering. A display of photos and news clippings tells the proud family's story of success.

SEA BREEZE. 8500 18th Ave., 259-9693, M–Th 8 a.m.–7 p.m.

There are lots of fish stores in this neighborhood, but Sea Breeze caught the attention of the first-ever Zagat guide to Brooklyn, and prices are low. A specialty is takeout platters of shrimp, baked clams, and other ready-to-eat dishes.

TRUNZO BROTHERS. 6802 18th Ave. corner of 68th St., 331-2111, M–Sa 8 a.m.–7 p.m., Su 8 a.m.–2 p.m., www.trunzobros.com.

Imagine all of those little mom-and-pop Italian food shops rolled into one *latticina fresca*-grocery-dairy-deli-*salumeria*. The sandwiches are mouthwatering. Also try the mozzarella rolled with spinach, the *soppressata*, and the ready-to-bake homemade minipizzas.

VILLABATE. 7117 18th Ave. bet. 71st and 72nd Sts., 331-8430, daily 7 a.m.–9 p.m.

A whiff of almond greets you when you walk in. Your eyes will spin from the swirls of vanilla, gobs of chocolate, and mounds of oversized strawberries in one display case, and spring-colored pistachio, lemon, and orange layer cakes. Oh, and grab some onion focaccia to take home.

86TH STREET—STREET MARKET AND STALLS

RUSSIAN VILLAGE SUPERMARKET. 3168 86th St. corner of Bay 31st St., daily 9 a.m.–7 p.m.

Ah! The wonderful excesses of capitalism! Not one iota like the old country. Russian Village sells cheaply priced fresh apricots and cherries in mid-December, alongside the root vegetables and *seven* different kinds of lettuce. The exuberance of food in the store is oddly matched by the Babel of languages on the street. Pretend for a moment you are in the exotic bazaar of some cosmopolitan crossroads in Eastern Europe, with a train rumbling overhead and next door to a riotous stall display of fake boas, fur caps, hats, leather gloves, belts, cheap leather jackets, and plastic toys . . . hello! it's Bensonhurst.

⊘ ☺ **T & H SUPERMARKET.** 2502 86th St. corner of 25th Ave. across from 25th Avenue W subway stop, 373-3366, daily 8:30 a.m.–8:45 p.m. Parking available.

This red-and-white building houses a massive Asian supermarket that's a full city block long—Chinatown all rolled into one. It's astonishing just to see all the different dried mushrooms, to look at the live fish in the tanks, to try to identify some of the exotic fresh Asian vegetables or to imagine how those dried fish could be made appetizing. There are a hundred choices of bottled sauces (light soy, stir fry, honey garlic, sweet and sour, to name a few). And, if you're inspired to try cooking your own Chinese food rather than ordering in, you can get any number of rice cookers, kitchen tools, and utensils. Kids will go for the alluringly packaged Japanese chocolates near the checkout.

Stores like this are *why* we live in the city. After all, where in the homogeneous 'burbs are you going to find six kinds of miso, an electric wok that fits in a suitcase, a huge, three-pound bag of bright green, fresh snow-pea tips, sheets of Tiang green-bean starch, and enormous fresh jumbo tiger shrimp for under $12 a pound?

Other Interesting Neighborhood Shops

ARCOBALENO. 7306 18th Ave. near 73rd St., 259-7951, daily 10 a.m.–10 p.m.

From CDs to videotapes, this store stocks a full line of imported Italian music and movies.

BATH BEACH CYCLES. 2156 Bath Ave. two blocks away from the Belt Pkwy. bike path near Exit 5 on the Belt, 265-2453, M–Sa 11 a.m.–6 p.m.

Former accountant Dominic Barilla opened this shop in 1990 to cater to cyclists looking for midlevel bicycles, and never looked back. He carries a huge inventory of all types of bikes from manufacturers like Giant, Haro, Jamis, and Signal, and his front showroom has more than two hundred BMX bikes on display. His mechanics can handle anything.

BOOKMARK SHOPPE. 6906 11th Ave. bet. 69th and 70th Sts., 680-3650, Tu–Sa 10 a.m.–7 p.m., Su 10 a.m.–4 p.m.

The area's first full-service independent bookstore opened in 2002, with a selection of best sellers, general fiction, biography, and travel guides. Plus, they run fun programs for children: monthly story time and special events such as a Harry Potter party.

FESTIVAL. 6412 18th Ave. near 64th St., 259-3811, M–W and F 10 a.m.–7 p.m., Th 10 a.m.–8 p.m., Sa 10 a.m.–8 p.m.

Better children's wear for both boys and girls from layette to size fourteen is sold here. Special items include boys' $200 white-silk communion suits, imported Italian christening gowns of organza and satin, and the Chico line, in addition to a good selection of everyday clothes.

FIORENTINO. 7102 18th Ave. corner of 71st St., 234-2861, M–Sa 10 a.m.–6 p.m.

A *serious* jewelry store, Fiorentino sells Italian-imported gold jewelry for men and women, as well as classy silver gift items. The family business started in Palermo in the 1920s.

HEALING TREASURE. 7618 18th Ave. at 76th St., 621-0889, M–Sa 10 a.m.–7 p.m.

Here's the scene: old Italian men buying herbal remedies for high blood pressure and getting acupuncture treatment at this typical Chinese herbalist, with Chinese writing on the walls. The owner claims that the cultures are similar, with a strong emphasis on extended family life and family loyalty.

LA CASA DE LA BOMBONIERA. 6915 18th Ave. bet. Bay Ridge Ave. and 70th St., 232-0230, M–W and F–Sa 10 a.m.–6 p.m., Th 10 a.m.–8 p.m.

For that special wedding present, you will find gifts, china, crystal, and collectibles at this store. Many items imported from Italy, including honeymoon lingerie, are sold upstairs.

MAGGIO MUSIC. 8403 18th Ave. corner of 84th St., 259-4468, M–F 1–9 p.m., Sa 10 a.m.–6 p.m., www.mag giomusic.net.

This father-son business has been in the Maggio family for over forty-five years. Electronic instruments are crammed into this small space, from electric guitars and beginner keyboards to top-of-the-line synthesizers. They also give lessons to kids ages six and up.

MALE ATTITUDE CLOTHING. 2084 86th St. near 20th Ave., 449-7518, M–W 10 a.m.–6 p.m., Th–F, 10 a.m.–8 p.m., Sa 10 a.m.–7 p.m.

Tired of looking like a trout fisher, a tennis pro, or a buttoned-up Wall Street lawyer? The fashionable, high-quality Italian men's sports clothes here are sharp and sexy.

MANZARI. 8512 19th Ave. at 85th St., 259-1949, M–F 10 a.m.–6 p.m., Sa 11 a.m.–7 p.m., www.manzari.com.

How about a pink sheared mink with chinchilla cuff and collar? Or a full Persian lamb with fox cuff and collar? The fur coats here are lush and expensive. Manzari is an upscale furrier with shops in Milan and Paris—and Bensonhurst.

S.A.S. ITALIAN RECORDS. 7113 18th Ave. near 71st St., 331-0539 or 331-0540, M–Sa 10 a.m.–9 p.m., Su 10 a.m.–8 p.m.

If you want the sounds, sights, and smells of contemporary Italian life, pop in here to pick up Italian popular music, videotapes, soaps, and toiletries.

SOMETHING ELSE. 2051 86th St. near 20th Ave., 372-1900, Tu–W and F–Sa 10 a.m.–6 p.m., Th 10 a.m.–8 p.m.

Trendy casual clothing for women is the specialty here. The look is young, with lots of cotton shorts and slacks, appliquéd denim jumpsuits, and party dresses. Prices range from $40 for pants to $130 and up for cocktail dresses.

PARK SLOPE, PROSPECT PARK

Greenwood
Cemetery

36th St.
37th St.
38th St.
39th St.
40th St.
41st St.
42nd St.
43rd St.
44th St.
45th St.
46thSt.

Fort Hamilton Pkwy.

M   M,W

Brooklyn
Public Library

BOROUGH

PARK

14th Ave.

Cortelyou Rd.

McDonald Ave.

Dahill Rd.

Ditmas Ave.

E. 5th St.
E. 4th St.
E. 3rd St.
E. 2nd St.
E.

12th Ave.

13th Ave.

New Utrecht Ave.

M   M,W

M   M,W

47th St.
48th St.
49th St.
50th St.
51st St.
52nd St.
53rd St.
54th St.
55th St.
56th St.
57th St.
58th St.
59th St.
60th St.

15th Ave.

16th Ave.

17th Ave.

18th Ave.

SUNSET PARK

FLATBUSH

Borough Park
Playground

61st St.
Tabor Ct.

N   M   M,W

61st St.
62nd St.
63rd St.
64th St.
65th St.

N   M

66th St.
67th St.
Ovington Ave.
Bay Ridge Ave.

11th Ave.

12th Ave.

13th Ave.

14th Ave.

15th Ave.

New Utrecht Ave.

Durrea
Ct.

Cameron Ct.

Ovington Ct.

Wallaston
Ct.

17th Ave.

68th St.

70th St.
71st St.
72nd St.
73rd St.

M,W

18th Ave.

Borough Park

Bounded by
Fort Hamilton Parkway,
18th Avenue, 38th Street,
65th Street, and New
Utrecht Avenue

BENSONHURST

5

Borough Park

ABOUT BOROUGH PARK

Those with an interest in things ethnically and religiously Jewish couldn't find a more authentic Orthodox community anywhere in the world. Borough Park is chockablock with synagogues, yeshivas (religious schools), many Jewish bookstores, and even the **Jewish Youth Library**. Kosher food stores aplenty offer the traditional chopped liver, chicken soup, eggplant salad, and baked goods. (We lament the closing of the acclaimed Ossie's Table restaurant.) Two new hotels, opened since 1999 and catering to Orthodox Jewish cultural requirements, are widely popular.

If we could use a single word to describe Borough Park's main attraction for most visiting shoppers, it would be "discount." You can find just about anything, from housewares to top-of-the-line silver, linens, and fine china, at 10 to 50 percent below department store prices. From top-quality children's clothing to women's undergarments, hats, and accessories, and designer sheets, Borough Park is a discount shopper's heaven. Some of the stores barely bother with window dressing, but you might be surprised by what you find inside.

Borough Park is a formidable Jewish melting pot of immigrants from Israel, Russia, and Europe, plus members of more than twenty Hasidic sects, such as the Satmar, Bobov, and Belz. The air is filled with a Babel of English, Yiddish, Hebrew, Russian, and various Eastern European languages. This is no accident—Borough Park is reputed to have the highest concentration of Orthodox Jews outside of Israel. The focus here, where four or more children per family is more the norm than the exception, is on family life.

If you want a feel for the pace of the Orthodox Jewish lifestyle, visit Borough Park early on a Friday afternoon. During this pre-Sabbath rush hour (several hours before sundown), scholarly-looking bearded men in black coats wait in line to buy foot-long challahs (traditional braided egg breads). Women with multiple children in tow rush to finish last-minute food shopping. Solemnly dressed schoolchildren, the boys in yarmulkes, play on the sidewalks. From the start of the Sabbath on Friday evening until its completion on Saturday evening, this community does not drive, turn on electricity, carry or use money, or conduct business. By late Friday afternoon, the streets are devoid of activity, save groups of men and some women walking to synagogue.

HOW IT GOT ITS NAME This area was named after a large real estate development, Borough Park, east of New Utrecht Avenue.

BY SUBWAY D or M train to Fort Hamilton Parkway.

STREET LIFE:
What's different in this picture?

Walking through this or other Brooklyn Orthodox neighborhoods, such as Crown Heights or the Hasidic part of Williamsburg, you'll get a sense that certain standard elements of New York street life are missing. That's because Jewish religious law strictly governs every aspect of daily life—eating, dressing, business and community relations, gender relations, and so on.

Accordingly, here's what you are *unlikely* to experience on the streets of Borough Park:

* people eating on the street, or food vendors on the street
* young couples (or couples of any age) holding hands or even touching in any way (and certainly not kissing)
* belly shirts, tattoos, piercings or green hair, short skirts or low-cut blouses
* young men hanging out at street corners
* loud music coming from cars, or rock and roll, Muzak, or hip-hop blaring from stores. (There are plenty of honking horns and sirens—the community has its own volunteer ambulance service, but otherwise it is very quiet.)

In the same vein, you are likely to find mostly women in the women's stores, and men in the men's stores. There are *no* stores specializing in clothing for the unisex look.

HISTORICAL NOTES

In the 1880s the Litchfield family, major landowners who also owned the vast area that became Prospect Park, developed a settlement in this area and called it Blythebourne. A nearby tract was called Borough Park. As the tale goes, a local realtor tried to convince Mrs. William B. Litchfield to sell Blythebourne, warning her that real estate values would plummet in rural Brooklyn as Jews fleeing pogroms in Eastern Europe invaded the area. She refused to sell. As it turned out, there was indeed an influx of refugee Jews into Borough Park. However, land values rose, and Borough Park expanded, eventually overtaking Blythebourne. Today the only trace of Blythebourne left is in the name of the Borough Park post office.

Borough Park has seen at least four waves of Jewish immigrants. The first group arrived at the turn of the century, marked by the construction of the synagogue that is now home of **Congregation Anshe Lubawitz,** at 4022 12th Avenue, and to Temple Emanuel, at 1364 49th Street. The second wave arrived after World War I, as new train and trolley tracks made the area more accessible to Jewish residents of Williamsburg and Manhattan's Lower East Side. Another group fled Europe before and after World War II and the Holocaust. Since the 1970s, immigrants from Russia, Hungary, Poland, Romania, and Israel have come to Borough Park.

☛ TIP

1. Don't even *think* of setting out for a shopping expedition to Borough Park on Friday night or Saturday. Everything shuts down for the Sabbath. Most shops close early on Friday, are closed on Saturday, and are very busy on Sunday. If you can, shop during the week.
2. To feel comfortable in this neighborhood, it helps to "go native" a bit. Both women and men are advised to avoid short shorts and other scanty clothing, in keeping with the modest dress code of Borough Park residents.
3. Be prepared for zany driving and competitive attitudes toward parking spaces, for instance, on 13th Avenue. It can be challenging.
4. In the kosher tradition, restaurants serving dairy meals, such as pancakes or blintzes, do not serve meat—and vice versa. If you have a meal with meat (or poultry), don't expect to get real milk in your coffee.

Kidstuff

☺ It would be an understatement to say that this is a neighborhood geared toward children; there are children absolutely everywhere. If you have little ones, bring a supply of quarters for the mechanical rides on just about every block along the main shopping drag, 13th Avenue. There are many informal, inexpensive places to eat, such as (kosher) pizzerias. If the shopping doesn't tire the kids out, there is a playground nearby.

POINTS OF CULTURAL INTEREST

SPECIAL EVENTS.
The springtime holiday of Purim is as close as Orthodox Jews, generally a serious and sober group, get to a carnival. During the autumn holiday of Sukkoth, stroll past the many sukkahs, small thatched-roof huts in which meals are eaten. Prior to Passover, Borough Park stores sell all kinds of provisions, from handmade matzohs to silver seder plates.

BOBOVER HASIDIC WORLD HEADQUARTERS. 4909 15th Ave. near 49th St., 853-7900.
The Bobover sect is one of the largest Hasidic groups in Borough Park. Hasidism was born around 1800 in Eastern Europe as a populist revolt against a stringently intellectual Talmudic tradition. Religious but unlearned Jews led by charismatic leaders (*rebbes*) created an alternative approach, stressing joyous prayer over scholarship and illustrative moralistic tales (*midrash*) over legalisms. Most of Borough Park's Hasidic population arrived here after World War II. Today many Hasidic sects have themselves become insular, differing from one another in ways only the initiated might appreciate. Unlike most large synagogues, this one has no fixed pews, platform (*bimah*), or tables. Instead, the abundant floor space better accommodates the crowds of men praying, singing, and dancing when the revered Bobover rebbe holds a gathering, which in these parts is called a *tish*.

CONGREGATION ANSHE LUBAWITZ. 4022 12th Ave. at 40th St., 436-2200.
This 1906 synagogue, originally known as Temple Beth El, was the first built in the area and became a haven for many Jews seeking to escape the overcrowding and slumlike conditions of Manhattan's Lower East Side. In 1916 the opening of the subway lines (B train) that connected Borough Park to Manhattan and Coney Island further increased the area's accessibility and created a housing boom. Today there are more than seventy-five active Orthodox Jewish congregations in Borough Park, including Russians, the most recent wave of Jewish immigrants to New York.

☺ **JEWISH YOUTH LIBRARY. 1461 46th St. bet. 14th and 15th Aves., 435-4711, open afternoons, closed Sa. Call to check hours.**
Jewish books for kids make this library unique. There are preschooler volumes in English that cover a wide range of Jewish topics. Visitors can use the comfortable reading room or borrow books with a modest annual membership. Some volumes are also available in Hebrew and Yiddish.

🎓 **PUBLIC SCHOOLS** PS 192 (4715 18th Avenue) is considered to be one of Brooklyn's best public elementary schools. (Source: *New York City's Best Public Elementary Schools*, 2002, by C. Hemphill with P. Wheaton.)

👉 **TIP**

KOSHER YELLOW PAGES. 877-WHY-KOSHER, www.kosheryellowpages.com or www.syny.com.
Forget the regular New York City Yellow Pages—in the banks here you can get freebie two-inch-thick Kosher Yellow Pages "serving New York, New Jersey, and Florida." An international multimedia company, based here in Borough Park, publishes the Jewish Yellow Pages and also a Sephardi Yellow Pages, geared to the community of Sephardi Jews who live in the Midwood section of Brooklyn.

SHMURAH MATZOH FACTORIES.

There are a handful of Orthodox handmade matzoh factories in Borough Park and Williamsburg, and it's worth a visit for those interested in TRADITION. Open only in the period before Passover, these bakeries produce the most kosher, expensive, and sought-after type of matzoh, called *shmurah. Shmurah* means "watched," and there is a complement of rabbis on hand to watch the clock and the workers: Jewish law stipulates that to be kosher, matzoh must be unleavened and cannot touch any leavened dough, and the entire process must not exceed eighteen minutes. Each time the dozens of workers complete a round, all utensils are changed, washed, and inspected, to avoid contact between batches. Don't expect to stay long; everyone is bustling about, and the place is not set up for tourists. No bare thighs or arms are permitted in this religious environment.

HADERIM SHMURAH MATZOH FACTORIES. 4312–14 New Utrecht Ave. and 43rd St., 436-9393 or 854-0597; 36th St. end of 13th Ave., 438-2006. Open in the pre-Passover season only (spring). Call for hours.

PARKS AND PLAYGROUNDS

☺ **BOROUGH PARK PLAYGROUND.** 18th Ave. bet. 56th and 57th Sts.

The kids will enjoy the climbing equipment and basketball courts here. Avid tennis players will be thrilled to discover nicely paved tennis courts that often sit empty.

☺ ✪ **HOCKEY RINK.** Joseph diGilio Park, McDonald Ave. bet. Ditmas and 18th Aves.

There's a story behind this spanking-new renovated hockey rink, tucked under the elevated F train. It's about Joe Natoli, the handyman and fireman at local Brooklyn Public School 321. Joe was the driving force behind the South Brooklyn Hockey League, which has grown over the decade from a bunch of roller hockey nuts to a dedicated four-hundred-person league of five- to seventeen-year-olds who play every weekend. Joe and a few buddies spent about seven years in the 1990s negotiating to get the city to allow them to renovate a beat-up rink, and finally, with several hundred thousand dollars of city money and zillions of hours of free labor, hammered and sawed and poured concrete at this site.

BOROUGH PARK CAFÉS AND RESTAURANTS

Note: If you are interested, there's a Kosher Referral Service: 877-WHY-KOSHER.

GLATT À LA CARTE. 5502 18th Ave. off 55th St., 621-3697, Su–Th 1–10 p.m.

An upscale Hungarian restaurant offering a selection of good wines, as well as relaxed atmosphere and decent kosher Eastern European fare.

MILLER'S RESTAURANT. 5602 New Utrecht Ave. off 56th St., 438-9594, 24/7, www.MillersFamousRest.com.

On the outskirts of Jewish Borough Park, Miller's is a three-generation family restaurant established in 1947, right during the height of the post–World War II boom in Brooklyn. The restaurant Web site evokes some nostalgia for that era: *"Some can still remember my grandmother . . . Electra Miller would always give you your order, even if you did not have the exact change. She knew sooner or later your mom or dad would be in to eat and pay your balance or tab."* Today, Miller's still cooks its own briskets, roasts, and turkeys. Kids will enjoy watching the working model train that runs overhead on a one-hundred-foot-long track. No, they're *not* kosher.

PLAZA DINING, AVENUE PLAZA HOTEL. 47th St. and 13th Ave., 552-3222, www.machers.com/plazadining. Kosher.

Go downstairs at the spiffy Avenue Plaza Hotel and you'll stumble into an old-fashioned, sit-down dining hall with a big menu that offers kosher variations on many cuisines: Italian, Israeli, and American Jewish (don't miss the "This Lox Rocks" platter).

SHOPPING

Specialty Food Shops

A TOUCH OF SPIRIT. 4720 16th Ave. near 47th St., 438-2409, Su–Th 11 a.m.–6 p.m., F 10 a.m.–2 p.m., closed Sa. Kosher.

Manischewitz wine is not the only game in town. Hundreds of different kinds of kosher wine are assembled here, including Italian, French, and Californian varieties—and most won't remind you of the Passover seders of yesteryear. They also sell hard liquor.

CANDY MAN. 4702 13th Ave. corner of 47th St., 438-5419, Su—Th 10 a.m.—6 p.m., F 10 a.m.—2 p.m., closed Sa. Kosher.

Candy Man calls itself "the Sweetest Place in the Kosher World," and indeed, elegantly arranged, customized baskets and platters of chocolate, candies, dried fruit, and nuts can be purchased here or ordered for delivery.

COLUCCIO'S. 1214 60th St. bet. 12th and 13th Aves., 436-6700, M—Sa 8 a.m.—6 p.m., Su 9 a.m.—2 p.m.

Here is a fabulous Italian market, a reminder that even Borough Park is a multicultural community. Food-loving bargain hunters avail themselves of huge vats of canned fish, a wide variety of pastas, cheeses, meats, and even cooking utensils.

GREENMARKET. 14th Ave. bet. 49th and 50th Sts., Th 8 a.m.—3 p.m., July—Oct.

A new Greenmarket has recently opened here, with lots of wonderful produce from local farms.

KORN'S. 5004 16th Ave. near 50th St., 851-0268 or 633-7466, M—Th and Su 6 a.m.—9 p.m., closes F in mid-afternoon, closed Sa. Kosher.

Korn's has all of those Jewish baked goodies your bubbie used to bring over, like great rye breads and huge challahs. For dessert try the *rugalach, babka,* and other freezable noshes. There are other branches on 16th Avenue near 50th Street, and 18th Avenue near 41st Street.

OSSIE'S. 1314 50th St. near 13th Ave., 436-1151 or 877-GEFILTE, M—Th 7 a.m.—7 p.m., closes F in mid-afternoon, Su 8 a.m.—4 p.m., closed Sa. Kosher.

There's plenty that's fishy here—and it comes fresh, smoked, frozen, and ready to eat. This terrific fish store does considerable wholesale as well as retail business. On one side, you'll find excellent take-home items made here: many different kinds of chowder, dozens of parve salads, as well as sushi—all kosher. On the other side of the store there's a wide selection of fish. But come early, the place is cleaned out by 3:30 or 4 p.m.

SCHWARTZ APPETIZING. 4824 16th Ave. near 48th St., 851-1011, Su—Th 9 a.m.—6 p.m., F 9 a.m.—2 p.m., closed Sa. Kosher.

"Herring has been good to us, thank G-d." Schwartz Appetizing started with herring a generation ago, and today they still sell famously delicious herrings as well as over a dozen special homemade dips. Fresh lox is about $20 a pound, or you can get cooked carp and whitefish, salmon caviar, fat-free kugel, as well as vegetarian pâté, spinach or tomato dip, and fresh salads made daily.

SCOTTO'S BAKERY & PASTRY. 3807 13th Ave. corner of 38th St., 438-0889, daily 7 a.m.–9 p.m. Cash only.

On the outskirts of Borough Park, here's a gorgeous, classical Italian bakery in its full splendor, with cakes covered in white, creamy icing and filled with chocolate crèmes, butter cookies, extraordinary pastries, and refreshing cappuccino.

STRAUSS BAKERY. 5115 13th Ave. near 51st and 52nd Sts., 851-7728, M–Th and Su 6 a.m.–7 p.m., closes early on F, closed Sa. Kosher.

Yum—cream cakes! Napoleons! Strauss has arguably the best cheese Danish for miles around. Everything here is kosher, to boot.

TIFERES HEIMISHE BAKERY. 4016 13th Ave. near 40th St., 972-6026, Su–Th 8 a.m.–6 p.m., F 8 a.m.–2 p.m., closed Sa. Kosher.

"Heimishe" means "family-ish" in a warm and loving sense—just like the Old World Hungarian baked goods in this tiny mom-and-pop bakery. "Everything by the hand, like my own grandmother's recipe," is how the grandfatherly owner describes his irresistible pastries called "flakes," and "kokosh" (cocoa) cakes. Cholesterol watchers note: the goods are parve, so eggs may be used but not butter.

WEISS HOMEMADE KOSHER BAKERY. 5011 13th Ave. near 50th St., 438-0407, M–Th and Su 6 a.m.–8 p.m., closes F in midafternoon, closed Sa. Kosher.

The building façade has had a makeover, with a tasteful beige and turquoise, with fake Corinthian columns and awnings over second-floor windows—reminiscent of Georgetown in Washington, DC. What's inside is just as tasteful—cookies and pastries, cakes and breads. The home-baked six-grain bread is particularly healthy and delicious.

⭐ **YEFRAIM KOSHER TANDOORY BREAD.** 1311 48th St. off 13th Ave., 437-2264, Su–Th 4 a.m.–8 p.m., F 4 a.m.–2 p.m., closed Sa. Kosher.

Rorschach test: If someone says "Bukhara," what do you think? Rugs, if anything, right? Well, stop in and see the huge, tasty Bukharan breads baked here by newly arrived Jewish immigrants from Uzbekistan, who congregate at a Bukharan synagogue in the neighborhood. Using three simple rounded ovens in the back room, brothers Moshe and Ephriam produce a gorgeous, semi-circular bread called *toekey* that's wafer thin, highly decorative, and scores a 10 for exotic.

Clothing and Accessories for Men and Women

ALL THAT GLITTERS. 4705 18th Ave. near 47th St., 853-8789, Su–Th 11 a.m.–6 p.m., F 11 a.m.–1 p.m., closed Sa.

Gents, here's a good place to look for a special piece of jewelry for that gal in your life. (Or ladies, for yourself.) Upscale and up-to-date, these 14- and 18-karat gold necklaces, diamond pins, and pearl earrings are contemporary classics designed by impressive names. You can count on getting a good price.

A TOUCH OF CLASS. 4921 16th Ave. bet. 49th and 50th Sts., 854-6814, Su–Th, 11:30 a.m.–6 p.m., F 11:30 a.m.–2 p.m., closed Sa.

A Touch of Class sells top-of-the-line women's imported suits and sports clothes at prices that are high but not quite stratospheric. Suits start at $900, sportswear at $300. Founded over twenty years ago by a trio of housewives named Bayla, Chedva, and Miri, this boutique's high style makes it one of Borough Park's more unusual finds.

HATS, HATS, AND MORE HATS

Romantic hats, practical hats, mannish hats, quirky hats, colorful hats, hats with veils, brims, flowers, polka dots, wraps. Hats for men. Hats for women. Strolling down 13th Avenue, notice the remarkable number of shops selling wigs, hats for men, and hats for women.

What's this hat thing all about?

Local residents tend to cover their heads *whatever* the weather. More specifically, when they are outside, men of all ages (boys, too) often wear black hats of a distinctly old-fashioned kind, or a yarmulke. Indoors, according to Jewish law, men usually cover their heads with a yarmulke.

There's a code in this. The kind of hat—the color, the shape, and the way it is worn—often has significance for those in the community, indicating what town in Europe the wearer's religious sect originated from, and therefore what specific variations on a custom he might follow. (Similarly, precisely how a man wears his white socks—with the pants tucked in or not, and so on—is also an indication of place of origin and related customs and traditions.)

Young women are not obligated to cover their heads, but the minute they get married (and in this community, where few women continue their education beyond high school, girls often marry by their early twenties) they are religiously obligated to cover all of their hair when in public. Why? Traditionally, a woman's hair is viewed as attractive to men—and, of course, once married, a woman has no business being attractive to any male other than her husband.

All of this explains why there are so many hatters and wig shops in this and other Orthodox Jewish neighborhoods. Some stores you might want to check out: **Beauty Fashion Wigs, Gold's Trimmings,** and **Headlines** (see pg. 106), or **Better Hat Boutique** on 42nd Street and 13th Avenue and **Yaffa and Perry Wigs** on 41st Street.

BEAUTY FASHION WIGS. 4517 13th Ave. near 45th St., 871-1366, M–Th 10 a.m.–6 p.m., closes F in mid-afternoon, closed Sa.

If you want or need a high-quality wig, this is a good place to go. Reputed to be one of the best of its kind in the neighborhood.

BRENDA'S. 4518 18th Ave. bet. 45th and 46th Sts., 435-1073, M–Th 10:30 a.m.–6 p.m., F 10 a.m.–2:30 p.m., Su 10 a.m.–5:30 p.m., closed Sa.

Brenda's carries brand-name clothing for the woman with a modest style, catering to the religious customer. The store is run by three siblings, and it is now named after their deceased mother, Brenda, who started the business some twenty years ago.

COAT PLAZA. 4414 13th Ave. bet. 44th and 45th Sts., 972-2682, M–Th and Su 10 a.m.–6 p.m., closes F in midafternoon, closed Sa.

Coat Plaza has a good selection of classic raincoats and conservative wool coats at 25 percent or more below department store prices. The inventory changes frequently.

GOLD'S TRIMMINGS & ACCESSORIES. 4710 13th Ave. near 47th St., 633-3009, M–Th 10 a.m.–7 p.m., closes F in midafternoon, Su 10:30 a.m.–5 p.m., closed Sa.

Don't be surprised at the high-fashion numbers sold here in Borough Park. This store appeals not just to the local Orthodox women for whom covering the hair is de rigueur—hat lovers come from all over to get simple $20 berets or exuberant, flashy styles costing well over $100. Go downstairs for an excellent sewing-and-notions department.

✪ **HEADLINES.** 4717 13th Ave. off 47th St., 436-4466, Su–Th 10:30 a.m.–6 p.m.

Hats off to Headlines, a long, deep store stuffed with women's hats, handbags, and accessories of all kinds. They also custom-make any kind of hat you want, including brand-new renditions of your favorite but battered old one. "A hat has to fit your personality," one of the co-owners explains confidently.

HINDY'S MATERNITY. 4902 New Utrecht Ave. corner of 49th St., 438-3840, M–Th and Su 11 a.m.–5:30 p.m., closes F in midafternoon, closed Sa.

Expecting a baby? This cramped New Utrecht Avenue location sells it all, from bathing suits and underwear to coats—in modest style typical here. They'll also sew fancy maternity clothes in fine fabrics to order. Other maternity stores are clustered in the 45th–47th Street, 12th–13th Avenue area nearby.

M & H COSMETICS. 4911 13th Ave. near 49th St., 871-6600, M–Th and Su 10 a.m.–6:30 p.m., closes F in midafternoon, closed Sa.

This enormous store resembles a cosmetics department at Macy's or Bloomingdale's, complete with a salon. However, many prices are pure Brooklyn—meaning, discounted. And they have their own CMK cosmetics line—which are kosher for Pesach!

M & M SHOE CENTER. 4526 13th Ave. near 45th St., 972-2737, Su–Th 10 a.m.–6 p.m., F 10 a.m.–2 p.m., closed Sa.

Shoe lovers will enjoy the shoe stores along 45th and 47th Streets on 13th Avenue, and especially M & M (also on the Lower East Side). The styles tend toward classic, with a practical emphasis on comfort and durability. The prices are lower than most Manhattan stores, with a special section for clearance sales.

MARCY CLOTHING, BOYS CLUB. 4409 13th Ave. near 44th St., 854-3977, Su–Th 10:30 a.m.–6 p.m., F 10:30 a.m.–2 p.m., closed Sa.

The clothes make the man, right? And so it goes for boys, too, at this serious, old-fashioned men's clothing store. On the main floor, there are hundreds of high-quality suits for men, with tailoring on the premises. Upstairs, second-generation owner Gary Stern oversees a Ralph Lauren–look-alike shop, featuring size 8–20 boys' clothes.

S AND W. 4217 13th Ave. bet. 42nd and 43rd Sts., 421-2800, Su–Th 10 a.m.–6 p.m., closes early on F, closed Sa.

In the tradition of Loehmann's, the great Brooklyn-born discount store, this women's clothing store is a big discounter of both American and European fashions. Note that even the separates tend to be dressy rather than sporty, and all items have long sleeves and high necklines. There's also an **S and W women's shoe store** down the block, at 4209 13th Avenue.

SIMPSON JEWELERS. 4922 13th Ave. bet. 49th and 50th Sts., 872-0120, Su–Th 10:30 a.m.–6 p.m., F 10:30 a.m.–2 p.m., closed Sa.

"Forty years in the business," Simpson's carries a wide assortment of high-quality watches, gold bracelets, necklaces, earrings, and brooches, as well as pearl and diamond pieces. The staff is knowledgeable and patient. And prices are low.

SYLVIA'S. 5101 13th Ave. corner of 51st St., 436-4771, Su–Th 10:30 a.m.–6 p.m., F 10:30 a.m.–2 p.m., closed Sa.

Elegant shoes, elegant clothes, and an elegant setting describe the newly revamped Sylvia's. You will find both stylish and practical shoes here.

UNDERWORLD PLAZA. 1421 62nd St. corner of New Utrecht Ave., 232-6804, M–Th and Su 10 a.m.–6 p.m., closes F in midafternoon, closed Sa.

What **Train World** is to model trains, Underworld is to those little unmentionables. Despite its Nowheresville location, this is one store to visit at least semiannually to rejuvenate a worn collection of underwear or look for a romantic teddy that won't break the bank. The selection of name-brand merchandise is vast. Parking is free.

Clothing and Equipment for Kids

JACADI BROOKLYN. 5005 16th Ave. at 50th St., 871-9402, Su–Th 10 a.m.–7 p.m., closes early on F, closed Sa.

Lovely, high-quality French imported children's clothing, from infant to age ten, is sold here at the same prices as in similar stores found in Manhattan.

JUDY'S NOOK. 4610 16th Ave. near 46th St., 633-4340, M–Th and Su 11 a.m.–5:30 p.m., closes F in midafternoon, closed Sa.

Shop here for a tasteful selection of upper-end children's clothing, from infant to preteen. Prices generally discounted at least 10 percent.

LE PETIT. 4619 18th Ave. bet. 46th and 47th Sts., 851-2921, M–Th and Su 11 a.m.–7 p.m., closes F in midafternoon, closed Sa.

The owners travel to Italy and France to select these top-of-the-line clothes for infants through juniors. For special occasions there are black velvet dresses, satin jumpsuits, fur-collared wool coats, and tailored, classic clothing for boys. Coats are $250 and up; dresses start at $150. Even the play clothes are elegant.

LITTLE KING AND QUEEN. 4415 13th Ave. bet. 44th and 45th Sts., 438-2007, M–Th and Su 10 a.m.–7 p.m., closes F in midafternoon, closed Sa.

Just start with the baby carriage—Maclaren, Inglesina, Chico, Silver Cross—and you'll know you've found a huge selection of furniture and equipment for your little royals. The prices are discounted 10 percent or more, and the salespeople couldn't be nicer. Imported cribs are from $190 to upwards of $500; carriages start at $200.

RACHEL'S BOUTIQUE. 4218–22 13th Ave. bet. 42nd and 43rd Sts., 435-6875, M–Th and Su 10 a.m.–6 p.m., closes F in midafternoon, closed Sa.

It's a good thing that some things just never change. Rachel's continues to display a truly huge inventory of top- and mid-tier children's clothing, all heavily discounted. Pick a size and you'll find about 150 outfits available for your toddler (we know, we counted).

☺ **TEACHER'S PET.** 4809 16th Ave. bet. 48th and 49th Sts., 436-6600, M–Th and Su 10 a.m.–7 p.m., closes F in midafternoon, closed Sa.

Teacher's Pet sells inexpensive, practical arts-and-crafts and school supplies.

☺ **TRAIN WORLD.** 751 McDonald Ave. near Ditmas Ave., 436-7072, M–Sa 10 a.m.–6 p.m., www.trainworld.com.

A fabulous store for train buffs or beginners, loaded with hundreds of trains, pieces of scenery, miniature figures, and lots of track. You'll think you've landed in Penn Station. One of the biggest train stores in New York City, Train World carries Lionel, American Flyer, and LGB, among others. You can get a medium-priced set starting at $100, but prices range from under $10 to over $300. Bring children, but expect to go home with something on wheels. A wide range of discounts, closeouts, and sales.

☺ **WHISPERS 'N' WHIMSIES.** 4919 16th Ave. bet. 49th and 50th Sts., 633-3174, M–Th and Su 10:30 a.m.–6 p.m., F 10:30 a.m.–2 p.m., closed Sa.

The housekeeping may be just a tad helter-skelter (like a teenage girls' camp bunk before cleanup time), but don't be discouraged. Unusual toys, books, funny pencils, and well-designed backpacks, lunchboxes, and other practical gear for kids are sold here at reasonable prices.

WONDERLAND. 5309 13th Ave. near 53rd St., 435-4040, Su–Th 10 a.m.–6 p.m., closes early on F, closed Sa.

Like Rachel's but in more modern facilities, this huge, busy, and very popular clothing store has better-quality merchandise for children at a hefty discount. Sizes range from newborn to preteen.

YEEDL'S. 4301 13th Ave. corner of 43rd St., 435-5900, M–Th and Su 11 a.m.–6 p.m., F 11 a.m.–3 p.m., closed Sa.

There's stroller gridlock here for a reason: good prices on imported, top-drawer strollers, cribs, and other juvenile furniture. Note that you are likely to see only women, not men, in this shop.

Other Interesting Neighborhood Shops

BRITISH SILVER. 4922 16th Ave. bet. 49th and 50th Sts., 436-2800, M–Th 10:30 a.m.–8:30 p.m., closes F in midafternoon, Su 11 a.m.–7 p.m., closed Sa.

You could put this very upscale, two-story building—with Tiffany-style full showcase windows on two sides—anywhere on Fifth Avenue in Manhattan. It's hard to believe that anybody these days buys such ornate, old-fashioned silver candelabras, but clearly there's a big market for these expensive, weighty pieces. The store also sells modern designs along with tea sets, serving trays, and an extensive collection of Judaica, ranging in price from $200 to $2,000. And if you've always wanted silver settings like Grandma's, note that the proprietor buys his flatware from estates, polishes it, and sells it for between $100 and $250 for a five-piece setting.

CONTINENTAL TABLESETTINGS. 4622 16th Ave. near 46th St., 435-1451 or 438-2522, M–Th 11 a.m.–6 p.m., closes F in midafternoon, closed Sa.

You wouldn't travel all this way for one fork, but you'll save a bundle if you're looking for a set of new crystal, china, or silver from top brands. Some are discounted 25 percent below department store prices.

D'ROSE LINENS. 1315 47th St. off 13th Ave., 633-0863, Su–Th 10:30 a.m.–6 p.m., closes early on F, closed Sa.

Better-quality sheets, towels, tablecloths, bedspreads, and comforters are all sold at 30 percent off department store prices. Name brands include Luxor, Springmaid, Martex, and Dan River. Got a pear-shaped or half-oval table? If they don't have a tablecloth for it here, they can order it for you, or custom-sew it.

EAGLE ELECTRONICS. 5005 13th Ave. corner 50th St., 438-4401, Su–Th 10 a.m.–6 p.m., F 10 a.m.–2 p.m., closed Sa.

Eagle is home-electronics heaven, selling everything you might need, from cellular phones to Cuisinarts. It's also an interesting place to shop for a gift, such as an electric dog-hair clipper or keyboard. You can find here a large range of 220-volt appliances, popular among locals who travel frequently to Europe and Israel. The prices are good and, after thirty-plus years in business, service is reliable.

EAST SIDE CHINA. 5002 12th Ave. at 50th St., 633-8672, M–Th 10 a.m.–6 p.m., closes F in midafternoon, Su 10 a.m.–6 p.m., closed Sa.

For more than two decades this store has made its reputation on discounted giftware, china, and dinnerware with names such as Wedgwood, Lenox, and Mikasa. Discounts are substantial, starting at about 25 percent.

EICHLER'S RELIGIOUS ARTICLES, GIFTS AND BOOKS. Corner of 50th St. and 13th Ave., 800-883-4245, Su–F 10 a.m.–6 p.m., closes early on F, closed Sa., www.eichlers.com.

They call themselves a "Judaica superstore," and, fittingly, this huge modern shop is located in the Solomon Plaza. You can find gift items, books, candelabras, wine cups, and ritual objects, as well as tapes, videos, and more. These folks have a sense of humor; in the display window they once featured potholders that read "oy vey"—with a picture of a chicken going headfirst into (chicken) soup pot.

ELEGANT LINENS. 5719 New Utrecht Ave. bet. 57th and 58th Sts., 871-3535, Su–Th 10 a.m.–6 p.m.,
F 10 a.m.–2 p.m., closed Sa.

If you spend one-third of your life in bed, why not do it with style? Elegant
Linens sells major brands from Canon to Springmaid, priced at one-half to one-
third of comparable items in Manhattan. But what really sets them apart is their
custom manufacture of bed linens, dust ruffles, and pillow shams. "We can
make whatever you want" is what they say, and they mean it.

FLOHR'S. 4603 13th Ave. at 46th St., 854-0865 or 800-JUDAICA, M–Th and Su 10 a.m.–6 p.m., closes F in
midafternoon, closed Sa.

There are at least eight bookstores in this neighborhood—many more than in
Brooklyn's gentrified brownstone communities. Although you won't be able to
read these tomes, called *sphorim,* unless you're fluent in Hebrew or Aramaic, the
sheer volume is impressive. The store's slogan says it all: "In Our Family & Yours,
Since 1892." Which is to say, for centuries, Orthodox Jewish communities and
bookstores go together. Flohr's also sells a wide range of religious gift items suit-
able for a Jewish wedding or bar/bat mitzvah—such as candelabras, Passover
plates, vases, *kiddush* cups, tapes of Jewish tunes, and other Judaica. (See their
new store, **Impressions,** p. 288.)

GAL.PAZ. 4616 13th Ave. bet. 46th and 47th Sts., 438-0631 or 438-9414, Su–Th 10:30 a.m.–6 p.m., F 10:30
a.m.–2 p.m., closed Sa, www.galpaz.com.

You'll find a vast and sophisticated world of Jewish music here. It's organized
alphabetically, as in "C" for "cantorial," "Carlebach," "Chassidic," "child," and so
on. This is one of a series of stores in Israel (Jerusalem, Bnei Brak, and Haifa) as
well as in London and Paris.

GRAND STERLING. 4921 13th Ave. near 49th St., 854-0623, Su–Th 10:30 a.m.–6 p.m., F 10:30 a.m.–2
p.m., closed Sa.

Grand Sterling claims to be one of the largest silver stores in the nation, and
it sells top-of-the-line brand names at discounts that can run as deep as 50
percent off regular retail. An elegant street-level showroom displays hundreds
of silver items, including candelabras, bowls, knickknacks, coffee sets, and, of
course, flatware. This three-generation business prides itself on reliability and
service. There are other similar but smaller silver stores in Borough Park.

LAMP WAREHOUSE. 1073 39th St. corner of Fort Hamilton Pkwy., 436-2207, M–Tu and F–Su 10 a.m.–
5:30 p.m., Th 9 a.m.–8 p.m.

Here's a bright idea: reduced prices on all major names in lamps. One of New
York's largest discount lamp stores, they also fix antique lamp wiring. Staff have

a creative flair for finding just the right Schonbek chandelier or shade for your favorite lamp. Note: Open Saturdays.

MILDRED'S FOR FINE LINEN. 4612 13th Ave. near 46th St., 435-2323, M–Th and Su 10 a.m.–6 p.m., closes F in midafternoon, closed Sa.

If you want your bedroom to look like that luscious magazine picture, with just a phone call Mildred's can ship the goods to you—at up to a 25 percent discount. There are half a dozen curtain and linen shops in Borough Park, but Mildred's claim to fame is a big phone-and-mail business on duvets, sheets, bath accessories, shower curtains, and other linens. The store itself has two floors crammed with attractive name-brand items and includes an extensive bath shop.

ROYALTY TABLEWARE. 1845 50th St. bet. 18th and 19th Aves., 854-6689, by appointment.

You'll have to put up with the limited hours here if you want to find stainless-steel and silverplated tableware at 25 to 60 percent discounts. But at $150 for twelve place settings, it's worth the hassle.

SEW SPLENDID TRIMMINGS AND NOTIONS. 5016 13th Ave. near 50th St., 437-5154, Su–Th 11 a.m.–6 p.m., closes before sunset on F.

Old women, young women, babies, strollers—there's lots of motion in this store selling notions: buttons, lace, appliqués, rhinestones, ribbons, pleating, hair ornaments.

THE PEPPERMILL. 5015 16th Ave. corner of 50th St., 871-4022, Su–Th 11 a.m.–6 p.m., closes before sunset on F, www.thepeppermill.com.

One of the best cook and kitchenware stores in Brooklyn, the Peppermill has an unusually wide selection of upscale cook- and bakeware, kitchen tools and equipment, and a sensible selection of cookbooks and kosher condiments. It's an airy, friendly place with a stove in the back for numerous classes offered by well-known chefs. It's run by two sisters-in-law, Debby and Karen, and, not surprisingly, their *spécialité de la maison* is kosher cookery.

Underground Stores

Only the UPS delivery man knows for sure how many underground businesses exist in Borough Park. We found at least a dozen home-based stores run by women, literally underground, in the basements of their homes. These are not fly-by-night operations, but well-run outfits that have, in some cases, been in business for decades. They pay taxes, take credit cards and phone orders, and are open regular, if truncated, hours (usually 11 a.m.–5 p.m.). For these Orthodox women, whose first priority is family life, basement stores are a sensible business solution. And shoppers enjoy the steep discounts, often 20 percent off regular store prices.

It's hard to find out about who sells what, except by word of mouth. The best strategy is to talk with some of the store owners who sell women's clothing. Then you can say someone sent you, which helps in this usually close-knit community. These stores are all closed Friday afternoons, Saturdays, and on Jewish holidays.

Shoes and Handbags

SOL'S DOLLS. 1624 48th St. off 16th Ave., 435-9444, Su–Th midday, but call ahead for hours. Use middle door.

For over two decades, Channi and her family have sold handbags from home, as well as shoes. There are over one hundred different styles of bags, including exquisite evening bags and everyday soft leather satchels. Shoes include well-known European names. Prices run at least 20 percent less than regular store prices.

Lingerie

SARA SAPOSH CORSET SHOPPE. 1730 46th St. bet. 17th and 18th Aves., 438-9497, Su–Th 10 a.m.– 5 p.m.

Mrs. Saposh sells bathing suits, undergarments, and nightgowns, both imports and top-quality made-in-America brands, at a fraction of the retail price. With a ton of merchandise jammed into a small space, it can get very busy.

Evening Wear

GOLDIE. 1436 46th St., 436-5781.

Walk down a few dimly lit steps to a boutique of expensive gowns and party dresses made of satin, brocade, lace, and silk.

Tablecloths

GITTA STEINMETZ TABLECLOTHS. 1729 46th St., 871-6964, M–Th 10 a.m.–6 p.m. Across the street from the basement lingerie shop (see above).

All sizes of tablecloths are sold here, including some for king-sized, sixteen-foot tables! Some are imported, some are American, and both the price and quality can't be beat.

6

Brighton Beach, Coney Island, and Sheepshead Bay

nug against the Atlantic Ocean at Brooklyn's southern end, Brighton Beach, Coney Island, and Sheepshead Bay offer an unparalleled combination of fun, food, and fashion. Because you can spend a full day here, combining a walk on Brighton's Boardwalk with a roller-coaster ride in Coney Island and dinner in Sheepshead Bay, we've included all three neighborhoods in this single chapter. Also included, for good measure, are some destinations in Mill Basin and Marine Park.

BY SUBWAY Q and B trains to Brighton Beach Avenue (Brighton Beach), or Sheepshead Bay Road (Sheepshead Bay). F train to West 8th Street (Coney Island). Check the NYC MTA for F train updates and construction.

Kidstuff

☺ Spend a day at **Coney Island, Brighton Beach,** or **Manhattan Beach Park.** Visit the **New York Aquarium.** Have fun on the rides at **Astroland amusement park** and **Deno's.** Ride the **Carousel.** Cheer your team at a **Cyclones game** at **KeySpan Park.** Watch the fishing boats come in, or go fishing from **Emmons Avenue fishing pier.** Play at **Marine Park.** Ride bikes and stargaze at **Floyd Bennett Field.** Learn to sail, walk the **Boardwalk,** go to the **beach!**

Brighton Beach

ABOUT BRIGHTON BEACH

At Brooklyn's southernmost end is a seaside neighborhood you won't want to miss. Commonly referred to as "Little Odessa," Brighton Beach is a Russian enclave in New York. Since 1989, over two hundred thousand people from the old Soviet Union have settled in New York City, and many of them started here.

MANHATTAN BEACH ↑

KINGS HIGHWAY, MIDWOOD, FLATBUSH ↑

Brighton Beach

Bounded by Ocean Parkway,
the Atlantic Ocean, Shore
Parkway, and 15th
Street/Westend Avenue

SHEEPSHEAD BAY

Sheepshead Bay

BRIGHTON BEACH

CONEY ISLAND

ATLANTIC OCEAN

Seaside Park

Ocean Ave.
Voorhies Ave.
Sheepshead Ave.
Bay Rd.
Emmons Ave.
Shore Blvd.
Ocean Ave.
Exeter St.
Dover St.
Coleridge St.
Beaumont
Amherst St.
Hampton Ave.
Oriental Blvd.
Westend Ave.
Shore Blvd.
E 13th St.
Cass Pl.
Corbin Pl.
Corbin Pl.
Esplanade
Br. 15th St.
Br. 14th St.
Brightwater Ave.
Ocean View Ave.
Brighton 13th St.
Brighton 11th St.
Brighton 10th St.
Br. 10th Ct.
Br. 10th Path
Br. 10th Ter.
Br. 10th La.
Shore Pkwy. (Belt Pkwy.)
Voorhies Ave.
Blake Ct.
Lawn Ct.
Coney Island Ave.
Brighton Beach Ave.
Oceana development
Millenium Theater
Br. 8th St.
Brighton 7th St.
Brighton 6th St.
Brighton 5th St.
Brighton 4th St.
Brighton 3rd St.
Br. 2nd St.
Br. 1st Pl.
Banner Ave.
Br. 8th La.
Br. 7th La.
Br. 4th Rd.
Br. 4th St.
Br. 4th Ter.
Br. 4th La.
Br. 3rd La.
Br. 3rd Rd.
Br. 3rd La.
Br. 2nd La.
Br. 2nd Pl.
Br. 1st Ct.
Br. 1st St.
Br. 1st La.
Br. 1st Rd.
Ocean View Ave.
Brighton 1st St.
Banner 3rd Rd.
Nixon Ct.
West Ave.
Belt Pkwy.
Neptune Ave.
Ocean Parkway
Brooklyn Public Library
Brightwater Ct.
Boardwalk East
W. 5th St.
W. 3rd St.
W. 2nd St.
W. 2nd Pl.
W. 1st St.
W. Brighton Ave.
Seabreeze Ave.
Shore Blvd.

If fifty years of the Cold War didn't rouse your curiosity about the former Soviet Union, a trip to Brighton Beach will.

The main thoroughfare, Brighton Beach Avenue, is peppered with Russian delis and restaurants, Russian-run clothing shops, and Russian-language-newspaper stores and shop signs in Cyrillic. During the winter months, an amazing number of both men and women do their daily errands dressed in heavy fur or leather coats. Residents of Brooklyn, surrounding suburbs, and even Manhattan trek here to ooh and aah over the delicious authentic Russian foods and wild nightclubs.

Food mavens will find a foray to Brighton Beach satisfying. The array of sausages, cheeses, and breads is mind boggling. You can stock up on a year's supply of exotic dried fruits and flavored bonbons. Visitors may be surprised by the number of vegetable stands—there are at least two on every block. As one local summed it up: "They are hungry from Russia still. One vegetable stand would be for a whole town there."

Demographically, the neighborhood is diversifying, with the arrival of American yuppies, Mexican, Pakistani, Afghan, and Indian workers, and the return of Americanized Russians as well. But the mix of restaurants and shops retain the flavor of Odessa, and it's still one of the most entertaining, eye-popping neighborhoods of Brooklyn to visit.

HOW IT GOT ITS NAME Named after England's most distinguished seaside resort, Brighton Beach was developed in the 1880s as a posh competitor with nearby Coney Island.

 ## What's **NEW?**

Yuppies Discover High-Priced High-Rises on the Oceanfront

What's new here is the Oceana, a sixteen-building luxury condo on the Atlantic beachfront. With luxury condos already up along the Boardwalk, and crummy old beach shacks being purchased and torn down for more, a new reality is sinking in: this is New York, and there's affordable oceanfront property, folks. It remains to be seen how, and when, improvements in Coney Island will spill over to Brighton Beach, but the rediscovery of Brighton's natural assets now seems more a matter of "when" than "if."

HISTORICAL NOTES

Like the Cyclone in nearby Coney Island, Brighton Beach has had its ups and downs. In the 1880s it was an affluent seaside resort complete with casino, racetrack, and a major hotel. It remained that way for decades; in 1907 the new Brighton Beach Baths (now the site of Oceana, a major residential development) boasted several swimming pools, a beach, and nightly entertainment by the country's top performers. These included John Philip Sousa's band and the first Yiddish vaudeville theater (and, in later years, Milton Berle, Lionel Hampton, and Herman's Hermits). By the 1930s Brighton Beach had become a densely populated year-round residential area with a sizable Jewish community, but after World War II the area went into decline along with Brooklyn's economy and an aging local population.

In the mid-1970s, the neighborhood was, as one local leader puts it, "like a dried-up sponge." That sponge has since absorbed nearly one hundred thousand immigrants, most of them Russian. In the seventies and eighties, these Russians were mostly working-class Jews, many of them from Odessa, hence the neighborhood's nickname.

In the early nineties, the collapse and fall of the Soviet Union opened the doors of Russian emigration, and a new wave of immigrants—mostly white-collar professionals from Moscow, Saint Petersburg, and Kiev—began to arrive, transforming the area.

POINTS OF CULTURAL INTEREST

SPECIAL EVENTS.

Brighton Jubilee, a street fair along Brighton Beach Avenue featuring local crafts, international food, and four stages of entertainment the last Sunday in August. Check www.brightonbeach.com or call 891-0800 for information.

ABRAHAM LINCOLN HIGH SCHOOL. 2800 Ocean Pkway., 372-5474.

Graduates include Arthur Miller, Joseph Heller, Neil Sedaka, Neil Diamond, Elizabeth Holtzman, and Harvey Keitel. Today the student body is comprised of a small United Nations of students from dozens of countries, with some classes in Russian, and an accelerated math and science program. Their renowned photography program is open to kids across the borough.

ART DECO APARTMENTS. 1120–40 and 1150–70 Brighton Beach Ave. across from Brighton 14th St.

Check out the entrances to these classic Art Deco buildings, remnants from the 1920s and 1930s when several dozen six-story deluxe apartment buildings were built here along Brighton Beach Avenue. Some boasted a special amenity: a salt-water spout in the bathtub. The original residents were immigrants who had made enough money to escape from the crowded tenements of the Lower East Side.

BRIGHTON BALLET THEATRE (SCHOOL OF RUSSIAN BALLET). 3300 Coney Island Ave. near Brighton Beach Ave., 769-9161 or 996-2486, www.brightonballet.com.

Russian director Irina Roizin seeks to bring together young dancers who are "the best and brightest of the former Soviet Union and the United States." According to some observers, that mission's been accomplished. You can some-times catch a performance at the **Millennium.**

• So Long, Brighton Beach Bath and Racquet Club •

If you grew up in Brooklyn and haven't been back for a few years, you'd be surprised to see not only that the Brighton Beach Bath and Racquet Club is gone, but that the huge, upscale **Oceana** complex is there in its stead. For them whose don't knows, the Brighton Beach Bath and Racquet Club was "sumptin' else." According to the *Encyclopedia of the City of New York,* the club was founded in 1907 and occupied fifteen acres on the Atlantic Ocean. It was "advertised as the world's largest beach resort," and boasted thirteen thou-sand members as late as the 1960s. "The Baths" were where families went in the summer to take a beach cabana, socialize with other immigrants, and enjoy beach sports—not just swimming but also knish-eating competitions and mah-jongg.

OCEANA CONDOMINIUM AND CLUB. Brighton Beach Ave. at Coney Island Ave., 332-0002, www.oceanausa.com.

Miami Beach has arrived in Brooklyn. Replacing the old **Brighton Beach Bath and Racquet Club** is a new sixteen-building, 850-apartment luxury devel-opment on the Atlantic Ocean.

It took decades for this $325 million development, one of the largest market-rate housing projects in the outer boroughs, to get off the ground. But it has, and as of this writing, half the buildings are up, and sold. Residents include Russians and Americans, professionals and businesspeople—computer experts, physi-cians, entrepreneurs. Some are New Yorkers who grabbed a rare chance for affordable beachfront property that's a subway ride away.

🎓 PUBLIC SCHOOLS.

PS 225 (1075 Ocean View Avenue) is considered to be one of Brooklyn's best public elementary schools. (Source: *New York City's Best Public Elementary Schools,* 2002, by C. Hemphill with P. Wheaton.)

SHOSTAKOVICH MUSIC, ART AND DANCE SCHOOL. 297 Ave. X, 376-8056.

Music, drama, theater, classical ballet, modern, jazz, and ballroom dance classes are offered here, in a Russian-run school that's named after a famous Russian composer. There are three locations.

"RUSSIAN BEAT" AT NEW YORK *DAILY NEWS*

The New York *Daily News* has a column called "Russian Beat," featuring outstanding Russian artists, businesspeople, and educators. According to one local, "It's time that Americans stopped thinking of Russians as just the mafia, because there's a lot of gifted Russians, too."

RUSSIAN—NEW YORK WEB SITE: WWW.RUSSIANNY.COM

Click on the "English" link for this mother lode Web site for New York's Russian community. Hint: There's lots of information, listings, funny chat—and a contest for the "sexiest Russian man."

ENTERTAINMENT

♫ **MILLENNIUM THEATER.** 1029 Brighton Beach Ave. near Coney Island Ave., 615-1500. Call for show information. Get tickets at the booth downstairs.

This restored old movie theater is the cultural center of Brighton Beach. Seating 1,800 people, Millennium has hosted such shows as **Brighton Beach Ballet,** opera, the Moscow Circus, top Russian singers, dancers, and theater troupes. But it's not just high culture. You might find yourself at a boxing match or a stuff-your-face-with-*pelmeni* contest. What's *pelmeni?* Russian meat dumplings, dummy.

Russian Restaurant-Nightclubs

There are over a dozen Russian nightclubs in Brooklyn, many of them within the half-mile stretch along Brighton Beach Avenue. Make sure you book ahead and ask whether they take credit cards.

♫ **ATLANTIC OCEANA.** 1029 Brighton Beach Ave. near Coney Island Ave., 743-1515.

This is a club downstairs, with the 1,800-seat theater and cultural center upstairs. It's all housed in an old renovated movie theater. You can have the Russian nightclub experience here, or host a catered event, Russian-style.

THE RUSSIAN NIGHTCLUB EXPERIENCE

You start off the night with a smoked-fish platter the size of an aircraft carrier, a little caviar here, a lot of citrus-infused vodka there, and a tremendous dollop of sour cream. At about nine o'clock, the band takes the stage—real Russian rock 'n' rollers sporting black leather jackets and distant, world-weary stares. They power up the synthesizers and slide into the "Macarena," followed by "Jailhouse Rock." Russians from all walks of life storm the dance floor—matrons in furs, elderly gentlemen in corduroy suits, young hipsters in white dinner jackets and gold plastic sunglasses. Onstage, things start to get weird: a young Harlemite emerges in a shimmering zoot suit, microphone in hand, and dives into a soulful version of "I Just Called to Say I Love You." Russian girls from all over the hall scream in unison and rush the new singer, forming a circle around him and jump up and down. In the middle of the song, he points to one of the girls and croons, "I just called to say I love you, Marina." The adolescent beauty squeals and giggles. It's her birthday. The song will be requested five more times that night. Unbelievable? Yes. Utter confusion? Only on your part. But are we serious when we tell you there's no better place to try out your latest moves? Absolutely. Brighton Beach's restaurant/dance halls are beyond doubt the best place to experience the strange and joyful mishmash that is Russian-American immigrant culture.

♫ **DE RIBAS RESTAURANT—NIGHTCLUB.** 706 Brighton Beach Ave. at Brighton 7th St., 934-5900. Check out Tuesday jazz jams. Call for a schedule of performers.

Something new is happening at this Brighton Beach restaurant and nightclub: hot jazz. There's something particularly poignant about a thickly accented Russian immigrant trumpet player who introduces his act, "Now that we are in the free world, we can be free, even in our music." De Ribas participates in the **Brooklyn Jazz Festival.**

♫ ✆ **NATIONAL RESTAURANT.** 273 Brighton Beach Ave. bet. Brighton 2nd and 3rd Sts., 646-1225, F–Sa 9 p.m.–3 a.m., Su 7 p.m.–1 a.m. Reservations are recommended.

When you walk into the National—the largest and, some say, tamest of Brighton Beach's nightclub/restaurants—the banquet-style tables are already set with about twenty cold appetizers, including eggplant salad, cold duckling, pickled vegetables, pâté, big plain boiled potatoes, and, of course, a cold bottle of vodka. That's just for starters—wait until the entrées arrive. The live entertainment is more "floor show" than "cover band," but the dance floor is still packed. The building is huge; it used to be a movie theater, and accommodates more than 350 people. The National gained some fame in the eighties as Robin Williams's haunt in *Moscow on the Hudson*. Average main course is about $25, banquets on Friday and Sunday run $45, and the full bash on Saturday is $55.

♫ ☺ **ODESSA.** 1113 Brighton Beach Ave. bet. Brighton 13th and 14th Sts., 332-3223, Tu–Th 10 a.m.–midnight, F–Sa 9 p.m.–3 a.m., Su 8 p.m.–2 a.m. Reservations required.

Odessa has atmosphere, lively dancing, terrific food, and the vodka keeps flowing. While more family-style than the National, Odessa is still huge; one flight above street level, it occupies the space taken up by a half-dozen shops, and seats more than three hundred people. The Odessa is a favorite of Russian locals, who congregate here at lunchtime. Try the chicken Kiev, meat loaf, and potato salad with meat. Dinner and entertainment run about $55 per person on the weekend; during the week the Russian foods are à la carte and cost about $30 for dinner, sans music.

♫ **PRIMORSKI.** 282 Brighton Beach Ave. near Brighton 3rd St., 891-3111, M–Th 11 a.m.–midnight, F–Sa 11–3 a.m., Su 11–2 a.m., www.primorski.com.

With capacity for about eighty people, Primorski is one of the more intimate Russian restaurants, but still is a spot for a boisterous evening. The eclectic mix of covered tunes tends toward fabulously schmaltzy renditions—go ahead and sing along, no one will mind. Entrées here, priced at about $14, are very tasty, and a fixed-price dinner is about $35 per person. During the day, you can get an enormous lunch for under $6. Reservations are recommended.

♫ **ST. PETERSBURG.** 223 Brighton Beach Ave. at Brighton 2nd St., 743-0880, daily 2 p.m.–3 a.m., www.SanktPetersburgNY.com.

The menu is Russian, by way of France, with a twist of American thrown in. Boogey to live music on Thursday, Friday, and Saturday nights; Tequila Sunday you get free tequila drinks and Latin dancing.

♫ **WINTER GARDEN RESTAURANT, LOUNGE & BAR.** 3152 Brighton 6th St., 934-6666, daily 10 a.m.–midnight in summer, later on weekends, call for winter hours, www.RussiaNY.com.

Big glass front doors swing open in the summer, offering 180-degree ocean views and people watching. Grab an umbrella table and choose from an extensive menu of Russian and French dishes. In the evening enjoy one of those indescribable live Russian stage shows, and dance to live music late into the night. The crowd at this two-hundred-seat restaurant is mostly Russian, with a sprinkling of visitors. The lunch special is $9; dinner runs about $30. Or, for a truly authentic experience, come for Thursday regional theme nights, with food and dance reflecting Georgian, Uzbek, and other ethnic cultures that were once part of the USSR.

PARKS AND PLAYGROUNDS

BRIGHTON BEACH AND BOARDWALK.

Ocean air! Seagulls! Avrum from Vladivostok! One block from Brighton Beach Avenue is the Boardwalk, the sand, the surf, and human geography.

☺ **BRIGHTON BEACH PLAYGROUND.** Bet. the Boardwalk and Brightwater Court, near Brighton 2nd St.

BRIGHTON BEACH RESTAURANTS

NOTE: *For Russian nightclubs, see Entertainment, above.*

Russian immigrants may have extravagant taste, so local cafés may tout their lobster and foie gras. Our advice: skip the haute cuisine and stick to the *vareniki,* borscht, and blini. Pedestrian as they may seem to the average Russian-American, these are the dishes local chefs know best, and are almost certain to provide an exotic treat for the visitor. Most of the dinner clubs listed in the **Entertainment** section above also serve lunch and dinner.

♫ **ART CAFÉ.** 1005 Brighton Beach Ave. off Coney Island Ave., 646-1900, daily 11 a.m.–11 p.m., www.art cafeonline.com.

Strategically located across from the Oceana luxury condo complex, Art Café takes a more European approach to food and entertainment than some of the more hard-core Russian spots. There's cool jazz (piano and sax) and pink walls. The menu is filled with rich items such as tomatoes stuffed with shrimp, red and black caviar; lamb chops served with baked apple; filet mignon in caviar sauce with shrimp and goose liver. It's new; the jury's still out.

CAFÉ GLECHIK. 3159 Coney Island Ave. bet. Brighton Beach Ave. and Brighton 10th St., 616-0494, daily noon–midnight.

On a Saturday evening, Café Glechik is packed as tightly as a can of smoked mackerel. That's because locals come here for traditional Russian dishes, at low prices.

CAFÉ PEARL, also known as the **BEST PEARL CAFÉ.** 303 Brighton Beach Ave. near Brighton 3rd St., 891-4544, 24/7.

For thirty bucks a head you can get Georgian cooking at this highly rated Brighton Beach eatery. There are lamb dumplings that some reviewers rave about, "cheesy rolls," and, on a more traditional Russian note, herring with pota-toes, eggplant, fish, and more Russian delicacies.

GAMBRINUS. 3100 Ocean Pkwy. corner of Brighton Beach Ave., 265-1009, daily noon–midnight.

Gambrinus is named after a beer bar in Odessa, Ukraine. This popular spot is decorated like a sunken ship, with rigging and buoys and mizzenmasts strewn about. Try the salty-sweet pickled herring, which comes with sugary onions and a heaping plate of roasted potatoes, and the generous seafood salad (order the dressing on the side if you don't like it drenched). If you stick to appetizers—more than enough food for the average North American—dinner will run you about $15.

GINA'S CAFÉ/CAFFE CAPPUCCINO. 409 Brighton Beach Ave. bet. Brighton 4th and 5th Sts., 646-6297, daily 11 a.m.–11 p.m.

Check out how the locals live. Nibble a little caviar and soak up some Russian rock and roll (or is it hip-hop?) while you're at it. You can get potato pancakes, and blinis with caviar that are straight from heaven. This small European-style café offers (relatively) light Russian food—you won't need a three-hour nap after eating here. There are *vareniki* (Russian-style pierogi), pickled vegetables, Ukrainian borscht, schnitzel, cheesecake, baba au rhum pastries, and excellent coffee. Lunch costs less than $10.

OCEANVIEW CAFÉ. 290 Brighton Beach Ave. near Brighton 3rd St., 646-1900, M–F and Su 11 a.m.–10 p.m., Sa 11 a.m.–11 p.m.

For a quick, informal bite while you're visiting the neighborhood, stop here for a $4 bowl of borscht and a main course of blinis or chicken that will cost you only $7.

VARENICHNAYA. 3086 Brighton 2nd St. off Brighton Beach Ave., 332-9797.

This small joint on a side street sells all the usual Russian dishes at prices so low that they must be in rubles, not dollars. An entrée of grilled chicken is under $5, a cup of borscht is $3.50, lamb kebabs $2.50, and the *vareniki* (Russian pierogi), after which the café is named, come stuffed with mushrooms and pota-toes, cabbage, cherries, and apple and strawberries for under $4.

On the Boardwalk Between Brighton 4th and Brighton 6th

Summertime tip: Check out the several big restaurants on the Boardwalk, where you can sit in a fine-dining atmosphere, have some Russian or American food, and people watch. Like all waterfront restaurants, they're expensive. But what fun!

CAFÉ VOLNA. On the Boardwalk and bet. Brightwater Ct. and Brighton 4th St.

SHOPPING

Specialty Food Shops

EFE INTERNATIONAL. 243 Brighton Beach Ave., 891-8933, daily 8 a.m.–9 p.m.

EFE specializes in dried fruits, nuts, and chocolates of wonderful quality and variety. Unusual dried fruits like cherry apples, yellow prunes, and black currants are reasonably priced, as are chocolate cordials of cognac, plum brandy, and other liqueurs, and dark chocolate bonbons with apricot and pineapple centers.

LA BRIOCHE CAFÉ. 1073 Brighton Beach Ave. bet. Brighton 10th and 11th Sts., 934-7709, daily 9 a.m.–7 p.m.

La Brioche is crammed with breads, coffees, and fresh pastries as well as chocolates, some imported from Russia.

⊘ **M & I INTERNATIONAL.** 249 Brighton Beach Ave. bet. Brighton 2nd and 3rd Sts., 615-1011 or 615-1012, daily 8 a.m.–10 p.m.

The labels on M & I's store brand of sausages feature old-fashioned black-and-white photos of smiling babies, as if to say, "We'd feed our child this two-foot bologna, wouldn't you?" A homey feel permeates this, the best and largest of a dozen local Russian food stores. In addition to cured meats of all kinds, you'll find a dizzying array of farmer, feta, and other cheeses; smoked fish and herring; prepared salads; and, of course, caviar, borscht, and sour cream. Prepared foods include kebabs, stuffed cabbage, chicken Kiev, and eggplant in garlic sauce. Don't miss the bakery upstairs. The local color is so compelling it's hard to know what to check out first, the people or the food. For takeout, try a potato or cheese *pierogi*.

If M & I is too overwhelming, try **Southern Gastronom** at 239 Brighton Beach Avenue, down the block.

⊘ **MRS. STAHL'S KNISHES AND NEW YORK BAGELS.** 1001 Brighton Beach Ave. corner of Coney Island Ave., 648-0210, daily 10:30 a.m.–6 p.m., www.mrsstahl.com.

The old Mrs. Stahl's sign on this storefront has made room for a new roommate, New York Bagels (yes, of Manhattan), which moved in during 2003. The bagels are good, but, hey, it's the knishes that are historic.

Mrs. Stahl's used the same recipe for these famous low-cholesterol knishes since 1935. The original knishes are kasha or potato filled, but by the late 1990s, Mrs. Stahl's menu included a rainbow of more than twenty fillings, including spinach, cabbage, cherry cheese, and chili. There's a small space for eating on the premises, but you're better off enjoying your knishes on the Boardwalk or at home. Shipping to knish-starved friends can also be arranged: the minimum order is one dozen. Tip: Never, ever heat your knish in a microwave.

ODESSA GASTRONOM. 1117 Brighton Beach Ave. bet. Brighton 13th and 14th Sts., 648-6044, daily 8 a.m.–7 p.m.

It's Mini Me of M & I. This food store has great cheeses, sausages, Russian-imported dry goods, caviar, fresh meats, and smoked fish. It's newly opened and fabulous.

SOUTHERN GASTRONOM. 239 Brighton Beach Ave. corner of Brighton 2nd St., 891-6569, daily 8 a.m.–10 p.m.

Straight from Eastern Europe: sausage, pastry, chocolates, and more. This is one of several such stores on the Brighton Beach Avenue strip. There's a café with pastries on the second floor.

Men's, Women's, and Children's Clothing, Accessories

CLASSIC FUR. 221 Brighton Beach Ave. near Brighton 2nd St., 332-5138, M–Sa 10 a.m.–7 p.m., Su 10 a.m.–6 p.m.

Here, second-generation Kiev furrier Anatoly Alter and his wife, Raya, have assembled a beautiful collection of mink, fox, lamb, lynx, raccoon, and other furs, as well as suede, with a European flair at good prices, starting at $800 and going up to several thousand. Tailoring is done on the premises, along with monogramming, cleaning, and storage.

GOLDEN DOOR. 256 Brighton Beach Ave. near Brighton 2nd St., 615-4050, daily 10:30 a.m.–6:45 p.m.

Golden Door showcases designer jewelry that brings out the vamp in you. It's part of a new wave of affluence that's hit Brighton Beach.

ITALIAN SHOE WAREHOUSE. 515 Brighton Beach Ave. bet. Brighton 4th and 5th Sts., 934-4812, daily 10:30 a.m.–7 p.m.

Bring your poor, tired dogs for a retread at this family emporium of high-quality, low-cost imported men's and women's shoes. (There are about eight such stores scattered through Brooklyn.)

LILY'S GIFTS AND JEWELRY. 1055-A Brighton Beach Ave. bet. Brighton 10th and 11th Sts., 615-0940, daily 10:30 a.m.–6:45 p.m.

Lily's displays of coral, gold, and diamond jewelry are like a siren's song, luring visitors and the well-heeled residents of Oceana across the street. Italian imports of high-end designers, such as Falcinelli, are showcased.

LITTLE ITALY BOUTIQUE. 291 Brighton Beach Ave. near Brighton 3rd St., 934-9337, M–F 11 a.m.–7 p.m., Sa 11 a.m.–6 p.m., Su 11 a.m.–5 p.m.

If you need fabulous dressy wear, come to Little Italy, where there's a terrific selection of sexy numbers for women by designers such as Sonia Rykiel, Blumarine, and Moschino—at full price.

MAJESTIC FASHION. 3165 Coney Island Ave. off Brighton Beach Ave., 743-7734, daily 11 a.m.–7 p.m.

Fur, fur, and more fur. You walk in this store, located on a noisy, trafficky, hard-core Brooklyn thoroughfare with the elevated Q train rumbling overhead every few minutes. Inside, there's a heavyset saleswoman smoking her one hundredth cigarette of the day, while a svelte young woman wearing skintight jeans and accompanied by a much older man (clearly not Dad) tries on fabulously flashy fur coats.

MILENA. 3169 Coney Island Ave. off Brighton Beach Ave., 648-1551, daily 11 a.m.–7 p.m.

This women's fashion store, owned by immigrants from Tashkent, Uzbekistan, for over two decades, has been renovated to look like a glitzy Milano fashion boutique, with lots of black, tight, expensive ladies' wear.

PELAME STUDIO. 272 Brighton Beach Ave., daily 11 a.m.–7 p.m., www.pelame.com.

How much is that fur coat in the window? At Pelame Studio, you can get furs, shearling, and leather for men, women, and children. They also custom-make furwear, so, if you are interested in a certain look or style, come here. Prices are good, and you can try to negotiate.

Books, Music, Gifts, and Other

BLACK SEA BOOKSTORE. 3175 Coney Island Ave. near Brighton Beach Ave., 769-2878, daily 11 a.m.–7 p.m.

Two doors down from **Mrs. Stahl's Knishes** (see above) is this one large room, stuffed with CDs, videos, audiotapes, and rows and columns of Russian tomes. Black Sea is different from most American bookstores: low on knick-knacks and flashy promotional displays, high on cover drawings of Boris Yeltsin, nude. Twenty minutes spent scanning the book jackets here will give you invaluable insight into the Russian sense of humor, adventure, and sexuality. If this puts you in the mood to learn more, you can also purchase tickets to occasional cultural events, such as poetry readings in Russian.

BRIGHTON FABRICS. 301 Brighton Beach Ave. bet. Brighton 3rd and 4th Sts., 769-1479, daily 11 a.m.–7 p.m.

Reminiscent of an earlier generation of immigrant Russian Jews who came to the United States and scraped together a living by selling sewing notions, the smiling owner of this crammed little store sells hundreds of different ribbons, seam bindings, buttons, and bolts of inexpensive cloth. Some of the goods are imported. Tailoring is an international language, which is helpful, as not much English is spoken here.

MALMAR. 258 Brighton Beach Ave. bet. Brighton 1st and 2nd Sts., 368-2516, daily 11 a.m.–7 p.m.

Malmar is one of several Madison Avenue–style boutiques in Brighton Beach, specializing in high-end Italian imported linens, table settings, handblown Murano glass from Venice, and other gift items for the home. There is also a small but excellent selection of pricey, sexy lingerie.

RBC VIDEO. 269 Brighton Beach Ave., 769-8605, daily 10 a.m.–9 p.m., www.RbcVideo.com.

Most Russian teens will only sheepishly admit to liking Russian pop music, but someone must be buying it, as RBC is the largest of several shops hawking Russian, European, and American CDs. Indeed, they claim to have "the largest Russian music and video collection in the United States."

ST. PETERSBURG BOOKSTORE. 605 and 230 Brighton Beach Ave. at Brighton 6th and 2nd Sts., respectively, www.ruskniga.com.

Karl Marx would roll over in his grave if he heard the motto of this Russian bookstore empire that markets in bookstores, on the Internet, and through direct mail: "We Easily Compete With Any Large Store in Russia." A capitalist success, St. Petersburg opened in 1994 in Brighton Beach, as a small mail-order Russian-language bookseller. By 1997 it claimed to be the largest bookstore in the United States specializing in Russian literature. The four locations in Brooklyn sell books, video, music, and DVDs—some airmailed from Russia so people can keep up with current trends. St. Petersburg stores also host cultural events and evenings with Russian music stars and writers, and serve as centers of Russian culture for the expatriates in their neighborhoods.

Coney Island

ABOUT CONEY ISLAND

Step right up, ladies and gentlemen! Keep your eye on Coney; things are changing. Meanwhile hipsters, artists, kids, fun lovers, the curious, and people with Brooklyn in their blood still flock here. Coney Island is as well known as Times Square. But, unlike Times Square, it hasn't experienced "revitalization," so don't expect to find a sanitized, corporate-owned amusement park. Yet.

Coney is a dreamland of fun and the press of human flesh, one of those magical places where a vivid past—known from movies, books, some collective American memory—crowds out today's lesser reality. When you go to Coney Island, you see the **Boardwalk,** the distant beach, and four blocks of amusement park. And your imagination adds what your eyes miss—the raw immigrant energy, amusement arcades as far as the eye can see, the kaleidoscopic images of an old New York, and the cacophony of barkers announcing their attractions, laughter, lovers' kisses, children crying, couples screaming, "Cumm'on over here." Just standing here stirs up a thick soup of memories, even among people too young ever to have come to Coney in its heyday.

There are plenty of ways to spend an afternoon or a day. Coney Island attracts a mishmash of tourists, locals, working people, artists, eccentrics, and parents with children; that it is a little tacky and very mixed appeals to bohemians. It is one of New York's safest spots, with an extremely low crime rate due to a beefed-up police presence.

HOW IT GOT ITS NAME However ridiculous it may sound, the story goes that when the Dutch first discovered this area, it was overrun with rabbits. They called it "Rabbit Island"—in Dutch, Konjin (Coney) Eiland.

BY SUBWAY D trains to Stillwell Avenue–Coney Island. Due to subway construction, check the MTA Web site for any service changes (www.mta.nyc.ny.us/nyct/subway/coney_island.htm). During construction, trains end a few stops away and offer shuttle bus service to Stillwell Avenue.

Coney Island

Bounded by Ocean Parkway, the Atlantic Ocean, Shore Parkway, and Nortons Point

↑ SHEEPSHEAD BAY

↑ TO MANHATTAN

GRAVESEND

E 3rd St.
E 2nd St.
E 1st St.
West St.
Ave. W
Ave. X
Ave. Y
Ave. Z
W 1st St.
W 2nd St.
W 3rd St.
McDonald Ave.
86th St.
Boynton Pl.
Murdock Ct.
Nixon Ct.

Shell Rd.
Ocean Pkwy.
West Ave.
Neptune Ave.

Br. 2nd St.
Br. 1st Pl.
Brighton 1st St.
Ocean View Ave.
Brightwater Ct.
Boardwalk E

BRIGHTON BEACH

Q

W Brighton Ave.
Seabreeze Ave.
W 5th St.
Seaside Park
Surf Ave.
Riegelman Boardwalk

Ave. X
W 8th St.
N
W 8th St.
Ave. X
W 11th St.
W 12th St.
W 13th St.
Stillwell Ave.
W 13th St.
Stillwell Ave.
W

BENSONHURST

New York Aquarium
Deno's Wonder Wheel, Cyclone, and Astroland

W 8th St.
Jones Wk.
W 10th St.
W 12th St.

F, N, Q, W
Coney Island Museum
Henderson Wk.
Bowery St.
Schweikerts Wk.
Kensington Wk.

Amusement Parks

C O N E Y I S L A N D

W 15th St.
W 16th St.
W 17th St.
W 18th St.
W 19th St.
W 20th St.
W 21st St.
W 22nd St.
W 23rd St.
W 25th St.
W 27th St.

Brooklyn Public Library

Keyspan Park & Cyclones
Steeplechase Park

Bath Ave.
Harway Ave.
Bay 41st St.
Bay 43rd St.
Bay 44th St.
Bay 46th St.
27th Ave.
26th Ave.
Cropsey Ave.
16th St. W
17th St. W
15th W
Bay 18th St.
Bay 20th St.
Bay 22nd St.

Bayview Shore Rd.

Bay 41st St.
Bay 43rd St.
Bay 50th St.

Bay 52nd St.
Bay 53rd St.
Bay 54th St.
W 16th St.
W 20th St.
W 21st St.
W 22nd St.

Dreier-Offerman Park

Gravesend Bay

Coney Island Creek

W 27th St.
W 28th St.
W 29th St.
W 30th St.
W 31st St.
W 32nd St.
W 33rd St.
W 35th St.
W 36th St.
W 37th St.

Mermaid Ave.
Neptune Ave.
Surf Ave.

Riegelman Boardwalk

Bayview Ave. W

W 36th St.
Canal Ave.

Sea Gate Ave.

Ocean View Ave.
Poplar Ave.
Maple Ave.
Cypress Ave.
Laurel Ave.
Lyme Ave.
Neptune Ave.
Nautilus Ave.
Oceanic Ave.
Atlantic Ave.
Surf Ave.
Manhattan Ave.
Beach 40th St.

Beach 50th St.
Beach 49th St.
Beach 48th St.
Beach 47th St.
Beach 46th St.
Beach 45th St.
Beach 44th St.
Beach 43rd St.

Nortons Point

A T L A N T I C   O C E A N

👁 What's **NEW?**

Coney's Comeback

Those in the know say anything could happen here in the next few years: big, upscale residential developments near the ocean; or the arrival of new entertainment clubs and venues; or opening of new, privately owned parks with rides and a water park.

Big-picture dreamers talk about the following possibilities: rezoning of parts of Surf Avenue to permit live-work lofts for artists and musicians, together with performance and exhibition spaces; upgrading the Aquarium and building a ferry pier there; luring a hotel to the area; adding a new tourism kiosk and a year-round sports park; restoration of the Parachute Jump; creating a bike path along the beach; opening a seasonal food court on Stillwell Avenue; and, most spectacular, building a modern sky ride looping around the whole amusement district for both rapid transit and fun. Some, none, or all may turn into reality.

If the Olympics come to New York City in 2012, a **Sportsplex** would host Olympic volleyball at Coney Island and subsequently be used for basketball and ice hockey competitions, and community recreation. Olympic planners envision Olympic sailing in the Atlantic Ocean. Just like the good ol' days.

While dreamers dream, here's what's *already* changed:

- **KeySpan Park**
- Lots more entertainment: Concerts at Asser Levy, the **Siren Music Festival,** sponsored by the *Village Voice*, **film festivals**, and, of course, the **Mermaid Parade.**
- There are even clean new bathrooms on the beach—and the beach itself is in better condition thanks to an Army Corps of Engineers environmental upgrade a few years ago.
- New York City has paid for an incredible renovation of the Stillwell Avenue and West 8th Street subway stations.

HISTORICAL NOTES

Coney Island's sensational era as a seaside resort lasted for more than a hundred years. As early as the 1830s, the rich and famous played here—from writer Herman Melville and poet Walt Whitman to actress Lillian Russell. When the subway gave millions of working-class New Yorkers access to Coney Island in the 1920s, the crowd changed, the entertainment cheapened, and it became the "playground of the people." On summer weekends, thousands of people of all ages, sizes, shapes, and nationalities poured through the subway turnstiles for entertainment and relief from the city's crushing heat. Among the most famous restaurants of the time was the German-owned Feltman's, whose founder reputedly claimed to have invented the notion of serving a sausage in an elongated roll, thereby inventing the hot-dog-in-a-roll.

Coney Island declined after World War II, and Steeplechase Park finally closed in 1965. Much of the bungalow housing around Coney Island was bulldozed and replaced with large public high-rises that remain today. The old feisty Coney Island of Steeplechase and Luna Park fame, the rides like the Thunderbolt and the Mile Sky Chaser, the racetracks, huge beach pavilions, flashy hotels, dozens of honky-tonk restaurants, and championship prizefights between muscle men in striped bathing suits exist mostly in memory and the movies. Meanwhile, Coney Island is more Brooklyn than Brooklyn itself. Don't miss it, ladies and gentlemen.

POINTS OF CULTURAL INTEREST

SPECIAL EVENTS.

Polar Bear Club Atlantic Ocean swim (January 1); Mermaid Parade (June); Brooklyn Cyclones Season Kickoff (June); Nathan's Hot Dog Eating Contest (July 4); Siren Music Festival (mid-July; www.villagevoice.com/siren); Seaside Concerts at Asser Levy Park (summer); Irish Fair (September).

AMUSEMENT PARK LANDMARKS: CONEY ISLAND.

The **Parachute Jump, Cyclone**, and **Wonder Wheel** are official New York City landmarks; the latter two dating from the 1920s are still in operation. The **recently restored Parachute Jump** was built for the New York World's Fair of 1939–40, and then transported to Steeplechase Park. The original steel tower is still visible from the Belt Parkway, Verrazano-Narrows Bridge, and many other vantage points.

CHILD'S RESTAURANT BUILDING. Boardwalk and W. 21st St. (one block west of KeySpan Park).

A reminder of the days when Coney Island was "the world's largest playground," this grand old building was designated a New York City landmark in 2003. Child's, replete with elaborate terra-cotta ornamentation, seashells, wriggling fish, gargoyles, sailing ships, and even a seaweed-draped sea god Neptune, opened in this fanciful building in 1923.

This was one of a chain of hundreds of self-service cafeterias started in 1889 by brothers Samuel and William Child. The restaurants, which were precursors to today's fast-food industry, were designed to look spiffy and clean, with white-tiled floors, marble countertops, and white starched uniforms on employees. After Child's closed, the building was used as a candy manufacturing facility, but Child's may once again become a restaurant or catering hall.

CONEY ISLAND, USA. 1208 Surf Ave., 372-5159, www.coneyislandusa.com.

Since 1982, Coney Island, USA, has made its mark by resurrecting fading Coney traditions: freak shows, vaudeville, and other forms of old-fashioned, hard-biting, sometimes corny working-class entertainment. This unusual non-profit arts organization has created the **Sideshows by the Seashore,** the **Coney Island Museum, summer films,** and the **Coney Island International Film Festival,** not to mention the spectacle of the **Mermaid Parade.** They've amassed a collection of Coney memorabilia, mounted art exhibits with a Coney theme, and hosted cutting-edge theater and music. Who makes all this honky-tonk? It is powered by a polyglot mix—people with academic credentials (the founder, Dick Zigun, has a degree from Yale in theater), Coney credentials (grandparents and parents who worked at Coney Island), artists, enthusiasts of the bizarre, and a multicultural mix of local residents. Coney Island, USA, *is* what they say they want to do: use Coney Island to "champion the honor of American popular art forms." Stay tuned for their next act. See "Entertainment" for details on all these great events.

IS 239 MARK TWAIN INTERMEDIATE SCHOOL FOR THE GIFTED AND TALENTED. 2402 Neptune Ave., 266-0814.

One of the city's most desirable public middle schools, Mark Twain is located on a lonely stretch in Coney Island—but the kids are bright, entrance is competitive, and many go on to excellent high schools. (Source: *New York City's Best Public Middle Schools,* 1999, by C. Hemphill.)

OCEAN PARKWAY SCENIC LANDMARK. From Seabreeze Ave. to just north of Coney Island.

Brooklyn's premier park architects, Frederick Law Olmsted and Calvert Vaux, envisioned Ocean Parkway as the link between green Prospect Park and the Atlantic Ocean waterfront. The tree-lined parkway has a bike path (once a bridle path), walkways, and wide drives. Check out the huge murals erected under the Ocean Parkway Viaduct at the intersection of Ocean Parkway and Brighton Beach Avenue. Commissioned by the MTA, Williamsburg-based artist Deborah Masters created 128 giant reliefs depicting the parade of humankind on Coney Island—fat, skinny, young, old, ugly, and beautiful.

PUBLIC SCHOOLS.

Among those considered to be New York City's best public elementary schools are PS 97 (1855 Stillwell Avenue) and PS 100 (2951 West 3rd Street). (Source: *New York City's Best Public Elementary Schools,* 2002, by C. Hemphill with P. Wheaton.)

STILLWELL AND 8TH STREET SUBWAYS: ARTISTIC RENOVATIONS.

If you haven't been to the Stillwell Avenue station for a while (or you have bad dreams about your last trip there), you won't recognize the place. Scheduled for completion in 2005, the renovated Stillwell station will boast a glass-block wall with sculpture by Robert Wilson, internationally famous director and theater man. The West 8th subway stop, across from the **New York Aquarium**, is getting a similar facelift, thanks to the artistic vision of Vito Acconci.

ENTERTAINMENT

> ☛ **TIP: The Perfect Summer Friday Family Outing**
> Take the kids and head down to the foot of Ocean Parkway. Bring a picnic, let the kids play in the sand until the Friday fireworks display starts about 9:30—and then walk down the Boardwalk for some great French fries.

Special Once-in-a-Season Events

☺ *Free!* **CIRCUS WEEKEND IN CONEY ISLAND.** Bet. W. 10th St. and Stillwell Ave., Astroland Amusement Park, 265-2100, www.astroland.com. July.

This *free* weekend-long event made its debut in 2003, and we hope it becomes an annual. Bringing the circus back to Coney Island, it featured small circus acts (such as Winn's Thrills of the Universe and their amazing circus and high-wire motorcycle), as well as local performance troupes such as Circus Amok and The Hungry Marching Band. Artists offered free face paintings to children while stilt walkers, jugglers, and clowns roamed throughout.

● *Free!* **MERMAID PARADE.** Surf Ave. and W. 12th St. June.

Combine raucous theater, tacky taste, and trendy hipsters with good clean fun, and what you get is a Brooklyn original, the Mermaid Parade. A good-natured, somewhat disorganized affair, the midafternoon parade gets bigger and better every year. Dozens of gorgeous vintage cars lead the procession, followed by mermaids, mermen, and merkids in sometimes freaky, always fishy costumes and floats. It is a photographer's delight of sequins, scant costumes, and corny humor.

NATHAN'S ANNUAL HOT DOG EATING CONTEST. Surf Ave. near Stillwell Ave., 946-2202, www.nathansfamous.com.

This twelve-minute contest that's held every Fourth of July gets television and print coverage from around the world.

♪ ◉ *Free!* **SIREN MUSIC FESTIVAL AT CONEY ISLAND.** www.villagevoice.com/siren. Mid-July.

Free music, all day, for all ages! Launched in the millennial year 2000, the Siren Music Festival is a free noon–9 p.m. indie music extravaganza, with two stages, sponsored by the *Village Voice.* About fifty thousand people crowd in to hear live national and local bands, DJs, carnival gaming, and much more throughout Coney Island's several indoor and outdoor venues. In the past, groups have included names such as Idlewild, The Datsuns, and Dirtbombs.

Summer-long Entertainment

☞ **TIP:** Don't miss 'em!
Cyclone, engineered in 1927, is a rare wooden roller coaster. Cars are pulled up by a chain pulley to the top, and gravity pulls them down nine spectacular drops and around six curves, reaching a speed of up to sixty-eight miles per hour.
Wonder Wheel was built in 1918–20 by the Eccentric Ferris Wheel Amusement Company. It is unusual in that eight of the cars are stable, while sixteen of them swing on tracks, enhancing the thrill of this 150-foot Ferris wheel.

♪ **AQUANIGHTS ⊅ NEW YORK AQUARIUM.** Surf Ave. at W. 8th St., 265-3474 (265-FISH), www.nyaquarium.com. July. Tickets are $15 general admission and $8 for kids 2–12 and seniors.

AquaNights concerts feature swing, Latin, and 1950s bands, and fun family music every Friday night in July. So you can relax in the plaza area and get a front view of the fireworks, or boogey through the Aquarium's grounds viewing penguins, beluga whales, and those funny, moustachey walruses. Evening ends at 10:30 p.m.

☺ ◉ **ASTROLAND AMUSEMENT PARK.** W. 12th St. bet. the Boardwalk and Surf Ave., 372-0275, weekends in April and daily mid-June to September, noon–midnight, www.astroland.com. One price for all rides, $13 at selected times. Ten kiddie rides cost $15.

Astroland is the bigger of the two amusement parks here, with about thirty rides and games for adults and older kids. The wood-framed **Cyclone** roller coaster, considered one of the best by roller-coaster aficionados, and featured in Woody Allen's classic movie, *Annie Hall,* is a screamer's delight.

☺ **B & B CAROUSEL.** 1043 Surf Ave., daily noon–10 p.m. Each ride costs $2.50.

Take the kids for a ride on a classic painted pony. The carousel's current owner, a rumpled senior citizen who sells tickets at nearby Hilo Kiddie Park and who says the carousel has been a family business for three generations, recalls that the fifty-five old-fashioned painted horses and carriages, with a classic central organ, were put in place in the mid-1930s or earlier. His family was connected with the people who ran the famous, long-defunct Steeplechase, making him Coney royalty.

☺ **BATTING RANGE, ROCK CLIMBING, MINIATURE GOLF, GO-CARTS.** Stillwell Ave. bet. Surf Ave. and Boardwalk, 449-1220, in season, daily 11 a.m.–11 p.m.

There's a new, small climbing wall here ($5 for three tries), miniature golf, go-carts, and nine batting cages ($2 for fourteen pitches), plus thrill rides.

> ☛TIP: Beach Fun (besides just hanging out)
> • **Sand Sculpting Contest on the beach.** 265-2100, www.astroland.com. July.
> • **Wrestling Championships on the Boardwalk.** 265-2100, www.astroland.com. July.

☺ ● **BROOKLYN CYCLONES.** KeySpan Park, 1904 Surf Ave., 449-8497, box office M–Sa 10 a.m.–4 p.m., www.brooklyncyclones.com. (See also **KeySpan Park** below.)

The kids pig out on curly fries. Everybody yells and cheers with abandon. Old men wear Cyclones T-shirts. There's a race between three big stuffed hot dogs (OK, people in full-body hot dog costumes) called Mustard, Ketchup, and Relish, between innings. The outfield wall is plastered with ads, one for a catering hall that says, "Only one wedding at a time!" You haven't been to Brooklyn if you haven't attended a Cyclones game. They play in **KeySpan Park**, a gorgeous small stadium with a hugely spirited crowd, views of the amusement park rides in motion and Atlantic Ocean breezes—and endless goofy shtick that keeps the crowd entertained.

The Cyclones are a Class A affiliate of the New York Mets. Players, generally aged 18–23, are scouted from around the world. They can be assigned to any of the Mets' farm teams, located in Tennessee, South Carolina, Florida, or Virginia. Home and away, the Cyclones play a seventy-six-game season.

Autographs: Cyclones' players and coaches are usually available before and after the games.

Team Store: The Cyclones store at KeySpan Park is open M–F 10 a.m.–5 p.m., Sa 10 a.m.–4 p.m., Su 11 a.m.–5 p.m.; you can shop at the team store on the Web and at a Kings Plaza Team Store, too.

Birthday fuss: Give twenty-four-hour advance notice and you might get a "Happy Birthday" on the video board or over the PA system (e-mail info@brooklyncyclones.com).

Rent-a-space: The Party Deck is available for rental on a nightly basis.

CONEY ISLAND MUSEUM. 1208 Surf Ave., 372-5159, Sa–Su noon–5 p.m., www.coneyislandusa.com.

For just 99 cents, you can check out this little museum of Coney Island memorabilia: a Steeplechase horse, the Boardwalk "rolling chair," fun-house distortion mirrors.

On a practical note, there's a clean bathroom here, some souvenirs, and a friendly person to answer questions about the neighborhood. Be a sport, join the museum; that gives you access to memorabilia in archives, for instance, a postcard collection, books about Coney Island, and material related to the history of Coney Island, USA. Future plans include walking tours and educational programs. Summer programs include "Ask the Experts," a Sunday-night series featuring Coney Island historians, and the new **Saturday Night Film Series,** featuring "historical, odd, colorful and informative films."

DENO'S WONDER WHEEL AMUSEMENT PARK. W. 12th St. bet. the Boardwalk and Surf Ave., 372-2592, Memorial Day to Labor Day 11 a.m.–midnight; April, May, September, October, weekends and school holidays only 11 a.m.–midnight, weather permitting, www.wonderwheel.com. Ten rides for $15.

Right next door to Astroland is a family attraction: an amusement park featuring the stomach-churning, sea-green **Wonder Wheel**, an official New York City landmark, which since 1920 has towered 150 feet over the Boardwalk, giving thrill-riders a tremendous view of the ocean and Brooklyn's rooftops and streets. You can also take younger kids on about two dozen juvenile rides here, visit the spook house, and play video games.

Deno's is named after Deno Vourderis, a Greek immigrant who jumped ship, swam to Coney Island, sold hot dogs, and bought the Wonder Wheel years ago. His sons run the amusement park today, and they're always there.

• *Films* •

⬤ **CONEY ISLAND SHORT FILM FESTIVAL.** www.indiefilmpage.com

Film festivals are sprouting up all over Brooklyn, but Coney's has a particular flair. Content-wise, anything goes, and some films resonate thematically with Coney Island, freaks and oddities, burlesque, and carnivals.

SUMMER SATURDAY NIGHT FILM SERIES AT THE CONEY ISLAND MUSEUM. June–Sept. Tickets are $5.

If you have a taste for strange and hilariously offensive movies, check out these Saturday-night specials. Some recent features included *Girlquake*—about "five Amazons from the center of the Earth who erupt into the desert one day and start doing the pony on a mountaintop"—and films by Nick Zedd, an underground filmmaker known for "violent, naked, perverted art films."

☺ ⬤ *Free!* **FIREWORKS ON FRIDAY NIGHTS.**

Sponsored by Astroland, Deno's, and others, these great Friday-night fireworks are visible from the beach, the ballpark, and the street. There's also a free, kid-pleasing karaoke show at the stage in front of Astroland kiddie park.

KEYSPAN PARK. 1904 Surf Ave., 449-8497, box office M–Sa 10 a.m.–4 p.m. Games are broadcast on Sporting News Radio 620AM WSNR or www.brooklyncyclones.com. (See **Brooklyn Cyclones** above.)

Home of the minor league **Brooklyn Cyclones,** KeySpan Park is a 7,500-seat ballpark located just steps from the Boardwalk. It opened in 2001—and in its first season began to transform Coney Island, bringing hundreds of thousands of people to the area on a weekly basis. (The Cyclones shattered the New York–Penn League attendance record in their first season, with 289,381 fans in thirty-seven games—a 7,821 average.) The opening of KeySpan marked the first time professional baseball's had a home in Brooklyn for almost fifty years—since dose bums, the Dodgers, quit for Los Angeles in 1957.

NEW YORK AQUARIUM. Surf Ave. at W. 8th St., 265-3474 (265-FISH), daily 10 a.m.–5 p.m., until 7 p.m. on summer weekends and holidays, wcs.org/home/zoos/nyaquarium. Admission is $11 for adults and $7 for children under 12 and seniors 65+. (Tip: It is economical to get a Wildlife Conservation Society membership if you plan to visit repeatedly, or visit other New York City area zoos.) Parking is additional. Call for directions.

Located at the foot of the Boardwalk in Coney Island, the New York Aquarium is home to giant sea turtles, tiger sharks, sea otters, beluga whales, and ten thousand other species. Rated one of the best aquariums in the nation, it is a year-round, indoor-outdoor facility that draws over three-quarters of a million visitors annually. Expanded facilities include Conservation Hall, which focuses on worldwide conservation concerns; Explore the Shore, a sophisticated display of coastal ecosystems, complete with miniature crashing wave which dumps four hundred gallons of water every thirty seconds in a simulated wave motion; the popular Aquatheater, an open-air amphitheater with a sea lion show; Sea Cliffs, a re-creation of a rocky Pacific coast habitat in which sea otters, walruses, penguins, and seals frolic; and Alien Stingers, which features the beauty of sea jellies and anemones.

Check out the seasonal programs for Halloween, winter holidays, and, of course, summer family camp. You can have birthday parties here, as well as private events, and get lots of information on shipwreck snorkeling off Long Island Sound, setting up home aquariums, and other terrific family activities.

♫ *Free!* **SEASIDE CONCERTS.** The band shell in Asser Levy "Seaside Park," Seabreeze Ave. and Ocean Pkwy., across from the Boardwalk and New York Aquarium, Th 8 p.m.

Here's one of the greatest rockin' summertime outings in the city. One summer's lineup included: Frank Sinatra Jr., followed by "world-class rockers" such as Randy Meisner of The Eagles, Denny Laine of Moody Blues and Wings fame, and Ron Wisko of Foreigner. Who could miss "A Tribute to Motown" with The Four Tops and Dennis Edwards' Temptations?

SIDESHOWS BY THE SEASHORE. 3006 W. 12th St. and Surf Ave., 372-5159, summer weekends, F 7 p.m.–midnight, Sa–Su 2 p.m.–midnight, www.coneyislandusa.com. Run by Coney Island, USA.

Part nostalgia, part freak show, part fun, this is a 1990s version of an old-time Ten-in-One Sideshow—that is, ten acts in one show. There are sword swallowers, a "bearded lady with an attitude," snake charmers, and other celebrations of a certain bizarre, seedy, curious side of life. Sometimes it's hilarious, sometimes raunchy—but it's never, ever sanitized like Disney.

PARKS AND PLAYGROUNDS

ABE STARK ICE-SKATING RINK. Bet. Surf Ave. and the Boardwalk at W. 19th St., 946-6536, Oct.–March. Call for hours and fees.

This indoor ice-skating rink is part of a huge New York City Parks and Recreation Department sports complex. The property is owned by the city, but operation of the facility is subcontracted, so double-check the hours before you go. There is parking on the premises.

CONEY ISLAND BOARDWALK. Along the Atlantic Ocean bet. Coney Island and Brighton Beach.

Coney Island's massive wooden boardwalk is as much a symbol as the Brooklyn Bridge. This big, beautiful boardwalk extends all the way from Brighton Beach through Coney Island. The natural scenery is as you would expect: the crashing Atlantic, a somewhat littered, broad beach—and the people watching is good too. Old-timers and retirees stroll and converse on the benches along the route, parents push carriages, and joggers speed past. In the winter, the Polar Bear Club has been known to take an icy dive here. This is a well patrolled and safe stroll during the day, which makes it perfect for a walk after eating in either Brighton Beach or Coney Island. By order of the Parks Department, it's also a "quiet zone," which means that loud radios are prohibited. Biking is allowed from 5 to 10 a.m. only.

KAISER PARK. W 31st St. and Neptune Ave.

This park has basketball and baseball facilities, a playground, and a fishing pier with a terrific view of the Verrazano-Narrows Bridge. The Gravesend Bay side of the park is famous for watching migrations in the spring and autumn of red-winged blackbirds, red-crested mergansers, buffleheads, double-crested cormorants, and marsh hawks.

♪ ☻ **SEASIDE-ASSER LEVY PARK.** Next to the **New York Aquarium**, bet. the Boardwalk and Seabreeze Ave., 946-1364.

This little twenty-two-acre park is a good place to let kids run off some steam after an afternoon at the **New York Aquarium**, and it's also notable for summer performances in its band shell (see p. 137). These shows are arranged in cooperation with **BAC**, the Brooklyn Arts Council (call 783-3077 to get a schedule). History buffs: Asser Levy was a Jewish New York social activist, and this park was originally created in 1908 when it housed a bathhouse, now a historic landmark that is located across from the Aquarium, near the entrance to the Boardwalk.

CONEY ISLAND RESTAURANTS, CAFÉS, PIZZERIAS, BEACH FOOD STANDS

CAROLINA. 1409 Mermaid Ave. bet. W. 15th St. and Stillwell Ave., 714-1294, M–Sa noon–10 p.m., Su 1–10 p.m.

Carolina was founded in 1928, just seven years after the Boardwalk opened. Along with **Gargiulo's**, Carolina is one of the few surviving eateries from that era, which included the now-defunct **Child's** and Feltman's, Coney Island's largest restaurant at the time. There is a lot of colorful history here, and the food is good, with big portions of old-fashioned Neapolitan home cooking. The interior sports lots of mirrors, a glass wall, and seats for three hundred people. Prices are moderate (entrées range from $10 to $18), and you're just a few blocks from the ocean. Valet parking is available.

GARGIULO'S. 2911 W. 15th St. between Surf and Mermaid Aves., 266-4891, W–M 11 a.m.–10:30 p.m., www.gargiulos.com.

This large family-run Italian restaurant is so popular that regular customers come from as far as New Jersey and Long Island. Don't be shy about asking for something you don't see on the menu—they'll prepare almost any dish you can think of. One final note: you can eat here for free if you're lucky. At the meal's end, your waiter will ask you for a number from one to ninety. He'll then produce a bucket of small chips, shake it up, and pull one from inside. If the numbers match, the meal is on the house (only applies to groups of ten or fewer, drinks excluded). Reservations are necessary.

GREGORY AND PAUL'S BEACH FOOD STANDS. Two locations: Surf Ave. facing the Cyclone, and 1001 Boardwalk East, 449-4252.

Those in the know claim that Gregory and Paul's serve the best French fries in town. Rumor has it that their secret recipe calls for only Yukon potatoes. Go try for yourself! Open when you'd expect them to be.

⚫ NATHAN'S FAMOUS RESTAURANT. Surf Ave. near Stillwell Ave., 946-2202, Su–Th 8–4 a.m., F–Sa 8–5 a.m., www.nathansfamous.com.

This is *THE original* Nathan's. Fans contend that the fries, hot dogs, and corn on the cob here are still better than those at the franchised Nathan's. You can just stand here munching while imagining the days when shrieking riders enjoyed the Thunderbolt, the Mile Sky Chaser, and the Loop-o-Plane. Or come on the Fourth of July for the twelve-minute Annual Hot Dog Eating Contest.

PEGGY O'NEILL'S CONEY ISLAND AT KEYSPAN PARK. 1904 Surf Ave. corner of W. 19th St., 449-3200, www.peggyoneills.com.

Burgers, mozzarella sticks—and, of course, shepherd's pie—are the fare at this new bar/restaurant, opened to serve the enthusiastic Cyclone baseball team fans. An offspring of the popular bar by the same name in Bay Ridge. Friday night is karaoke night, and on Tuesdays, they sponsor a **summer film festival.**

TOTONNO'S. 1524 Neptune Ave. bet. W. 15th and 16th Sts., 372-8606, W–Su noon–8:30 p.m. Cash only.

Founded in the 1920s, this Brooklyn institution serves what many consider to be the best brick-oven pizza in the entire Big Apple (except for their new Upper East Side location—maybe). Otherwise sane and sober men have been heard to compare eating **Totonno**'s pizza with having a religious experience. Used to stay open only as long as the dough lasted, but a changing of the guard means they actually keep normal hours.

AND THEN THERE'S . . .

☻ **LOLA STAAR.** On the Boardwalk, 855-8773, www.lolastaar.com. Irregular hours.

Nice or naughty? Decide for yourself. Lola Staar is a teen-oriented vampy souvenir shop that sells take-homes like T-shirt designs inspired by the old Coney Island amusement parks. Lola Staar shirts pop up in the strangest places, including on the cover of *Teen People.*

Sheepshead Bay

This subchapter is a pastiche, combining Sheepshead Bay and some bits of Manhattan Beach, Marine Park, Mill Basin, and Garristen Beach, as well. It also lists Canarsie Pier and the Gateway Center Mall.

ABOUT THE NEIGHBORHOODS

Sheepshead Bay

Emmons Avenue is out of this world. The pressure of New York's urban hustle fades quickly amid piers and fishing boats, dressed-down seafood restaurants, and the lovely beach breezes of Sheepshead Bay. The waterfront at Sheepshead Bay feels as if it belongs in Rhode Island.

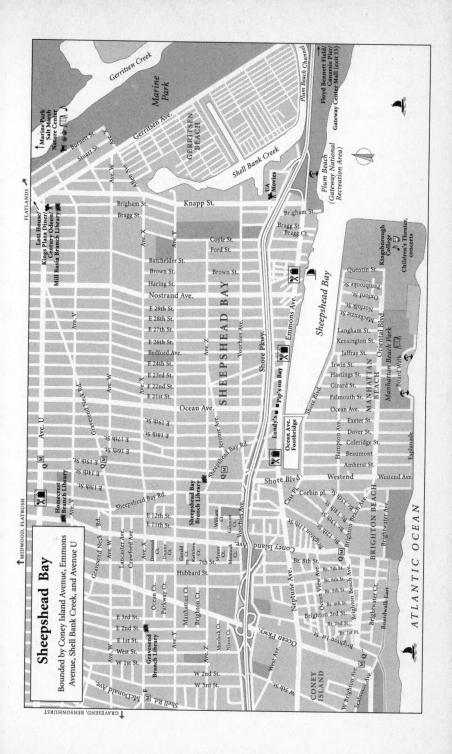

You can go out with a half-day fishing boat from the Emmons Avenue piers in the morning, or come around one or four p.m. to purchase the day's catch. There's a wonderful lobster-and-fish shop called **Jordan's Lobster Dock**, and a ten-screen movie theater in Sheepshead Bay. **Randazzo's** continues to do a land office business in fried seafood, and **Pips on the Bay** is still keepin' them laughing. (This pioneer comedy club gave the young Joan Rivers, David Brenner, and Rodney Dangerfield their early breaks.) **Loehmann's,** a started-in-Brooklyn institution, is a discount shopper's paradise, and when you're starved from all that shopping you can try out one of the large cafés right downstairs from the store.

HOW IT GOT ITS NAME Sheepshead Bay is named for the sheepshead, a once-common fish in nearby waters, now long gone due to urban pollution. The shape of the fish's head and teeth resemble a sheep's head. Marine Park is named for the public park it its midst, near the water.

☛ **TIP: For parents.** Plan a nice day trip for young kids. You can get some quick food near the water, and around one p.m. or four p.m. watch a few afternoon boats come in and the fish prepared and sold. Or, put the bikes in the back of the car and take a little ride along the piers (about a mile).

Manhattan Beach

Across the water from Sheepshead Bay is **Manhattan Beach**. Manhattan Beach started, and remains, quite separate from more rough-and-tumble Sheepshead Bay nearby. This little area (between Amherst Street and Pembroke Street and the ocean blocks of Corbin Place and West End Avenue) was home in the late nineteenth century to big, fancy hotels. Alas, there's no place you can go today to see what Manhattan Beach once was. The elite, exclusive summer resort area was developed by one Austin Corbin, who was given to labeling Brooklyn streets with upper crust–sounding British street names. There's an entertaining history of class conflict occurring between the two neighborhoods over the now-**Ocean Avenue Footbridge** connecting them. If you're interested, read *Swept by Ocean Breezes,* published in 1989, by one-time Brooklyn official historian, and Manhattan Beach resident, John B. Manbeck.

Today, homes here are still luxurious; many have views of the ocean or the bay. Residents include a growing number of Russians spilled over from nearby Brighton Beach. At its eastern end, **Kingsborough Community College** occupies a stunning piece of real estate, bounded on three sides by the water. The view alone is reason enough to attend a free outdoor summer concert.

Avenue U: Another Brooklyn Chinatown

Melting pot indeed! Second only to Sunset Park, this is a burgeoning China-town, with Chinese trading stores, Chinese fish stores, Chinese travel agents—and, of course, Chinese restaurants. Instead of granola and waffles for breakfast on the weekend, try dim sum specials, a little duck, or spare ribs and sauce.

And Then Some

East of Sheepshead Bay are a number of attractions, including **Marine Park**, the **Jamaica Bay Riding Academy**, and **Gateway National Park**.

In the **Mill Basin** area you will find **Villa Bay Ristorante and Pizzeria**. Visit **Mill Basin Kosher Deli and Fine Art Gallery**, perhaps the only delicatessen in New York City that boasts a real art collection. There are old-fashioned neighborhood Italian food places on Avenues N and T. Inexpensive authentic Italian cuisine can be found at **Prima Pasta and Café** or **Massimo's Ristorante,** or food to take home at **La Torre Pork Store** and **Moretti's Bakery**. Marine Park offers a full day's worth of outdoor fun; don't miss a visit to the **Salt Marsh Nature Center** here.

HISTORICAL NOTES

Sheepshead Bay: A bit of colorful history graces Sheepshead Bay. Most of Brooklyn was rural farmland in the nineteenth century. By the 1870s streetcar lines and railroads were extended to the hotels, stimulating a real estate boom in the area. During the late nineteenth century, wealthy Manhattanites frequented the many fancy Manhattan Beach hotels and resort homes. In the late 1800s a horseracing track ran along Ocean Avenue between Jerome Avenue and Neck Road. After racetrack betting was outlawed, the racetrack tried unsuccessfully to shift from horses to cars, but the Sheepshead Speedway lasted briefly, giving way in 1923 to residential development. In decades to follow, the area benefited greatly from two municipal building programs. In the 1930s the piers along Emmons Avenue were built as part of a Works Progress Administration project. In the 1950s the new Belt Parkway vastly improved access to Sheepshead Bay, which stimulated the growth of the middle-class Jewish and Italian community.

Marine Park: Now, a word on how Brooklyn's early history was intimately tied up with that of Native Americans and the colonial Dutch. Of course, Native Americans lived in this gloriously fertile coastal area, too, as was documented in the late 1970s by Professor H. Arthur Bankoff and other Brooklyn College archaeologists who found three sites with shells, pottery, and beads, dated to about 1400. A large swath of land was purchased in (est.) 1636 from local Canarsee Indians by the Dutch government (who paid in clam shells), who in turn granted a large tract to a Dutch settler named Garretson. Garretson built a farm and the first gristmill in the area, which survived to be the longest-standing tide mill in Kings County. The descendants of the original settler (known as Gerritsen) kept the homestead and land until 1876, and the mill remained in operation until the late nineteenth century, explaining why the area became known as Gerritsen Creek. In the early twentieth century, the wetland north of Avenue U was filled in and is today housing. (In a genius stroke of urban recycling, the landfill came from the New York area, from all the digging around bridge-and-tunnel construction of that era.) In the 1920s, 150 acres of Gerritsen's remaining land was purchased by New York City as the core parcel for a public park. Within a decade, both the area and the park became officially known as Marine Park. For more information, contact the Brooklyn Historical Society, Brooklyn College Archaeological Research Center, or Museum of the American Indian. (See also: **Lott House**, p. 146).

(Based in part on "Marine Park" by Dr. H. Arthur Bankoff, Christopher Ricciardi, and Alyssa Loorya—a summary of the official site report on file at Brooklyn College.)

POINTS OF CULTURAL INTEREST

SPECIAL EVENTS.

Bayfest—live music, rides, diving and sailing demonstrations, parades of historic boats (May); art shows along Emmons Avenue (May and September); summer concerts at Kingsborough Community College. *In Marine Park:* Back to School Festival (September); Santa in the Park (December); and Music in the Park concerts (summer). *In Floyd Bennett Field:* Many special events, including September Antique Auto Show; call for calendar.

BAY ACADEMY OF ARTS AND SCIENCES. Emmons Ave. at Shore Blvd.

Intermediate School 98, also known as Bay Academy of Arts and Sciences, is a magnet school for gifted students, which accepts only a fraction of applicants.

F.W.I.L. LUNDY BROTHERS RESTAURANT. Emmons Ave. corner of Ocean Ave.

A New York City landmark, Lundy's of Sheepshead Bay was considered America's largest restaurant when it was built in 1934. An earlier restaurant opened in 1907 on the bay side of Emmons Avenue. It is said that the restaurant could serve as many as five thousand meals a day, and fifteen thousand on a major holiday. Closed in 1979, it remained an empty shell for many years, and a smaller, renovated Lundy's reopened in one half of the building in 1999. The rest of the huge structure houses offices. F.W.I.L. are the initials of the founder, Frederick William Irving Lundy. The two-story stucco Spanish Mission–style building is unusual for the area.

HOT ROD SHOW. Diehard Cruisers, St. Columbus Church, 2245 Kimball Street at Ave. V, 917-406-0611. June, www.diehardcruisers.org.

Vroom, vroom, vroom, deep in the heart of Brooklyn. A person might live in Brooklyn Heights, say, for thirty-five years, in blissful ignorance of the annual all-day hot-rod show where hard-core Brooklynites of the James Dean persuasion (if not, perhaps, looks) show off about a hundred cars.

HOLOCAUST MEMORIAL MALL PARK. Emmons Ave. at Shore Blvd.

Thousands of Holocaust survivors live in the area—some say more than in any other part of the world outside of Israel. This small mall was the first memorial in New York City to commemorate those who perished in the Holocaust.

KINGSBOROUGH COMMUNITY COLLEGE. 2001 Oriental Blvd. off Quentin Ave., 368-5000, www.kbcc.cuny.edu.

Wow, what a campus—some of the top schools in the country can't match it. Founded in 1963, Kingsborough is one of twenty colleges in the City University of New York (CUNY) system, the third largest system in the United States. It is located on a 72-acre waterfront campus in Manhattan Beach, on the southern peninsula of Brooklyn. The college serves more than 35,000 credit and continuing-education students per year, accepting all students with a high school diploma or GED. It offers a range of academic programs and given its waterfront location and full marina, it's not surprising that one of their focuses is teaching waterfront job skills.

You have to pass a security guard to enter (and if you come with a bike group, call ahead for clearance, 368-4800).

LEON M. GOLDSTEIN HIGH SCHOOL FOR THE SCIENCES. On campus of Kingsborough Community College, 1830 Shore Blvd., 368-8500.

This high school is set right on the college campus, with views of fishing boats bobbing in Sheepshead Bay. The fewer than two hundred students per grade enjoy use of the college library and gym, and have their own new building, well equipped with science labs and rooms for the arts. The school has associations with Lincoln Center and the Brooklyn Botanic Garden and rates "very good" college admissions. (Source: *New York City's Best Public High Schools: A Parents' Guide: Second Edition,* by C. Hemphill with P. Wheaton and J. Wayans).

LOTT HOUSE. 1940 E. 36th St. bet. Fillmore Ave. and Ave. S., 375-2681. Not currently open to public.

Officially known as the **Hendrick I. Lott House**, this rambling old Colonial-style farmhouse was first built in 1720 by Dutch farming settlers named Lott. It had been occupied continuously until 1989, and in sheer physical size was a major presence in an otherwise unremarkable tract of modest homes.

Kings County was the second largest slave-holding area in the nation before New York State abolished the practice in 1827. An excavation conducted from 1997 to 2001 by a team led by Professor H. Arthur Bankoff of the Brooklyn College Archaeological Research Center discovered some intriguing finds. Bankoff's archaeological team discovered a trap door in the ceiling of a lean-to connected to one section of the rambling house. The trap door led to a tiny, cramped living space. Under the old floorboards was what, to the untrained eye, might look like junk: some old corncob husks shaped in what appears to be a five-pointed star, a shell, pieces of an animal's pelvic bone, and a cloth pouch. However, these objects bear similarities to items used in spiritual practices of both slaves in the Deep South and of the West African tribes from which many slaves were taken. One interpretation is that African spiritual traditions survived outside the Deep South and were practiced in the north despite the isolation that slaves endured.

But it's a bit of a detective story, due to this twist: The Lott family are identified through historical records as having been among the area's early major slave owners. However, they freed their slaves prior to emancipation. So, were these quarters slave quarters? And, if so, who were the enslaved? The end of the story has yet to be written. (Thanks to Brooklyn College Archaeological Research Center, Department of Anthropology and Archaeology, for assistance).

☺ **MARINE PARKWAY—GIL HODGES BRIDGE.** South end of Flatbush Ave.

Most kids love bridges, and this is a pleasant one, connecting Brooklyn to the public beach at Jacob Riis Park and more secluded beaches off residential streets in Rockaway, Queens.

☺ **OCEAN AVENUE FOOTBRIDGE.**

In August 1880 the first simple drawbridge connecting Sheepshead Bay and Manhattan Beach was built by the Manhattan Beach Company. It's still a delight to walk across from one neighborhood to the other. The wooden planks have a nice feel, and often you'll see folks fishing from the bridge; one might pull a "bunker" out of the water! This is a nice little walk for young children.

🎓 **PUBLIC SCHOOLS.**

Among those considered to be among New York City's "best public elementary schools" are PS 251 (1801 Avenue Y); PS 195 (131 Irwin Street in Manhattan Beach); PS 222 (3301 Quentin Road); PS 236 (6302 Avenue U); PS 312 (7103 Avenue T). (Source: *New York City's Best Public Elementary Schools,* 2002, by C. Hemphill with P. Wheaton.)

VARUNA BOAT CLUB. 2806 Emmons Ave. off E. 28th St.

Today it's just a private club, engaged in football and dart tournaments. And no, tourists aren't welcome. But if it's true, as rumored, that the original club was founded in 1875, that date coincides with Coney Island–Sheepshead Bay's early heyday, just after the opening of railways reaching this far out.

WYCKOFF-BENNETT RESIDENCE. 1669 E. 22nd St. corner of Kings Hwy.

Admire this homestead, a national historic landmark, from the outside only; it is still privately owned. Built in the Dutch style, it was used by Hessian troops during the Revolutionary War. The date of its construction is discreetly carved into one of the wooden beams: 1766.

ENTERTAINMENT

CENTURY THEATER-CINEPLEX ODEON KINGS PLAZA. 5201 Kings Plaza at Flatbush Ave. and Ave. U, 253-1110, 253-1111, or 718-777-FILM.

There are four screens here, on the upper level of the mall.

☺ **CHILDREN'S THEATER FESTIVAL AT KINGSBOROUGH COMMUNITY COLLEGE.** 2001 Oriental Blvd. off Quentin Ave., 368-5596, www.kbcc.cuny.edu. Call for a concert schedule.

A *great* resource: you can get $8 tickets for shows like *Peter Pan* and *Amelia Bedelia.* Visiting troupes include Paper Bag Players, Story Salad Productions, and the Hudson Vagabond Puppets. Make a day of it: a walk around the campus, lunch near the boats across the way, and take in a kiddie performance. (See below for more on KCC.)

☺ **FISHING BOATS.** Emmons Ave. bet. Ocean and Bedford Aves.

For a wonderfully picturesque Brooklyn activity, walk along this pier at around four p.m. any afternoon and watch the fishing boats unload their daily haul of bluefish, flounder, and mackerel. You can buy fresh fish at rock-bottom prices.

Or, you can book onto any one of over a dozen party fishing boats, both half-day bay and full-day ocean boats. Half-day boats, more appropriate for families and casual fishermen, leave hourly from 7 a.m. to 1 p.m. for four-hour trips, and cost $17–$30 for adults, with discounts for kids under twelve. Try the *Pastime* (252-4398) or the *Dorothy B.* (646-4057). The *Amberjack V* also is available for cruises and charter.

Dorothy B. also makes sunset tours of the New York Harbor and Statue of Liberty.

☛ **TIP: Fishing Boats in Sheepshead Bay.**

Pier 1: *Bullet Fleet* (265-6915).
Pier 2: *Pastime Princess* (252-4398 or www.pastimeprincess.com).
Pier 3: *Royal Sunshine* (965-6931). Also *Explorer* (680-2207 www.explorerfishing.com). Also *Sea Queen* (646-6224).
Pier 4: *Captain Dave* (491-9702 or 251-2628).
Pier 5: *Ocean Eagle* (946-2614) and *Jeanne II* (332-9574) Also *Sea Queen:* "Family Friendly."
Pier 6: *Brooklyn Comfort* (743-8464) and *Dorothy B. VIII* (646-4057 www.dorothyb.com).
Pier 7: *Lark III* (645-6942).
Pier 8: *Navigator* (967-2131 or 917-609-7736).
Pier 10: *Amberjack V* (646-7753).

FUN TIME, USA. 2461 Knapp St. bet. Aves. X and Y, Su–Th 10 a.m.–10 p.m., F–Sa 10 a.m.–1 a.m., www.Funtimeusa.net. Entrance package about $15.

This large indoor amusement park offers over fifty thousand square feet of rides, including a maze, tornado ride, bumper cars, batting cages, and video arcade, with an additional fee for laser tag. It draws a diverse, urban crowd. Adults may find it a little tacky, but the kids don't seem to mind.

☺ **HITS & HOOPS.** 336 Ave. Y off McDonald Ave., 998-4000, M–F 11 a.m.–midnight, Sa–Su 10 a.m.–midnight, www.hitsandhoops.com/hits_n_hoops/home.html.

Newer than Fun Time, this facility offers 43,000 square feet of batting cages, basketball, hockey, instructional hitting and pitching, and video games. They throw children's parties with a choice of clowns, dance instructors, and more. There's a memorabilia shop on premises.

☺ ◉ ♫ 🎓 **KINGSBOROUGH COMMUNITY COLLEGE.** 2001 Oriental Blvd. off Quentin Ave., 368-5669, www.kbcc.cuny.edu.

For an oceanside Saturday evening, check out the free summer concerts at this community college. Bounded on three sides by water (Sheepshead Bay, Jamaica Bay, and the Atlantic Ocean) this modern seventy-two-acre campus with its own private beach is one of New York City's loveliest and most secluded spots. The concerts feature big band music, and the middle-aged, multiethnic audience loves to dance!

KCC also has open-to-the-public lectures, political forums, and great classes in those things you've always wanted to do (play the guitar, for instance). A new film festival is being planned. There are Saturday classes for youngsters, "College for Kids," and "Weekend College for Adults." Enrolling as a student gets you a beach pass. The college is exploring opening a new **Holocaust Resource Center.**

PIPS ON THE BAY. 2005 Emmons Ave. corner of Ocean Ave., 646-9433, F–Sa 9:15 p.m., 11:30 p.m.; special Th and Su shows, www.pipscomedyclub.com (might change to *.net* or *.org*).

Joan Rivers, David Brenner, Rodney Dangerfield, and Andy Kaufman all tried out their early comic routines at Pips. This club has hosted Woody Allen, Lenny Bruce, George Carlin, Jerry Seinfeld, and Adam Sandler. You never know what up-and-comer you may hear first at Pips, or what star may pop in to test a new bunch of jokes. It's basic humor, the human observation sort; wry understatement is not the *spécialité de la maison*. Up and comers? According to owner Roy Garvey, watch for Vic Di Bitetto, Jim Florentine, Joey Gay. Pips draws a rollicking outer-borough crowd (Brooklyn, Staten Island, Queens, and Long Island). And they get an inexplicably large number of bachelorette parties.

UA MOVIES AT SHEEPSHEAD BAY. 3907 Shore Pkwy. bet. Knapp St. and Harkness Ave., 615-1700, 718-777-FILM #786.

It seems like the suburbs here at Brooklyn's largest movie complex, a ten-screen theater easily reached from the Belt Parkway's Knapp Street exit. It's only twenty minutes from Brooklyn Heights in moderate traffic, so you may wait longer to get into the movie than to get to it. The picturesque harbor and **Jordan's Lobster Dock** across the street both contribute to a sense that you've left the city behind.

Russian Nightclubs

The Russians have arrived in Sheepshead Bay, as is evident by the two following nightclubs. Rumor has it that sometimes there are teen nights, but we haven't been able to confirm this. See page 120 in Brighton Beach for a general description of Russian nightclubs.

HEAVEN NEW YORK. 2814 Emmons Ave. at 28th St., 934-2283, Th–Su 9 p.m.–2 a.m., live music and DJs, www.heavenny.com.

Live it up! Life's short! Heaven is one of the Russian community's most popular Sheepshead Bay nightclubs. It's a sleek multilevel chrome-and-stainless-steel club with a "VIP lounge" that overlooks the water (where the old Paradise Club used to be). The club claims to have a multimillion-dollar light-and-sound system. Chilean chef German Caceres did a stint at the SoHo Grand Hotel. Average entrée about $20.

RASPUTIN. 2670 Coney Island Ave. at Ave. X, 332-8111 or 332-9187, M–Th noon–10 p.m., F–Su noon–4 a.m.

Since 1992, Rasputin has made a name for itself by treating customers to a lavish French-Russian version of a Las Vegas dinner, dancing, and floor show. It's larger (and louder) than life: the Russian clientele is outrageously flashy, the food is overwhelming, the cultural innuendo flows thick, and the icy-cold Absolut, well, just flows. It's an experience. About $65 per person.

Yacht Clubs and Sailing School

MIRAMAR YACHT CLUB. 3050 Emmons Ave., 769-3548, www.miramaryc.com.

Miramar's fleet of Ensigns, a one-design sailboat class, races regularly out of this club along with its larger sailboats, which compete with neighboring Sheepshead Bay Yacht Club. Miramar's club includes a swimming pool and a large outdoor sun deck for parties and barbecues, which are frequent during the summer months.

SHEEPSHEAD BAY YACHT CLUB. 3076 Emmons Ave., 891-0991, www.sheepsheadbayyc.org.

Established in 1908, the club offers facilities for sailing and motoring, including sailboat racing on weekends and Wednesday nights, a large outdoor pool, dining facilities, a well-stocked 29-foot bar, and pool table.

☻ **SHEEPSHEAD BAY SAILING SCHOOL.** 377-5140, mid-May through October.

You can learn to handle sails and moorings and to maneuver a sailboat right here in Brooklyn. Since 1966 Irving Shapiro has given private lessons to aspiring sailors ranging in age from thirteen to sixty. There are beginner, intermediate, and advanced sessions aboard his Ensign sloop, which leaves from one of the yacht clubs in Sheepshead Bay on Emmons Avenue. You can hire out a thirty-five-foot C & C sailboat on an hourly basis; call for rates.

PARKS, PLAYGROUNDS, AND BEACHES

☺ **BILL BROWN PARK PLAYGROUND.** Bedford Ave. at E. 24th St. bet. Aves. X and Y.

☻☺ **MANHATTAN BEACH PARK.** Oriental Blvd. bet. Ocean and Mackenzie Sts.

A favorite among families, Manhattan Beach is a forty-acre public park and beach area, complete with ball fields, surf and sand, concession stands, and room for parking.

☺ **MANHATTAN BEACH PARK PLAYGROUND.** Corner of Oriental Blvd. and Ocean Ave.

☻ PLUM BEACH. Along BQE, near Floyd Bennett Field, 338-3799. Accessible by car only from Shore Pkwy. going east, turn in past Exit 9. Or take the 235 bus from Flatbush Ave. to Floyd Bennett Field and walk the greenway. Dawn to dusk.

Stop for a beach walk along a mile and a half of protected shoreline along Dead Horse Bay and Sheepshead Bay. This is an environmentally protected salt-marsh area, under the joint jurisdiction of the New York City parks department and the federal park system. School groups often come to explore the salt marsh, which is an estuary for fish and mollusks. Although not allowed officially, some people go wind surfing and parasurfing here. Fishing is allowed, without a permit.

◑ ☺ TUCKER PLACE POCKET PARK. Emmons Ave. corner of E. 27th St.

J. Driscol Tucker, a Brooklyn politico known as the "Mayor of Sheepshead Bay," is memorialized in this small park with nice benches, aggressive pigeons, and a view of the boats.

The following parks are in nearby **Mill Basin** *or* **Marine Park**:

◑ ☺ ☻ FLOYD BENNETT FIELD. Flatbush Ave. past Ave. X and Belt Pkwy., 338-3799, daily 6 a.m.– 9 p.m. Take Exit 11S from Belt, go south of Flatbush Ave. for ¼ mile. To get a full calendar of what's going on here, get on their quarterly newsletter mailing list. *For aviation history* www.floydbennett.org. *Stargazing* www.aaa.org/events/floydbennett.html. *For bird-watching* www.brooklynbirdclub.org/floyd.htm.

This old, unused airfield from the 1930s takes up more than 1,500 acres and still rates as one of the city's scruffy rural treasures. There are rarely crowds here. You can zoom around on a bike, try out your homemade recumbent vehicle, or bring a bunch of kids for a birthday party with remote-controlled cars, or, even better, airplanes, on one of the long unused runways. There are four miles of paved bikeable paths, but no off-road biking.

Organized special events include everything from bike races to antique auto shows every September (see **Antique Automobile Association of Brooklyn**). In the summer, hundreds of people come to garden in a designated three-acre area comprised of over six hundred individual plots, under the aegis of the Floyd Bennett Field Gardening Association.

In the fall you can walk (not bike) the North Forty Nature Trail and get an eyeful of autumnal colors. The New York City Amateur Astronomers Association comes to stargaze, and the Brooklyn Bird Club organizes trips to bird-watch.

Who was Floyd Bennett anyway? The pilot who made the virgin flight over the North Pole with Admiral Richard Byrd in 1926. This airfield was built four years later as New York City's first municipal airport, but it was bypassed in favor of the more centrally located LaGuardia as the site for an expanded commercial airport. Floyd Bennett Field was used for several decades by the U.S. military, including during WWII. Since 1972 it has been part of the National Park Service.

⚫☺ **GATEWAY SPORTS CENTER.** 3200 Flatbush Ave. across from Floyd Bennett Field, 253-6816, daily 8 a.m.–11 p.m.

At Gateway you can brush up on your golf skills, hit a few tennis balls, or take a swing or two at some fastballs. Open year-round, this facility has a driving range, tennis courts, and batting cages. You can make an outing of it with the kids, as Gateway isn't far from Toys "R" Us, the huge Kings Plaza shopping mall or Marine Parkway Bridge, which leads to Jacob Riis Park Beach. There's a multisport pro shop on the premises.

⚫☺ **JAMAICA BAY RIDING ACADEMY.** 7000 Shore Pkwy. bet. Exits 11 and 12 (the exit for the riding academy is marked by a large horse), 531–8949, Tu–Th 9 a.m.–7 p.m., M and F 9 a.m.–5 p.m., Sa 9 a.m.– 5 p.m., Su 10 a.m.–7:30 p.m., www.horsebackride.com. Call for exact hours, options, and prices.

Your child can learn to ride a horse in Brooklyn. There are wonderful trails through three hundred acres of bird-watching country, including three miles along the beaches of Jamaica Bay. Kids as young as four can take lessons, the under-four set gets a twenty-minute pony ride—with Mom or Dad holding the horse ($10 for fifteen minutes), and teenagers can ride with a guide for nearly an hour ($25). There are group and private trail rides, pony rides, lessons, and ring rides. There's a summer camp and birthday party packages, too.

☺♣ **MARINE PARK.** Bounded by Flatbush Ave., Gerritsen Ave., 32nd St., Stuart St., Ave. U (Exit 11N off Belt Pkwy.), 965-6551/965-8973 (Marine Park Civic Assn. 336-7343), daily 6 a.m.–10 p.m.

At 798 acres, Marine Park is Brooklyn's largest outdoor recreation area, and it's worth a visit. There is a wonderful **Nature Center** (see p. 153), about a dozen tennis courts on Fillmore Avenue and Stuart Street, playgrounds at East 38th and East 33rd Streets, and a running track at East 33rd Street. There are lots of events, including a "haunted" twilight walk at Halloween, kite-flying, bird-watching, biking, bocci courts, and summertime concerts. Plans to reconstruct the eighteenth-century Gerritsen's gristmill and convert it into a museum are under consideration.

☺ *Special Events:* There's a Back to School Festival in September, Santa in the Park, and bocci tournaments (free). There are wonderful free concerts, including opera, in the summer. And kids love the annual **Clyde Beatty–Cole Brothers Circus.**

MARINE PARK GOLF COURSE. Corner of Flatbush Ave. and Ave. V, 338-7113, daybreak to sunset, spring to autumn. Free for New York City residents, non-residents fees M–F $34, Sa–Su $28.

Marine Park also is home to Brooklyn's largest full-length golf course. Experienced golfers report that because of its location near the water, this course can be windy, adding to the challenge. Not as landscaped as suburban courses, this nineteen-hole, 210-acre course can seem long. Rentals are limited; bring your own clubs. Motor carts are available for people over twenty-one. Facilities include a snack bar and locker rooms, but no showers.

♦☺ **SALT MARSH NATURE CENTER.** 3302 Avenue U. across from Marine Park, 421-2021, Th–Tu 9 a.m.–5 p.m. Call for library hours. Calendar available on site.

When you visit the multimillion-dollar Salt Marsh Center, you can play with the tidal tanks (you can raise and lower the tides), microscopes, fish tanks, decipher a stratigraphic map of the area, and peruse an environmental library. Outdoors, you can hike a one-mile walk on a nature trail through the salt marsh, stopping at little overlooks to peer at the wildlife living in and around Gerritsen Creek.

The Nature Center is engaged in habitat restoration projects to stabilize the shoreline and the ecobalance, for instance, by adding indigenous plantings to filter pollutants and attract wildlife. Locals use the Nature Center for square dances, arts and crafts workshops, art shows, and other community events, sometimes temporarily displacing the environmental exhibits, so call ahead.

See the end of this chapter for **Gateway National Park** and **Sebago Canoe Club.**

SHEEPSHEAD BAY RESTAURANTS

Emmons Avenue
Within walking distance of the piers you'll find the following:

BAKU PALACE. 2718 Coney Island Ave. at Emmons Ave., 615-0700, daily 11 a.m.–2 p.m., www.bakupalace. com. Free parking.

Across from both Lundy's and the waterway, there's a huge modern-looking building that's designed for festivities, Russian-style. The menu has a French twist, there's a spiffy Russian crowd, and lots of food. "Baku," by the way (for the geographically challenged among us), is the capital of Azerbaijan, a country on the Caspian Sea.

CAFÉ ISTANBUL. 1715 Emmons Ave. bet. Sheepshead Bay Rd. and E. 16th St., 368-3587, daily 11 a.m.–11 p.m.

This pretty little Turkish café with a red awning and Turkish artifacts on the walls has a brick oven that turns out great appetizers, *borekas*, and other bready specials. Try the Turkish-style pizza, called *"pide,"* or freshly made stuffed grape leaves and salads. For main courses, meat and chicken dishes are recommended. Some of the recipes are very traditional, such as the *lahmacun,* an ancient Turkish meat-pie dish. Very inexpensive, beer only.

IL FORNETTO. 2902 Emmons Ave. corner E. 29th St., 332-8494, daily noon–11 p.m.

Stop in for a drink at the bar, or very good traditional Italian foods at the large restaurant with windows facing the water. Entrees are under $15. Have a tartufo or gelato for dessert, and you're ready for more sightseeing!

🅿 ☺ JORDAN'S LOBSTER DOCK. 3165 Harkness Ave., 934-6300, Tu–Th, Su 11:30 a.m.–8 p.m., F–Sa 11:30 a.m.–11 p.m., www.jordanlobsterfarms.com.

An informal Cape Cod–style restaurant, Jordan's serves lobster dinners in three price ranges, starting with a $15 special for a one-pounder, as well as fried clams, flounder, soft-shell crabs, bay and sea scallops, homemade fish cakes, and a huge fisherman's-platter combo. It's all as fresh as can be; Jordan's runs the fish store next door, by the same name. Memorial Day to Labor Day, you can dine facing the waterfront, on the outdoor patio. Complete takeout menu available. Or, go next door to Jordan's Lobster Dock shop for a live one to take home.

☺ LUNDY BROTHERS. 1901–29 Emmons Ave. corner of Ocean Ave., 743-0022, M–Th 5–10 p.m., F–Sa 5 p.m.–midnight, Su 3–9 p.m., www.lundybros.com.

There's nothing fishy about this legend revisited. Just about anybody who was anybody in old Brooklyn (from the 1920s to the 1980s) ate at Lundy's, across from the fishing boats. It's a relic of the once-thriving fishing industry here.

The recently renovated Lundy's is smaller than the original—and surly waiters are no longer likely to insult you. For a walk down memory lane, come for their specialities of seafood, especially shellfish, or the big Sunday brunch buffet. You can't miss the huge lobster tank, pictures of old Coney Island hanging on the walls, and annotations on the menu describing the original Mr. Lundy's favorite dishes. For a quick meal, check out the raw bar.

MARIA'S RESTAURANT. 3073 Emmons Ave. near Brown St., 646-6665, M–Th noon–10:30 p.m., F–Su noon–11:30 p.m.

For more than sixty years Maria's has won the hearts of locals. The food is fresh, the service is friendly, and it is as good a restaurant for the entire family as you're likely to find. There are many seafood specials, along with traditional veal Milanese, chicken rollatini, and pasta dishes. Most entrées are about $10. And since the restaurant is just a few blocks from the fishing piers, you can take a stroll before or after you eat.

☺ **RANDAZZO'S CLAM BAR.** 2017–23 Emmons Ave. bet. Ocean and Bedford Aves., 615-0010, daily noon–midnight (sometimes later).

Randazzo's is still here. And it's still fabulous. Unpretentious, noisy, and fun, Randazzo's has been serving up fresh fish for more than twenty-five years. They specialize in fried calamari, scungilli, and baked clams—you won't find fresher or better anywhere. You can eat indoors or, in fine weather, on picnic tables outside. There are chowders and fresh blue-point clams, as well as stuffed shrimp and French fries and a few kinds of wine and beer. *Yes!*

🍴☺ **ROLL 'N' ROASTER.** 2901 Emmons Ave. bet. E. 29th and Nostrand Ave., 769-5831, daily 11–1 a.m.

The owners call this "a grown-up fast-food restaurant" serving roast beef, burgers, and fries. In business for more than thirty years, Roll 'N' Roaster is a good place to stop after a boating expedition when you're good and hungry—and tired of fish!

Other Restaurants and Cafés in Sheepshead Bay, Bath Beach, and Mill Basin

☺ **BRENNAN AND CARR.** 3432 Nostrand Ave. at Ave. U (Marine Park area), 769-1254, M–Th 10–1 a.m., F–Sa 11–2 a.m., Su 11 a.m.–1 p.m.

It's been extolled by just about every food writer in the city. Brennan and Carr has been around since 1938, and this is still one of the best places in Brooklyn for roast beef. The aroma of roast beef (thinly sliced, very lean) positively wafts out of this unassuming red-brick building. A good-size sandwich is about $4.50; a full plate that includes French fries and vegetables is under $8. You can take it out or eat in the small, pleasant back room.

BUCKLEY'S BAR AND RESTAURANT. 2926 Ave S at Nostrand Ave., 998-4242, M–Th lunch noon–3 p.m., dinner 5 p.m.–1 a.m.; Sa–Su lunch 11:30 a.m.–3 p.m., Sa dinner 5–11 p.m., Su dinner 3–9 p.m.

Popular with born-and-bred Brooklynites, this is a straight-ahead American-style restaurant specializing in well-made basics: meat, baked potatoes, and fish. Moderately priced.

☺🍴 **DOLLY'S ICES.** 5800 Ave. U at 58th St. (Mill Basin area), no phone.

Dolly's is nowhere—a little shack painted red, white, and green (the colors of the Italian flag), on a block where you can neither stop nor park, which is why cars double park, and the local cops don't give a darn. Because everyone loves

Dolly's $1.75 homemade ices. The strawberry cheesecake. The banana walnut chip. The Oreo. The chocolate hazelnut chip. Dolly's gives free sprinkles on ice cream.

GOURMET GRILL. Ave. N and 64th St. (Mill Basin area), 241-2345, M–Th 11 a.m.–9 p.m., F–Sa 11 a.m.–6 p.m.

As one of our food spies put it, "This is a very unusual type of restaurant for Brooklyn. It's *healthy*. Everything is grilled. The menu is out of the American Heart Association cookbook, neatly listing the calories, fat content, and sodium content of every dish. They use a little less cheese in the chicken parmigiana, a little less olive oil in the sauce." Open-air seating in the summer.

JOE'S BAR AND GRILL. 255 Ave. U near Van Sicklen St. (Mill Basin area), 372-9595, W–Su noon–11 p.m., M–Tu call ahead for hours.

This old-fashioned hangout of a bar is popular with locals, many of whom retreat here regularly. The rare specialty of the house is *campanula,* roasted lamb's head. It's a delicacy back home, but timid souls might stick with the fried calamari.

K.P.D. AKA KINGS PLAZA DINER. 4121 Ave. U near Flatbush Ave. (Mill Basin area), 951-6700, Su–Th 6–2 a.m., F–Sa 6–3 a.m.

As one grateful local put it, "It's an *amazing* diner. You can order fish from this diner and not worry that you may turn blue a few hours later." The menu includes gourmet quiche, broiled fish, oversized burgers, a big carving board, and ice cream made of tofu. WWII vets hold their monthly meetings here. The huge parking lot in the back is bigger than most stores in Brooklyn.

LA PALINA. 159 Ave. O bet. W. 4th and W. 5th Sts. (Mill Basin area), 236-9764, Tu–F noon–10 p.m., Sa noon–12 p.m., Su noon–10 p.m. Cash only.

The grandsons of founder Charles Vertolomo, who now run La Palina, know how to cook Neapolitan. That means large portions, lots of garlic, and an enthusiastic clientele. Reservations recommended on the weekends.

LA VILLA. 6610 in Key Food Plaza (Mill Basin area), 251-8030, M–Sa 11 a.m.–11 p.m., Su 11 a.m.–10 p.m. Also in Park Slope.

There's more than one reason to love La Villa. La Villa has *paninis* and heroes. Or could it be the pizzas with a large selection of toppings, or pastas, or desserts?

LENNY AND JOHN'S PIZZERIA. 2306 Flatbush Ave. bet. Ave. P and Flatlands (Mill Basin area), 252-9710, Su–Th 11 a.m.–2 p.m., F–Sa 11 a.m.–3 a.m.

Lenny and John's is a throwback from pizzerias of the past. It's been run by the same guys, Lenny and John, since 1969. There are just six tables (caved in from decades of use, once red but now an interesting shade of worn pink), and they still serve drinks from that red fruit-punch-and-grape drink dispenser that used to be ubiquitous. They are open really late on weekends, until three a.m. People actually line up for their Tuesdays 5–11 p.m. "Pick Up Only" special—a large pie for the yesteryear price of $5.25 (normally it is $1.35 a slice). "We Deliver in All Kinds of Weather."

MILL BASIN KOSHER DELI AND FINE ART GALLERY. 5823 Ave. T corner of 59th St., 241-4910, daily 11:30 a.m.–9 p.m., www.pastrami.net. or www.millbasindeli.com.

It's the oddest double-decker combo this side of a pickle. Mill Basin Deli is a Jewish deli. It's kosher, under the rabbinical supervision. They make old-fashioned Jewish sandwiches: roast beef, corned beef, and spicy pastrami. The stuff is so good that people ship it to friends all across the United States. Plus, they sell a few specials here that you *won't* find in many kosher delis, like Southern fried chicken made with Empire Kosher chicken. And art.

Www.pastrami.net speaks for itself: "Our Chopped Liver couldn't be fresher and our Matzo Balls are better than grandma's. Mill Basin Kosher Deli and Fine Art Gallery . . . has Great Kosher cuisine and it's a world-class gallery exhibiting works by many masters of today including a collection of original works by Erté, the father of Art Deco, which rivals the collection of the Metropolitan Museum in New York, turn-of-the-century posters by Alphonse Mucha, and 3-D works by James Rizzi, as well as works by Roy Lichtenstein, Marc Chagall, and other great artists."

MASSIMO'S RISTORANTE. 2147 Mill Ave. bet. Ave. U and Strickland Ave. (Mill Basin/Bergen Beach area), 968-1111, Su–Th 11:30 a.m.–11 p.m., F–Sa 11:30 a.m.–midnight.

Ornate wrought-iron chairs and an airy décor make this feel like Italy. Specifically, some small town in Italy, because at Massimo's, if they don't recognize you as being from the neighborhood, you might get a few stares. It's all-you-can-eat on Tuesdays 5–9 p.m. for just $14.50 per person—including pizzas, tortellini, and the whole typical Italian menu. Inexpensive and delicious.

FIORENTINO. 311 Ave. U near McDonald Ave., 372-1445, daily noon–midnight.

This large, noisy, busy, two-hundred-seat restaurant gets rave reviews. The reason is clear: excellent Italian fare at moderate prices in a very convenient location on one of Sheepshead Bay's neighborhood shopping strips. Weekend reservations are recommended. A branch of the family that owns Fiorentino started **Carolina's Restaurant** in Coney Island.

♫ **MICHAEL'S RESTAURANT.** 2929 Ave. R near Nostrand Ave. (Marine Park/Gravesend area), 998-7851, Su–Th noon–10 p.m., F–Sa noon–midnight, www.MichaelsOfBrooklyn.com. Reservations on weekends.

Savor the flavors of authentic twentieth-century Italian Brooklyn. The setting couldn't be nicer at this family-owned, 150-seat restaurant. Live music, moderately priced excellent food—the menu runs seven pages—and a steady clientele have contributed to its success since it opened in 1964. Check out **Michael's Pastry Shop** across the street.

NICK'S RESTAURANT. 2777 Flatbush Ave. bet. Kings Plaza and Belt Parkway, 253-7117, daily 11 a.m.–11 p.m.

The only thing missing from Nick's Cape Cod–like seafood restaurant is sand on the floor and sunburned kids in wet bathing suits. Everything else is straight out of an oceanfront fish shack, including the plastic cups and nearly frozen bottles of beer. The seafood is superfresh (you walk through the retail fish store to make your reservation), and kids will love the multiple televisions running old films nonstop.

PRIMA PASTA AND CAFÉ. 5821 Ave. T bet. 57th and 58th St. (Mill Basin area), 209-1030, Su–Th 11:30 a.m.–10 p.m., F–Sa 11:30 a.m.–11:30 p.m.

The menu reads like a tourist menu in Rome—organized both by main ingredient and price, with lots of options. Take your pick of a half-dozen chicken entrées listed under "Chicken $10." "Veal $11" includes veal *parmigiana, pizzaiola, sorrentino, marsala, francese,* and *primavera.* Pastas are $9 (choose from nine different shapes) and with that you get a choice of more than a dozen different sauces. There's not much atmosphere.

🌀 ☺ **SAHARA RESTAURANT.** 2337 Coney Island Ave. bet. Aves. T and U. 376-8594, winter 11–2 a.m., summer 11–4 a.m., www.saharapalace.com.

No, it's not a mirage: Sahara's undergone a lovely renovation and now feels like a restaurant, not a takeout place, with decorative tables and huge fish tanks. In the summer, there's an enormous garden patio under a very Mediterranean-looking grape arbor. Sahara still makes the same excellent low-cost, high-quality food: homemade kebabs and gyros made of finely chopped lamb, wonderful lentil soup, crunchy-fresh salads with lemon and parsley, stuffed *borekas,* eggplant done three ways, and an array of honey-rich sweets. Appetizers average about $3, and a kebab platter with rice is about $10. Portions are huge; consider sharing an entrée.

VERANDAH. 2423 Coney Island Ave bet. Aves. U and V, 376-0100, daily 11 a.m.–10 p.m.

Of the several Turkish restaurants in the Coney Island Avenue area, this is one that locals love to come back to, in part because there's almost as much seating in the garden as in the restaurant itself. You can get kebabs, freshly baked breads, and wonderful appetizers here.

☺ **VILLA BAY RISTORANTE AND PIZZERIA.** 2113 Ave. Z bet. E. 21 and E. 22 (Sheepshead Bay), 648-4400, W–Su 11:30 a.m.–9:30 p.m.

This is one of those places that you'd never know about unless your neighbor, a lifelong Brooklynite, told you it was golden. Villa Bay's a bargain—delicious Italian food, friendly service, family-style portions (they assume you're *big* eaters!), and a huge range of items on the menu. Note the supersaver: a $16 special dinner for two.

☺ Avenue U: Asian Restaurants

DA LAT VIETNAMESE RESTAURANT. 1243 Ave. U at East 12th St., 375-6702, Su–Th 11 a.m.–10 p.m., F–Sa 10 a.m.–10 p.m.

Westerners may know *pho* the best, but it's fun to peruse the vast variety of Vietnamese dishes, and Da Lat specializes in the country's authentic cuisine. Pair up their delicious BBQ shrimp roll on sugar cane with the spicy squid, chili sauce, and lemon grass. And don't miss their selection of refreshing and sweet beverages, like salty lemonade or soda with yolk and condensed milk. Seafood dishes start at $8, everything else starts at $5.

HOP SING SEAFOOD RESTAURANT. 1241 Ave. U at E. 12th St., 375-3388, daily 10:30 a.m.–11 p.m.

A highly rated Chinese restaurant, Hop Sing has wonderful duck and noodle dishes, soups, and tasty fish dishes. Daring customers might ask the waiter to bring some *ja g guy, seeaw ong, yow ja tofu,* or *chow fun naachoy* (and nope, we're not telling what they are!).

PHO HOAI. 1906 Ave. U bet. E. 19th and E. 20th Sts., 616-1233, Su–Th 10 a.m.–10:30 p.m., F–Sa 10 a.m.–11 p.m.

This authentic noodle house, specializing in Vietnamese *pho*, is a family hangout on the weekends. A specialty of the house are the "rice noodle beef" soup dishes; there are eighteen varieties. Prices are low, starting at $5 for a very filling meal.

⚙ **U NOODLE HOUSE.** 1241 Ave. U at E. 12th St., 375-3388 or 375-0623, daily 10:30 a.m.–10:30 p.m.

A testament to the international flavor of this burgeoning area, U Noodle House's menu is in three languages: Chinese, English, and Vietnamese. Don't let the name fool you, though; although the speciality is a steaming bowl of soup with noodles and a choice of meat, chicken, fish, or vegetables, there is an extensive menu to choose from—including spaghetti. A meal here is one of the best bargains in town: starting from $3 for lunch or dinner.

YUE HOI SEAFOOD RESTAURANT. 1321 Ave. U at E. 13th St., 336-3475 or 336-2875, daily 8 a.m.–8 p.m.

This is by far one of the largest menus you'll ever come across. Yue Hoi is the ultimate Chinese diner, offering everything from beef with scrambled egg on rice to Buddha's vegetables with noodles, to the various selections in their Szechuan dishes special. Rice dishes start at $4; lunch or dinner for two is about $25.

SHOPPING

Specialty Food Shops

🌀 ☺ **JORDAN'S LOBSTER DOCK.** 3165 Harkness Ave. off Belt Pkwy., 934-6300, Su–Th 9 a.m.–6 p.m., F–Sa 9 a.m.–7 p.m., www.jordanlobsterfarms.com.

You may feel as if you're in Seattle at this appealing shop that overlooks a harbor full of cabin cruisers. This is no average fish store—you can actually walk out with a complete meal. Jordan's sells delicious takeout Manhattan and New England clam chowder, lobsters steamed to order while you wait, fresh-cooked shrimp, and a full clam bar from which to select your evening appetizers. There's also plenty of fresh raw fish, baskets of clams, and frozen shrimp, octopus, Alaskan king crab claws, and squid, along with plenty of condiments. Kids will enjoy watching the staff clean and chop the fresh fish and catch live lobsters from a three-tiered holding pen.

You'll know it by the huge statue of a fisherman in foul-weather gear out front. Jordan's, by the way, has been a Brooklyn family business for over fifty years, and the owners hailed from—where else?—Boston. You can order your live or steamed lobsters by phone for next day FedEx delivery: 800-882-3314.

KINGLY BAKERY. 1505 Ave. U at E. 16th St., 339-3388, daily 7 a.m.–8 p.m.

With three sister stores on 8th Avenue in Sunset Park, this minichain is quickly becoming the location of choice for pastries in Brooklyn's Chinatowns.

LA TORRE PORK STORE. 4518 Ave. N at E. 45th St., 252-0546 (Mill Basin area), M–Sa 6 a.m.–6 p.m.

This Italian deli makes "pinwheels," a pretty preparation of thinly cut filets of meat rolled together with proscuitto or mozzarella that's often made with a special "Sunday sauce" for the Sunday family meal. Locals wait in line to buy flavored chicken and beef patties for summer BBQs. You can also pick up wonderful mozzarella balls marinated in garlic and olive oil, homemade manicotti and ravioli, olives, and condiments—everything for an Italian feast.

MORETTI'S BAKERY. 4524 Ave. N at E. 46th St. (Mill Basin area), 377-5364, M—Sa 6 a.m.—6 p.m., Su 6 a.m.—3 p.m.

Moretti's is one of the only bread bakery stores in the Mill Basin area. On Sunday morning, if you are not in line by eight a.m., you can just *fuggedaboutit*. The bread flies out the door, it's so good. They sell every type of bread here, including pizza dough.

Other Interesting Neighborhood Shops (Sheepshead Bay, Bath Beach, Mill Basin area)

❷ ☺ **HERE'S A BOOKSTORE.** 1989 Coney Island Ave. bet. Quentin and Ave. P, 645-6675, M—F 11 a.m.—6 p.m., Sa 11 a.m.—4 p.m., Su noon—4 p.m.

It's hard to maintain a mom-and-pop bookstore, but if you come in here and peruse the wide variety of kids' books, fiction, and nonfiction, you'll see what a labor of love means. It's one of the few remaining independent bookstores in Brooklyn, with tons of secondhand books. It's just a few blocks from **Lester's.**

INTIMATE FANTASIES. 2083 Ave. U bet. Kings Highway and Ave. R, 376-3689, M—Sa 1—7 p.m.

If you're about thirty years old and grew up in Brooklyn, chances are you know that Intimate Fantasies is a very large, unabashed sex shop situated on a busy intersection. They've got anything you might need (or *think* you need). You'll see John Q. Public here: the married guys in the business suits, the teenagers looking around with embarrassed curiosity, and a couple of young women doubled over in laughter as they consider flavored glow-in-the-dark condoms for a bachelorette party.

JAMAR. 1660 Sheepshead Bay Rd. at E. 16th St., 615-2222, M—Sa 11 a.m.—5:30 p.m., Th 11 a.m.—7:30 p.m.

Specializing in fine jewelry and giftware with brand names such as Movado, Lenox, and Waterford, this little store sells many of the better-quality items you'd expect to find only in larger Manhattan department stores. Some lines are discounted more than 10 percent.

JAZZ BOUTIQUE. 432 Ave U. bet. E. 3rd and 4th Sts., 627-0100, M—Sa 10 a.m.—6 p.m., Su noon—5:30 p.m.

Youthful styles for "sharp" dressers, with American and French designer sportswear. Sweaters are in the $100 range, shirt or pant sets about $140. Also in Bay Ridge, at 8813 Third Avenue (492-6606).

☺ **LEARNING WHEEL.** 1514 Ave. Z bet. E. 15th and E. 16th Sts., 934-5540, M—F 11:30 a.m.—6 p.m., Sa 11 a.m.—5:30 p.m., www.thelearningwheel.com.

It's the toy equivalent of a health-food store, full of educational supplies for schoolteachers. But kids and parents will find plenty of games, art supplies, books, flash cards, workbooks, math and language games, puzzles, stickers, posters, and other gizmos here. Phone orders are accepted.

🌑☺ **LESTER'S.** 2411 Coney Island Ave. near Ave. U, 336-3560 or 998-6829 (Layette, Toddler, Girls 4–14, Preteen, Juniors, and Ladies departments 645-4501), M–Sa 10 a.m.–6 p.m., Th 10 a.m.–9 p.m., Su noon–5 p.m.

Lester's is a famous Brooklyn discount family-clothing empire. Started in 1940 by Lester and Lil, now no fewer than seven separate stores feature trendy styles for girls, boys, and preteens. Other Lester's shops feature active wear, men's clothing and shoes, women's and kids' shoes, clothing for toddlers, and an extensive layette department. Prices on name brands are about 20 percent below department-store prices.

LOEHMANN'S AT LOEHMANN'S SEAPORT PLAZA. 2103-27 Emmons Ave., 368-1256, M–Sa 10 a.m.–10 p.m., Su 11 a.m.–6 p.m., www.loehmanns.com.

They call themselves an "upscale, off-price specialty retailer" with prices that are 30 to 65 percent lower than at department stores. Loehmann's has shoes, an extensive collection of women's suits, sportswear, and intimate apparel. Its famous Backroom is stuffed with designer clothing and expensive evening wear and dress suits. As always, there's the thoughtful comfort of the hubby lounge—overstuffed chairs for the guys to slouch in while the wives are busy shopping and spending.

Loehmann's, the store that breathed life into the word "discount," was itself born in Brooklyn in 1921. The old Duryea Place store is gone, and in its stead there's this spiffy two-story shop, opened in 1996.

NO LIMITZ SPORTS SHOP. 3179 Emmons Ave. near Batchelder St., 743-0054, M–Sa 11 a.m.–5 p.m., Su noon–5 p.m.

You can come here for all your sports needs, from skiing to snowboarding to scuba. They carry brands such as Obermeyer in winter sports, and Halcyon gear for divers. Speaking of which, you can rent scuba here, and get expert training from Captain Bob Hayes, a retired NYPD deputy inspector and former commanding officer of the NYPD Scuba Team. His dive boat *Karen* (421-5547) is a fast forty-two-foot crew boat with lots of high-tech gear.

🌑☺ **SAM ASH.** 2600 Flatbush Ave., 951-3888, M–F 10 a.m.–9 p.m., Sa 10 a.m.–7 p.m., Su noon–6 p.m., www.samashmusic.com.

Sam Ash is famous nationwide among musicians as a discounter of top-quality musical instruments. You will find plenty of top-of-the-line electric guitars, synthesizers, and high-tech equipment to choose from as well as more traditional instruments. A Brooklyn legend, it was founded by Sam and Rose Ashkenase (she reputedly pawned her diamond engagement ring to start the business), and their descendants now oversee an empire that has served the likes of Stevie Wonder and Garth Brooks.

SEAHORSE. 1622 Voorhies Ave., 646-9133, M–W 10 a.m.–7 p.m., Th 10 a.m.–8 p.m., F 10 a.m.–7 p.m., Sa 10 a.m.–6 p.m., Su noon–5 p.m.

Husband-and-wife team Marcel and Nancy Goldfarb have assembled an exciting range of imported Israeli, Italian, and Spanish swimwear for women, men, boys, and girls. They also sell beach shoes, bags, and other paraphernalia.

◐ ☺ STELLA MARIS BAIT AND TACKLE. 2702 Emmons Ave. at E. 27th St., 646-9754, daily 5 a.m.–8 p.m.

Fishermen can gear up at Stella Maris, a local fixture for over half a decade. They sell AVET, Shimano, and many other reels, as well as rods. Their motto: "Feel the Bite!" You can get tide charts here, too. It's a very friendly place, so if you or your kid needs some free advice, come during the day, but avoid 5–8 a.m. That's fisherman's rush hour, when the boats are leaving.

ACCOMMODATIONS

COMFORT INN. Emmons Ave. corner of Coyle St.

A new hotel is going in here. Call 800-COMFORT-INN for information.

AND THEN, A FEW EXITS FARTHER ON THE BELT PARKWAY . . .

Not too far away (but not that near, either), as you head from Brooklyn toward Canarsie or Queens on the Belt Parkway, there are several other attractions.

☺ CANARSIE PIER. South of the Belt, at the foot of Rockaway Pkwy.

It's about as far away from Times Square as you can get. Canarsie Pier was, and still is to some extent, a watery playground, a place where you can go fishing off the pier, feel close to the water, daydream while you gaze at the distance. There are wonderful pictures of the Pier from 1963 at http://members.aol.com/brookbourn/pier.html.

Free! **GATEWAY NATIONAL PARK.** 338-3799 or 354-4602, www.nps.gov/gate/

Welcome to America's largest national urban park. The entire expanse of Gateway stretches over 26,000 acres of coastline, marsh, and parks that include **Floyd Bennett Field** in Brooklyn, Jamaica Bay Wildlife Refuge in Long Island, Breezy Point in Queens, and Sandy Hook in New Jersey. Go on an adventure **stargazing** or **bird-watching,** or take a self-guided nature walk. You can get information at the **Ryan Visitor Center, Floyd Bennett Field,** or at the **Canarsie Pier Station** (Belt Parkway Exit 13, 763-2202).

SEBAGO CANOE CLUB. Ave. N and Paerdegat Ave. North, 241-3683, www.sebagocanoeclub.org. Belt Parkway to Exit 13 (Rockaway Parkway), follow Rockaway Parkway northwest ½ mile, turn left on Ave. M, turn left onto Paerdegat Ave. Entrance is bet. Diamond Point Yacht and Paerdegat Athletic Clubs.

OK, OK, it's really Canarsie. But neighborhood pride aside, this is a resource for the whole borough. For an annual fee of about $100 members of the seventy-year-old Sebago Canoe Club store their kayaks and canoes for trips out into Jamaica Bay. There are also instructional programs in sea kayaking, sailing, and flatwater racing—and members enjoy access to a cabin on Lake Sebago in Harriman State Park. Club members include kayakers, canoeists, sailors, rowers, and flatwater racers. Call for information on their open-to-the-public biweekly kayak trips on the bay.

GATEWAY CENTER. Exit 15 off the Belt Parkway (East New York).

This spanking new mall—the largest suburban-style retail mall in the City of New York—is huge: about the size of ten football fields. The $192 million center is home to ten national retail chains and three family-style restaurants. A new seventeen-acre public park—the first in New York City to provide a regulation cricket field—and a new wetland habitat are supposed to be built here soon, too.

7

Brooklyn Heights and Downtown Brooklyn

This chapter covers two neighborhoods that are dissimilar but linked geographically: Brooklyn Heights and Downtown Brooklyn.

> ☛ **TIP:** Parking during the week can be very difficult; use public transportation or be prepared to either look for a while or pay garage fees.

Brooklyn Heights

ABOUT BROOKLYN HEIGHTS

"The Heights," as this diminutive neighborhood is fondly called, is one Brooklyn neighborhood that most Manhattanites have heard of—and maybe even visited. (After all, the Manhattan skyline is reassuringly visible from here, and it only takes seven minutes by train to get to Wall Street.)

Locals describe their small (by Brooklyn standards) neighborhood in loving terms: urbane in its sophistication, yet provincial in its neighborliness. And from a quick visit, one can see why. The eminently walkable Brooklyn Heights is human-scaled, cultivated, and a fine place for a stroll in any season. The Heights is an obviously white-shoe neighborhood in a mostly middle- and working-class borough.

Some say the Heights, once bohemian, has become staid. And, true, one would best look to other Brooklyn neighborhoods for the *zing* of artistic energy or entrepreneurial excitement. The commercial rents on Montague and Court Streets have soared too high to support risky, innovative ventures. And the cost of buying or renting an apartment in the area matches that of better Manhattan neighborhoods.

If you're seeking history, architecture, and tony residential style (not to men-

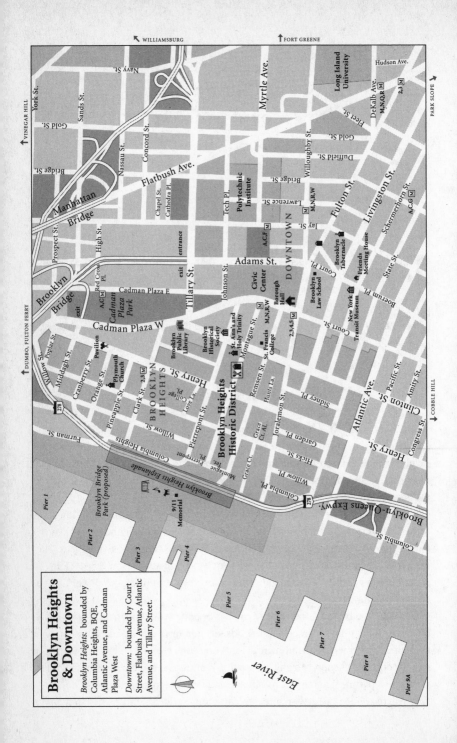

Brooklyn Heights & Downtown

Brooklyn Heights: bounded by Columbia Heights, BQE, Atlantic Avenue, and Cadman Plaza West

Downtown: bounded by Court Street, Flatbush Avenue, Atlantic Avenue, and Tillary Street.

WILLIAMSBURG

FORT GREENE

VINEGAR HILL

PARK SLOPE

DUMBO, FULTON FERRY

COBBLE HILL

East River

Pier 1
Pier 2
Pier 3
Pier 4
Pier 5
Pier 6
Pier 7
Pier 8
Pier 9A

Brooklyn-Queens Expwy.

Columbia St.
Henry St.
Clinton St.
Court St.
Boerum Pl.

Congress St.
Amity St.
Pacific St.
State St.
Schermerhorn St.
Livingston St.
Fulton St.
DeKalb Ave.
Hudson Ave.

Long Island University

Myrtle Ave.

Polytechnic Institute

Tech Pl.
Lawrence St.
Bridge St.
Willoughby St.
Gold St.
Duffield St.
Pearl St.

Jay St.
Adams St.

DOWNTOWN

Civic Center
Borough Hall

Brooklyn Tabernacle
Friends Meeting House
Brooklyn Law School
New York Transit Museum

Cadman Plaza E
Cadman Plaza W

Johnson St.
Tillary St.

Flatbush Ave.

Concord St.
Nassau St.
Chapel St.
Cathedral Pl.

Navy St.
Sands St.
York St.
Gold St.
Bridge St.
Prospect St.
High St.

Manhattan Bridge

Brooklyn Bridge

Cadman Plaza Park

entrance
exit
Red Cross Pl.

BROOKLYN HEIGHTS

Plymouth Church
Pavilion

Pineapple St.
Orange St.
Cranberry St.
Middagh St.
Poplar St.
Willow St.
Clark St.
Pierrepont St.
Monroe Pl.
College La.
Montague Ter.
Pierrepont Pl.
Columbia Heights
Furman St.

Brooklyn Public Library
Brooklyn Historical Society
St. Ann's and Holy Trinity
St. Francis College

Brooklyn Heights Historic District

Remsen St.
Montague St.
Grace Ct.
Grace Ct. Al.
Joralemon St.
Hunts La.
Sidney Pl.
Garden Pl.
Willow Pl.
Hicks St.
Columbia Pl.

Brooklyn Bridge Park (proposed)
Brooklyn Heights Esplanade

9/11 Memorial

tion convenient transportation back to Manhattan), it's here in abundance. Check out peaceful Willow Street, with its several Federal-style homes of architectural note (see particularly numbers 155, 157, and 159). Grace Court Alley, once used as a stable alley for fancy homes on Remsen Street, is a charming mews. Pierrepont Street is graced with some of New York City's most beautiful residences (numbers 2, 3, and 82), and Garden Place, Sidney Place, and Hunts Lane are pleasant detours from Joralemon Street. Saint Ann's church is home to sixty famous restored stained-glass windows, the first made in the United States. And, of course, the **Brooklyn Historical Society**, after a long-term renovation, is a treasure trove.

During the weekday, the Heights and the surrounding area, including the Fulton Mall, Metrotech, the Brooklyn Marriott, and the large municipal administration area, is an industrious workplace. Legions of office personnel are employed by major financial institutions that have located their back offices on these *un*mean streets of Brooklyn. The Mass Transit Authority, which oversees New York's subways and buses, is nearby, as are several institutions of higher education. Thousands of people pour into work in the state courts and civic administration at Borough Hall. And so, you'll find the predictable slew of coffee shops, restaurants, and clothing chain stores. Given the plans for Downtown Brooklyn, the pressure of commercialization will only increase.

On the other hand, in the evenings and during weekends and holidays, the residential backbone of the neighborhood is unmistakable. Like a stage set that's used for the next scene, these same locations—the park benches, the pizzerias, the much-coveted parking spaces—are filled with local families, the young kids dressed in soccer or baseball uniforms, the corporate lawyers and executives who live in the area now dressed down in khakis and sneakers, running off to play squash. The restaurants, outdoor cafés, and shops are filled with locals who stop for a friendly chat.

BY SUBWAY The following trains arrive at stations that are all within a ten-minute walk of each other, in and around the Heights: 2, 3, 4, 5, A, C, and F. The M and R trains stop at Court Street nearby. However, if you want to get to *North Heights* (Cranberry, Orange Streets, etc.), take the 2 or 3 to Clark Street; *Montague Street*, take the 2, 3, 4, or 5 train to Borough Hall; and *Downtown Brooklyn*, take the A, C, or F train to Jay Street, or 2, 3, 4, or 5 train to Borough Hall.

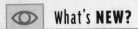

What's **NEW?**

BROOKLYN BRIDGE PARK. 802-0603, www.brooklynbridgepark.org and www.bbpc.net.

What's new—assuming that budget constraints don't put a crimp in the plans—is a fabulous new waterfront park with world-class views of Manhattan, the Statue of Liberty, and all that wonderful boat traffic in New York Harbor. A huge project undertaken by community residents, New York City, and the state government has produced plans for "greening" the waterfront stretching from Atlantic Avenue to the Manhattan Bridge.

HISTORICAL NOTES

An aristocratic urban center in the nineteenth century, it deteriorated after the 1930s until a vigorous preservation movement during the 1960s led to the designation of some thirty blocks as New York's first historic district in 1965. The renaissance started by preservationists was completed by an influx of Wall Street lawyers and bankers during the late 1970s and 1980s. But for many lean years Brooklyn Heights was a bohemian haven. The young artists and writers who lived amid its slightly seedy, decaying elegance and subsequently became famous include Hart Crane, W. H. Auden, Walker Evans, John Dos Passos, Richard Wright, Thomas Wolfe, Arthur Miller, Norman Rosten, Alfred Kazan, Truman Capote, Nobel Prize–winning poet Joseph Brodsky, and currently Norman Mailer.

First settled by the Dutch, Brooklyn Heights dates to the mid-1800s. It was the civic and commercial heart of the then-independent city of Brooklyn. Secluded from Manhattan by lack of transportation other than the Fulton Ferry or private boat, Brooklyn Heights was developed by wealthy Protestant bankers, industrialists, and shipping magnates whose piers and ships were nearby. The Heights was the home of the activist nineteenth-century **Plymouth Church**, where Charles Dickens spoke and abolitionist Henry Ward Beecher preached; Walt Whitman, editor of the *Brooklyn Daily Eagle*, first published *Leaves of Grass* here.

Many of Brooklyn's unique cultural institutions got their start here. The **Brooklyn Historical Society** was founded in the Heights under a different name in the 1860s, as were the Brooklyn Philharmonic and the original Brooklyn Academy of Music, first housed on Montague Street. **Packer Collegiate Institute**, housed in a fabulous Gothic building designed by Minard Lafever, and **Borough Hall**, which in the mid-nineteenth century was an elegant rival to Manhattan's City Hall across the river, were both built in this era. Among the prominent citizens who grew up here was Seth Low, who became mayor of Brooklyn, president of Columbia University, and finally mayor of New York City.

The opening of the Brooklyn Bridge in 1883 destroyed the exclusivity of this remarkable community. The elite retreated to fashionable Clinton Hill, Park Slope, or Manhattan's then-developing "Gold Coast" on upper Fifth Avenue. Brooklyn Heights lost its status as an independent municipal civic center in 1898 when New York City incorporated the city of Brooklyn. Fortunately, Brooklyn Heights's early, aristocratic architecture has been preserved for later generations.

• *Famous Writers' Homes* •

Lots of writers have lived in the area, according to Bill Morgan's book *Literary Landmarks of New York* (Universe Publishing 2002). Norman Mailer still resides at 142 Columbia Heights, as he has for decades. W. H. Auden lived nearby, on 1 Montague Street, and Thomas Wolfe at 5 Montague. Willow Street had more than its fair share: Arthur Miller lived at 155 Willow, Truman Capote at 70, and Hart Crane at 77.

Kidstuff

☺ Kids can play along the **Promenade**. Watch pizza being made at **Monty Q's.** Visit the **New York City Transit Museum** and **Heights Kids,** a great children's store.

POINTS OF CULTURAL INTEREST

SPECIAL EVENTS.

Summer concerts on the promenade; a brownstone tour through the interiors of restored private landmark homes (May).

BROOKLYN ARTS COUNCIL (BAC). 195 Cadman Plaza West off Pierrepont St., 625-0080, M–F 10 a.m.– 5 p.m., www.brooklynartscouncil.org.

BAC has a great Web site, which is an excellent place to start if you are interested in exploring culture and the arts in Brooklyn. Browse online through the "Directory of Brooklyn Arts Organizations" and "Registry of Brooklyn Literary, Performing and Visual Artists." Interested in oral history and folklore? Caribbean cultures? Eastern European immigrants and their dance? A Kurdish library? African diasporan music? The Brooklyn Arts Council can help you. Whether you are moving to Brooklyn, or are already here, BAC is a gem of a resource.

A major administrator of governmental grants for the nonprofit arts in Kings County, BAC also presents programs about those artists' necessities of life, such as funding, new technology, and legal matters.

BRIC (Brooklyn Information and Culture, Inc.) 30 Flatbush Ave., 855-7882. Call for quarterly calendar of events and information.

BRIC is the organizer of the summer **Celebrate Brooklyn** concerts in Prospect Park and **Welcome Back to Brooklyn** events. They also run **Brooklynx** Web site, the **Rotunda Gallery, BRIC Studio,** and **Brooklyn Community Access Television, BCAT.**

BROOKLYN HEIGHTS ASSOCIATION LANDMARK HOUSE AND GARDEN TOUR. 858-9193, www.brooklynheightsassociation.org. House tours are given every May and cost about $25. Call for a schedule.

Maybe you're a landmarks buff, or are interested in seeing what brownstone mansions look like from the inside. Either way, join the many veterans of Brooklyn Heights house tours as they visit area houses and their extraordinary gardens dating from 1800 to 1890.

• *Brooklyn Heights Historic District* •

This large, quaint, historic district—the first to be so designated in New York City—reads like a map of architectural history of early New York. The Heights was the first Brooklyn area to be settled after the Fulton Ferry made it easy to cross the East River, and in its row houses, brick buildings, old apartment buildings, and even a few old wooden homes, there are vestiges of almost every decade of the nineteenth century. A number of historically important buildings are listed in this book.

BROOKLYN HISTORICAL SOCIETY AND MUSEUM. 128 Pierrepont St., bet. Clinton and Henry Sts., 222-4111, www.brooklynhistory.org. Call for hours.

BHS houses the country's largest single collection of Brooklyn history in an elegant 1880 landmark building. The extensive array of artifacts and memorabilia offers an imagination-tweaking peek into the past. History buffs will revel in the richness of historical relics here: models of the Brooklyn Bridge; a huge zinc eagle from the *Brooklyn Daily Eagle*; documents about the Civil War–era Underground Railroad; photos of union workers; copies of early ethnic newspapers in the many languages of our forefathers, and zany remnants of Coney Island. BHS organizes mini–traveling exhibits. Tourists and locals recommend their **Brooklyn Walks and Talks** series.

HEIGHTS CASINO AND CASINO MANSION APARTMENTS. 75 Montague St. and 200 Hicks St., 624-0810, www.heightscasino.com.

In 1904, when Heights Casino was founded, social clubs were an essential part of life for the moneyed classes, and the Casino—located just a half block from the elegant **Promenade** and enviable views of lower Manhattan and New York Harbor—catered to the classiest clientele in Brooklyn Heights society. The adjacent building, Casino Mansion Apartments, built in 1910, boasted only two apartments per floor, and was considered one of the most prestigious addresses in Brooklyn.

Heights Casino is one of the few such buildings in Brooklyn to still be used as a private club. Today, patrons play tennis and squash, dine, and socialize, all for a hefty annual membership fee. (To learn the different fate of another Brooklyn social club, see **Montauk Club** in Park Slope, pg. 356.)

PACKER COLLEGIATE INSTITUTE. 170 Joralemon St. bet. Court and Clinton Sts., 875-1644. Tours by appointment.

It looks like an urban castle, with pinnacles, Gothic arches, and a tower. But look again, because Packer, founded in 1845 and the oldest independent school in Brooklyn, is a leading private school. Conceived as an institute for young ladies, the lovely building was designed by Minard Lafever; inside are original Tiffany windows. The school has expanded into the former Saint Ann's Episcopal Church building nearby.

The progressive, academically challenging school features small classes, community involvement, and serves a diverse student body of nine hundred students from kindergarten to twelfth grade. College admissions are excellent.

ROTUNDA GALLERY. 33 Clinton St. at Cadman Plaza W., 875-4047, www.rotundagallery.org.

Rotunda Gallery is a not-for-profit exhibition space that features the work of Brooklyn-affiliated contemporary artists in all media. Founded in 1981 and run by BRIC, its education program serves five thousand students from prekindergarten through high school, annually.

SAINT ANN'S SCHOOL. 129 Pierrepont St. corner of Clinton St., 522-1660, www.saintanns.k12.ny.us/home

Saint Ann's is a prestigious private school with an enrollment of about a thousand students, preschool through grade twelve, founded in 1965. Saint Ann's guiding light has been its iconoclastic headmaster, Stanley Bosworth, whose educational philosophy for thirty years has resulted in a program that's ungraded, intellectually rigorous, interdisciplinary, artistic, and wide-ranging in scope. Admissions are highly selective, and college admissions are excellent.

SAINT FRANCIS COLLEGE. 180 Remsen St. near Court St., 522-2300, www.stfranciscollege.edu.

Another old Brooklyn educational institution, Saint Francis College was founded by Franciscan Brothers in 1884 to educate children of the working class. For 120 years, Saint Francis College has pursued its Catholic-Franciscan mission to serve students from the five boroughs, especially those of limited means, first-generation Americans and first-generation college-goers. It recently received a half-million-dollar federal grant to upgrade its technology resources, including new laptops, microscopes, centrifuges, and spectrophotometers. The grant will enable Saint Francis to upgrade its technology-education programs serving high school students in the summer and senior citizens year-round.

SAINT GEORGE HOTEL (HISTORIC). The block bounded by Clark, Hicks, Henry, and Pineapple Sts.

The Saint George Hotel has had a presence in Brooklyn Heights for over 120 years. The first structure, designed by Augustus Hatfield, was a ten-foot-tall tower built on Clark between Hicks and Henry in 1885 by Captain William Tumbridge, an officer in the Union Navy during the Civil War. It's thought to have been one of the tallest buildings in Brooklyn at the time, and in 1931, with 2,632 rooms, it could boast being the largest hotel in all of New York City. And it must have been grand, with saltwater swimming pools, rooftop dancing, and elegant public rooms. An urban resort, it was comprised of eight separate units. The Saint George was extremely busy during and after World War II, due to the central role that New York Harbor played as a port of embarkation. After the war, the hotel, like the neighborhood, went into decline. In the 1980s some cooperative apartments were carved out of the building, and a devastating fire in 1995 destroyed some of the old hotel. The old site is now divided into college-student dorms, residential co-ops—and, possibly, a new **Hotel Saint George**.

CHURCH OF PILGRIMS, NOW OUR LADY OF LEBANON MARONITE ROMAN CATHOLIC CHURCH. Corner of Henry and Remsen Sts., 624-9828.

The first Congregational church in Brooklyn was built by New Englanders who brought with them their Yankee sense of democracy and community. According to the American Institute of Architects *Guide to New York City Landmarks*, it was a radical design. The church is the first round-arched, Early Romanesque Revival Ecclesiastical building in America and became a model for many buildings erected by evangelical Protestant congregations in succeeding decades. The building now serves a Roman Catholic Lebanese congregation. For related history, see **Plymouth Church of the Pilgrims**.

DANISH SEAMAN'S CHURCH. 102 Willow St., 875-0042, www.users.rcn.com/dankirke

Even if you're not Danish, don't miss the Christmas festivities at the Danish Seaman's Church, when about a thousand Danes descend on the Christmas Bazaar. You can also celebrate Midsummer ("Sankt Hans Aften") here with a jazz service followed by an outdoors jazz dinner.

FIRST PRESBYTERIAN CHURCH. 124 Henry St. corner of Clark St., 624-3770. Tours are by appointment.

Dating from 1846, the First Presbyterian Church is an early example of the many cultural, educational, and religious institutions built by the affluent mercantilists who first established Brooklyn Heights. It is located in an area settled because of its proximity to Fulton Ferry. Starting in 1814, the ferry provided fast boats from Fulton Street in Brooklyn to Fulton Street in Manhattan. First Presbyterian, which has six Tiffany windows, is across the street from the German Evangelical Lutheran Zion Church, built in 1840.

FIRST UNITARIAN CHURCH OF BROOKLYN. Pierrepont St. at Monroe Pl.

New Englanders who came to live in Brooklyn in the 1840s built a number of Brooklyn Heights churches, including this lovely Gothic-style church designed by Minard Lafever. Both the church and its one-hundred-year-old pipe organ have been restored. Note nearby Willow Chapel, on 26 Willow Place, which was built by Alfred Tredway White ten years later.

GRACE CHURCH. 254 Hicks St. corner of Grace Ct., 624-1850, www.gracebrooklynheights.org. Tours are by appointment.

Detour a few short blocks from commercial Montague Street and you'll stumble upon this lovely 1847 church, designed by the prolific Richard Upjohn and boasting several Tiffany windows. Even in the early twenty-first century, church tradition is carried on by a formidable Boys' and Men's Choir. If you visit, check out **Grace Court Alley** nearby—it was a true mews built for the mansions on Remsen and Joralemon Streets.

PLYMOUTH CHURCH OF THE PILGRIMS. 75 Hicks St. corner of Orange St., 624-4743, www.plymouthchurch.org.

Few national historic landmarks are known for their association with progressive social causes. This one, dating back to the mid-nineteenth century, is called the "Grand Central Terminal of the Underground Railroad," and it was used by American slaves seeking asylum in the North and Canada. Suffragist and abolitionist Henry Ward Beecher was a pastor here for some forty years. Prominent visiting speakers included Mark Twain, Clara Barton, Booker T. Washington, and Martin Luther King Jr. Look for the Tiffany windows and the sculpture of Beecher in the courtyard.

♫ **SAINT ANN'S AND THE HOLY TRINITY EPISCOPAL CHURCH.** 157 Montague St. corner of Clinton St., 875-6960.

This highly ornamented, red sandstone Gothic Revival landmark was designed by architect Minard Lafever. Its crowning jewels are soaring neo-Gothic ceiling vaults, unusual stucco work—and seven thousand square feet of stained glass by William Jay Bolton. The organ loft window is on permanent exhibition in the American Wing of the Metropolitan Museum of Art.

Historically, the parish of the Holy Trinity was considered a progressive force locally and even nationally, participating in national labor and civil rights movements. In 1959 the church closed for a decade, due to structural problems. In 1979 the New York Landmarks Conservancy became involved in saving the historic site.

A small congregation uses the church for religious purposes and occasional classical concerts that are open to the public. Stained-glass conservation continues off-site.

ENTERTAINMENT

♫ **BROOKLYN SYMPHONY ORCHESTRA.** www.brooklynheightsorchestra.org, info@brooklynsymphony orchestra.org.

This community orchestra performs free concerts at the Cadman Plaza library and some of the churches and schools. Founded in 1973, the orchestra is a mix of amateur, semiprofessional, and professional musicians, and is sponsored by the Brooklyn Heights Music Society.

HEIGHTS PLAYERS. Willow Place Auditorium, 26 Willow Pl. bet. Atlantic Ave. and Joralemon St., 237-2752.

The Heights Players produces nine shows over a series of three weekends each, from September to July. This lively community theater has an eclectic program of classics, comedies, dramas, and musicals.

♫ **ORCHESTRA OF THE SEM ENSEMBLE.** Willow Place Auditorium, 26 Willow Pl. bet. Atlantic Ave. and Joralemon St., 488-7659. Tickets about $7 for local concerts.

The SEM Ensemble debuted in 1992 at Carnegie Hall with a tribute to John Cage. Since then, the ensemble, under the direction of Petr Kotik, has performed major concerts in New York, Japan, and Europe, receiving positive critical reviews from key music critics.

🎬 **PAVILION BROOKLYN HEIGHTS, PREVIOUSLY THE BROOKLYN HEIGHTS CINEMA.** 70 Henry St., corner of Orange St., 369-0838.

This small, renovated movie theater is a local favorite. It is very close to DUMBO, as well as **Henry's End** and **Noodle Pudding,** and within easy walking distance of Montague Street restaurants.

■ UA CINEMAS: COURT STREET STADIUM 12. 108 Court St., bet. State and Schermerhorn Sts., 246-7459, 777-FILM.

A twelve-screen cinema that serves much of brownstone Brooklyn, this centrally located theater was, in its early planning phase, the source of much neighborhood contentiousness. It is usually busy.

WILLOW PLACE AUDITORIUM. 26 Willow Place, bet. Atlantic Ave. and Joralemon St.

A large performance space located in a building used by young children attending Saint Ann's school, the Willow Place Auditorium is also used occasionally by the **Heights Players** and **SEM Ensemble.**

PARKS AND PLAYGROUNDS
■ CADMAN PLAZA PARK. Bounded by Court St., Cadman Plaza West, Joralemon, and Adams Sts., 965-6980.

Cadman Plaza is not really a plaza as such, but rather a stretch of green that runs several blocks in length. Don't be confused by the fact that the park and the adjacent street are called by the same name. If you want to walk across the Brooklyn Bridge, you can reach **the Brooklyn Bridge Pedestrian Walk** from here.

9/11 MEMORIAL DAFFODIL PROJECT: See **September 11th Memorial Park at Pier 4.**

■ HILLSIDE PARK. Columbia Heights, along Middagh St., dusk–10 p.m.

This two-acre dog run, a local favorite, is neighborly and a great place to make new friends, both human and canine. Bring your own chair. **Friends of Hillside Park** organizes a Halloween dog costume party.

☺HARRY CHAPIN PLAYGROUND. Go one-half block past the Eagle Warehouse apartment building and left up Everitt St.

☺PIERREPONT PLAYGROUND. Columbia Place at the end of Montague St.

BROOKLYN HEIGHTS PROMENADE. Along the East River; access at the end of Montague and Orange Sts., and streets in between.

Take a stroll here for what may possibly be the most spectacular view of downtown Manhattan to be had with your feet still on the ground. Also visible are the Statue of Liberty, the Brooklyn Bridge, and a constant flow of tugs, barges, and other harbor traffic. There are outdoor concerts in the summer, and an art show. Take a walk on the wild side; it's less than a half mile long.

A memorial note: On September 11, 2001, many residents of the area stood here and watched in horror as the World Trade Center towers, visible just across the water, burned and collapsed.

SEPTEMBER 11TH MEMORIAL PARK AT PIER 4. Montague and Furman Sts., directly below the Brooklyn Heights Promenade. (Visit in early spring if possible.)

Come in the spring to see a daffodil memorial to the victims of the World Trade Center disaster. In 2002, 160 local school children worked alongside adult volunteers to clear an acre of decrepit Pier 4 and plant 25,000 white and yellow daffodil bulbs on the Brooklyn waterfront, across from where one once saw the World Trade Center twin towers. The garden design echoes the World Trade Center's two towers with two 20 by 180–foot beds of flowers. This was part of a post–9-11 citywide effort to plant over one million daffodils throughout New York City, facilitated by a Dutch bulb supplier who donated one-half million bulbs.

BROOKLYN HEIGHTS RESTAURANTS

♫ **GRAPPA CAFÉ.** 112 Court St. at State St., 237-4024, M–Th 11:30 a.m.–10 p.m., F 11:30 a.m.–11:30 p.m., Sa 5–11:30 p.m., Su 3–10 p.m., www.grappacafe.com.

Grappa is quiet, and the tables are well spaced for private conversations—a rarity in New York. Chef Anthony Parascondola of Remi and Maxim's whips up calamari, broccoli rabe, Black Angus shell steak, linguini vongole, and pan-roasted shrimp. There's a great selection of grappa liqueurs, of course. Live music on weekends. Entrées are in the $17 range.

HEIGHTS CAFÉ. 84 Montague St. near Hicks St., 625-5555, daily lunch noon–3 p.m., dinner 5–11 p.m. American Express and cash only.

Heights Café is a good place for a business meeting, a quick lunch while on a shopping spree, or a quiet dinner with a date. The eclectic, something-for-everyone menu includes such favorites as a hummus platter, seafood sausage, pizzas, pork chops, and Texas-style meat loaf. Upscale, modern, and big, it was designed by the same folks who brought you the Union Square Café in Manhattan. Dinner runs about $20 per person, without drinks.

HENRY'S END. 44 Henry St. corner of Cranberry St., 834-1776, Su–Th 5:30–10:30 p.m., F–Sa 11:30 a.m.–11:30 p.m.

Forever busy, forever noisy, forever crowded (and located at the end of Henry Street, of course), Henry's End is one of the finest restaurants in the Heights. The menu often includes unusual entrées of game, as well as carefully prepared poultry and sensational seafood dishes. The chef assumes that you are really hungry, so light eaters should order half portions. There is an extensive wine-tasting menu and several dozen varieties of beer. Entrées range from $15 to $22.

IRON CHEF. 92 Clark St, 858-8517, M–Th 11:30 a.m.–11 p.m. Sa 1 p.m.–midnight, Su 4–10:30 p.m.

Discreet, local, and delicious, this little Japanese restaurant serves high-quality sushi.

KAPADOKYA. 142 Montague St. (2nd floor) bet. Clinton and Henry Sts., 875-2211, M–Th 11:30 a.m.–11:30 p.m., F–Sa 11:30 a.m.–midnight, Su 11:30 a.m.–10:30 p.m.

Come for "Turkish cuisine and *narghile* bar" while you ogle the bellydancers (weekends only), snack on *tamara* (whipped red caviar), spicy vegetables, cheese-and-spinach pastries, and Sultan's Delight, a "classic Ottoman dish" of lamb or chicken baked over a smoky eggplant puree. A *narghila* is a hookah pipe, and you can smoke it (legally) with fifteen different-flavored tobaccos, like apple, rose, and peach, over burning wood charcoal on the back patio.

● **NOODLE PUDDING.** 38 Henry St. bet. Cranberry and Middaugh Sts., 625-3737, T–Th 5:30–10:30 p.m., F–Sa 5:30–11 p.m., Su 5–10 p.m. Cash only.

A light meal it's not, but Noodle Pudding is packed most nights. Families with kids, young couples, and retirees sometimes wait in line to eat at this storefront featuring dishes such as rigatoni with broccoli rabe, as well as brasciola with mushrooms, a lively bruschetta, and grilled portobellos. Though the signature dish is not often served, you'll have plenty to choose from. Entrées range from $8 to $20. Sometimes it gets crowded; no reservations.

QUEEN. 84 Court St. near Livingston St., 596-5954, M–F 11:30 a.m.–11 p.m. Sa–Su 2–11:30 p.m.

Queen is so low-key that even many gastronomically savvy Brooklynites forget it is there. Famous for drawing a big lunch crowd of lawyers and judges from the nearby Brooklyn courts, Queen is often pleasantly quiet—romantic even—at dinnertime. The décor isn't quite up to the food, which is excellent. Entrées start at $17.

TERESA'S RESTAURANT. 80 Montague St. corner of Hicks St., 797-3996, daily 7 a.m.–11 p.m. Cash only.

Located a block from the Promenade, Teresa's serves Polish-Euro food: banana pancakes, apple fritters, chicken-liver omelets for breakfast (served all day long), and borscht and other homemade soups, along with burgers, goulash, stuffed cabbage, fresh ham, roast beef, pork, and great veggies at lunch and dinner. You can also get a milkshake and a tuna sandwich on rye. It is clean, airy, and the food is always satisfying. The vegetarian options are right out of a health-food cookbook: spinach, corn, beets, sauerkraut, peas, and kasha. (Also in Manhattan, at 1st Avenue bet. 6th and 7th Streets.)

THE GREENS. 128 Montague St. (2nd fl.) corner of Henry St., 246-0088, daily 11 a.m.–10:30 p.m. Kosher.

Unusual vegan and vegetarian dishes—all kosher—are the specialty at this little second-floor Chinese eatery. In the evenings and on weekends you'll find lots of young people hankering for scallion pancakes and fresh vegetable dishes. Entrees under $10.

THAI GRILLE. 114 Henry St. off Clark St., 596-8888, M–F noon–10:30 p.m., Sa–Su 3:30–11 p.m.

Tucked away on a quiet street close to the Clark Street subway station, Thai Grille, with its welcoming bar, offers sustenance after a romantic walk over the nearby Brooklyn Bridge. Try the curry noodle soup.

FATOOSH. 330 Hicks St. corner of Atlantic Ave., 243-0500, daily 11 a.m.–10 p.m.

Tiny Fatoosh sells wonderful lentil soup, excellent baba ghanoush, and *fool* (which is fava bean salad), as well as falafel. Good for lunch and takeout.

☺ ◉ **MONTY Q'S.** 158 Montague St. bet. Henry and Clinton Sts., 246-2000, M–Sa 11 a.m.–10 p.m., Su noon–10 p.m.

The pizza comes in dozens of combinations of toppings. You'll also find salads, pasta, rolls stuffed with chicken, and eggplant parmigiana, plus a selection of desserts.

SHOPPING

Specialty Food Shops

GARDEN OF EDEN. 180 Montague St. near Clinton St. 222-1515, M–Sa 7 a.m.–10 p.m., Su 7 a.m.–9:30 p.m., www.edengourmet.com.

Expensive but incredibly convenient, this Manhattan-style emporium has wonderful breads, meats, fresh seafood, condiments, prepared foods, fresh veggies, and sweets. There are over six hundred varieties of fine cheeses and fifteen different types of lettuce—and extensive selections of takeout and gourmet packaged foods. It's the perfect place to find, say, fresh duck when you decide to throw a last-minute dinner party for eight.

GREENMARKET. Cadman Plaza, near Court and Remsen St., Tu and Sa 8 a.m.–6 p.m., 2nd week April–Christmas.

These outdoor stalls sell farm-fresh fruit and vegetables, fresh fish, assorted baked goods, and plenty of flowers and plants. On summer Fridays, there's a bazaar-like row of tents with vendors selling clothing and gift items.

HEIGHTS PRIME MEATS. 59 Clark St. bet. Henry and Hicks Sts., 237-0133, M–Sa 9:30 a.m.–7 p.m., Sa 9:30 a.m.–6 p.m.

You can tell a lot about a neighborhood by the local butcher shops. Polish Greenpoint and Italian Bensonhurst have at least six butchers each; PC Park Slope has nary a one. Like its upscale surroundings, this compact, top-notch butcher shop/deli would fit in just fine, say, in London's Knightsbridge, near Harrods. Located on a side street, it sells top-of-the-line products, including organic chickens; hot, freshly cooked turkey breasts; and other gourmet meat and poultry. A wonderful place to catch some local gossip.

LASSEN & HENNINGS DELI. 114 Montague St. bet. Henry and Hicks Sts. 875-6272, M–Sa 7 a.m.–11 p.m., Su 7 a.m.–10 p.m., www.lassencatering.com.

Get homemade seasonal soups, gorgeous sandwiches, stuffed wraps, hot and cold daily specials, or your choice of several dozen health-packed salads—for a walk on the Promenade or for dinner. There's imported chocolate, huge loaves of bread, a good cheese selection, and cheesecake and Black Forest cakes that you'd gladly die for.

PERELANDRA NATURAL FOOD CENTER. 75 Remsen St. bet Clinton and Court Sts., 855-6068, M–F 8:30 a.m.–8:30 p.m., Sa 9:30 a.m.–8:30 p.m., Su 11 a.m.–6 p.m.

Perelandra has been the mainstay health-food store in this area for over a decade. Named after the utopia described in C.S. Lewis's book by the same name, Perelandra is a big, clean, California-style health-food supermarket. In back, there's a small juice bar that serves shakes and daily specials.

Other Interesting Neighborhood Shops

✪ **BROOKLYN WOMEN'S EXCHANGE.** 55 Pierrepont St. near Hicks and Henry Sts., 624-3435, M–Sa 10 a.m.–4 p.m. Closed during the summer.

There's a great selection of charming quilts, sweaters, mittens, hats, stuffed animals, and children's clothes here. Almost everything is handmade. And it's especially heartwarming that this nonprofit store remains in business even as its better-known sister, the Manhattan New York Exchange for Woman's Work, closed in the winter of 2003. Both stores were founded in the nineteenth century as a way to provide Civil War widows a way to earn a "proper" living: selling their handicrafts. Of the seventy-five or so such stores that cropped up nationwide in the late nineteenth century, only a half dozen or so remain in business. A percentage of the proceeds go to the people who made the goods: the handicapped, the elderly, those in financial need, or artisans furthering American crafts.

HEIGHTS BOOKS. 109 Montague St., 624-4876, Su–Th 10 a.m–11 p.m, F–Sa 10 a.m.–midnight, heights books@aol.com.

Heights Books has a stunning range of gently used hardcovers and paperbacks covering the gamut: art, fiction, U.S., European, African, and Asian history, fiction, nature, mystery and sci-fi, as well as academic books on philosophy, linguistics, and religions. Opened in 1999 with a scant selection, Heights Books is now crammed to the hilt with miscellaneous treasures: rare books (including, on one visit, a book about Romare Beardon bearing the artist's signature), first editions, signed copies, and interesting collections (ranging from Civil War to rare smut). Locals are both the suppliers of and customers for their books. The store owners, co-owners of the old Mercer Street Bookstore, describe Brooklyn Heights as an incredible community of readers, writers, and book buyers. **Park Slope Books** is an affiliate (pg. 381).

HEIGHTS KIDS. Pineapple Walk bet. Cadman Plaza W. and Henry St., 246-5440, M–F 10 a.m.–6:30 p.m., Sa 10 a.m.–6 p.m., Su 11 a.m.–5 p.m.

Heights Kids and Toy Box have merged into one of the biggest educational toy stores to be found either in Brooklyn or lower Manhattan. The focus is on newborns to age ten. Strollers (mostly Maclarens), car seats, baby clothes, toys, accessories, and safety items are displayed on one side of this large store, while on the other there's an enticing range of puzzles, arts-and-crafts items, boxed sets, including brands such as Brio and Creativity 4 Kids, and more. Watch for a third storefront to be opening soon, and possibly an expanded line of books. Special services: twenty-four-hour turnaround on Maclaren stroller repair, and they'll ship a gift to that special out-of-town birthday boy or girl.

✪ **PEERLESS SHOE SERVICE.** 113 Montague St. bet. Henry and Hicks Sts., 855-4954, M–Sa 8 a.m.–6 p.m.

If the shoe fits, wear it. There's only one master craftsman in Brooklyn who has made thigh boots for Placido Domingo singing the role of Othello at Lincoln Center's Metropolitan Opera house. "Jimmy" Yefim Sluskel learned his craft at age eleven, from his father, a shoemaker living in Russia. Rumor has it that in a paper bag in his store he keeps a handwritten list of dozens of stars whose feet he's fit, along with their shoe dimensions. In between making $500 custom shoes from scratch out of sheets of dyed leather or, sometimes, expensive alligator skins, Jimmy is busy fixing straps, heels, and toes.

SEAPORT FLOWERS. 214 Hicks St. near Montague St., 858-6443, Tu–Sa 10:30 a.m.–7: 30 p.m., Su noon–5 p.m.

This is no shrinking violet of a flower shop. Seaport Flowers' arrangements are often in demand by the Heights' most elegant drawing rooms. Seaport Flowers has mastered that casual "cutting garden" Victorian look that complements the area's marvelous nineteenth-century architecture.

TAKES TWO TO TANGO. 145 Montague St. bet. Clinton and Henry Sts., 625-7518, M–F 10:30 a.m.–7 p.m., Sa 10:30 a.m.–6 p.m.

One of the classiest boutiques in Brooklyn, Tango has a full line of women's clothing, including an excellent selection of fine shoes, dressy work clothes, casual wear, lingerie, and handbags.

Downtown Brooklyn

ABOUT DOWNTOWN BROOKLYN

Things have been getting better and better for Downtown Brooklyn. In the late 1990s, **MetroTech Center** opened with six million square feet of office space, plus three and a half acres of open parklike space called the Commons. Brooklyn's first new hotel in decades, the **Marriott**, opened in 1998 in a mixed-use office and hotel complex. **Polytechnic University** moved into twenty-first-century facilities, the recipient of a huge, fairy-tale surprise endowment.

 What's NEW?

A Skyscraper of Its Own

In April 2003, city officials announced a new $100 million plan that will radically remake the face of Downtown Brooklyn. Look for a new park, lots of new office space, incredible traffic, some new underground parking lots, and Downtown Brooklyn positioning itself as a commercial and business center. And expect to see tall office buildings—perhaps taller even than the Williamsburgh Savings Bank, Brooklyn's tallest building at thirty-four stories and 512 feet. Meanwhile, the old House of Detention has been emptied, and its future is under discussion. And a spanking new YMCA is being built on Atlantic Avenue, replacing a big car garage.

What's ahead? A great deal more commercial development, so that Brooklyn rivals even Los Angeles for downtown office space. And, along with that, the standard amenities, including more services and major upgrade of the subway stations at Lawrence, Jay and Fulton Streets. These plans take years to evolve, but the initial vision was this:

WILLOUGHBY STREET PARK: A new 1.5-acre park west of the Flatbush Avenue extension.

LIVINGSTON STREET: A new residential development, from Smith Street to Flatbush Avenue.

FLATBUSH AVENUE EXTENSION AND WILLOUGHBY: Three large new office towers, with up to three million square feet of space.

FLATBUSH AND MYRTLE AVENUES: In the currently low-rent area east of Flatbush Avenue, from Tillary to Willoughby Streets and along Myrtle Avenue, new mixed-use residential and office space.

BOERUM PLACE: A large office tower near the Boerum Place entrance to the Fulton Mall, as big as 850,000 square feet.

STATE STREET: The new Brooklyn Law School dorms on 205 State Street, which will bring more students to the area.

SUBWAYS: Upgrades to subway entrances, and a possible plan to link the IND and BMT lines at Jay and Willoughby Streets by 2008.

PARKING: Construction of as many as one thousand new underground parking spaces, and a new traffic coordinator assigned just to this part of Brooklyn. Traffic might get worse. But you'll have somewhere to put the car.

STUDENT CENTER: Downtown Brooklyn is a de facto college town, with thirty thousand full-and part-time students attending seven different colleges and universities, so plans are under discussion to possibly construct some form of student center. (See **Like Boston, Brooklyn's a Multicollege Town**, p. 187.)

POINTS OF CULTURAL INTEREST

ABRAHAM & STRAUSS BUILDING—NOW MACY'S. 420 Fulton St. corner of Hoyt St.

True story: Abraham, a Bavarian immigrant, turned a small dry goods shop into a then-innovative concept in retailing: the one-stop department store. He chose this 1870s cast-iron building for his new store after correctly figuring that the area would flourish along with the opening of the new Brooklyn Bridge. The original store was fitted with stunning amenities and luxuries, such as lounging parlors for tired female shoppers, and a mineral spa. Renovated and enlarged in the 1920s, the Art Deco building boasted paned glass, twenty-foot ceilings, and brass-and-glass elevators. Macy's now occupies the historic Abraham & Strauss building.

BROOKLYN BOROUGH HALL. 209 Joralemon St. bet. Adams and Court Sts., 855-7882 ext. 51, M–F 9 a.m.–5 p.m. Free tours Tu 1 p.m.

A New York City landmark, Borough Hall was built in 1846–51, and is one of New York's most fabulous Greek Revival buildings. Dating from the era when Brooklyn was a city separate from Manhattan (they merged in 1898), it is larger than City Hall and considerably more sumptuous. High points include a hammered brass cupola restored by the same French craftsmen who restored the Statue of Liberty, a spectacular courtroom, grand rotunda, and portico, and a marble exterior. Today it is the office of Brooklyn's borough president and a new **Brooklyn Tourism and Visitors Center**. There are occasional public art shows here, too.

BROOKLYN TOURISM AND VISITORS CENTER AT BOROUGH HALL. 209 Joralemon St., M–F 9 a.m.–5 p.m.

Come on in! Volunteers in the new Tourism and Visitors Center will provide transit information, hotels, sites, and so on.

BROOKLYN FRIENDS SCHOOL. 375 Pearl St. near Willoughby St., 852-1029, www.brooklynfriends.org.

Brooklyn Friends School (BFS) was opened in 1867 by the descendants of early Quaker settlers. It was started in the basement of the nearby **Friends Meeting House** which it continues to use in addition to the main building on Pearl Street. The Pearl Street building was originally erected as **Brooklyn Law School**.

BFS is a highly regarded coed private school with a diverse student body from preschool to grade twelve. It has a strong academic program with extensive arts and theater options. BFS incorporates Quaker principles of truth, simplicity, and peaceful resolution of conflict. And amazing to see, all students observe the Quaker tradition of silence at regularly held communal meetings. BFS is home to the "Bridge Film Festival" for teen-produced films and was ranked one of "The City's 20 Most Sought-After Preschools" by *New York* magazine. Admissions are highly selective, and college admissions are excellent.

BROOKLYN LAW SCHOOL. 250 Joralemon St. off Court St., 625-2200, www.brooklaw.edu.

As its Web site notes, Brooklyn Law School, founded over a century ago and located just a sneeze away from the courts of Downtown Brooklyn, boasts a sixteen thousand-strong alumni body, which includes noted members of the bench and bar, and leaders in public service and private industry. The faculty includes internationally recognized scholars. Innovative teaching techniques augment traditional course offerings with instruction in emerging areas of law. Capitalizing on its location in New York City, the school has attracted speakers as such Noam Chomsky, Ruth Bader Ginsburg, and U.S. senators Charles Schumer and Hillary Clinton. Once a commuter school, Brooklyn Law is erecting new dormitories in the area, bringing new student presence to Downtown Brooklyn.

♫ **THE BROOKLYN TABERNACLE.** 17 Smith St. bet. Fulton and Livingston Sts., 290-2000, Su worship services 9 a.m., noon; gospel service Su 4 p.m.; prayer meeting Tu 7 p.m., www.brooklyntabernacle.org.

Known for its contemporary gospel music, Brooklyn Tabernacle's nondenominational Sunday services have a huge 250-person choir with musical backup equipment that is so high-tech it looks like a recording studio. They won a Grammy Award in 1996 for best gospel choir album. The service is spirited. It's a cross-cultural community, and not entirely without its commercial aspect. Tuesday prayer meetings can attract up to two thousand participants, so get there early for a seat (the doors open at 6 p.m.).

CITY OF BROOKLYN FIRE HEADQUARTERS. 365–67 Jay St. bet. Willoughby and Myrtle Aves.

"This is a building to write home about" is what the late Elliot Willensky, Brooklyn's official historian and coeditor of the authoritative *AIA Guide to New York*, said about this little building. Go see for yourself.

FIRST FREE CONGREGATIONAL CHURCH, now part of Polytechnic Institute, 311 Bridge St.

A historical gem. From the mid-nineteenth century until the early twentieth century, this church was home to Brooklyn's oldest African-American congregation known as the **Bridge Street African Wesleyan Methodist Episcopalian Church** (AWE). After the congregation moved to Bedford-Stuyvesant, the church was used as a factory. It was renovated by Polytechnic, and is now used as a student center.

FRIENDS MEETING HOUSE. 110 Schermerhorn St. off Boerum Pl., 625-8705.

Quakers have been worshipping in Brooklyn since 1657. This landmark building reflects the values of Quakerism: simplicity and democracy. It is still used by the Brooklyn Monthly Meeting of the religious Society of Friends, founded in 1837, and is affiliated with **Brooklyn Friends School.**

DUFFIELD STREET HOUSES. Duffield Pl.

Originally located on Johnson Street in downtown Brooklyn, these four houses were erected between 1835 and 1847 on farmland. As described by the New York City Landmarks Commission, they "are unusually intact survivors from the early 19th century residential neighborhood that once flourished on the blocks east of Brooklyn's civic center. In contrast to wealthier Brooklyn Heights and the working class district near the Navy Yard, this neighborhood evolved between the late 1820s and 1840s as a upper middle-class enclave and remained downtown Brooklyn's leading middle-class neighborhood throughout the nineteenth century." During the nineteenth and early twentieth century, these houses were occupied by merchants, lawyers, brokers, engineers, teachers, builders, and shipmasters. The houses were moved two blocks to their present site in 1990, as part of **MetroTech,** and were designated official landmarks in 2001.

🎓 LONG ISLAND UNIVERSITY. University Plaza—Flatbush Ave. bet. Willoughby and DeKalb Aves., 488-1015, www.liu.edu.

Since LIU's founding in 1926, many students have been immigrants, or the first in their families to seek higher education. Today, eleven thousand students at LIU represent over forty nationalities. A private university, it offers academic programs such as nursing, pharmacy, health professions, business, education, media and liberal arts, with Ph.D.-level study in several areas.

LIU houses one of the few remaining grand theaters from Brooklyn's past. Metcalf Hall, at the corner of Flatbush and DeKalb, was once the **Brooklyn Paramount,** which staged big-name shows with performers like Frank Sinatra. In 1933 scenes from the original King Kong movie were filmed here.

The nationally famous **George Polk Awards** for excellence in journalism were established by LIU in 1949. One of America's most coveted journalistic honors, the award memorializes a CBS correspondent slain in Greece while covering Greek Civil War after writing critically about the brutal fascist government. They acknowledge journalists and "those who have risked their lives in covering a story . . . those who have exposed corruption, crimes and injustice in city halls and world capitals . . ."

LIU's Spike Lee Screening Room has played host to the **Brooklyn International Film and Video Festival,** the Brooklyn Young Filmmakers Film Series, and film festivals about minority women organized by Reel Sisters of the Diaspora. Outdoor sculpture exhibitions have been curated by cutting-edge **Smack-Mellon Studios** in DUMBO.

🎵 METROTECH CENTER. Bounded by Flatbush Ave., Willoughby St., Jay St., and Tech Pl., 488-8200.

This sixteen-acre office and retail facility is located just minutes from the Brooklyn and Manhattan Bridges. Built in the 1990s, it is occupied by large corporate employers, such as Verizon, KeySpan, J. P. Morgan Chase Bank, Bear Stearns, and a number of city agencies, whose employees, taken together, number about twenty thousand. MetroTech is also the site of Polytechnic University and the Marriott Hotel at the Brookyn Bridge. There are summer lunchtime concerts, displays of public art, festivals, and other events in the **MetroTech Commons.**

🎓 NEW YORK CITY COLLEGE OF TECHNOLOGY. 300 Jay St. near Tillary St., 260-5500, www.citytech.cuny.edu. Some lectures open to the public.

City Tech is a branch of the City University of New York. It's the only state-assisted college of technology in New York City with a focus on applied technology, a melting pot where 10,500 students study in over forty degree programs.

☺ **NEW YORK CITY TRANSIT MUSEUM.** Corner of Boerum Pl. and Schermerhorn St., 694-1600, Tu–F 10 a.m.–4 p.m., Sa–Su noon–5 p.m., www.mta.info/museum.

Kids of all ages will love pretending they are passengers in this subway museum, authentically located underground in a historic 1936 IND subway station. One exhibit, called *Steel, Stone and Backbone,* recounts the tale of building New York City's nearly one hundred-year-old subway system. There are interactive exhibitions, too, such as *On the Streets,* which has a simulated traffic intersection complete with traffic lights and coordinated Walk/Don't Walk signs, parking meters, fire hydrants, and other street "furniture." Kids of all ages can climb up, get in, and pretend to drive a twelve-seat refurbished vintage bus. You can board the museum's vintage collection of subway and elevated trains, and visit a working signal tower. Plus, there's an exhibit of different collection devices used throughout history: paper ticket–choppers used in 1904, coin and token turnstiles, and a fifty-year history of the subway token.

NEW YORK MARRIOTT AT THE BROOKLYN BRIDGE. Brooklyn Renaissance Plaza, 333 Adams St., 246-7000 or 800-228-9290, www.marriott.com.

Normally, a hotel wouldn't be listed as a "cultural attraction," but this one, opened in 1998, was the first major hotel built in Brooklyn in sixty years–since the 1930s.

♫ **OPERA COMPANY OF BROOKLYN.** 986-3294, http://members.aol.com/operabrooklyn.

The newly formed Opera Company of Brooklyn seeks to makes opera accessible through a diverse, affordable selection of classic opera productions. They produce about ten operas a season (check Web site for venues) and offer educational programming for school children. They ruffled some feathers and created interest when, in 2003, they performed Mozart's *Magic Flute* with a "virtual orchestra."

🎓 **POLYTECHNIC UNIVERSITY–CENTER FOR ADVANCED TECHNOLOGY IN TELECOMMUNICATIONS.** 333 Jay St. near Flatbush Ave., 260-3087, www.poly.edu.

Many Brooklynites aren't even aware that there is a leading engineering institute in our midst. Polytechnic was founded in 1854 in Brooklyn, and, as the nation's second oldest private engineering and science center, boasts over 37,000 alumni. Today it is training a diverse student body in telecommunications, information science, and technology management, with additional campuses located in Manhattan, Westchester, and Long Island. Poly's engineering doctoral program has been rated in the nation's top ten by the American Society of Engineering Education.

Since 1998, when Polytechnic received a surprise endowment of more than

$150 million from a retired faculty member, it has opened a new academic building, an athletic center, and a four-hundred-bed residence hall, renovated their academic hub building, and upgraded communications systems throughout. Polytechnic has raised over $10 million in scholarships and supported over two thousand students, most from immigrant families who are the first generation to earn a college degree.

U.S. POST OFFICE AND COURT HOUSE, BROOKLYN CENTRAL OFFICE. 271-301 Cadman Plaza West.

Still in use after over a century of stamping, sending, and dispatching, this ornate Romanesque-style building is a Brooklyn, and an official New York City, historic landmark. The Philatelic Center inside has interesting displays of commemorative stamps and offers a free booklet for kids on how to start a stamp collection.

DOWNTOWN BROOKLYN RESTAURANTS

ARCHIVES RESTAURANT AND BAR. Marriott Hotel, 333 Adams St., 222-6543, M–Sa 7–10:30 a.m., 11:30 a.m.–2:30 p.m., 5–10 p.m., Su 7–10:30 a.m., 12–4:30 p.m., 5–10 p.m., www.marriott.com.

This large, carpeted dining room and bar makes the perfect meeting place for a Brooklyn version of the corporate hotel experience. An eclectic menu reflects the local culture, offering jerk chicken wings and "Sheepshead Bay fish chowder." It's a great place for a business meeting, or to bring out-of-towners. There's a dedicated kosher kitchen for special events.

LIKE BOSTON, BROOKLYN'S A MULTICOLLEGE TOWN

Brooklyn's downtown area has a college-age student population of over thirty thousand. That's almost as many students as attend big state universities like Ohio State. Count 'em:

- Brooklyn Law School
- Long Island University, Brooklyn Campus
- Polytechnic University
- Pratt Institute
- St. Francis College
- St. Josephs College
- NYC Technical College

GAGE & TOLLNER. 372 Fulton St. bet. Boerum and Smith Sts. Closed as of Valentine's Day, 2004.

A New York City landmark, Victorian-style Gage & Tollner was established in 1897, when Brooklyn was a bustling port—and an independent city. It was known for its turn-of-the-century ambience, with mahogany tables, gas chandelier lighting, old-fashioned mirrors, and old-time waiters. Patrons included such celebrity notables as Diamond Jim Brady, Jimmy Durante, and Mae West.

✪ **JUNIOR'S.** 386 Flatbush Ave. corner of DeKalb Ave., 852-5257, Su–W 6:30–12:30 a.m., Th 6:30–1 a.m., F–Sa 6:30–2 a.m., www.juniorscheesecake.com.

Roll across the Manhattan Bridge and up Flatbush Avenue on the Brooklyn side; you can't miss big, brightly lit Junior's. The menu lists just about every deli item your hungry heart could desire: cheese and cherry blintzes, hamburgers, corned beef, good pickles, and ice cream sundaes. It is clean, urban, and bright, and at any time of day the customers might include cabbies, students from Pratt Institute and Long Island University across the street, artsy types from BAM, and people who just absolutely need a piece of Junior's famous cheesecake (best when plain). Entrées run about $12; cheesecakes to take home are $13 to $15, and you can FedEx a cheesecake anywhere in the country. If you get one of their huge deli sandwiches to go, plan to share it with a friend, unless you are a football linebacker or very, very pregnant.

SHOPPING

BARCLAY SCHOOL SUPPLIES. 166 Livingston St. (2nd floor) at Jay St., 875-2424, M–F 9 a.m.–5 p.m., www.barclayschoolsupplies.com.

Parents of preschool through high school students, take note: Barclay's School Supplies is where the teachers shop for their classrooms, and where you, too, can purchase durable, reasonably priced educational gear for your favorite youngster. Among the thousands of items they sell are maps and globes, flash cards for math and foreign languages, books, art supplies, wall calendars, English writing workbooks, and much more.

BRIDGE STREET FABRIC SHOPS. Bridge St. off Willoughby St.

You'll have to look long and hard before you find a better collection of good, cheap fabrics and sewing notions. Some are 100 percent cotton (including eyelet in a half-dozen colors) and some are poly blends (with wool, satin, cotton), but the prices are all very low, ranging from $1 to $5 a yard. Among the half-dozen other fabric shops on this strip are Fabric Discount Stores at 392 Bridge St. (625-

7200) and SewRite at 388 Bridge St. (522-2525), which sells $10-per-yard upholstery fabric.

⊘ FULTON MALL. Between Flatbush Ave. and Boerum Pl., Schermerhorn St., MetroTech, www.fultonstreet mall.com.

The Fulton Mall, anchored by Macy's, includes about two hundred stores, many of which are chains. Fulton Mall is often disregarded because of a low-income, almost bazaar-like quality to the storefronts, but things may change in the twenty-first century: an improvement campaign is underway by the local business association and MetroTech to upgrade the mall's image and to publicize to major retailers the extraordinary volume of shoppers who pass through here daily.

GREENMARKET. MetroTech at Lawrence and Willoughby Sts., Th 8 a.m.–5 p.m., May–Nov.

As of 2003, there's a new Greenmarket here at MetroTech.

SAVE-A-THON. 411 Bridge St. off Willoughby St., 852-5757, M–Sa 9 a.m.–7 p.m.

One of a chain, Save-A-Thon advertises itself as "New York's Largest Sewing Machine, Fabric and Craft Center." It's a handy, inexpensive place for doll molds, fake flowers, baskets, T-shirt paints, $3-per-yard juvenile print fabrics, foams, sewing machines, and related repairs and accessories.

SID'S HARDWARE AND HOME CENTER CORP. 345 Jay St. off Willoughby St., 875-2259, M–F 8 a.m.–6 p.m., Sa–Su 9 a.m.–5 p.m.

Some people just *love* hardware stores. If you count yourself among them, stop in at Sid's. Sid's is the place to go when you need a wrench, garden hose, duct tape, and even a two-by-four piece of lumber. Some people have been known to buy Sid's gift certificates to give as birthday presents.

W.C. ART & DRAFTING SUPPLY CO. 1 MetroTech Center at Jay St., 855-8078, M–F 9 a.m.–6 p.m., Sa 9 a.m.–5 p.m.

W.C. sells fine art and drafting supplies, computer papers, and offers a ton of hobby-and-craft supply items that are often difficult to find elsewhere. And it is conveniently located next to Sid's Hardware, a long-standing Brooklyn institution.

YOLY FABRICS. 226 Livingston St. bet. Hoyt and Elm Sts., 596-4668, M–F 9 a.m.–6 p.m., Sa 10 a.m.–6 p.m.

Yoly Fabrics has a limited but highly unusual collection of imported African fabrics and exclusive screen prints. Some of the Senegalese and Nigerian fabrics cost $5 per yard. In addition, there are a half-dozen bolts of gorgeous decorative materials used for African ceremonial dress.

ACCOMMODATIONS

AWESOME BED AND BREAKFAST (see p. 14)

DIANA'S B&B (see p. 15)

HOTEL AT SAINT GEORGE (under construction—see p. 172)

MARRIOTT BROOKLYN (see p. 12)

MERZ HOUSE (see p. 16)

8

The Greater Carroll Gardens Area

Carroll Gardens, Cobble Hill and Boerum Hill, Gowanus, and Atlantic Avenue

ABOUT THE AREA

Smith Street is the tail that wagged the neighborhood dog. Years ago, it wouldn't have seemed right to lump these five neighborhoods—Carroll Gardens, Boerum Hill, Cobble Hill, Gowanus, and Atlantic Avenue—into one big chapter of a Brooklyn guidebook. Each little subneighborhood had a distinctive character and different histories. And in the 1980s and early 1990s, an income disparity separated genteel Cobble Hill, middle-class Carroll Gardens, and sometimes scruffy, more heterogeneous Boerum Hill. As for Gowanus, *fuggedaboutit*. And Columbia Street is still considered by many to be Red Hook.

But there's been a whirlwind of change along Smith Street since our 1999 edition, and Smith Street's defined the neighborhood. Some locals say they take a walk once a week down Smith Street, just to see what's new, as though this restaurant-and-boutique-row were a hothouse garden, with new shops and eateries popping open like summer flowers. Of course, the old thoroughfares, such as Court Street, are still lined with small bakeries, restaurants, and shops, and are plenty interesting and busy. But Smith Street, once low-rent, abandoned at night, and occasionally dangerous, is the late-blooming star of the neighborhood. With dozens of highly rated restaurants, popular bars, and interesting little boutiques, Smith Street has become urbane, hip, and fun.

Armchair visitors: This is typical Brooklyn, with street after street of brown and red-toned nineteenth-century homes no taller than three or four stories. There are few big apartment buildings in the area, save the historic, architecturally significant **Home and Tower Apartments.** Conversions from church rectories into apartments, and some discreet smaller apartments do exist. But it is the sturdy, practical, sometimes elegant houses, the tree-lined narrow streets, the huge front gardens on some blocks, and pocket parks here and there, which define the feel of the place. There's no *room* in this area for overpopulation. The

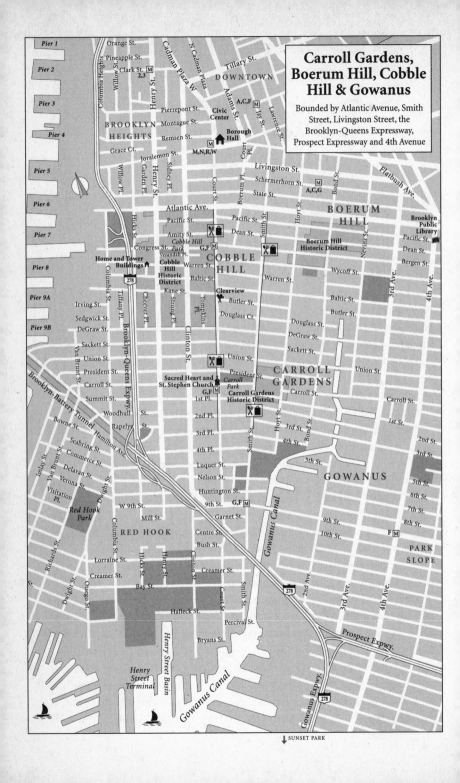

Pier 1
Pier 2
Pier 3
Pier 4
Pier 5
Pier 6
Pier 7
Pier 8
Pier 9A
Pier 9B

Orange St.
Pineapple St.
Clark St. M 2,3
Catman Plaza W
N Catman Plaza
Tillary St.
DOWNTOWN
Adams St.
Pierrepont St.
Montague St.
Civic Center
A,C,F M
Lawrence St.
Jay St.
BROOKLYN HEIGHTS
Remsen St.
Borough Hall
M
Court Pl.
Livingston St.
Flatbush Ave.
Grace Ct.
Joralemon St.
M,N,R,W
Schermerhorn St.
State St.
A,C,G M
Bond St.
Hoyt St.
BOERUM HILL
Nevins St.
Brooklyn Public Library
Atlantic Ave.
Pacific St.
Pacific St.
Dean St.
Dean St.
Amity St.
Cobble Hill Park
G,F M
Dean St.
Smith St.
Bergen St.
3rd Ave.
4th Ave.
Congress St.
Verandah Pl.
COBBLE HILL
Warren St.
Boerum Hill Historic District
Home and Tower Buildings
278
Cobble Hill Historic District
Warren St.
Wycoff St.
Baltic St.
Kane St.
Strong Pl.
Clearview
Butler St.
Baltic St.
Butler St.
Columbia St.
Irving St.
Tompkins Pl.
Douglass Ct.
Douglass St.
DeGraw St.
Sedgwick St.
Butler St.
DeGraw St.
Sackett St.
Van Brunt St.
Sackett St.
Union St.
Clinton St.
Union St.
CARROLL GARDENS
Union St.
President St.
President St.
Sacred Heart and St. Stephen Church
Carroll Park
G,F M
Carroll Gardens Historic District
Carroll St.
Carroll St.
Summit St.
1st Pl.
Hoyt St.
Bond St.
1st St.
Woodhull St.
2nd Pl.
2nd St.
Bowne St.
Rapelye St.
3rd Pl.
3rd St.
4th Pl.
4th St.
3rd St.
Seabring St.
Luquer St.
5th St.
GOWANUS
Commerce St.
Nelson St.
5th St.
Delavan St.
Huntington St.
6th St.
Verona St.
9th St.
G,F M
7th St.
Visitation Pl.
Garnet St.
8th St.
Red Hook Park
W 9th St.
9th St.
F M
Mill St.
10th St.
PARK SLOPE
Centre St.
RED HOOK
Bush St.
Lorraine St.
Creamer St.
Creamer St.
278
Richards St.
Hicks St.
Henry St.
Clinton St.
Bay St.
2nd Ave.
Dwight St.
Osego St.
Halleck St.
Court St.
Smith St.
3rd Ave.
4th Ave.
Percival St.
Bryans St.
Prospect Expwy.
Henry Street Terminal
Henry Street Basin
Gowanus Canal
278
Gowanus Canal
↓ SUNSET PARK

Carroll Gardens, Boerum Hill, Cobble Hill & Gowanus

Bounded by Atlantic Avenue, Smith Street, Livingston Street, the Brooklyn-Queens Expressway, Prospect Expressway and 4th Avenue

commercial streets, mainly Court Street and now Smith, are also defined by older buildings. There's virtually no modern commercial architecture in the area; it is a stage set for what neighborhoods used to be like in the nineteenth century. Like much of brownstone Brooklyn, it is the human scale here that's so appealing. And you can see the sky.

Carroll Gardens used to be a mixed Italian neighborhood, known as much for its rough-and-tumble atmosphere as its rows of nicely kept homes. It was a tight-knit community where the little old ladies in black leaned out the brownstone windows and knew everything that went on up and down the street. Fathers and sons worked hard at the nearby docks. Although there is nothing of interest to see in the old **Longshoremen's Union Building** on Court Street, those who know their union history can sit, stare, and savor the fact that right here, along the Brooklyn waterfront, some big battles were fought. The strikes, the graft, the ups and downs of the longshoremen weren't just stories in the newspaper—they were often very personal matters, sometimes of life or death. That's all a thing of the past, now, with the waterfront no longer a very active port, and consideration being given to turning the piers into a big park or a dock for cruise ships.

The little old Italian ladies in black aren't so numerous anymore; visitors will have to work a little harder than in the past to feel the Italian history here. But you get the flavor of it watching a game of bocci, or noting the statues of the Virgin in many front yards. There's a colorful Good Friday parade and brightly lit displays of the Christmas epic every winter. Speaking of flavor, the Italian legacy lives on, where else, in food. It's hard to resist the taste of fresh pasta sauce and soft, warm mozzarella, or the aroma of coffee newly roasted in an old cast-iron roaster. Mixing old and new, there's a wonderful neighborliness here, with street fairs, block parties, book clubs, active neighborhood associations, and community activities.

It's daunting to try to list the range of culinary options; you'll also find lots of options for a quiet drink, a noisy bar scene, a game of pool, a jukebox, or DJs.

There's a certain style that the new Smith Street has brought: sophisticated, urbane, uncluttered, and—with lots of bright colors and clean lines—upbeat. Many of the boutique owners both work and live in the area. Local stores and restaurants receive favorable reviews so regularly in *Time Out* and *New York* magazines that one has to believe that half their staff writers live here, too.

BY SUBWAY Take the F or G train to Bergen Street for Smith Street and Cobble Hill, to Carroll Street for Carroll Gardens, or to Smith and 9th Street for Smith Street. Other subway stops are about six blocks on the other side of Atlantic Avenue: take the 2, 3, 4, or 5 train to Borough Hall, the M or R to Court Street, or the A or C to Jay Street.

In the pages below, we've sliced and diced the area into unorthodox sections. With apologies to purists, most restaurant and shopping listings for Carroll Gardens/Cobble Hill/Boerum Hill are lumped together under **Carroll Gardens**. And we've taken a separate look at **Gowanus** and the **Atlantic Avenue** area. As for the Columbia Street area, you will find it in a separate section in the Red Hook chapter.

WHAT'S "BOCOCA"?

As the area has gentrified, it's given itself a new name: Bococa. This made-up word combines the first two letters of three neighborhoods: BO-erum Hill, CO-bble Hill, and CA-rroll Gardens. At the time of this writing, it is too early to say whether the name will take root in the popular vocabulary, as Manhattan's SoHo and Brooklyn's DUMBO have done. The parameters of this area are geographic, but Bococa is about a quantum leap into a new state of mind, not just an additive connecting of old Italian Carroll Gardens with genteel Cobble Hill. The shopkeepers in the area are, of course, tickled pink to be part of something than might generate more attention and business; many advertise in a spiffy map-and-brochure called "Bococa." Real estate agents, too, welcome the verbal face-lift. But Brooklyn's true neighborhood identities have evolved out of long histories, local politics, housing price differentials, and demographic trends. Only time will tell whether the urbane, eclectic, artistic, youthful 'hood that the name "Bococa" suggests, will, in fact, meld together the existing neighborhoods—and endure.

What's **NEW?**

Smith Street Is So Happening, It's Happened; the Action Shifts

The "yuppification" of this large, popular residential area continues with lightning speed, driven by the success of Smith Street's little restaurant-and-boutique row. Housing prices are so far up that even longtime realtors are agape. It's likely that this area will continue to gain steam as an appealing place for young singles and families to live. It's hip, energetic, friendly, and, with many landmark buildings and well-kept front gardens on brownstone-lined streets, it's beautiful. Even the old subway station at Smith and 9th is slated for a major overhaul and upgrade around 2006.

Three little pockets to watch: the area around the Gowanus Canal, Atlantic Avenue, and Columbia Street.

☛ **TIP:** Pick up the annual *Shopping Guide and Walking Guide* by the Atlantic Avenue Betterment Association (*www.atlanticave.org*) as well as two BOCOCA brochures for restaurants and shopping (*www.bococa.com*).

HISTORICAL NOTES

The first Europeans to settle here were seventeenth-century Dutch farmers and middle-class English who moved in through the early 1800s. But it was the immigrant sailors and longshoremen—initially Irish, but overwhelmingly Italian by 1900—who labored on the nearby docks that gave the neighborhood its flavor. In those days the entire area was simply called "Red Hook," and it covered present-day Red Hook, Carroll Gardens, and parts of nearby Boerum Hill (but not the more rarefied Cobble Hill).

The ports of the Atlantic and Erie Basins, the busy State Barge Canal Terminal, and the connecting railways made this one of the nation's busiest shipping centers for more than a century. It is no accident that the headquarters of the Longshoremen's Union was, until recently, right here on Court Street. The passions and raw energy of Red Hook were captured in Arthur Miller's *A View From the Bridge* and Elia Kazan's *On the Waterfront*; its worst aspects were epitomized by Al Capone, who plied his trade as petty thief here before moving to Chicago.

After World War II the entire area declined, as Brooklynites raced to the suburbs. The newly built Brooklyn-Queens and Gowanus expressways and Brooklyn Battery Tunnel separated the industrial waterfront from the residential areas farther inland. Shipping and related businesses moved out to more modern facilities in New Jersey, when containers revolutionized the industry in the 1960s. Old Red Hook was ruined by the highway construction and loss of jobs. The row houses were razed, isolated low-income projects erected in their place. Cobble Hill and Carroll Gardens also declined, but retained their core Italian community, and then began to revive in the 1960s, fueled by activist residents and an influx of younger newcomers. (Indicative of recent changes are the churches-turned-condos at 360 Court Street and 450 Clinton Street.) Commercial growth in the nearby downtown area has also helped. In the 1990s, as real estate prices in Cobble Hill and Carroll Gardens have begun squeezing people out, the gentrification frontier has pushed farther south along Smith Street, into Gowanus, across to the waterfront side of the BQE to the Columbia Street area, and south along Van Brunt Street into Red Hook.

Kidstuff

☺ **Playgrounds, bookstores,** and **pizza places,** oh my! Make some pottery at the **Painted Pot.** Look at the bridges on the **Gowanus Canal.** Go to a street fair in the summer!

Carroll Gardens Area

HOW IT GOT ITS NAME Carroll Gardens was originally a section of Red Hook, and was given its current moniker by real-estate brokers in the 1960s, after the neighborhood was cut off from the waterfront by the construction of the BQE. "Carroll" refers to Maryland's Charles Carroll, an Irishman and the only Roman Catholic signer of the Declaration of Independence, in honor of the Maryland regiment that defended the Old Stone House at Gowanus, a local landmark, against the British in the Revolutionary War. And "Gardens" refers to the many deep, front-yard gardens in the neighborhood.

POINTS OF CULTURAL INTEREST

SPECIAL EVENTS.
Court Street Summerfest (summer), Court Street Crawl (September); call 858-0557 for dates. Smith Street Fun-Day Sunday (second or third Sunday in June); call 852-0328.

♪ ☺ ✪ **BROOKLYN YOUTH CHORUS.** 179 Pacific St., 243-9447, www.brooklynyouthchorus.org. By appointment.

Founded by Diane Berkun, who launched her dream over a decade ago while teaching at nearby Brooklyn Friends School, the Brooklyn Youth Chorus is a success story built on tenacity and talent. Melding the voices of some of New York City's multiracial, ethnically and culturally diverse youth, the chorus has traveled to Europe, sung for presidents, and performed at Carnegie Hall.

CARROLL GARDENS HOMES. 1st Pl. through 4th Pl. bet. Henry and Smith Sts.

It is no accident that Carroll Gardens has the word "garden" in its name. The homes on these blocks have unusually large front yards, thanks to an innovative surveyor, Richard Butts, who mapped out this area for development in 1846.

CARROLL GARDENS HISTORIC DISTRICT. President and Carroll Sts. bet. Hoyt and Smith Sts.

This small residential area of nineteenth-century brownstones is a lovely remnant of local architecture from 1870 to 1885. The front yards are particularly deep, and the street design minimizes traffic.

CUYLER WARREN ST. PRESBYTERIAN CHURCH. 450 Warren St. near Nevins St.

Completed in 1892, this church is the only twentieth-century site in New York

State associated with Mohawk Indian history to be listed on the New York State and National Registers of Historic Places. It had the largest Native American community in New York City, as families of Mohawk Indian ironworkers came here between the 1930s and 1950s to work at high altitudes on the construction of New York City skyscrapers. A prominent pastor of the church, Reverend David Munroe Cory, who died in 1996, is said to have learned the Mohawk language and translated religious tracts into Mohawk.

☺ **DOLL AND TOY MUSEUM OF NEW YORK CITY.** Currently inside P.S. 42 at 610 Henry St. but see the Web site, 800-99-DOLLS, www.dollandtoymuseumofnyc.org. By appointment.

The only doll-and-toy museum in New York City was started in 1999 by a local resident and author of several books about dolls.

Bet you didn't know that the first-ever teddy bear was a born Brooklynite? Well, as the story goes, Morris Michtom, a Russian immigrant and novelty-store owner in Brooklyn who started Ideal Toy Company, the world's largest purveyor of toys, created the bear in 1902, after reading a story in the *Washington Post* about President Theodore Roosevelt's refusing to shoot a bear cub while on a hunting expedition in Mississippi. The toy was named "Teddy's bear," after the president's nickname, and later changed to teddy bear.

440 CLINTON STREET HOUSE. 440 Clinton St. off Court St.

F. G. Guido Funeral Home occupies this 1840s New York City landmark building, which was one of the biggest of its time in Brooklyn. Note the fine old granite entrance.

INTERNATIONAL LONGSHOREMEN'S UNION BUILDING (former). 343 Court St. at Union St. Now part of Long Island College Hospital.

This official-looking building used to house the headquarters of Longshoremen's Union, once a powerful force on the Brooklyn waterfront and in local and national politics. The tumultuous, sometimes violent history of the union reflected the brutal physical demands on the longshoremen, whose backbreaking work required loading and unloading shipments of sugar, coffee, and other goods. Sometimes colorful, sometimes corrupt, always noisy, the longshoremen were a tremendous influence on Carroll Gardens and the neighboring waterfront community of Red Hook, which was built primarily by and for the people who worked at the Brooklyn ports. The introduction of containerization in the 1960s precipitated a rapid decline of the longshoremen industry, which explains why the building is now part of Long Island College Hospital's complex—currently the School of Nursing and soon to be home to the Stanley Lamm Institute for Child Development and Neurology.

MICRO MUSEUM. 123 Smith St. bet. Dean and Pacific Sts., 797-3116, www.micromuseum.com. Open by appointment only.

Look for the solar-powered kinetic sculpture in the window. Exploring the intersection between technology and art, this little mom-and-pop gallery (it's not a "museum," really) presents such projects as interactive online streaming video with long-distance audience participation. There are occasional exhibits of mixed media (including sound) and artwork.

Free! **OPEN STUDIO TOUR OF CARROLL GARDENS.** www.jonathanherbert.com.

In the spring, the Brooklyn Working Artist Coalition of Carroll Gardens, Cobble Hill, and Red Hook organize a free, self-guided art walk through dozens of working artists' studios. For information, call **Brooklyn Arts Council** (625-0080) or check Web site.

PUBLIC SCHOOLS.

Among those considered to be New York City's "best public elementary schools" are the gifted program at PS 38 (450 Pacific Street); PS 146, also known as the Brooklyn New School (610 Henry Street); PS 32 (317 Hoyt Street); PS 29 (425 Henry Street); and PS 261 (314 Pacific Street). (Source: *New York City's Best Public Elementary Schools*, 2002, by C. Hemphill with P. Wheaton.)

SACRED HEARTS AND ST. STEPHEN CHURCH. 108 Carroll St., 596-7750.

Considered Brooklyn's oldest Italian Catholic parish, it sponsors a traditional Good Friday procession through the neighborhood streets, reminiscent of medieval Italy and old Carroll Gardens.

SOUTH CONGREGATIONAL CHURCH. Court St. corner of President St.

Built in stages from 1851 to 1893, this Romanesque Revival church, now residential apartments, is a New York City landmark. It once housed an active congregation of South Brooklynites, including longshoremen, merchants, and tradespeople. It housed a church, ladies parlor, and rectory.

PARKS AND PLAYGROUNDS

CARROLL PARK. Carroll St. corner of Court St.

Once a private garden, this park was built in the 1870s and rapidly became a centerpiece of the neighborhood. Carroll Park has swings and seesaws as well as a bocci game on a nice afternoon. It's a very safe, neighborhood environment, and while there's not much shade in hot weather, the sprinkler keeps the kids cool.

👻 **DIMATTINA PARK AND DOG RUN.** Hicks and Rapelye Sts., 965-6980, daily 6 a.m.–10 p.m.

CARROLL GARDENS AREA RESTAURANTS, BARS, AND CAFÉS

The term "Smith Street restaurants" is so common that we listed them separately, below. But there are lots of other good restaurants in the neighborhood, on Court Street and Columbia Street, too. Quick bites and bars are also listed separately. Most of these establishments are within a ten-minute walk of each other.

Smith Street Restaurants

BANANIA CAFÉ. 241 Smith St. at Douglass St., 237-9100, M–Th 5:30–11 p.m., F lunch 11 a.m.–3 p.m., dinner 5:30–11:30 p.m., Sa–Su lunch 10:30 a.m.–3 p.m., dinner 5:30–11:30 p.m. Cash only. Reservations for larger parties.

Smack in the middle of the action, Banania was one of the pioneering Smith Street eateries, and it still attracts a loyal clientele to its cheerfully crowded bistro. It consistently delivers delicious French-inspired food and good service at moderate prices. Try the winning calamari, soup of the day, and pork chops. About $30 per person.

💲 **BAR TABAC.** 128 Smith St. at Dean St., 923-0918, Su–Tu 11–1 a.m., W–Th 11–2 a.m., F–Sa 11–3 a.m., www.bococa.com/restaurants.

One of Smith Street's great success stories, Bar Tabac not only turns out reliably good French bistro food but, *mon Dieu*, it's open late! It's informal but sophisticated, relaxed, and hip, a home away from home for the world-weary seeking refuge from the office, computer, their love life, and urban strife. Bar Tabac produces an outstandingly tasty meal, from bistro bites to winter stews to summer salads. Save room for dessert, notably anything chocolate or lemon.

Owners Jacques and George Forgeois have created a popular neighborhood bar scene. A seat at a sidewalk table is prized on a balmy summer night.

🎵 **BOUDOIR BAR AT THE EAST END ENSEMBLE.** 273 Smith St. bet. Baltic and Butler Sts., 624-8878, 6 p.m.–3 a.m., www.eastendensemble.com.

Come ready to chuckle. Boudoir is a wine bar with theme nights, live music, comedy, open mic nights, independent films, and burlesque shows. Their boast: "Our Bartenders Wear Vintage Lingerie and Silk Pajamas. Anyone Emulating Us Gets a Free Drink Without Question." They've called themselves "The Sexiest L'il Bar in All of Brooklyn." There's a Sunday open jazz jam.

CAFÉ KAI. 151 Smith St. bet. Bergen and Wyckoff Sts., 596-3466, M–F 8 a.m.–7 p.m., Sa 10:30 a.m.–7.p.m., Su 11.a.m.–5.p.m.

Vegan and vegetarian fare is what makes this tiny, sunny café and garden spot (named after the West African Yoruba word for "lovable) such a popular shop. The ingredients are seasonal and pesticide-free. Café Kai has only a few small tables inside (with a few more in the garden). But you can take out freshly squeezed vegetable and fruit juices, soy shakes, and heartier fare like curried couscous, or pita sandwiches with veggies and miso dressing.

CAFÉ LULUC. 214 Smith St. bet. Baltic and Butler Sts., 625-3815, M–Th 7:30 a.m.–midnight, F–Sa 8–2 a.m., Su 8 a.m.–midnight, www.cafeluluc.com. Cash only.

Outside of your local diner (*boring*), how many restaurants serve breakfast, lunch, *and* dinner? Not many. That's why this cheery French-Cuban restaurant is popular among the off-peak people: writers, local entrepreneurs, artists, and moms. Café LULUc dishes out eggs and pancakes for breakfast, fat sandwiches stuffed with fresh ingredients for lunch (try the Cuban pressed sandwich with pork, melting cheese, and *aioli*), and, at dinner, more serious entrées of meats and fish. There's a practical, everyday ambiance, and a garden—not to mention a popular Sunday brunch. Sandwiches with salad run about $10.

CASERTA VECCHIA. 221 Smith St., 624-7549, Tu–Th, Su noon–10:30 p.m., F–Sa noon–11 p.m., www.caser tavecchiarestaurant.com. Cash only. Reservations recommended.

Thin-crust lovers alert! This Neapolitan establishment welcomes with its white tablecloths, blond-wood furniture, and a brick oven visibly blazing in the back. The owner Alfonso Carusone is a third-generation pizza man. Caserta Vecchia offers classic toppings and a half-dozen "pizza fantasie" options: smothered in Nutella chocolate-hazelnut spread and shaved pear slices, or pineapple and ham. There's also grilled calamari, wood oven–grilled vegetables, and non-pizza entrées. Pizza pies and entrées both in the $8–$13 range.

EL CIBAO. 172 Smith St. near Bergen St., 596-1501, M–Th 7 p.m.–9 p.m., F–Sa 7 p.m.–10 p.m.

Check out this little place that harkens back to the days before Smith Street became a hot spot. It's a plain eatery where you can get huge quantities of food for under $10. Try the pork, or inquire as to what is the best dish of the day.

☺ ❀ **FAAN.** 209 Smith St. at Baltic St., 694-2277, 11 a.m.–1 a.m., www.bococa.com/restaurants.

Neighborhood kids like Faan's brightly colored storefront. Faan's Asian-fusion food—sushi rolls, stir fries, and the like—is inexpensive and plentiful, combining popular Thai, Vietnamese, and Japanese dishes. In the summer, you can eat on sidewalk tables. It's about $10 per entrée. Downstairs, **Bar Below** has a DJ dancing scene (after the kids are fast asleep).

♫ ⊘ **HALCYON.** 227 Smith St. bet. Butler and Douglass Sts., 260-9299, M–Th 11–1 a.m., F–Sa 10–2 a.m., Su 10 a.m.–midnight, www.halcyonline.com.

Every so often, something truly *original* comes along, which helps define a neighborhood. Halcyon, opened in 1999, is just that. It started life as a multitasker: café, retro-record shop, kitsch furniture shop, and performance-art space. Halcyon hosts live performances, spoken word, fashion shows, and more. Meander over to the back and put some vinyl on the record players, pop headphones on your noggin', and groove to oldies-but-goodies. Or buy a portable Vestax turntable for vinyl records at home. One of the best places in the neighborhood to pick up fliers about local events, Halcyon is postcollege, neighborhood Brooklyn at its very best.

Schedule: They book a seasonal schedule. New events are presented every four months. A few DJ events are permanent, and there's a different DJ for every mood: smooth drum and bass "Acupuncture" on Fridays, tech house music on "THC" Thursdays, etc. Every other Wednesday there are celeb guests who take a spin as DJs, including Tina Weymouth and Chris Frantz of The Talking Heads, Chocolate Genius, and Julie Cruise of Twin Peaks.

PANINO'TECA. 275 Smith St. bet. DeGraw and Sackett Sts. 237-2728, Su and Tu–Th noon–midnight, F–Sa noon–2 a.m., www.bococa.com/restaurants. Cash only.

Va bene, a whiff of Italy! Perfect for a tasty lunch or an inexpensive informal dinner, this darkly lit café serves outstanding Italian cheeses, sandwiches, soups and salads, Italian-style coffees, and imported sodas. For just $6 or so, you can get a freshly prepared panino (a hot pressed sandwich on ciabetta bread) with artful insides, such as a combo of soppressata, roasted garlic, artichoke, and fontina. Or a salad of arugula, fennel, and *pancetta* in a pumpkin dressing. With only about a dozen tables and as many seats at the bar, it's intimate.

PATOIS. 255 Smith St. bet. DeGraw and Douglass Sts., 855-1535, Tu–Th 6–10:30 p.m., F–Sa 6–11:30 p.m., Su brunch 11:30 a.m.–3 p.m., dinner 5–10 p.m. Reservations recommended.

Smith Street pioneer Alan Harding's Patois got a huge welcome from Brooklynites when it opened in 1998. This little bistro is moderately priced (entrées from $10 to $16) but offers a fantastically tasty French and American menu that changes seasonally. The chef (known to wear a beret *inside* the kitchen) produces excellent fare, including grilled meats and fish, and flavorful sauces and sides. There's a decent wine list. The interior is cozy, with tin ceilings and exposed-brick walls. The thirty-person capacity expands somewhat in the summer with garden seating. (See **Schnäck**, page 408).

♩ **PROVIDENCE.** 225 Smith St. at Butler St., 522-9060, M–F 6 p.m.–midnight, Sa–Su brunch 10 a.m.–3 p.m., dinner 6 p.m.–midnight, DJs Th–Su 9:30–3 p.m.

Smith Street's biggest and loudest place for dining and dancing, Providence rocks from Thursday to Sunday. The cuisine is Mediterranean (try the mussels gratin), with a wide range of entrées. There are several different spaces here: a street-level bar, a dining room, and another bar downstairs.

RED ROSE. 315 Smith St. bet. President and Union Sts., 625-0963, M and W–Th 4:30–10:30 p.m., F–Sa 4:30–11 p.m., Su 2–10:30 p.m.

This old-fashioned restaurant with hearty food and good prices caters primarily to locals. You can have a bowl of soup and pasta for less than $10, and the food is well prepared and fresh. Come early on Sundays and you'll dine among Carroll Gardens' older Italian crowd.

RESTAURANT SAUL. 140 Smith St. bet. Bergen and Dean Sts., 935-9844, M and W–Sa 5:30–11 p.m., Su 5:30–10:30 p.m., www.bococa.com/restaurants.

Restaurant Saul gets high marks for ambiance, food, wine list, and service. Plus, the tables are set far apart enough so you can indulge in an intimate personal or business conversation while chef-owner Saul Bolton turns out excellent, creative French and American dishes. Average entrées are in the $20-up range.

SAVOIA. 277 Smith St. bet. DeGraw and Sackett Sts., 797-2727, M 5:30–10:30 p.m., Tu–W noon–10:30 p.m., Th noon–11 p.m., F–Sa noon–midnight, Su noon–10 p.m., www.bococa.com. Cash only.

As an alternative to the usual greasy $2.60 slice-and-a-soda, Savoia has made a reputation for itself for great wood-oven pizzas. There are lots of other entrées, as well. Come with the family. *Mangia!*

SHERWOOD CAFÉ (AKA ROBIN DES BOIS). 195 Smith St. bet. Baltic and Warren Sts., 596-1609, M–F noon–midnight, Sa–Su 11 a.m.–midnight, www.bococa.com.

Sherwood Café is worth a visit just for the fun of it. The owner has transformed his antiques shop into a venue that's simultaneously a bar, café, antique store, and occasional gallery. The food is traditional French fare; you can get a *croque monsieur* or cheese and charcuterie board while contemplating buying that chair. In the winter months, there's hot spiced wine and an indoor fireplace; in summer, the garden is fabulous for brunch or an early evening drink.

SUR. 232 Smith St. bet. Butler and Douglass Sts., 875-1716, M–Th 6–11:30 pm, F 6 p.m.–midnight, Sa brunch 11 a.m.–4:30 p.m., dinner 6 p.m.–midnight, Su brunch 11 a.m.–4:30 p.m., dinner 5:30–11 p.m.

This Euro-Argentinean restaurant serves Argentinean imported beef, along with special *chimichurri* sauce, and a variety of delicious empañadas, pasta dishes, and other entrées. Vegetarian friends can find some tasty alternatives. Things get busy around eight p.m., and there's sometimes live music in the bar area. The weekend brunch can be a long, lingering affair. Entrées average about $15.

3 BOW THAIS. 278 Smith St. bet. DeGraw and Sackett Sts., 834-0511, Su–Th 11:30 a.m.–10:30 p.m., F–Sa 11:30 a.m.–11 p.m. Cash only.

Pocketbook-friendly is an understatement. Distinguishing itself from its Smith Street comrades, this Thai restaurant lets you have it all: a great meal, quick service, and enough piggy-bank money left over to save for a summer trip to—well, Thailand. The owners also run Greenpoint's **Amarin** (itself an offshoot of Williamsburg's **Planet Thai**). What they don't spend on frills and décor, they do on fresh ingredients. There are surprisingly good, un-Thai, key lime pie and chocolate mousse. Salads are under $4, and curries or noodle dishes are about $7.

THE GROCERY. 288 Smith St. bet. Union and Sackett Sts., 596-3335, M–Th 6 a.m.–10 p.m., F 6 a.m.–11 p.m., Sa 5:30 a.m.–11 p.m.

At this little nipper of a restaurant, very welcoming co-chef-owners Charles Kiely and Sharon Pachter dish up healthful, inventive concoctions, such as duck breast with bulgur or Arctic char. It's tiny, seating only about thirty people. About $35 for dinner. The Grocery was highly rated by Zagat 2003.

♩ TUK TUK. 204 Smith St. bet. Baltic and Butler Sts., 222-5598, Su–Th noon–10:15 p.m., F–Sa noon–11:15 p.m. Cash only.

Tuk Tuk's owners, also of Manhattan's Chelsea Thai, dish up such specials as a *tom yum* soup, *khao soy*, crisp noodles served in a yellow curry with vegetables, a good hot green chili dish, and a tasty Thai ice cream dessert. Peaceful for lunch and sometimes crowded at dinner time, the simple décor at this new Thai restaurant is matched by the weekend live jazz. What's a *"tuk tuk"*? It's a little three-wheeled taxi commonly used in Thailand, and you can see a dozen little toy models on a shelf here. Entrées are in the $10 range.

VINNY'S OF CARROLL GARDENS. 295 Smith St. near Union St., 875-5600, M–Sa 11 a.m.–10 p.m.

Old-timers love Vinny's. Ask them to recommend a local eatery, and they'll say, "Vinny's, of course." Some newcomers aren't so sure. If you like lots of red sauce, low prices, and a clientele that mixes old and new, try 'em.

WASABI SUSHI. 213 Smith St. bet. Baltic and Butler Sts., 243-2028. (See Williamsburg listing, p. 455.)

ZAYTOONS. 283 Smith St. at Sackett St., 875-1880, M–F lunch 11 a.m.–4 p.m., dinner 5–11 p.m., Sa 11 a.m.–11.p.m., Su 11.a.m.–9 p.m., www.zaytoons.com. (Also at 472 Myrtle Ave. in Fort Greene.)

Really authentic Middle Eastern food can be found at this Smith Street fave. It's on a par with the more traditional Middle Eastern places on Atlantic Avenue, but the ambiance is brighter. There's an energetic local buzz here, very youthful and upbeat. The pita is served fresh, and the dishes are satisfying. Entrées average under $9.

Other Notable Area Restaurants

CAFÉ ON CLINTON. 268 Clinton St. bet. Warren and Congress Sts., 625-5908, M–Th 5–11 p.m., F–Su lunch 11 a.m.–3:30 p.m., dinner 5–11 p.m.

Warmth pours forth from this intimate little restaurant, with its oak-and-exposed-brick walls and beautifully restored pressed-tin ceilings. The menu features fresh-from-the-market grilled fish plus Mexican, Oriental, and Italian dishes, with entrées priced from $8 to $15. Don't miss the hand-wrought-iron brain-teaser puzzles hanging near the bar. They'll keep you busy for hours.

CAFFÈ CARCIOFO. 248 Court St. corner of Kane St., 624-7551, daily 5:30–10:30 p.m., Su brunch 11 a.m.– 3 p.m. No credit cards.

Despite the name, artichoke (*carciofo* in Italian) is not a theme of the menu. The eclectic Northern Italian fare is good and reasonably priced, and the menu changes daily. But the real star here is the restaurant itself, with its bright tile floor, exposed-brick walls, and muted dark-wood accents. When the weather permits, the restaurant opens onto the sidewalk. Entrées from $10 to $16.

CASA ROSA. 384 Court St. bet. Carroll and President Sts., 625-8874, daily 11:30 a.m.–11 p.m.

Good, solid Italian fare in a simple, old-fashioned setting. The sort of place where you can still get a full (and filling) dinner—including antipasto and coffee—for less than $20.

HARVEST. 218 Court St. bet. Warren and Baltic Sts., 624-9267, Tu–Th lunch 1:30 a.m.–3 p.m., dinner 5:30–11 p.m., F–Sa 6 p.m.–midnight, www.bococa.com/restaurants.

Harvest's hearty food, large portions, and reasonable prices continue to draw loyal customers. There's something for everyone here: crayons for the kids, a bar for the adults, great desserts, and, of course, Southern comfort food. The cuisine includes fried catfish, meat loaf, and jambalaya. Entrées from $9 to $15.

♪ **JOYA.** 215 Court St. bet. Warren and Wyckoff Sts., 222-3484, Su–Th 5–11 p.m., F–Sa 5 p.m.–12:30 a.m. Cash only. Reservations on weekends.

Cheap. Fun. Popular. Joya's Thai food is fresh, and prepared with panache. A weekend DJ draws a young singles crowd, and there's some outdoor space, too.

♪ **LATIN GRILL.** 254 Court St. bet. Kane and DeGraw Sts., 858-0309, M 5–11 p.m., Tu–Th lunch 11 a.m.–3 p.m., dinner 5–11 p.m., F lunch 11 a.m.–3 p.m., dinner 5 p.m.–midnight, Sa–Su brunch 10 a.m.–3 p.m., dinner 5 p.m.–midnight.

Latin Grill takes its inspiration from Cuba and Mexico. The attractively tiled, simple décor is the backdrop for an unusual menu of excellent "Nuevo Latino" dishes. Aficionados rave about the excellent ceviche, grilled shrimp and chorizo, Cuban-style roasted pork, and Mexican grilled corn. Latin Grill is a good place for drinks, too. And there are salsa lessons on the first Saturday of the month. Moderately priced.

MARCO POLO RESTAURANT. 345 Court St. corner of Union St., 852-5015, M–Th 11:30 a.m.–11 p.m., F 11:30 a.m.–11 p.m., Sa 3 p.m.–midnight, Su 1–10 p.m., www.marcopoloristorante.com.

Want to get a sense of the Carroll Gardens of yesteryear, when little old ladies in black used to hang out the windows on 3rd Place? An old-fashioned favorite of locals, Marco Polo competently turns out about fifteen seafood and an equal number of meat entrées, with specialties like porcini mushroom pasta, and black pasta with scallops and shrimp, just like it did before Smith Street became Brooklyn's hottest dining destination. The pasta is made in-house, and the bread is from a local bakery. There's live piano every night, an enclosed sidewalk café, valet parking, and a fireplace in the winter. Make reservations for weekend dinners. Entrées cost from $15 to $20.

♪ **MAX COURT.** 394 Court St. at Carroll St., 596-9797, M–F 4 p.m.–midnight, Sa–Su noon–midnight, www.bococa.com/restaurants. Cash only.

This downtown Manhattan restaurant has an appetite for expansion, with branches in Harlem and Carroll Gardens. Popular dishes include the lasagna, osso buco, and stuffed meat loaf. A meal costs about $17 per person.

OSAKA. 272 Court St. bet. Kane and DeGraw Sts., 643-0044, M–Th noon–10 p.m., F 11:30 a.m.–11 p.m., Sa 5 p.m.–11 p.m., Su noon–10 p.m.

One of the pioneers in the ever-expanding world of sushi in Brooklyn, Osaka offers a wide range of appetizers, a sake bar, and a Japanese garden out back. Prices are reasonable, at $12 for a sushi meal.

Quick and Casual Meals

BUDDY'S BURRITO AND TACO BAR. 260 Court St. bet. Baltic and Kane Sts., 488-8695, M–Sa 11:30 a.m.–11 p.m., Su 11:30 a.m.–10 p.m. Cash only.

Definitely worth a visit for those with big appetites and small budgets, Buddy's is as informal as can be, and you can't beat it for basic good Mexican food for under $8. Stop in and stuff your face before going to the movies (the theater is right across the street) or hitting the local watering holes.

CALIFORNIA TAQUERIA. 187 Court St. corner of Bergen St., 624-7498, Su–Th noon–10 p.m., F–Sa noon–11 p.m. No credit cards. (Branches in Park Slope.)

The food is filling and not overwhelmingly spicy. Standard Mexican fare is made with your choice of stewed or grilled meats (don't miss the tangy *chile Colorado*). Six bucks buys you a burrito the size of your head, or a huge platter with a taco, enchilada, or chile relleno (sort of a cheese-and-pepper omelet here), plus rice and beans, guacamole, nacho chips, and *pico de gallo*.

JOE'S. 349 Court St. bet. Union and President Sts., 625-3223, daily "five or six-ish" a.m.–7:30 p.m. No credit cards.

Joe's old luncheonette attracts the locals for breakfast and lunch. The prices are low, the food is hearty, and the owners and clientele are as down to earth as you can get. Joe's serves a mean cup of espresso.

LEONARDO'S BRICK OVEN PIZZA. 383 Court St. corner of 1st Pl., 624-9620, daily 3–11 p.m. No credit cards.

You can't throw a rock in Carroll Gardens without hitting a pizzeria, and Leonardo's is one of the best in the neighborhood. The crust is thin, comes with lots of different toppings, and is cooked in an old-style brick oven. There is outdoor seating in good weather, and children are welcome.

NINO'S RESTAURANT AND PIZZERIA. 531 Henry St. at Union St., 834-0863, daily 10:30 a.m.–10 p.m.

If you want to have a good slice and also hear the local gossip among shopkeepers, Columbia Street artists, and urban soccer moms, come here.

SAM'S RESTAURANT. 238 Court St. bet. Kane and Baltic Sts., 596-3458, W–Su noon–10:30 p.m. Call ahead to check hours. No credit cards.

For over seventy years, Sam's has been turning out *rollatini,* spaghetti, and brick-oven pizzas. It's still a favorite with some of original, pregentrification, three-generation Italian families who used to give Carroll Gardens that authentic Italian neighborhood flavor. Prices are low.

TABOULEH. 136 Smith St. near Bergen and Dean Sts., 797-3313, daily 1–11 p.m.

You can see what you'll be eating at this little low-key place: Middle Eastern spinach pies, pita sandwiches stuffed with spicy chicken or lamb shish kabob, falafel and tabbouleh, of course. There are only a half dozen tables. Specials are only $8.

Bars and Cafés

ANGRY WADE'S. 222 Smith St. at Butler St., 488-7253, M–F 3 p.m.–4 a.m., Sa–Su noon–4 a.m. Cash only.

Angry Wade's provides a full weekly schedule of theme nights (pool night, ladies' night, karaoke, and more) and drink specials to lure you in. During football season, the bar is packed, with avid fans watching a choice of games on one of five TV screens with the NFL Sunday ticket; additional perks are free snacks and half-price drinks until one p.m. on game days. A pool table, dart board, fireplace, self-serve popcorn machine, along with a well-stocked jukebox of comfort music for those in their thirties and late twenties, make this a friendly spot.

♩ **BAR BELOW.** 209 Smith St. at Baltic St., 694-2277, daily 6 p.m.–3 a.m.

Following the upstairs restaurant's penchant for unusual décor, Bar Below follows an aquatic theme, with waterbed cushions and lots of greens. There's a full schedule of DJs, and Tuesday and Thursday nights are especially popular. The bar gets a mixed crowd of fashionistas.

THE BOAT. 175 Smith St. bet. Warren and Wyckoff Sts., 254-0607, daily 5 p.m.–4 a.m. Cash only.

This red-faced bar has no sign out front. But don't get hung up on that for too long—this is a great, reasonably priced hangout with plenty of seating (tables up front, couches and fireplace in the rear, bar in the middle). The one-hundred-disc jukebox filled with indie and alt-rock tunes provides an uptempo soundtrack to the evening. By the way, they know that "Guinness" is spelled wrong.

BROOKLYN INN. 148 Hoyt St. corner of Bergen St., no phone. Daily, "whenever someone walks in lookin' for a drink" until 4 a.m. No credit cards.

A no-nonsense neighborhood bar, the Brooklyn Inn has no TVs and no food, but it doesn't need them; it has a pool table, a great jukebox full of country, old R&B, and jazz, and an eclectic clientele of local writers, artists, and other creative types. Featured in the movie *Smoke,* the bar itself is turn-of-the-century, made all the more dramatic by a huge mirror and beautifully carved wood detailing. Brooklyn Inn is usually packed.

♩ **COUSINS II.** 160 Court St. at Amity St., 596-3514, M–Tu 4 p.m.–2 a.m., W–Th noon–2 a.m., F–Sa noon–4 a.m., Su 11:30–2 a.m.

This popular corner bar had a face-lift a few years ago; its huge plate-glass windows make for excellent people-watching. Cousins (named after the two co-owner cousins) serves inexpensive sandwiches, burgers, and other pub fare, as well as steaks and veal dishes that run up to $17. You can catch brunch on weekends and a game on one of the bar's TVs anytime. Friday-night karaoke and live-music Saturdays, except during the summer months.

FALL CAFÉ. 307 Smith St. bet. Union and President Sts., 403-0230, M–F 7:30 a.m.–9 p.m., Sa 8 a.m.–9 p.m., Su 9 a.m.–8 p.m. No credit cards.

Furnished in Salvation Army–style armchairs, this coffee bar has become a center of life in Carroll Gardens for Generation-Xers, writers, and moms of preschoolers desperate for a good latte and adult conversation. There's nice comfort food here: hot oatmeal in the morning, chilis and vegetarian soups, and sandwiches. They display locals' artwork and feature music on many weekend evenings, from jazz to baroque, as well as poetry readings. The prices are low.

GOWANUS YACHT CLUB AND BEER GARDEN. 323 Smith St. Open June through Halloween.

Name aside, it's really on Smith Street. You can't beat this for local color. Come and sit outside for cheap beers in disposable cups, and hot dogs, and ask some old-timer (if you can find one) how this all got started.

♫ **LAST EXIT.** 136 Atlantic Ave. bet. Clinton and Henry Sts., 222-9198, daily 5 p.m.–4 a.m.

This is a terrific bar. There's great music with a DJ on the weekend and a hip, local crowd. The drinks are just $6. Last Exit's owned by some of the same long-time local residents who brought us **Flying Saucer Café** on Atlantic Avenue.

MAZZOLA. 295 Court St. bet. Bergen and Wyckoff Sts., 797-2385, M–F 7 a.m.–8 p.m., Sa–Su 8 a.m.–7 p.m. No credit cards.

Owned by Mazzola's Bakery in Carroll Gardens, this little café offers tea and coffee (of the drinkable and by-the-pound varieties), as well as a variety of Italian cakes, cookies, and pastries. Of course, they also have scones, croissants, muffins, and other de rigueur café munchies.

P. J. HANLEY'S TAVERN. 449 Court St. near Nelson St., 834-8223, M–W 5–11 p.m., Th–Su noon–11 p.m. Cash only.

Hanley's Tavern claims to be the oldest bar in Brooklyn, dating from 1874. Today it's a low-key sports bar, with a fireplace that lends a nice atmosphere on winter nights.

QUENCH. 282 Smith St. at Sackett St., 875-1500, daily 6 p.m.–4 a.m. Cash only.

This slick-looking bar brings a little piece of Manhattan to Smith Street. You might feel compelled to dress up a bit, and the wildly eclectic jukebox may confuse you, but those looking for a more upscale drinking experience on the sunny side of the East River should be happy quenching their thirst here.

ROXY. 144 Smith St. at Bergen, 802-9686, daily noon—4 a.m. Cash only.

This bar is owned by the same folks who run three other Brooklyn bars: The **Boat, Buttermilk,** and **Great Lakes,** attracting a similar crowd of twenty- and thirty-something locals. Roxy is simple, but good enough for the casual afternoon or evening, with a decent selection on the jukebox of new wave, punk, rock, jazz, and country music, a pool table, and $3 pints until eight p.m. If you're feeling socially desperate midweek, there's a *Wednesday* night DJ. Ask at the bar for the *real* story behind the bar's name and old sign.

☻ SPARKY'S ALE HOUSE. 481 Court St. corner of Nelson St., 624-5516, Su—Th 4 p.m.—2 a.m., F—Sa 4 p.m.—4 a.m. Cash only.

One of a half-dozen Irish pubs in Carroll Gardens, Sparky's is the least slick and pretentious of the bunch. Just good people and lots of good brews (Irish, English, and American) in a small, friendly corner pub. You can also play darts or the jukebox here. Broadway wanna-bes will appreciate the monthly open-mic evening. It's dog-friendly.

UNCLE LOUIE G'S. 517 Henry St. bet. Union and Sackett Sts. (See Park Slope listing, p. 374.)

ZOMBIE HUT. 261 Smith St., 875-3433, daily 6 p.m.—4 a.m. Cash only.

Tired of the city scene? Take a step into the Zombie Hut and transport yourself to a tropical-drink paradise decorated with a fake bamboo canopy over the bar, and ocean and beach-themed wall hangings. This is the home of the "Suffering Bastard," "Gilligan," and "Frozen Zombie," among other cleverly named intoxicants. Drinks are a little on the pricey side for Brooklyn (the one exception is $2 cans of PBR), but they're strong enough that you'll only need a couple before your head is spinning.

SHOPPING (BOERUM HILL, COBBLE HILL, AND CARROLL GARDENS)

Specialty Food Shops

BOERUM HILL FOOD COMPANY. 134 Smith St. bet. Bergen and Dean Sts., 222-0140, daily 8 a.m.— 10 p.m., www.bococa.com/restaurants.

That Boerum Hill Food Company boasts one of the best community bulletin boards in the neighborhood is a telltale sign of its popularity. All day long, locals pop in to this postage stamp–sized eat-in/takeout store for food. They sell big, fresh sandwiches on freshly baked breads (try the seared chicken breast with fontina cheese and arugula), crepes, and dinner entrées such as duck confit. Sides of macaroni and cheese, broccoli and mashed potatoes, not to mention a killer chocolate fudge cake, all satisfy. And they do a nice weekend brunch. The average main course is $10.

BROOKLYN BREAD CAFÉ. 436 Court St. bet 2nd and 3rd Sts., 403-0234, M–F 6 a.m.–10 p.m., Sa and Su 7 a.m.–10 p.m.

Hands down, the best bread in Brooklyn is sold here, imported from the Royal Crown Bakery in Bensonhurst. Stop in for a sandwich, lunch, or a good cup of Italian coffee and a pastry. Newly arrived in mid-2003, this is great news for bread lovers. There's a sister store, **Paneantico**, in Bay Ridge; watch for more popping up in a neighborhood near you.

CAPUTO'S BAKE SHOP. 329 Court St. bet. Union and Sackett Sts., 875-6871, M–Sa 6 a.m.–7 p.m., Su 6 a.m.–5 p.m. No credit cards.

Caputo's fourth-generation family bakery (the centennial is in 2004) is a great place for bread. About ten different kinds are baked on the premises, and you can make a meal out of a special bread filled with salami and provolone.

CAPUTO'S FINE FOODS. 460 Court St. bet. 3rd and 4th Pls., 855-8852, M–Sa 8:30 a.m.–7 p.m., Su 9 a.m.–2:30 p.m.

How do you spell "heaven" to a working mother with hungry kids at home? C-A-P-U-T-O'S.

Part of the Caputo family food business, this hearty, old-fashioned takeout can't be beat. You'll find over a dozen sauces to heat and serve on that fresh pasta, ready-to-go soups, and some sides as well.

COLLEGE BAKERY. 239 Court St. bet. Warren and Baltic Sts., 624-5534, Tu–Su 7 a.m.–8 p.m. No credit cards.

Not much of the original German population is left in this neighborhood, but one survivor is this nearly seventy-year-old, family-run German bakery. It makes old-fashioned whipped-cream birthday cakes, chocolate layer cakes, and rye and sourdough breads, as well as snack-sized tarts, strudels, *hamantaschen*, and other delicacies. Their prices, like the decor, remain in the 1950s.

☻ COURT PASTRY SHOP. 298 Court St., bet. DeGraw and Douglass Sts., 875-5403. Daily, 8 a.m.–8:30 p.m.

Wonderful traditional Italian sweets are the treat here, from cannoli to *sfogliatella* (huge lobster-tail pastries filled with cream) and *sfinge,* also known as "Saint Joseph's pastries." Seasonal holiday treats like *strufoli* and *cassata* are also available. In the summer, don't miss the chocolate and vanilla spumoni ices here, which taste like cannoli because they're made with *cremolata*. They give very hearty portions, one ice piled high will feed three small kids, for just $1.75.

CURRYSOURCE. 88 Bergen St. at Smith St., 797-9719, M–F 4–10 p.m., Sa–Su 2–8 p.m., info@curry source.com. Cash only.

What an innovative concept. This tiny takeout food store specializes in prepared Indian dishes that you can take home and heat up. The tastes are "Anglo-Indian," as the proprietors hail from the UK. (There's an informative little explanation on the menu of the British perspective on curry.) Try the *pakora* or vegetable *korma*, pork *vindaloo* and chicken *tikka masala*.

D'AMICO FOODS. 309 Court St. bet. DeGraw and Sackett Sts., 875-5403, M–Sa 9 a.m.–7 p.m., www.damicofoods.com.

D'Amico's has been in biz since 1948—over a half century. What could be more authentic and scene-setting than a huge old-fashioned cast-iron coffee roaster and grinder smack-dab in the middle of a food shop? That's why ABC TV featured them in a segment on how to make the perfect cuppa coffee. More than sixty different kinds of coffee are roasted on the premises. You'll also find large jars of olives, pimientos, spices, cheeses, and biscotti. Order from the Web site, or in person.

DELICATESSEN AT VERANDAH PLACE. 264 Clinton St. bet. Baltic St. and Verandah Pl., 852–1991, M–F 7 a.m.–8:30 p.m., Sa–Su 8 a.m.–7 p.m. No credit cards.

This is one of those urban niceties that make Brooklyn home-sweet-home: world-class food across the street, nestled on a pretty corner in a residential neighborhood. The French owner-and-chef Christian Barbier counts the prime minister of France and the Paris Hotel Ritz as previous employers. Try whatever is home-cooked, as it's bound to be delicious. And the sandwiches are normal deli prices, *mon Dieu*!

FISH TALES. 191A Court St. bet. Bergen and Wyckoff Sts., 246-1346, M–F 9 a.m.–8 p.m., Sa 9 a.m.–6 p.m.

Fish Tales, which opened in 1996, specializes in gourmet, sushi-quality fish and live shellfish, brought in daily. Fish Tales also sells prepared takeout dishes (including crab-stuffed sole and grilled salmon and swordfish) and soups, and is planning a sit-down raw bar. The staff is extremely friendly and knowledgeable and more than willing to offer serving suggestions (or cautions).

G. ESPOSITO PORK STORE. 357 Court St. near President St., 875-6863, M—Th and Sa 8 a.m.—6 p.m., F 7 a.m.—7 p.m., Su 9 a.m.—2 p.m. No credit cards.

Esposito's family-owned shop has been selling homemade sausages since 1922. Among the varieties are sausages flavored with fennel, pepper and onion, and cheese and parsley. You can pick up ingredients for a feast here—three kinds of mozzarella; eggplant, olive, or mushroom salad; delicious milk-fed veal; rice-and-prosciutto balls; and, if you're in the mood, pigs' feet.

JIM AND ANDY FRUIT AND PRODUCE MARKET. 208 Court St. bet. Wyckoff and Warren Sts., 522-6034, M—Sa 9 a.m.—6 p.m., closed Tu during July and August. No credit cards.

Welcome to *the* classic Brooklyn vegetable stand. In the heart of Cobble Hill for three decades now (and we hope they don't retire to Florida anytime soon), Jim and Andy's small, selective store sells handpicked fresh fruits and vegetables, from apples to zucchini. It's an unassuming old place, the proprietors are not chatty, and the prices are on the high side. But Jim and Andy are true food professionals, and their produce is of the highest quality.

KIMBERLY'S SWEET SHOP. 575 Henry St., 855-3129. Call ahead.

A proud winner of the first Egg Cream Extravaganza 2003, held at Brooklyn Borough Hall to decide the best makers of Brooklyn's official drink.

LOS PAISANOS MEAT MARKET. 162 Smith St. bet. Wycoff and Bergen Sts., 855-2641, M—Sa 8 a.m.—7 p.m.

Los Paisanos used to carry a limited selection of meats, geared to the working-class Latino residents. But reacting to the changes along Smith Street, they've removed that "pigs' feet" sign from the window and now sell aged steaks, organic eggs and meat products, homemade sausages, and nitrate- and antibiotic-free franks.

MARQUET PATISSERIE. 221 Court Street. corner of Warren St., 852-9267, daily 7:30 a.m.—8 p.m. (Also, Fort Greene, 680 Fulton St.)

Started by neighborhood residents Jean-Pierre Marquet and his wife, Lynne Guillot, over a decade ago, this little French pastry shop continues to turn out first-class lemon tarts, spectacular croissants, and gorgeous cakes. When it opened, the *New York Times* rated Marquet Patisserie "one of the finest pastry shops in New York City," and the quality remains high.

MAZZOLA'S BAKERY. 192 Union St. corner of Henry St., 643-1719, M—F 6 a.m.—8:30 p.m., Sa 7 a.m.—8 p.m., Su 7 a.m.—6 p.m. No credit cards.

For more than seventy years in the same location, Mazzola's has specialized in bread. The loaves stuffed with pepperoni and provolone (sold under the unfortunate name "lard bread") are delectable, as are the extra-fluffy *torrese* bread and magnificent raisin bread.

MONTE LEONE'S PASTRY. 355 Court St., 624-9253, M–Th 8 a.m.–8 p.m., Sa and Su 8 a.m.–9 p.m., in summer ices are available until 10 p.m., www.Monteleonepastry.com.

Established in 1902 by the family of a well-known actress, this shop offers such specialities as cookies, cheesecakes, biscuits, napoleons, and cannoli. (You can get a do-it-yourself cannoli kit here, with cream and shells.) Try their chocolate cookies, with bittersweet chocolate folded into the cookie, so that it's not too sweet, just dangerously enticing.

PASTOSA RAVIOLI. 347 Court St. near Union St., 625-9482, M–F 9 a.m.–7 p.m., Sa 9 a.m.–6 p.m., Su 9 a.m.–2 p.m.

The original Pastosa opened more than thirty years ago, and another dozen or so have since been launched by members of the Ajello family throughout New York City (one is Fratelli Ravioli at 200 Court St.). They sell a great variety of classic (four-cheese, spinach) and eclectic (pumpkin, sun-dried tomato, and lobster in squid's-ink dough) ravioli and tasty homemade sauces (tomato, vodka, pesto, marinara, etc.), along with gourmet pastas, olives, and other delicacies.

SCOTTO'S WINE CELLAR. 318 Court St., 875-5530.

A fixture of Carol Gardens since 1935, this good local wine store bears the same name as Buddy Scotto, one of the movers and shakers behind the cleanup of the once-putrid Gowanus Canal waters and rejuvenation of the surrounding area.

STAUBITZ MARKET. 222 Court St. bet. Baltic and Warren St., 624-0014, M–F 9 a.m.–7 p.m., Sa 8 a.m.–6 p.m. Delivery available.

An institution for more than eighty years, Brooklyn's most upscale butcher shop carries a wide selection of "health-food meats"—nitrate-free turkey and hot dogs; mousses, pâtés, and sausages by Les Trois Petits Cochons; hormone-free chicken and veal; organic beef; and a good selection of standard meats. The store also sells top-quality gourmet foods, such as imported cheese, pasta, chutney, barbecue sauce, fresh-ground coffee beans, and bread. Call in your freezer orders, and they'll pack it for instant storage.

SWEET MELISSA PATISSERIE. 276 Court St. bet. Kane and DeGraw Sts., 855-3410, Su–Th 8 a.m.–10 p.m. F and Sa 8 a.m.–midnight. No credit cards.

For a cup of tea, a back-garden reverie, and great pastries, try this little

French-style café. The elegant goodies are made by a pastry chef who used to work for a well-known Manhattan restaurant, and you'll enjoy the lemon tart and croissants, among other treats. The menu has expanded to include some salads and pâtés. The wait for Sunday brunch is worth it, but you can also try Melissa's sweet version of British afternoon tea.

TULLER PREMIUM FOOD. 199 Court St., 222-9933, M–Sa 10 a.m.–8 p.m., Su 11 a.m.–6 p.m.

Over a hundred kinds of cheeses, dozens of freshly prepared foods, free-range rotisserie chickens, takeout gourmet soups and sandwiches, to-die-for cupcakes, and a rare line of Il Laboratoria ice cream by the founder of Ciao Bello make Tuller's a favorite stop on the way home. The cheeses selection includes hard-to-find imports, such as Humbold and Fog goat cheese and Dutch three-year-old gouda. Tuller's isn't cheap by any means, but you're paying for high quality and informed staff. If you live nearby, they deliver. Catering available.

UPRISING BAKERY. 210 Court St. near Warren St., 422-7676, daily 7:30–9 p.m. (See Park Slope listing, p. 374).

Contemporary Home Furnishings, Antiques, and Collectibles

ASTRO-TURF. 290 Smith St. bet. Union and Sackett Sts., 522-6182, Tu–F noon–7 p.m., Sa 11 a.m.–8 p.m., Su 10 a.m.–7 p.m.

They call it "twentieth-century furniture and objects," and if you're into fifties and sixties haute kitsch, this antiques store is a little slice of heaven. Plastic and Formica dominate, and any of the Rocket Age glasses, containers, wall decorations, and other knickknacks would be at home in the Cleaver household.

✪ **BROOKLYN ARTISANS GALLERY.** 221A Court St. corner of Warren St., 330-0343, Tu–Sa 11 a.m.–7 p.m. Su 11 a.m.–6 p.m., www.brooklynartisans.com.

Cooperatively owned by six local artists and craftspeople, this shop showcases handmade glassware, ceramics, candles, jewelry, textiles, books, picture frames, and other objets d'art, including wearables. The owners also handle consignment sales and show rotating exhibitions of work by local and national artists. Ahead of its time, the collective started the shop in 1994, and was one of the few places then in Brooklyn to feature local artists' work.

DAVID ALLEN. 331 Smith St. bet. President and Carroll Sts., 488-5568, W–Su noon–6 p.m., davidallengallery.com.

David Allen is the only authorized Brooklyn dealer for furniture designed by Herman Miller. Remember the 1960s marshmallow sofa? The Eames chair? The amoeba-shaped Noguchi coffee table? *That* Herman Miller. You can choose a piece from the collection, select your own fabric, and negotiate the price, too.

There's also a gallery side to this business, with an opening every six to eight weeks of art that is described by the owner as "between decorative and conceptual." Downstairs, see edgier installations.

ENVIRONMENT337. 337 Smith St. bet. Carroll and President Sts., 522-1767, Tu–Sa 11 a.m.–7 p.m., Su 11 a.m.–5 p.m.

Upbeat, colorful, functional: that's the kind of items for home, bath, and bedroom that Environment sells. There's a seasonally changing palette of dishes, glasses, and items such as throw pillows, as well as an appealing section for both children and gardens. If you are in the market for an unusual table design, check out their locally made Nollette tables, of steel and concrete, selling in different sizes from $700 to $2,000. And there's a line of Mrs. Meyers cleaning products scented with stress-reducing aromatherapy oils, so you can whistle while you work.

MAI MAI. 251 Smith St. bet. DeGraw and Douglass, 624-4620, Tu–Su noon–7 p.m.

The South African owner of Mai Mai has brought an artist's sensibility to her selection of South African contemporary handmade crafts. The inventory, which is replenished every few months, includes high-end (but not prohibitively expensive) artifacts, some of museum quality. There are brightly colored telephone wire baskets of varying sizes, beadwork items, traditional clay pots and wooden bowls, unusual Christmas decorations, fabrics, large Zulu mat-racks (good for your yoga mat), and a particularly lovely selection of very fine traditional wooden headrests. The store, which opened in 1999, is named after a migrant-laborer market in Johannesburg where the proprietor used to find Zulu artifacts. A great place for a gift or something unusual to spruce up your home.

MAIN ST. EPHEMERA. 272 Smith St. bet. Sackett and DeGraw Sts., 858-6541, W–F 3–7 p.m., Sa, 11 a.m.–7 p.m., www.analogguy.com. No credit cards.

If you're looking for twentieth-century movie posters, ads, postcards, magazines, or other paper collectibles, you'll be thrilled at this selection. Also available: Gowanus Canal Yacht Club T-shirts.

✪ **ROUX ROUX DESIGNS.** 243 Smith St., corner of Douglass St., 875-0351, W–Sa noon–7 p.m., www.rouxroux.com.

Small *is* beautiful. Roux Roux's unique designs will add a humorous and entertaining touch to liven up your home. Designer Steve Vaubel has come up with some whimsical originals: 100 percent lead-free pewter drawer knobs made in a wide range of irresistibly wonderful, fanciful shapes of faces, ships, animals, and more. They cost from about $20 to $45. And there's a new and very interesting line of unusual gold-plated and silver jewelry pieces, some with glass and stone, ranging from $40 to $300. Make sure you ring the bell, as sometimes the staff gets busy in the workshop, in the back.

✪ **SWALLOW.** 361 Smith St. bet. Carroll and President Sts. 222-8201, Tu–Su noon–7 p.m., www.swallowglass.com.

A California mellowness hits you the minute you walk into Swallow, a specialty shop that features handblown and artisanal glass, from local and other glass artists. The forms and colors of the glass suggest a harmony of whispering wind, water, sunlight—all that West Coast stuff New Yorkers are accused of ignoring. So, stop in and expand your horizons. A wonderful place to buy a wedding present, or pick up some unusual jewelry, Asian ceramics, or small glass items. Prices range from $5 to $500.

✪ **ZIPPER.** 333 Smith St. bet. President and Carroll Sts., 596-0333, W–Sa 11 a.m.–7 p.m., Su noon–5 p.m., www.zippergifts.com.

Whether you're feeling up or down about life, Zipper's probably got something to put the teeth back into your quest for a tastefully decorated home. This playful store is buttoned up when it comes to design, showcasing "personal accessories, spa products, sensuous home, entertaining, kids toys and books, with a focus on design and architecture." The parent store is in Los Angeles, and their Web site must be a first: "Brooklyn and LA." As Austin Powers might say, it's bicoastal, baby.

Books and Music

BOOKCOURT. 163 Court St. bet. Pacific and Dean Sts., 875-3677, M–Sa 10 a.m.–10 p.m., Su 11 a.m.–8 p.m.

Comfortable and filled with a good selection of contemporary paperbacks, new hardcovers, and local-interest books, this pleasant independent bookstore also has an attractive children's room in the back, with cute seats for the little browser. The staff know their literature, and can always point you toward new and interesting authors. Check their newsletter to get the pulse of what the neighborhood is reading. There's a Reading Series schedule for author readings and book signings.

COMMUNITY BOOKSTORE. 212 Court St. corner of Warren St., 834-9494, M–Sa noon–10:30 p.m., Su noon–10 p.m. ("No Web site; we're Luddites here.")

Don't let the messy housekeeping deter you from exploring this funky Court Street bookshop. It's a very full and old-fashioned store that offers you the opportunity to roam through stacks and stacks of discounted hardcover bestsellers, both new and used books, and a good selection of kids' books and even toys. The owner often can direct you to just the right pile to find a very inexpensive copy of whatever book you might be seeking.

DON'S MUSIC. 192 Amity St. bet. Court and Clinton Sts., 246-0458, daily noon–8 p.m.

Don sells used LPs (a great selection of which cost only $1) and cassettes from a cramped store that spills onto the sidewalk when it's not raining. You'll also find tons of rock and roll, cutting-edge, esoteric, and unusual CDs, underground music, jazz, hip-hop, and more. Don's has amps, guitars, and other stuff musicians need. This tiny, off-the-beaten-track shop was rated "Best Record Store Named After Its Memorable Owner" by the veteran hipmeister the *Village Voice* in 2000.

✪ SHAKESPEARE'S SISTER. 270 Court St., 694-0084, M–Sa 10 a.m.–6:30 p.m., Su 11 a.m.–5 p.m.

Tucked behind the displays of cards, candles, and the like, Shakespeare's Sister has a back room where you can settle down for a quiet cup of coffee. They call it the "ArtBack," and it's an informal gallery for local artisans who make pocketbooks, earrings (there's a big selection of Gina Rosencrantz), silk sachets, and small cute gift items, most priced at under $20. There are very popular paintings here of the neighborhood, and of the Gowanus, with a price range from $200 to $1,000. It's very low-key, Vermontish.

SOFT SKULL SHORTWAVE. 71 Bond St. at State St., 643-1599, M–Sa 11 a.m.–7 p.m., Su noon–5 p.m., www.softskull.com.

The Lower East Side literary scene has arrived in Brooklyn. Soft Skull is one of a new wave of small, independent publishers who moved to Brooklyn as a respite from high Manhattan rents. Soft Skull dares to publish where other, more conservative houses fear to tread.

Drop in for a dose of activist politics with your Zapatista coffee. They sell all Soft Skull Press publications here, as well as literary journals and magazines, used books, CDs and vinyl records, and a selection from other small independents, such as Open City, Small Beer, New Press, and many others. And there are Sunday readings.

MUSICIAN'S GENERAL STORE. 207–213 Court St., Tu–F noon–8 p.m., Sa 10 a.m.–7 p.m., Su noon–5 p.m., www.musiciansgeneralstore.com.

Musician's General has built a small musical empire here, like a miniature version of Manhattan's famous Musicians' Row in the mid-40s. You'll find just about anything you need: sheet music, software, and novelties at #207; various popular-brand-name pianos, keyboards, brass, and woodwinds at #209; and guitars, amps, percussion, and lessons at #213.

For the Kids

☺ **GREEN ONION.** 274 Smith St. bet. Degraw and Sackett Sts., 246-2804, Tu 11 a.m.–6 p.m., W 11 a.m.–6 p.m., F 11 a.m.–7 p.m., Sa 10:30 a.m.–6 p.m., Su 10:30 a.m.–6 p.m.

Green Onion is for the sweet little people in your life. It sells wonderful toys, tiny-sized clothing from Petite Bateau and other good brands, and silly irresistibles like junior-sized sunglasses. It's across the street from **Savoia,** so you can pop over here while waiting for your pizza.

☺ **LAUGHING GIRAFFE AT MONKEY'S WEDDING.** 324 Court St. corner of Baltic St., 852-3635, M–Sa 11 a.m.–4 p.m.

Here's a little toy store that's chock-full of children's toys, including "educational" toys mixed in with more pedestrian offerings like crayons, paper, and other basics. Literary quiz: What does the name of the store refer to?

☺ **THE PAINTED POT.** 339 Smith St. bet. Carroll and President Sts., 222-0334, Su–M 11 a.m.–7 p.m., Tu–W 11 a.m.–9 p.m., Th–F 11 a.m.–10 p.m., Sa 11 a.m.–9 p.m., www.paintedpot.com. Also 8009 3rd Ave., in Bay Ridge.

At Painted Pot you (and the kids) can paint your own ceramics, take pottery-wheel and hand-building classes, learn to make mosaics, and create jewelry and cool items from their new bead bar. There's a lovely community sensibility here, with special "moms' nights out," "bring a bottle of wine" Fridays, and other fun meet-your-neighbor events. Call for a variety of value-for-money package deals, including children's party deals named "Van Gogh" and "Matisse."

☺ **TOONS & TEENS.** 168 Court St. bet. Bergen and Dean Sts., 488-0698, daily 10 a.m.–7 p.m.

Children and preteens love this store, which carries a full line of Hello Kitty products, stickers, stuffed animals, and cute puppets.

Women's Clothing & Accessories

DIANE T. 174 Court St. at Congress St., 923–5777, Tu–F 11 a.m.–7 p.m., Sa 11 a.m.–6:30 p.m., Su 1–5 p.m.

The closest thing you'll find in brownstone Brooklyn to a personal shopper, Diane T. has a terrific eye for the elegantly casual, good-looking clothes that working women need. You'll find name brands here, with a tasteful selection of shoes, daytime and evening handbags, jewelry, and accessories. Diane T.'s style is simultaneously classic and classy; you won't go wrong.

★ **FLIRT.** 252 Smith St. at Douglass St., 858-7931, W–Sa noon–8 p.m., Su noon–6 p.m.

Just the name of this store gives you the idea of its style. You can find tops, skirts, and dresses that work in any setting except maybe at your own wedding. Some of the higher-priced dresses, at $250, can be dressed up or down nicely. The majority of pieces here are one of a kind and are made by designers in the tristate area, including, of course, Brooklyn.

✪ **FRIDA'S CLOSET.** 296 Smith St. off Union St., 855-0311, Tu–F 1–8 p.m., Sa 11 a.m.–9 p.m., Su 11 a.m.–7 p.m.

The window display is likely to feature a coy black skirt, sassy knitted hat, and a sweet, fragile necklace. Sophisticated, feminine one-of-a-kind clothes with novelty trim and great buttons are sold here by Mexican-born designer Sandra Paez. Tops start at $60, skirts at $110. Along with Refinery, hats off to Frida's Closet for being one of Smith Street's fashion pioneers. Custom work by appointment.

✪ **HABIT.** 231 Smith St. bet. Douglass and Butler Sts., 923-0303, Tu–W noon–8 p.m., Th–Sa noon–9 p.m., Su noon–7 p.m.

An attractive shop with contemporary clothing and accessories for urbane women who like to dress creatively for work and play. There are hipster tops and jeans, and handbags, and shawls here. Some items are by designers waiting to be discovered. A lot of the moderately priced jewelry is one of a kind, and made in Brooklyn. Prices start at $40.

✪ **HANDMADE NEW YORK.** 251 Smith St. bet. Douglass and Butler Sts., 694-9336, Tu–Su noon–7 p.m., Su noon–6 p.m., www.handmadenyc.com.

Handmade is a carefully curated shop that specializes in unusual items for the home and the body. Here you'll find jewelry for men and women, glass pieces, decorative pillows, lighting, and a range of personal scent items. Most of the jewelry, which starts at $20 and averages about $100 a piece, is Brooklyn-made by people who live in the area, trained at Pratt, and work here. Handmade just opened a new store in Greenwich Village.

HENNA K. 165 Court St. bet Bergen and Dean Sts., 852-5777, M–Th noon–7 p.m., Su noon–5 p.m.

This light, airy jewelry store is one of the best in Brooklyn, selling a range of gold and silver pieces, some with gems. It's well worth a visit.

◗ **LILY.** 209 Court St. bet. Warren and Wyckoff Sts., 858-6261, M–Sa 11 a.m.–7 p.m., Su noon–6 p.m.

Much appreciated by local moms and their daughters, Lily's has been selling affordable casual clothing and accessories since 1999. Scarves, bags, special T-shirts, skirts, and lots more is available here, including brands such as Juicy Couture, Flax, Michael Stars, and Free People, as well as the indispensable Dansko clogs. Brooklyn artists contribute T-shirts and jewelry. Most items are well under $100.

⭐ **REFINERY.** 254 Smith St. corner of DeGraw St., 643-7861, Tu–Sa noon–8 p.m., Su noon–6 p.m.

This small artisanal handbag gallery was one of the pioneers that helped launch Smith Street into the trendy restaurant-and-fashion strip it's become. Owner Suzanne Bagdade's winsome totes made from vintage fabrics sell in the $50–$100 range. Refinery was also first on the block to sell boasty T-shirts with a Brooklyn area code, 718, which now come in infant sizes, too.

⭐ 🌀 **STACIA.** 267 Smith St. corner of Degraw St., 237-0078, Tu–F noon–8 p.m., Sa 11:30 a.m.–8 p.m., Su 11:30 a.m.–6 p.m., www.stacianewyork.com.

You gotta love a place that sells a delicate $125 "overnight bag" stuffed with the following: a camisole, thong, toothbrush, and candle. Stacia sells sexy, one-of-a-kind women's clothing. The clothes—and even the fabric—are designed by the owner, who cut her fashion teeth working for the likes of Calvin Klein, J. Crew, and Cynthia Rowley. The boutique is decorated with antique photos and chandeliers, and also features jewelry, sandals, swimsuits, and (bagged or otherwise) some intimate apparel. Prices for dresses are in the $200–$380 range, skirts start at $150, and tops cost between $50 and $125.

Cobble Hill

ABOUT COBBLE HILL

Historically, Cobble Hill shares more with patrician Brooklyn Heights than with working-class Carroll Gardens. Defined by a twenty-block officially designated New York City landmark district north of DeGraw Street, its elegant town houses were mostly built between 1840 and 1880 by members of the upper middle class, including distinguished architect (and resident) Richard Upjohn, of Trinity Church fame. A significant Middle Eastern immigration began in the early twentieth century; many of their descendants remain, as is obvious from the variety of food shops and restaurants along Atlantic Avenue and Court Street. After a period of economic decline, Cobble Hill has gone through an upswing, largely due to an influx of affluent young professionals, an activist community, and the brownstone-revival movement. Residents managed to secure landmark status and block public housing, and real estate values have risen sharply since the 1970s.

In Cobble Hill, visitors can wander lovely, tree-lined streets, stroll past pre–Civil War architecture, walk by the nineteenth-century "socially enlightened" low-income housing at **Workingmen's Cottages** (also known as Warren

Place and Cobble Hill Tower) built by philanthropist Alfred Tredway White, or rest in lovely Cobble Hill Park. Those looking for the footsteps of the famous can see Thomas Wolfe's Verandah Mews row house, and the childhood home of Churchill's mother at 154 Amity Street.

HOW IT GOT ITS NAME The name was revived in the 1950s by brownstone enthusiasts who discovered that the area had been designated "Cobbleshill" on a 1766 map of New York. The map referred to a long-gone hill near the modern intersection of Court Street and Atlantic Avenue.

POINTS OF CULTURAL INTEREST

COBBLE HILL HISTORIC DISTRICT. Along Clinton St. near Henry St.

Take a walk along Clinton Street to get a taste of the history of this neighborhood:

- Number 296 Clinton was the residence of Richard Upjohn and his son, both famed turn-of-the-century architects who built **Grace Church** in Brooklyn Heights.
- Numbers 301 through 311 Clinton St. are Italianate-style houses built about 1850 by lawyer and developer Gerard Morris.
- Number 334 was built in 1850 by established Brooklyn architect James Naughton, who also built the architecturally acclaimed **Boys' and Girls' High School** in Bedford-Stuyvesant.
- Number 340 is the widest house in the area, built for Dr. Joseph Clark in 1860.
- Verandah Place, between Clinton and Henry Streets, is a lovely mews full of carriage houses, in one of which writer Thomas Wolfe lived for a time.

KANE STREET SYNAGOGUE. 236 Kane St. bet. Court and Clinton Sts., 975-1550.

Founded in 1856, the congregation housed here, Beth Israel, claims to be the oldest Jewish congregation in Brooklyn. Its fate followed that of the neighborhood, prospering through the 1920s, languishing until the 1960s, and coming to life again as the brownstone gentrification movement brought in younger members. The original synagogue was located on the site now occupied by the Brooklyn House of Detention; the current synagogue building was erected in 1855 as a Dutch Reformed church.

MODEL TENEMENTS: HOME AND TOWER BUILDINGS. Warren Pl. bet. Hicks and Henry Sts.

Make a short detour to visit two of the nation's first low-rent housing units. Philanthropist Alfred Tredway White built these units in 1877 as an innovation to provide decent, affordable housing for workers. The design was inspired by

London's Victorian apartment buildings, and incorporated modern concepts of ventilation, plumbing, and natural light, which were then uncommon in working-class housing. They are considered unique and important architectural innovations of the nineteenth century.

One of White's innovations was to put the stairways and halls on the outside of the building, opening up the inner apartment windows to more light and air from a common internal courtyard, which doubled as a safe play space for children and a communal meeting area. Note the playful decorative detail in the brick and ironwork; this, too, was a gift of artistry and design meant to uplift the working poor.

The nearby tiny Workingmen's Cottages—each less than twelve feet wide—line a lovely mews, on Warren Place, which runs one block from Warren to Baltic Street, between Henry and Hicks Streets.

The Home and Tower apartment buildings were restored in the late 1970s as Cobble Hill Towers. The three original Towers apartments are located at 417–35 Hicks Street, 136–42 Warren Street, and 129–35 Baltic Street. The original Home Buildings apartments are located at 439–45 Hicks Street and 134–40 Baltic Street.

See also the **Astral Apartments** in Greenpoint.

ENTERTAINMENT, PARKS, AND PLAYGROUNDS

CLEARVIEW COBBLE HILL CINEMAS. 265 Court St. at Butler St., 596-9113, call for show times.

This multiscreen theater shows blockbusters as well as independent films, and there is always at least one kids' movie playing. A ticket to the first show every day costs $5.

COBBLE HILL PARK. Enter on Clinton and Henry Sts. between Congress St. and Verandah Pl.

One of the first "vest-pocket" parks in the city, this park was created by community activists who wanted to prevent construction of a supermarket in this residential section. One of the loveliest parks in Brooklyn, it has antique-style benches and tables and marble columns at the entrances. It is near Thomas Wolfe's Verandah Place home. If you are hungry, walk over to Court Street or stop at the nearby Delicatessen at Verandah Place.

Gowanus

ABOUT THE GOWANUS AREA

Romance is inspired by the most curious conditions. The long-putrid, small canal named Gowanus (after the displaced Native Americans who presumably enjoyed a cleaner stream of water) has a fan club. Many are unusual enthusiasts of one sort or another: a self-made millionaire, a devotee of canoe paddling, a photographer with a jones for capturing on film the changing environment around this most urban of canals. What they have in common is a passion for the Gowanus, and a vision of what it might become.

To get the facts straight, there is both a canal, and a neighborhood by the name Gowanus. The neighborhood isn't really a neighborhood at all. Gowanus is more of a geographic district that encompasses bits and pieces: a large public-housing area, several light industrial areas and parking lots for large vehicles, some heavily trafficked thoroughfares, several little residential streets, mostly disconnected from each other, two grand old canal bridges—and, of course, the **Gowanus Canal.**

Those who try to draw serious parallels with either Venice, Italy, or Venice, California, deserve a Bronx cheer. Gowanus is uniquely Brooklyn! While you can get a canoe tour with the **Gowanus Dredgers Canoe Club** or BCUE there are no gondolas, palatial mansions, barely even a home along the Gowanus, unless you count the occasional mysterious houseboat. The joke probably began at the local Italian restaurant, **Monte's Italian.**

But water has a magic all its own, and the intersection between the stark-urban landscape and the water of the Gowanus has inspired more artists than one might, at first glance, suspect. There are painters and photographers obsessed with capturing the canal in its changing visages. Enough artists have been attracted to it to form an arts organization or two. You can see some of the canal-inspired work at the annual **Gowanus Open Studio Tour.** In fact, rumor has it that some local Brooklyn artists are trying to arrange a little showing of the Gowanus work in Venice, contrasting the seediness of the Brooklyn canals with those in Venice. There may be some artists' exchanges in the works.

What could the canal become? Many hope for a long stretch of landscaped waterfront along a canal that's brimming with fresh fish and water fowl—a bit of waterside nature in the city center. That prospect seemed impossible a few years back, when from blocks away you could smell the Gowanus stench on a hot summer day. Now, with a cleanup that's still only halfway home, it just might come to pass. There are some little signs of new life, as well, including a fashion atelier and a wonderful outdoor garden store, **Gowanus Nursery.** Meanwhile, some intrepid boaters take to the water in their little motor boats or paddle canoes, and, starting in Carroll Gardens, float out through the Gowanus Canal to the Gowanus Bay.

☞ **TIP** To find out what's going on,
www.waterfrontmuseum.org/dredgers/
www.gowanusartists.com
www.gowanus.org
www.gowanusdevelopmentcorp.com

POINTS OF CULTURAL INTEREST

SPECIAL EVENTS.

EcoCruises (spring); annual bike tours (May, June, October); block party (July); Gowanus Open Studio Tour week (October); annual Gowanus Earth Day (April); OktoberFest (October).

OLD AMERICAN CAN FACTORY. 232 3rd St. corner 3rd Ave., 237-4335, www.xoprojects.com.

From industrial to artistic. This historic, 140,000-square-foot, six-building complex was built from 1860 through 1905. It's an interesting space, with an internal courtyard and alleyways. Renamed the "Old American Can Factory," it's been renovated as a mixed facility that rents to business tenants as well as arts groups such as **BAX**. A company called Xø Projects Inc. operates it.

CARROLL ST. BRIDGE. Bet. Hoyt and Nevins Sts.

Declared a landmark and renovated in 1989, this historic bridge spans the **Gowanus Canal,** built in 1889 as part of Brooklyn's network of industrial water-ways. The bridge is unusual: it opens by sliding along the tracks on the shore to a perpendicular angle, allowing boats and ships to pass below. It is the oldest of four such "retractile" bridges, as they are called, in the United States, and, as such, is both a city and national landmark. Note the sign reading "Any Person Driving Over This Bridge Faster Than a Walk Will Be Subject to a Penalty of Five Dollars for Each Offense." It's a replica of the original sign that, one guesses, was needed to slow down those impatient horse-and-buggy drivers of the nineteenth century.

543 UNION ST. BUILDING. 543 Union St. at Nevins St.

There are a lot of artists working in this building, including **Porcelli Art Glass Studio** and Elizabeth O'Reilly, whose work is shown at George Billis in Manhattan.

Free! **GOWANUS OPEN STUDIO TOURS.** 789-7243, www.gowanusartists.com. Last weekend in October. Free.

Over seventy artists open their galleries and studios during this weekend studio tour. It began in 1997, showing the work of just fifteen artists, and has grown in participation and stature, drawing visitors not only from local communities, but also from DUMBO, Williamsburg, Manhattan, and the suburbs. Most artists have a sample of their work and direct contact information on the site.

Private tours of artists' studios can be arranged, as well. Contact regina@gowanusartists.com or info@gowanusartists.com

GOWANUS DREDGERS CANOE CLUB. 243-0849, www.waterfrontmuseum.org/dredgers/.

For local ecotourism, check out the volunteer-run Dredgers Canoe Club, a group of paddlers, who are committed to the cleanup of the Gowanus. Things are progressing, too; seagulls, oysters, and mussels have reappeared in the once-fetid waters. Gowanus Dredgers participate in an annual Gowanus Earth Day, Spring Cleaning, the Red Hook Earth and Surf Parade, and paddle in flotillas at various citywide events. Call if you're interested in arranging a canoe trip down the Gowanus, a truly Brooklyn experience.

Community involvement has been essential to the rejuvenation of the Gowanus area. Bike enthusiast and original Dredger Owen Foote and some pals have organized an annual bike tour of the area, in conjunction with the Gowanus Open Studio Tour week.

THE STORY OF GOWANDA AND THE GOWANUS CANAL

Once upon a time, there was a terribly stinky old canal called the Go-On-Us. It was so dirty that some people swore you'd turn green, too, if you stuck your pinky toe in that water. Then some nice people who lived nearby got determined to clean it all up. After lots of meetings and years of telephone calls, they finally got some help and turned on a big flusher system. New, clean water came into the canal. Slowly the floating shoes, and old tires, and crushed-up soda cans floated out to sea. Then, one day, surprise! A fish was sighted in the canal! And oysters! And some water birds, too! Most recently a baby seal! (Nobody had ever seen a seal in the canal before.) They gently, carefully pulled it out of the canal water. Before releasing the seal, what do you think they named it? Gowanda!

Gowanus Canal

The Gowanus Canal was created in the late 1840s, when a natural creek, named after the local Gowanus tribe, was widened to about a mile-and-a-half-long canal. The canal provided access for commercial barges to transport goods to and from Brooklyn via the Gowanus Bay, New York Bay, and beyond. In the mid-twentieth century, when trucking became cheaper than shipping (and with trucks able to access the nearby Gowanus Expressway) the canal fell into disuse and disrepair, with multiple sources of pollution.

For several decades in the late twentieth century, the Gowanus Canal was scorned as an odiferous (Brooklynese translation: "stinking") industrial waterway.

It has long divided brownstone Carroll Gardens from brownstone Park Slope. Now it seems that a thirty-year cleanup campaign is paying off. In 1998, a $450-million sewage treatment plant was installed to clean up the canal, and a tunnel to circulate the water opened. And it's true: fish, oysters, waterfowl, and a baby seal, named Gowanda, have been sighted. Although it is still rudely industrial here, visionaries imagine a multiplex theater, tree-lined walkways, parks, and waterside housing on both sides of a clean-water canal. Fish in the canal are a sure sign of an ecological success. When (not "if" anymore) the Gowanus is fully cleaned up, the waterfront access could benefit an estimated quarter of a million residents who live within walking distance.

Of the five crossings, the ones at 3rd and Carroll Streets still have old bridges; other crossings are at Union Street, 9th Street, and Hamilton Avenue.

Gowanus Canal Tours and Events

Increasing numbers of organizations are offering tours. See **BCUE, Gowanus Dredgers.** And, there are lots of interesting events created to monitor and contribute to the canal's environmental improvement, from Earth Day cleanup to EcoCruises in the spring and OktoberFest in the autumn.

GOWANUS RESTAURANTS

MONTE'S ITALIAN RESTAURANT. 459 Carroll St. bet. Nevins St. and 3rd Ave., 625-9656 or 624-8984, M–Th 11 a.m.–10 p.m., F 11 a.m.–11 p.m., Sa noon–midnight, Su 2–10 p.m.

Tucked away on a tiny strip of trendy Carroll Street, Monte's lays claim to being the oldest Italian restaurant in Brooklyn, having opened in 1906. The hand-painted Venetian scenes on the walls of the single small dining room reflects wishful thinking, although the nearby deputrified and rapidly gentrifying Gowanus Canal is no longer likely to turn up tires and even mysteriously dumped bodies, as once rumored. Years back, locals joked that it's best to sit facing the door; if you have to ask why, don't.

SHOPPING

✪ **CLAIREWARE STUDIO.** 543 Union St. corner of Nevins St., 875-3977, www.claireware.net. Call for an appointment.

New York–born potter Claire Weissberg calls her work "urban folk pottery." Her porcelain cups and saucers, plates, serving bowls, and other items have been carried by gift shops at the Guggenheim and other leading museums. You can buy them directly from her studio. Seconds run $5 to $50, top-quality products start at about $20. There's a terrific annual Christmas sale; call to get on Claire's mailing list.

GOWANUS NURSERY. 102 3rd St. bet. Bond and Hoyt Sts., 852-3116, Th–F 11 a.m.–7 p.m., Sa–Su 9 a.m.–7 p.m., www.gowanusnursery.com.

Just opened in 2003, this fabulous nursery, owned by a woman who cared for Martha Stewart's garden, sells hard-to-find beauties to help make your garden a pleasure.

✪ **KEUR DJEMBE.** 568 Union St. bet. 3rd and 4th Aves., 522-7324, daily 11 a.m.–8 p.m., www.keurdjembe.com

Senegalese-born Ibrahima Diokhane has a passion: drums. His store, Keur Djembe (which means "House of Drums" in Wolof), is filled to the brim with djembes and other African drums, which he handcrafts on the premises. Made of authentic materials—imported woods, animal skins, shells, and other traditional pieces—his creations will entice both novices and experienced drumming-circle types. The $100–$400 drums include traditional *sabar* drums that are played at all occasions; *tama*, a two-sided lizard-skin drum; *coutirou* from Cassamace in southern Senegal; and several sizes of *djun djun*, which are used to keep the rhythm during performances. You'll find classes for kids and adults, repairs, and information about drumming circles here.

✪ **PORCELLI ART GLASS STUDIO.** 543 Union St. at Nevins St., #3A, 596-4353, www.ernestartglass.com. by appointment only.

Ernest Porcelli runs a full-service stained-glass studio here, doing commissions and restorations. There are weekend classes. You can buy original art-glass works at reasonable prices, as well, including large, colorful glass plates and decorative items.

☺ ✪ **TIKI ATELIER.** 267 Wyckoff St. at Nevins St., 797-2677, M–F, call for hours.

This little children's boutique makes cheerful clothing for little Brooklynites with interesting, inventive printed material designed by the owners, a husband-and-wife team. Their clothes are sold at better Manhattan children's shops, such as Space Cadet, and some Brooklyn boutiques.

Atlantic Avenue

ABOUT ATLANTIC AVENUE

Strictly speaking, Atlantic Avenue isn't a neighborhood. It's a major thoroughfare that starts at the edge of New York Harbor, where you can see the Statue of Liberty, and transverses some of Brooklyn's grittier neighborhoods. The section we include here belongs, respectively, to three official neighborhoods: Boerum Hill, Carroll Gardens, and Cobble Hill. Atlantic Avenue doesn't have brownstone

Atlantic Avenue
From the East River to
Flatbush Avenue

PARK SLOPE

CLINTON HILL

DUMBO

CARROLL GARDENS

5th Ave.

4th Ave.

3rd Ave.

Carlton Ave.

Cumberland St.

S Oxford St.

S Portland Ave.

S Eliott Pl.

Fort Greene Pl.

St. Felix St.

Ashland Pl.

Rockwell Pl.

Hudson Ave.

Hanson Pl.

Flatbush Ave.

Q,2,3,4,5

Brooklyn
Public Library

M,N,R,W

Washington
Park

Fort Greene
Park

FORT GREENE

Lafayette Ave.

Fulton St.

C G

Long Island
University

DeKalb Ave.

2,3,4,5

M,N,Q,R,W

Nevins St.

BOERUM
HILL

Bond St.

Dean St.

Bergen St.

Wycoff St.

Pacific St.

Douglass St.

Willoughby St.

Flatbush Ave.

Myrtle Ave.

Fleet St.

Gold St.

Duffield St.

Bridge St.

Lawrence St.

Jay St.

M,N,Q,R,W

2,3

M

A,C,F

Livingston St.

Schermerhorn St.

State St.

291-324 State St.

Hoyt St.

Smith St.

F G

DeGraw St.

Sackett St.

DOWNTOWN

Al Farooq
Mosque

Court
Pl.

Boerum Pl.

Warren St.

Baltic St.

Butler St.

Douglass Ct.

Adams St.

Tillary St.

A,C,F

Civic
Center

M,N,R,W

2,3,4,5

M

Court St.

Atlantic Ave.

Pacific St.

Amity St.

Congress St.

Verandah Pl.

Warren St.

Baltic St.

Kane St.

Tompkins Pl.

Clinton St.

Strong Pl.

COBBLE
HILL

Cadman
Plaza
Park

Cadman Plaza E

Cadman Plaza W

Clinton St.

Sidney Pl.

Henry St.

Cheever Pl.

Henry St.

Clark St.

2,3

M

Pineapple St.

Willow St.

Montague St.

Remsen St.

Joralemon St.

Garden Pl.

Brooklyn-Queens Expwy.

Tiffany Pl.

278

278

BROOKLYN
HEIGHTS

Pierrepont St.

Hicks St.

Willow Pl.

Columbia Pl.

Exit 27

Columbia St.

Irving St.

Sedgwick St.

DeGraw St.

Columbia Heights

Pierrepont
Pl.

Montague
Ter.

Grace Ct.

Brooklyn Heights Esplanade

278

Pier 1

Pier 2

Pier 3

Pier 4

Pier 5

Pier 6

Pier 7

Pier 8

Pier 9A

Pier 9B

East River

houses or historic landmarks. But Atlantic Avenue has a definite urban personality. And it's in play.

A flurry of high-end, stylish home-furnishing and clothing stores has arrived. The *New York Times* flagged the trend early on, pegging Atlantic Avenue as "a new destination for modern furniture, lighting and rugs as well as antiques." A fraction of its former size, Atlantic Avenue's "antique row" is mostly concentrated on the three-block strip between Bond and Smith Streets.

There are also two little Middle Eastern enclaves, located a mile apart. The tourist section is just one block long, a little row of restaurants and specialty food stores, notably **Sahadi's.** The other enclave, near **Al Farooq Mosque,** caters to immigrants who work in nearby shops, restaurants, and car services. Drivers racing to beat the long traffic lights at the congested intersection of Atlantic and Flatbush Avenues have been known to jump when they hear the *muezzin*, broadcasting a call to prayer loudly from the mosque. The street scene is New York, but, five times a day, the soundtrack is straight out of Cairo.

BY SUBWAY 2, 3, 4, or 5 train to Borough Hall; or M, N, or R train to Court Street.

POINTS OF CULTURAL INTEREST

SPECIAL EVENTS.

Atlantic Antic (October); Sidewalk Market, once a month, May–September, call 596-1866 (Atlantic Avenue Betterment Association) for information.

AL FAROOQ MOSQUE. 544 Atlantic Ave. bet. 3rd and 4th Aves.

This modest, orange-and-gold-trimmed mosque sits next door to a large post office on a busy thoroughfare. It's a religious home to many Muslims who work and live in the area, but it has been in the news from time to time. It was briefly visited by the blind Egyptian sheik Omar Abdel Rahuian, convicted in the 1993 WTC bombing, and also by El-Sayid Nosair, the man convicted of killing radical rabbi Meir Kahane in 1990. Al Farooq Mosque again became the subject of government interest in the post-9-11 era.

ISLAMIC MISSION OF AMERICA. 143 State St. off Bond St., 875-6607.

A few blocks down from the historic State Street Houses, the Islamic Mission of America has transformed a brownstone into what is now the oldest mosque in Brooklyn.

"THAT BILLBOARD." Atlantic Ave. and Nevins St.

You're driving down Atlantic Avenue toward Flatbush Avenue, and suddenly there's a huge billboard with what looks like a color magazine ad from the 1950s or earlier. But it's not really an ad, it's more like a private joke. This is the work of Jerry Johnson, sign painter and billboard guerrilla, who has been entertaining locals for years with his offbeat, social-commentary message on a billboard. Yes, it's legal. Yes, it's a little obscure. And yes, of course, he's a Brooklynite.

☺ **SHADOWBOX THEATER.** YWCA Memorial Hall, 30 3rd Ave. bet. Atlantic Ave. and State St., for schedule call 212-724-0677; YMCA is 875-1190, www.shadowboxtheatre.org.

With its original scripts and contemporary themes, this children's puppet repertory company has been a staple for New York City schools for over thirty years. The Shadowbox Theater performances have a range of small and large puppets, actors, and shadow puppets in shows that convey a social message, such as "Sing Out for Peace." Shadowbox is available for private parties, too.

STATE STREET HOUSES. 291–99 and 290–324 State St. bet. Smith and Hoyt Sts.

Tucked away just one block from the bustle of Atlantic Avenue's antiques stores is this lovely stretch of twenty-three neatly kept historic row houses. Built in the period from 1840 to 1870, they are New York City landmarks that reflect the evolving architectural styles of that era, from early Greek Revival to Italianate ornamentation. Built as homes for the prosperous merchants who "urbanized" this part of Brooklyn, today they are still private residences, lovely to walk by while conjuring up the past. Indeed, these blocks are award-winners for their lovely gardens.

ATLANTIC AVENUE RESTAURANTS
BACCHUS. 409 Atlantic Ave. near Bond St., 852-1572, Tu–Th 9 a.m.–11 p.m., Sa–Su 11–1 a.m.

Newly opened in 2003, Bacchus brings "bistro and vins" to Atlantic Avenue. With pale yellow walls, a lovely back garden, a huge selection of French wines, and entrées such as grilled tuna and hanger steak at about $13, it's likely to be a hit.

BRAWTA CAFE. 347 Atlantic Ave. corner Hoyt St., 855-5515, Su–M noon–10 p.m., Tu–Th noon–11:30 p.m., F–Sa noon–11:30 p.m. Takeout: "Brawta Outpost" in Park Slope, 447 7th Avenue bet. 15th and 16th Sts., 788-4680. www.bococa.com/restaurants.html. Under construction: www.brawta.com.

This popular Jamaican joint is often crowded, and with good reason. Try the "Rasta Pasta," plantains in spicy sauce, codfish cakes—and don't miss a special drink of ginger beer and sorrel, or sea moss. There's an unusually varied menu of fish entrées, all freshly made to order, as well as chicken dishes and a veggie stew. The menu lists entrées, which range from $14 to $15, as "Big Tings," explaining: "All big tings are served with rice & peas or white rice and Brawta's salad or steamed cabbage." BYOB.

BROOKLYN GRILL. 320 Atlantic Ave. bet. Hoyt and Smith Sts., 797-3324, M–Sa 3–10 p.m., Su 11:30 a.m.–3 pm., www.bococa.com/restaurants.html.

If you want to get away from it all, there's good American-style food here, a roomy bar, and a relaxed garden in the summer.

CARAVAN. 193 Atlantic Ave. near Court St., 488-7111, M–Sa noon–11 p.m. Su 2–10 p.m.

Even fussy food writers give a "thumbs up" to this restaurant, which specializes in Moroccan dishes. You can get a full, freshly prepared, and tasty meal of chicken, lamb, veal, or fish, along with rice, vegetables, and salad for two for about $28. Highly recommended: an appetizer, *mohammarah,* which is a spicy puree of sweet red peppers, walnuts, pomegranate, and molasses.

DOWNTOWN ATLANTIC. 364 Atlantic Ave. bet. Hoyt and Bond Sts., 852-9945, M–F, 11 a.m.–11 p.m., Sa–Su brunch 11 a.m.–4 p.m., dinner 4–11 p.m.

A comfortable new eatery with great coffee and pastries and good crab cakes, Downtown Atlantic dishes up the American basics. Rib-eye steak, tagliatelle, and free-range chicken keep drawing the area's new crowd of savvy, well-heeled young professionals and artists. Entrées under $12.

LA BOUILLABAISSE. 145 Atlantic Ave. bet. Clinton and Henry Sts., 522-8275, M–Th noon–10:30 p.m., F noon–11 p.m. Sa–Su brunch 10:30 a.m.–3 p.m.

A meal at La Bouillabaisse is worth the occasional wait. They serve tastefully prepared French dishes, simple robust seafood entrées (including, what else?, a terrific bouillabaisse) and zesty, garden-fresh vegetables. Trekking to almost the end of Atlantic Avenue, sometimes waiting in line (there are no reservations here), and sitting elbow-to-elbow with your neighbor in a modest little room are all part of the adventure.

MESON FLAMENCO. 135 Atlantic Ave., 625-7177, Tu–Su noon–11:30 p.m. Su 4–11:30 p.m.

Olé! It's not Barcelona exactly, but you can find tapas and live entertainment—yes! flamenco dancing!—on weekends. Mouthwatering tapas—Spanish antipasti, heavy on garlic and seasonings—almost make a meal. Or try the excellent shrimp dishes, *tortilla de patatas*, or seafood salad for a full dinner that will cost under $20.

MEZCAL'S. 151 Atlantic Ave. bet. Henry and Clinton Sts., 643-6000, daily noon–midnight, www.mezcals restaurant.com.

Most Mexican restaurants get by with frozen margaritas and chips, but Mezcal's food is both tasty and creative. Try the sizzling fajitas, or the *camarón ameyal*—a garlic-and-lemon-flavored mix of garbanzo beans and shrimp. Other locations: Bay Ridge, Carroll Gardens, and Park Slope.

MOROCCAN STAR. 148 Atlantic Ave. off Clinton St., 643-3042, daily 1–11 p.m.

A bargain hunter's delight, to eat in or take out. Entrées run about $7, and soups and appetizers hover in the $2 range. Moroccan Star serves traditional Moroccan and Middle Eastern comfort food, such as lamb stew and chicken with vegetables, prunes, and almonds; kibbe and, of course, the standard hummus, baba ghanoush, tabbouleh, and stuffed grape leaves. The shish kebab is usually a hit with the kids.

PETITE CREVETTE. 127 Atlantic Ave. bet. Henry and Clinton Sts., 858-6660, daily noon–11 p.m.

Fish lovers take note! You can eat in, take out, or buy fish at the highly regarded European-style Petite Crevette. The chowders and stews are fresh and wonderful, as are the fish cakes and seafood linguini. There's a children's menu with fish-and-chips, and a bargain lunch special for under $5.

TRIPOLI. 156 Atlantic Ave. corner of Clinton St., 596-5800, M–F 11 a.m.–11 p.m., F–Sa 11 a.m.–midnight, Su 11 a.m.–10:30 p.m., www.tripolirestaurant.com.

The Salem family, originally from the Lebanese city of Tripoli, established Tripoli restaurant in 1973, and for over a quarter of a century have been serving up reliable if literal renditions of Lebanese cuisine. There's a new juice bar, a good selection of vegetarian platters, and many satisfying traditional lamb dishes. Entrées average $9 to $12.

WATERFALLS CAFÉ. 144 Atlantic Ave. bet. Clinton and Henry Sts., daily 11 a.m.–11 p.m.

Here's something new under that hot Mediterranean sun: an original approach to Middle Eastern cookery. Food critics rave about "spectacular" appetizers and "fantastic" specials of the day. Try the brick-oven gourmet pizzas (some with salmon, hot dog, and chicken toppings), the tuna or shrimp kabobs, or the appealing array of veggie dishes, and wash it all down with one of a dozen fresh-squeezed juices. You can easily get a meal for two for $20.

YEMEN CAFÉ. 176 Atlantic Ave. bet. Court and Clinton Sts., 834-9533, daily 10 a.m.–10 p.m. Cash only.

There's an Indian twist on the Middle Eastern food here. The cuisine of Yemen has elements of Indian cooking, including nan-like breads and deliciously mild curried dishes served with basmati rice. The soups are wonderful, and if you are lucky, you can get a slow-roasted lamb dish that's off the menu.

Bars, Cafés, and Quick Meals

BEDOUIN TENT. 405 Atlantic Ave. bet. Bond and Nevins Sts., 852-5555, daily 11 a.m.–11 p.m., www.bococa.com/restaurants.html.

The name has changed (it used to be called Moustache), but this wonderful small café still serves very fresh hummus, tabbouleh, and other Middle Eastern standards. However, it is known for its unusual pizza (made of pita dough) with interesting toppings, such as shrimp or garlicky chicken. It is owned by the same Lebanese family that runs the Olive Vine Café in Park Slope, and the quality of its food is consistently high. The back garden, mint tea, and Arabian music will transport you to the Middle East. BYOB.

FLYING SAUCER CAFÉ. 494 Atlantic Ave. bet. Nevins St. and 3rd Ave., 522-1383, M–F 7:30 a.m.–7 p.m., Sa–Su 8:30 a.m.–7 p.m.

A great place to come before BAM or while exploring Atlantic Avenue. Here you can get soups, H&H bagels, salads, and Hale and Hearty soups. The leafy garden beckons in the summer. If you want to read your poetry here and can guarantee that a crowd of a couple dozen guests will come, they're happy to accommodate.

♪ **KILI.** 81 Hoyt St. bet. State St. and Atlantic Ave., 855-5574, Tu–Th 5 p.m.–4 a.m., Sa–Su noon–4 a.m.

There's live soul music here on Tuesdays, weekend brunch, and late night DJs during the week. Check out the cool young crowd, most of whom are Brooklyn newbies who are picking up the pace in this once-staid neighborhood.

MONTERO'S BAR & GRILL. 73 Atlantic Ave. off Furman St., 624-9799, M–Sa 10–4 a.m., Su noon–4 a.m.

An innocuous local bar frequented by aging longshoremen and miscellaneous elderly locals, Montero's received a write-up in a 1998 *New York* magazine, which said, "this place isn't just about nostalgia: some of the local literati come by to soak up stories for their next novel (along with some of the cheapest beer in town)."

♪ **WATERFRONT ALE HOUSE.** 155 Atlantic Ave. bet. Clinton and Henry Sts., 522-3794, daily 11:30 a.m.–1:30 p.m., later on weekends, www.waterfrontalehouse.com.

Brooklyn's closest match to Boston's Cheers. Previously known as "Pete's," this popular bar and eatery is a friendly local place with a good selection of new microbrews, single-malt scotches, small-batch bourbons, tequilas, and vodkas. Families nip in with the kids for a quick, light dinner. Some foodies have been known to recommend the *landjaeger* sausage. Live music on weekends features jazz and blues musicians, many drawn from local talent. There's another Water-front Alehouse on 2nd Avenue and 30th Street in Manhattan.

SHOPPING

Specialty Food Shops

The Middle Eastern enclave in the block between Court and Clinton Sts. is a colorful remnant of the days when Brooklyn's waterfront was a bustling international seaport.

CHERYL KLEINMAN CAKES. 448 Atlantic Ave. bet Bond and Nevins Sts., 237-2271, by appointment only.

Let them eat cake, indeed. You could walk right by this modest door a hundred times without guessing that inside is one of the city's finest fancy-cake-makers. If you have a really special occasion—wedding, major birthday, or anniversary—and want a gorgeously decorative cake, the much-acclaimed Cheryl Kleinman can make it for you.

DAMASCUS BREAD & PASTRY. 195 Atlantic Ave. bet. Clinton and Court Sts. 625-7070, M–Sa 8 a.m.–5 p.m. No credit cards.

If you live in New York, you've probably seen packages of Damascus pita bread in your local supermarket. Inside this small shop is a vast selection of freshly baked plain, whole wheat, sesame, garlic, onion, and even oat-bran pitas. The business was started in 1933 by Grandpa Hassan Halaby, who hailed from Damascus.

ORIENTAL PASTRY AND GROCERY. 170 Atlantic Ave. bet. Clinton and Court Sts., 875-7687, daily 10 a.m.–8:30 p.m. No credit cards.

The Syrians have been perfecting the sweet ancient taste of pistachio, honey, and dough for more than a thousand years, and here you'll benefit from all of that experience. Try the *burma* (shredded dough filled with honey and nuts) or the Turkish delight. All baking is done on the premises. For something more substantial, there is takeout hummus, lebany yogurt, and falafel mix, along with dozens of spices and other accoutrements of Middle Eastern cooking.

SAHADI IMPORTING COMPANY. 187–189 Atlantic Ave. bet. Clinton and Court Sts., 624-4550, M–Sa 9 a.m.–7 p.m., www.sahadis.com.

An institution that for over fifty years has attracted shoppers from the tristate area. Part gourmet food store, part exotic takeout deli, this is the largest and best stocked of the Middle Eastern food emporiums in New York City. There is an admirable selection of freshly prepared take-home foods, including soups, *tab-*

bouleh, stuffed vine leaves, *imjadara* (a dish made of rice and lentils), apricot-currant chicken, hummus, curries, and couscous. Check for seasonal specials, such as Middle Eastern turkey stuffing and an edible almond Christmas wreath. There are often crowds at holiday times, but the fabulously cheerful owner, Charlie Sahadi, keeps everyone smiling. You can order gift baskets from the Web site, which also gives a true-to-life self-portrait.

Antiques

ANTIQUE ROOM. 412–16 Atlantic Ave. bet. Bond and Nevins Sts., 875-7084, W–Su noon–6 p.m., www.antiqueroom.com.

Previously called the Upholstered Room, this shop showcases nineteenth-century American furniture, some of it museum-quality. One room shows Victorian tables, sofas, and chairs. The back room features period furniture, perfect for that historically correct renovated brownstone. The styles range from American Federal to Empire. Everything is in mint condition and priced accordingly, in the $1,000-and-up range. The owners' personal collection of American Gothic Revival furniture has been featured in *Victorian Homes* and *House Beautiful*.

CIRCA ANTIQUES AND CIRCA RESTORATION. 374 and 377 Atlantic Ave. bet. Bond and Hoyt Sts., 596-1866, Tu–F 11:30 a.m.–5:30 p.m., Sa 11 a.m.–6 p.m., Su noon–6 p.m., www.circaantiquesltd.com.

There are restored Empire tables, chairs, and beds of walnut, rosewood, and other fine woods here. Prices for sets range from $1,000 to $7,000. The store has been here for thirty years, so you can be assured of its good reputation. Circa Restoration also does refinishing and restoration of fine furniture.

HORSEMAN ANTIQUES. 351 Atlantic Ave. bet. Bond and Hoyt Sts., 596-1048, daily 10 a.m.–6 p.m.

There are four floors of turn-of-the-century and Art Deco pine and oak furniture here, plus a fairly large collection of stained glass. In addition, you will find an eclectic collection of new brass headboards and beds. Prices here are moderate, which may be one reason this store has been in business for over forty years. If you are interested in selling or consigning appropriate furniture, call.

IN DAYS OF OLD, LIMITED. 357 Atlantic Ave. near Hoyt St., 858-4233, Tu–Sa 11 a.m.–5 p.m., Su 1–5 p.m.

Lots of late-Victorian and turn-of-the-century oak, walnut, and mahogany pieces are sold here—armoires, desks, and tables—along with turn-of-the-century lighting fixtures. The friendly owner has restored several Brooklyn brownstones himself, and he has an eye for unusual pieces. This is a good place for people redecorating or renovating their own homes in period style.

TIME TRADER ANTIQUES. 368 Atlantic Ave. bet. Bond and Hoyt Sts., 852-3301, M–F 11 a.m.–6:30 p.m., Sa–Su noon–6 p.m.

The excellent and fairly priced merchandise here spills over into several store-fronts along Atlantic Avenue. This is one of the largest importers of English and European furniture in the tristate area. There are original armoires, sofas, chairs, and tables, Victorian to Deco, as well as less expensive reproduction pine and oak furniture.

Contemporary Home Furnishings

BARK. 369 Atlantic Ave. bet. Hoyt and Bond Sts., 625-8997, Tu–Su noon–7 p.m., Su noon–6:00 p.m.

This high-end bath-and-linen shop is seductively luxurious. Thick cotton towels and robes, wonderful soaps, delightful bathroom ornaments, and more, ooze relaxation and delicious, harmless self-indulgence. And why not? Bark is definitely a great place to find a gift to pamper that someone special in your life—whether it's you or someone else you love.

And they sell certain made-in-Brooklyn items, for instance, glassworks by John Pomp, who has done exclusive lines for Donna Karan and Tiffany. His work is sold at Barneys New York and Colette's in Paris. And at Bark.

⭐ **BREUKELEN.** 369 Atlantic Ave. bet. Hoyt and Bond Sts., 246-0024, Tu–S noon–7 p.m., www.brooklyn gifts.com.

It looks a bit like the MoMA store, but much more laid back. Breukelen (named after the borough's original Dutch name) sells artfully displayed, beau-tifully designed functional objects. Thomas Gibson and John Snyder have put together a terrific collection of classic and modern design objects for the home, priced from $20 on up. Breukelen is straight out of Manhattan's Tribeca or SoHo—*New York* magazine recently rated it "best curated shop."

⭐ **KEA CARPETS & KILIMS.** 477 Atlantic Ave., 222-8087, W–Su noon–7 p.m., www.keacarpesandkilims.com.

Wonderful, visually appealing rugs and kilims are found here. You can browse through an interesting collection of antique, exotic, and hand-designed carpets. Or have a consult, and design a custom piece to fit your new brownstone apart-ment. Prices range from $700 into thousands of dollars.

⭐ **RICO.** 384 Atlantic Ave. bet. Hoyt St. and Bond St., 797-2077, W–F noon–7:00 p.m., www.shoprico.com.

In the 1980s, Rico created rock-and-roll stage lighting for the likes of Madonna, Sade, Sonic Youth, and the Beastie Boys, and was an award-winning lighting consultant for Bergdorf Goodman, Barneys New York, and Ralph Lauren. Today, Rico designs affordable lighting (costing between $100 and $200) for home use, along with a line of sofas and accessories.

House and Kitchenwares

A COOK'S COMPANION. 197 Atlantic Ave. bet. Clinton and Court Sts., 852-6901, M–Sa 11 a.m.–7 p.m., Tu by appointment.

In 1997, retailer Jennifer Baron set out in an entrepreneurial venture to market cookware and tools for the home and professional chef. She was so successful that within a few years she opened **A Perfect Setting**, nearby. There's a zestful display of high-end cookware (with discounts on such brand names as Le Creuset), kitchen knives (made by Wusthof and Global, also discounted), an intelligent collection of cookbooks, and assorted kitchen must-haves, from oddly sized bundt pans to fresh-pepper grinders to practical-yet-pretty oven mitts to marble rolling pins. She organizes occasional cooking classes, teaching basic knife skills; sushi for parties; pie making; and Thanksgiving cookery.

A PERFECT SETTING. 140 Atlantic Ave. near Clinton St., 222-1868, M–Sa 11 a.m.–7 p.m., Tu–Su noon–7 p.m.

There's so much great tableware jammed into this 450-square-foot space that you don't know what to buy first: the wineglasses, French country-style tablecloths, serving dishes, colorful candles, or vases. For pots, pans, and other truly practical kitchenware, check the sister store, **A Cook's Companion**. Gift certificates available.

TWO FOR THE POT. 200 Clinton St. corner of Atlantic Ave., 855-8173, T–F noon–7 p.m., Sa 10 a.m.–6 p.m., Su 1–5 p.m. Mail order available, but no credit cards.

Savor the aroma of freshly roasted coffees here. While you are buying, check out the assortment of coffee makers, herbs, spices, and barbecue equipment. The personable owner, a former cartoonist, is ready with suggestions and information.

Clothing

BUTTER. 389 Atlantic Ave. bet. Hoyt and Bond Sts., 260-9033/858-8214, daily, noon–7 p.m.

The Manhattany boutique sells a fine collection of modern classic clothing for the independent woman. You won't find these brands in department stores: Kristensen, Martin Margiela, and others. T-shirts run from $50 to $150, and cashmere sweaters start at about $300; there's a small selection of shoes, too. Run by sisters, this is a shop for gals who love to shop.

GUMBO. 493 Atlantic Ave. bet. Nevins and 3rd Ave., 855-7808, T–Sa 11 a.m.–7 p.m., Su 11 a.m–6 p.m.

What a fun, wonderful store! You can find a little bit of everything, with women's fashions and jewelry, infant and children's wear and gear, and crafts. Gumbo also holds story hours and craft classes.

✪ **KIMERA.** 366 Atlantic Ave. bet. Hoyt and Bond Sts., 422-1147, M–F call for hours, Sa–Su noon–6 p.m. Also at 274 5th Ave., 965-1313, M–F call for hours, Sa noon–8 p.m., Su noon–6 p.m., www.kimeradesign.com.

If you love deep warm colors and the luxury of silk, drop by. Kimera designer Yvonne Chu opened here in 2002 after a successful start on 5th Avenue. This much larger store shows her entire collection, plus a new line of furniture and home accessories, including Kimera's own silk-shantung-and-brocade pillows and Asian furniture and baskets. Kimera is a favorite among bridesmaids who are buying bridesmaids' dresses.

LEGACY. 362 Atlantic Ave. bet. Hoyt and Bond Sts., 403-0090, W–Su noon–7 p.m., www.legacy-nyc.com.

High-quality vintage designer clothing and handbags are sold at this store, a sister to the hip Legacy on Thompson Street. You might luck out and get a $130 1960s Pucci, or a new dress made from vintage fabric, priced at $180 and up.

☺ ✪ **MELTING POT.** 492 Atlantic Ave. near Nevins St., 596-6849, Tu–Su noon–7 p.m.

You'll find great gift items for children at this little batik-boutique. It's a mother-daughter operation (started when the now-adult daughter was a small child), in which simple T-shirts, aprons, bibs, dresses, hats, baby quilts, and so on are hand-batiked in bright, cheery colors that will never run when washed. The folk-art motifs include lots of stars, moons, polka dots, dinosaurs, and friendly flowers.

✪ **MICHELLE NEW YORK.** 103 Bond St. off Atlantic Ave., 643-2230, Th–Sa 11 a.m.–7 p.m., www.michelle newyork.com

The deft hand of a Parsons-educated designer is apparent in the unique "bustle back" skirts, eyelet blouses, and clever wrap tops. Shirts start at about $100.

✪ **SCARLET GINGER.** 376 Atlantic Ave. bet. Hoyt and Bond Sts., 852-8205, T–Sa 11 a.m.–6 p.m., Su noon–6 p.m., www.brooklynboutique.com.

From frilly knickers to 1950s fashions, fun's the name of the game at this eclectic, edgy ladies' clothing boutique, and Brit owner Charlie brings more than a charming accent with her. She uses vintage materials in new clothing (ladies blouses made out of men's tux shirts; handbags made of paint canvasses) and rents out funky cocktail-party outfits (dress, shoes, bag) by the weekend; see the "frocks box" in the back of the shop.

✪ **SILVER TAO.** 394 Atlantic Ave. bet. Hoyt and Bond Sts., 422-7700, W–Su, noon–7 p.m., www.suzansilver design.com.

Breathtakingly beautiful kimonos are on display here. You can wear them, if that's your cup of tea. Or owner Susan Silver will help you select the fabric to decorate pillows, cover a duvet, or make into decorative curtains. The inventory changes regularly.

✪ **SIR.** 360 Atlantic Ave. bet. Hoyt and Bond Sts., 643-6877, W–Su, noon–7 p.m.

Watch the creative process as you shop at this boutique/workshop. Wearable, original women's and men's clothing, some of vintage fabrics, are made here. You won't see this raw, deconstructed edge at Macy's. Priced from $75 to $250.

URBAN MONSTER. 396 Atlantic Ave. bet. Hoyt and Bond Sts., 855-6400, M noon–6 p.m., Tu–Th 11 a.m.– 6 p.m., F 11 a.m.–7 p.m., Sa noon–7 p.m., Su noon–6 p.m., www.urbanmonster.com.

Everything is cute in this children's gear shop: the babies, the clothes, bibs, tiny socks and colorful toys, diaper bags, even the funny Web site. There's a wide range of brands geared for the hip mommy and baby, and some gently used designer items on consignment. You can get on a mailing list for new parent support groups, and workshops.

Other Interesting Neighborhood Shops

KNITTING HANDS. 398 Atlantic Ave. bet. Hoyt and Bond Sts., 858-5648, M 11 a.m.–6 p.m., Tu–Th 11 a.m.–6 p.m., F 11 a.m.–7 p.m., Sa 10 a.m.–7 p.m., Su noon–6 p.m., www.knittinghands.com.

Knitting Hands is such a winsome place that the colors, textures, and range of choice of yarns and crocheting materials will inspire even beginners to get clickety-clacking with those needles. After all, it's not the product, it's the process. Lots of classes, books, and support.

SCUBA NETWORK. 290 Atlantic Ave. corner of Smith St., 802-0700, Tu–F 11 a.m.–7 p.m., Sa 10 a.m.–6 p.m.

Amid the antique dealers and Middle Eastern food merchants is this store catering to water lovers. You can get all the gear you'll need for snorkeling or scuba diving, sign up for classes for your next trip south, or even book a tour to Cozamel and other diving destinations.

ACCOMMODATIONS

ANGELIQUE BED & BREAKFAST (see p. 14)
BAISLEY HOUSE (see p. 14)
MONSIGNOR DEL VECCHIO PLACE (see p. 17)
SAINTS AND SINNERS (see p. 17)

9

DUMBO

Fulton Ferry Waterfront
and Vinegar Hill

ABOUT DUMBO

Whether you are interested in history, great views of Manhattan, Brooklyn's emerging art scene, or a respite from the urban fray, a trip to DUMBO and the waterfront can be just what the doctor ordered. If you are traveling with children, the open spaces and fresh breezes are wonderful for an urban romp. Music buffs can take in a concert at the old-barge-turned-concert-hall, Bargemusic, or a summer outdoor movie shown against a dramatic backdrop of two historic bridges and a twinkling Manhattan skyline. And it's the perfect place to start, or end, a walk across the Brooklyn Bridge.

At any time of the year, it's fun to walk around this neighborhood, with its intense concentration of old warehouses and industrial buildings, and wonder at the vastness (and noise) of the Brooklyn and Manhattan Bridges overhead. These days, you never know what little shop, gallery, or restaurant you might bump into around the next corner.

A great deal of creative work is going on in this contained ten-block area, although not necessarily at eye level. Behind an innocuous door and up a few flights, electric guitars are being fashioned by hand; customers include many famous rock-and-roll stars. Up a few blocks, there's a company that specializes in ice sculpting, whatever the weather, using ton-weight blocks of ice and chain saws to create enormous, magnificent pieces for special events. The size of the studio spaces, in these old industrial buildings, invites artists to think big and work on large projects, whether paintings, mixed media, or sculpture.

Only about three thousand people live in DUMBO today. Many are well-known artists, including Vito Acconci, Tom Otterness, and photographer Renee Cox. An estimated thousand artists work here, double the number there were just a few years ago.

Don't miss several special art events: the October **Open Studio Tour**, when

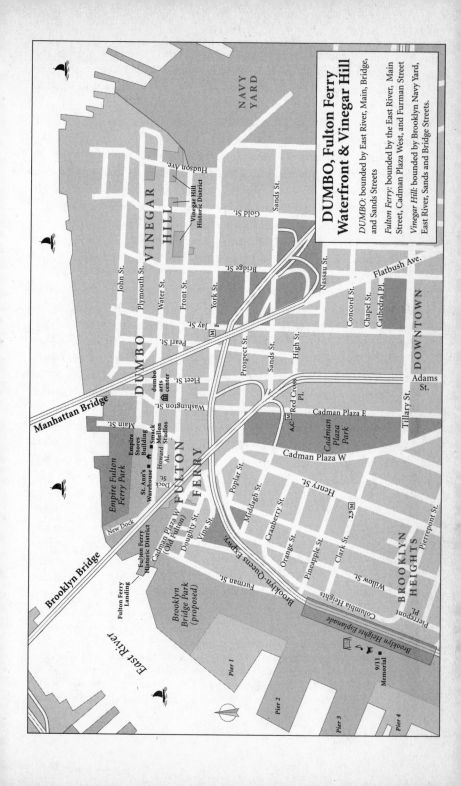

DUMBO, Fulton Ferry
Waterfront & Vinegar Hill

DUMBO: bounded by the East River, Main, Bridge, and Sands Streets.

Fulton Ferry: bounded by the East River, Main Street, Cadman Plaza West, and Furman Street

Vinegar Hill: bounded by Brooklyn Navy Yard, East River, Sands and Bridge Streets.

NAVY YARD

VINEGAR HILL

Vinegar Hill Historic District

Hudson Ave.

Sands St.

Gold St.

John St.

Plymouth St.

Water St.

Front St.

Bridge St.

York St.

Nassau St.

Flatbush Ave.

Concord St.

Chapel St.

Cathedral Pl.

DUMBO

Pearl St.

Jay St.

Prospect St.

Sands St.

High St.

DOWNTOWN

Fleet St.

Manhattan Bridge

dumbo arts center

Washington St.

Red Cross Pl.

A,C

Adams St.

Cadman Plaza E

Main St.

Empire Stores Building

St. Ann's Warehouse

Howard Mellon Studios

Smack

A,L.

Dock St.

FULTON FERRY

Cadman Plaza Park

Cadman Plaza W

Tillary St.

New Dock

Empire Fulton Ferry Park

Cadman Plaza W (Old Fulton)

Doughty St.

Vine St.

Poplar St.

Middagh St.

Cranberry St.

Henry St.

Orange St.

Pineapple St.

Clark St.

2,3

Pierrepont St.

Brooklyn Bridge

Fulton Ferry Historic District

Fulton Ferry Landing

Brooklyn Bridge Park (proposed)

Furman St.

Brooklyn-Queens Expwy.

Willow St.

BROOKLYN HEIGHTS

Pierrepont Pl.

Columbia Heights

Brooklyn Heights Esplanade

9/11 Memorial

Pier 1

Pier 2

Pier 3

Pier 4

East River

over a hundred artists open their studios to the public, and the summer "Between the Bridges" Outdoor Sculpture Show. The **d.u.m.b.o. arts center** organizes periodic **Art Walks**, and there are great shows, too, at **Smack Mellon** gallery.

As we go to press in 2003, DUMBO is undergoing a metamorphosis. As recently as 1998, it was desolate, decrepit, even creepy sometimes. There were some studios, some artists, a restaurant and a bar or two, and a lot of dreams for the neighborhood. *Now,* those million-dollar views are fetching million-dollar condo prices. Some of the old industrial buildings have been converted into fabulous apartments. There's a burgeoning center of high-end contemporary furniture here, showcased by a well-received curated show, *Brooklyn Designs,* held here in 2003. The ferry link to Manhattan, new bars and eateries, a wonderful ice cream place, and a high-visibility chocolatier, have helped transform DUMBO into a hip destination.

HOW THEY GOT THEIR NAMES *DUMBO:* An acronym for Down Under the Manhattan Bridge Overpass. *Fulton Ferry:* Named after Robert Fulton's *Nassau,* the first steam-powered ferry, which first plowed the waters of the East River between Manhattan and a landing here. The ferries transported both people and produce; at their busiest, in the 1870s, they made about 1,200 crossings a day. *Vinegar Hill:* Called Irishtown in the late 1700s, the area was renamed Vinegar Hill by a large landowner, John Jackson, in commemoration of a battle fought as part of the Irish revolution of that era.

BY SUBWAY *Fulton Ferry* and *DUMBO:* Take the A or C to High Street or the 2 or 3 to Clark Street. *Vinegar Hill:* In order of proximity, closest train is F to York Street, A or C to High Street, 2 or 3 to Clark Street, a twenty-minute walk from the 4 and 5 at Borough Hall.

 What's NEW?

A New Park, Sitting Pretty from the Bridges to the Piers

The rate of change in DUMBO seems to be exponential now, with the arrival of **ABC Carpet,** some new restaurants, and the development of the huge, historic **Empire Stores** site. And then there's the **Brooklyn Bridge Park!**

The earliest that construction is likely to begin on the much discussed Brooklyn Bridge Park is 2004. Here's the plan as it currently stands:

Brooklyn Bridge Park will be a seventy-acre waterfront recreation area offering diverse experiences. Most of the park will be open space, about fifty acres. This will include the existing Empire Fulton Ferry Park (see below), the Main Street lot and adjacent property, as well as Piers 2 and 3, half of Pier 1, and the uplands between Pier 2 and Pier 5, plus the ConEd lot to the north of the Park. What will be replaced are acres of parking and old sheds, which currently enjoy waterfront views. The park will feature a waterfront esplanade, with a natural area at the north end. Ideally, public recreation facilities will include children's playgrounds, a great lawn with informal playing fields, a walled garden, swimming pool, skating rink, basketball, tennis and handball courts, boat docks, a fishing pier, and a skateboard/rollerblade venue. Revenue-generating uses will be confined to less than 20 percent of the site, and possible uses include a hotel at Pier 1, restaurant, and an indoor recreation center. The River Café and Bargemusic will remain at Fulton Ferry Landing.

For information, call 802-0603, www.brooklynbridgepark.org.

HISTORICAL NOTES

Originally a waterfront hamlet, the Fulton Ferry area was the site from which Brooklyn's Dutch settlers embarked for Manhattan. The little hamlet became a bustling commercial and residential area in the nineteenth century, when steam ferries began transporting people and produce across the East River.

Many historical figures lived here: Thomas Paine lived in a house at the corner of Sands and Fulton (now Cadman Plaza West). Talleyrand once lived in a Fulton Street farmhouse opposite Hicks Street. Walt Whitman set type for the first edition of *Leaves of Grass* in 1855 at 170 Fulton Street, on the corner of Cranberry. But with the completion of the Brooklyn Bridge in 1883, and the loss of ferry traffic, the neighborhood went into decline.

DUMBO, as the buildings suggest, was an industrial area, and it can claim to be the place where corrugated cardboard was first manufactured.

Vinegar Hill evolved as a waterfront working-class residential neighborhood. In the nineteenth century, the row houses still standing today were built, and small industries thrived. (It was here that the New York Chewing Gum factory first put chicle on the map as a chewable treat.) It was a raucous boomtown during the heyday of the adjacent Brooklyn Navy Yard. The area thrived through the end of World War II, but thereafter the Navy Yard itself declined, affecting the surrounding neighborhood. Since the 1980s, Vinegar Hill has been on a gentle upswing.

Starting in the 1980s, a fair amount of abandoned industrial loft space underneath the bridges was resuscitated by artists, and, more recently, developers. The architecture and scale of these buildings reflects their original use as sites for the construction of large metal units ordered by the nearby Navy Yard. For big-scale painters and sculptors, they offered ideal spaces. A few artists and artisans moved here for the spectacular light, the views, the proximity to the bridges, and the river. But most came for the low rent, and, while enjoying the views, they also endured inconvenience, rough conditions, and desolation. Some residents contributed a tremendous amount of physical labor to improving their buildings—they built bathrooms, erected walls, and installed heating, even as renters. Until about 2000, there were few amenities here, other than Grimaldi's, Pete's, and the River Café; the nearest supermarket was a hike away, in Brooklyn Heights. In our 1999 edition we noted that while Manhattan was just a short walk away, artists in DUMBO could work in "splendid isolation." That era is fast becoming history.

POINTS OF CULTURAL INTEREST

Performance and Art

SPECIAL EVENTS.
Outdoor Sculpture Show (July), d.u.m.b.o. Art Center festival (October).

ANCHORAGE. Cadman Plaza W. and Front St., under the Brooklyn Bridge, 625-0080. Call for information.
Alas, since the terrorist attacks on the World Trade Center and related threats to the Brooklyn Bridge, this gallery is closed. It was housed in eight 55-foot-high stone chambers that hold the Brooklyn Bridge suspension cables.

ARTS ∂ ST. ANN'S. See **St. Ann's Warehouse** (below), www.artsatstanns.org.

BARGEMUSIC. Fulton Landing, at the end of Cadman Plaza W., 624-4061/2083, concerts Th–Su, www.barge music.org. Call for the schedule; ticket $35. Reservations are a must.
Here's a place that knows when to celebrate, say, Bach's birthday. Or Piatigorsky's. Keeping a staccatto pace of at least four concerts weekly for fifty weeks a year, Bargemusic arguably presents more chamber music than any other venue not only in the United States, but in the world. And it's very cool. The concerts are held in a renovated Erie-Lackawanna coffee barge, floating in the water but anchored, with zillion-dollar views of Lower Manhattan. Since 1977, noted individual soloists with experience at places such as the New York Philharmonic come together here to play in a lovely wood-paneled hall that has great acoustics—and a fireplace. Since the boat is just 102 feet long, and there's seating for only 125, you virtually sit in the musicians' laps. Founder and violinist Olga Bloom is now a senior citizen and is one of the borough's great waterfront pioneers.

Free! **"BETWEEN THE BRIDGES" OUTDOOR SCULPTURE SHOW.** Empire Ferry Park, 596-2507, www.bwac.org. July.

Every July for about twenty years now, a most unusual sculpture garden is temporarily erected at the Empire Fulton Ferry Park between the Manhattan and Brooklyn bridges, organized by the **Brooklyn Waterfront Artists Coalition, BWAC.** Most of the sculptures are designed specifically for this venue, and must meet certain practical criteria: it must be sturdy enough to withstand the vicissitudes of weather, and be vandal-resistant, as well as removable without a trace at the end of the show. Of the entries, only a handful are chosen for the show. It's wild and wonderful, and worth a trip.

BIG DANCE THEATER, INC. 303 Clinton St., 875-0202, www.bigdancetheater.org.

Big Dance Theater is an Obie Award–winning company that creates dance performances frequently based on literary sources. In 2003, their *Antigone* won rave reviews. They work out of **Nest** (see below).

BROOKLYN UNDERGROUND FILM FESTIVAL. www.brooklynunderground.org.

What starts small can eventually make an impact. Founded in 2002 by a group of passionate young filmmakers, the Brooklyn Underground Film Festival (BUFF) is an outlet for emerging and radical new voices.

⦿ **d.u.m.b.o. ARTS CENTER (DAC).** 30 Washington St., 624-3772 (office), 694-0831 (gallery), www.dumboartscenter.org.

The mission of the d.u.m.b.o. arts center, launched in 1997, is to foster creative expression in this part of Brooklyn, and to promote the work of local artists to a national and international audience. Their exhibits, mounted five or six times a year, are selected by celebrity guest curators, for instance, from the Weatherspoon Gallery in North Carolina, or the Museum of Contemporary Canadian Art. Their **Art Walks,** run in conjunction with exhibit schedules, offer a rare opportunity to talk with DUMBO area artists. For $35 per person, you can have a wonderful three-hour experience: visit the exhibits, then walk to the studios of five local emerging artists, and return to the d.u.m.b.o gallery for wine and cheese and a discussion with some of the artists whose work is being shown. They also host an annual **Artists Talk** as part of the October festival, a two-or three-hour dialogue with well-known artists, and have a slide registry. Their annual auction often includes pieces by internationally known artists, such as Alexander Calder and Robert Rauschenberg. Also, dac organizes the **d.u.m.b.o. art under the bridge festival.**

ART UNDER THE BRIDGE FESTIVAL AND OPEN STUDIOS, sponsored by **d.u.m.b.o. arts center,** 624-3772, www.dumboartscenter.org. October.

Don't miss it. Over three days in October, performances and events take place in DUMBO's galleries and streets, while hundreds of artists open their studios for public viewing. In 2002, 150,000 visitors enjoyed such events as Live-Action Painting, with a wet auction to follow, and the Parade of Concept, featuring art, light, and sound in motion. Two hundred and fifty open studios, gallery exhibitions, theater, dance, spoken word, a fashion show, an experimental short-film and video festival, and much more. Organized by **d.u.m.b.o. arts center (dac)** (see above).

DUMBO ART EXPO. www.dumboartexpo.com.

All the world's a gallery. In 2002, enterprising local sculptor Jan Larsen persuaded a dozen local retail stores to display the work of local artists. As you walk around the area, notice the photography, silk screens, paintings, and digital work on the walls of wherever you might be. Everything's for sale—you might discover the next big talent. They also organize a **DUMBO "Expo Show"**—monthly installations with DJ music.

HOWARD SCHICKLER FINE ART. 45 Main St. near Front St., Studio #402, 212-431-6363, Tu–F 10 a.m.–5:30 p.m., Sa 11 a.m.–3 p.m., www.schicklerart.com.

Originally specializing in nineteenth and twentieth-century photography, the gallery now includes paintings, drawings, and rare books.

JAZZREACH AND METTA QUINTET. 55 Washington St. near Water St., 625-5188, www.jazzreach.org.

Jazz is something that Americans of diverse backgrounds can share, but can music bring us *together*? Maybe. JazzReach, a nonprofit organization, has been traveling the country to venues such as Washington DC's Kennedy Center, and Boston's Berklee Performance Center, doing multimedia educational programs on the heritage of jazz, reaching over ten thousand young people with concerts by their Metta Quintet.

MASTEL + MASTEL GALLERY. 70 Washington St. #700, 646-452-1300, www.mastelgallery.com.

It's worth looking up at some of the big old buildings in DUMBO and wondering what's inside. Because you might miss this nonprofit gallery, showcasing "art on the verge": video, visual arts, and interesting exhibits.

THE MYSTERIOUS METAL ARTIST

Nobody knows who's doing this. But there's metal graffiti welded to surfaces here and there, in a display of anonymous public art. Check the railing at Adams

Street between Front and Water Streets, and the south side of Water and Adam, halfway down the block, chest-height.

NEST. 88 Front St. corner of Front and Washington Sts., www.nestARTS.org.

What an inventive idea. Nest is an interdisciplinary nonprofit arts organization dedicated to activating idle real estate for artistic purposes. It has temporarily occupied a thirty-thousand-square-foot former corrugated cardboard factory to present film, theater, music, dance, and party events. Some groups using the Nest are **Big Dance Theater** and the **Brooklyn Underground Film Festival.**

ONE ARM RED. 45 Main St. near Front St., 797-0046, www.onearmred.com.

This inventive theater company works in mixed media, combining drama, music, and interactive forms of presentation.

ST. ANN'S WAREHOUSE/ARTS AT ST. ANN'S. 38 Water St. bet. Main and Dock Sts., 858-2424, www.artsatstanns.org.

One of Brooklyn's treasures, Arts at St. Ann's has long been recognized for its inventive concerts and music-theater collaborations. ASA has produced many new works of distinction, often in partnership with others, including Lou Reed's and John Cale's *Songs for 'Drella* and David Byrne's *Forest.* ASA is also the home of **The Lab,** an acclaimed puppet theater workshop led by Dan Hurlin and Theodora Skipitares. The organization established itself over several decades as Arts at St. Ann's in Brooklyn Heights.

● **SMACK MELLON STUDIOS.** Office 70 Washington St., 422-0989, W–F 11 a.m.–6 p.m.; Gallery 56 Water St., 834-8761, W–Su noon–6 p.m., www.smackmellon.org.

Nonprofit Smack Mellon, billed as a "multidisciplinary exchange between visual artists and musicians," opened its doors in 1995. It's a home away from home for artists who undertake projects that don't fit neatly into one category or another. It's geared both to new artists and midcareer artists who need a space to grow.

TOURISM KIOSK.

Look for the tourism pushcart at the Brooklyn Bridge in DUMBO.

Architecture and Real Estate

BROOKLYN BRIDGE. Walkway entrance is at Adams and Tillary Sts.

Walk it, drive it, bike it, or just admire it—the Brooklyn Bridge soaring over the East River is one of the greatest of New York City's bridges. An architectural beauty designed by John A. Roebling, at the time of its completion in 1883 it was the world's longest suspension bridge, connecting Manhattan at City Hall Park to Brooklyn's Cadman Plaza. It is an icon of the borough as well as the picturesque subject of paintings, photos, and movie sets, not to mention a few time-worn jokes. With spectacular views of Manhattan's skyline, the river, and the Statue of Liberty, the bridge is the place for one of the most romantic and inspiring strolls in all New York.

The opening of the Brooklyn Bridge was the first of several major changes that transformed Brooklyn from a rural farming area with scattered neighborhoods into a popular Manhattan suburb. Land speculators and developers brought new residents to established, if scattered, neighborhoods, such as Brooklyn Heights, Fort Greene, and Bedford, and also carved out new residential areas in Carroll Gardens, Cobble Hill, and Boerum Hill.

COMMANDER'S QUARTERS, also known as Matthew C. Perry House

Tucked away on a bluff in Vinegar Hill, this breathtaking gated mansion was built in 1805 by Charles Bulfinch, architect of the U.S. Capitol building. It was built as the home of Captain Matthew C. Perry, associated with the **Brooklyn Navy Yard,** and is on the National Register of Historic Places. It's a private home today; no tours. If you want to see it, walk down Ashland Place, which becomes Navy Street, which in turn becomes Hudson Street, then turn right up the hill before you get to the power plant.

EAGLE WAREHOUSE. 28 Old Fulton St., corner of Elizabeth Pl., 855-3959.

In 1980 this elegant medieval-style warehouse was renovated into expensive cooperative apartments, many with spectacular views of Manhattan, the Brooklyn Bridge, and the East River. Built in 1893, it is one of Brooklyn's few remaining buildings by Frank Freeman, who was dubbed "Brooklyn's greatest architect" by the *AIA Guide to New York*. The arched entry bears large bronze letters reading "Eagle Warehouse and Storage Company"; atop the building is a huge clock, now situated in a studio loft.

EMPIRE STORES BUILDING. 53–83 Water St. bet. Dock and Main Sts.

This hulking nineteenth-century warehouse built circa 1885 was recently purchased and is slated to undergo renovation. Watch for a new row of retail shops on the ground level.

MANHATTAN BRIDGE. Spans the East River bet. Canal St. in Manhattan and Flatbush Ave. in Brooklyn, north of the Brooklyn Bridge and south of the Williamsburg Bridge.

Built in 1909, this two-level suspension bridge with spectacular views of

Manhattan was designed by Leon Moisseiff. It is over 6855 feet long and carries cars, truck traffic, and a subway line. The upper deck has a pedestrian walkway. It leads directly into Canal Street and Manhattan's Chinatown.

Other Points of Interest

🎓 **DUMBO SCIENCE SKILLS CENTER,** 49 Flatbush Ave. Extension, under Manhattan Bridge, 788-1514.

Founded in 1993 with grants from the National Science Foundation, among others, this public high school of seven hundred students encourages kids to consider careers in medicine, engineering, and other scientific fields. Experts call it "a school to watch."

(Source: *New York City's Best Public High Schools: A Parents' Guide*—Second Edition by C. Hemphill with P. Wheaton and J. Wayans.)

NEW YORK WATER TAXI. 212-742-1969, M–F 6:30 a.m.–7 p.m., Sa–Su 11 a.m.–8 p.m., www.nywater taxi.com. Stops include Fulton Ferry Landing (Brooklyn), Wall St./South St. Seaport (Pier 11), Battery Park (Pier A), World Financial Center (North Cove), West 22nd St. (Chelsea Piers), West 44th St. (Pier 84), and Brooklyn Army Terminal.

This is a really fun way to get around, for both visitors and New Yorkers. You can take a New York Water Taxi to neighborhoods, parks, and cultural attractions along the West Side, Lower Manhattan, and Downtown Brooklyn waterfronts. The yellow catamarans with black and white checks offer comfy seats, spectacular views, and a small café/bar. A number of passes exist to suit your needs, such as the "All-Day Pass" that allows a rider to hop on and off anytime during a twenty-four-hour period. Call or check Web site for routes, prices, and schedules.

ENTERTAINMENT

Free! 🎬 **BROOKLYN BRIDGE PARK SUMMER FILM SERIES.** Empire-Fulton Ferry State Park, Old Fulton St. (toward the waterfront). Free admission. Movies begin at 8:45 p.m.

Great summer fun: a series of free feature movies shown on the waterfront between the Brooklyn and Manhattan Bridges. Short independent films, all with a Brooklyn connection, are often run before each feature. There's "valet parking" for bicycles, and a free shuttle bus runs along Clark Street, High Street, and York Street.

PARKS AND PLAYGROUNDS

Free! **BROOKLYN BRIDGE PEDESTRIAN WALK.** Accessible at end of Cadman Plaza Park.

Paris has its Pont Neuf, Florence its Ponte Vecchio. How can you live in New York (or visit) and never walk across the city's most soulful bridge? It's a twenty-

or thirty-minute stroll, with fabulous views. If you walk from Brooklyn into Manhattan, you'll end up at City Hall.

☺ **EMPIRE FULTON FERRY PARK.** New Dock Rd., by Water St. and the East River. Walk, drive, or ride the B41 bus.

You'll almost forget you're in New York City when you visit this sizable grassy meadow along the East River, sandwiched between the Brooklyn and Manhattan Bridges. While the kids run around or picnic, you can treat yourself to views of Manhattan in front, fabulous Civil War–era spice warehouses and turn-of-the-century industrial lofts behind, and the bridges on either side.

DUMBO RESTAURANTS, CAFÉS, AND BARS

BETWEEN THE BRIDGES. 63 York St. corner Adams St. 237-1977, M–Th 2 p.m.–midnight, F–Sa 2 p.m.–2 a.m.

We don't know if it will survive gentrification. The *only* bar in the neighborhood back when struggling artists were pretty much the only ones crazy enough to live here, Between the Bridges is just a small working-class bar. It's incredibly noisy when the trains rumble nearby every few minutes.

☺ ⚫ **BROOKLYN ICE CREAM FACTORY.** 1 Old Fulton St. at Water St., 246-3963, Tu–Su 1–10 p.m.

Life is wonderful. Fresh ice cream—made in small batches to capture the flavor, with handmade waffle cones—can be purchased in this little historic building, and then you can either hop on the ferry to Manhattan or stroll around the wooden platform overlooking the river and admire your free Manhattan views.

BUBBY'S. 1 Main St. at Plymouth St., 222-0666, M–Th 11:30 a.m.–p.m., Sa–Su 9 a.m.–11 p.m.

Tribeca has arrived in DUMBO in the form of popular Bubby's restaurant. A favorite for weekend brunch, you can get a nice assortment of homemade baked goods, and comfort food, with fabulous Manhattan views.

D SPACE. 68 Jay St. at Front St., 522-7599, M–Th 11 a.m.–10:30 p.m., F–Sa 11 a.m.–11 p.m., Su 1–9:30 p.m.

A local hangout.

FIVE FRONT. 5 Front St., 625-5559, M, W–Th noon–3 p.m., 5:30–11:30 p.m., F–Su 11 a.m.–9 p.m., 5:30 p.m.–midnight. Reservations recommended for garden seating (summer).

In contrast to the bigness all around DUMBO—the giant Anchorage, the huge bridges, the large old industrial buildings, Five Front offers an appealing sense of intimacy. There are burgers and French fries for the kids, and more sophisticated French-style mussels, chicken, and meat dishes for you. Check out the occasional prix fixe and a lovely garden.

FRONT STREET PIZZA, DELI AND GRILL. 80 Front St. at Washington St., 875-3700, M–F 6 a.m.–9 p.m., Sa–Su 10 a.m.–9 p.m.

You can nip in for an unpretentious quick American-food snack and watch TV, too. The guys behind the counter will gladly cut your toddler's slice into thirds. Grab a slice of New York cheesecake or a blueberry muffin, a burger or even a Philly cheese steak hero. Eggy breakfasts are available until 11 a.m. Check out the bargain $6 lunch specials.

GRIMALDI'S. 19 Old Fulton St. bet. Front and Water Sts., 858-4300, M, W, F, 11:30 a.m.–11 p.m., Sa–Su 2 p.m.–midnight, www.grimaldisbrooklyn.com. No deliveries; cash only.

Grimaldi's is a tourist favorite—a reason, even, to travel to Brooklyn. But what explains the Saturday-night queues of *Brooklynites* waiting outside (aside from great people-watching and even better views of Manhattan)? It's the absolutely fresh, deliciously thin-crusted pizza topped with homemade sauce and your choice of toppings, churned out by this unassuming pizzeria. Inside, the joint looks like a pizzeria out of the flicks: it's got the jukebox, red-checkered tablecloths, Sinatra photos, and a nice Brooklyn buzz.

LOW BAR. 81 Washington St. bet. Front and York Sts., 222-1LOW, W–Sa 7 p.m.–3 a.m., www.riceny.com/low.

The hipster *Black Book*'s take on Low Bar (located below **Rice Restaurant**,) is "dope little spot" with "retro-futuristic electro-pop" and a house magician. But that's not the whole picture. They also host playwrights' readings and other interesting art/performance events. It's sleek, trendy, and über cool. And one of the few places in the borough that puts on burlesque, too.

LUNATARIUM. 10 Jay St. near John St., 813-8404, www.lunatarium.com. Check Web site for events.

There are great views of Manhattan, and twenty thousand square feet of penthouse space in what was once a typical DUMBO industrial building. It's now used for parties, events, and mixed-media installations and performance art. Book here when you want to invite your one thousand best friends for a great party.

PEDRO'S. 73 Jay St. bet. Front and Water Sts., 625-0031, daily 11 a.m.–8 p.m.

This is a fantastic dive. So go in for the chicken anything (the chicken tacos are good), rice 'n' beans, and a Budweiser beer—'cause that's what they've got. Pedro's is what DUMBO was like in the old days, before gentrification reared its moneyed head.

PETE'S DOWNTOWN. 1 Old Fulton St. at Water St., 858-3510, Tu–Th, noon–10 p.m., F noon–11 p.m., Sa noon–11 p.m., Su 1–9 p.m., www.petesdowntown.com.

Reserve a window-side table here: the spectacular Manhattan skyline is just across the river from this quiet, moderately priced Italian continental restaurant, sandwiched between the River Café and Grimaldi's. It's good for a large party, or as a place to bring the kids. Outside seating and parking is available.

⊘ **RICE.** 81 Washington St. bet. Front and York Sts., 222-9880, daily noon–11 p.m., www.riceny.com.

Rice is based on a novel mix-and-match concept. It specializes in eclectic dishes from different international cuisines—all based on rice. Try the Indian curry with Persian rice or Thai black rice with a chicken kebab. If the Atkins diet is your thing, there's also a range of non-rice-o-centric dishes. Check out the great patio and **Low Bar** below. With the average entrée about $8, the price is nice at Rice.

RIVER CAFÉ. 1 Water St. at end of Cadman Plaza W., 522-5200, M–Sa lunch noon–2:30 p.m., dinner 6:30–11 p.m., Sun lunch 11:30 a.m.–2:30 p.m., dinner 6–11 p.m., www.rivercafe.com.

Famous for its breathtaking views of the Manhattan skyline—for the River Café is perched right *on* the East River—this tony, intimate New York City classic has an excellent menu, lots of romantic ambience, and valet parking. Don't be put off by the whine of cars crossing the Brooklyn Bridge overhead; it's all part of the charm. This is the perfect place to pop the question, celebrate a special occasion, or have a drink before heading off to eat somewhere else (that's cheaper). Dinner at the River Café is $70 for prix fixe menu and more for the tasting menu; brunch and lunch are à la carte, with most entrées costing about $23. For the gents, jackets are required and ties preferred at dinner. Reservations are absolutely, unequivocally necessary.

66 WATER ST. 66 Water St. bet. Dock and Main Sts., 625-9352, daily 11:30 a.m.–11 p.m., bar open until 4 a.m.

You'll be met with a friendly Irish charm here, and so don't be surprised that you can get **perfectly** chilled beers. The menu has something for everyone, which explains the popularity of this local spot. Check the schedule for performances—dance, live bands, comedy, and more—held downstairs.

☺ ♫ **SUPERFINE.** 126 Front St. bet. Jay and Pearl Sts., 243-9005, Tu–Th lunch 11 a.m.–3 p.m., dinner 6–11 p.m., bar till 2 a.m., F lunch 11:30 a.m.–3 p.m., dinner 6–11 p.m., bar till 4 a.m., Sa dinner 6–11 p.m., bar 3 p.m.–4 a.m., Su brunch 11 a.m.–3 p.m., dinner 6–10 p.m., bar till 2 a.m. Reservations recommended.

Much beloved by DUMBO locals and Lower Manhattan hipsters, Superfine is located directly under the Manhattan Bridge in a partially renovated industrial loading dock. The minute you walk in, you're hit with an eyeful of cool architectural vestiges, such as a ramp walkway, a half-wood half-cement flooring behind the long, inviting bar, and enormous exposed ductwork. Come see occasional music, performance art, open mike night, and even fashion shows.

And the food? Eclectic, interesting, and, for dinner, vaguely Mediterranean, with lots of fish and fresh vegetables. The **Sunday Bluegrass Brunch** (live bands, sometimes wearing cowboy hats) offers you options like mahi mahi tacos with salsa fresca or huevos rancheros with chili flown in from New Mexico weekly. Service can be uneven when it's busy, but who cares? The place is quintessentially DUMBO.

SHOPPING

ABC CARPET & HOME. 20 Jay St. at Plymouth St., 643-7400, daily 11 a.m.–6 p.m., www.abccarpet.com. Call for a schedule of events held at ABC.

New York's premier home fashion megaboutique, ABC Carpet opened this cavernous warehouse store in 2002. Here are 32,000 square feet of furniture—beds, tables, armoires, desks, chairs, and more—imported from the four corners of the world and artlessly arranged near mountainous piles of handmade rugs from Persia, India, Pakistan, and China. DUMBO's ABC Carpet doesn't have anywhere near the flagship's huge selection of glam-fabulous soft goods—the pricey Egyptian cotton linens, bedspreads, and $200 silk throw pillows. But there are bargains to be had; ABC says that all items are discounted 25 percent or more.

✪ **CITY JOINERY.** 70 Washington St., Suite #711, 596-6502, www.cityjoinery.com.

One of Brooklyn's best contemporary designers, City Joinery makes new furniture of solid hardwoods, using traditional craftsmanship. The dining tables, sofas, chairs, desks, armoires are exquisite. Collectibles start at $1,000.

✪ **INSIDERSNY.** 65 Washington St. bet. Front and York Sts. (inside the Overpass Flowers shop), 422-0700, www.insidersny.com.

Here's the ideal hip New York gift item. You can browse a photography-based line of bags, accessories, and clothes with photos cleverly printed on leather. You can get gloves that have a map of Canal Street, handbags with photos of the New York City skyline or subway, and great messenger bags featuring the #6 subway pulling out of a station.

JACQUES TORRES CHOCOLATE. 66 Water St. bet. Dock and Main Sts., 875-9772, M–Sa 9 a.m.–7 p.m., www.mrchocolate.com.

Jacques Torres, former pastry chef at Le Cirque, is a well-known high-end chocolatier, and his little DUMBO shop won't disappoint, which explains the lines out his door on Saturdays. The displays are gorgeous, and you can watch, through a glass window, as the kitchen turns out his fresh goodies. It's hard to say what's more exciting, the taste of the chocolate, or their beautiful little shapes and decorations. There are no preservatives, no additives. You can order online for overnight delivery. Buy a gift for someone you love. Hint: Some folks are addicted to the chocolate mudslide cookies, others to the "Wicked Hot Chocolate" mix. Oh, and if you can't decide, you can nab one of the little tables here and have a hot chocolate and a rich pastry while you think.

Stay tuned: There may soon be a new furniture store next door, run by the same company.

☺ **RECYCLE-A-BICYCLE.** 55 Washington St. near Front St., 858-2972, M–Sa noon–7.

The fancy exterior at 55 Washington Street belies the mission of Recycle-A-Bicycle, which takes used and neglected bicycles, clothing, and accessories, including helmets, and restores them for sale at reasonable prices. This store's mission is to reduce not only landfill waste but smog as well. Plus it puts a lot of happy faces on kids and adults who otherwise might not be able to afford two-wheeled transport.

✪ **SADOWSKY GUITARS.** 20 Jay St. near Plymouth St., 422-1123, M–F 9 a.m.–6 p.m., www.sadowsky.com.

Talk about top brass. The customer list for Sadowsky's custom guitars is jaw-dropping: Bruce Springsteen, Keith Richards, Pat Metheny, Lenny Kravitz, and Lou Reed, among others. One defining characteristic of Sadowsky guitars is that they are made with wood selected for acoustic resonance (such as alder, southern swamp ash). These guitars, which cost $3,000 and up, transcend what is available in music stores. Serious hobbyists and professional musicians alike come to the showroom, settle into a private sound room, and try some of the sixteen fabulous-looking model guitar and basses on display. Out-of-towners should check the Web site for the seven-day trial offer. An affable master craftsman of electric guitars and basses for over twenty years, Roger Sadowsky recently moved his Manhattan production studio and a showroom to DUMBO.

WEST ELM. 55 Washington St., 875-7757, www.westelm.com.

West Elm is a brand that helps young homeowners furnish and accessorize their apartments at affordable prices but in high style. Their first retail operation is opening as we go to press.

10

Flatbush—More or Less

Caribbean and African-American; Jewish, Muslim, Christian, and Rastafarian; Turkish, Pakistani, and Israeli—a cacophony of cultures and religions greets you in Flatbush. A trip to Flatbush is a healthy reminder of the sturdy immigrant backbone of New York, historically and today.

This chapter provides a bird's-eye view of several strikingly different areas in the center of Brooklyn: Flatbush.

Starting from the areas closest to Prospect Park and moving south, it encompasses a large district, including the residential areas near Prospect Park, such as Ditmas Park, Prospect Park South, Prospect-Lefferts Gardens, and Albemarle-Kenmore; East Flatbush, a center of Caribbean-American life; Midwood, covering Avenues J and M near Coney Island, currently populated by many Orthodox Jews, Syrian Jews, and Israelis, among others; the Kings Highway retail center; and the Coney Island Avenue area that's home to immigrants from Bangladesh, Pakistan, Afghanistan, and other Muslim nations, as well as Russia and China. Flatbush is a fascinating pastiche of cultures, food, shopping, and history.

OVERVIEW OF FLATBUSH

There is a wonderfully urbane incongruity in contemporary Flatbush.

Hungering for Caribbean flavors and sounds? Take Flatbush Avenue to the Caribbean community in East Flatbush. West Indians from more than thirty Caribbean nations reside here. Who said peace in the Middle East is impossible? In Midwood, there are thousands of traditional Muslim immigrants living cheek-by-jowl with several large Orthodox Jewish communities—for the most part, ignoring one another, but doing so peaceably. Both groups stand out for their customs. You can see Orthodox Jews dressed in black Hasidic clothing on one block of Coney Island Avenue. And nearby, in a vibrant Pakistani community, conservative Muslims dress in colorful *shalwar kameez* robes, some men in

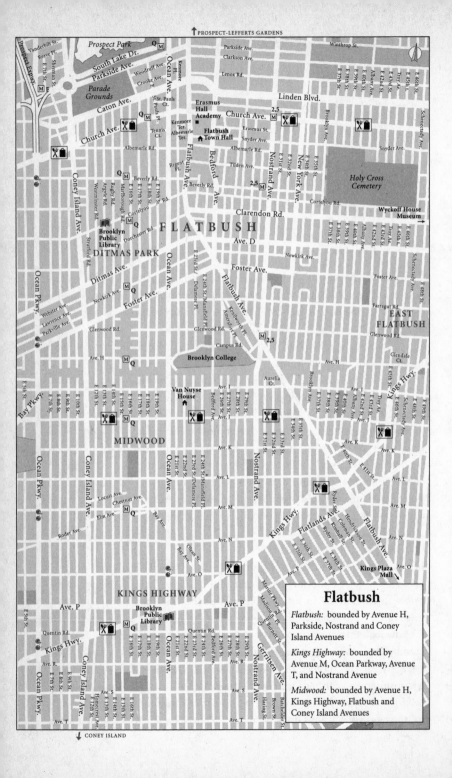

Flatbush

Flatbush: bounded by Avenue H, Parkside, Nostrand and Coney Island Avenues

Kings Highway: bounded by Avenue M, Ocean Parkway, Avenue T, and Nostrand Avenue

Midwood: bounded by Avenue H, Kings Highway, Flatbush and Coney Island Avenues

white *kufi* caps or turbans, and the women in *dubattas* scarves in brilliant hues. Midwood may be one of the few places in the world where it's not surprising on a Friday to see pious Muslim men, who've finished their prayers at the mosque down the block, standing chatting in front of a halal butcher—while nearby Jewish men are emerging from the **Kosher Gym** that's near the kosher butcher, heading toward synagogue for evening Sabbath prayers.

There are, as a result of this ethnic hodgepodge, lots of ethnic eating places and interesting shopping opportunities.

After all this culture shock, you may need a respite. A half dozen blocks down Coney Island Avenue from Prospect Park is the peaceful residential area of **Prospect Park South**, and, a bit farther, **Ditmas Park**. Even Brooklynites are surprised to find block after block of turn-of-the-century urban mansions here. If you've only got time for a quick look-see, go down East 17th Street between Dorchester and Ditmas Avenues, to see a row of breathtakingly lovely suburban-style homes.

Who needs an airline ticket to experience world culture? It's cheaper to take a subway to Flatbush.

HOW IT GOT ITS NAME Reflecting Brooklyn's early Dutch settlers, Flatbush derives from the Dutch word for wooded area, *Vlackebos*.

BY SUBWAY Take the B or Q train to Church Avenue (Prospect Park South), Newkirk Avenue (Ditmas Park), or the Q to Avenue J or Avenue M. Take B or Q to Kings Highway (Midwood and Kings Highway). Or take the 2 or 5 train to Sterling Street (Prospect-Lefferts Gardens) or to Flatbush Avenue (Brooklyn College), or the 2 or 5 train to Church Avenue (East Flatbush).

☛ **TIP:** Born-and-bred Brooklynites will split hairs over whether something is in Gravesend or Kings Highway, and residents of Ditmas Park may never have been to Avenue M. Because our guide is written with the casual tourist and Brooklyn novice in mind, the following is an unconventional stew of what we have dubbed "Flatbush—More or Less."

HISTORICAL NOTES

With thousands of single-family homes and well over thirty thousand apartment buildings in Flatbush today, it is hard to imagine this as farmland, but that's what it was just 150 years ago. The area was first settled in 1652 by Dutch farmers, remaining a sleepy backwater until the opening of the Flatbush and Coney Island Railroad in 1878. Access to transportation "suburbanized" the northern parts of Flatbush, drawing middle- and upper-middle-class New Yorkers from

Manhattan and brownstone Brooklyn to what, literally, were greener pastures. The opening of a subway line in 1920 to the Atlantic Ocean beaches and nearby amusement park attractions sped the development of residential areas deeper into Brooklyn. Large apartment buildings, many of which still line Ocean Parkway, were erected. Their early occupants were mainly Jewish, lending the area its mid-twentieth-century association with Jewish mores, New York Jewish humor, and Jewish delis.

In the decades after World War II many Jewish residents of Brooklyn relocated to the suburbs. A large immigration of Caribbean islanders moved in, along with other immigrant groups from Asia, Central America, and Russia, transforming Flatbush. Today, Flatbush is a fascinating pastiche of immigrant and old New York cultures, ethnic foods, discount shopping, and New York City history.

Kidstuff

☺ **Just walking around the area** is a lesson in diversity. **Family Time** has kids' shows. Check out some **urban playgrounds and basketball courts.** Call for a performance schedule of the **Russian/American Kids Circus.** Visit historic **Wyckoff House Museum** and **Prospect Park.** See wholesale **Terminal Market.**

POINTS OF CULTURAL INTEREST

SPECIAL EVENTS.

Mardi Gras (Avenue M, June); historic house tours of Victorian Flatbush (spring, call 859-3800).

BROOKLYN COLLEGE. 2900 Bedford Ave. (Flatbush Avenue/Brooklyn College stop on the 2 train), 951-5000, www.brooklyn.cuny.edu.

Brooklyn College, founded in 1930, has long enjoyed the reputation as the "poor man's Harvard." And it sort of resembles Harvard University, with its leafy quadrangle surrounded by stately neo-Georgian brick buildings hung with ivy. A $70-million library renovation was completed in 2003. Watch for more improvements here, due to gifts of $6.5 million from former philosophy professor Walter Cerf to the arts program, and $10 million from alumni Claire and Leonard Tow.

The roster of its graduates from the mid-twentieth century is replete with an extraordinary number of Nobel Prize winners, U.S. senators, artists, actors, and authors. And Brooklyn College's time-honored tradition of providing a top-flight education to otherwise disadvantaged students continues today. More than half of Brooklyn College students qualify for financial aid. The college's creative writing program, deemed one of the best in the city, is led by Pulitzer Prize–winning novelist Michael Cunningham.

For the public at large, old flicks, theater, dance, lectures, and even job seminars are available at Brooklyn College. There are wonderful inexpensive performances for children and adults at **Brooklyn College Performing Arts Center,** also known as **BCBC** (see below). Area residents can get a community membership allowing limited access to the library.

🎓 BROOKLYN COLLEGE ACADEMY, 350 Coney Island Ave.

They jokingly call it the "big island school," because this high school draws many immigrants from Trinidad, Jamaica, the Dominican Republic, and Puerto Rico (although also from Bangladesh, Pakistan, and India). Students start at a different campus, called Bridges to Brooklyn, on Coney Island Avenue, and, in eleventh grade, classes move to the Brooklyn College campus. (Source: *New York City's Best Public High Schools: A Parents' Guide*–Second Edition, by C. Hemphill with P. Wheaton and J. Wayans.)

🎭 BROOKLYN CENTER FOR THE PERFORMING ARTS. Whitman Hall, Brooklyn College, intersection of Hillel Pl. and Campus Rd. For a season brochure and subscription, call 951-4600 ext. 25. For single tickets, call 951-4500, Tu–Sa 1–6 p.m. Select performances at Ticketmaster: 212-307-7171. For all info: www.brooklyn center.com.

More than eighty excellent and affordable classical and world music, dance, family, and theater performances make their way here each year. Well-known names have included Alvin Ailey, Itzhak Perlman, Dionne Warwick, and the New York Philharmonic. (See Family Time below)

BROOKLYN DODGERS AND EBBETS FIELD. Empire Blvd.

The Jackie Robinson Apartment complex, so-called after America's first, and legendary, black major league baseball player (a Brooklyn Dodger), covers over most of what was the home ballpark for the Brooklyn Dodgers. Ebbets Field, opened in 1913 in Flatbush, remained home to "dem bums" until they moved to Los Angeles in 1957. Both the ballpark and the team are Brooklyn cultural icons.

As for the mythology of the Brooklyn Dodgers—and their enthusiastic, eccentric fans—entire books have been devoted to the subject. With all their foibles and antics, they were the most human of competitors, they were beloved—and they are sorely missed. (See **Brooklyn Cyclones**, in the Coney Island chapter.)

⊘ ☺ BROOKLYN TERMINAL MARKET. Main gate is on Foster Ave. near E. 87th St., 444-5700 or 968-8434, daily 7 a.m.–6 p.m. (Take Exit 13 off the Belt Pkwy., go north on Rockaway Pkwy., then left on Foster Ave. to the main gate.)

This market actually is in Canarsie, but close to Flatbush. This big, bustling wholesale food and plant market, in operation since 1945, is a great place for showing kids where the store owners go shopping. Lots of people like the pickles and ambience here better than what they find on Manhattan's Lower East Side.

🎓 EDWARD R. MURROW HIGH SCHOOL. 1600 Ave. L., 258-9283, www.murrowhs.org.

About 3,500 kids attend this ethnically and socially diverse, progressive public high school. There are strong programs in music and art, with screened admissions, an award-winning chess team, no team sports, more girls than boys, and "very good" college admissions. Any student living in Brooklyn may apply. (Source: *New York City's Best Public High Schools: A Parent's Guide*—Second Edition, by C. Hemphill with P. Wheaton and J. Wayans.)

ERASMUS HIGH ACADEMY/ERASMUS HIGH SCHOOL MUSEUM OF EDUCATION. 911 Flatbush Ave., bet. Church and Snyder Aves., 282-7804, The museum is open during school hours; for more info, call 282-8079, ext. 67160 or 47200 www.erasmushall.org.

Once called "the Eton of High Schools," Erasmus is one of New York's most famous high schools. Opened by the Flatbush Reformed Dutch Church in 1786, it became a public school one hundred years later, as part of the nation's emphasis on providing education for all children. Thousands of ambitious, upwardly mobile, sometimes brilliant children of European immigrants were educated and Americanized here. Its alumni include a veritable Who's Who list of achievements, from Alexander Hamilton to Barbara Streisand. Inside the original Georgian-Federal building with a columned porch, visitors can view old yearbooks, desks, and framed photos of famous alumni.

☺ FAMILY TIME Performances. Brooklyn Center for the Performing Arts. Whitman Hall, Brooklyn College, intersection of Hillel Place and Campus Rd., 951-4500, www.brooklyncenter.com.

From puppet shows to musical concerts, this is a wonderful program for children and parents. Subscriptions are available. (See **Brooklyn Center for the Performing Arts**, above).

FLATBUSH REFORMED DUTCH CHURCH. 890 Flatbush Ave. corner of Church Ave., 284-5140.

A New York City landmark, the Flatbush Reformed Dutch Church was built in the 1790s. It has the unique distinction of occupying the site of one of the longest continuous religious congregations in the City of New York.

FLATBUSH TOWN HALL. 35 Snyder Ave. near Flatbush Ave.

This New York City landmark is a remnant of the days when Flatbush was an independent community, two decades before Brooklyn made the fateful decision to become part of New York City (which some Brooklynites now regret).

FLATLANDS DUTCH REFORMED CHURCH. 3931 Kings Hwy. at 40th St., 252-5540.

The original congregation in 1654, but the existing structure was built in 1796. This New York City landmark church has held a Sunday service every week for the last 345 years!

HOMES OF ARTHUR MILLER. 1277 Ocean Pkwy. bet. L and M Aves. and 1350 E. 3rd St.

Acclaimed author Arthur Miller moved here as a teenager with his family from Manhattan's Upper West Side in the 1920s. They lived here briefly and then moved to nearby 1350 E. 3rd St., which reportedly became the setting for *Death of a Salesman.*

JAMES MADISON HIGH SCHOOL. 3787 Bedford Ave., 758-7200, www.nycenet.edu/hs_directory.

Another Flatbush institution, James Madison is a well-regarded public high school. However, it gets less attention than others, because Madison takes few students from outside the neighborhood school zone.

JOHANNES VAN NUYSE HOUSE. 1041 E. 22nd St. bet. Aves. J and I.

Travel back in time, away from the cars and commerce, to this typical Dutch Colonial farmhouse, a New York City landmark that was erected in 1800. It was built by the son of Joost and Elizabeth Van Nuyse, whose house, remarkably, is also still standing in this area.

JOOST AND ELIZABETH VAN NUYSE HOUSE (COE HOUSE). 1128 E. 34th St. near the intersection of Kings Highway and Flatbush Ave.

Built before 1792, the Dutch Colonial–style Joost and Elizabeth Van Nuyse House is the sole remnant of what was Joost's eighty-five-acre farm in this area. It is a New York City landmark.

KOSHER GYM. 1800 Coney Island Ave. off Ave. N, 376-3535, www.machers.com/KosherGym/.

Mostly, this book doesn't list gyms and health clubs. But what in the world makes a gym kosher? Is it the kosher snack bar? Maybe a curtain between men and women's workout spaces? Neither. Kosher Gym just has different hours for men and women.

☛ **TIP: Machers Web site** http://www.machers.com/tour/midwood
Check out this Web site for a video street tour of Midwood, virtual shopping, humor, directories of stores, restaurants, places of worship, and more, geared to the Orthodox Jewish community.

LOEW'S KING. Flatbush Ave. corner of Beverly Rd.

Anyone who grew up in Jewish Flatbush will remember Loew's. It was a fabulous, ornate, enormous movie house built with all the panache of the Roaring Twenties.

MADRASSAS AND YESHIVAS

Curiously, there are probably more orthodox Muslim and Jewish schools in the Midwood and Coney Island Avenue sections of Flatbush than in any other single area of New York City. There are a dozen or more schools for religious Jewish boys, from pre-K to college, called yeshivas, and several Muslim religious schools, called madrassas. In many such schools of both religions, boys and girls are educated separately.

MAKKI MASJID AND MUSLIM COMMUNITY CENTER. Coney Island Ave. bet. Glenwood and Parkville.

One of many mosques in Brooklyn, Makki Masjid and Muslim Community Center is reportedly the largest Pakistani mosque in New York City. You'll know it by its size, and the eye-catching green columns and signage that's been affixed to an otherwise unremarkable brick building. The mosque is in the center of several blocks of Muslim shops, with colorful signs in Arabic script over the barbershop, sari store, and jewelry stores as well.

After the September 11 attacks, this section of Brooklyn underwent dramatic changes, with some residents leaving, some staying discreetly indoors. Police were stationed at the mosque for protection after children had been harassed.

♫ **MARTIN LUTHER KING JUNIOR CONCERT SERIES.** Wingate Field. Winthrop St. bet. Brooklyn and Kingston Aves., across from Kings County Hospital, 469-1912, www.brooklynconcerts.com.

There are seven summer concerts held in Flatbush's Wingate Field, featuring such headliners as Gladys Knight, The Count Basie Orchestra, and The Brooklyn Philharmonic. Don't miss the July annual gospel night, or the classical soul night with such performers as the Isley Brothers, or the August Caribbean Carnival.

🎓 MIDWOOD HIGH SCHOOL. 2839 Bedford Ave., 487-7000.

This public high school is a hybrid. It's simultaneously a neighborhood school and home to several selective science and humanities programs. It draws 3,760 ethnically and socially diverse students borough-wide, and occasionally receives national acclaim.

There are extensive programs in sports, theater, and extracurricular activities. Advanced students take courses at Brooklyn College across the street. About 325 students are admitted each year to the prestigious medical science program, from which participants are also drawn for Midwood's often-successful Intel Science Talent Search. College admissions are "very good." It's overcrowded, however, say the experts, which results in complicated scheduling.

(Source: *New York City's Best Public High Schools: A Parents' Guide: Second Edition,* by C. Hemphill with P. Wheaton and J. Wayans.)

NBC STUDIOS. E. 14th St. off Ave. M, 780-6400. For information, call NBC public relations in Manhattan 212-664-4444.

Some of the earliest silent films were made in this building, the old Vitagraph Studios. Mary Pickford had a house built on the corner of nearby Ditmas Avenue and Rugby Road, so she could live it up in style while filming here. The original *Peter Pan* was filmed here in the 1950s. Sammy Davis Jr. recorded shows here in the 1960s, and this also was the base of operations for *The Cosby Show* during its heyday in the mid-1980s. The soap opera *Another World* was video-taped and edited here for over thirty-five years.

🎓 PUBLIC SCHOOLS.

Among those considered New York City's "best public elementary schools" are PS 230 (1 Ablemarle Road), PS 139 (330 Rugby Road), PS 217 (1100 New Kirk Avenue), PS 193 (2515 Avenue), and PS 6 (43 Snyder Avenue). Call 927-5125 for information about programs for gifted children. (Source: *New York City's Best Public Elementary Schools,* 2002, by C. Hemphill with P. Wheaton.)

🎪 ☺ RUSSIAN/AMERICAN KIDS CIRCUS. 266-0202, www.rakidscircus.org.

Who doesn't love a circus? But this is something special: the performers are kids, and their trainers award-winning pros from the old-school Russian circus. If you can, get a ticket to one of these shows, to watch a group of ten or twenty young performers (many of them Russian émigrés), ages six to sixteen, juggle, clown around on unicycles, spin plates, and do amazing acrobatics.

Here's the story: Award-winning Russian circus pro and former star of the world-famous Moscow Circus, Alex Berenchtein came to the United States in 1990. By 1994, along with his wife and mother-in-law, he'd started a circus school in Brooklyn, with the dream of transplanting the discipline and skills of the old Russian circus. The performance troupe, now known as the Russian/American Kids Circus, practices and performs under the expert guidance of several Moscow Circus veterans. The kids perform in venues across North America.

SEPHARDIC COMMUNITY CENTER. Ocean Pkwy. at Ave. L, 627-9567.

The local Jewish Sephardic community built this multimillion-dollar community center, in part as a way to keep the young people close to home—and likely to find spouses in the community. Traditions remain strong here; young women often marry right out of high school, while men go into business or pursue higher education and professions.

SHAARE ZION CONGREGATION. 2022 Ocean Pkwy. bet. Ave. T and U, 376-0009.

A large synagogue that's central to the life of the Syrian Jewish community. (See box, p. 280.)

SINGER AND SINGER HARDWARE. 1266 Flatbush Ave., 859-7700, M–Sa 8 a.m.–4:45 p.m.

This hardware store is, reputedly, the place where the great escape artist of all time, Harry Houdini, bought his locks, chains, and other props for his bizarre escapades.

SUBWAY STATION AT AVENUE H.

This subway station (the Q train) is nearly a hundred years old, one of a handful of remaining wooden stations in New York City. The community is attempting to get the circa-1906 building designated a historic landmark, but the MTA considers the station a fire hazard. Stay tuned.

VIDEO CENTER OF ARTS PERFORMANCES IN THEATRES, INC. (VIDCAPT). 1350-A Flatbush Ave., 338-9120, www.caribbeanamericanfoods.com.

The mission of this nonprofit organization is to promote Caribbean culture and experience. They put on great events, such as **Caribbean Craft and Food Fair in Prospect Park** and a new program of biweekly food tours, called **Caribbean Spice Tours**. Contact them for their directory of Caribbean restaurants. (See E. Flatbush section, page 270.)

WATT SAMAKKI DHAMMIKARM. 26 Rugby Rd. off Caton Ave.

A Cambodian temple and related school, indicative of the diversity of the neighborhood, sit on this residential street, one block away from historic nineteenth-century homes of industrial barons.

☺ **WYCKOFF HOUSE MUSEUM.** Clarendon Rd. and Ralph Ave. at E. 59th St., 629-5400, M–F by appointment. Call for schedule of events.

One of the oldest buildings in New York City, restored to reflect the lifestyles of wealthy Dutch settlers of the 1650s, this historic oasis is worth visiting. Today there are lectures, weekend craft sessions, children's story hours, and outdoor programs held on a large lawn. Standing here all those years, the Wyckoff House is a remainder of all the social configurations Brooklyn has witnessed: from a rural Dutch colonial farming settlement to a retreat for wealthy nineteenth-century industrialists, to a haven for Jewish, Italian, and other immigrants in search of the American dream, to today's urbanized hodgepodge of yentas, yuppies, Caribbean islanders, African-Americans, and Eastern European immigrants. Cultural events are held here, including summer concerts.

YESHIVA OF FLATBUSH. 919 E. 10th St.

This is one of New York's best-known Jewish day schools, where students study in both English and Hebrew.

ENTERTAINMENT

✪ 🎬 **BROOKLYN CENTER CINEMA.** Whitman Hall, Brooklyn College, intersection of Hillel Pl. and Campus Rd., 951-4610 or 951-4600. Call for show times. Tickets are only $5; free for sneak previews.

Film buffs! In an era when many Manhattan revival theaters are closing down, Brooklyn's Walt Whitman Hall is going strong. This is Brooklyn's first and only retrospective movie house, complete with seating for thousands and a forty-foot-wide-by-two-story-high CinemaScope screen.

🎬 **KENT TRIPLEX MOVIE THEATER.** 1170 Coney Island Ave. near Ave. H, 338-3371. Call for show times.

This local triplex is close to both the Ditmas Park and Midwood areas and not far from Prospect Park. Ticket prices are reduced substantially for matinees.

🎬 **LOEWS CINEPLEX KINGS PLAZA SIXPLEX.** 5201 Flatbush Ave. at Ave. U. at Kings Plaza, 253-1111.

A six-theater movie house that is close to Kings Plaza shopping and area restaurants.

PARKS AND PLAYGROUNDS
✪ ☺ **BIKE PATH.**

A bike lane runs down a special sidewalk path along Ocean Parkway all the way from Prospect Park to the Atlantic Ocean Boardwalk, accessible at the corner of Brighton Beach Avenue and Ocean Parkway. It's a wonderful, if slow, ride (due to many traffic lights) and safe for accompanied kids, or teens riding alone. Bike riding on the Atlantic Ocean Boardwalk is not allowed after 10 a.m.

☺ **COLONEL DAVID MARCUS PARK.** Ave. B bet. E. 3rd St. and Ocean Pkwy.

This spacious and recently renovated playground is a wonderful find, and close to several interesting shopping areas, such as Avenue M and Kings Highway.

☺ **KOLBERT PLAYGROUND.** Aves. L and M bet. E. 17th and E. 18th Sts.

OCEAN PARKWAY MALL. Ocean Pkwy. from Prospect Park to the Atlantic Ocean.

Ocean Parkway is one of the finest boulevards for riding or strolling in New York City. It was designed by Frederick Law Olmsted and Calvert Vaux, creators of Central Park and Prospect Park. Along the way you'll pass through a middle- and upper-middle-class, largely Orthodox Jewish, area.

ACCOMMODATIONS

DEKOVEN SUITES (see p. 15).

EVE'S BED & BREAKFAST (see p. 15).

HONEY'S HOME BED & BREAKFAST (see p. 16).

MIDWOOD SUITES (see p. 16).

STRANGE DOG INN (see p. 17).

WESTMINSTER SUITES (see p. 18).

Prospect Park South, Ditmas Park, Prospect-Lefferts Gardens, Albemarle-Kenmore Terraces, and Coney Island Avenue

ABOUT THE NEIGHBORHOOD

If you have the idea that Brooklyn is all old brownstones, a trip to Prospect Park South, Ditmas Park, and the other nearby historical areas will turn that notion on its head. You'll think you're dreaming when you first spot elegant Victorian mansions with spacious porches, decorative turrets, bay windows, stained glass, and well-kept lawns throughout the area. Busy two-career couples of the twenty-first century can only imagine the pampered lifestyle once enjoyed here. The architecture says it all: sweeping mahogany-banister staircases lead to sumptuous bedroom suites; steep backstairs ascend from the kitchen to third-floor servants' rooms. If you can, book onto the **House Tour of Victorian Homes in Flatbush**. Otherwise, note the addresses of **Historic Homes** below, and take a walk.

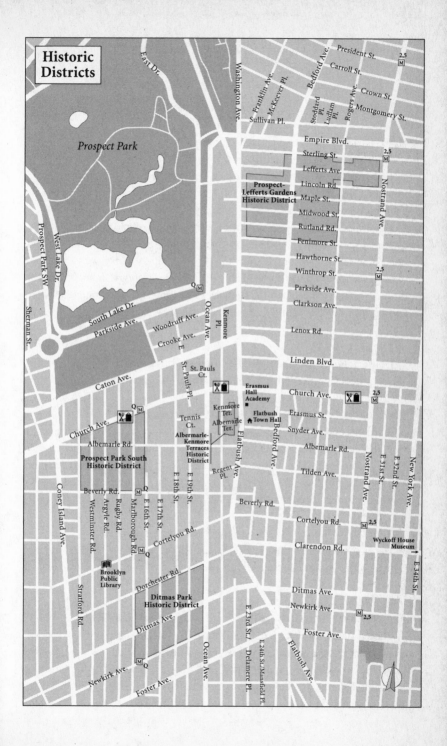

Historic Districts

Prospect Park

East Dr.

West Lake Dr.

Prospect Park SW

Sherman St.

South Lake Dr.

Parkside Ave.

Caton Ave.

Washington Ave.

Franklin Ave.

McKeever Pl.

Sullivan Pl.

Bedford Ave.

Carroll St.

President St.

Crown St.

Rogers Ave.

Montgomery St.

Stoddard Pl.

Ludlam Pl.

Empire Blvd.

Prospect-Lefferts Gardens Historic District

Sterling St.

Lefferts Ave.

Lincoln Rd.

Maple St.

Midwood St.

Rutland Rd.

Fenimore St.

Hawthorne St.

Winthrop St.

Parkside Ave.

Clarkson Ave.

Lenox Rd.

Linden Blvd.

Nostrand Ave.

Woodruff Ave.

Crooke Ave.

Ocean Ave.

Kenmore Pl.

St. Pauls Ct.

St. Pauls Pl.

Tennis Ct.

Kenmore Ter.

Albemarle Ter.

Albemarle-Kenmore Terraces Historic District

Regent Pl.

Flatbush Ave.

Erasmus Hall Academy

Flatbush Town Hall

Church Ave.

Erasmus St.

Snyder Ave.

Albemarle Rd.

Tilden Ave.

Bedford Ave.

Church Ave.

Albemarle Rd.

Prospect Park South Historic District

Beverly Rd.

Coney Island Ave.

Westminster Rd.

Argyle Rd.

Rugby Rd.

Marlborough Rd.

E 16th St.

E 17th St.

E 18th St.

E 19th St.

Cortelyou Rd.

Beverly Rd.

Brooklyn Public Library

Dorchester Rd.

Ditmas Park Historic District

Stratford Rd.

Ditmas Ave.

Newkirk Ave.

Foster Ave.

Ocean Ave.

E 23rd St.

Delamere Pl.

E 24th St./Mansfield Pl.

Flatbush Ave.

Cortelyou Rd.

Clarendon Rd.

Wyckoff House Museum

E 34th St.

Ditmas Ave.

Newkirk Ave.

Foster Ave.

Nostrand Ave.

E 31st St.

E 32nd St.

New York Ave.

2,5 M

POINTS OF CULTURAL INTEREST

Historic Homes

Take your pick from among many delicious fantasies: the so-called Japanese house (131 Buckingham Road); the lovely home where the movie *Sophie's Choice* was filmed (101 Rugby Road); the "Honeymoon Cottage" (305 Rugby Road), built for one of the Guggenheim daughters; and for gardeners, the private botanic gardens at the rear of 145 Argyle Road. Or walk down Albemarle Road, off Stratford Road, to see former homes of the industrial elite. Number 1519 Argyle Road was built by the president of the American Can Company in 1905; down the street at 1505 is a Queen Anne–style home built by Elmer Sperry, of Sperry-Rand fame, back in 1990. The architect of Manhattan's famous Chrysler Building designed the Spanish-style home at number 1215, for the Fruit of the Loom family. It's small wonder that lots of movies and even commercials are filmed in these picturesque homes. For a self-directed walking tour, contact the **Flatbush Development Corporation** (859–4831) and ask for their "Flatbush" brochure, or e-mail guide@fdconline.org.

SPECIAL EVENTS.

House Tours of the landmarked districts are run in the spring. Call Flatbush Development Corporation, 859-4632, or e-mail guide@fdconline.org.

HOUSE TOUR OF VICTORIAN HOMES IN FLATBUSH. To book, call 859-3800. April.

Residents open the doors of their historic homes one day a year for the Victorian Flatbush House Tour. See for yourself how splendidly the well-heeled early Brooklynites lived. The Flatbush Development Corporation organizes this four-hour shuttle-bus tour of a dozen private homes that are restored, and original mansions dating from the turn of the twentieth century.

JAZZ@FOUR. 856-7436, 797-0635, 3rd Sunday of each month, jazzatfour@nyc.rr.com.

Here's something unusual: jazz performed in the parlor of a house every third Sunday of the month. About forty people come to sit and listen to live jazz. It's cozy and accessible.

KNICKERBOCKER FIELD CLUB. 114E. 18th St. at Church Ave. and Tennis C., 856-5098.

Tucked away behind some drab residential blocks in the heart of Brooklyn's Caribbean community is one of the most unusual nooks and crannies in Brooklyn: an old tennis club from the 1880s that's still in operation. The city has grown up around it. But as you walk through the gates at the end of Tennis Court Road and down a rutted driveway, you are suddenly in an older, greener, more genteel

Brooklyn of the past. Tennis balls plop contentedly, and the train rattling by might as well be on its way to the Hamptons. Pictures of the old wooden Victorian clubhouse, which burned down, can be seen inside the new, more utilitarian, cinderblock, fireproof one. Classes are available. If you're not taking a class, you need to join as a member, but as the place is indifferently managed, you may need to go in person to get the details. See old photos at www.knic.com/PostCard/9.htm.

PROSPECT LEFFERTS GARDENS HOUSE AND GARDEN TOUR. 284-6210 or 462-0024, 1st Su in June, noon–5 p.m., $15 in advance, $20 day of tour.

The annual house tour is an opportunity to discover what's behind closed doors. In 2003 it included a classical revival row house with a red-tile roof and tinted plaster, and an Arts and Crafts house with tiled fireplaces, ornate entry hall, and a twenty-foot-wide parlor.

AREA RESTAURANTS

♪ **LOS MARIACHI'S.** 805 Coney Island Ave. near Cortelyou Rd., 826-3388, Su–Th 10:30 a.m.–11:30 p.m., F–Sa 10:30–1 a.m.

Gringos love the big portions of authentic Mexican food and live mariachi music (weekends only; call ahead to make sure), which make for a festive ambience. Entrées run from $5 to $15.

● **MIKE'S INTERNATIONAL.** 552 Flatbush Ave. bet. Lincoln and Maple Sts., 856-7034, M–W 8 a.m.–11 p.m., Th–Sa 8 a.m.–midnight, Su 8 a.m.–9 p.m.

Anyone who knows anything about Jamaica knows about spicy jerk chicken and pork. Mike's serves a full menu of specialties, such as oxtail stew, curries, and powerful-tasting juices of sorrel and soursop, along with live music on summer weekends.

PUNJAB RESTAURANT. 691 Coney Island Ave. near Ave C., 856-6207, 24–7.

This bare-bones joint (with $5 entrées) caters to local immigrants from the Indian subcontinent with curries and kebabs. The twenty-four-hour **Punjab Grocery** sells spices, rice, and other ethnic foods a few blocks down Coney Island Avenue (434-9310).

RUG-B. 1301 Cortelyou Rd. at Argyle Rd., 284-0024, daily 5 p.m.–midnight.

Families, businesspeople, and groups of friends have welcomed this airy corner restaurant, which specializes in sophisticated Caribbean food and combinations of European and Caribbean dishes. It's conveniently located next to a playground, so there's somewhere fun to take the little ones who get bored with dinner-table conversation.

SHOPPING

BANIA. 602 Coney Island Ave. near Beverley Rd., 853-2525, M–Th 10 a.m.–midnight, F–Su 8 a.m.–midnight.

Steam your heart out in an old-fashioned Russian-style *schvitzer*, located closer to Prospect Park than Brighton Beach. The clientele is about 75 percent European and Russian at this new bath house, which offers you a full day of steam rooms and dunk baths for $20. The steam rooms are coed, so bring a bathing suit or a cover-up. For extra, you can get a massage or chow down on borscht, herring, and shish kebab.

BICYCLE LAND. 424 Coney Island Ave. bet. Church and Caton Aves., 633-0820, M–F 11 a.m.–7 p.m., Sa 11 a.m.–6 p.m., Su 11 a.m.–4 p.m.

BMXers will go crazy at Bicycle Land—this family-owned and run shop is chock-a-block with gear that will have hot-doggers spinning out the door and around Prospect Park. While BMX bikes dominate, owner Carlos Cortes, a former Colombian bike racer, also sells several high-end road bikes, as well as kiddie bikes.

GREENMARKET. 330 Rugby Rd. near Cortelyou Rd., Sa 8 a.m.–6 p.m., July–Nov.

A new greenmarket has recently opened here, with lots of wonderful produce from local farms.

East Flatbush

ABOUT EAST FLATBUSH

American vacationers by the millions have fallen in love with the Caribbean. Music born of the islands seems almost as American as apple pie, from Harry Belafonte's calypso "Day-O" in the "Banana Boat Song" to the reggae and salsa beats that influence modern jazz and permeate rock and roll. This cultural and human traffic travels a two-way street; today Brooklyn is home to hundreds of thousands of pizza-eating, subway-riding islanders from more than thirty different nations.

For the attentive visitor, it's the music here that is most surprising. First of all, there are a *lot* of music stores—more along a mile-long strip than in just about any other neighborhood in Brooklyn or in most of New York City, outside the professional music district in the West 40s. Among them are a half dozen very specialized **Caribbean music shops,** some with hard-to-find vintage recordings, and others with music from Nigeria, Ghana, Zaire, Cameroon, Ethiopia, and South Africa, along with reggae, *compa* and *zouk,* and *soca* and *calypso* from the islands.

Another attraction is unquestionably culinary, if you don't mind eating in simple places with no formal décor. It's exciting that **Caribbean Spice Tours** now offers guided tours of Caribbean eateries. On your own, a walk along **Church Avenue** will bring you to small, informal, and inexpensive eating establishments bubbling over with the true Caribbean flavors. Start at Flatbush Avenue and make your way down a half dozen blocks of this busy street. Be adventuresome: tiny hole-in-the-wall places sometimes do the most serious down-home cooking.

STEEL BANDS

You hear them on Sundays at Drummer's Grove in Prospect Park, in some clubs, in the subway stations, and walking down certain streets where people are practicing. Steel drums are a memorable feature of the **West Indian American Labor Day Parade**.

Steel drums, more correctly known as "pans," are a particularly Caribbean form of music. Unlike most drums, they are not only percussive but can carry a melodic tone. A versatile instrument, pans can be played in groups as small as four or in orchestral groupings upward of a hundred musicians. Some groups play simple tunes; others play classic rock songs. Some pan orchestras have mastered Bach. Often, the pan players are not formally trained musicians; they learn pieces by heart (a prodigious task, if you're playing classical music). This is a tradition that is passed on from generation to generation.

Pans are a new and nonelectronic twentieth-century instrument. There's some disagreement about who, how and when it all started, but one accepted version is that pans were first used as crude metal drums by some rebellious, noise-seeking teenagers in Laventille, a low-income suburb in Trinidad in the late 1930s. One of the youths realized that if he thinned out the metal and made bumps in it, he could make the pans carry a musical pitch.

The trend caught on. By the 1940s, Trinidadians were converting discarded fifty-five-gallon oil-drum barrels into musical instruments, using concave shapes to broaden the musical range of the instruments. Many people, now recognized as pan innovators, contributed to expanding the range of the steel drums. A single pan might have a full chromatic scale. Tuning them is far beyond the "beating of metal" and is considered an art. Born as an invention of poverty, the success of the steel drum as an instrument is a case history of both good musicianship and entrepreneurship.

Steel drum bands debuted as an international sensation in 1951 at a London music festival, leading to exposure on the BBC and a tour in France. Today there are several hundred steel-drum bands in the USA; many are located in Brooklyn. They have colorful names, such as Crossfire Steel, Moods Pan Groove, Tommy Baptiste's Pan Phonicks, and Women in Steel. (See www.WIADCA.com/steel bands.htm for local bands.)

Some of the ingredients of West Indian cuisine reflect the combined African and Indian origins of this culture. *Bammy* is a flatbread made of the cassava root (also the basis of tapioca), which is indigenous to the West Indies; Columbus reportedly feasted on cassava bread given to him by the local Indians. A spinach look-alike called *callaloo* is an indigenous African vegetable said to have been introduced to the Caribbean islands by African slaves. An okra dish with the wonderful name *coo-coo* also has African origins. And exactly what goes into the soft drinks with such erotic names as *Agony: Peanut Punch Plus* and *Front End Lifter and Magnum Explosion Combo*, which are sold at some of the bakeries, is anybody's guess.

HISTORICAL NOTES

Of three hundred thousand West Indian immigrants who arrived in the United States between 1900 and the 1930s, tens of thousands ended up in Brooklyn. Many had a strong work ethic, and they scrimped and saved and eventually bought homes in such neighborhoods as Bedford-Stuyvesant, East Flatbush, and Crown Heights. Following World War II, the flow of immigrants picked up again. Since 1960 well over a half million Caribbean immigrants have sought their fortunes in New York City. According to 2000 Census figures analyzed for the *New York Times*, the West Indian population citywide grew in a decade to comprise a quarter of the city's black population. But they are hardly one united community. Rivalries and tensions are said to run strong, which is not surprising, given the diversity of their backgrounds and native tongues: English in Trinidad, Jamaica, Grenada, and Barbados; Dutch in Aruba and Curaçao; Spanish in Puerto Rico and the Dominican Republic; and French and Creole dialects in Martinique, Guadeloupe, and Haiti. There are many authors who've written well about this community as it has experienced the throes of immigration, including Magdalene Elaine Robinson's poignant *Mama in America*.

POINTS OF CULTURAL INTEREST AND ENTERTAINMENT

SPECIAL EVENTS.
    West Indian American Day Parade.

BAMBOO GARDENS RESTAURANT. E. 95th St. at Ave. L, 272-3175, M–F 11 a.m.–noon, F–Sa 11–12:30 a.m.

    You can get a combo of West Indian and Chinese food here, and live bands playing Caribbean music on some weekend nights, DJs on others. It's in Canarsie, not East Flatbush, but Bamboo is one of the musical hot spots in the community.

Caribbean Culture Organizations

Many nonprofit organizations work to share Caribbean cultures with the American mainstream, bringing art, dance, and theater performances to audiences nationwide. The best known are the organizers of the incredible **West Indian American Labor Day Parade**. Other groups may specialize in a certain island and cultural heritage, such as the **Trinidad and Tobago Folk Arts Institute** (3522 Farragut Rd., 783-6161) and a Haitian drum-and-dance ensemble called **La Troupe Makandal** (621 Rutland Road #4C, 953-6638). Many of the Caribbean culture organizations are located in East Flatbush or nearby Crown Heights. For information on Caribbean folk culture, contact **Brooklyn Arts Council** in Brooklyn Heights.

CARIBBEAN SPICE TOURS. 338-9120.

Launched in 2003, this is a great way to get to see the neighborhood and taste some Caribbean foods. You can choose one of several different routes. Each route will have four or five destinations, for instance, an ice cream factory, a store that carries Caribbean food products you can purchase, and places where you can sit down and eat, too. Organized by **VIDCAPT** (p. 264).

GUYANA FOLK FESTIVAL. Held at **Brooklyn Children's Museum,** 763-6313. August.

This daylong festival of Guyanese culture features masquerade bands, steel bands, dances, and storytelling, as well as delicious ethnic foods. It coincides with the fabulous **West Indian American Carnival** and festivities.

🎓 **PUBLIC SCHOOLS.**

PS 135 (684 Linden Boulevard) and PS 235 (525 Lenox Road) are considered to be among New York City's best public elementary schools. (Source: *New York City's Best Public Elementary Schools*, 2002, by C. Hemphill with P. Wheaton.)

TEMPTATIONS. 2210 Church Ave. bet. Flatbush and Bedford Avs. 856-5946. Th–Su.

Temptations boasts an active list of entertainers, including, for instance, in a given evening, *Fun Factory, Soca Ambassador*, and *Music Research Lab*. The folks at Temptations are deeply involved in the West Indian reggae and dance-hall music scene; they are one of the organizers of the annual Reggae Carifest.

RESTAURANTS AND SPECIALTY FOOD SHOPS

B AND H FRUIT AND VEGETABLE. 5012 Church Ave. corner of Utica Ave., 345-7839. 24/7.

To get the flavor of the neighborhood, check out the wonderful Korean-run multiethnic grocer next to **Hammond's Bakery** (see below). It sells not only the standard array of grapes, carrots, and kiwis one finds everywhere in New York, but also breadfruit, a mind-boggling array of yams with such foreign names as *dasheen* and *edo*, plus salted beef, plantain flour, palm oils, and an international assortment of packaged goods.

BLUE STAR FOOD AND PAPER. 1233 Utica Ave. corner of Ave. D, 629-1250, M–Sa 7 a.m.–4:15 p.m.

Get that BBQ fanatic in your life a small truckload of jerk sauce and Caribbean condiments without going broke at your local gourmet-food store. Blue Star is a wholesale and retail operation that provides a lot of the canned, jarred, pickled and packaged food products that makes this neighborhood a culinary destination for Carib-food junkies.

CHEFFY'S JAMAICAN. 707 Nostrand Ave. corner of Park Pl., 363-9515, M–Sa 10 a.m.–9 p.m.

If you're in the mood for authentic Jamaican food, the locals say you should try Cheffy's. This hole-in-the-wall restaurant in Crown Heights is one of several in the area serving fried dumplings, oxtail stew, fish cakes, cow's feet, goat curry, and more. A full meal runs less than $10 per person.

DANNY & PEPPER JERK CHICKEN. 771 Flatbush Ave. bet. Lenox and Clarkson Aves., 940-9717, daily 9 a.m.–1 a.m.

Just a stone's throw from Parkside side of Prospect Park is one of the two local contenders for the best jerk chicken place in Brooklyn. **Jamaica Inn**, a half mile up Flatbush, is the other. Try them out and choose for yourself!

FLATBUSH FOOD COOPERATIVE. 1318 Cortelyou Rd. bet. Argyle and Rugby Rds., 284-9717, daily 7 a.m.–10 p.m.

Started in 1976, this health-food cooperative has a large selection of organic produce and specialty natural and kosher foods. The co-op is owned and operated by members who get discounts off shelf prices. Unlike in the Park Slope Food Co-op, you don't have to be a member to shop here.

GOLDEN CRUST. 931 Flatbush Ave. at Church Ave., 856-2991, daily 9 a.m.–8 p.m.

A popular Jamaican restaurant, Golden Crust serves home-style meals. Specials are tasty stews of curried goat, curried chicken, or curried oxtail, rice with peas and plantains. The cuisine is authentic—and so is the cooking! There's another, in Downtown Brooklyn on Flatbush Avenue.

🌀 **HAMMOND'S FINGER LICKIN' BAKERY.** 5014 Church Ave. near Utica Ave., 342-5770, M–Sa 8:30 a.m.–7:30 p.m., Su 8:30 a.m.–5 p.m.

While cruising Church Avenue in search of a Caribbean taste, stop here for

Jamaican cinnamon buns, tropical-fruit turnovers, beef patties, and more. All goodies are under $1. The food made at this small bakery is traditional and very tasty. There's another Hammond's, at 1436 Nostrand Avenue.

ITAL SHAK VEGETARIAN RESTAURANT. 989 Nostrand Ave. corner of Empire Blvd., 756-6557, 24/7.

Located near the Sterling Plaza subway stop in Crown Heights, this vegetarian restaurant serves an international menu of vegetarian dishes. It's popular with Rastafarians. The food includes mac cheese, *callaloo*, lo meins, and West Indian stews. If you're into reggae, note that this restaurant hosted a concert by the St. Croix group Midnite, who also appear at S.O.B.

JAMAICA INN. 1135 Flatbush Ave. at Clarendon Ave., 856-4638, daily 9 a.m.–1 a.m.

Food fanatics hell-bent on finding the best jerk chicken takeout joint in Brooklyn swear that Jamaica Inn is one of the two very best, by leaps and bounds. Compare with **Danny & Pepper Jerk Chicken** a half mile down Flatbush.

SYBIL'S BAKERY AND RESTAURANT. 2210 Church Ave. near Flatbush Ave., 469-9049, daily 8 a.m.–11 p.m.

This clean, friendly West Indian (Guyanese) restaurant and bakery is centrally located if you happen to be driving down Flatbush Avenue. The bakery section is filled with sweet coconut bread, doughy cheese rolls, glazed jelly-filled triangles, and *salaras*, red coconut cookies. Sit at the counter, or at one of the green-and-white tables for a meal of baked chicken, stewed fish, codfish cakes, and goat roti curry. Try a few drinks: cane juice, sorrel, ginger beer, *mauby* (from a bark akin to cinnamon). There are Guyanese newspapers, too, for a change of perspective.

VEGGIE CASTLE. 2242 Church Ave. bet. Bedford and Flatbush Aves., 703-1275, daily 9 a.m.–11 p.m.

Surprisingly cheap, healthy vegetarian specials can be found at this local Jamaican eatery, for eating here or taking home. You can get meatless West Indian specials, such as curried stews. The spicy okra is out of this world, and the juice concoctions are worth the trip, if just for a chuckle at their names. It's a colorful, mixed crowd of West Indian Brooklynites.

SHOPPING

THERE'S GREAT MUSIC ON NOSTRAND AVENUE.

Check out the one-and-a-half-mile strip of Nostrand Avenue from Maple Street down to Newkirk Avenue, or from the Sterling Street stop on the 2/5 train to the Newkirk Avenue stop.

For the curious, the adventurous, but particularly the African and Caribbean music enthusiast, Nostrand Avenue offers a wealth of possibilities. There are little music stores that don't advertise what their specialty is, so you'd never guess, until you venture inside, that each offers a highly specialized collection of, say, reggae, or vintage African LPs, or music from Ghana, Nigeria and Senegal—in addition to the latest African and West Indian mega hits that you might find in a chain music store.

Here are a few specialty music shops. Don't be shy about asking questions; the staff know their music and are happy to pop on anything that you might want to hear. The listings are organized by street number, along Nostrand Avenue, for a tour down the street.

🎵 **TIGER'S REGGAE HUT.** 1092 Nostrand Ave. bet. Lincoln Rd. and Maple St., 469-1325, M–Sa 10 a.m.–10 p.m., Su 12 P.M.–7 P.M. Cash only.

Tiger's specializes in anything that has to do with reggae, from live Bob Marley bootlegs to Jamaican flags. The tiny shop is packed with videos and DVDs—comedies, documentaries, carnival recordings, and even porno—from just about every island in the Caribbean. The owner is proud of his collection of "dance-hall videos," which are videotapes of dance parties and events (his are from Haiti, Aruba, St. Lucia, Barbados, Trinidad, and Brazil). These tapes are in high demand, as that's how folks pick up the latest dance moves and hottest fashion tips from back home. Prices are $5–$15.

AFRICAN RECORD CENTRE, MOKASSA DISTRIBUTION LTD. 1194 Nostrand Ave. bet. Fenimore St. and Hawthorne St., 493-4500, daily 9 a.m.–6:30 p.m.

For the vintage and rare African record collector, this store is a gem. African Record Centre, Mokassa Distribution, Ltd. has been around for decades, as have most of its records. Be prepared to do a little digging and you will find a wealth of compact discs, music videos, records, and tapes from Nigeria, Ghana, Zaire, Cameroon, Ethiopia, and South Africa by such prominent Third World artists as Fela Kuti, Franco, and OK Jazz group. There's an extensive collection of popular Haitian music. The knowledgeable staff will play demonstration tapes for you. One of New York City's largest importers and producers of pan-African sounds for over thirty-five years, this shop is a central resource for many musicians. The LPs range from $15 to $20, depending on how rare the item is.

ORIGINAL AFRICAN CARIBBEAN CLOTHING, FOODSTUFF & ACCESSORIES. 1321 Nostrand Ave. bet. Clarkson Ave. and Lenox Rd., 940-8966, daily 10 A.M.–9 P.M. Cash only.

The store's name speaks for itself, and they carry a small but choice selection of African CDs, cassettes, and music videos, mostly from Nigeria, Ghana, and Senegal. Go in and poke around, or watch their newest video from the sidewalk on the TV perched in the window. At $5 a cassette, $7 a videotape, and $10 a CD, this store's a bargain.

PUMPKINS. 1448 Nostrand Ave. bet. Martense St. and Church Ave., 284-9086, M–F 7–11 p.m., Sa 9 p.m.–1 a.m., Su 6 p.m.–10 p.m. No cover, drinks start at $5.

Pumpkins claims to be the longest-running jazz bar in Brooklyn, and it's a jazz haven. It's a place where jazz artists get together after work, that is, after they are finished playing gigs for pay in Manhattan. If you are not familiar with the area, car service is recommended.

FACTOR ANTILLES MIZIK, LTD. 1698 Nostrand Ave. bet. Cortelyou Rd. and Clarendon Rd., 287-9320, M–Sa 11 A.M.–9 P.M. Cash only.

Compa (Haiti) and *zouk* (especially from Martinique and Guadeloupe) are the specialties here, plus a handful of French, Spanish, and African CDs, along with a few posters, cassettes, and flashing earrings. This small space is as much a neighborhood hangout as a music store—the majority of people inside are men with beers, not customers. Don't go if you're in a hurry, because the employees are on island time, and just getting their attention can take a few minutes. CDs cost $10; cassettes are $5.

JW PRODUCTIONS. 2833 Church Ave. bet. Nostrand Ave. and Lloyd St., 693-9261, M–Th 10 A.M.–8 P.M., F–Sa 10 A.M.–9 P.M.

This is the place to go for *soca* and *calypso* from all the islands, particularly Trinidad. JW feels like a Midtown Manhattan shop, with higher prices but a wider selection. JW also has a sizeable collection of African and American LPs and CDs. Prices are moderate (CDs $13–$25; LPs $8).

Also:

♫ ✪ **RUDY KING, STEEL DRUM MAKER.** www.WIADCA.com.

This elderly gentleman was honored by City Lore, an nonprofit organization, for bringing steel drums to New York over fifty years ago. He's still making them.

DISCMART BLACK MIND. 610 New York Ave. corner of Rutland Rd., 774-5800, Tu—Sa 11 a.m.—7 p.m.

African and world culture books and records are sold at Discmart, one of Brooklyn's premier black book shops. In tune with cultural trends in the intellectual and spiritual life of diasporan Africans, the store has a large collection of books on the Nigerian-based Yoruba religion and its manifestations in the New World, including Cuba and Brazil. The store receives inquiries from major museums, scholars, and Europeans who are interested in the syncretism of this religion. There is also a good selection of African writers and sounds, some produced by Mokassa Distribution Company, in addition to Caribbean and Haitian imports.

DORSEY'S PICTURE FRAME AND ART GALLERY. 553 Rogers Ave. bet. Hawthorne and Fenimore Sts., 771-3803, daily 1—8 p.m.

Framing is the business at hand at Dorsey's, but there's also a small display of artwork by Caribbean and other African diasporan artists.

STRAKER RECORDS. 242 Utica Ave. bet. Lincoln and St. John's Pl., 756-0040, M—F 11 a.m.—8 p.m., Sa—Su 10 a.m.—8 p.m.

There's a good selection of calypso, reggae, and soca sounds. At this and other select area stores, you can often buy tickets for local entertainment.

Midwood

ABOUT MIDWOOD

This middle swath of Brooklyn is a complex layering of different ethnic groups across a wide range of nationalities: Pakistani, Israeli, Bangladeshi, Russian, Afghani, Chinese, Syrian, Turkish, and American, to cite a few. English may be the common language here, but it is certainly not the mother tongue of many residents.

There's economic diversity, too. Within five minutes, you can drive from million-dollar homes on Ocean Parkway to divey apartments under a rumbling railroad bridge. Gritty Coney Island Avenue has a jumble of functional businesses: tire and car-repair shops, mom-and-pop grocery stores, insurance companies, plumbers, funeral homes, and discount shoe outlets. Yet between Coney Island Avenue and Ocean Parkway there are some breathtakingly beautiful homes, with small manicured lawns and separate garages. And, abutting them, are many blocks of plain working-class housing. We've included several interesting pockets within Midwood:

CONEY ISLAND AVENUE The blocks between Avenue H and Parkville on Coney Island are intensely Middle Eastern. This area is quite different from the Atlantic Avenue Middle Eastern strip anchored by **Sahadi's,** where most of the businesses are owned by people who hail from the Levantine Middle East. Here the immigrants are more recently arrived, and tend to come from Bangladesh, Pakistan, and Afghanistan. Less English is spoken. The exotic condiments, enormous sacks of rice, and bulk containers of strong spices sold here are like those sold on Atlantic Avenue. But these are meant not for tourists and Anglos, but rather for the kitchens of the local residents. Family networks are strong: there's a small empire of shops and eateries by the same name: **Punjab Grocery, Punjab Sweets,** and **Punjab Restaurant.**

OCEAN PARKWAY Drive along Ocean Parkway on a Friday or Saturday evening and you'll see a constant flow of Jewish families shuttling back and forth between home and one of Midwood's many synagogues. Dubbed "kosher yuppie land" by one New York daily, Midwood recently has undergone a youthful gentrification.

There is a great deal of Jewish cultural life here. Midwood, where actor-director Woody Allen went to high school, is home to both Sephardic (Middle Eastern and South European) and Ashkenazic (Northern European) Jews. The Ashkenazic presence is visible in Midwood's old German bakeries and the world-famous Flatbush and Mirrer yeshivas (religious schools). Members of the wealthy Jewish community that have settled around Ocean Parkway are mainly Syrians from Aleppo and Damascus. Their style and affluence are apparent in the **Sephardic Community Center** and **Sha'are Zion Synagogue** on Ocean Parkway. Demand for housing within walking distance of the Sephardic synagogues is so strong that the prices of some homes have shot easily past the million-dollar mark.

AVENUES J AND M Tevye of *Fiddler on the Roof* would have felt at home here. Avenue J reflects old Jewish Flatbush. In its past, Avenue J served a thriving German and Eastern European Jewish community; it still helps to know a little Yiddish here. In the clothing shops you are likely to hear talk of *hassanas* (weddings) and *shidduchs* (arranged marriages) as well as bar mitzvahs. Typical of Brooklyn, where Jews and Italians have lived side by side for decades, the neighborhood used to be partly Italian.

Avenue M is a thriving shopping street with a mix of local stores and expensive boutiques catering to both the affluent Syrian community and escaped-to-the-suburbs ex-Brooklynites—many of whom still make shopping pilgrimages back to Brooklyn in search of good prices and storekeepers who know them on a first-name basis. Incongruously located near a kosher fast-food joint called Chapanosh (which in Hebrew translates to "Grab-a-Bite") is the old Vitagraph movie studio, now used by **NBC**. Silent-movie stars Mary Pickford and Laurel and Hardy filmed at the Vitagraph; later, *The Perry Como Show*, *The Steve Allen Show*, and *The Cosby Show* were produced here. The nearby **Edward R. Murrow High School** specializes in communications.

KINGS HIGHWAY Kings Highway has been a major shopping thoroughfare for decades. The two-story buildings that line the avenue date from the 1930s, when the strip was first built; note the decorative Alexandria at 809 Kings Highway. The section of Kings Highway from about East 2nd Street to East 9th Street is part of the Syrian Jewish enclave; among expensive clothing shops, Middle Eastern grocery stores carry the names of Israeli and Lebanese cities: Bat Yam, Holon, and Beirut. On Saturday most stores in this area are closed for the Sabbath. Past East 9th Street, the numerous clothing and shoe stores serve the general public and are open on Saturday.

HOW IT GOT ITS NAME From the Dutch Midwout, or "Middle Woods." In fact, many streets are still tree-lined.

POINTS OF CULTURAL INTEREST

There's a ton of local color in this neighborhood, from the **Kosher Gym** to the **Makki Mosque.** And you will find such New York City historic landmarks as

THE SMALL WORLD OF SYRIAN JEWS

A remarkable community of Syrian Jews has made the area near Ocean Parkway their home. Clannish, enterprising, and with a proud sense of their three-thousand-year Jewish tradition, this community has built its own schools, synagogues, and a cemetery, a large community center, and even summer-resort communities where entire extended families retreat to the beach, such as Deal, New Jersey. The Syrian Jews of Brooklyn, who trace their roots to Damascus and Aleppo, are known for large, sometimes lavish weddings unusual both in size (typically, hundreds of guests) and duration (they often start at 10 p.m. and last for hours). Many have become successes in business; household-name companies from Jordache Jeans to Duane Reade were started by Syrian Jews.

The first wave of Syrian Jewish immigrants arrived in the United States in the early twentieth century, seeking economic opportunity and relief from conscription, and many settled in Bensonhurst; a second wave fled persecution after the birth of the State of Israel in 1948. There are only several dozen Sephardic communities in the United States; the Brooklyn group is the largest Syrian Jewish community outside Israel.

Johannes Van Nuyse House, Joost and Elizabeth Van Nuyse House, and the old Flatlands Dutch Reformed Church, all remnants of Brooklyn's earliest days. More contemporary sites include the NBC Television Studios and Midwood High School, at Bedford Avenue and Glenwood Road, which is one of New York City's premier public high schools.

SPECIAL EVENTS.

Believe it or not, a Mardi Gras along Avenue M (June).

MIDWOOD RESTAURANTS

☛ TIP: If you are looking for a kosher meal, you can find one on Kings Highway. Or dial 877-WHY-KOSHER to find out about a directory of kosher restaurants.

Avenues J and M

CARAVILLE. 1910 Ave. M near E. 19th St., 339-2540, daily 6 a.m.–midnight.

Caraville serves good kosher-style food and a wide range of other dishes, ranging from Italian veal dishes to crab-meat salad and pancakes. A dead ringer for a Greek diner in terms of low prices and vast menu, but with more comfortable ambience.

⭐ DIFARA'S PIZZERIA. 1424 Ave. J near E. 15th St., 258-1367, daily 11 a.m.–10 p.m. Cash only.

Amazingly, this pizzeria near Brooklyn College hasn't received the same accolades as Grimaldi's, because everyone who's tried DiFara's incredibly fresh sauces and handmade pizzas with fresh mozzarella agrees it is one of the borough's best pizzerias. Don't come with a date if he/she is more impressed with décor than food, but this joint is a foodie's heaven.

ESSEX ON CONEY DELI. 1359 Coney Island Ave. corner of Ave. J, 253-1002, Su–Th 9 a.m.–12 a.m., F 9 a.m.–2:30 p.m., Su noon–5 p.m., closed Sa. Kosher.

Wonder of wonders, the corned beef is lean, the pickles are just right, and the service is peppered with friendly wisecracks. You can get heroes by the foot, 1950s-style Jewish chicken chow mein, fresh chicken soup, of course, and a dozen overstuffed combo sandwiches named after Coney Island rides. New York has just a fraction of the number of kosher delis it did thirty years ago, so come, *fress*, and enjoy Essex on Coney.

FAMOUS PITA. 935 Coney Island Ave. near Newkirk Ave., 284-0161, Su–Th 10a.m–3 a.m., closed F before sundown and Sa until an hour after sunset. Kosher.

It's *seriously* no-frills. But for a fresh pita and a quick takeout meal, you can't beat Famous Pita's falafel and turkey *schwarma*, made with an Iraqi-recipe hot sauce called *umba*. Pay a dollar extra, and you can get a bigger size, wrapped in a *laffa*, which is a big fluffy (also very fresh) flatbread. Famous is cheap, kosher, and open very late.

Kings Highway Area

ADELMAN'S KOSHER DELI FAMILY RESTAURANT. 1906 Kings Hwy. bet. E. 19th St. and Ocean Ave., 336-4915, M–Th 7 a.m.–10 p.m., F 7 a.m.–4 p.m., Su 7 a.m.–10 p.m. Kosher.

Adelman's menu says, "All Deli Mavens Agree That Adelman's Is One of the Finest Kosher Delis in the New York Area." And it probably is. The menu starts with chopped liver, Hungarian goulash, and fried kreplach, moves onto matzo ball soup, and then presents you with the misery-making choice of a hot tongue sandwich, corned beef, salami, or rolled beef "overstuffed combo sandwich" and, for variety, hot Oriental beef on garlic bread.

MABAT. 1809 E. 7th St. off Kings Hwy., 339-3300, Su–Th 11–2:30 a.m., closed midday F, closed Sa until one hour after sundown. Kosher.

Mabat is not your average place. They serve authentic dishes familiar to North African Jewish communities, such as okra and rice, turkey with onions, lamb soup, tahini, and various grilled meats. Their meat dishes are excellent. At about $20 per person for a full meal, it will cost you more than a few lira. Not only kosher, but glatt kosher.

SUNFLOWER CAFÉ. 1223 Quentin Rd. corner Kings Hwy., 336-1340, Su–Th, 9 a.m.–2 a.m., closed early Fr, closed Sa. Kosher.

Always busy, usually with a crowd of young Orthodox men and women, some dating, some with babies in carriages, Sunflower Café feels like it could be on Dizengoff Street in Tel Aviv. Even the foods are reminiscent of Israeli cafés, with many different kinds of smoothies and frappes, fresh juices (try "Isaac's Health Juice") and coffees, including "Israeli Nescafé with steamed milk."

Coney Island Avenue

BAHAR RESTAURANT. 984 Coney Island Ave. near Newkirk Ave., 434-8088, daily 11 a.m.–11 p.m.

Located on a three-block strip of Pakistani and Afghani stores, Bahar is one of the biggest restaurants in the area, and they claim to be the only "authentic" Afghan eatery in the borough. The chicken kebab, cooked over coals, is tender, the *ashak* appetizer delicious, and the eggplant appetizer is tantalizing. As you might imagine, *haute* it's not. But judging from the extended-family clientele, Bahar is authentic enough. Entrées run about $9.

BUKHARA RESTAURANT. 1095 Coney Island Ave. bet. Glenwood and Ave. H., 859-8033, daily noon—1 a.m. Cash only.

There's a strip of Pakistani restaurants here, and it's impossible from the outside to tell which is a good bet. Bukhara gets high marks for Punjabi-Pakistani. Cheap.

NINO'S RESTAURANT. 1971 Coney Island Ave. bet. Ave. P and Quentin Rd. (Gravesend area), 336-7872, daily noon—11 p.m.

Moderately priced Nino's ranks high for tasty northern and southern Italian cuisine. Pasta dishes run about $10-$12.

TACIS BEYTI TURKISH RESTAURANT. 1955 Coney Island Ave. bet. Ave. P and Quentin Rd. (Gravesend area), 627-5750, daily 10 a.m.—11 p.m.

This family-oriented Turkish restaurant, one of several in the area, serves kebabs, good rice dishes, excellent eggplant salad, slightly sweet stuffed grape leaves, and delicious breads. Avoid the "caviar," a poor man's version made mostly of mayo. Entrees cost about $8.

SHOPPING

Specialty Food Shopping

BACK TO NATURE. 535 Kings Hwy. bet. 3rd and 4th Sts., 339-0273, M—Th 11:30 a.m.—10 p.m., F—sundown, Su noon—10 p.m.

Satisfy all your kosher health-food needs here.

CHIFFON'S BAKE SHOP. 1373 Coney Island Ave. bet. Aves. J and K, 258-8822, M—Th 6 a.m.—8 p.m., F, closes early; closed Sa. Kosher.

Your Jewish grandmother would be at home here. Chiffon's has been turning out baked goodies—rye breads, challahs, and cheesecakes—for years, using the same time-tested recipes.

GREENMARKET. PS 139 schoolyard at 330 Rugby Rd., Sa 8 a.m.—6 p.m., July 12—Nov 22, www.cenyc.org.

Opened in 2003, there's a new greenmarket here.

HIGHWAY BAGELS CORP. 1921–23 Kings Hwy. bet E. 19th and E. 20th Sts., 336-9200, 24/7.

Get 'em while they are hot—bagels, bialys, rolls, croissants, and more. Locals recommend this twenty-four-hour bagel shop, which makes everything on the premises.

LE CHOCOLATIER EXTRAORDINAIRE. 1711 Ave. M off E. 18th St., 258-5800, M—W 10:30 a.m.—6 p.m., Th until 7 p.m., F 10 a.m.—2 p.m., Su 10 a.m.—2 p.m.; closed Sa. Kosher.

Le Chocolatier Extraordinaire is a study in contrasts: high-priced Godiva (yes, they are kosher) chocolates in a helter-skelter, ribbons-on-the-floor workshop environment. Most customers order gift baskets by phone.

MOISHA'S DISCOUNT SUPERMARKET. 325 Ave. M. off E. 4th St., 336-7563, M—Th 8 a.m.—8 p.m., F closes early; closed Sa. Kosher.

When the going gets tough and the Jewish shoppers get going, there's a good chance you'll find them at Moisha's. During the holidays, Moisha's may be the last-minute shopper's saving grace. Where else can you find *schmurra* matzoh two days before Passover? It ain't fancy but it meets your needs.

Great for your inner Bubbi.

MANSOURA'S ORIENTAL PASTRY. 515 Kings Hwy. bet. E. 3rd and E. 4th Sts., 645-7977, Su—Th 8 a.m.—6 p.m.; F, closes early; closed Sa. Kosher.

A fifth-generation family business, run by Sephardic bakers from Aleppo, Syria, Mansoura's uses centuries-old recipes for their bird's-nest honey-and-pistachio-filled pastry, Turkish delights, and other specialties.

MILLER'S MARKET. 914 Kings Hwy., 336-8100, Su—Th, 8 a.m.—8 p.m., F closes early, closed Sa.

Reflecting the Eastern European bent of the neighborhood, this local supermarket sells Russian cheeses, blinis in six flavors, and cookies and cakes baked on the premises.

NEGEV. 1211 Ave. J bet. E. 12th and E. 13th Sts., 258-8440 or 800-834-NEGEV, Su—Th 9 a.m.—6 p.m., F, closes early, closed Sa, www.negev.com. Kosher.

A takeout kosher deli, Negev has smoked salmon, herring, and whitefish salads, kosher honey-roast chickens, and pastrami. You can order holiday dishes here.

OSTROWSKI BAKERY. 1201 Ave. J corner of E. 12th St., 377-9443, Su—F 8 a.m.—7 p.m., F closes early, closed Sa. Kosher.

Jewish European-style Ostrowski bakers turn out kosher chocolate rolls, babkas, cookies, and loaves of bread big enough to feed any army.

PUNJAB SWEETS. 1083 Coney Island Ave. bet. Foster Ave. and Ave. H, 434-5972, 24/7.

Do you like *gulab jamun,* the sweet cheese balls cooked in cardamom syrup that often come after an Indian meal? Come to Punjab Sweets for this and other specialties.

PUNJAB GROCERY. 1071 Coney Island Ave. at Foster Ave., 434-9310, daily 6 a.m.–2 a.m.

Punjab is a good place to come for large quantities of fresh, inexpensive spices, as well as unusual types of flour, imported goods, and a sense of what food shopping is like back home in Bangladesh, Pakistan, and Afghanistan.

PRESSER'S BAKERY. 1720 Ave. M bet. E. 17th and E. 18th Sts., 375-5088, Su–Th 8 a.m.–7 p.m. F, closes early, closed Sa. Kosher.

Ah, the chocolate rolls, brimming fruit pies, and babkas, all baked on the premises. In keeping with most of the neighborhood's shops, the food is kosher.

Clothing and General

BROOKLYN JUNCTION RETAIL CENTER. Corner of Flatbush and Nostrand Aves. and Ave. H.

About 250,000 square feet of new retail space has opened up here, across from Brooklyn College, with decking over the Long Island Rail Road. Plans include a family style sit-down restaurant, and a dozen or so retail stores that will face Flatbush and Nostrand Avenues.

⚫ **CANAL JEAN.** 2236 Nostrand Ave. bet. Aves. H and I, 421-7590, M–Sa 10:30–8:30 p.m., Su noon– 7:30 p.m., www.canaljean.com. Call or check the Web site for directions.

Their slogan reads, "Anti-established Since 1973." This cheeky purveyor of retro-overalls, vintage bomber jackets, racy lingerie, and racks of other alternative gear was once a fixture of Lower Broadway in SoHo until it closed recently. Their Brooklyn satellite has now taken over selling the same great, cheap merchandise.

Menswear

CHUCKIES. See below.

CLOTHING CONNECTION. 508 Kings Hwy. near E. 2nd St., 375-5893, Su–Th 10 a.m.–6 p.m., F 10 a.m.–2:30 p.m., closed Sa.

Updated classic Italian suits in fine lightweight wools are sold here at at least a 15 percent discount, including the top Italian brands.

CROWN CLOTHIERS. 1434 Coney Island Ave. near Ave. J, 252-6666, Su–Th 11 a.m.–7 p.m., F, closes early, closed Sa.

Crown has a complete line of discounted medium- and high-quality menswear that includes a big selection of sports jackets and slacks, suits, sweaters, leather jackets, and accessories.

WASSERBERGER. 1709 Kings Hwy. corner of E. 17th and 18th Sts., 998-2300, M, W, F 10 a.m.–6 p.m., Tu and Th 10 a.m.–7 p.m., Sa 10 a.m.–5 p.m., Su 11:30 a.m.–4:30 p.m.

The best of both worlds, Wasserberger stocks a huge selection of ready-made designer garments—over ten thousand suits!—and custom-makes coats, suits, jackets, trousers, even tuxedo shirts, sewn on the premises by trusted tailors. A custom suit starts at $650; its off-the-rack counterpart costs from $250 to $650. As colorful as a tailor's thread box, the clientele runs from African-Americans to Orthodox Jews to Russian immigrants, with businessmen and office professionals included. One of few remaining custom stores in Brooklyn, this three-generation business was started by a Holocaust survivor who arrived here in 1948.

Women's and Children's Clothing

CAROLE BLOCK. 1413 Ave. M bet. E. 14th and E. 15th Sts., 339-1869, M–Th 10 a.m.–6 p.m., F 10 a.m.–2:30 p.m., closed Sa. Su noon–5 p.m.

Carole Block is known to carry one of the largest selections of fine leather handbags this side of Manhattan. Prices range from $50 to over $1,000.

CHUCKIES. 1304 Kings Hwy. near E. 13th St., 376-1003, M–Sa 10 a.m.–7:30 p.m., Su noon–6 p.m. (Another store in Manhattan.)

Chuckies sells top-of-the-line imported shoes for both men and women. Don't expect to pound the pavement in them, though—these are knockout, special-occasion fashion shoes.

ESTI'S. 1888 Coney Island Ave. off Ave. P, 645-2600, Su–Th 10 a.m.–5 p.m., 10 a.m.–4 p.m., or 2 hours before sundown, closed Sa.

You can't miss this huge shop, one of Brooklyn's biggest designer-name discount clothing stores for women—with gowns, sportswear, suits, skirts, blouses, shoes, bags, jewelry, and other accessories, even stockings. Most women will find a good range of beautiful options, although some styles are geared to the über-modest Orthodox crowd. Just for fun, go ogle the wedding wear.

JIMMY'S. 1226 Kings Hwy. near E. 13th St., 645-9685, M–Sa 10 a.m.–6 p.m., Su noon–5 p.m. (Other locations in Manhattan.)

Jimmy's is in a class all by itself in Brooklyn. Their specialty is top-of-the-line, this-season fashion by European designers for both men and women, and accessories such as bags and shoes. What makes shopping here different from an upscale department store is the family-style service: regular customers are greeted on a first-name basis. You'll find Manolo Blahnik, Christian Dior, Gucci, and more.

LAHORE FASHIONS 1067 Coney Island Ave. near Glenwood Ave., 940-1099, daily 10 a.m.–6 p.m.

Lahore's colorful window display has drums, bright fabrics, and *shalwar kameez* (the traditional tunic and pajama-style pants frequently worn by Pakistani women) in flamboyant reds and blues and purples. A sign outside advertises a sale on fabric: 99 cents a yard.

LAVENDER LACE LINGERIE. 1318 Ave. M bet. E. 13th and E. 14th Sts., 382-9349, M–Fr 10 a.m.–6 p.m.

Peignoir sets in silk, delicate white nightgowns, and thick terry robes are the specialty at this enticing lingerie shop. The selection is small but moderately priced.

PAK JEWELERS. 1072 Coney Island Ave. near Glenwood Ave., 859-545, daily 10 a.m.–6 p.m.

Gold, gold, and still more gold. Large, heavy gold necklaces, traditional gold bangles, and enormous ornate earrings made of 22- and 24-karat gold flash in the display window.

TUESDAY'S CHILD. 1904 Ave. M bet. E. 19th St. and Ocean Ave., 375-1790, Su–M and W–Th 10 a.m.–6 p.m., Tu 10 a.m.–8 p.m., F, close early, closed Sa, www.tuesdayschild.com.

Exclusive, expensive, and elegant imported children's clothing ranging from layette through junior size for both girls and boys fill this upscale establishment. Many items are manufactured in Italy especially for this store. There's a sale shop at 1624 Ave. M (338-7022).

YELLOW DOOR. 1308 Ave. M bet. E. 13th and E. 14th Sts., 998-7382, M–F 10 a.m.–5:30 p.m., Su 11 a.m.–5 p.m., closed weekends in summer, www.theyellowdoor.com.

Perfect items for weddings, anniversaries, Mother's Day, or birthdays include fine crystal, unusual table linens, and decorative boxes. The Yellow Door also has a huge selection of high-fashion costume jewelry in the $50 to $1,000 range, by well-known designers. Some items are sold below retail prices.

Other Interesting Area Shops

AMAZING SAVINGS OF AVENUE M. 1415 Ave. M corner of E 15th St., 998-2020, Su–W 10 a.m.–7 p.m., Th 10 a.m.–9 p.m., F 10 a.m.–7 p.m.

Bargains galore: toys, books, baby clothes, kitchen items, cosmetics, and much more. If you're doing a monster shop for, say, cosmetics for a preteen dress-up party for twenty kids, or getting functional pots and pans for your new post-divorce apartment, you can find brand-name items at half to a third the price at the local drugstore or hardware store. There's another store on Ave. I, at 1080 McDonald Ave. (253-2244).

EICHLER'S RELIGIOUS ARTICLES, GIFTS AND BOOKS. 1401 and 1429 Coney Island Ave., 258-7643 and 800-883-4245, Su–Th 10 a.m.–6 p.m., F, closes early, closed Sa, www.eichlers.com. (Also in Borough Park.)

Eichler's is the largest of several Brooklyn shops specializing in Judaica. There are tomes of the Talmud in Aramaic, Passover *Haggadoth,* holiday tapes in English and Hebrew, *tifilin,* and reference guides on how to teach your kid to be a Jewish *mensch.*

HARNIK'S HAPPY HOUSE OF BOOKS. 1403 Ave J. corner of E. 14th St., 951-9805, M–Th 10 a.m.–7 p.m. F 10 a.m.–several hours before sundown, Su noon–6 p.m., www.harnikbk.com.

For decades, Harnik's has served the mostly Orthodox Jewish Avenue J community. It's a remarkable place; they sell books, but for years have offered a lending library of new hardcovers. Independent-minded, Harnik's also issues their own *neighborhood* best-seller list. The staff is warm and knowledgeable—it's hard to tell which they love more, people or books. Harnik's helped organize a low-cost SAT prep course for local students. Harnik's Web site lists the New York Board of Education suggested reading list for elementary, middle, and high schools and offers "genre lists" to choose a book by theme—and also has a place for kids to write book reviews. Harnik's is an original, and it's terrific.

HECHT'S HEBREW BOOK STORE. 1122 Ave. J near Coney Island Ave., 254-9696, Su–Th 10 a.m.–6 p.m., F 10 a.m.–2:30 p.m., closed Sa.

This is a pleasant Judaica store where you will find books, records, and religious items.

IMPRESSIONS. 1436 Coney Island Ave. near Ave. J, 338-4438, Su–Th 11 a.m.–7 p.m., F 11 a.m.–4 p.m.

Discount china, silver, crystal, and upscale gift items are sold at Impressions, a 2003 offshoot of the well-respected **Flohr's.**

URDU BAZAAR. 1080 Coney Island Ave. near Glenwood Ave., 421-1917, daily 9 a.m.–10 p.m.

Urdu Bazaar is a 99-cent store where the staff speaks multiple languages that many Americans have never heard of, starting with Urdu, the official language of Pakistan. You can find the usual housewares, jewelry, underwear, and school supplies here, with some unusual additions, such as historical and Arabic books, plus Islamic religious tracts.

11

Fort Greene and
Clinton Hill

ABOUT FORT GREENE AND CLINTON HILL

Fort Greene and Clinton Hill are subtle kinds of places. Unlike with Park Slope (stroller gridlock) or Smith Street (restaurant row) or Williamsburg (postcollege town with abundance of galleries), it takes a while to get to know these two neighborhoods. There are five different factors that make the area so special:

- Fort Greene Park—a wonderful swath of green that lends gentility to the area.
- Pratt Institute—the entire complex of fabulous nineteenth-century buildings, plus the artistic professors and students associated with Pratt and surrounding historic Clinton Hill.
- BAM—the megawatt cultural magnet that's attracting artistic energy and raw talent to the area, from performers to investors to back-office arts administrators.
- The visual beauty of the neighborhood—streets with rows of brownstones in Fort Greene, and the elegant mansions in Clinton Hill.
- An ethnic and racial diversity here—all the more remarkable for its seeming so unremarkable.

HOW IT GOT ITS NAME: Fort Greene was named after Fort Greene Park. Clinton Hill, literally just up the hill from Fort Greene Park, was a fashionable nineteenth-century residential area named for New York governor DeWitt Clinton.

How to get there:

BY SUBWAY: 2, 3, 4, 5, or Q train to Atlantic Avenue; B, M, N, or R train to Pacific Street; C train (A on weekends) to Lafayette Avenue.

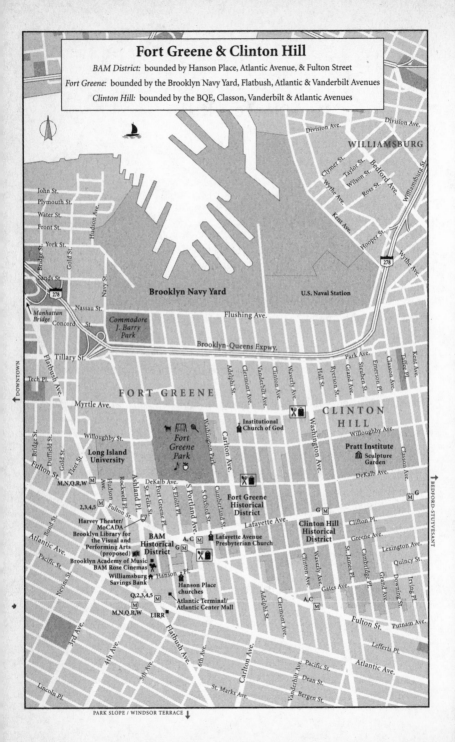

Fort Greene & Clinton Hill

BAM District: bounded by Hanson Place, Atlantic Avenue, & Fulton Street

Fort Greene: bounded by the Brooklyn Navy Yard, Flatbush, Atlantic & Vanderbilt Avenues

Clinton Hill: bounded by the BQE, Classon, Vanderbilt & Atlantic Avenues

BY CAB: Atlantic Avenue Car Service (797-5666). Fares are about $7 to Brooklyn Heights, $18 to Grand Central Station.

THE AFRICAN DIASPORA—A NEW LENS

It feels like a hand reaching around the globe. You are standing on Fulton Street or DeKalb Avenue in Brooklyn, New York. Yet within a few blocks there are restaurants specializing in Senegalese, South African, *halal,* Caribbean and Southern black foods, sprinkled among the predictable bistros and Chinese and Thai eateries. Fashion boutiques feature artisanal work made with printed fabric imported from Ghana. Some of the clothing emulates the draped, flowing lines of traditional African robes. Down the street a shop sells African herbal remedies. A gift-shop window displays chess sets with intricately carved African large-game animals for pieces—lions, tigers, and elephants. A postcard advertising a nearby nightclub invites you to evening entertainment that combines hip-hop and Afro-Cuban beats. Entrepreneurs choose to use African words, like "Moshood" and "Akwaaba," as the names of their Brooklyn-based businesses. Clothing stores feature T-shirts bearing the map of the African continent and pictures of Nelson Mandela, as well as the words of Martin Luther King Junior and rap stars. Not one, but three or four major summer festival events are dedicated to African and diasporan art and culture; so is an entire new museum.

There's an embrace of "world culture" with an African theme.

When people speak of Brooklyn as the "International Capital of the African Disapora," they are not only thinking of migrants from the Caribbean and the American South, who were largely descendants of involuntary migrants, but of voluntary immigrants from West, East, South, and North Africa. In Brooklyn today, there are people from RSA (Republic of South Africa), Ghana, Nigeria, Senegal, Sierra Leone, Guinea, and many, many others.

To connect to the African Diaspora is to connect to the cultures of tens of millions of people of African descent in the Caribbean, Latin America, the United States, and beyond. In neighborhoods like Fort Greene and nearby Bedford Stuyvesant, there's a process of joyous discovery going on as Brooklynites dip into the broad, rich stream of both African and "African Diasporan" cultures.

. . . And More About the Neighborhood . . .

With its rows of renovated nineteenth-century brownstones and sycamore-lined streets, Fort Greene/Clinton Hill is one of Brooklyn's loveliest landmark brownstone areas to wander in. The neighborhood is blessed with historic charm and lovely housing stock, excellent transportation options, and easy access to

Manhattan. Manhattanites tired of the pressure have been known to come for a night and never want to leave.

The area breeds talent: residents have included poet Walt Whitman, who penned *Leaves of Grass*, author Richard Wright, who wrote *Native Son*, poet Marianne Moore, who rhymed that "Writing is exciting, and baseball is like writing." Octogenarian and accomplished artist Ernie Chrichlow lived in Fort Greene for many years, as did jazz saxophonists Steve Coleman and Branford Marsalis, film director Spike Lee, jazz vocalist Betty Carter, and trumpet master Lester Bowie. Today, Chris Rock, Cecil Taylor, and Rosie Perez reportedly live in Fort Greene homes, as do up and coming artists, such as filmmaker Thomas Allen Harris. Spike Lee's Forty Acres and a Mule still operates, in part, out of a renovated firehouse.

Clinton Hill: Once a silk-stocking, mansion-filled retreat for wealthy industrialists, it is home to **Pratt Institute.** On a fine day, you can't beat taking a break at the **Pratt Sculpture Garden.** Tour Pratt's campus if you can; it's a maze of treasures, including a nineteenth-century engine room, a hidden fountain, and covered passageways. Rain or shine, and especially in the snow, it's inspiring to stroll along Clinton or Washington Avenues and enjoy the palatial streets with wide front gardens and fine buildings.

Brooklyn Navy Yard: At the outer edge of the neighborhood, the historic, hulking Navy Yard looms behind gates. It has been transformed from one of the nation's foremost shipyards into a hotbed of small businesses including the newly built **Steiner Studios,** a massive Hollywood-style film and TV studio.

HISTORICAL NOTES

After the Dutch sailed into New York Harbor in 1624, a few of them built farms in "Breuckelen," stretching uphill from the East River to about Greene Avenue today. The initiation of Fulton Ferry transportation from Manhattan to Brooklyn sparked the suburbanization of nearby farmlands.

Shipbuilding at the Brooklyn Navy Yard was the main occupation here for over a century, as it was through much of coastal Brooklyn. The Navy Yard remained an important source of jobs until the yard finally closed in 1966.

From its earliest beginnings, there was an independent black community in this area. In the 1840s a free-black community of shipbuilders lived here—that was before the Civil War brought widespread emancipation. The Hanson Place Baptist Church, now known as the Hanson Place Seventh Day Adventist Church, was an important stop for slaves fleeing the South via the Underground Railroad. More than half of the black population in Brooklyn lived in Fort Greene by 1870.

European immigrants arrived, too. Upper-class street names, such as Portland and Oxford, reminiscent of London, were given to the newly created nineteenth-century developments to attract new residents. Irish, German, and English settlers occupied some of the row houses still seen today. In 1848, Fort Greene Park was opened as part of the grand scheme to create urban oases of green throughout New York City.

Lower Fort Greene was settled by the middle and working class. But the neighborhood's most desirable residential location—up the hill on Clinton and Washington Avenues—was the site of sumptuous villas with great lawns, backed by elegant carriage houses like those that still line Waverly Avenue. Clinton Hill became known as a fashionable district of great mansions designed by famous architects of the era. (See **Clinton Avenue homes,** below).

At the turn of the century, the area down the hill was developed further. Fulton Street thrived, and the **Brooklyn Academy of Music (BAM)** was built in 1907 along with the Martyrs Memorial in Fort Greene Park (1907) and the Masonic Temple (1907). In her essay "Brooklyn from Clinton Hill," Pulitzer Prize–winning poet Marianne Moore captured the elegance of the era from her home at 260 Cumberland Street. By the 1920s, with the surge of the film industry, great movie palaces such as the **Paramount** (now Long Island University) brought in crowds to see the likes of Al Jolson. The **Williamsburgh Savings Bank** went up in 1929.

In the Depression years, much of the era fell into disrepair, and during World War II many brownstones were subdivided into rooming houses to accommodate the seventy thousand workers laboring at the nearby **Brooklyn Navy Yard.** Many mansions in nearby Clinton Hill were razed; a precious few were incorporated into **Pratt Institute** and **St. Joseph's College.** Gentrification began in the late 1960s and 1970s, leading to renovation and rising real estate values. The area bounded by Willoughby and Vanderbilt Avenues and South Elliot Place, Fulton Street, and Fort Greene Park is now a landmark district.

Kidstuff

☺ Take the kids to **Fort Greene Park** and **BAM.** Check out **Greenmarket** on Saturdays. Visit a Sunday open house at **Urban Glass.** See "haunted houses" on Halloween on Clinton Avenue.

POINTS OF CULTURAL INTEREST

SPECIAL EVENTS.
Fort Greene historic home tour (May every other year); SONYA Studio Stroll (May); Cultural Crossroads Fair (May); Garden tour (June); Juneteenth Festival (June); Dance Africa at BAM (June).

BROOKLYN NAVY YARD. Bounded by Hudson Ave., Navy St., Flushing Ave., Kent Ave., and the East River. There is no public access.

Talk about recycling! Behind those forbidding gates, this old place is buzzing, with over 3,500 people working in hundreds of firms, including Sweet'N Low, thirty furniture makers, jewelry makers, ship repair, plus high-tech and printing firms. By 2005, **Steiner Studios** are expected to start operations.

The colorful history of the Brooklyn Navy Yard reads like a roster of America's maritime adventures. Ships destined for raids against the Barbary pirates were fitted out here. Similarly, seagoing vessels designed to encounter British merchant ships in the War of 1812 were built or overhauled here. Among the ships built or worked on at the Brooklyn Navy Yard were the oceangoing steamship pioneers *Fulton* and *Niagara*, and ships that fought in the Civil War (including the *Iron Monitor*). It was a key supply station during the Spanish-American War.

In World War II, thousands of people came to New York to find work in its dry docks, piers, buildings, and railroads and related businesses, creating housing shortages in nearby residential neighborhoods, such as Bedford-Stuyvesant. The Brooklyn Navy Yard rapidly became the largest of the U.S. Navy's construction facilities.

During the mid- to late-twentieth century, the Brooklyn Navy Yard experienced severe cutbacks as shipbuilding moved to other centers. When the Navy finally closed the facility in 1966, selling the area to the New York City government, it closed a chapter on 150 years of shipbuilding at this location.

Navy Yard landmarks include the Surgeon's House, the U.S. Naval Hospital, and Dry Dock #1, considered a great accomplishment of nineteenth-century engineering.

STEINER STUDIOS. Brooklyn Navy Yard, 15 Washington Ave. at Flushing Ave., 858-1600. No public tours.

Godzilla would be *thrilled*. In 2005, Steiner Studios will open a fifteen-acre studio complex with high-ceiling stages that can accommodate humongous stage sets (for instance, the Empire State Building) otherwise unavailable in New York City. Steiner says this will be one of the largest film production facilities ever built, with five soundstages ranging up to 27,000 square feet, grid heights of 45 feet, and enough power to light big-budget features, plus state-of-the-art production services.

The Brooklyn Navy Yard is like one big backlot, with the *real* stuff: historic Civil War– and World War II–era buildings, awe-inspiring dry docks, and views of Manhattan.

BROOKLYN TECHNICAL HIGH SCHOOL. 29 Fort Greene Pl. to So. Elliott Pl. off DeKalb Ave., 858-5150, www.bths.edu.

Brooklyn Technical High School is one of New York City's specialized public high schools. That means, to be admitted, students must take the same demanding competitive examination as at Stuyvesant and Bronx High School of Science. Brooklyn Tech was founded in 1922 and moved to this site in the 1930s. About four thousand students, representing a wide variety of races and nationalities, attend, studying an advanced curriculum in science, math, computer science, premedical education, as well as liberal arts. Brooklyn Tech has received several private endowments and has an active alumni fund-raising campaign, so, despite its old building, the students enjoy well-equipped labs. College admissions are "excellent." (Some information from *New York City's Best Public High Schools: A Parents' Guide: Second Edition,* by C. Hemphill with P. Wheaton and J. Wayans.)

CLINTON AVENUE HOMES OF CHARLES PRATT.

Charles Pratt of the Standard Oil Company catalyzed the neighborhood by building a home at 252 Clinton Avenue in 1874. Each of Pratt's sons also was presented with a fine home along the avenue, as a wedding present. Number 229 recalls a Tuscan villa; 241 is a brick Queen Anne with a glistening green-tile roof and a porte cochere, now the home of the Roman Catholic bishop of Brooklyn; 245 is a neo-Georgian, owned today by St. Joseph's College. Other merchants and industrialists who followed Pratt's lead in building fine homes here included Cuban coffee magnate John Arbuckle; members of the Underwood family of typewriter fame; lace manufacturer A. G. Jennings; and D. R. Hoagland, a baking-soda merchant.

HOUSE AND GARDEN TOURS. Tickets cost $10–20, depending on the tour.

You can go on tours of fabulous **Fort Greene** homes and also of **Clinton Hill** (789-5492). About eight houses are shown, dating from the nineteenth and early twentieth century. If you're a garden buff, take the **Brownstone Brooklyn Garden District Sunday Garden Walk Tour** (717-1277). For art tours, see **SONYA Studio Stroll** (see below).

☺ FEDERATION OF BLACK COWBOYS. 925-0777, www.federationofblackcowboys.com.

Don't pinch yourself; you're not dreaming. Those really *are* African-American men in full-dress cowboy hats and gear, riding horses down Flatbush Avenue. Members of the Queens-Based Federation of Black Cowboys, they participate in events in Brooklyn parks, Macy's Thanksgiving Day parades, Black World Championship Rodeo, and school programs. They're "keeping alive the legacy of America's forgotten Black Cowboys"—and educating inner-city youth to the care and handling of horses. They focus on the role of black Americans on the American frontier, including the 1879 post-Reconstruction exodus when many freed slaves fled West, finding jobs as cowboys. Cedar Lane Stables in Queens is home to their forty horses and rodeo equipment for the sports of bull-riding, bucking horse–riding, bulldogging, and calf-roping. Some of the kids who benefit from working with these urban cowboys and their horses live in Brooklyn's tougher areas, so we've adopted the federation as honorary Brooklynites!

40 ACRES AND A MULE FILMWORKS. Firehouse # 256, DeKalb Ave., 624-3703, M–F 9 a.m.–5 p.m. By appointment only.

Spike Lee's production company has used this renovated firehouse as a Brooklyn home for over a decade. Lee lived in Fort Greene from the age of two, and has employed local residents and used Brooklyn as a setting in such films as *She's Gottta Have It*, *Do the Right Thing*, and *Crooklyn*, which view the ironies, injustices, humor, and challenges of life from an African-American urban perspective. Lee's administrative offices dealing with scripts, music labels, and other enterprises have spilled out of this old firehouse and into nearby offices.

HOME OF RICHARD WRIGHT, AUTHOR. 175 Carleton Ave. bet. Myrtle and Willoughby Aves.

Richard Wright (1908–1960) wrote his famous book *Native Son* while living in this house in the 1930s and early 1940s with his wife and child. He later moved to other homes in the area.

JUNETEENTH FESTIVAL. HTTP://LETTIE.COM/JUNETEENTH/

Juneteenth is a daylong festival of African-American art and culture, a joyous celebration of the end of slavery in the United States. Centered in Fort Greene, it's a community-wide celebration that attracts thousands. What's Juneteenth? It's a commemoration of June 19, 1865, when freedom for Texas slaves was officially announced, and spontaneous celebration erupted in the African community. This Texas tradition has spread nationwide and is growing as a major cultural festival akin to Cinco de Mayo, Passover, and other celebrations of liberation. For a fuller history, see the Web site.

LEFFERTS-LAIDLAW HOUSE. 136 Clinton St.

Built in phases from 1825 to 1874, this Greek Revival landmark typifies the residences that were constructed during a period of suburban development in the Brooklyn Navy Yard environs. You can still see much of the historic clapboard siding and molding. Civil War commander Marshall Lefferts originally occupied it, and today it remains a private home.

PARAMOUNT THEATER. DeKalb Ave. at Flatbush Ave., 488-1015.

There's just memories here, really. In the 1920s and 1930s, the Paramount was a hot spot for big-name performers: Mae West, Bing Crosby, Rudy Vallee, Ginger Rogers. The theater, closed in 1962, now belongs to LIU. The original Wurlitzer pipe organ can still be played.

PRATT INSTITUTE. 200 Willoughby Ave., gateway at DeKalb Ave. and Hall St., 636-3600.

More than a century old, the pioneering educational institution Pratt was founded in 1887 by oil baron Charles Pratt, a pragmatist who recognized the growing need for trained industrial workers in a changing economy. Pratt encouraged students in the study of mechanical drawing, engineering, sewing, and typing. The school was progressive for its day, admitting both men and women of all races, and opening the first free library in Brooklyn—Pratt's Free Library.

Today, Pratt's schools of Architecture, Art and Design, Information and Library Sciences, and Liberal Arts and Sciences enroll 4,300 undergraduate and graduate students from fifty states and approximately seventy countries. Pratt also hosts college prep programs; a Saturday art program; and an art therapy program created in the aftermath of September 11, 2001. Pratt's twenty-five-acre campus provides a leafy oasis where neighbors come throughout the year to relax, visit campus galleries, and attend performances in Memorial Hall.

Pratt is expanding. A new building for its School of Architecture was designed by Steven Holl—one of the architects chosen to submit plans for a new World Trade Center complex. There are also plans to build a fifteen-thousand-square-foot **Pratt Art Supply and Bookstore** on Myrtle Avenue, to open in 2004. See also **Pratt Institute's Sculpture Park**.

PUBLIC SCHOOLS.

Community Partnership Charter School (171 Clermont Avenue) is considered "worth watching" by experts. (Source: *New York City's Best Public Elementary Schools*, 2002, by C. Hemphill with P. Wheaton.)

Free! **SONYA STUDIO STROLL.** (May) 789-2545, www.sonyany.com.

An increasingly visible nonprofit artists' organization, SONYA (an acronym for South of the Navy Yard) has in a few short years made some great contributions to the community at large. Don't miss their annual weekend-long free SONYA Open Studio Tour in May. Started in 1999, it has grown to include visits by over two thousand people to nearly a hundred different studios in Fort Greene, Clinton Hill, and Bedford-Stuyvesant. Their motto: "Great Art at Affordable Prices."

STEELE HOUSE. 200 Lafayette Ave., diagonally across from Queen of All Saints Church at Vanderbilt Ave.

As though plucked from a Massachusetts seacoast town, this nineteenth-century frame house with its small widow's walk stands out from the surrounding brownstones and churches in the area. It is a landmark of architectural interest, since successive owners combined Federal, Greek Revival, and Italianate elements, and the small eastern wing may date to 1812. Originally built for Joseph Steele, it was later owned by the first president of Brooklyn Union Gas Company.

Churches

Of the numerous churches in Fort Greene Clinton Hill, we've listed a few, chosen for their architectural heritage, community involvement, or gospel choir.

CHURCH OF ST. LUKE AND ST. MATTHEW. 520 Clinton Ave. bet Atlantic Ave. and Fulton St., 638-0686. Phone for hours.

Described as a "voluptuous Victorian valentine," this church is distinguished by a long porch, sculpted teak columns, and Tiffany windows. Designed by architect John Welch and built by Episcopalian industrial barons, the hundred-year-old Romanesque church, erected between 1900 and 1924, is a landmark listed on the National Register of Historic Places. It is located not far from **Pratt Institute** and the mansions along Clinton Avenue, where some of the church's original congregants lived in splendor.

EMMANUEL BAPTIST CHURCH. 279 Lafayette Ave. at St. James Pl., Clinton Hill, 622-1107. Phone for hours.

This large French Gothic church, with its twin towers and triple entrance, is reminiscent of a medieval cathedral. Completed in 1887, it is a notable landmark contributing to the nineteenth-century ambience of the neighborhood. The church was built with financial support from Charles Pratt, industrialist and founder of **Pratt Institute.**

HANSON PLACE CENTRAL METHODIST CHURCH. 1 Hanson Pl. at St. Felix St., 783-0908. Phone for hours.

This 1929 "Art Deco–Gothic" wonder, located in the BAM historic district and designed by the same firm as designed BAM itself, has been called the Cathedral of Methodism. Nearby are streets of row houses with cast-iron railings and wooden doors, reminiscent of the time when Fulton Street was a major commercial center.

HANSON PLACE SEVENTH DAY ADVENTIST CHURCH. 88 Hanson Pl. at So. Portland Ave. 789-3030. Phone for hours.

Monumental in scale, this Greek Revival and Italianate church is of the same 1850s and 1860s architectural generation as **Borough Hall** and the landmark **State Street Houses.** Once a Baptist congregation, this church welcomed southern slaves traveling the Underground Railway to Fort Greene's community of free blacks, many of whom were employed in the nearby **Brooklyn Navy Yard.**

♩ **INSTITUTIONAL CHURCH OF GOD IN CHRIST.** 170 Adelphi St. bet Willoughby and Myrtle Aves., 625-9175. Phone for hours.

The nationally known Institutional Choir performed on Broadway in *Gospel at Colonus,* and in Europe. There are services three times a week, often in collaboration with other American and international choirs.

♫ **LAFAYETTE AVENUE PRESBYTERIAN CHURCH.** 102 Lafayette Ave. at So. Oxford St., 625-7515.

Depending on your bent, this church offers spiritual uplift, social action—and joyful gospel from the choir and four-keyboard organ. Pulitzer Prize–winning poet Marianne Moore called this her church. A leader in progressive social causes for over a century, this church was an abolitionist headquarters, and more recently was an instigator of the public education campaign to halt abusive labor practices in textile factories in El Salvador. It was also the birthplace of publishing company Kitchen Table: Women of Color Press, founded in 1981 and dedicated to publishing writings of lesbians and women of color. They published where commercial houses dared not tread; for instance, now-classic *This Bridge Called My Back: Writings by Radical Women of Color* and *Home Girls: A Black Feminist Anthology*.

It's not all highbrow. The church sponsors an annual **Brooklyn Bombazo,** an Afro-Latin drum-dance event and many other fun community activities.

And it's a New York City architectural landmark. Glorious, pastoral windows in the Underwood Chapel of this 1864 Romanesque building are among the last completed by the Tiffany Studio about 1920. In 2002, a new program designed to preserve the Tiffany windows at Lafayette Presbyterian Church was initiated. This is an interesting three-way collaboration with the World Monuments Fund and an innovative program to teach high school kids about historic preservation—including stained-glass conservation.

QUEEN OF ALL SAINTS ROMAN CATHOLIC CHURCH. 300 Vanderbilt Ave. at Lafayette Ave., 638-7625. Call for hours.

HELLO, MYRTLE AVENUE!

Once sleepy, working-class Myrtle Avenue is suddenly seeing new stores and especially restaurants opening, such as **Karrots, Peaches N Cream, Thai 101**, and **Zaytoons**. See if you can identify the graphically sophisticated new store signs, a special project by those talented kids at Pratt. In 2004, a vast **Pratt Art Supply and Bookstore** is scheduled to open, to satisfy the growing community of supply-starved Brooklyn artists. This step-by-step neighborhood face-lift is good for some people, but bad for others. Meanwhile, veterans like **Clinton Simply Art and Frames** are absolutely worth a visit.

A flamboyant Gothic nave in this 1913 church, heightened by lavish windows, takes its inspiration from the Sainte Chapelle in Paris.

PARKS, PLAYGROUNDS, AND COMMUNITY GARDENS

BROOKLYN BEARS COMMUNITY GARDEN. Flatbush Ave. and Pacific St., Green Thumb Project, 212-788-8070, www.greenthumbnyc.org.

Saved more than once from threatened "urban renewal," the now five-hundred-square-foot garden has become something of a cause célèbre among green-minded folks. It's one of hundreds of community gardens in Brooklyn, most of which were derelict, ugly lots that were "adopted" by gardening volunteers.

🐾 ☺ ♫ 🎨 **FORT GREENE PARK.** Bounded by Washington Park, DeKalb, and Myrtle Aves., www.fortgreenepark.org.

Sledding in winter. Concerts and films in summer. Blooms in spring. Swirling leaves underfoot in autumn. One of Brooklyn's loveliest, Fort Greene Park cuts a natural swath through the heart of downtown urban Brooklyn. Thought to have the world's only all-marble bathrooms, this park designed by Olmsted and Vaux of Prospect Park and Central Park fame is topped by a 148-foot Doric column, built in 1908 as a monument to the Prison Ship Martyrs. There are six tennis courts.

DOGS IN FORT GREENE PARK. Fort Greene Park Users and Pets Society (P.U.P.S.) is a collective group of dog owners. www.fortgreenepups.org.

PRATT-CLINTON HILL COMMUNITY GARDEN. St. James Pl. and Hall St.

This lovely green space is a community project, with a popular Halloween walk for the little ones.

☺ *Free!* **PRATT INSTITUTE'S SCULPTURE PARK.** 200 Willoughby Ave., entrance at DeKalb Ave. and Hall St., 636-3000, www.pratt.edu/campus/directions.

Enter another world, one of the largest sculpture parks in the Big Apple. You can sit on a large, tree-shaded lawn and soak up the vibes of aesthetically placed sculptures. Some are suspended, while others seem to grow from walls and borders. The works change every year or two. It's peaceful.

☺ **UNDERWOOD PLAYGROUND.** Washington Ave. at Lafayette Ave.

The land under this big playground used to be the site of a mansion belonging to typewriter baron John T. Underwood. As the story goes, his widow had it demolished so that her precious home would not fall into the "wrong hands" when she thought the neighborhood was deteriorating. She really needn't have worried.

FORT GREENE RESTAURANTS

À TABLE. 171 Lafayette Ave. at Adelphi St., 935-9121, M–F 8 a.m.–3:30 p.m., 5:30–11 p.m., Sa–Su 8 a.m.– 3 p.m., 5:30–11 p.m.

One of the prettiest of the little French bistros to have flowered in Fort Greene, À Table gets A ratings for décor, ambiance, and authentic French food (and occasionally for authentic French attitude as well). The big, long, country wooden tables and authentic country décor lull you into feeling that you're vacationing in Provence, a sensation that only increases when you're rubbing elbows with a fellow named Hervé who is asking, in impeccable French, that waitstaff bring forth wine, mussels, and juicy shell steak—toot-sweet. If it feels like you've walked into a little town where people know each other, you're probably reading things right: À Table is very popular with a local crowd. Vive le Brooklyn. It runs about $30 per meal, including a drink and tip.

☺ **BLACK IRIS.** 228 DeKalb Ave. corner of Clermont Ave., 852-9800, daily noon–midnight.

Black Iris serves Middle Eastern spinach-and-cheese pie, chicken ouzi (a phyllo pocket filled with grilled chicken, carrots, almonds, and raisins), and basmati rice. There are also "pitzas" with unconventional toppings, such as lamb, shrimp, and chicken. You can eat in, come with a date, or bring the kids.

BROOKLYN MOD. 271 Adelphi St. corner of DeKalb Ave., 522-1669, daily 6 p.m.–4 a.m.

Brooklyn Mod is a "scene" to be seen in, in Fort Greene—just take a look at their hours. This self-styled champagne bistro in a beautiful old brownstone is a good place to have a drink and engage in some heavy-duty socializing and people-watching. The food, however, is of uneven quality.

♪ **BUTTA'CUP LOUNGE.** 271 Adelphi St., 522-1669, Tu–Th 11 a.m.–midnight, F–Sa 11 a.m.–2 a.m., Su 11 a.m.–4 p.m., 6 p.m.–11 p.m., www.buttacuplounge.com.

It's a quiet, friendly nonscene. Butta'Cup Lounge has excellent jazz, good food (and an all-you-can-eat Sunday jazz brunch), and great atmosphere. Downstairs there's a bar, some tables, and spacious booths with a hint of leopard skin that somehow fits with the pressed tin walls and old, high windows. Climb up the old wrought-iron staircase, and you're in an intimate living room–style arrangement that invites conversation, family quality time, and relaxed dining. Check the Web site for performance schedule.

CAFÉ LAFAYETTE. 99 So. Portland Ave. at Fulton St., 624-1605, daily 11 a.m.–midnight.

Brought to you by the owner of the popular Chez Oskar, tiny subterranean Café Lafayette has instant appeal. The pressed tin on the ceiling and walls, tight seating, and a makeshift feel impart a gritty, casual charm. A basic menu—of dishes such as ravioli, mussels, veggie burgers, and salads—and wine list don't always live up to the restaurant's romantic promise, though.

CAMBODIAN CUISINE. 87 So. Elliot Pl. at the intersection of Lafayette Ave. and Fulton St., 858-3262, daily 11 a.m.–10:30 p.m.

Do you like it hot? Lovers of tingling-hot chicken, veggies, or seafood will be in heaven. And if your palate is more reserved, don't fear—the menu's more than 140 different items guarantee there's something here for everyone. Both the food and its tasteful presentation have won accolades since the restaurant opened in the mid-1990s. Cambodian Cuisine's motto is "No Pork, Less Fat, Better Than Chinese Food." It's low on ambience, and inexpensive.

CASTRO'S CAFÉ. 511 Myrtle Ave. bet. Grand and Ryerson Sts., 398-1459, daily 7 a.m.–11 p.m. Cash only.

This Castro's is Mexican, not Cuban. Local students and art teachers from Pratt come for the *mole poblano,* and delicious burritos. Aficionados say their authentic spicy stew, *tinga,* is a rare find. The menu itself isn't what's special—what's special is how well cooked and spiced the food *is.* As for the ambience, *no hay.*

♫ **CHEZ OSKAR.** 211 DeKalb Ave. at Adelphi St., 852-6250, M–Th 6 p.m.–midnight, F 6 p.m.–1 a.m., Sa brunch 11 a.m.–4 p.m., dinner 6 p.m.–1 a.m., Su brunch 11 a.m.–4 p.m., dinner 6 p.m.–midnight.

Chez Oskar is a crowd-pleaser that's won recognition from *New York* magazine as "best Fort Greene restaurant." The bar scene is active and easygoing during weekends. The kitchen is oriented toward creative French cookery, and you can trust that the classic mussels, pâtés, roast chicken, and other dishes will be excellent. Or you can build a whole meal out of appetizers. Brunch on weekends is popular, as is Thursday-night jazz. A full meal with one drink runs about $35.

CINO'S. 243 DeKalb Ave. bet. Claremont and Vanderbilt Aves., 622-9249, M–Sa lunch 11:30 a.m.–2:30 p.m., dinner 4–10:30 p.m.

Cino's Italian food is so homey that it's survived for over fifty years here. Nouvelle cuisine and all the other cooking styles du jour have bypassed this kitchen, so stick to the Neapolitan tried-and-true, like spaghetti with garlic, stuffed mushrooms, and clams casino. Entrées run about $15.

DAKAR RESTAURANT. Clifton St. at Grand Ave.

Opened in 2003, an outgrowth of Sage Catering Company, Dakar offers café food, with breakfast items, sandwiches, and salads. There's ethnic cuisine here with an African twist. Too new to have a phone number.

GREEN APPLE CAFÉ. 110 DeKalb Ave. off Ashland Pl., 625-1248, M–F 8 a.m.–10 p.m., Sa–Su 9 a.m.–10 p.m.

It's hipper than Junior's. (So what *isn't?*). Wander a few blocks up DeKalb into this charming hole-in-the-wall café. The artfully mismatched furniture invites you to sit down and have a friendly heart-to-heart talk. For breakfast you can get pancakes and eggs, and for lunch, salads, homemade hummus, fresh soups, and burgers.

HALL STREET COFFEE SHOP. 47 Hall St. off Kent Ave., 222-3119, M–F 7 a.m.–4 p.m.

Across from the Brooklyn Navy Yard, this dumpy little diner is popular with local workers. (After all, there's *nuthin'* around there!) So it's a good thing you can get delicious calzones, cheese blintzes, potato latkes, and a variety of fish dishes and tuna wraps. The food is kosher, and the area is a mini–United Nations.

JOLOFF. 930 Fulton St. at St. James Pl., 636-4011, M–Sa noon–10:30 p.m., Su noon–10 p.m.

This Senegalese restaurant gets high marks for the filling food and cozy atmosphere. And you won't have to pay much for a couple of fish or veggie patties, or the vegetarian dishes cooked in a mélange of spicy sauces. Try the bean pie with cinnamon, and a sip of sorrel, a beet-red drink not unlike cranberry juice. Entrées are about $8.

KEUR N' DEYE. 737 Fulton St. bet. So. Elliot and So. Portland Sts., 875-4937, Tu–Su, noon–10:30 p.m.

Proprietor Salif Cissé transported the dishes of his native Senegal to Fort Greene, and the lines outside the door of this small, handsome restaurant are testimony to the wondrous tastes and reasonable prices. *Tiebou dieun* is the national dish of fish and rice, and it takes center stage. But don't miss the peanut chicken, *mafe guinaar*, or the curried vegetables. The spicy ginger drink is refreshing, as is the sorrel, which is sweeter and will please the kids. Keur N'Deye is simple, clean, and filled with Senegalese art and music.

KUM KAU KITCHEN. 465 Myrtle Ave. corner Washington Ave., 638-1850, M–F 11–1 a.m., Sa–Su 11–2 a.m.

Terrific and cheap, cheap, cheap, this no-frills Chinese restaurant has an extensive menu. It offers such entrées as BBQ boneless spare ribs, fantail shrimps, over fifty different kinds of Hunan/Szechuan dishes, and combination platters of a main dish, egg roll, and pork fried rice, all for about $7.

♫ **LIQUORS.** 219 DeKalb Ave. bet. Adelphi St. and Clermont Ave., 488-7700, M–Th 5:45–11 p.m., F 5:45 p.m.–midnight, Sa brunch 10:30 a.m.–4 p.m., dinner 5:45 p.m.–midnight, Su brunch 10:30 a.m.–4 p.m., dinner 5:45–11 p.m.

Considering that it's named after the old liquor store that was here forever, it's appropriate that this small, often jam-packed restaurant serves knockout drinks. The menu offers an interesting selection of foods from the African diaspora, displays of art change monthly, the clientele is diverse, and weekend DJs play mellow jazz. By the same owners, **Bodega**.

LOCANDA VINI & OLII. 129 Gates Ave. corner of Cambridge Pl., 622-9202, Tu–Th 6–10:30 p.m., F–Sa 6–11:30 p.m., Su 6–10 p.m. www.locandavinieolii.com.

Sophisticated, interesting Italian food, intimate décor in a beautifully renovated antique pharmacy, a good wine selection, and an informal Clinton Hill ambiance conspire to make this a popular stop for locals as well as tourists from Manhattan (about ten minutes away, if you have great traffic karma). Owners François Louy and Catherine de Zagon live nearby and walk to work; both have pedigree résumés from working at places such as Balthazar. They imported a young Italian chef, Michele Baldacci, about whom the James Beard Foundation raves: "his food is rigorously authentic and unlike almost anything on the menu in Italian restaurants across the city." A three-course meal with wine comes to about $30, but you can get away happily with several antipasti.

LOULOU. 222 DeKalb Ave. bet. Adelphi St. and Clermont Ave., 246-0633, M and W–Sa 6–11 p.m., Su brunch 11:30 a.m.–3:30 p.m., dinner 6–11 p.m.

That Loulou is packed on a dismally rainy Saturday evening is proof of the popularity of this tiny romantic restaurant. There's a small menu, with one or two options for fussy eaters (as in, don't-eat-meat-hate-garlic types). Mussels are recommended. The tables are closely spaced, inviting people-watching of the most upfront kind. In fine weather, enjoy outdoor dining. Entrées start at about $16.

MO-BAY. 112 DeKalb Ave. bet. Ashland and Rockwell Pl., 246-2800, M–F 11 a.m.–11 p.m., Sa noon–11 p.m., Su 3–10 p.m., www.mobayrestaurant.com.

Reminiscent of your last Caribbean jaunt, with a little soul food tossed in, Mo-Bay is informal and fun. Sit under a thatched roof and wait for a delicious snapper *escovitch* while you drink a Jamaican concoction, and enjoy the traditional *bammie,* a cassava-flour fried bread. Put aside your diet and try the Rummy Rum cake. In good weather you can eat outdoors by a fountain. Pleasant, with lots of vegetarian options, and moderately priced at $12–$15 an entrée.

RUTHIE'S SOUL FOOD. 96 DeKalb Ave. at Rockwell Pl., 246-5189, M–Sa 11:30 a.m.–10 p.m.

Across from Brooklyn Hospital, this teensy takeout place with seating for about twelve serves up the flavors of the Deep South: BBQ, sweet potato pie, fried chicken, and candy yams. Hush now, Ruthie's is a well-kept secret.

SCOPELLO RISTORANTE LOUNGE BAR. 63 Lafayette Ave. off Fulton St., 852-1100, M–Th 5–11 p.m., F–Sa 5 p.m.–midnight, Su 10 a.m.–11 p.m.

Scopello's spare, sophisticated bar, airy dining room, and huge front windows are a welcome addition to the Fort Greene restaurant scene. The cuisine is healthful Italian, featuring, for instance, a salad of green pears, fresh mushroom ravioli served in a truffle-essence sauce; and pork loin with brandy, orange juice, and pistachio nuts. Entrées in the $15 range.

SOL. 229 DeKalb Ave., at Clermont Ave., 222-1510, M–Th 6 p.m.–1 a.m., F–Sa 6 p.m.–4 a.m., Su brunch 11 a.m.–4 p.m., dinner 6 p.m.–1 a.m.

Sunny Sol is popular with the local black entrepreneurial and artistic crowd, people who live in this neighborhood. There's a DJ on weekends, and a busy calendar of entertainment. It's open late, and you can enjoy yourself at the bar or in the garden. Entrées run about $15.

MADIBA. 195 DeKalb Ave. at Carlton Ave., 855-9190, M–Th 5:30–midnight, F–Sa 5:30 p.m.–1 a.m., Su 1–11 p.m.

Nelson Mandela looks down on you from the walls. You may be only on DeKalb Avenue, but with all the interesting artifacts from South African life at Madiba, you feel transported to another reality, perhaps a (stage-set version) shantytown outside Johannesburg. Madiba serves an eclectic menu of delicious dishes, from all over South Africa. An international waitstaff who are far from home seem eager to describe the dishes and where they come from. There are excellent fish dishes, curries, and specials such as ostrich; portions are large. This is a must-visit for armchair travelers and the culinarily curious.

TILLIE'S. 248 DeKalb Ave. at Vanderbilt Ave., 783-6140, M–F 7:30 a.m.–10 p.m., Sa 9 a.m.–10 p.m., Su 9 a.m.–8 p.m.

Tillie's is a college town–style coffeehouse that might easily be in Madison, Wisconsin. There's a friendly scene here, with live jazz, open mic nights, readings, and a bulletin board covered with flyers about local happenings. Outdoor seating makes for good people-watching on summer weekends.

THOMAS BIESL. 25 Lafayette Ave. bet. Ashland Pl. and St. Felix St., 222-5800, M–F 4 p.m.–midnight, Sa–Su brunch 10 a.m.–4 p.m., dinner 4 p.m.–midnight.

The chef at the new restaurant across the street from BAM spent over a decade at Café des Artistes, and now brings fabulous Viennese foods to Brooklyn. Try the sauerbraten, onion soup, eggplant terrine, and, of course, the incredible coffee and deserts.

☺ **PEACHES & CREAM CAFE.** 436 Myrtle Ave. near Clinton Ave., 852-2243, M–Th 7:30 a.m.–9 p.m., F–Sa 7:30 a.m.–10 p.m., Su 7:30 a.m.–8 p.m.

Who said hot summer in the city couldn't be fun? You can get made-on-the-premises homemade ice creams at this little coffee shop, along with a variety of frozen desserts and baked goods. Owner Bob Morris personally is fond of ginger-honey-graham and banana-pudding flavors. But basic chocolate and strawberry are good, too.

SPRINKLES RESTAURANT AND BAKERY. 466 Myrtle Ave., bet Washington and Hall Sts., 399-3085, Su–Th 11 a.m.–11 p.m. F–Sa 11 a.m.–midnight.

Sprinkles is an old-fashioned eatery that serves such West Indian dishes as curries, oxtail stew, jerk chicken, roti, and patties, as well as homemade breads and pastries. Eat here or, better yet, take some home.

THAI 101. 455A Myrtle Ave. bet. Washington and Waverly Aves., 855-4615 daily 11 a.m.–11 p.m.

Is the name a joke with the nearby student community? Thai 101 serves the basics: basil fried rice, shrimp fritters, and curries, both fiery and not. At night, with candles on the table, it's a nice neighborhood spot. Check out the $4.95 lunch special.

♫ **TWO STEPS DOWN.** 240 DeKalb Ave. bet. Clermont and Vanderbilt Aves., 399-2020, W–Sa 5–11:30 p.m., Su brunch 11:30 a.m.–3:30 p.m., dinner 4–11:30 p.m.

Two Steps Down's been around for over a decade. Tucked into a brownstone on DeKalb, it was one of the earliest of this busy thoroughfare's now-thriving string of restaurants. The menu offers Louisiana specials and lots of seafood. Upstairs there's often live music and spoken-word performances.

ZAYTOONS ON MYRTLE. 472 Myrtle Ave. bet. Hall St. and Washington Ave., 623-5522, M–Th 11 a.m.–11 p.m., F–Sa 11 a.m.–midnight, www.zaytoons.com.

An offshoot of the popular Smith Street restaurant, Zaytoons serves great ten-inch "pityZas"—with toppings of sun-dried tomato, ground lamb and beef, or shrimp. House specials are spinach pie, couscous, *malphouf* (Middle Eastern stuffed cabbage.) *Zay-toons,* by the way, in Arabic means (1) olives, (2) an offering of peace, (3) a garnish to wonderful food, and (4) a lifelong dream of childhood friends.

Jazz in Fort Greene

♩ **FIVE SPOT SUPPER CLUB.** 459 Myrtle Ave. at Washington Ave., 852-0202.

Not related to the original 5 Spot of Monk, Coltrane, and Coleman fame, this soul-food joint has become a supper club with a Sunday jazz brunch and live music (soul, R&B) during the week, starting at 9 or 10 p.m. Call after 4 p.m. for information on who's playing.

♩ **NIGHT OF THE COOKERS.** 767 Fulton St., 797-1197, M–Th 5 p.m.–midnight, F–Sa 5 p.m.–2 a.m., Su noon–4 p.m.

There's a simple menu here, in this large, airy restaurant. On Thursdays, Fridays, and Saturdays, there's live jazz, and a popular jazz brunch on Sundays as well. It's named after the Blue Note album *Night of the Cookers.*

♩ **PO'K KNOCKERS.** 956 Atlantic Ave. bet Washington and Grand Aves., 638-0727, daily, 5 p.m.–4 a.m.

This restaurant is located on a fast-moving thoroughfare, and you'd probably never stop unless someone told you there was a sixteen-piece jazz orchestra playing every Wednesday from nine p.m. till midnight. Po'k Knockers offers an eclectic roster of live performances, ranging from *soca* and calypso to reggae and comedy to karaoke and R&B. The Jamaican food served includes vegetarian, seafood, spicy chicken, *escovitch* fish, and curry goat.

♩ **BROOKLYN MOON.** 745 Fulton St. bet. So. Elliot and So. Portland Sts. 243-0424, Tu–Su 10 a.m.–10 p.m. Cash only.

You may think you've wandered into a private party in this small, living room–like café and arts salon. Some nights poetry is read, while on others a guitarist may be performing. The menu is simple sandwiches and the like—but fresh and good. Relax on the sofa, pull up a chair, put up your feet, have a bite, and enjoy the evening. There's a great weekend brunch and a Friday-night open mic. People come to hear contemporary open readings, as well as live music. If you want to get to know some locals, this is a good first stop.

BARS, NIGHTLIFE, DANCING, AND SCENES

♪ **DUPLEXX.** 46 Washington Ave. bet. Park and Flushing Aves., 643-6400, www.theduplexx.com.

This nightlife spot caters to a late-night crowd, with dancing, reggae, and drinks. It's on a desolate, rough-around-the-edges, empty block near the Navy Yard.

♪ **FRANK'S COCKTAIL LOUNGE.** 660 Fulton St. at So. Elliott Pl., 625-9339, Su–Th 3 p.m.–2 a.m., F–Sa 2 p.m.–4 a.m. Happy hour 4–7 p.m., call for schedule of guest DJs and live performances.

When Jen, your lithe twenty something Pilates instructor swears that Frank's is Brooklyn's *best* place for dancing, now that's a recommendation. Resurrected from a sleepy neighborhood bar, Frank's has morphed into a rocking, multiethnic dancing scene. There's hip-hop and Motown, and everything in between.

♪ **OVERTIME CAFÉ.** 327 Myrtle Ave. next to White Castle bet. Grand and Steuben Aves., 974-8144 or 857-2908 or 284-0024. Call for hours.

This little café's card says it all: "No hats, bandanas, du-rags, throwback jerzees, timbs, sports paraphernalia, sweat suits, or sneakers. PEACE." There's all kinds of music here, too: "Afrobeat, Afrofunk, Compa, Soul, Reggae, Hip-hop, Bhangra, Zouk, Black Rock, Samba." It is near Pratt.

♪ **MOE'S BAR.** 80 Lafayette Ave at So. Portland Ave., 797-9536, daily 5:30 p.m.–3:30 a.m.

Despite it's faux-fifties plastic seating, this simple bar is a newcomer. Reportedly the brainchild of actor Chelsea Altman and Ruby Lawrence, producer-star of a TV show called *Thrush TV*, it attracts a sophisticated, urbane local clientele. Check out the monthly jam.

♪ **667 BAR GALLERY LOUNGE.** 6567 Fulton St. bet. Ashland and Rockwell Pls., 855-8558, Tu–Su 5:30 p.m.–3:30 a.m.

Popular with folks who love to dance, this place often boasts a weekend scene. Wednesday nights there's a midweek party with a live DJ, and local hip-hop music.

SHOPPING

Food Shops

BERGEN BAGELS. 486 Myrtle Ave. corner of Hall St., 789-9300, daily 6 a.m.–11 p.m.

Bergen's Bagels sells typical New York deli food, like smoked fish platters of whitefish and smoked sable, and tons of thick, $6 sandwiches. At 55¢ apiece, the baked-on-the-premises bagels are cheap, too.

BODEGAS. 501 Clinton Ave, corner Fulton St., 230-3728.

Opening in 2003, Bodegas is an upscale newcomer to the area. It provides a full-service café with buffet area, and a food market that's a "restaurant in a bottle," so you can come in and pick up all ingredients for a dinner, including produce and fresh meats and fish, specialty gourmet oils, and so on.

CAKE MAN RAVEN CONFECTIONERY. 708 Fulton St. corner of So. Oxford St., 694-CAKE, M–F 10 a.m.–10 p.m., Sa 10 a.m.–midnight, Su 4–10 p.m., www.cakemanraven.com.

A hip bakery with delicious soft huge oatmeal cookies and a mouthwatering exuberance of devil-may-care-about-calories cakes. For instance, peach upside-down cakes, beautiful cheesecakes, Caribbean black cake, carrot cake, cinnamon swirl loaf, German chocolate cake, strawberry shortcake, and an intriguing Watergate cake. Some say that their Southern Red Velvet cake (it's red) is possibly the best cake they've ever tasted.

Cake Man had the honor of doing a fantastic, enormous replica of the Brooklyn Bridge, arches and all, for the 120th anniversary of the bridge in 2003; it was big enough to serve more than three thousand people.

GREENMARKET. Fort Greene Park/Washington Park bet. DeKalb Ave. and Willoughby St., Sa 8 a.m.–5 p.m., second weekend of July through Thanksgiving.

There was a grand opening of the Fort Greene Greenmarket in 2003, featuring fresh fruits, veggies, flowers, baked goods, and so on.

JIVE TURKEY. 441 Myrtle Ave. corner of Washington Ave., 797-1688, M–F 1 a.m.–10 p.m., Sa–Su 11 a.m.–7 p.m.

Come on in for a fried turkey sandwich, turkey wings, turkey legs, turkey sandwich, turkey salad. Or there's also chicken, catfish, meat loaf, ribs, mashed potatoes, yams, sweet salad, and desserts. It's so good you'll want to g___e it right up.

KARROT. 431 Myrtle Ave. corner of Clinton St., 522-9753, M–Sa 8:30 a.m.–8 p.m.

This cute new shop sells organic and gourmet foods, vitamins, books, art, incense—and a fabulous concoction called Mambo juice.

L'EPICERIE DU QUARTIER. 270 Vanderbilt Ave., 636-1200, Tu–Su 11 a.m.–9 p.m.

This French-style grocery sells an appealing selection of breads (from Blue Ribbon bakery), meats and charcuterie, cheeses, imported and domestic organic produce, and Jacque Torres chocolates. You can get great takeout foods as well. It was started by the owner of the popular nearby restaurant À Table.

Other Interesting Neighborhood Shops

⭐ **ASADA.** 1001 Fulton St. off St. James, 399-9488, M—Sa noon—9 p.m., www.asadanewyork.com.

If it's good enough for the entertainment star Usher, it's good enough for you, right? This talented husband-and-wife designer duo from Atlanta makes a line of sexy men's and women's wear. Men can buy off the rack or get custom tailoring.

BIG DEAL BOOKS. 973 Fulton St., 622-4420, daily 9 a.m.—9 p.m., www.sevendollarbooks.com.

Don't be surprised if you stop in for a book and emerge a full hour later, having gotten into the middle of an intense political discussion here. Big Deal seems to invite conversation and reflection. It carries a good selection of books concerned with the African diasporan experience, from politics to novels to children's books to how-tos on hair, cooking, and home décor.

⚫⭐ **CAROL'S DAUGHTER.** 1 So. Elliot Pl. corner of DeKalb Ave., 596-1862, M—Tu and Th 10 a.m.—7 p.m., W and F—Sa 10 a.m.—8 p.m., Su noon—6 p.m., www.carolsdaughter.com. Order online or from catalogue.

Think Kiehl's or Origins for an African-American market. Carol's Daughter ("discovered" by both Oprah *and People* magazine in 2002) makes and sells fabulous, mega-moisturizing, all-natural, hair and body products that are geared to an African market. They've been a word-of-mouth success for a decade. With edible names like "Hyacinthe & Pear with Lady Day" shampoo, "Amaretto Trufle Coconut Body Milk," and "Jamaican Punch" bath salts, who could resist? No wonder orders for sumptuous gift baskets roll in from Japan and Europe, and from celebrities such as Erykah Badu, David Sanborn, Jada Pinkett-Smith, Halle Berry, Gary Dourdan, and Oprah. Check out the full line of yummy-scented products for men and women as well as for pregnant women, babies, and young kids—including "honey pudding" cream to combat eczema.

CLINTON HILL SIMPLY ART AND FRAMING GALLERY. 583 Myrtle Ave. near Classon Ave., 857-0074, Tu—Su 11 a.m.—7 p.m.

At first glance, this is just another framing shop. But if you are a beginner art collector, and want a friendly, down-to-earth place to learn about and buy African diasporan art, drop by Lurita Brown's successful gallery, located one block from **Pratt Institute**. Since 1991, Lurita has focused on what she describes as the "beginner collector of ethnic art." Her gallery includes original artwork by selected African-American, Caribbean, and Native American artists. Her clientele are businesspeople and professionals who are interested in developing their eye—and who are willing to pay for a sound investment in up-and-coming artists. There's also a collection of fine-art reproductions and posters, ranging up to $65. And you can get good prices for framing!

✪ **COURTNEY WASHINGTON.** 674 Fulton St. bet. So. Elliot and So. Portland Aves., 852-6899, Tu–Su noon–7 p.m., www.courtneywashington.com.

Jamaican-born Courtney Washington designs flowing styles for men and women from fine fabrics, often linen in the summer and light wools in the winter. The look is elegant, yet easy fitting, priced at about $220 an outfit. You can wear these clothes at home or at an evening party—and be assured of compliments. Courtney Washington's work has been featured in *Essence* magazine, among others.

DA SPOT 88 UNDAGROUND BOUTIQUE. 88 So. Portland Ave. bet. Fulton St. and Lafayette Ave., 222-1947, Su–Th 1–8 p.m., F–Sa 1–9 p.m., http://daspot88.tripod.com.

A really interesting vintage shop, Da Spot also has a sense of humor ("Undaground"?). There's new and old stuff here. It's stylish, funky, and reasonably priced.

✪ **EXODUS INDUSTRIAL.** 771 Fulton St., bet. So. Portland and So. Elliot Pl. 246-0321, daily noon–8 p.m., www.exodusindustrial.com.

Come here if you want something that's really excellent—and *not* mass-produced. This small collection of edgy clothes—linen tops, layered tops, patchwork shirts—helps if you want to stand out from the crowd. Prices start at $150 for a dress. Special-occasion wear, including wedding gowns, can be made to order. There's casual elegant clothing for men, too.

✪ **4W CIRCLE OF ART & ENTERPRISE.** 704 Fulton St. near So. Oxford St., 875-6500, Tu–W 11 a.m.–7 p.m., Th–F 11 a.m.–8 p.m., Sa 10 a.m.–8p.m., Su 1–5:30 p.m.

4W stands for "Women Working and Winning the World." This is an artists' collective, started in 1991. Based on the model of an African marketplace, it has served as an incubator for many local artists whose work you may find yourself ogling in the windows of Manhattan boutiques. There's always a fresh supply of interesting and affordable jewelry (some designed by recent Pratt graduates), clothing, leather goods, wedding accessories, and children's gear, as well as unusual hand-designed cards and stationery. Some of the work has an African bent; this is a great place to shop for Kwanzaa and, year-round, for one-of-a-kind items. As the neighborhood and artists' work change and evolve, so do the collections in this bellwether boutique.

☺ **HOT TODDIE.** 741 Fulton St. bet. So. Portland and So. Elliot Pl., 858-7292, Tu–F 10 a.m.–6 p.m., Sa–Su 11 a.m.–6 p.m., www.hottoddieonline.com.

Unabashedly romantic boys' and girls' clothes for infants to size 8 are artfully displayed on nostalgic props like sleds and antique baby strollers. Brands include the likes of Betsey Johnson, Dolce & Gabbana, Diesel, and more, plus some shoes to match, and a smattering of creative toys. Brooklyn-based designers are featured as well: Tiki wear by local Linda Grady was presented here before it got picked up by large Manhattan stores. And little girls go nuts for the locally designed Loolie jewelry of sterling silver and semiprecious stones. Check the schedule of family-friendly story readings, book signings, CPR classes, and so on.

♫ **INDIGO BOOKS.** 672 Fulton St. bet. So. Elliot and So. Portland Aves., 488-5934, Tu noon–8 p.m., W–F noon–9 p.m., Sa noon–10 p.m., Su 12–9 p.m.

Indigo Books is more than a bookstore: it's an invitation to think. This independent bookstore-café has an African and political emphasis. It also boasts community spirit, a back garden, and a schedule of special events that are related to books and contemporary social issues, including author readings, readings by local poets, and free Sunday jazz in the summer. There's a living room–like setting (not to mention muffins, soup, and Free Trade coffee) and warm welcomes to new and old friends. The owner has recreated the ambiance of an independent bookshop in Cambridge, Massachusetts, her hometown.

You can also find here some CDs cut by local up-and-coming musicians and vocalists.

★ **MALCHIJAH HATS.** 225 DeKalb Ave. near Clermont Ave., 643-3269, Su–Th 11 a.m.–8 p.m., F–Sa 11 a.m.–10 p.m.

Genius blooms in strange places. The handcrafted hats, made on the premises here, are like a colorful fantasy garden. Summer straw hats in fabulous shapes and boisterous colors are invitations to play, flirt, and prance. Winter hats in more durable fabrics continue the fanciful theme. Prices range from $50 to $125. Their motto: "Get the Hattitude!"

★ **MOSHOOD CREATIONS.** 698 Fulton St. near So. Oxford St., 243-9433, M–Sa 10 a.m.–10 p.m., Su noon–8 p.m., www.afrikanspirit.com.

For twenty-five years Moshood Afariogun, an award-winning designer from Nigeria, has been a pioneer in styles based on African clothing design. Here, in his original boutique (there are now stores in Atlanta and Harlem), you will find his contemporary, sophisticated, urban clothing made of linen, silk, cotton, and wool, adapting traditional West African designs. There are colorful, flowing dashikis and drawstring pants, and *buba* tops and wrap skirts for women, all moderately priced. The store logo, imprinted on everything from little hats to full-length garments, means "faith" in Yoruba. Moshood acts as an informal cultural hub.

Hair Styling

Corn rows, Rasta locks, weaves, lock extensions, invisible braids, kinky twists, sister locks, wraps. What's this hair thing? To learn more about it, log onto www.modernbraid.com or www.designerbraid.com. Or just walk up Flatbush Avenue to find any number of salons. Some specialize in specific kinds of extensions and braiding; prices range from $75 to over $250 for the most extensive "do's" which can take six hours. In the neighborhood: Designer Braids, 922 Fulton St. (783-9078), and Tendrils, 154 Vanderbilt Ave. (875-3811).

PREMIUM GOODS. 694 Fulton St. bet. So. Portland and So. Elliot Pl., 403-9348, Tu–Sa noon–7 p.m., www.premiumgoods.net.

Sneaker-collectors alert: This sparely decorated shop sells sneaker exclusives—limited editions imported from Europe and Japan—as well as Brooklyn-designed T-shirts. Brands include Nike Quickstrike, Nike UK and French exclusive, Adidas originals, and vintage.

★ **RAIFA ATELIER.** 887 Fulton St. corner Vanderbilt Ave., 622-2377, M–Sa 9 a.m.–9 p.m., www.raifatelier.com.

Divas such as Queen Latifah, Angie Stone, and gospel singer Donna Lawrence buy their clothes here, as you can see from their photos on the walls. Raifa designs ethnic formal wear here, such as long drapey gowns and outfits for special occasion wear, many in large sizes. There's a tasteful selection of affordable jewelry. The shop is run by a West African immigrant husband-wife team who hail from the nations of Togo and Guinea, respectively.

SISTERS HARDWARE. 900 Fulton St. near Washington Ave., 399-7023, M–F 8 a.m.–8 p.m., Sa 8 a.m.–7 p.m., Su 10 a.m.–3 p.m.

Why go to a chain store when you can keep the business right in the 'hood? Sisters Hardware has got it all, from hardware to paint to good advice—along with a sense of humor and the resourcefulness of an entrepreneur-owner. Bring your questions to Ms. Barkr, a lifelong Brooklynite, or her knowledgeable staff.

SOUTH PORTLAND ANTIQUES. 753 Fulton St. corner of So. Portland Ave., 596-1556, M–F 9 a.m.–7 p.m., Sa 11 a.m.–7:30 p.m., Su noon–6:30 p.m.

You can find Victoriana and other furniture to befit a brownstone here. There are dressers, chairs, and chests, all tastefully displayed, along with paintings, china, and other European and American items.

THE STORE AT URBANGLASS. 647 Fulton St. corner Rockwell Pl., 625-3685, M–F 9 a.m.–5 p.m., www.urbanglass.org/glass.

Opened in 1998, this little store on the premises of UrbanGlass Studio sells handmade glass objects ranging in price from $5 to $500.

MY LITTLE INDIA. 96 So. Elliot Pl. corner Fulton St., 855-5220, Tu–F noon–8 p.m., Sa 10 a.m.–7 p.m., Su noon–8 p.m.

You can browse through an interesting selection of heavy wooden bed frames, tables made from decorative doors imported from India, and large functional baskets here.

★ **TRIBAL IMPRESSIONS.** 921 Fulton St. bet. Clinton and Waverly, 622-4500, www.jointhetribe.com.

Casual clothing for men and women, designed by husband-wife team of Jayson and E'treea Tropp-Abram, is sold here. Their line includes well-conceived linen shirts with crocheted trim, elegant skirts, and, for men, casual pants and shirts, and kufi—colorful knitted hats. Individual pieces range from $20 to over $100. There's an African ethnic flair and logo, and this gear will look good on you whether you're black, white, or green.

★ **TRIBAL TRUTHS COLLECTION.** 117 So. Oxford at Fulton St., 643-8322, Tu–Su noon–8 p.m.

Designer Brenda Brunson-Bey's extravagant, elegant designs have won her a following in African fashion–conscious circles. This is a fun store, with lots of possibilities for gift items and one-of-a-kind clothes.

Malls

ATLANTIC TERMINAL. Bounded by Atlantic Ave., Flatbush Ave., Hanson Pl. Open daily.

It's *huge*. Slated to open in 2004, Atlantic Terminal is a 400,000-square-foot office building with a capacity for 1,700 employees, above a four-story, 375,000-square-foot retail center. It will be home to Bank of New York, Target, Bath and Body Works, The Children's Place, DSW, Outback Steakhouse, Red Lobster, and Starbucks. Under the whole complex is a renovated Long Island Rail Road and a hub for nine subway lines.

ATLANTIC CENTER MALL. Bounded by Atlantic Terminal, Atlantic Ave., Hanson Pl. Open daily.

Opened in 1988, this mall has 380,000 square feet of large chain stores. There's a large, inexpensive underground parking area. Atlantic Center is a mixed-use residential and commercial project.

ACCOMMODATIONS

There's an informal network of B&Bs in the area. We list only two:

GARDEN GREEN BED & BREAKFAST (see p. 16).
SADDLE DOWN BED & BREAKFAST (see p. 17).

12

Greenpoint

ABOUT GREENPOINT

Suddenly, there's a buzz going on about—of all places—Greenpoint. For years "Greenpernt" as it was pronounced by true Brooklynites, was dispatched with an airy wave of the hand. Greenpoint, a destination? No way.

Real estate trends have a life of their own in the Big Apple. The decade-long incubation during the 1990s of Williamsburg as a youthful, arty—and increasingly expensive—neighborhood has created new demand for property in nearby Greenpoint. Plus, major economic powers in New York City are finally interested in developing a natural asset with which Greenpoint is graced aplenty: waterfront property. (See **What's New,** below.)

Greenpoint has long been home to a thriving, industrious little community of Polish immigrants and a smaller influx of Latino residents. This tidy neighborhood of about forty thousand people is not run down, as Williamsburg was before the college-educated aesthetes and musicians moved in. Many of the homes are owned by Greenpoint residents, not absentee landlords. You see tender, loving care everywhere—in the freshly painted houses, flowerboxes, and swept sidewalks. There's cheap food, and a decent, if small, park.

For fun, compare Greenpoint with the Upper East Side for a moment. Subway access isn't the city's best, but you're not much worse off than living on York Avenue and 81st Street. And the views here (of Manhattan) are far, *far* superior.

There are lots of reasons to come and explore Greenpoint. History and architecture buffs come because of Greenpoint's recently landmarked district. Sociologists study Greenpoint as the American Dream in bloom. Europeans come and stay because, well, it feels like Europe. Young Americans come to live here because it is inexpensive and neighborly (and their parents come here to see where that expensive college education has led to . . . Brooklyn?) And, in the late

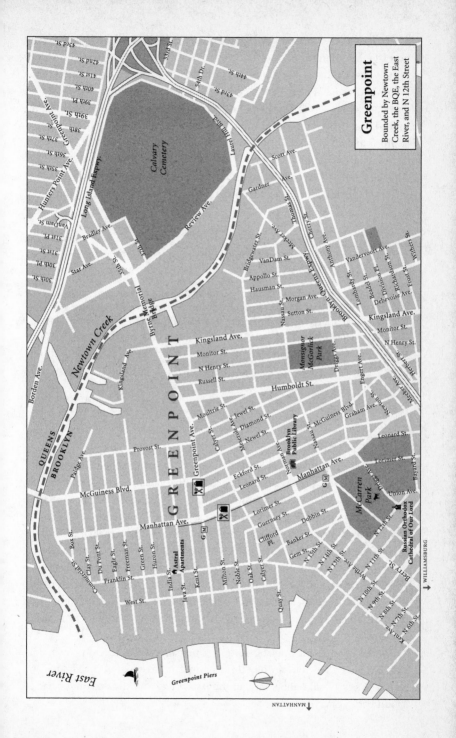

1990s, real estate developers started to come, too, sensing opportunities for the next Brooklyn waterfront frontier.

HOW IT GOT ITS NAME Not surprisingly, Brooklyn's northernmost point was once covered in trees, hence "Green Point," now Greenpoint.

BY SUBWAY From Manhattan ride the L crosstown train from 14th Street to the Lorimer Street stop and transfer to the G subway heading north, or L to Bedford and then buses B61, B48, or B43. Get off at the Nassau Avenue or Greenpoint Avenue stops. (Note: The G train has no Manhattan stops.) Or take the 7 train to Vernon Boulevard/Jackson Avenue, walk a few blocks, cross the bridge walkway, and go down the stairs to Ash Street in Greenpoint.

STUDENTS, ARTISTS, HIPSTERS ARRIVE

There's a growing population of generally affluent and well-educated twenty- or thirty-something Americans in Greenpoint. The rents are a little cheaper. It is quick and easy to hop on a bike to Williamsburg, or take the L train to Union Square in Manhattan. The local crime rate is among the lowest in New York City. There's even a fun softball league in **McCarran Park,** some new bars, and a few galleries, too. (See below for galleries.)

Polish Greenpoint

Take a quiet stroll down Kent Street between Manhattan and Franklin Avenues, or along Java and Calyer Streets. Appreciate the industrial-residential mix on charming Milton Street, in the historic district—and don't be surprised to see a delivery truck labeled "Family's Pierogi" in a driveway.

With an estimated 35,000 Polish residents, it's no surprise that Polish culture is everywhere in Greenpoint. There's a two-inch-thick Polish Yellow Pages that you can get at the bank, the newsstands carry dozens of Polish glossy magazines and newspapers, and the local travel agent's signs are in both English and Polish. There is, it seems, a babka in every kitchen, a kielbasa in every pot, with delis and small restaurants seemingly just around the corner of every residential street.

The basics of life are available for prices that almost don't seem to be in dollars. For under $10 you can buy three pastries, a large loaf of bread, and two babkas. A hearty, substantial meal of soup, stew, and a small salad can be had at a local Polish eatery for under $8.

From many places in Greenpoint—from the still-decrepit waterfront, from the top floors of rental apartment buildings, and from certain corners on the main shopping drag, Manhattan Avenue—you can see the Manhattan skyline like a distant mirage.

What's **NEW?**

Out of Obscurity: Manhattanites May Soon Discover Where Greenpoint Is.

Does a green swath along the Greenpoint waterfront sound unlikely? Does high-speed ferry access to Manhattan sound improbable? Well, they are not. If all the city's plans come to fruition, there'll be public access—a park, a promenade, a playground, maybe a museum—every few blocks along the water, transforming Greenpoint's acres of wasteland property into something beautiful, wonderful, world-class.

Greenpoint is poised on the brink of a lot of changes, IF the following things happen: accelerated gentrification of Williamsburg (almost a certainty); further waterfront development in Brooklyn (highly likely); ferry transportation to Midtown Manhattan (long overdue); a change in housing options as Williamsburg wanna-bes move into Greenpoint and some of the Polish community relocates to nearby Queens (already happening); a 2012 Olympics in New York City, transforming the waterfront (which is boggling).

May we please go near the water?
Zoning changes in the works would enable:

A PARK AT THE END OF MANHATTAN AVENUE. Expect to see boat access for kayaks in a small vest-pocket park at the tip of Manhattan Avenue, expansion of Barge Park Playground, creative recycling of the big old circular sludge tank off DuPont Street for a community facility.

APARTMENTS IN THE OLD GREENPOINT LUMBER EXCHANGE AND TERMINAL MARKET AREAS: Think high-rise. A now-unappealing twenty-four-acre area that starts at West and Freeman and ends at the water—with spectacular views of the East River and Manhattan—has been optioned to a residential developer. The old Greenpoint Terminal Market site is owned by a residential developer considering a fourteen-acre project, including a public waterfront promenade.

PUBLIC ACCESS PIER AND WALKWAY ON THE WATERFRONT AREA BETWEEN JAVA AND KENT STREETS. The New York City Environmental Development Corporation owns this land and has slated it for a recreational pier and esplanade.

A MONITOR MUSEUM AND PARK, BETWEEN OAK AND QUAY STREETS, AND WEST STREET AND THE EAST RIVER. Long-term, watch for a new park and museum to commemorate the Civil War ironclad USS *Monitor*, built and launched on this site.

For information, call Greenpoint Williamsburg Waterfront Task Force at the Community Board. Or subscribe to the *Greenpoint Gazette.*

HISTORICAL NOTES

Purchased by the Dutch in 1638 from the Indians, Greenpoint, along with Williamsburg, was part of the mid-seventeenth-century town known as *Bos-ijck* (Bushwick), meaning "the wooden district." Real development began only in the early and mid-1800s.

Greenpoint became a center for what were known as the "five black arts": glass and pottery making, printing, refining, and the manufacture of cast iron. Charles Pratt's Astral Oil Works refined kerosene here. In addition, a shipbuilding industry arose; the iron Civil War gunship, the *Monitor,* launched in 1862 from a site near the intersection of Oak and West Streets, was fabricated in Greenpoint by Continental Iron Works at West and Calyer Streets. Greenpoint's only better known offspring, actress Mae West, was born here in 1893.

Greenpoint was settled by Northern Europeans, until the arrival of Polish, Russian, and eventually Italian immigrants in the 1880s and thereafter. Despite the downturn in local industry after World War II, immigration continued, and Greenpoint became the unofficial "Little Poland" of New York City. Immigrants from Puerto Rico also settled here.

We can't actually prove this bit of Greenpoint lore, but it is said that Brooklyn's famous and distinctive accent was born here in "Greenpernt." (It is linguistically similar-sounding to the accent that developed in Flatbush, which also lays claim to having the original Brooklyn twang.)

An interesting note: the streets running roughly perpendicular to the East River are named alphabetically, from Ash to Box, Clay, Dupont, Eagle, Freeman, Green, Huron, India, Java, Kent, Greenpoint (formerly Lincoln), Milton, Noble, and Oak Streets.

Kidstuff

☺ Greenpoint is a teaching opportunity. **Have a chat about immigration and U.S. history, look at Polish magazines,** try some new foods at a **Polish restaurant.** Show the kids **Greenpoint Manufacturing and Design Center** and explain what it was and how it's been recycled into twenty-first-century uses. At **Astral Apartments,** imagine life without indoor plumbing, toss a ball in **McCarren Park,** take camera buffs to see the window at **Albert Photo Centrum.**

POINTS OF CULTURAL INTEREST

SPECIAL EVENTS.

Parade of Ships honoring *Monitor* (March 9th); Festival of Polish Culture and Polish film festival at Polish and Slavic Center (October–November, 383-5290);

Greenpoint International Festival, in the summer, with bands, Ferris wheel, crafts fair.

ASTRAL APARTMENTS. 184 Franklin Ave. bet. Java and India Sts.

Like the "model tenements" of Cobble Hill, the Astral apartment complex represented an important step in socially progressive architectural planning. Charles Pratt's Astral Oil Works refined kerosene in Greenpoint, and this huge apartment house was built in 1886 to house Astral's workers. At the time it was built, the provision of light, indoor plumbing, and both hot and cold water were unusual amenities for laborers. Also note the patterned brickwork, brownstone lintels and arches, and multiple entrances. See also the **Home and Tower Buildings** (p. 221).

CONGREGATION AHAVAS ISRAEL. 108 Noble St.

A thread from the century past, this Romanesque Revival-style synagogue was opened for prayer in 1904, and has been home to Jewish congregations ever

---

• *Galleries Arrive in Greenpoint* •

FRANKLIN AVENUE GALLERIES. Bet. Kent and Huron Sts., Check out numbers 112, 150, 213. Open, working galleries.

MARTINEZ GALLERY. 37 Greenpoint Ave. near West St., 706-0606, www.martinez gallery.com. Call for hours or check Web site.

Bearing the pedigree of one of its owners, a well-known graffiti art dealer and historian, Martinez Gallery opened to excited reviews in 2002. It is located way down toward the waterfront, and combines a gallery, bar, and entertainment space. New shows are often launched with a DJ party; multicultural glitterati have been known to show up.

GARAGE GALLERY. 135 A India St. off Manhattan Ave., 349-2738 (upstairs from bookstore). Open weekends and by appointment.

This European-style gallery specializes in post—World War II "Polish School of Poster" art. It's a famous genre that is best-known for the surprising creative associations of its artists, interpreting theater, movies, and cultural events.

SAFE-T-GALLERY. 134 Bayard St. corner of Graham and Manhattan Aves., 782-5920, www.safetgallery.com.

An alternative to the alternative? Safe-T-Gallery bills itself as "the alternative to the general Williamsburg alternative space." They have a special interest in conceptual and personal documentary photography. The gallery is psychologically in Williamsburg, but geographically just a hundred feet across the Williamsburg-Greenpoint border—in Greenpoint.

since. For much of the last half of the twentieth century, the rabbi here was a Polish Holocaust survivor. There's been a recent renaissance of the community here.

GLASSWORKS, THEN AND NOW. 99 Commercial St.

This old building was once home to a fine glassware maker, Christian Dorfinger. According to the Brooklyn Historical Society, President Lincoln's wife once bought a set of glasses made here. The building is once again in use as a center for artists and sculptors.

GREENPOINT INTERNATIONAL FESTIVAL. www.greenpointfestival.com.

A summer street fest with bands, Ferris wheel, crafts fair.

GREENPOINT MANUFACTURING AND DESIGN CENTER (GMDC). 1155–1205 Manhattan Ave. at Ash St., 383-3935.

Williamsburg's craftsmen and artists have recycled a hulking old nineteenth-century industrial complex that once housed a rope factory and die works into New York State's largest industrial cooperative for artisans. It's a visionary project, based on the simple concept of community: many artists, craftspeople, and small businesses have similar needs for technical equipment, marketing, and loans. GMDC (to whom they pay rent) helps provide it. Among the estimated five hundred tenants are painters, sculptors, jewelry makers, restorers, and other specialists. Interestingly, a number of Eastern European immigrants also work here, using Old World skills to make high-end furniture and other non-mass-produced products. This innovative project involved a multimillion-dollar renovation, financed in part by government funds.

GREENPOINT SAVINGS BANK. 807 Manhattan Ave.

It's the architecturally classic, yeah even ponderous, New York City bank.

GUERNSEY STREET. bet. Meserole and Norman Aves.

It's a gem of a street. The sight of this long, seamless block of nineteenth-century apartment buildings lined with tall honey locust trees makes you almost gasp out loud—especially right after a fresh snowstorm. But it's the remarkable visual impact of standing on one end of this street and looking down the block, that makes it worth the visit.

NEZIAH BLISS HOUSE. 130 Kent St. bet. Manhattan and Franklin Aves.

A bit of history lives in this house. It was built in 1859 by Neziah Bliss, a Greenpoint industrialist whose company, Novelty Iron Works, built the *Monitor*'s famous revolving gun turret.

POLISH AND SLAVIC CENTER. 177 Kent St. off Manhattan Ave., 349-1033 (Polish) or 383-5290 (English). (See **Polish Slavic Center Cafeteria.**)

A testimony to the local community's cohesiveness, this large social service center (located in what was once an Italian church) provides a host of facilities for new and established Polish residents, from an inexpensive cafeteria to English classes to a credit union. It serves both as a welcoming committee and a vehicle for acculturation.

BEYOND CYRK
Polish Poster Art

It's easy to forget that immigrants came from somewhere. Polish poster art gives you an idea of what the Polish population here in Greenpoint left behind. During the forty-five-year Communist era in Poland (from the end of WWII to 1989), the walls of building sites throughout a strife-ridden postwar Poland were often plastered with posters announcing films, rallies, operas, theaters, concerts, and festivals. As with television and print ads in the United States, you can get the feel of the times just by flipping through the images. It's a surreal, often harsh worldview. See www.contemporaryposters.com and www.polbook.com/polishartgallery.

PUBLIC SCHOOL 34. 131 Norman Ave. corner of Eckhart St., 389-5842.

One of the top-ranked elementary public schools in Brooklyn, PS 34 is also a New York City Landmark. It is one of the city's few remaining nineteenth-century school buildings—one of the oldest schools in continuous use in New York City.

This early Romanesque Revival building was erected in 1867 just after the end of the Civil War and the assassination of President Lincoln. It was named after Oliver Hazard Perry, an American naval officer whose fleet defeated the British in the Battle of Lake Erie during the War of 1812.

Public education was a major force in nineteenth-century Brooklyn. Brooklyn established its first public-education system as early as 1816.

PUBLIC SCHOOLS.

Among those considered to be New York City's best public elementary schools are PS 31 (75 Meserole Avenue) and PS 34 (131 Norman Avenue). (Source: *New York City's Best Public Elementary Schools,* 2002, by C. Hemphill with P. Wheaton.)

RUSSIAN ORTHODOX CATHEDRAL OF THE TRANSFIGURATION OF OUR LORD. 122 No. 12th St., at Driggs Ave.

Even though Brooklyn is considered the "city of churches," you won't want to miss this official landmark Eastern Orthodox beauty, built in 1921. Its five copper-clad, onion-shaped domes, typical of Russian Byzantine style, tower over the neighborhood. When the structure was built, Greenpoint was one of several thriving industrial belts in Brooklyn, with a large Eastern Orthodox population working in nearby factories.

ST. STANISLAUS KOSTKA CHURCH. 607 Humboldt St. corner Driggs Ave., 388-0170.

The main church for Greenpoint's Polish community and a vital participant in community affairs. Come at Easter or Christmastime to get the full flavor of active European Catholic worship. Many New Yorkers recalled the visit here of Pope John Paul II when he was still a cardinal.

SIDEWALK CLOCK. 753 Manhattan Ave. bet. Norman and Meserole Sts.

Like the famous clock on Fifth Avenue and 23rd Street in Manhattan, this sidewalk clock was erected as an early form of advertising for jewelry and other stores. It is made of cast iron and is a New York City landmark. There are only seven such clocks extant in New York City. This is the only one in Brooklyn.

STORAGE TANKS.

Whoops, they're gone! There were once enormous Brooklyn Union Gas Company storage tanks here, visible from most of Greenpoint. Some people mourned their recent removal, the loss of a gritty old landmark reminiscent of the area's industrial past.

USS *MONITOR*. Old Piers, end of Huron St.

The ironclad USS *Monitor* was built right here. Use your imagination, though, because the launch site on Bushwick Creek is inaccessible, not to mention dangerous. (As of this writing, the area is mostly used by scruffy kids, local fishermen, and nocturnal drinkers, at their own risk.) But the old manufacturing buildings, which once produced ropes for the shipbuilding industry, still stand nearby. There are plans afoot to construct a 150-foot boardwalk here—and possibly a *Monitor* Museum, preservation of the launch site, and formal commemoration of Greenpoint's contribution to American maritime history. (See **What's New** box.)

WINTHROP PARK SHELTER PAVILION, MONSIGNOR McGOLRICK PARK.

A New York City landmark, the lovely curved pavilion is reminiscent of eighteenth-century formal gardens. That's no accident; it was designed in 1910 after the Trianon at Versailles by Helmle and Huberty, who were also the architects for the Prospect Park Boathouse and several other Brooklyn historic landmarks.

PARKS AND PLAYGROUNDS

☺ **McCARREN PARK.** Bounded by Manhattan Ave., Berry St., No. 12th St., and Bayard St.

A large, well-used urban park that is home to serious soccer and baseball games, extended family BBQs, and very sociable dog-walking, McCarren Park is the dividing line between Williamsburg and Greenpoint, and is used by residents of both communities. Meanwhile, those with young kids should beware broken glass in the grass. There's a summer greenmarket here.

☺ **McCARREN PARK POOL AND BATHHOUSE.**

There's a huge Art Deco–era swimming pool, bathhouses, and a beautiful arched pavilion entrance here—closed and decrepit. There's pressure in the community to renovate and reopen this WPA showcase and perhaps create a skate park or upgrade the soccer fields; stay tuned.

☺ **MONSIGNOR McGOLRICK PARK.** Along Nassau and Driggs Aves., bet. Monitor and Russell Sts., daily 6 a.m.–10 p.m.

Monsignor McGolrick park is reminiscent of a small, quiet European urban park. On a warm afternoon you will find moms strolling with babies, lovers holding hands, and gaggles of older men sitting and talking. The square is ringed with modest, two-story homes sporting aluminum siding, mostly owner-occupied (and likely to appreciate in value greatly if and when the much-discussed gentrification of parts of Greenpoint actually occurs). For a game of soccer or baseball, go instead to nearby **McCarren Park.**

History buffs will be interested in the **Winthrop Park Shelter Pavilion** in the center of the park (see p. 324). Note also the statue of the naked sailor pulling on his mooring rope, a memorial to the *Monitor*, a Civil War ship built locally.

GREENPOINT RESTAURANTS

AMARIN. 617 Manhattan Ave. bet. Driggs Ave. and Nassau St., 349-2788, daily 11 a.m.–10:30 p.m. Cash only.

This Thai restaurant with light, very fresh food, started by folks who used to work at **Planet Thai** nearby, is noisy, crowded, and generally popular with locals.

CHRISTINA'S. 853 Manhattan Ave. corner of Milton St., 383-4382, daily 8 a.m.–8 p.m. Cash only.

One of the neighborhood's two better bets for Polish food. Ten booths and a counter are all there is to Christina's, and that intimacy, plus good-value, good-tasting, home-cooked food, are the reasons this little Polish diner is busy with local patrons. Try the Hungarian pancakes. You can get a substantial meal for less than $8 per person, and "Christina's Sunday Special" brunch is a bargain at $6.25.

OLD POLAND BAKERY AND RESTAURANT (AKA RESTAURACJA PIERKRNIA STAROPOLSKA).
190 Nassau St. corner of Humboldt St., 349-7775, daily 11 a.m.–9 p.m. Cash only.

A guy jumps out of the passenger side of a delivery truck and enters the restaurant. A mom pushing a stroller goes in. Two young men stop in. What's the attraction? Supertasty home-style foods: a dozen kinds of rich soups (fruit soup, sauerkraut soup, borscht, for starters) and an equal number of different fillings for blintzes and pierogi; mounds of mashed potatoes and fresh vegetables; cooked-to-a-T cutlets, dumplings, and meat loaf. Euro-deli style here; you wait in line to place your order, then sit down, and they will call you when your order is ready.

OTT. 970 Manhattan Ave. at India St., 609-9495, 11 a.m.–11 p.m.

What a curious mix of cuisines on Manhattan Avenue: Polish and Thai. OTT serves basic country Thai food at low prices, across the street from the Thai Café.

PSC (POLISH SLAVIC CENTER) CAFETERIA. 177 Kent St. bet. Manhattan Ave. and McGuinness Blvd.,
349-1033, M–F 11 a.m.–7 p.m. Sa 11 a.m.–4 p.m. Cash only.

Nostalgic for your school days of yore? The PSC Cafeteria has everything you could hope for: plastic trays, women in white uniforms, fluorescent lighting, and a little window where you bring your dirty dishes. The lace curtains and the plants atop the Pepsi machine add a homey touch to the otherwise institutional vibe. The food is way better than the average cafeteria sludge; in fact, they claim that everything is made fresh. The $1 soups are quite good (especially the unbelievably creamy dill soup with noodles), the $4 meatballs taste like Mom's, and the $4 cheese blintzes are a must.

POD WIERCHAMI. 119 Nassau Ave. corner of Eckford St., 347-296-0191, daily 10 a.m.–9 p.m. Cash only.

Taxidermy shop or restaurant? This cafeteria-style Polish eatery is decorated with a selection of stuffed elk, deer, and birds adorned with Christmas lights, fake flowers, and jewelry. The picnic tables, wooden carvings, and amateurish landscape paintings complete the trippy lodge aesthetic. Try the kasha-and-vegetable plate—a heaping plate of buckwheat, pickled beets, cooked cabbage, and carrots. Or stick to the homemade blintzes (delicate and delicious) or pierogies (fried to perfection). Every order comes with a free cold raspberry drink—and a warm smile from the Polish lady behind the counter. Entrees range from $4 to $6.

POLSKA RESTAURANT. 36 Greenpoint Ave. near Manhattan Ave., 389-8368, daily noon–9 p.m.

Generous servings of entrées such as chicken cutlets, goulash with barley, and beef Stroganoff cost less than $10. The $2 homemade soups—Russian borscht, sorrel soup, vegetable soup—are excellent, as are the potato pancakes, and, if you dare, the herring and onions. This Polish restaurant is one that's recommended by locals.

SUN VIEW LUNCHEONETTE. 221 Nassau Ave. corner of N. Henry St., 383-8121, daily 6 a.m.–10 p.m. Cash only.

Remember the popular *Cheers* sitcom lyric "where everybody knows your name"? Sun View's owner seems familiar with at least half of the clientele, and is equally friendly with the other half, chatting it up about the vintage phone booths in the back or her hometown in Greece—which explains the languid service. But where else can you still get coffee for 50 cents or a burger for $1.15?

THAI CAFÉ. 925 Manhattan Ave., 383-3562, M–W 11:30 a.m.–10:30 p.m., Th–Sa 11:30 a.m.–11 p.m., Su 1–11 p.m.

This absolutely no-frills Thai restaurant has more tables, fewer crowds, the same great food, low prices, and, for the time being, shorter lines than Williamsburg counterparts. With entrées in the $8 range, the price is right, but bring your rose-colored glasses; it's time for a décor makeover here.

WASABI. 638 Manhattan Ave. See Wasabi in Williamsburg.

BARS AND NIGHTLIFE

♫ **EUROPA.** 765 Manhattan Ave. corner of Meserole Ave., 383-5723, www.europaclub.com.

A hot spot. East meets West. Europa draws a cosmopolitan crowd of local Polish twenty-somethings, European visitors, artists, and hipsters from the Williamsburg scene. You can buy $15 tickets online for jazz and other live performances—and check out the photos of Europa's owner with the president of Poland and various New York City politicos.

♫ **ENID'S.** 560 Manhattan Ave. at Driggs Ave., 349-3859. Cash only.

Enid's is inexpensive, artsy, and unpretentious—with a good jukebox. Sunday brunch attracts a relaxed, urbane young crowd, dressed almost entirely in funereal black. There're DJs several times a week, and an occasional country night.

GREENPOINT TAVERN.

Gotcha. It's not in Greenpoint, but in Williamsburg. See **Rosemary's Greenpoint Tavern** (page 461).

IRENE'S PUB (AKA MURPHY'S). 156 Calyer St. corner of Lorimer St., 383-8833, daily 8 a.m.–2 to 4 a.m. Cash only.

Oozing with history and old-time charm, Irene's Pub is the type of joint where every drink has a special name—even tap water is called "city gin." Irene's has a rich and sordid past—as an ice-cream parlor, a speakeasy, and a brothel. The original mahogany bar and wood paneling may explain a recent surge of movie directors and crews filming here, seeking authentic old Brooklyn sets.

LE CUE BILLIARDS & CAFÉ. 213 McGuinness Blvd. bet. Greenpoint Ave. and Calyer St., 349-1445, M–Th noon–1 a.m., F–Sa until 3 a.m. From $7.60 per hour.

At this old-fashioned billiards place, you're likely to meet a cross-cultural mix of old-time *Greenpernt* folks, Polish immigrants, and hipsters.

PENCIL FACTORY. 142 Franklin St. at Greenpoint Ave., 609-5858, M–F 2 p.m.–4 a.m., Sa–Su 1 p.m.–4 a.m.

Greenpoint was a blue-collar area, and this bar is aptly named after the building's original business. It used to be the Eberhard Faber pencil factory. You'll know it by the giant decorative yellow pencils at the top of the building façade. Come for a drink (no food) and check out the old photos in the back, of Brooklyn mid-twentieth century.

SPLENDID. 132 Greenpoint Ave. bet. Franklin and Manhattan Sts., 383-1900, Tu–Th and Su 6:30 p.m.–2 a.m., F–Sa 6:30 p.m.–3 a.m.

Just a stone's throw from the Greenpoint Avenue stop on the G train, Splendid is a local hangout popular with Americans and Europeans born in the 1970s and 1980s. There's local art on its walls, a pool table, and a jukebox full of faves. It's a low-key, friendly bar scene.

♫ **WARSAW AT THE POLISH NATIONAL HOME.** Polish National Home, 261 Driggs Ave. at Eckford St., 387-5252, daily 5 p.m.–midnight, www.polishnationalhome.com.

A few nights a week you can come here for a drink at the bar and some sets of music by indie rockers. Wander in at the wrong evening, though, and you might feel like you're in, well, Warsaw. On weekend nights the large meeting hall doubles as a club for artists and hipsters who can enjoy the pre–World War I architecture—high ceilings, decorative walls—and the sheer size of the place. (It accommodates one thousand people, enough for a party.) During the week you might find yourself at a social function or political meeting to discuss the rezoning of the waterfront and local school budgets. There's a bar on the premises, too, with pretty good snacks; after a few beers and a pierogi or two you might find yourself homesick for the Poland depicted on the wall mural, even if you've never been there. It's the perfectly odd meeting place for two different cultures, a Greenpoint highlight. Call ahead or check the Web site to find out who's playing; gigs are organized by the same bookers used by the Village Underground. It's near G train Nassau Avenue stop, and close to **Splendid.**

SHOPPING

Specialty Food Shops

> ☛ **TIP: Bakeries and Sausages** There are more sausage makers and bakeries in Greenpoint than you can shake your *paczki* at, and that's with or without the hole in the middle. And if you think that's jabberwocky, that's because you haven't tried *paczkis*, the Polish version of the doughnut. The following lists a few bakeries and meat markets—and other food emporiums—that will transport you far from your diet into *paczki* and babka heaven.

ERIC GIRERD CHOCOLATE FACTORY. 609-6064, www.ericgirerd.com.

Eric Girerd is a world-class pastry chef and award-winning genius for exquisite, detailed sculpting in chocolate. "I like to make chocolate because chocolate makes people happy," says the jovial, gray-haired French chef. Girerd's forte is combining chocolate with unusual spices and flavors: lavender, raspberry, curry, Szechuan peppers, fennel, coriander, licorice, coffee, tea, even wasabi, and, special for **Bierkraft,** Brooklyn beer. There's not a store here, just a kitchen (it's not set up for retail business, so please don't drop in). Sold in **Bierkraft, L'Epicerie du Quartier,** and many Manhattan stores. A tiny delicate box of chocolates costs $6.50.

FORTUNATO BROTHERS. 289 Manhattan Ave. near Devoe St., 387-2281, daily 8 a.m.–9 p.m., Su 1–5 p.m. Cash only.

Classic Italian desserts are made here, from wedding cakes to spumoni to pastries. Stop in for a cappuccino or espresso, and enjoy! Oh, an insider's tip: the café is reportedly owned by the Genovese family, associated with headline news, jail sentences, and the like.

> ☛ **TIP: Greenmarkets** There's a big greenmarket on Saturdays 8 a.m.–3 p.m. at Lorimer Street and Driggs Avenue, and a smaller seasonal greenmarket (July–October), at Havemeyer Street and Broadway, Th 8 a.m.–5 p.m.

POZNANSKI'S BAKERY. 668 Manhattan Ave. near Greenpoint Ave., 389-5252, daily 8 a.m.–7 p.m. Cash only.

Poznanski's sells good, fresh babka (go for the cheese kind), *challah*, and pastries. They also have just about the best *hamantaschen* (triangular pastries filled with prune, apricot, or poppy-seed paste) in town.

STAR MARKET. 176 Nassau St. bet. Humboldt and Jewel Sts., 383-6948, daily 8 a.m.–7 p.m. Cash only.

Another throwback to your Polish grandma's pantry, this tiny, no-frills food store is crammed with long-shelf-life delicacies, such as smoked fish, baked goods, rows of berry jams, and boxes of herbal teas.

STEVE'S MEAT MARKET. 104 Nassau bet. Leonard and Eckhart Sts. corner of Leonard St., 383-1780, M–F 8 a.m.–8 p.m., Sa 8 a.m.–6 p.m. Cash only.

Steve's claims to have the best kielbasa in America. His salted, smoked sausages have won kudos from wiener-lovers, and the fact that there are a half-dozen different kinds of horseradish casually displayed in the window suggests that Steve takes his sausages seriously.

SYRENA. 207 Norman Ave. corner of Humboldt St., 349-4560, M–F 6 a.m.–9 p.m., Sa 6 a.m.–8 p.m. Cash only.

Ask a Polish restaurateur who makes the bread they serve with their borscht, and they're likely to answer, Syrena. Wait in line to choose from an impressive selection of *wiejski* (a Polish bread), babkas, Danishes, poppy-seed cake, or *chruschiki*—rectangular treats that taste like fried dough but crunch like a cookie. Prices are cheap, with big loaves of bread under $2.00 and cookies just $5.00 a pound.

THE GARDEN. 921 Manhattan Ave. bet. Kent and Greenpoint Aves., 389-6448, M–Sa 8 a.m.–8 p.m., Su 9 a.m.–7 p.m., www.thegardenfoodmarket.com.

The Garden is an upscale, health-oriented supermarket that sells a wide variety of foods, from fresh vegetables to prepared salads to dozens of different kinds of cheeses, to entire lines of packaged health-food goods. And then there's the chocolate mousse. The store is big, so wear your roller skates: five thousand square feet of shopping heaven.

W. NASSAU MEAT MARKET. 915 Manhattan Ave. near Greenpoint Ave., 389-6149, M–F 8 a.m.–8 p.m, Sa 8 a.m.–6 p.m. Cash only.

Don't be shy. Even if you don't know what something in the window is, wander in and ask. These Greenpoint butchers are so friendly you are likely to get several samples of their freshly made, spicy meat loaf. This shop is great for bacon, sausages, and kielbasa, plus things to go with them, such as huge loaves of fresh rye bread, imported mustard, horseradish, and canned cherries.

WEDEL. 772 Manhattan Ave. corner of Meserole Ave., 349-3933, M–Sa 10 a.m.–8 p.m., Su 10 a.m.–6 p.m. Cash only.

Polish Willy Wonka's on speed. Chocolate animals, candy with cartoons, floral wrappers—it's a wild, colorful kingdom of confections. With towering shelves of sweets in every possible shape and size, it would take more than a few visits to nibble your way through all of Wedel's treasures. If you don't speak Polish, you won't be able to read the labels, so here's a tip: try the chocolate-covered prunes ($4.99/lb). Prices are cheap to moderate.

Other Interesting Neighborhood Shops

ALBERT PHOTO CENTRUM. 662 Manhattan Ave. bet. Nassau and Norman Sts., 383-1585, M–Sa 11 a.m.–8 p.m. Su 11 a.m.–5 p.m.

One of New York's largest displays of vintage cameras graces the store window and shelves of this surprisingly upscale camera shop. The collection—which is not for sale—totals over a thousand old cameras, including two large antique "accordion"-style view cameras dating from the late 1800s. What you can buy are new cameras and equipment from top-line manufacturers such as Nikon, Leica, and Minolta, at low prices. The owner, a Polish-born photographer/collector whose demeanor suggests the Left Bank of Paris, also has a commercial photo lab on the premises.

BI MUSIC RECORDS. 735 Manhattan Ave. bet. Norman and Meserole Sts., 389-1376, M–Sa 11 a.m.–8 p.m., Su 1–6 p.m.

Here's where you can find CDs, cassettes, video tapes, and DVDs—all in Polish.

CHOPIN CHEMISTS. 911 Manhattan Ave. off Greenpoint Ave., 383-7822, daily 9 a.m.–7 p.m.

Women will find an extensive line of preservative-free, all-natural Polish-imported cosmetic products for all skin types in this otherwise fully Americanized pharmacy. There's an interesting line of natural products by a Dr. Irena Eris, and another called "Satysfakcja," plus herbal teas, chamomile, and extracts.

OAZA. 928 Manhattan Ave. corner of Kent St., 349-0694, M–F 11 a.m.–7 p.m., Sa 11 a.m.–5 P.M. Cash only.

Shut your eyes, click your heels, and you're not in New York anymore. Oaza is one of those eclectic gift shops that make you wonder *who* buys the stuff: a bird made out of pipe cleaners, a $4 soapstone elephant, and a bronze statue of a Chinese goddess priced at $400.

POLONIA. 882 Manhattan Ave. bet. Greenpoint St. and Milton Ave., 389-0684, M–Sa 11 p.m.–6 p.m., librrros@masn.com.

Polish music, videos, kids' books, dictionaries, imported vases, and magazines are all sold in this little gem of Polish cultural pride. In the window you are likely to see books in Polish about a broad range of topics, from the much beloved Pope John Paul II, to the famous artist Frida Kahlo, to horoscopes in Polish.

POLISH BOOKSTORE & PUBLISHING INC. 135 A India St., 349-2738, M–Sa 11 a.m.–7:30 p.m., Su 11 a.m.–5 p.m., www.polbook.com.

An intellectual's bookstore and a cultural hub, this well-stocked shop has contemporary fiction and nonfiction, action novels, and classics. If you'd like to ship your college roommate a Polish care package, see their specialty food line at www.SweetPoland.com; their Web site also has links to Polish cultural events in the United States, including classical concerts, Roman Polanski movies, and contemporary European theater productions.

● **POP'S POPULAR CLOTHING.** 7 Franklin St. bet. No. 15th St. and Meserole Ave., 349-7677, M–Sa 9 a.m.–6 p.m., Sa 9 a.m.–4 p.m.

Pop's sells new and used clothing, mainly for men. Authentic navy pea coats, gas station jackets (many prepatched with names like "Ed" and "Larry" for those days you feel like being someone else), blue jeans, boots, belts, and a slew of thoroughly original shirts and ties. (For more listings nearby, see **Williamsburg Vintage and Collectibles.**)

WIZARD ELECTROLAND. 863 Manhattan Ave., 549-6889, daily 10 a.m.–7 p.m.

Spacious and inviting, this large, upscale consumer electronics store is an independent company, run by Robert Pastuszak, who was born in Warsaw and educated in Europe. Upstairs you'll find brand-name keyboards, boom boxes, CD players, and high-end televisions, and downstairs there's a whole room full of DVDs, videos, and music, as well as PlayStations. The staff is friendly, helpful, and, of course, Polish-English bilingual. They offer a thirty-day guarantee to match the lowest price of your purchase, so prices are competitive.

☺ **ZAKOPANE.** 714 Manhattan Ave. bet. Norman and Meserole Sts., 389-3487, daily 11 a.m.–8 p.m. Cash only.

A woodcarver's paradise, the jumble of wooden bowls, jewelry boxes, and enormous carved eagles make this a must-stop in Greenpoint. Everything is imported from Poland.

ZIOEA HERBAPOL. 178 Nassau St., bet. Humboldt and Jewel Sts., 383-5892, M–Sa 10 a.m.–6 p.m. Cash only.

Interested in fragrant soaks for sore feet, syrups to calm the nerves, or concoctions to increase libido? For maladies beyond your HMO's limited horizons, you might venture here to seek some old-fashioned herbal remedies.

ACCOMMODATIONS
PSC GREENPOINT YMCA BED & BREAKFAST (see p. 17).

13

"Heart of Brooklyn"

The Museums, Central Library, Prospect Park, and Zoo

 ## What's NEW?

Brooklyn's Getting a New Heart

Some of the borough's biggest cultural institutions, located quite close to one another, have joined together in a collaboration they call the **Heart of Brooklyn: A Cultural Partnership**. It includes the Brooklyn Botanic Garden, the Brooklyn Children's Museum, the Brooklyn Museum of Art, the Brooklyn Central Public Library, Prospect Park, and the Prospect Park Zoo. Watch for a new magazine, user-friendly information (look for their calendars)—and maybe even a few food kiosks to fuel you as you make the rounds. As tourism increases, also watch for street improvements along Washington Avenue. Check www.heartofbrooklyn.org for events at all six institutions.

BY SUBWAY *To Prospect Park and Zoo:* Take the 2 or 3 train to Grand Army Plaza, or the B or Q train to 7th Avenue and walk up Flatbush Avenue. Or, for the zoo, you can also take the Q train to Parkside Avenue. *To the Brooklyn Museum of Art and Brooklyn Botanic Garden:* Take the 2, 3, or 4 train to the Eastern Parkway/Brooklyn Museum stop, or take the Q to the Seventh Avenue, walk around Grand Army Plaza, and one block up Eastern Parkway. *To the Brooklyn Children's Museum:* Take the 3 or C train to Kingston Avenue (but be prepared to walk).

SPECIAL EVENTS All institutions have a busy schedule of cultural events. Call the main numbers, check Web sites, or watch listings in the newspapers and local magazines.

☛ **TIP: Trolley Around the Park** Get a free ride year-round to all of the Heart of Brooklyn institutions on weekends from noon–6 p.m. Call 965-8999 for the trolley schedule.

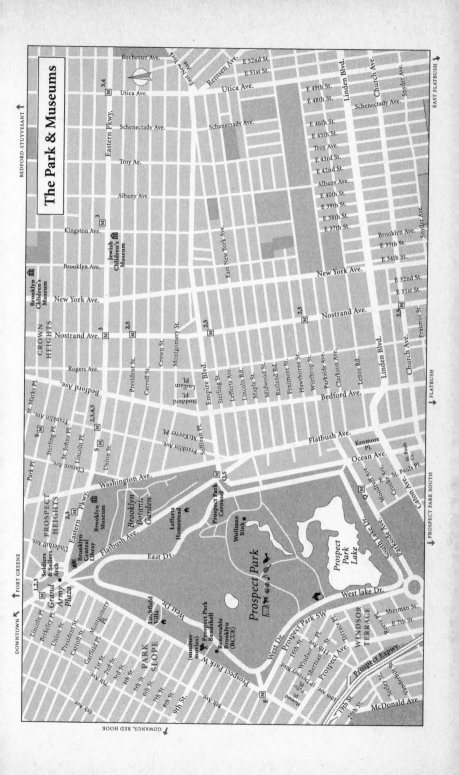

The Park & Museums

BEDFORD-STUYVESANT

EAST FLATBUSH

FLATBUSH

PROSPECT PARK SOUTH

DOWNTOWN

FORT GREENE

GOWANUS, RED HOOK

CROWN HEIGHTS

PROSPECT HEIGHTS

PARK SLOPE

WINDSOR TERRACE

Prospect Park

Prospect Park Lake

Rochester Ave.
Remsen Ave.
E 52nd St.
E 51st St.
Utica Ave.
Utica Ave.
Schenectady Ave.
Schenectady Ave.
Schenectady Ave.
E 49th St.
E 48th St.
E 46th St.
E 45th St.
Troy Ave.
E 43rd St.
E 42nd St.
Albany Ave.
E 40th St.
E 39th St.
E 38th St.
E 37th St.
Linden Blvd.
Church Ave.
Snyder Ave.
Brooklyn Ave.
E 35th St.
E 34th St.
Eastern Pkwy.
Troy Ae.
Albany Ave.
Kingston Ave.
Jewish Children's Museum
Brooklyn Ave.
New York Ave.
Brooklyn Children's Museum
East New York Ave.
New York Ave.
E 32nd St.
E 31st St.
Erasmus St.
Nostrand Ave.
Nostrand Ave.
Nostrand Ave.
President St.
Crown St.
Montgomery St.
Empire Blvd.
Sterling St.
Lefferts Ave.
Lincoln Rd.
Maple St.
Midwood St.
Rutland Rd.
Fenimore St.
Hawthorne St.
Winthrop St.
Parkside Ave.
Clarkson Ave.
Lenox Rd.
Linden Blvd.
Church Ave.
Rogers Ave.
Bedford Ave.
Carroll St.
Stoddard Pl.
Ludlam Pl.
Bedford Ave.
St. Marks Pl.
Sterling Pl.
St. Johns Pl.
Lincoln Pl.
Franklin Ave.
Classon Ave.
Union St.
Park Pl.
Washington Ave.
Sullivan Pl.
McKeever Pl.
Franklin Ave.
Kenmore Pl.
Ocean Ave.
Woodruff Ave.
Clarkson Ave.
St. Pauls Pl.
St. Pauls Ct.
Caton Ave.
Brooklyn Botanic Garden
Prospect Park Carousel
Lefferts Homestead
Brooklyn Museum
Brooklyn Central Library
Soldiers & Sailors Arch
Grand Army Plaza
Eastern Pkwy.
Underhill Ave.
Flatbush Ave.
East Dr.
Wollman Rink
West Dr.
West lake Dr.
South Lake Dr.
Parkside Ave.
Lincoln Pl.
Berkeley Pl.
Union St.
President St.
Carroll St.
Garfield Pl.
Montgomery Pl.
Litchfield Villa
West Dr.
Prospect Park Bandshell
Celebrate Brooklyn (BCUE)
(summer movies)
6th Ave.
7th Ave.
8th Ave.
9th St.
8th St.
7th St.
6th St.
5th St.
4th St.
3rd St.
2nd St.
1st St.
Prospect Park W
Prospect Park SW
8th Ave.
Windsor Pl.
16th St.
10th Ave.
Windsor Ave.
Sherman Pl.
Prospect Ave. Terrace Pl.
Reeve Pl.
Sherman St.
E 7th St.
Howard Pl.
Fuller Pl.
Vanderbilt Ave.
Prospect Expwy.
McDonald Ave.
19th St.
20th St.
Seeley St.
Prospect Ave.

THE MUSEUMS

Brooklyn Botanic Garden

☺ 1000 Washington Ave. along Eastern Pkwy., 623-7200, www.bbg.org. April–Sept. Tu–F 8 a.m.–6 p.m., Sa–Su and holidays (incl. M, except Labor Day) 10 a.m.–6 p.m., Oct–March Tu–F 8 a.m.–4:30 p.m., Sa–Su and holidays (incl. M.) 10 a.m.–4:30 p.m. Closed Thanksgiving, Christmas, and New Year's Day. Adults 16 and over $5; seniors and students with valid IDs $3; free for children under 16; free to the public every Tuesday and every Saturday (until noon); and free for seniors every Friday.

Special events: There are many, including the annual **Brooklyn Botanic Garden Plant Sale**, spectacular **Cherry Blossom Festival, Springfest, Sunday** performances, and more. Check the Web site.

A refuge, a garden, a place of beauty and wonder: that's the Brooklyn Botanic Garden, located in the heart of Brooklyn.

Outside, there are over fifty acres of carefully designed and meticulously maintained environments: lilac and daffodil hills, rose gardens, a blossoming Japanese cherry orchard (and an annual festival with drumming and performances that's not to be missed), a children's garden, a fragrance garden, and a garden for the blind. A favorite is the enclosed **Japanese Garden,** with footbridges, paths, and a Shinto shrine. Kids will love discovering the wildlife and running along the walkways, including Celebrity Walk, which has names of famous Brooklynites inscribed on it. The summertime Children's Garden is a local institution.

Inside, the new and architecturally acclaimed **Steinhardt Conservatory,** designed by Davis, Brody and Associates and completed in 1988, is a must-see. It houses the Trail of Evolution, the Aquatic House, a bonsai pavilion, and special rooms with tropical, desert, and temperate environments. The Botanic Garden was founded in 1910, and is a New York City landmark. Call for information about the famous annual plant sale, tours, classes, and festivals.

TERRACE CAFÉ. Brooklyn Botanic Garden, 622-4432, 623-7200. For hours, see above.

Lunch in May or June is heaven in this informal outdoor café in one of New York City's two major botanical gardens. Just getting there, walking past the Japanese gardens, Daffodil Hill, and rows of spring flowers is half the fun. It's jammed on the weekends, so aim for late breakfast or late lunch.

☺ **MOUNT PROSPECT PLAYGROUND.** Eastern Pkwy. bet. Brooklyn Museum of Art and Central Library.

Said to be Brooklyn's second highest natural vantage point, this is the site of a Continental Army lookout post prior to the infamous Battle of Brooklyn in 1776. There's a secluded little eight-acre park and playground here.

Brooklyn Children's Museum (BCM)

☺ I-45 Brooklyn Ave. corner of St. Marks Pl., 735-4400, fall/winter/spring hours: Tu–F 2–5 p.m., Sa–Su 10 a.m.–5 p.m., summer hours: Tu–F noon–5 p.m., Sa–Su 10 a.m.–5 p.m., www.brooklynkids.org. Admission $4.00. Call for special events.

If you were designing a children's museum, where would your imagination take you? The Brooklyn Children's Museum, which has literally been underground for years, is about to blossom—into an undulating, two-story, daffodil-yellow building. In 2006 the museum will double its space, growing into over a hundred thousand square feet, in a new edifice designed by world-renowned architect Rafael Vinoly. Come see for yourselves!

Elementary-school kids love it here. There's an exhibit called *Totally Tots,* just for kids under five; *Music Mix,* an exhibit of musical instruments from around the world, where kids can create their own music; a plant-education area, greenhouse, and garden in which kids build their own ecosystem and plant their own seedlings; and *Together in the City,* where kids can go on parade or become pizza-shop owners as they explore an urban cityscape. In *Collections Central,* kids can string a beaded necklace, create a superhero, and get up close to the museum's collection of natural history and cultural artifacts. Plus, the museum has a traveling exhibit space with ever-changing exhibits, from dinosaurs to castles. In the summer, don't miss the Friday rooftop music jam!

The kiddie clientele, a wonderful mix of races and backgrounds, is itself an education. The museum's inspired, exuberant, curiosity-provoking exhibits include multicultural artifacts, ethnomusical instruments, experiments that relate to concepts of space, measurement, and weight, and activities designed to teach peaceful collaboration between different cultural groups.

One of the few children's museums with a permanent collection, BCM has over 27,000 objects ranging from baskets and costumes to musical instruments. About 250,000 people visit every year.

The Brooklyn Children's Museum was the world's first children's museum, pioneering in the nineteenth century a concept that is still valuable today: hands-on, interactive installations. In 1999 it celebrated its centennial birthday. And there's still a lot to celebrate at the Brooklyn Children's Museum. Please, "DO touch!"

Brooklyn Museum of Art

☺ ◉ 200 Eastern Pkwy. corner of Washington Ave., 638-5000, W–F 10 a.m.–5 p.m., Sa–Su 11 a.m.–6 p.m., closed major holidays, www.brooklynmuseum.org. The museum's popular, admission-free **First Saturday** program features art, live music, films, and dancing, on the first Saturday of each month, 5 p.m.–11 p.m. **Museum Café** open until 4 p.m. **Museum libraries and archives** are open by appointment. **Museum shops** 10:30 a.m.–closing time. Admission is $6 contribution.

You *won't* believe what you will find here: a world-class museum in which you can prowl and browse in peace, to your heart's content.

The BMA is spectacular. The Brooklyn Museum of Art is one of the premier art institutions in the world, with a permanent collection that represents almost every culture and includes more than one million objects, from ancient Egyptian masterpieces to contemporary art. It ranks as the second largest museum in the United States, in terms of square footage of museum space.

The BMA is an increasingly important venue for contemporary and emerging artists nationally. Some hail from New York City, including, of course, Brooklyn, which has been called the nation's epicenter of new art. The curator of this department, Charlotta Kotik, is considered by many to be one of the most innovative curators of contemporary art in the United States.

BMA's collection of ancient Egyptian art is generally acknowledged to be one of the finest in the world, rivaling that of the Metropolitan Museum in terms of quality. The second phase of a major reinstallation of this collection, titled *Egypt Reborn: Art for Eternity*, opened in 2003 on the third floor. It includes approximately six hundred additional works—some not on view since the early twentieth century. There are now over eleven hundred objects on permanent display, including masterpieces from every period in ancient Egyptian history.

To get an idea of how Americans lived in previous centuries, check out the extraordinary collection of nineteenth-century American paintings, sculpture, and decorative arts featured in the recently reinstalled American galleries on the fifth floor, under the title *American Identities: A New Look.*

The fourth floor contains decorative arts and over a dozen period rooms, including an elaborate 1864 Moorish-style room from the New York City home of John D. Rockefeller, and an important collection of Royal Worcester porcelain.

The first museum in the United States to display African objects as art rather than as ethnological artifacts in 1923, the BMA today boasts a collection of African art, particularly strong in works from central Africa, that is one of the largest and most important in the United States. There are also arts of the Pacific, including Melanesia, and a collection of Andean textiles. The Asian art collection, started in 1903, includes the art of many cultures. And there are small, specialized gems: the Korean art collection is one of the most important in the United States, and the art from Iran's Qajar dynasty is the only serious collection of its kind on display in the country.

Planned by its founders to be the largest museum in the world, the Brooklyn Museum would have surpassed the Louvre in size had it been completed. A dramatic glass entrance pavilion and public plaza, designed by architects James Stewart Polshek and Partners in collaboration with Arata Isozaki & Associates, will open in the spring of 2004.

The BMA's origins date to 1823, when it was founded as the Brooklyn Apprentices' Library Association. Walt Whitman was one of its first librarians. During the nineteenth century it occupied locations in downtown Brooklyn, and by 1890 it had evolved into the Institute of Arts and Sciences, with departments ranging from anthropology to zoology. The Brooklyn Museum of Art, Brooklyn Botanic Garden, the Brooklyn Academy of Music, and the Brooklyn Children's Museum arose out of the new institute, and, by the late 1970s, each of these institutions became a separate corporate entity. Since the 1930s the BMA had established a new collecting policy focusing exclusively on art.

BMA has a track record as a social innovator, pioneering the field of museum education, including interactive, computer-based arts education programs. It helped the Adopt-a-School program, and made a significant investment of expertise in the creation of the innovative New York City Museum School, a public high school.

Check out the BMA interactive Web site.

BROOKLYN MUSEUM GIFT SHOP. 200 Eastern Pkwy. corner of Washington Ave., 638-5000, W–Su Daily 10 a.m.–5 p.m., www.brooklynmusuem.org.

Unusual among museum shops for its large collection of handmade items and antiques (rather than reproductions), this is a wonderful source for gifts. You'll find contemporary and antique jewelry here, plus handmade African masks, quilts, rugs, and textiles; Japanese porcelain, and items that reflect the work shown in current exhibits. With plenty of items under $20, this is the place to shop for the holidays. A museum membership entitles you to discounts. There is also a special shop for children, **ArtSmart.**

BROOKLYN MUSEUM CAFÉ.

It's the café that dared to be whimsical. The menu changes to reflect the cuisine of the museum's main show. That means that during the *Jewels of the Romanov* show, there was Russian food, including salmon and "Georgian Chicken Salad." Whatever the show, the food is tasty, and the art-food synergy is fun.

☺ ❂ **"FIRST SATURDAY" AT BROOKLYN MUSEUM OF ART.** First Sat. of every month, 6–11 p.m. Free. Parking $4, starting at 5 p.m. Kids under 12 must be accompanied by an adult.

Want to see Brooklyn at its multicultural best? Come to the Brooklyn Museum of Art's First Saturday, a free program of art and entertainment each month. The programs vary, but there are often films, live music, dancing, and the galleries are open for viewing. The **Museum Café** serves a wide selection of sandwiches, salads, and beverages, and a cash bar offers wine and beer. One spring Saturday in 2003, ten thousand people attended, a cross section of families, young and older couples, and singles.

FILM FESTIVALS.

There are various film festivals held here, including the **African Film Festival,** the **Brooklyn International Film Festival,** and **Jewish Film Festival,** among others.

CENTRAL LIBRARY

Brooklyn Public Library

☺ ✆ Grand Army Plaza, corner of Flatbush Ave. and Eastern Pkwy., 230-2100. Call for hours and locations of other branches.

Brooklyn's sixty-branch public library system is the fifth largest in the United States, and one of the oldest. Central Library, which opened in 1940, is a glorious Art Deco building that is shaped like an open book. Be sure to note the bronze panels depicting American literary characters, which decorate the library's entranceway.

In addition to a fine traditional collection, Central Library features a Youth Wing that includes a state-of-the-art computer Technology Loft, and a Multilingual Center with materials in over thirty languages. It is also home to the Brooklyn Collection, the premier resource on Brooklyn history, including the "morgue" of the *Brooklyn Daily Eagle* (1841–1955), the newspaper where Brooklyn's most famous poet, Walt Whitman, served as editor. Exhibitions of paintings, photographs, and sculptures, usually by Brooklyn artists, are mounted bimonthly in Central Library's Grand Lobby; and scores of lectures, author talks, movies, and other performances are presented each year at various venues in the library.

☺ **BROOKLYN EXPEDITION.** www.brooklynexpedition.org.

The Brooklyn Public Library, the Brooklyn Children's Museum, and the Brooklyn Museum of Art are collaborators on this great, child-oriented Web site. The site introduces different "themes," including Brooklyn.

"BROOKLYN WRITERS FOR BROOKLYN READERS" PROGRAM.

This is a free reading and discussion series hosted by WNYC's "New York and Company." Writer-speakers have included Rob Reuland, Alexander Chee, Martha Southgate, Alician Erian, and Jennifer Egan among others. Call for schedule.

Grand Army Plaza
Intersection of Flatbush Ave., Prospect Park W., Eastern Pkwy., and Vanderbilt Ave.

If the hair-raising traffic circle around the Grand Army Plaza makes you feel, for better or worse, that you're in Paris, it's for good reason. Look up. The famous 1870 monumental arch was designed by Frederick Law Olmsted and Calvert Vaux, after what's now known as the Place Charles de Gaulle, surrounding the Arc de Triomphe.

SOLDIERS AND SAILORS MEMORIAL ARCH. Flatbush Ave. at Eastern Pkwy., 788-0055, Sa–Su only.

Known as America's "Arc de Triomphe," this imposing structure was built at a cost of $250,000 and unveiled in 1902 to celebrate the fallen heroes of the Civil War. The six-story spiral staircase to the "Quadriga," the horse-drawn chariot sculpture at the top of the arch, is a fairly easy climb. From the top you'll get an idea of the urban vision that park designers Olmsted and Vaux had in 1860 for bringing European-style greenery and airiness into cramped city life. You can see the landmark entrance to **Prospect Park**, the Manhattan skyline, the monumental **Brooklyn Central Public Library**, and the first few blocks of Eastern Parkway, built in 1870 as the first American tree-lined promenade with benches and plantings. Bas-reliefs of presidents Lincoln and Grant decorate the inner sides of the archway.

☺ ❂ **GREENMARKET AT GRAND ARMY PLAZA.** Sa 8 a.m.–4 p.m.

There's a wonderful greenmarket here on Saturdays, with fresh fruit, vegetables, healthy baked goods, incredible fresh fish, organic meats, handspun yarn, fresh organic cheeses, and plenty of flowers and plants on sale as well. (For other locations, see Index, Greenmarkets.)

Jewish Children's Museum
☺ 332 Kingston Ave. off Eastern Pkwy., 467-0600, www.jcmonline.org Scheduled to open late 2003–early 2004.

The first-of-its-kind Jewish Children's Museum aims to present Jewish history, values, and traditions through playful, highly interactive, hi-tech exhibits designed to fascinate and educate children. Non-Jewish children will gain some understanding of the Jewish experience, too. One pavilion called The World of Good celebrates universal values of faith, charity, justice, kindness, and not speaking poorly of others. The museum expects to welcome two hundred thousand visitors a year, Jewish and non-Jewish. Check the Web site; the music alone gives you the flavor of this unique institution.

This new project was inspired by the Hasidic community of Crown Heights, but support for the Jewish Children's Museum is widespread among people with diverse ethnic backgrounds. On a poignant note, a prominent supporter is Devorah Halberstam, whose young son Ari was shot to death while riding on a school bus across the Brooklyn Bridge in 1994, the victim of a hate crime.

PROSPECT PARK

The main entrance to Prospect Park is at Grand Army Plaza, at the intersection of Flatbush Avenue, Prospect Park West, and Eastern Parkway.

SPECIAL EVENTS.

These include **Celebrate Brooklyn!** Performing Arts Festival (summer); Halloween Walk and Carnival; New Year's Fireworks; Art in the Arch exhibits at **Grand Army Plaza**; Discover Nature tours and Hawk Weekend (late September) at the Audubon Center; Macy's **Fishing Contest**; Harvest Fair (September) and Pinkster Day (May) at **Lefferts Historic** House. Call for information on special events, exhibits, races.

> ☛ **TIP:** You can begin your park visit by picking up a free map of the park at the **Audubon Center, Litchfield Villa, Wollman Rink,** or the **Carousel.** Or check the Web site (www.prospectpark.org), or call for a listing of current, free events, from free tours to bird-watching to gardening clubs to lectures (965-8999).

Prospect Park is Brooklyn's flagship park. Frederick Law Olmsted and Calvert Vaux, who designed Manhattan's Central Park, said they considered Prospect Park to be their best work (experts say they didn't make the same mistakes twice). Designed in 1866, and now a historic landmark, the 526 acres of rolling green lawns, wooded areas, streams, brooks, and lake make this a great environment for biking, boating, walking, romancing, and relaxing. The heart of the park includes over 150 acres of native woodlands featuring a manmade but completely natural-looking Ravine that recently underwent elaborate landscape restoration.

In spring and summer, you can rent a pedal boat, ride the glamorous electric boat, and see an outdoor concert. You can listen to outdoor performances of the Metropolitan Opera and New York Philharmonic, or attend a **Celebrate Brooklyn!** concert. In winter there is ice-skating at the outdoor Wollman Rink, and cross-country skiing in Long Meadow. Year-round, there are festivals, birdwatching tours, soccer and volleyball games, dog-walking, and horseback-riding lessons. In autumn the foliage is gorgeous, and at Halloween there's a Haunted Walk and Carnival on Lookout Hill.

Car traffic is restricted in daytime hours and weekends along the park drive, making these good times to run or bike.

Free! **CELEBRATE BROOKLYN! PERFORMING ARTS FESTIVAL.** Prospect Park Bandshell, summers, www.brooklynx.org or www.bricanline.org, 885-7882.

One of the great pleasures of living or visiting Brooklyn in the summer, Celebrate Brooklyn! organizes outdoor concerts and an outdoor movie series at the Prospect Park Bandshell. Bring a blanket and picnic dinner for the grass, or come early for a seat. Programs are as diverse as the borough itself, offering something for everyone: an all-star tribute to Leonard Cohen with Rufus Wainwright, among others; the Lincoln Center Jazz Orchestra with Wynton Marsalis; Dance Brazil; Derek Trucks Band playing jazz/rock fusion; African Festival with Salif Kieta of Mali and Zimbabwean Oliver Mtukudzi and Salsa diva India, to name just a few. Outdoor films shown here might include *Creature from the Black Lagoon* in 3D, with the Jazz Passengers; *Black Pirate* with Alloy Orchestra, and Alfred Hitchcock's *Vertigo* accompanied by live chamber music. Founded in 1979, Celebrate Brooklyn! is one of New York City's longest-running, free, summer outdoor performing arts festivals. Over two hundred thousand people attend each season. Its huge success is a testimony to the vision, talent, and tenacity of a group of hardworking Brookynites led by director Jack Walsh, to whom a standing ovation is due.

AUDUBON CENTER AND CAFÉ AT THE BOATHOUSE. Near Lincoln Rd. and Ocean Ave., 287-3400, June 5–Sept. 1 Th–Su noon–6 p.m., www.prospectparkaudubon.org.

Opened in 2002 as the nation's first urban-area Audubon Center, this state-of-the-art facility is housed in the park's newly restored, landmarked 1905 Boathouse, an architectural masterpiece based on the design of a sixteenth-century Venetian library. Hands-on exhibits allow children of all ages to investigate nature through interactive technology. A rustic arbor on the shore of the park's Lullwater serves as an outdoor classroom for nature tours and educational programs. A friendly staff of educators lead public programs that expose urban kids to the wonders of nature.

There are also arts classes for adults, like Introduction to Landscape Drawing. Try the weekly Introduction to Bird-watching Tour, Saturdays at noon, where you'll learn how to spot some of the nearly two hundred bird species that inhabit the park or make a rest stop here as they fly along the **Atlantic Flyway.** (Atlantic Flyway is the I-95 for birds migrating north or south—and one major Brooklyn rest stop is right here.) Prospect Park, Jamaica Bay, and other parts of Brooklyn are interesting places for bird-watchers to spy some feathery friends en route.

Birdsong Café serves light snacks. Hours are the same as the Audubon Center hours.

While you're at the Audubon Center, don't forget to take a tour on the **electric boat** *Independence,* a replica of a touring boat from 1910. The silent launch glides under bridges through the serene Lullwater, a meandering waterway that is home to hundreds of wildlife species, including ducks, turtles, and fish. Boat rides are $5 dollars ($3 for ages 3–12, free for ages 2 and under).

DOGS, UNLEASHING, AND THE DOG BATH. 888-604-3422, www.fidobrooklyn.com.

Dogs can roam free off-leash in three areas of Prospect Park: Long Meadow, Nethermead, and Peninsula. Off-leash hours: *Apr. 1–Oct. 31* before 9 a.m. and after 9 p.m.; *M–F* after 5 p.m. in the Nethermead; *Nov. 1–March 31* before 9 a.m. and after 5 p.m.

There's a huge, happy dog scene here in the early mornings, when Fido can roam unleashed on the meadows. The dogs make friends, and so do their owners.

On the first Saturday of every month, dogs and their owners gather in the Long Meadow near the Picnic House for Coffee Bark, where the FIDO organization provides coffee, muffins, and dog biscuits for early-morning dog walkers. Ask about the little corner of the pond marked "Dog Bath" where dogs can splish-splash.

Bark! The Herald Angels Sing is an amusing Christmas-season "sing-and-bark-along" in Long Meadows, near the Tennis House.

DRUMMERS GROVE. Opposite Wollman Skating Rink.

Every Sunday there's African drumming and dancing. It's a long-standing Prospect Park tradition.

FISHING CONTEST. Lakeside near Wollman Rink, 965-8999, July, www.prospectpark.org.

R.H. Macy's sponsors an annual fishing contest in July. They provide the poles, but you have to find the fish. Kids age fifteen and younger are eligible to participate. Prizes include fishing gear and modest gift certificates from Macy's. All fishing is catch-and-release only. Weekdays are the quietest and least crowded times. Call for the shuttle bus schedule (287-5538).

HORSE-RIDING AT KENSINGTON STABLES. E. 8th St. and Caton Pl. near Park Circle—Coney Island Ave., 972-4588, daily 10 a.m.–sunset. Call for rates.

It may seem incongruous to ride a horse in Brooklyn, but there is a stable here with about twenty horses for rentals or lessons, and a 3.5-mile bridle path through Prospect Park.

ICE SKATING AT WOLLMAN RINK. Near Parkside Ave., 287-6431, www.prospectpark.org. Thanksgiving–March. Call for hours.

This outdoor skating rink draws a friendly crowd of kids and adults. There's parking right next to the rink; hot chocolate, instant soups, and hot dogs are available.

• *Playgrounds* •

3rd Street off Prospect Park West
Vanderbilt Street off Prospect Park Southwest
Lincoln Road off Ocean Ave.
Garfield Place off Prospect Park West (Tot Lot)
Parade Place off Caton Avenue (in the Parade Ground)

☺ **IMAGINATION PLAYGROUND.** Ocean Ave. bet. Lincoln Rd. and Parkside Ave. entrance.

The award-winning Imagination Playground uses architecture to stimulate children's imaginations. Instead of slides and swings, there's an open stage for arts and culture programs, clusters of body masks in the shape of cats and ducks, and three playhouses decorated in black-and-white optical patterns.

☺ **HARMONY PLAYGROUND.** Prospect Park W. and 11th St.

Recently renovated, Harmony Playground takes the theme of the nearby Bandshell and transforms it into inventive play equipment, such as a giant xylophone. There are also plenty of swings and a roomy sandbox.

Also special for kids is

☺ **PROSPECT PARK CAROUSEL.** Near Empire Blvd. and Ocean Ave., 965-8999, Apr.–Oct. Th–Su noon–5 p.m. (until 6 bet. Memorial Day and Labor Day,) www.prospectpark.org. Reservations for private parties and school groups.

A relic from the past, the Prospect Park Carousel reopened in 1990. For a mere 50 cents, you can ride on this beautifully restored masterpiece, which cost more than half a million dollars to bring back to life, in a program run by the **Prospect Park Alliance.** Choose from among fifty-one Coney Island–style horses, lions, giraffes, goats, and chariots, all restored according to original designs created in a Brooklyn shop around 1912 by Charles Carmel, one of the world's foremost carousel designers of the era. The Wurlitzer organ has been rebuilt, too.

• *Tennis* •

PROSPECT PARK TENNIS. Coney Island Ave. at intersection of Parkside Ave. Outdoor tennis, April–Nov. contact Brooklyn Parks Department for hours, fees, and permits information, at 95 Prospect Park West, 965-8993 or 965-8914, M–F 9 a.m.–4 p.m., closed most weekends. For indoor tennis, Nov.–March, see below.

Local tennis buffs know the seasonal indoor/outdoor arrangement here. In the summer, take your racquet to **Prospect Park Parade Ground,** where you'll find courts. Management of the courts reverts to the city in the summertime, and you can play on the ten outdoor courts during the day for free, on a first-come, first-served basis, after obtaining a tennis permit for a nominal fee from the Brooklyn Parks Department. It's a good idea to call ahead to check office hours and procedures, such as whether you need to bring photo ID and whether you can obtain a permit for another family member. In the winter, you can play at the same location, but under different management, at the Tennis Center, see below.

TENNIS CENTER. 305 Coney Island Ave. near Parade Grounds, 965-8951, daily 7 a.m.–midnight. Call for information on hours, prices, and credit cards.

In the winter there's a "tennis bubble" at the far end of Prospect Park, with adult and junior programs, and men's and women's leagues. You can get individual or group lessons, or just rent a court.

PEDAL BOATS. Lakeside near Wollman Rink, 965-8999. May–Oct., weather permitting, Th–Su noon–5 p.m. (6 p.m. in summer), www.prospectpark.org. $10 per hour plus $10 refundable deposit for a four-person boat.

One of the park's loveliest features, the sixty-acre lake comes almost as a surprise as you walk, bike, or roller-blade down the long hill. Kids love to watch the waterfowl here, and there's not a prettier place in Brooklyn in the spring or autumn. And although you can't walk on water, you can bike on it. The pedal boats in Prospect Park are good family fun. Kids under age sixteen must be accompanied by an adult.

☺ **PROSPECT PARK ZOO** (formally known as the Wildlife Center). 450 Flatbush Ave. near Empire and Ocean Aves., 399-7339, April–Oct. M–F 10 a.m.–5 p.m.; Sa–Su and holidays 10 a.m.–5:30 p.m., Nov.–March daily 10 a.m.–4:30 p.m., www.prospectpark.org. Admission $2.50 for adults, $1.25 for seniors, 50 cents for kids ages 3–12. *Note:* Zoo hours may change due to New York City budget cuts.

Rain or shine, there's nothing better for kids than a trip to the zoo. This little twelve-acre wonder run by the New York City Wildlife Conservation Society, a nonprofit conservation organization based at the Bronx Zoo, was reopened in 1993 after extensive renovation. Kids love the pop-up prairie dog display (they duck into and out of little gopher holes, and you can, too), the sea lions swimming in a circle, the baboons picking one another's fur, and the red panda, which is as nice as nice can be.

Other Attractions in Prospect Park

Many buildings within Prospect Park have been designated as historic landmarks, and you can get full information from the **Prospect Park Alliance**. Two that people often ask about are:

Free! ☺ **LEFFERTS HISTORIC HOUSE.** Flatbush Ave. near Empire Blvd., 789-2822. Memorial Day–Labor Day Th–Su and holidays noon–6 p.m., Labor Day–Nov and April–Memorial Day Th–Su and holidays noon–5 p.m., Dec.–March Sa–Su and holidays noon–4 p.m., www.prospectpark.org. Call for schedule of special programs.

Lefferts Historic House is one of the few surviving Dutch-American farmhouses in Brooklyn. Built circa 1783 for Pieter Lefferts, a prominent eighteenth-century Flatbush landowner, it was donated to New York City in 1918 and moved to Prospect Park. Operated by the **Prospect Park Alliance,** it's a museum for families and children that shows everyday life in the nineteenth-century farming village of Flatbush, especially as it was experienced by the Dutch-American, African-American, and Native American people of the area. The house has period rooms, interactive exhibits, reproduction objects, and a working garden that includes vegetables, herbs, and medicinal plants. There's a flax plot on the grounds, where flax is planted, harvested, and prepared for spinning by a "spinster" during the museum's Harvest Fair and Winter Festival. There are terrific free programs in the arts, crafts, and work of yesteryear here: ice cream–making, quilting, weaving, cooking, and farming.

LITCHFIELD VILLA. Prospect Park W. bet. 4th and 5th Sts., 965-8999, M–F 9 a.m.–5 p.m., www.prospect park.org.

Ah, for the good old days when one's mansion had a commanding view! Built between 1855 and 1857 for land baron Edwin Clarke Litchfield by architect A. J. Davis, this lovely stuccoed mansion was only one of many estates built in "rural Brooklyn" by wealthy industrialists as a getaway from Manhattan. Shortly after the villa was completed, the City of Brooklyn paid the Litchfield family about $4 million for the more than five hundred acres that now constitute Prospect Park, and acquired the mansion itself in 1892. The villa is now the Brooklyn Parks Department and **Prospect Park Alliance** headquarters.

THE RAVINE. Enter from Long Meadow near the Pools or start at Audubon Center.

With its craggy terrain, spectacular waterfalls, and more than ten thousand trees, a walk through this area can make you feel like you are hiking through the Adirondack Mountains. Still recovering from decades of overuse that caused soil compaction and erosion, the Ravine and surrounding woodlands were under lock and key since 1996 while undergoing intensive landscape restoration. Park designers Olmsted and Vaux considered the Ravine to be the heart of Prospect Park.

PARADE GROUND. Parkside and Coney Island Aves., 965-8951.

After undergoing a four-year, $14 million reconstruction by the **Prospect Park Alliance,** the Parade Ground reopens in spring 2004 as the home turf of local high schools and countless baseball, basketball, football, and soccer clubs. Now featuring several Astroturf fields and a premier baseball diamond with night lighting and concessions, the Parade Ground is legendary for launching the baseball careers of Sandy Koufax, Joe Torre, and others.

And Several Great Services:

BROOKLYN CENTER ON URBAN ENVIRONMENT (BCUE). Tennis House, Prospect Park, 788-8500, www.bcue.org.

Cited as a "national exemplar in *urban* environmental education," BCUE is an award-winning urban environmental education program. Founded over twenty-five years ago by a visionary urban scholar, John Muir, BCUE runs inventive youth programs on urban environmental issues serving over fifty thousand children and adults annually, as well as recycling and neighborhood-based environmental programs. In 1997 the center began an initiative on environmental injustice and degradation. BCUE runs some of the best tours available of such Brooklyn areas as Coney Island, Gowanus, DUMBO, Red Hook, Smith Street, and many others.

Recyclers Note: if you have used laser and inkjet toner cartridges, or old cell phones, give them to BCUE. BCUE participates in a program called **Renewable Brooklyn** and exchanges these discards for free educational and computer equipment. (M–F 2–6 p.m., Sa–Su noon–5 p.m.)

An independent nonprofit organization, BCUE is headquartered in the Tennis House, an architectural landmark building with Palladian columns that's nestled in the park, a five-minute walk from the Bandshell.

PROSPECT PARK ARCHIVES. Picnic House near Prospect Park W. and 3rd St., 965-7722. By appointment.

Ever wonder what Brooklyn looked like back in the day when thousands of gown-wearing, croquet-playing pleasure-seekers rode their horse-pulled carriages into Prospect Park for a concert on the now-vanished Music Island? The Prospect Park Archives have an extensive collection of materials documenting the history of Prospect Park and Brooklyn.

PROSPECT PARK ALLIANCE. Litchfield Villa, 965-8951, M–F 9 a.m.–5 p.m., www.prospectpark.org.

This is the organization that manages many of the activities in Prospect Park. If you have any questions, this is the place to call.

🌀 **YOUTH RESOURCE CENTER.** The Parade Ground. Corner of Caton and Coney Island Aves., 854-4901.

The Prospect Park Youth Resource offers training, special events, and job opportunities to area teenagers. Walk-ins are encouraged.

Last But Certainly Not Least . . .

🌀 **WEST INDIAN AMERICAN DAY CARNIVAL.** Utica Ave. down Eastern Pkwy., from Utica Ave. to Grand Army Plaza, Labor Day, noon–6 p.m., www.WIADCA.com.

The **West Indian American Day Carnival** in Brooklyn is a must-see. It's fun, beautiful, musical—so *alive*. There's literally dancing in the streets. One of the nation's most colorful, festive parades, this event has been an annual Labor Day highlight for over thirty-five years.

A friendly crush of people (by some estimates, the 2001 crowd topped 4 million) starts lining Eastern Parkway's broad boulevard early in the day for the noontime start. If you come early, rest assured there's plenty of good ethnic food available from street vendors. You can hear the parade before you see it, the contagious calypso music, melodious tinkling of steel bands, followed by fabled costumes, over sixty extravagant floats, and a parade of community groups and politicians of all stripes, from New York's mayor to members of Congress. It's a huge parade, it lasts hours.

Some of the traditions you'll enjoy in Brooklyn echo Trinidad's Carnival. In colonial Trinidad, this festivity became a politically rebellious and wickedly humorous mimicry of the imperial French, who brought the European fad of the fancy masked costume ball to the new world. It's a rare treat in New York to see the extraordinary masquerade bands (masbands), musicians in costumes, swirling and dancing down Eastern Parkway. Certain costumes, including the bats, midnight robbers, red-and-black devils, and Red Indians, have long folk histories in West Indian culture. In Trinidad, masbands perform prior to Ash Wednesday, when there are parades and the crowning of a "king" and "queen."

For onlookers, the parade is a one-day affair. But for the participants, this is Carnival, and it lasts five days, with pre-parade costume competitions and band performances, and a Sunday children's carnival and competition. These private festivities are held at the Brooklyn Museum grounds. The nonprofit West Indian American Day Carnival Association, WIADCA, is the organizer.

14

Park Slope

ABOUT PARK SLOPE

Fondly referred to as simply "the Slope," this neighborhood has become one of Brooklyn's most famous. When young, city-loving couples in Manhattan decide to have children, they often think first of moving to Park Slope. People *do* know their neighbors, *do* shop in the neighborhood, and *do* vote. Widely known as one of the city's most liberal communities, Park Slope has more than its fair share of professionals, writers, artists, successful businesspeople, and work-at-home entrepreneurs—of various ethnicities and sexual orientations. There are tellingly disproportionate numbers of bookstores and real estate agents. The rapid gentrification of 5th Avenue from a working-class Latino section to a hot new strip of trendy restaurants and boutiques has attracted a younger generation, probably lowering the average age of the neighborhood by a decade or so.

What first draws new residents and visitors alike is the well-preserved brownstones and town houses on Park Slope's many tree-lined streets, as well as the proximity to some of Brooklyn's grandest attractions: heavenly Prospect Park, the main branch of the Brooklyn Public Library, the Brooklyn Museum, and the Brooklyn Botanic Garden. (See the Heart of Brooklyn chapter.) What keeps people here is the sense of community. Along the main commercial streets, now both 7th and 5th Avenues, you invariably see small clusters of people chatting, having just bumped into each other in the park, running errands, or getting a cappuccino. Parents gratefully acknowledge that Park Slope is the kind of "village" that, magically, helps to raise a child.

In recent years, the rejuvenation of 5th Avenue has, literally, expanded the neighborhood's shopping and restaurant capacity. The half-mile stretch from about Sterling Place to about 4th Street has sprouted a cornucopia of restaurants, artisanal shops, and interesting food stores.

Park Slope boasts twenty-four blocks of landmark buildings and charming

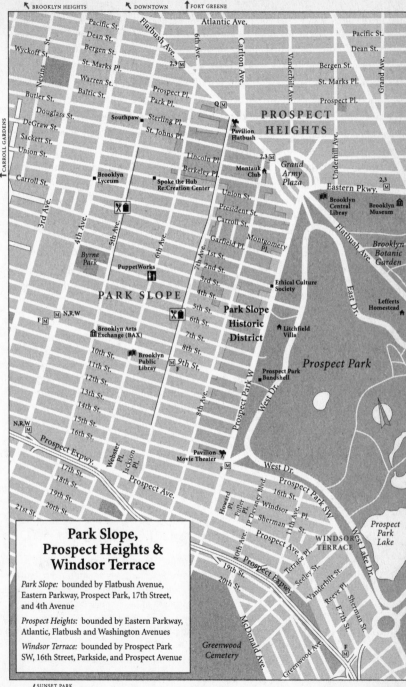

Park Slope, Prospect Heights & Windsor Terrace

Park Slope: bounded by Flatbush Avenue, Eastern Parkway, Prospect Park, 17th Street, and 4th Avenue

Prospect Heights: bounded by Eastern Parkway, Atlantic, Flatbush and Washington Avenues

Windsor Terrace: bounded by Prospect Park SW, 16th Street, Parkside, and Prospect Avenue

shops. Amid spires, turrets, bay windows, and rows and rows of evenly matched brownstone stoops are architectural treasures reflecting Italianate and French Second Empire as well as Greek and Romanesque Revival styles. Among the most outstanding are the mock-Venetian palazzo Montauk Club, and the parkside mansion in which Brooklyn Poly Prep is housed. Just walk along Montgomery Place, Carroll Street, or 6th Avenue to get a sense of the variety and beauty here. The landmark district goes from Park Place to Union Street between 6th and 8th Avenues, then from Union Street to 4th Street between Prospect Park West and 7th Avenue.

HOW IT GOT ITS NAME Any neighborhood that slopes downhill from Prospect Park could logically be known as Park Slope.

BY SUBWAY The 2 and 3 trains go to Bergen Street and Grand Army Plaza, and the B or Q train goes to 7th Avenue, all at the north end of Park Slope. The F train will take you to the 7th Avenue stop at 9th Street or 15th Street and Prospect Park (Windsor Terrace). The F, M, and R go to 9th Street and 4th Avenue and the M and R stop at Union and 4th Avenue, both close to interesting shops and restaurants on 5th Avenue, depending on their address (see below, Tip).

☞ **TIP:** If you're not sure what subway to take, use this rule of thumb: For 7th Avenue destinations: below 270 7th Avenue, closest are B and Q trains at 7th Avenue or 2, 3 at Grand Army Plaza; above 270 7th Avenue, closest are F, M, R trains at 9th Street. For 5th Avenue destinations: below 100 5th Avenue, closest are subways 2, 3 Bergen Street; 100–350 5th Avenue, closest is M, R at Union Street, above 350 5th Avenue, F, M, R trains at 9th Street and 4th Avenue. Having said that, everything is within about a fifteen-minute walk, if you're wearing sneakers.

  ## What's **NEW?**

Just When You Escaped Manhattan, Here It Comes All Over Again

Over the next few years, the place to watch for new development is along 4th Avenue and, to a lesser extent, along 3rd Avenue. In 2003 city government rezoned 110 blocks of Park Slope, permitting construction of twelve-story high-rises along 4th Avenue from Union Street to 15th Street, and development of 3rd Avenue between 7th and 12th Streets. A new "canyon of housing" along 4th Avenue will likely bring increased demand for shopping, parking, and public facilities in the Slope, a transformation of 4th Avenue, more traffic on the N and R trains, the continued gentrification of 5th Avenue, and the knitting together of Park Slope, Gowanus, and Carroll Gardens.

HISTORICAL NOTES

Settled in the seventeenth century by Dutch farmers, Park Slope remained the province of two large families until the mid-1800s, when developers began subdividing the area into neat rows of streets and avenues. The Litchfield family's mansion still presides over Prospect Park; today it is the headquarters for the Parks Department.

When developers first began selling homes here in the mid-1800s, German and English upper-middle-class families settled in the brownstones in what is now Park Slope's landmark district. The area came to be known as a "streetcar suburb," a pleasant place to live with easy access to Manhattan, just two miles away. (The description is still apt today.) Park Slope even gained its own version of Central Park: completed in 1873, Prospect Park was the masterwork of Calvert Vaux and Frederick Law Olmsted, the team that had collaborated on Manhattan's rural jewel. In the latter quarter of the nineteenth century, Italian and Irish working-class immigrants settled in more modest homes in what came to be known as the "South Slope," below broad, tree-lined 9th Street.

Just before the turn of the twentieth century, the impressive new mansions being built across from Prospect Park on Prospect Park West and Plaza Street came to be dubbed "Millionaires Row," or "Brooklyn's Gold Coast." Development in the area continued after World War I, with large apartment buildings rising on Plaza Street. After World War II the entire neighborhood went into a brief decline—but, as with the rest of brownstone Brooklyn, a revival started in the 1960s that led to the renovation of many homes in Park Slope and the surrounding areas. And so it continues.

Kidstuff

☺ Romp in **Prospect Park**. Read at the **Central Library**, **Community Bookstore**, or **Kids on 7th**; take in a show at **PuppetWorks** or the **Brooklyn Family Theater**. Get creative at **Pottery Café**. . . . Play with dough while you wait to eat at **Two Boots**, go shopping while you get a haircut at **Lulu's Cuts and Toys**. Take wonderful classes at the **Brooklyn Arts Exchange** and **Spoke the Hub**.

LIVING IN BROOKLYN
(from a Park Slope fifteen-year-old's perspective)

To live in Brooklyn is to be colorblind. The borough is a kaleidoscope of ethnicity, with a daily flow absolutely undisturbed by racial boundaries. While it is true that there are communities where one race may predominate, as the barriers have been crumbling over the years so have the ethnic divides. Park Slope has slowly been edging toward the East River, almost hopping 4th Avenue in proximity to the Gowanus housing projects. In Williamsburg, the Hasidic community intermingles with both Latinos and upper-class hipsters, mostly without strife. For teenagers, the public high schools reflect this. What are considered "minority" races across the rest of the country are generally the majority in Brooklyn's public schools.

For Brooklynites, everything you'll ever need to know you learn growing up here. In a borough where concrete is more common than grass, the streets are the playgrounds as well as the after-school activity. Kids in Brooklyn aren't driven to school every day—commuter rush hour is not only for business workers but also for the multitudes of grade-school kids riding the subways and buses each morning with their parents, with their friends, or solo. In the warmer months, the streets are bright with sidewalk chalk and lopsided hopscotch courses. Burst fire hydrants not only benefit those trying to escape the heat, they're also the neighborhood car wash.

Unlike in the suburbs, in Brooklyn there are almost no malls to go to, and you cannot get a driver's license in New York City until you are eighteen. Hanging around Starbucks pretty much signals a self-inflicted life of loneliness. So, rather than chill in front of the TV at home, lots of Brooklyn high school kids tend to get together in small groups outside of the local pizza shops and ice cream emporiums. People-watching is a popular pastime, as is sitting on brownstone stoops talking and waiting for more of your friends to wander by. Playgrounds tend to draw small crowds of teens after dark, for entertaining, albeit sketchy, activities. There's at least one movie house in each neighborhood, as well as a few teen-oriented dance clubs in Brooklyn. For the more alternative crowd, there is always The Punk Temple in Bensonhurst, or the occasional subway trip to a Manhattan club to see a pop or indie concert. In winter, generally the merriment moves to individual houses, or to pizza places. And, of course, there are always the parks, the skating rink, different cool shops in each neighborhood, the library, hobbies—and homework.

POINTS OF CULTURAL INTEREST
ANSONIA CLOCK FACTORY CO-OPS. 420 13th St. along 7th Ave.

This four-story red-brick apartment building was once an abandoned clockworks factory that had employed many Polish and Irish immigrants in the nine-teenth century. It is one of five hundred projects undertaken since the 1960s by the Brooklyn Union Gas Company through its "Cinderella" program to help revitalize Brooklyn neighborhoods.

🎓 BERKELEY CARROLL SCHOOL. 181 Lincoln Pl., bet. 7th and 8th Aves., 789-6060, www.berkeley carroll.org.

Berkeley Carroll has a visible presence in Park Slope, with its two large school buildings on Lincoln and Carroll Streets, new gym, and lots of happy students walking in groups along 7th Avenue. An independent college-prep co-ed day school, enrolling eight hundred students from pre-K to twelfth grade, Berkeley Carroll offers small classroom size, community service, and extensive extracur-ricular activities, including a strong theater program. Admissions are selective; college admissions are excellent.

BROOKLYN ARTS EXCHANGE (BAX). 421 5th Ave. bet. 7th and 8th Aves., 832-0018, www.bax.org.

This spirited nonprofit community arts institution offers programs in avant-garde dance, theater, performance art, and music for young students, artists-in-residence, and others. BAX, formerly Gowanus Arts Exchange, hosts annually as many as seventy performances by an ethnically diverse crop of new artists.

🎵 BROOKLYN CONSERVATORY OF MUSIC. 58 7th Ave. at Lincoln Pl., 622-3300, www.brooklynconser vatory.com. Call for schedule of classes, concerts, and other events.

Do you hear music wafting down 7th Avenue? It's likely to be coming from a gracefully restored 1881 Victorian mansion that houses the Brooklyn Conserva-tory of Music, founded in the nineteenth century by German-American immi-grants as a classical European conservatory. Today it offers instruction in Broadway melodies, jazz and gospel singing, Latin jazz, and African drumming. Take a class, enjoy the jazz concerts, bring your toddler to the popular children's program. The "Find a Musician" referral service is useful for parties and special events.

BROOKLYN JEWISH ARTS GALLERY. Congregation B'nai Jacob, 401 9th St. bet. 6th and 7th Aves., 965-9836, www.bjag.org. Call or check the Web site for shows and hours.

Launched in 2003 by Congregation B'nai Jacob, this unusual gallery presents artists from different backgrounds and places whose work deals with Jewish themes.

🎵 GOOD COFFEEHOUSE, ETHICAL CULTURE SOCIETY. 53 Prospect Park W. at 2nd St., 768-2972, F 11:15 p.m., www.bsec.org. $10 per performance.

A wholesome scene with a slightly rustic sensibility prevails at the Good

Coffeehouse, held in a landmark building with a large side garden. Good Coffeehouse is a product of the 1980s and still runs an active program of live folk, rock, jazz, cabaret, classical, bluegrass, and poetry. If you're looking to meet people, this is as nonthreatening a crowd as you'll find this side of the moon.

GILDA'S CLUB, BROOKLYN CLUBHOUSE. 502 8th Ave. bet 5th and 6th Sts., www.gildasclub.org (no phone yet as this writing).

The poignantly named cancer-support organization, Gilda's Club, founded in 1991 in honor of *Saturday Night Live* star Gilda Radner ("Roseanne Rosannadanna"), opened this satellite center in 2003 in conjunction with Gilda's Club of New York City and local hospitals.

MONTAUK CLUB. 25 8th Ave. at Lincoln Pl., 638-0800, www.Montaukclub.com. Not open to the public.

One of Park Slope's finest old buildings, the 1891 Venetian Gothic palazzo is surrounded by a narrow moat of neatly trimmed green grass. The brass rails up the steps to the entrance are usually well buffed. The Montauk Club houses both a private social club (and it is often used as a set by film crews in need of a beautiful manor-house interior) and five gorgeous apartments. In true Victorian tradition, the club once had a private parlor and separate entrance set aside for the female set.

OLD STONE HOUSE MUSEUM. J.J. Byrne Park bet. 4th and 5th Aves. and 3rd and 4th Sts., 768-3195, www.oldstonehouse.org.

Imagine cannons blazing and scruffy American troops fighting against the British. The Old Stone House, also known as the Vechte-Cortelyou House, is a replica of a Dutch stone farmhouse originally built by a Dutch immigrant beside the Gowanus Creek in 1699. The Vechtes farmed the hills of Park Slope, harvesting oysters in the Gowanus Creek and ferrying produce to market in Manhattan. During the battle of Brooklyn, Long Island, on August 27, 1776, the sturdy house and its strategic position made for a dramatic battle. Rebuilt in the 1930s, with original stones from this Revolutionary War–era site, the Old Stone House Museum celebrates Brooklyn's role in the American Revolution. Special events include an alternative press fair, Father's Day, and June Tara Irish Tea Festival.

PARK SLOPE CIVIC COUNCIL HOUSE TOUR. 832-8227, www.parkslopeciviccouncil.org. Fourth Su in May, noon–5 p.m., $15 in advance, $20 day of tour.

The Park Slope house tour, popular since 1959, is the oldest of its sort in all of New York City. Each of the ten to fifteen homes on the tour is staffed with knowledgeable volunteers to answer questions.

POLY PREP (LOWER SCHOOL). Prospect Park West at 1st St., 768-7890, www.polyprep.org.

Looking over Prospect Park, this fabulous 1883 Romanesque Revival mansion has a double outdoor staircase and turret windows. It originally was the home of Henry Carlton Hulbert, a vice president of the South Brooklyn Savings Institution. Today it houses a private school, so plan to appreciate it mainly from the outside.

PROSPECT HALL. 263 Prospect Ave. bet. 5th and 6th Aves., 788-0777, www.grandprospect.com.

Built before the turn of the twentieth century, this old opera house, restaurant, and speakeasy fell into disrepair until its new owners restored it as a catering hall. The Grand Ballroom, complete with two balconies, holds up to 1,500 people and was the scene of a wedding celebration in the film *Prizzi's Honor.* The Men's Card Room, a former speakeasy, appears in the film *The Cotton Club.* The hall also contains the first elevator ever installed in Brooklyn (it still works).

⊗ **PUBLIC BATH HOUSE NO. 7 AKA BROOKLYN LYCEUM.** 227 4th Ave. at President St., 866-GOWANUS, www.brooklyceum.com.

Built in 1911 as part of a citywide campaign to improve public health, this old bathhouse—an architectural landmark—sat empty for decades. In 1998 a private owner renovated it into two performance spaces, the sixty-seat Geloscopic, and an immense, four-thousand-square-foot Downstairs. Programs include a weekly comedy troupe, improv jams, a monthly ten-minute play tournament, and jazz.

Brooklyn Lyceum's "Only the Dead" is an inventive collaboration with **Green-Wood Cemetery** (see p. 415). It's a series of brief dramatizations, held in the **1911 Chapel,** of the stories of people buried in Green-Wood, including "Mile-a-Minute Murphy," who raced a locomotive on a bicycle; John Matthews, "soda fountain king," and Kate Claxton, an unlucky actress who was caught on stage during the tragic Brooklyn Theater Fire.

🎓 **PUBLIC SCHOOLS**

Among those considered to be New York City's best public elementary schools are PS 321 (180 7th Avenue) as well as PS 282 (180 6th Avenue), PS 372 (372 Carroll Street), and PS 107 (1301 8th Avenue). (Source: *New York City's Best Public Elementary Schools*, 2002, by C. Hemphill with P. Wheaton.)

SPOKE THE HUB RECREATION CENTER. 748 Union St. between 5th and 6th Aves., also 295 Douglass St. bet. 3rd and 4th Aves., 857-5158, www.spokethehub.org. Call for calendar of events and programs.

One of the neighborhood's creative whirling dervishes, Elise Long has created an eclectic, soul-warming institution that gives creative arts and fitness classes and performances. **Local Produce Performing Arts Festival** showcases local artists in April in various community gardens, Prospect Park's Tennis House, and in indoor venues around Brooklyn.

SQUAD ONE SEPTEMBER 11 MEMORIAL SCULPTURE. Union St. bet. 6th and 7th Aves.

This huge wooden memorial sculpture, titled "Out of the Rubble," was sent by N. Thomas and R. Boswell of Portland, Oregon. On September 11, 2001, the specialized Squad One of the New York City Fire Department lost twelve firemen who raced to the World Trade Center; a total of 343 New York City firemen died, along with thousands of other victims.

TOURISM KIOSK. Look for the tourism pushcart at Grand Army Plaza.

WILLIAM B. CRONYN HOUSE. 291 Ninth St.

A stucco-covered house with a slate roof built in the 1850s in French Second Empire style. When built, the house was surrounded by farms; later it was transformed into the headquarters of an ink company, and today it is again in use as a private home.

Other Points of Interest

CHASSIDIC ART INSTITUTE (CHAI). 375 Kingston Ave. bet. Carroll and Crown Sts. in Crown Heights, 774-9149 or 778-8808, Su–Th noon–7 p.m., F closes early, closed Sa.

Jewish, and specifically Hasidic folk art and paintings have been shown for over twenty years in this unusual gallery located in nearby Crown Heights. The art is fervent and emotional, exploring Jewish themes. The nonprofit gallery was founded by community leaders after a 1977 Brooklyn Museum show on Hasidic art drew ten thousand visitors. More than one hundred artists are represented. Posters start at $10; paintings go up to $10,000.

ENTERTAINMENT

☺ ♫ **BROOKLYN FAMILY THEATER.** 1012 8th Ave. at 10th St., 670-7205, www.brooklynfamily theatre.

Think off-off-off-Broadway. In 2001, two longtime staff members of the New York Youth Theater started this family-oriented community theater that puts on four productions a year, each running for five weeks. The shows, enthusiastically reviewed by local papers, are appropriate for all ages: *Godspell, Wiz, Charlie Brown,* and other Broadway musicals, produced with energy and a funky attitude. BFT has outfitted the 140-seat performance space in a local church with theater lights and a new sound system. Local kids often help with costumes and tech. It's fun, convenient, and just $12 a ticket.

BROWNSTONE BILLIARDS. 308 Flatbush Ave. at 7th Ave., 857-5555, Su–Th noon–2 a.m., weekends later. $3.95 per person per hour.

A favorite weekend hangout for the local private school teenage set.

GALLERY PLAYERS OF PARK SLOPE. 199 14th St. bet. 4th and 5th Aves., 595-0547, Shows Th–Sa 8 p.m. Su 3 p.m., www.galleryplayers.com. Call for reservations; seats on first-come, first-served basis.

In 2003, the Gallery Players, a "showcase" theater located in Park Slope, celebrated its thirty-fifth anniversary. A combination of professional and aspiring actors put on satisfying shows for a mostly local Brooklyn audience. Most seasons include an eclectic mix of musicals and classics, plus a June "Black Box" series of new works, and "Bare Bones," a series of tried-and-true plays with just the bare essentials. Tickets are $15; discounts for kids and seniors.

PAVILION MOVIE THEATER. 188 Prospect Park West bet. 14th and 15th Sts., 369-0838.

Opened in the late 1990s, this renovated old movie house shows first-run flicks, and often has lines around the block.

PAVILION FLATBUSH (formerly the Plaza Twin Cinema Park Slope). 314 Flatbush Ave. near 7th Ave., 369-0838.

One of Park Slope's two movie houses.

☺ **PUPPETWORKS.** 338 6th Ave. at 4th St., 965-3391, Sa–Su, call for show times, www.puppetworks.org. Tickets $6 for children, $7 for adults.

The true art of puppetry might be lost if it were not for marionette makers and performers like these seasoned professionals who have helped create, among other things, Macy's annual Christmas and Easter puppet shows. The new one-hundred-seat theater is air-conditioned.

♪ **SOUTHPAW.** 125 5th Ave. near Sterling Pl., 230-0236, daily 8:30 p.m.–4 a.m., www.spsounds.com.

Southpaw is the first venue to slowly bring underground rock above ground and into the welcoming arms of Park Slope hipsters. The Slope's answer to the East Village and Williamsburg, and host to many local independent rock groups, Southpaw multitasks as an art gallery/dance floor/bar. It's become a trendy place to be on Saturday nights, drawing audiences from other parts of the city. Admission is in the $10 range, and occasionally shows are listed and/or reviewed in the likes of *Time Out New York*, and (gasp!) the *New York Times*.

NEW SPORTSPLEX AT 14TH REGIMENT ARMORY. 8th Ave. bet. 14th and 15th Sts.

As we go to press, it looks like plans are under way to turn the old Armory into a public sports facility.

PARKS, PLAYGROUNDS, COMMUNITY GARDENS

THE GARDEN OF UNION AND ANNIE'S GARDEN. Union St. bet. 4th and 5th Aves., Sa–Su 10 a.m.–2 p.m., Th 4 p.m.–dusk, www.choplogic.net/garden_web. Children must be accompanied by a parent or guardian. Membership is open.

Annie's Garden was started in 1977 and has grown to include two additional lots. It's a community-based garden run by several dozen volunteer members who use organic principles of gardening.

J.J. BYRNE PARK. Bet. 4th and 5th Aves. and 3rd and 4th Sts.

This little park is home to a playground, some refreshing benches, and the historic **Old Stone House** (see p. 356).

PROSPECT PARK. See p. 342.

PARK SLOPE RESTAURANTS AND CAFÉS

AL DI LA. 248 5th Ave. off Carroll St., 783-4565, M, W–Th 6–10:30 p.m., F–Sa 6–11 p.m., Su 6–10 p.m.

Consistently rated as one of the borough's best under-$25 restaurants, al di la's chef changes his trattoria-style Northern Italian cuisine daily to make best use of what's fresh at the market. Also sponsors prix-fixe wine-tasting dinners. Entrées range $10–$15.

AUNT SUZIE'S KITCHEN. 247 5th Ave. bet. Carroll St. and Garfield Pl., 788-2868, Su–Th 5–10 p.m., F–Sa 5 p.m.–midnight.

Child-friendly and inexpensive, Aunt Suzie's settled on 5th Avenue well before it became trendy. The Italian fare tastes home-cooked, and the mismatched furniture is charming. Specials are likely to include several fish dishes and pastas. A selection of plate-sized games and kiddie books is available.

BISTRO ST. MARK'S. 76 St. Marks Ave. at 6th Ave., 857-8600, M–F 5:30–11 p.m., Sa–Su brunch 11 a.m.–4 p.m., dinner 5:30–11 p.m.

Acclaimed for its excellent seafood and contemporary French cuisine, Bistro St. Mark's is close to the Brooklyn Academy of Music and a perfect place for a date or late dinner. There's a nice bar scene, too. Entrées about $18. Reservations recommended. Stay tuned for new developments at their next-door "Market."

BLUE RIBBON BROOKLYN. 280 5th Ave. bet. Garfield Pl. and 1st St., 840-0404, Tu–Th 6 p.m.–2 a.m., F 6 p.m.–4 a.m., Sa brunch noon–4 p.m., dinner 6 p.m.–4 am, Su brunch noon–4 p.m., dinner 6 p.m.–midnight. No reservations; come early on weekends.

Wait a minute. Is this Manhattan or the Slope? Blue Ribbon's raw bar, crowded bar scene, and tasty menu explains why Brooklyn foodies give it high marks. The eclectic menu covers a range of seafood, meat, and vegetarian dishes. Save room for the even-better-than-mom's Americana desserts. Entrées around $20.

BLUE RIBBON SUSHI. 278 5th Ave. bet. Garfield Pl. and 1st St., 840-0408, Tu–Th 6 p.m.–2 a.m., F 6 p.m.–4 a.m., Sa brunch noon–4 p.m., dinner 6 p.m.–4 a.m., Su brunch noon–4 p.m., dinner 6 p.m.–midnight.

Unlike its boisterous sibling next door, Blue Ribbon Sushi is an oasis of calm, with a wood-and-brick, low-light interior that complements the understated but extensive menu. Sushi and sashimi are offered from both the Atlantic and the Pacific. The presentation is first-rate.

BLUE SKY BAKERY. 53 5th Ave. off Bergen St., 743-4123, daily 7 a.m.–7 p.m.

Wonderful pastries, coffee, and an artistic European décor make this little garden café feel like it's spring all year round. In summer, sit under a peach tree and munch on an egg-toast sandwich.

BONNIE'S GRILL. 278 5th Ave. bet. Garfield Pl. and 1st St., 369-9527, M–Th 5–11 p.m., F–Sa 1–midnight, Su 1–10 p.m.

"American food with a hot and spicy twist" is how staff describe Bonnie's Grill. With its diner-like counter, Bonnie's looks like it might do no better than milkshakes and grilled cheese sandwiches. Take a table or enjoy the show at the counter as expert chefs work their magic. Excellent, inexpensive.

BRAWTA OUTPOST. 447 7th Ave. bet. 15th and 16th Sts., 788-4680. See **Brawta**, page 230.

⊘ CAFÉ AT COMMUNITY BOOKSTORE. 143 7th Ave., 783-3075, M–F 9 a.m.–9:45 p.m., Sa 9 a.m.–10 p.m., Su 10 a.m.–10 p.m.

A classy little café, with a postage-stamp garden that includes a dwarf-sized pond, makes this bookstore nook a favorite meeting place for locals.

CAFÉ STEINHOF. 422 7th Ave. at 14th St., 369-7776, M 5 p.m.–2 a.m., Tu–Su 11 a.m.–2 a.m.

Wunderbar! When a middle-aged German woman concedes, "This schnitzel is almost as good as mine," you know you're in for a *serious* meal. Prices are low, and portions are sizable. Viennese café-style dishes include cheese *spaetzle* with salad, sautéed dumplings with wild mushrooms, smoked salmon and *liptauer* on toasted bagel.

❸ CHIP SHOP/CURRY SHOP. 383 5th Ave. at 6th St., 832-7701, M—W noon—10 p.m., Th noon—10:30 p.m., F noon—11 p.m., Sa 11 a.m.—11 p.m., Su 11 a.m.—10 p.m. Cash only.

Can bangers and mash make it in New York? You bet. Traditional British fish and chips, funny posters and memorabilia plastered on the bright yellow walls, and a cute little Mini Cooper delivery vehicle that bops around the neighborhood, conspire to make this a local favorite. They're also famous for fried Mars Bars, Twix, Bounty, Snickers, Reeses, and Twinkies, a hit with kids of all ages, their dentists, and the media. The **Curry Shop** next door specializes in "British-style curry."

CHRISTIE'S. 334 Flatbush Ave. at Sterling Pl., 636-9746, M—Sa 9 a.m.—10 p.m., Su 9 a.m.—5 p.m.

This hole-in-the-wall takeout serves some of the best homemade beef, chicken, and spicy vegetable Jamaican patties in New York. And their coconut turnovers will have you *oohing* and *ahhing* for more.

COCINA CUZCO. 222 7th Ave. at 3rd St., 788-5036, daily 11:30 a.m.—10:45 p.m.

From fresh ceviche to tuna-wrapped crab in an avocado-lime sauce, the food here is hearty. Ask for the vegetable plate (it's not on the menu)—a delicious corn-and-cilantro combo wrapped in plantain leaves and fried banana. The garish wall mural is a downside, but after a couple shots of tequila, who cares? Entrées run $10–$15.

COCO ROCO. 392 5th Ave. bet. 6th and 7th Sts., 965-3376, M—Th noon—10:30 p.m., F—Sa noon—11:30 p.m., Su noon—10:30 p.m.

Always busy, always good, Coco Roco serves Peruvian food with a coastal twist. Favorites include ceviche papaya (red snapper marinated in papaya, ginger, and lime sauce) and *tacu-tacu con pescado*, a sweet potato–crusted fish with Peruvian rice-and-bean risotto, salsa, and yucca fritters. The chefs have toned down the spiciness for gringo palates, but will happily add more chilies upon request. Portions are huge, the presentation is colorful, but service can be *mañana*. Entrées run about $13.

COCOTTE. 337 5th Ave. at 4th St., 832-6848, M and W—Th 6—11 p.m., F—Sa 6 p.m.—midnight, Su brunch 11 a.m.—3 p.m., dinner 6—11 p.m. Reservations recommended.

Cocotte is owned by the same folks who brought Loulou's to Fort Greene. In the front, the crowded French-American restaurant has unusual vegetarian options, like a dynamite mushroom strudel, with a broader-than-usual selection of seafood entrées, including a bouillabaisse that gets rave reviews. It's pleasant in warm weather, when the entire restaurant front opens up. A bar, with a separate entrance on 4th Street, is in the rear.

CONVIVIUM OSTERIA. 68 5th Ave. bet. Bergen St. and St. Marks Pl., 857-1833, T–Th 6–10 p.m., F–Sa 5:30–11 p.m., Su 5:30–10 p.m.

Convivium's tiny, perfectly appointed dining room has been done up to look like an old European country inn. The menu offers sophisticated Portuguese, Spanish, and Italian specialties, and there's a little garden for al fresco dining.

COUSIN JOHN'S BAKERY. 70 7th Ave. bet. Berkeley Pl. and Lincoln Pl., 622-7333 or 768-2020, Su–Th 7 a.m.–11 p.m., F–Sa 7–1 a.m.

The smell of croissants, scones, and muffins will make your mouth water. Kids will love watching the action in the open kitchen.

CUCINA. 256 5th Ave. bet. Carroll St. and Garfield Pl., 230-0711, M–Th 5:30–10 p.m., F–Sa 5:30–10:30 p.m., Su 5–10 p.m.

Like many of the brownstones around it, the ambience in this large, popular, two-dining-room restaurant is elegant but informal.

DIZZY'S. 511 9th St. at 8th Ave., 499-1966, M–F 6 a.m.–10 p.m., Sa–Su 9 a.m.–10 p.m.

Dizzy's calls itself a "finer diner"—and that it is. The French fries are hand-cut, the designer omelets use plum tomatoes and sweet onions, and the house salad is mesclun greens. Sunday brunch is popular with the locals, so come early and grab the sofa seating or an outside table.

GINKO LEAF STORE AND CAFÉ. 788A Union St. bet. 6th and 7th Aves., 399-9876, Tu–Sa noon–11 p.m., Su noon–10 p.m.

Slope resident and artist Toshio Sasak, along with his wife, Miyo, serve traditional home-cooked Japanese fare in a deliciously quiet atmosphere. There's cool jazz, a gurgling fountain, paper lighting fixtures, and a large garden in the back. White tablecloths and discreet service are a nice benefit. Entrées about $15.

JAVA. 455 7th Ave. at 16th St., 832-4583, M–Tu 5–11 p.m., W–Su 1–11 p.m.

This plain-Jane Indonesian restaurant serves both mild and spicy delicacies. For a sampler, order the *rijsttafel* for two, consisting of twelve or so mini-dishes. Or try the pastel appetizer—a patty stuffed with rice noodles and vegetables; it's light, tasty, and a wonderful starter—your choice of great entrées, and an exotic drink, like Jakarta Green Light.

JOHNNY MACK'S BAR AND GRILL. 1114 8th Ave. at 12th St., 832-7961, daily 4–11 p.m., Su brunch noon–3:30 p.m., dinner 5–10 p.m.

Mack's is a warm and cozy place to stop in for a meal, a drink, and refuge. The menu isn't extensive, but you're bound to find a fish or meat dish to suit your fancy. Good bets include the steamed dumplings in ginger sauce, pan-seared crab cakes, or grilled fish. The prix-fixe brunch is about $11.

LA TAQUERIA. 72 7th Ave. bet. Berkeley and Lincoln Pls., 398-4300, M–F 11 a.m.–10 p.m., Sa–Su 11 a.m.–11 p.m.

The long lines at dinner and on weekends tell the tale: cheap, plentiful, tasty California Mexican food that satisfies. There's a takeout joint with a few tables on the right, and a larger sit-down restaurant on the left. Hungry folks go for the enormous burritos, and in the winter the soups are a fave. Vegetarians will find plenty to satisfy.

LEMONGRASS GRILL. 61A 7th Ave. bet. Berkeley and Lincoln Pls., 399-7100, daily 11 a.m.–10 p.m.

Part of the large Thai chain.

LONG TAN. 196 5th Ave. bet. Berkeley Pl. and Union St., 622-8444, Su–Th 5:30 p.m.–midnight, F–Sa 5:30 p.m.–2 a.m., www.long-tan.com.

Southpaw (see p. 359) patrons and other peckish night owls will love Long Tan's late hours. You can savor an intimate moment in a dark lounge area or small garden—or people-watch in the large dining area. Ruby Foo chef Jeff Hardinger's contemporary Thai dishes are both tasty and tastefully presented. Entrées are $10–15.

LOS POLLITOS. 148 5th Ave. bet. Douglass and 5th Ave., 623-9152, M–Th 11:30 a.m.–11 p.m., Sa–Su 11:30 a.m.–midnight.

Authentic Mexican cuisine is inexpensive and good, and really cold *cerveza* hits the spot. The chicken dishes and guacamole are outstanding; outdoor seating is prime for people-watching.

LUCE. 411 11th St. at 6th Ave., 768-4698, T–F 5:30–11 p.m., Sa–Su brunch 11 a.m.–3:30 p.m., dinner 5:30–11 p.m.

If comfort is an excellent Italian restaurant within walking distance, then Luce is one of those elements that makes the Slope homey. With pressed-tin ceilings, large windows, and a pleasant atmosphere, Luce offers a diverse menu of modern Italian dishes, with plentiful seafood, and vegetarian and salad options. Average entrées is about $16.

MARIA'S MEXICAN BISTRO. 669 Union St. off 4th Ave., 638-2344, daily 5 p.m.–midnight.

Forget humdrum fajitas and refried beans. And the fact that you are sitting right on top of 4th Avenue (which will strike some as bizarre). Because Maria's Mexican food is sophisticated, international cuisine, drawing from Mexico City's finest eateries. Try the salmon ceviche or quesadillas with zucchini flowers, and wash it down with one of the more than eighty different tequilas offered.

MEXICAN SANDWICH SHOP. 322 5th Ave. bet. 2nd and 3rd Sts., 369-2058, daily 11 a.m.–11 p.m.

Creative-fusion Mexican sandwiches with flavorful insides, such as fresh salsas, duck, and good cheeses, make this a favorite little eat-in or takeout.

MILAN'S. 710 7th Ave. bet. 22nd and 23rd Sts., 788-7384, T–Su noon–9 p.m. Cash only.

If you guessed that "Milan" is Italian, it would be understandable—but wrong. Hearty Slavic comfort food is served at this restaurant on Park Slope's outer edge. Try the pierogi, goulash, or potato pancakes. There's no wine or bar; a meal is under $8 a person.

THE MINNOW. 442 Ninth St. bet. 6th and 7th Aves., 832-5500, M and W–F 5:30–11 p.m., Sa 5–11 p.m., Su brunch 11:30 a.m.–2:30 p.m., dinner 5–9:30 p.m.

Health-conscious Slopers have given a whale of a warm welcome to tiny seafood restaurant, Minnow. You'll find inventive and tasty options, or you can select your fish and have it prepared as you like. A tiny garden offers seating in nice weather. Average entrée $16. Reservations recommended.

MR. FALAFEL. 226 7th Ave. bet. 3rd and 4th Sts., 768-4961, Su–Th 11 a.m.–11 p.m., F–Sa 11 a.m.–midnight.

If you're a falafel purist, this is the real thing, straight from the streets of Cairo or Jerusalem. Other Middle Eastern specialties here are good—but the falafel sandwich is perfect.

MODA CAFE. 294 5th Ave. bet. 1st and 2nd Sts., 832-8897, M–Th 8 a.m.–midnight, F–Sa 11 a.m.–1 a.m., Su 11 a.m.–8 p.m.

Warm up at this tiny place with a cuppa cappuccino—and try the tapas.

MOUTARDE. 239 5th Ave. at Carroll St., 623-3600, M–Th 11 a.m.–midnight, F 11–2 a.m., Sa 8–2 a.m., Su 8 a.m.–midnight.

From the smoked-salmon appetizer sliced paper-thin, to the classic desserts (don't miss the chocolate cake "ancienne"), Moutarde provides a French bistro experience, replete with its signature palette of mustards, in a charming environment of yellow walls and zinc bar. (Things weren't always so cheery here; a decade ago this was a funeral parlor.) Entrées hover around $16.

NANA. 155 5th Ave. bet. St. John's Pl. and Lincoln Pl., 230-3749, Su–Th 5 p.m.–1 a.m., F–Sa 5 p.m.–2 a.m. Kitchen closes one hour before the restaurant closes. Cash only. Weekend reservations recommended.

What do you get when you mix Thai, Malaysian, and Japanese food into an Asian fusion? Nana. The "steamed emerald vegetable" dumplings are not just green, but tender and perfectly seasoned; "crispy Taro duck roll" comes as a cocktail hotdog–sized nugget that's stuffed with flavorful duckling, and don't say they didn't warn you about spicy with the "hot hot hot *japjai* shrimp with pumpkin." There's a large selection of sake (try it cold) and very good sushi. The large backyard draws languid summer crowds and people-watchers, as does a separate bar up front. Reasonably priced.

NAIDRE'S. 384 7th Ave. bet. 11th and 12th Sts., 965-7585, M–F 6:30 a.m.–9 p.m., Sa–Su 7:30 a.m.–10 p.m.

A faithful following flocks to Naidre's for college-eatery fare of fresh smoothies, comforting brownies, flavored coffees, healthful soups, and salads. Sandwiches include vegan egg salad, prosciutto and smoked mozzarella, or peanut butter, Nutella, banana, and honey. Coffees are sold by the pound.

⊘ **OLIVE VINE.** 81 7th Ave. bet. Berkeley Pl. and Union St., 622-2626, daily 11 a.m.–11 p.m. Cash only. Other locations: 362 15th St. at 7th Ave., 499-0555.

Homemade lentil soup, superb falafel and hummus, and freshly made puffy pita bread beckon at this informal Middle Eastern café. Folks keep coming back for the individual pizzas, which will satisfy an adult, or two children, for just $8.

⊘ **OZZIE'S COFFEE.** 57 7th Ave. at Lincoln Pl., 398-6695. daily 8 a.m.–midnight; also at 249 5th Ave. at Garfield Pl., www.ozziescoffee.com.

This gourmet-coffee café is the "in" local hangout and meeting place for Slopers of all types. Ozzie's business reflects the pattern of the neighborhood: the early-to-work crowd gives way to moms with toddlers and writers with laptops, followed by high school students on lunch break, and the postwork crowd again. The larger 5th Avenue store, where the owner roasts his beans, often hosts readings, has wireless Internet access, and also runs the "Empty Bowl" project, which enables customers to make a contribution to the local soup kitchen.

PRESS 195. 195 5th Ave. bet. Sackett and Union Sts., 857-1950, M–Th 11:30 a.m.–10 p.m., F 11:30 a.m.– 11 p.m., Sa noon–11 p.m., Su 10 a.m.–9 p.m., www.press195.com.

Come when you're hungry—the hot and cold sandwiches are he-man–sized, yummy concoctions on fresh loaves of ciabatta bread from the local **Uprising Bakery.** Wine, a latte, or ginger beer are available, as are tons of vegetarian dishes (including soy pizza) or a homemade roast pork, ham, and Swiss. Big eaters: Save room for the cheesecake of the day. Sandwiches run about $7, appetizer platters of black-bean hummus or bresaola are about $5.50. Service can be slow.

ROSE WATER. 787 Union St. bet. 5th and 6th Aves., 783-3800, M 5:30–10 p.m., T–Th 5:30–10:30 p.m., F 5:30–11 p.m., Sa brunch 11 a.m.–3 p.m., dinner 5:30–11 p.m., Su brunch 11 a.m.–3 p.m., dinner 5:30–10 p.m. No reservations; come early on weekends or be prepared to wait.

Rose Water continues to stun its patrons with out-of-this-world Mediterranean-style food. Chef and co-owner Neil O'Malley relies on locally grown produce for his artistry. Whether it's a plate of greens with goat-cheese dressing, chicken, or desserts, it's mouth-watering. The restaurant is quite tiny, with sidewalk tables in the summer. Brunch servings are ample. Entrées around $16.

SANTA FE BAR AND GRILL. 60 7th Ave. at Lincoln Pl., 636-0279, M–F 5–11 p.m., Sa–Su 3 p.m.–midnight.

Frozen margaritas, cold beer, and chips with salsa make this a popular hangout for young Slopers after work and on weekends. On cool nights, the doors and windows are flung wide open, making the street scene a part of the dinner scene. The food is average Mexican, but the activity at the bar is top-shelf.

2ND STREET CAFÉ. 189 7th Ave. at 2nd St., 369-6928, daily 8 a.m.–10:30 p.m., www.2ndstreetcafe.com.

Locals like this diner-cum-bistro for breakfast, lunch, and dinner, especially the salads, crab cakes, and variety of vegetarian options. The most expensive entrée, a grilled rib-eye in a red-wine-and-shallot sauce, is $12.50. Crayons and paper table coverings will keep young budding Da Vincis busy. Weekend brunch is wildly popular.

STAR OF INDIA. 232 5th Ave. bet. President and Carroll Sts., 638 0555, Su–Th noon–11 p.m., F–Sa noon–11:30 p.m.

This family business arrived in 2003, as part of a miniwave of new Indian restaurants that suddenly seem to have discovered curry-deprived Slopers. You can get traditional pakoras, soups, kebabs, curries, and more here. Finally!

♪ **SUGARCANE.** 238 Flatbush Ave. at Bergen St., 230-3954, M–W 4 p.m.–midnight, Th–Sa 4 p.m.–4 a.m., Su brunch 11 a.m.–4 p.m., dinner 5:30 p.m.–midnight. Reservations recommended.

Things are poppin' here on weekends. Caribbean foods (plantain-crusted red snapper, spicy-sauced codfish, soursop flan) in a small, elegantly spare dining room draw a young, diverse crowd. The high-tech bar is crammed from Thursday through Saturday evenings, as live music, from reggae to hip-hop to calypso, plays until the wee hours. Check out the Sunday jazz brunch.

◉ TEA LOUNGE 350 7th Ave. and 10th St., 768-4966, M–F 7 a.m.–1 a.m., Sa–Su 9 a.m.–2 a.m. Also, new site at 839 Union St. bet. 6th and 7th Aves.

If you're looking to warm up, cool down, or just play a quick game of chess with a stranger, the Tea Lounge is the perfect spot. There's stroller gridlock here during the weekday mornings as moms with young children gather. With a setup that looks like a fusion of several already mismatched living rooms, it's hard not to feel comfortable. There are over sixty teas with tantalizing names such as "Red Shakra." Single cups ($2.50) can be ordered to stay or to go, but the best way to take your tea is in a pot for two ($5.00). Tea can also be ordered in bulk.

12TH STREET BAR & GRILL. 1123 8th Ave. at 12th St., 965-9526, M–Th 5:30–11 p.m., F–Sa 5:30 p.m.–midnight, Su brunch 11:30 a.m.–3 p.m., dinner 5:30–11 p.m.

12th Street Bar & Grill serves eclectic American-style cuisine with items like "grilled shrimp with a slightly spicy tomato jam, topped with leeks on an Israeli couscous salad," as well as a Brooklyn steak sandwich with "sautéed onions and peppers on French bread topped with Swiss and provolone." Grilled, homemade duck *saucisson*, and sliced-fennel-and-orange salad are also good. Friendly, noisy, and busy, the bar next door serves from this excellent kitchen. Entrées about $15.

♫ TWO BOOTS. 514 2nd St. just off 7th Ave., 499-3253, Su–Th 10:30 a.m.–4 p.m., 5–11 p.m., F–Sa 10:30 a.m.–4 p.m., 5 p.m.–midnight.

Like its popular Manhattan locations, this zany, eclectic restaurant combines moderately priced food with kiddie accoutrements: coloring books and crayons, kid-level tables and coat hooks, pizza dough "play doh," and a pizza decorated like a face. It's not just a kids' place, though: there's a bar area, and dishes like sweet-potato-and-scallion omelettes with salsa verde will appeal to adults. Come Friday and Saturday nights for live jazz, blues, Latin and African rhythms, and more. No cover, no minimum.

TWO TOMS. 255 3rd Ave. at Union St., 875-8689, T–Sa 5–9:30 p.m., Su 3–7 p.m.

Two Toms is an undeniably Italian, working-class, family-oriented, no-nonsense restaurant where the specialties—huge portions of steak and chops—

get raves. Ditto for the enormous antipasti. Good for kids and large groups. Low prices. Drive here if you can, since it's located in a somewhat isolated area between an auto body shop and a launderette near the Gowanus Canal. Weekend reservations recommended.

Bars

Of course, many area restaurants listed above, such as Blue Ribbon, Santa Fe, and others, have busy bar scenes, as well.

♫ **BAR 4.** 444 7th Ave. at 15th St., 832-4800, daily 6 p.m.–4 a.m. DJ most nights.

Red lights, electronic music, and plenty of old, assorted sitting-room furniture pieces give this place a very mellow and upbeat atmosphere. The people usually look hip, the music is soothing and danceable, and you'll be comfortable sitting on a plush sofa (that seems like it belongs somewhere on Park Avenue forty years ago), with a multiracial Gen-Y crowd doing their thang all around you.

♫ **BARBÈS.** 376 9th St. at 6th Ave. 965-9177, Su–Th 5 p.m.–2 a.m., F–Sa 5 p.m.–4 a.m., www.barbesbrook lyn.com.

It's more than a bar, it's a gestalt. Cozy and cool, exuding hipness, this bar is a venue for live jazz and bluegrass music almost every night of the week. Covers are usually $5–$10 for shows (but you can also hear the music from the bar without paying). Recent performances included a Slavic soul party with Balkan dance music, readings by local authors, performances, by guitar, cello, and trombone, and the Zagnut Circus Orkestar. **Barbès is** named after a Parisian neighborhood known for its low rent and North African immigrant population.

♫ **BAR REIS.** 375 5th Ave. bet. 5th and 6th Sts., 832-5716, M–F 5:30 p.m.–3 a.m., Sa–Su 2 p.m.–3 a.m. DJs, karaoke, live music (occasionally).

An interesting space, with two bars (one on ground level, and another in the basement of the building next door) and a large patio out back, Bar Reis brings in a multiracial, twenty-something, local assembly nightly. On the walls you'll find a rotating crop of local artwork. Theme nights include Thursday karaoke and weekend DJs.

BLAH BLAH LOUNGE. 501 11th St. bet. 7th and 8th Aves., 369-2524, M–Th 6 p.m.–1 a.m., Sa–Su 3 p.m.–2 a.m.

Relax on a sofa in this living room–like bar where you can hang out around a working fireplace, enjoy a few drinks, and blah, blah, blah with your pals, both old and new. They have readings, DJs, open mic, and lots of special events.

• *Gay/Lesbian Cafés and Bars* •

Park Slope has gained the reputation as being a gay-positive place to live. Each June, the Brooklyn Gay Pride celebration parades down 7th Avenue and into Prospect Park, where local performers do their best Gloria Gaynor or Tina Turner imitations. A couple of local places:

EXCELSIOR. 390 5th Ave. bet. 6th and 7th Sts., 832-1599, M–F 6 p.m.–4 a.m., Sa–Su 2 p.m.–4 a.m.

The crowd here is predominantly male, gay, and young. From outside, Excelsior seems a bit of a mystery, with perpetually drawn black blinds and discreet lighting. Inside, it's got a certain aesthetic: a large mirror behind a wide selection of liquors and a buff bartender. There's not a lot of seating, but a balcony and garden out back offer escape on hot summer nights.

GINGER'S BAR. 363 5th Ave. bet 5th and 6th Sts. 788-0924, M–F 6 p.m.–4 a.m., Sa–Su 2 p.m.–4 a.m.

Formerly known as Carrie Nation, this is perhaps the best known lesbian bar in the 'hood, and as such gets a good crowd. Female patrons seem to be on the plus side of thirty, and you will see an occasional guy or two mixed into the swarm. There's a pool table in the back, a patio that closes at eleven p.m., and a jukebox filled with up-tempo pop music.

BUTTERMILK BAR. 577 5th Ave. at 16th St. 788-6297, daily 6 p.m.–4 a.m. Cash only.

A lone oasis on a nighttime deserted stretch of 5th Avenue, Buttermilk's warm lighting and spacious seating area attracts local tipplers looking for a cheap beer ($4 draughts and bottles) and a low-key place to enjoy it.

♪ **GREAT LAKES.** 284 5th Ave. corner of 1st St., 499-3710, daily 6 p.m.–4 a.m.

Come for the jazz and to hang, but don't plan on food. Great Lakes serves up live music Sunday to Tuesday, often performed by recent music-school grads. The rest of the week, it's a bar. It's a twenty- and thirty-something scene. A good place to meet people.

THE GATE. 321 5th Ave. off 4th St., 768-4329, M–F 4 p.m.–4 a.m., Sa–Su 1 p.m.–4 a.m.

Two dozen draft beers, twenty-eight single-malt scotches, twenty American whiskeys, and half a dozen different bottlings in other categories is what pulls in the crowds at The Gate. Not to mention a spacious outdoor seating area, games of chess, backgammon, or darts—and a staff who know their customers well enough to take calls, hold keys, and the like.

♪ **LOKI.** 305 5th Ave. at 2nd St., 965-9600, M–F 3 p.m.–4 a.m., Sa–Su 1 p.m.–4 a.m. F–Sa DJs.

There's a long bar and sideboard running back from the door to greet you as you come in, leading to a pool table, dart board, lounge area, fireplace, and garden—this place is bigger than the average Brooklyn bar. On weekends, loads of young neighborhood professionals show up, talking, drinking, and lounging to the jukebox rock, reggae, country, punk, and dance music. Happy hour 3–6 p.m.

O'CONNOR'S. 39 5th Ave., 783-9721, daily noon–4 a.m. Cash only.

Dive into this bar for a cheap-'n-sturdy drinking experience and have a chat with the moose head hanging over the bar. The crowd is of the hard-drinking variety and generally made up of people in their thirties & forties.

SHOPPING

Specialty Food Shops

A. S. FINE FOODS. 274 5th Ave., bet. Garfield Pl. and 1st St., 768-2728, M–Th 7:30 a.m.–6 p.m., F 7:30 a.m.–7 p.m. Sa 7:30 a.m.–6 p.m. (Other locations: 8614 5th Ave. and 361 Ave. X.)

For those seeking genuine Italian provisions from rolled veal with garlic to chicken stuffed with mozzarella and prosciutto, the people at A.S. have been perfecting the art of Italian cooking for more than fifty-five years.

ANDY'S FRUIT & VEGGIE TRUCK STAND. Parked corner of 7th Ave. and President St. most weekdays, 8 a.m.–6 p.m. in spring, summer, and autumn.

"Hello, darlin'," "How are you today?," "How 'bout a strawberry for you, junior?" Andy, as everyone calls him, pulls up in his beat-up red truck every day, as he has for decades, parks on a busy corner, and sets up boxes of precious perishables: oranges, apples, grapes, berries, bananas, tomatoes, and whatever else he got fresh that morning at the market. He can judge when a cantaloupe is ripe (very hard to do): "For today, perfect." Or "wait until ta-*marrah*." Andy's reappearance every spring is a welcome signal: summer—and Andy's friendly cornucopia of fresh produce—are just around the corner.

BLUE APRON FOOD. 814 Union St. at 7th Ave., 230-3180, M–Sa 10 a.m.–7 p.m.

When Blue Apron Food first opened, they were promptly deluged by what seemed like an entire neighborhood longing for gourmet, imported, high-end, artisanal, sophisticated cheeses and foods. This "purveyor of cheese, charcuterie, and fine foods" is a wonderful store with a fine selection of breads, handmade mini-pizzas, gourmet chocolates, oils, and condiments, and excellent specialty pâtés, sausages, and olives. At the register, little, freshly baked banana or pumpkin breads are hard to resist. But ah! The cheeses! The cheeses! Even the fussiest French guests won't complain.

BIERKRAFT. 191 5th Ave. bet. Berkeley Pl. and Union St., 230-7600, M—Th 11 a.m.—8 p.m., F—Sa 11 a.m.—10 p.m., Su noon—6 p.m.

Bierkraft's arrival on 5th Avenue was tantamount to an engraved announcement reading, "5th Avenue has arrived! Artisanal foods!" They sell over six hundred craft beers. They stock dozens of cheeses, sliced nitrate-free turkey, grass-fed roast beef, fresh pâtés, Peet's coffee, and incredibly good, if expensive, breads. There are sixty-five different kinds of imported chocolates—including some beer-flavored gems by Brooklyn's own **Eric Girerd.** On Tuesdays there's a free beer tasting 7–8 p.m.

CONNECTICUT MUFFIN. 171 7th Ave. at 1st St., 768-2022, M—Th 6 a.m.—10:30 p.m., F—Su 6 a.m.—11 p.m. Other locations: 206 Prospect Park West near the Pavilion movie house (965-2067); at 115 Montague St. in Brooklyn Heights (875-3912), and at 423 Myrtle Ave. in Fort Greene (935-0087).

There are forty different muffins, cakes, and bagels to choose from, and on warm days the outdoor benches welcome the mix of singles, marrieds, and kids.

EAGLE PROVISIONS. 628 5th Ave. at 18th St., 499-0026, M—Sa 6 a.m.—7 p.m., Su 6 a.m.—5 p.m.

This small, ultraclean supermarket with its international flavor and large selection of high-quality Eastern and Western European items seems to belong in Manhattan's Yorkville section. In addition to fresh produce, you'll find smoked meats made on the premises, from juicy hams to no-preservative sausages and oven-ready fresh stuffed chicken breasts and brisket.

ERICA'S RUGELACH AND BAKING COMPANY. 265 5th Ave. bet. 1st and Garfield Sts., 965-3657 and 499-0445, M—F 9 a.m.—5 p.m., www.ericasrugelach.com.

They make mountains of *rugelach* here, and ship nationwide. You have to order a day ahead, but it's worth advance planning to get these fabulous *rugelach*, brownies, macaroons, linzer tarts, and hamantaschen.

CHEZ ISABELLE. 427 7th Ave. bet. 14th and 15th Sts., 832-0127, M 7:30 a.m.—3 p.m., T—F 7:30 a.m.—8 p.m., Sa 9 a.m.—8 p.m., Su 8:30 a.m.—8 p.m. Cash only.

Chez Isabelle would be right at home in the West Village, or, for that matter, the Left Bank, with its French pastries, cakes, and delicious sandwiches. Chez Isabelle adds welcome leavening to what used to be a flatly grubby strip of the Slope's famous 7th Avenue.

FRATELLI RAVIOLI. 169 Lincoln Pl., 783-7833, daily 9 a.m.—7 p.m., www.fratelliravioli.com. (Another location: 169 7th Ave. bet. Garfield Pl. and 1st St., 369-2850.)

The original Carroll Gardens shop opened more than thirty years ago, and has since expanded into a small retail empire. Besides the incredible made-on-the-premises fresh mozzarella cheese, classic (four-cheese, spinach) and eclectic (pumpkin, and lobster in squid's-ink dough) ravioli and tasty homemade sauces, you can get a great sandwich here, summer ices, and new fresh pizzas that you can pick up and cook when the kids come home. With a day's notice, Fratelli's can produce hero sandwiches six feet long!

LA BAGEL DELIGHT. 252 7th Ave. at 5th St., 768-6107, M–Th 6 a.m.–7 p.m., F–Su 6 a.m.–10 p.m. (Another location: 122 7th Ave. at President St., 398-9529.)

It isn't hard to find bagels in Brooklyn, but finding really good bagels is more of a challenge. Although there will always be those who disagree, many locals consider these baked-on-the-premises bagels some of the best around.

PARK SLOPE FOOD CO-OP. 782 Union St. bet. 6th and 7th Aves., 622-0560, M–Th 8 a.m.–9:45 p.m., Sa 9 a.m.–7:30 p.m., Su 8 a.m.–5 p.m., www.foodcoop.com.

The place is simply remarkable. An *institution*. You can't believe it actually functions on 90 percent volunteer labor—but it does, and beautifully. If you want to understand Park Slope, check out the co-op. You can't shop here unless you are one of the more than nine thousand members who belong to this unique institution. And if you do take a tour, expect to hear an erudite conversation about jazz, recipes for jicama-and-orange salad, or the health benefits of chlorella.

This is the country's largest member-run food cooperative, founded back in 1973. Members do 80 percent of the labor (paid employees handle the rest) and commit to two hours and forty-five minutes of work every four weeks. The co-op caters to a wide range of tastes and offers a diversity of products with an emphasis on organic, minimally processed and healthful foods. A big attraction is the extensive produce section, which includes many organic items, and prices at just 17 percent above cost. Handwritten signs explain environmentally sound foods and staples to buy and to avoid.

POLLIO. 398 5th Ave. bet. 6th and 7th Sts., 768-6887, M–F 7 a.m.–8:45 p.m., Sa 7 a.m.–8 p.m., Su 8 a.m.–7 p.m.

Pollio is a great little Italian store that makes fresh mozzarella and sells sundried tomatoes, fresh basil, terrific sandwiches, and homemade ravioli.

RUSSO & SONS. 363 7th Ave. bet. 10th and 11th Sts., 369-2874, M–Sa 8:30 a.m.–7 p.m., Su 10 a.m.–4 p.m.

Russo's sister is over ninety years old—that is, the sister store in Manhattan, on East 11th Street. Russo & Sons has been voted "best cheese and pasta shop" by Jack Robertiello, author of *Mangia*, a guidebook to the best Italian food in the Big Apple. But don't take anybody else's word, see for yourself what the secret to longevity is: try their homemade mozzarella and frozen stuffed pastas.

SECOND HELPINGS. 448 9th St. at 7th Ave., 965-1925, T–F 11 a.m.–8:30 p.m., Sa–Su 10:30 a.m.–8 p.m.

Oddly, it's hard to find vegan foods in the Slope. Second Helpings has a good selection of salads, sandwiches, wraps, and vegan desserts, in addition to nicely prepared nonvegetarian dishes—but they don't come cheap. You can eat in at one of two tables inside or get takeout for dinner or a picnic at nearby Prospect Park.

TROPICAL FRUIT STAND. 4th Ave. bet. 2nd and 3rd Sts., spring, summer, 7 a.m.–6 p.m.

Like a tropical landmark in the heart of Brooklyn, in the summer there's always a parked truck loaded with fresh sugar cane, papayas, mangos, small sweet bananas, and plantains at this corner.

TWO LITTLE RED HENS. 1112 8th Ave. bet. 11th and 12th Sts., 499-8108. M–F 7 a.m.–7 p.m., Sa 8 a.m.–7 p.m., Su 8 a.m.–5 p.m. (Another location: Manhattan, 1652 2nd Ave. at 85th St, (212) 452-0476.)

Park Slopers line up on weekends for eat-in (if they can get a seat) or take-home goodies. The best-seller at this little gem of a bakery is the Brooklyn Black-out Cake, a dark-chocolate confection filled with chocolate pudding and covered with chocolate icing and chocolate crumbs. If you aren't a chocoholic, go for the raspberry tart or the most extraordinary Key lime pie. Pricey, but you get what you pay for.

UNCLE LOUIE G'S. 41 Union St. at 5th Ave., 965-4237, Su–Th 11 a.m.–11 p.m., F–Sa 11 a.m.–1 a.m.

Uncle Louie G's started out a few years back on Coney Island Avenue, on a funky block, but word spread fast of the cornucopia of delicious homemade ice cream and gourmet Italian ices. If you haven't had a cremolata ice, try it, or dive into the apple-pie-à-la-mode ice cream (yes, it's an ice-cream flavor, and darned tasty). With more than fifty flavors, everyone will be satisfied. There are multiple locations in Brooklyn and around the nation.

UPRISING BAKERY. 328 7th Ave. bet 8th and 9th Sts., 499-8665, daily 8 a.m.–7 p.m. (Other locations: 138 7th Ave. bet. Carroll and Garfield Sts., 499-5242; Court St. in Carroll Gardens.)

Uprising is a family-owned bakery that has a production facility in nearby Sunset Park, started by a husband-and-wife team. They produce a range of nat-urally leavened breads, rustic styles that are hand-crafted and hearth-baked, with no additives, no dairy, no eggs. Delicious.

Clothing and Shoes

AARON'S. 627 5th Ave. near 16th St., 768-5400, M–Sa 9:30 a.m.–6 p.m., www.aarons.com.

Their slogan says it all: "You Won't Do Better Unless Your Husband's in the

Business." Inside Aaron's innocuous, windowless storefront, you'll find discounts on leading designer sportswear, dresses, and coats at 25-to-50-percent savings. Look for labels like Harvé Bernard, Albert Nipon, Blassport, and Henry Grethel. There's parking across the street, and the salespeople are attentive.

ALMOST NEW. 68 St. Marks Ave. off 6th Ave. near Flatbush Ave., 398-8048, M—Tu noon—7 p.m., F—Su noon— 6 p.m.

Really great vintage jewelry, elegant suits and dresses, boas, furs, handbags, and other "finds" await at Almost New. Teenage girls who are into vintage will adore this store—and moms who want to play dress-up will, too.

BABY BIRD. 428 7th Ave.bet. 14th and 15th Sts., 768-4940, Tu—Th 11:30 a.m.—7:30 p.m., F—Sa noon— 6:00 p.m., www.shopbird.com.

One of the nicest baby-clothing shops in Brooklyn, Baby Bird sells dressy wear for infants through age six, including almost the entire Petite Bateau line. In addition, you'll find Cotton Kaboodle and Cocoli and Lucky Wang. It's adorable stuff, and the kids won't mind coming here, either, as there's a beautiful aquarium built at child's-eye level, and lots of toys. Don't miss the line of locally made hipster T-shirts with pitchers of Bob Marley and other stars, $26 each.

◉BEACON'S CLOSET. 152 5th Ave. bet. President and Carroll Sts., 789-3447, M—F noon—9 p.m., Sa—Su 11 a.m.—8 p.m., www.beaconscloset.com.

A Williamsburg favorite, this "clothing exchange" shop appeals to hip moms and cool teenagers who love gently used and vintage clothing. (See description of flagship store, 88 No. 11th St., 486-0816, in **Williamsburg** chapter).

◐ ✪ BIRD. 430 7th Ave. bet. 14th and 15th Sts., 768-4940, Tu—Th 11:30 a.m.—7:30 p.m., F—Sa noon— 6:00 p.m., www.shopbird.com.

Bird's developed a nice line (pants and a dress and skirt) under its own brand name in sunny bright colors, thanks to the creativity of their designer, trained at the Rhode Island School of Design. An appealing collection of unique casual wear, from independent European designers, makes for comfortably feminine styles. Dresses start at $130, and locally made jewelry starts at $80.

☺ BOING BOING. 204 6th Ave. corner Union St., 398-0251, M—F 11 a.m.—7 p.m., Sa—Su 10 a.m.—6 p.m.

Pregnancy and new babies have a way of creating new shopping needs, like bigger clothes (how much bigger *can* one get?) and other maternity needs, including nursing gear and infant toys. Books about babies and pregnancy and lots of good networking can also be found at this helpful store.

⊘ ✪ **BROOKLYN INDUSTRIES.** 152 5th Ave. bet. Douglass and Degraw Sts., 789-3447, M–F noon–9 p.m., Sa–Su 11 a.m.–9 p.m. www.brooklynindustries.com

A newcomer from Williamsburg, with "Brooklyn" T-shirts galore.

CITY CASUALS. 223 7th Ave. bet. 3rd and 4th Sts., 499-5581, M–F 10 a.m.–7 p.m., Sa 10 a.m.–6 p.m., Su noon–5 p.m.

Working women are regulars at this shop stuffed with relaxed yet professional fashions. Among the store's loyal customers are dentists, doctors, lawyers, writers, professors, and therapists. The dresses and two-piece outfits start at around $130. The shoes are good-looking and comfortable, with many imports ranging from $45 to $150.

✪ **DIANA KANE.** 229 Fifth Ave. bet. President and Carroll Sts., 638-6520, Tu–Sa noon–8 p.m., Su 11 a.m.–6 p.m.

Lovers and those who would woo, take note: There's wonderful lingerie and great jewelry, made by the owner, in this store. Teddies galore and femme fatale gear make this a neighborhood hit.

⊘ ✪ **EIDOLON.** 233 5th Ave. bet. Carroll and President Sts., 638-8194, Tu–Sa noon–8 p.m., Su noon–7 p.m., www.eidolonbklyn.com.

Eidolon represents the work of three designers. There are lots of skirts and frocks; in the winter look for corduroy and wool skirts. Prices range from $120 for shirts to $150 for dresses. Funky wrap bracelets made of colorful stones ($40) or jeweled drop earrings ($25) top off any outfit with pizzazz. Also check out the line of hand-knit lingerie. This is a wonderful place to shop for one-of-a-kind, made-in-Brooklyn pieces. Custom tailoring.

☺ **FIDGETS.** 169 7th Ave. bet. 1st and 2nd Sts., 788-2002, M–Sa 10 a.m.–7 p.m., Su 11 a.m.–6 p.m.

Perfectly in tune with the neighborhood's tastes, Fidgets sells fun, practical, crayon-box colored clothes for babies to tweens, at reasonable prices.

⊘ **4PLAY OKAY.** 360 7th Ave. bet. 10th and 11th Sts., 369-4088, Tu–Sa 11 a.m.–8 p.m., Su noon–6 p.m.

Quirky and colorful, 4Play is Park Slope's version of Urban Outfitter meets St. Marks. Pairs of tight jeans and hip-hugging Dickies pants line the walls, intermingling with lacy dresses and cotton vintage-style tees. Elevated red velvet–draped dressing rooms make anyone feel like a supermodel, but the trendy hipsters working behind the counter will give their honest opinion. Pants are priced $40–$60; tops $20–$50. Check out the $5 bin.

JUMPIN' JULIA'S. 240 7th Ave. bet. 4th and 5th Sts., 965-3535, M–Sa 10 a.m.–7 p.m., Su 11 a.m.–6 p.m.

Clothing for babies and small children in rainbow colors and practical styles are Jumpin' Julia's specialty.

✪ **KIWI.** 78 7th Ave. off Berkeley Pl., near 7th Ave. 622-5551, Tu–F noon–7 p.m., Sa 11 a.m.–6 p.m., Su noon–5 p.m., www.kiwidesignco.com.

Hopelessly romantic and deliciously feminine, Kiwi's style feels like retro-1940s. The designer, whose apprenticeship to Parisian masters shows in her attention to detail, adds a personal twist to the most basic classics. In summer, you can't do better than with their sundresses, and in winter, the made-to-order cashmere coats. Pants and dresses start at over $100. Custom tailoring.

✪ **KIMERA.** 274 5th Ave. bet. Garfield and 1st Sts., 965-1313, www.kimeradesign.com. (Another location: 366 Atlantic Ave., 422-1147.)

This little store is not much bigger than some people's closets, but it's stuffed with very feminine clothing in shimmering colors. You can find locally made jewelry and handbags here as well. Check the back for a small select collection of vintage clothing. Custom tailoring.

✪ **MADORAN.** 449 7th Ave. bet. 15th and 16th Sts., 768-4935, W–F noon–8 p.m., Sa 11 a.m.–6 p.m., Su noon–6 p.m.

"It's a wonderful time in Brooklyn for women's clothes," says the Madoran's owner and designer. She's right. This little store sells one-of-a-kind hats, playful, feminine casual clothes for twenty- and thirty-somethings on a budget. Handmade T-shirts cost about $30 and skirts about $80, dresses are under $100. Utilitarian hobo bags are $60 and up. There are whimsical prints, appliqués, and gear for casual dressing up. Custom tailoring.

OTTO. 348 10th St. off 7th Ave., 788-6627.

Fine lingerie, bathing suits, jewelry, and cute objects for the home make little Otto, tucked away on a side street, a favorite among women.

☺ **PLAY IT AGAIN SAM.** 732 Carroll St. bet. 6th and 7th Aves., 499-8589, T and Th–Sa 10 a.m.–6 p.m., W 10 a.m.–8 p.m.

When owner Pamela Sherid's own children started to get too big for their britches, she transformed her brownstone basement into a secondhand children's shop. It's a great place to buy and sell children's clothes, equipment, and maternity clothes.

SLANG BETTY. 172 5th Ave. bet. Lincoln and Berkeley Pls., 638-1725, Su–M noon–6 p.m., T–Sa 11 a.m.–7 p.m.

This little boutique specializes in feminine, fun, inexpensive clothing and accessories. You won't find any name brands, but the styles are trend-setting. A summer top sells for $20; winter pants for $40. Accessories include jewelry, handbags, and occasional must-haves.

TRIANGLE CLOTHING. 182 Flatbush Ave. at 5th Ave., 638-5300, M–F 9:45 a.m.–6:30 p.m., Sa 9:45 a.m.–5:30 p.m.

In business since 1917, Triangle is a potpourri of sporting goods, work clothes, and sports clothes. There's a large inventory, so ask for help. Prices can be lower than most chain stores; last year's $100 ice skates can be found here for as little as $60.

Other Interesting Neighborhood Shops

BOB AND JUDI'S COLLECTIBLES. 215 5th Ave. bet Union and President Sts., 638-5770, W–Su 11 a.m.–7 p.m.

Photos of old Brooklyn and a small antique barn's worth of interesting vintage items are neatly crammed into this little store. Bob and Judi's is a good place to start if you're looking for little old-fashioned lamps, wonderful vintage jewelry, including antique diamond rings, interesting glassware, framed pictures, and eclectic silver and pewter bowls, pitchers, and other service pieces. Prices are reasonable, and the knowledgeable owners, named guess-what, are helpful.

COG & PEARL. 190 5th Ave. at Sackett St., 623-8200, W–Sa noon– 8 p.m., Su noon–6 p.m., www.cogandpearl.com.

Advertised as selling "handmade stuff to give or keep," most of what you'll pick up here will fall into the latter category. Check out the crocheted bobby pins ($9), restructured T-shirts ($44), handmade bath soaps (especially the soy line!), and beautifully crafted picture frames. They also sell high-end handcrafted articles made by Brooklyn-based designers, including very lovely art glass pieces.

COMMUNITY BOOKSTORE OF PARK SLOPE. 143 7th Ave. bet. Carroll St. and Garfield Pl., 783-3075, M–F 9 a.m.–9 p.m., Sa–Su 10 a.m.–9 p.m.

Locals are intensely loyal to this decades-old independent bookstore with its enticing café and back garden. The reason has to do with sensibilities—and service. Community has an intelligent selection of both contemporary and classic literature and nonfiction, as well as poetry, mysteries, travel guides, and gift items. A welcoming corner of the store is reserved for children's books. The staff is eager to offer literary suggestions; in this writerly neighborhood, Community Bookstore is a bibliophile's haven; as one customer summed: "they sell books with a tenderness you'd expect from people selling puppies." In addition to a lively calendar of author readings, they advise on the selections of local book clubs, post community notices in the window, and generally serve as a community hub.

In the days after the September 11th World Trade Center attack, the bookstore volunteered its space and quickly became a key center for collection and distribution of a small avalanche of contributed relief supplies. (See **Café at Community Bookstore**, page 361).

⭐ **CLAY POT.** 162 7th Ave. bet. Garfield Pl. and 1st St., 800-989-3579 or 788-6564, M–F 11 a.m.–7:30 p.m., Sa 10 a.m.–6:30 p.m., Su noon–6 p.m., www.clay-pot.com.

Clay Pot features the work of hundreds of artisans in one-of-a-kind and unusual jewelry, pottery, weaving, lamps, and woodcrafts. They are known for their wedding and engagement rings.

The store's Web site tells a nice little tale: In 1969, Clay Pot started as an urban ceramics studio. A trunk show of engagement rings in 1989 was such a smashing hit that the store started to cultivate its now-extensive collection of handcrafted engagement and wedding rings. The selection represents the work of over seventy-five goldsmiths nationwide. Ring prices range from $1,500 to $8,000.

ECCO HOME DESIGN. 232 7th Ave. at 4th St., 788-1088, M–Sa 10:30 a.m.–7:30 p.m., Su 11 a.m.–6 p.m.

Ecco is an elegant home-furnishing store selling interesting designer lamps, rugs, picture frames, and a limited selection of lovely furniture. You can hire Ecco's interior designers to transform a plain-Jane room into an opulent, sensual setting.

GINKO LEAF. 788A Union St. bet. 6th and 7th Aves., 399-9876, Tu–Sa noon–11 p.m., Su noon–10 p.m.

A tasteful collection of home décor, dining-room accoutrements, and creature comforts is sold in this unusual Asian-themed store.

JOURNEY. 158 Berkeley Pl. off 7th Ave., 638-3330, T–F 11:30 a.m.–7 p.m., Sa 11 a.m.–7 p.m., Su 11 a.m.–5:30 p.m. Warehouse at 254 3rd Ave. bet. Union and President Sts.

Owned by one of the Slope's friendliest proprietors (and her husband, a New York City fireman) Journey sells an appealing variety of imported antique and reproduction furniture, such as wooden benches, hand-painted cabinets, and attractive coffee tables made of old wooden doors. There's quick turnover with new items all the time, including smaller pieces: French dinnerware, Moroccan tea glasses, vases, and old powder boxes. Ask to see what's in the two-thousand-square-foot warehouse on 3rd Avenue nearby.

☺ **LITTLE THINGS.** 145 7th Ave. bet. Carroll and President Sts., 783-4733, M–F 10:30 a.m.–7 p.m., Sa 10 a.m.–6:30 p.m., Su 11 a.m.–5 p.m.

The purple-and-yellow storefront is startling enough, but once inside Little Things you will find a good range of children's and babies' toys, educational toys, crafts, and knickknacks for party bags.

☺ **LULU'S CUTS AND TOYS.** 310 5th Ave. bet. 2nd and 3rd Sts., 832-3732, M–Sa 10 a.m.–6 p.m., Su 11 a.m.–5 p.m.

Lulu's turns a childhood fear into an entertainment extravaganza. Personal TVs are stationed in front of every mirror, constantly aglow with Disney classics. The barbershop doubles as a bookstore/toy store, giving the little ones a strong incentive to get that treacherous trim. There are toys, puzzles, treats, and more here. A kiddie destination!

✪ ◉ **NANCY NANCY.** 244A 5th Ave. bet. Carroll and President Sts., 789-5262, Tu–Sa 11 a.m.–8 p.m.

Nancy Nancy seems to specialize in kitsch so brilliantly over-the-top that you need to have it. Things tend to be slightly pricey, but hey, packaging is half the charm. Nancy Nancy is the best place to go for cute, original, and, of course, aesthetically irresistible gifts.

PS 321 FLEA MARKET. 7th Ave. bet. 1st and 2nd Sts., 833-9864, Sa–Su 9 a.m.–6 p.m.

Rated one of the best flea markets in the city. About fifty vendors sell vintage clothes, antiques, furniture, jewelry, postcards of old New York, collectibles, and lovely junk at this popular weekend institution.

PARK SLOPE BARBERSHOP. 223 7th Ave. corner 4th St., 965-4366, M–F 10 a.m.–6:30 p.m., Su noon–5 p.m.

A local institution, this old-fashioned barbershop does its bit for Park Slope's cozy quality of life. It's been here since 1906, and is run by three Italian brothers who snip, chat, and joke while Sinatra croons in the background (and they croon along, sometimes). They serve cookies and always put up a great window display of electric trains at Christmas. Their shop, replete with antique fixings, has been used as a movie set to capture the mood of old New York. Here you're as likely to see babies having their first locks snipped as octogenarians who've been coming here for years.

PARK SLOPE BOOKS. 202 Seventh Ave. bet. 2nd and 3rd Sts., 840-0020, Su–Th 10 a.m.–11 p.m., F–Sa 10 a.m.–midnight.

You'll find a wide range of offerings in this multilevel, multiroom browser's delight, including a large selection of used paperback best-sellers. Park Slope Books is the sister shop to **Heights Books** in Brooklyn Heights (see p. 180).

PATRIAS. 167 5th Ave. bet. Berkeley and Lincoln Pls., 857-9091, Tu–Su, noon–7 p.m., www.patrias.com.

As you wander through the authentic Latin American art, jewelry, and home furnishings here, you'll get a quick education from various explanations posted alongside the displays. The black pottery is not only functional but microwaveproof, you learn; it is handcrafted from a certain clay in Colombia. This is a wonderful store owned by folks who know and love Latin American folk art.

⊘ ☺ **POTTERY CAFÉ.** 129 6th Ave. bet. Park and Sterling Pls. Studio: Tu–Sa 10 a.m.–8 p.m., Su 10 a.m.–6 p.m. Café: Tu–Su 7 a.m.–8 p.m.

Two-thirds paint-your-own-pot, and one-third cappuccino-muffin café, Pottery Café welcomes artists as young as two years old to come and paint a pot or two. Nice for parties; there are classes in mosaic and handbuilding, too.

REVERSE AND A UNTO Z BOOKS. 176 5th Ave. bet. Sackett and DeGraw Sts., 638-2252, daily noon–7 p.m.

A combo bookstore and vintage treasure trove, this shop opened in September 2001. You might find Fiestaware, a book on British and Irish folk music, an old Electrolux vacuum cleaner, and retro clothing from the 1970s.

⊘ **RUMBLESEAT MUSIC.** 327 5th Ave. bet. 3rd and 4th Sts., 369-7646, Tu–W and F–Sa 11 a.m.–7 p.m., Th 11 a.m.–9 p.m., Su noon–5 p.m., www.rumbleseatmusicbrooklyn.com.

Opened in 2003, this branch of a well-known Ithaca, New York vintage guitar store buys and sells used and collectible guitars. Brands include Fender, Gibson, and Gretsch. (Gretsch, incidentally were originally made in Brooklyn. You can see the Gretsch signs on some buildings as you take the train over the Williamsburg Bridge.) Instruments range from $90 used guitars to $4,000 collectible guitars. There are accessories for guitars and drums, as well as lessons for all levels, and repair services. Rumbleseat also buys vintage instruments.

⊘ ✪ **SCAREDY KAT.** 229 5th Ave. bet. Carroll and President Sts., 623-1839, Tu–Sa noon–8 p.m., Su noon–6 p.m.

Specializing in newly made goods with an old-time bent. Relax to jazz as you browse through children's toys (albeit with a strong vintage feel) and journals covered in foreign roadmaps ($25). Find the perfect thing to smoke away your nostalgia with—an ashtray made from a melted record ($10–$25). Rolls of fresh, quirky giftwrap line the walls.

7TH AVENUE BOOKS. 300 7th Ave. bet. 7th and 8th Sts., 840-0188, daily 10 a.m.–10 p.m.

It would be enough if this bookshop was simply clean, well-lit, and easy to browse. But what adds to its utility is the extremely knowledgeable proprietor who can find you that classic or political tome in a flash. Related to **7th Ave. Kid's Books** (below), this shop has a membership club—$25 per year—that entitles you to 25 percent off adult titles and 10 percent off kids' books.

7TH AVENUE KID'S BOOKS. 202 7th Ave. bet. 2nd and 3rd Sts., 840-0020, M–S 10 a.m.–8 p.m., Su 10 a.m.–6 p.m.

Spacious, uncluttered, and teeming with kids' books, grouped by age and reading ability, this fun little new-and-used bookstore is replete with beanbag chairs, carpeting, and extremely friendly staff. Parents will want to know about the Tuesday and Thursday storytelling hour, beginning at 10:30 a.m. Prolific readers and buyers should pay the $25 annual membership fee that entitles you to 10 percent off all kids' books and 25 percent off adult titles here or at the sister store, **7th Avenue Books** (see above).

☺ ⊘ **SEVENTH AVENUE ART SUPPLIES.** 376 7th Ave. bet. 11th and 12th Sts., 369-4969, daily 10 a.m.–6 p.m.

Check out the full inventory of supplies for fine artists, graphic artists, students, and children.

✪ **SERENE ROSE.** 331 5th Ave. bet. 3rd and 4th Sts., 832-3224, M–Th noon–8 p.m., F–Sa 11:30 a.m.–9:30 p.m., Su 11:30 a.m.–7 p.m., www.serenerose.com.

New in 2002, Serene Rose has become a rare hit with both moms and their older teenage daughters. For moms: classic dresses and sophisticated cocktail dresses with nice detail, some imported from France, between $150 and $300. For older teens: flirty tops, starting at $40, and coy skirts. The clothing is dressy but easy to wear. In the winter they carry dramatic opera coats. Designers include Max Studio, Laundry, Easel, and Cousin Johnny's, and you can find unusual made-in-Brooklyn items, too.

STANLEY'S PLACE. 329 5th Ave. bet. 3rd and 4th Sts., 832-0239, M–F 1–7 p.m., Sa 10 a.m.–7 p.m., www.stanleysplaceusa.com.

Brooklyn is known for its defunct Dodgers, but there's a parallel universe of black baseball players, who, until Jackie Robinson, had been denied the opportunity to play in the major leagues. For years, Stanley's Place, a family business that's a labor of love, has collected items from the era of the Negro Baseball League.

THREE PEDLARS. 176 Lincoln Pl. near 7th Ave., 638-6889, M–Sa 11–7 p.m., Su noon–5.

Tucked away on a little side street across from Ozzie's Café, Three Pedlars sells a multihued riot of rich, vibrant, home-decorating fabrics for furniture, drapes, pillows, and throws. The expert staff will consult.

TRAILER PARK. 77 Sterling Pl. off 6th Ave., 623-2170, T–Su 11 a.m.–7 p.m., www.trailerparkslope.com.

Specializing in 1950s furniture and country collectibles, Trailer Park is one of the few New York City stores where you can find sturdy Amish farm tables made of recycled barn lumber (costing about $500). Plus there's a small but interesting selection of fun, functional, and funky shabby chic items here—at reasonable prices—for instance, an oak hutch, a little quirky hand-painted kitchen stool, wrought-iron chairs, and many decorative items. The amiable owners will keep their eyes open for special items if you ask.

WALTZING MATILDA AND CO. 447 1st St. off 7th Ave., 965-9088, M–Sa 10 a.m.–7 p.m.

Tucked away on a side street, this little upstairs-downstairs shop has great vintage clothes, some interesting secondhand furniture, and a fast-changing inventory. It's across from PS 321.

☛ **TIP: Stoop Sales and Bargain Hunters** Brooklyn's answer to a yard sale, the stoop sale is a time-honored spring and fall tradition in much of the borough, when people clean out their stuff to make way for growing families, moving, or eliminating clutter. Park Slope may have the best stoop sales for kids' stuff, housewares, and clothing. Prices can be as low as 50 cents for a book, or $2 for a shirt.

ACCOMMODATIONS

BED AND BREAKFAST ON THE PARK (see p. 15).

FOY HOUSE (see p. 16).

THE HOUSE ON 3RD ST (see p. 18).

Prospect Heights

ABOUT PROSPECT HEIGHTS

Prospect Heights encompasses some of the best of Brooklyn: the Brooklyn Museum, Botanic Garden, and street after street of nineteenth-century brownstone homes. It's also more diverse in terms of income, ethnicity, and age than better-known and pricier Park Slope, across Flatbush Avenue. You're apt to find physicians and teachers living within blocks of people barely above the poverty line. There's a friendly racial mix, with the majority of residents of African-American and Caribbean descent.

Increasingly, young couples in their twenties and thirties move here from Manhattan, having heard about Park Slope first and recoiled from the sticker shock. It's a family-oriented, leafy neighborhood, one of the few in Brooklyn where autumn leaves actually pile up enough for a child to hear them swish and crunch underfoot. Far more residential than commercial, Prospect Heights breeds Brooklyn neighborliness. There's **Parlor Entertainment**, a home-based occasional jazz series, and neighborhood-based book clubs and dinner clubs, block associations, and lots of information exchanged about the best way to fix up that brownstone. This is important, because unlike some other neighborhoods, Prospect Heights went into a steep depression in the post-WWII era, and for several decades these blocks upon blocks of homes were partly abandoned, unkempt, and unsafe. A renaissance began in the 1980s and is still going strong. Every street is a little different, with a blend of apartments, houses, condos, co-ops, and carriage houses.

POINTS OF CULTURAL INTEREST (SEE page 354 as well.)

BROOKLYN ARENA STADIUM.

Where: On a three-block parcel of land at the intersection of Flatbush and Atlantic Avenues, the same area where Walter O'Malley, the legendary owner of baseball's Brooklyn Dodgers, had envisioned a home for his team nearly half a century ago. When: Arena development is to begin at the end of 2004.

Brooklyn never recovered from losing the Dodgers in the 1950s, but finally we may be getting a team of our own. Metrotech developer Bruce C. Ratner has, as we go to print, just contracted to buy the New Jersey Nets. (There's a name change in their future.) As the plan goes, they'll play at a new, 19,000-seat Brooklyn Arena stadium, designed by acclaimed architect Frank Gehry, as the focal point of Brooklyn Atlantic Yards, a new urban complex of housing, commercial, and retail space. It's steamingly controversial, as the plans call for homes and stores to be destroyed to make room for the development. Preliminary sketches promise six acres of landscaped public open space, including a park on the Arena's roof, ringed by an open-air running track that doubles as a skating rink in winter with Manhattan views. As for the Nets, a kid quoted in the newspaper got it right: "If they come to Brooklyn, they better not lose." The stadium could open as early as 2006, with the rest of the complex scheduled for completion in 2014.

NEWSWALK CONDOS. 535 Dean St., 788-8200.

This hulking big building, facing desolate railroad tracks on one side, and an undistinguished stretch along residential Dean Street on the other, was built in 1927 as a New York *Daily News* printing plant. After churning out thousands of newspapers every night, the plant finally closed in 1998. In 2002, it reopened— revamped as a 140-unit upscale condominium residence, with a showy external elevator and pricey top-floor apartments boasting a broad overview of downtown Brooklyn, including BAM, the Williamsburgh Savings Bank tower, and lots and lots of sky. And it's near the Atlantic Terminal Mall and Atlantic Center Mall, as well as the Long Island Rail Road.

We include this here because NewsWalk represents a trend evident in DUMBO, Williamsburg, Red Hook, and now the outskirts of brownstone neighborhoods, as well. Brooklyn's stock of once-abandoned commercial buildings represents a gold mine for residential developers. The conversion of an old **Spalding Ball Factory** in the area was similarly successful.

PARLOR ENTERTAINMENT, IN THE MOMENT. 119 Vanderbilt Ave., 855-1981, lower duplex, first and third Saturdays of the month, www.Parlorjazz.com.

Those in the know call this jazz-in-the parlor experience "magical" and "a class act." And indeed, you can't beat the setting—an 1850s, Gothic Revival, brick-row-house parlor—or the intimate environment. You're almost close enough to the musicians to pluck those bass strings yourself. Well worth the $15 suggested contribution. Call or check the Web site for details.

♫ **UP OVER JAZZ CAFÉ.** 351 Flatbush Ave. bet. 7th and 8th Aves., 2nd fl., 398–5413. Show times 9 p.m., 10:30 p.m., and midnight. Cash only. Cover $10–$15. Reservations recommended. www.upoverjazz.com.

It's like having the Blue Note, sort of, in your neighborhood. One flight upstairs from noisy, trafficky Flatbush Avenue, and you've entered a pristine world of jazz. There's a small room with cheerful yellow walls featuring a gallery of photos of jazz musicians, a bar and nondescript tables—and a couple of guys jamming in front of no more than four or five dozen people. It's all about the music here. The sets are satisfyingly long, and Up Over Jazz gets some highly reputable jazz musicians.

✪ **VIOLIN MAKER, SAM ZYGMUNTOWICZ.** 475 Dean St., 636-4671.

These violins were good enough for Isaac Stern. A violin maker with an international reputation for excellence, Sam Zygmuntowicz has a genius for making fine, orchestra-quality reproductions of famous Guarneri- and Stradivari-crafted violins. He works on commission only, with a three-year backlog of orders.

PROSPECT HEIGHTS RESTAURANTS

ALISEO OSTERIA DEL BORGO. 665 Vanderbilt Ave. at Park Pl., 783-3400, Tu–Su 6–11 p.m., Su 11–10 p.m. Cash only.

Romantic, inventive, yet strangely familiar, this little nook of an Italian restaurant serves up interesting dishes in a welcoming atmosphere.

GARDEN CAFÉ. 620 Vanderbilt Ave. at Prospect Pl., 857-8863, Tu–Sa 6–9:30 p.m. Call for reservations; street parking available.

A wonderful place, the Garden Café is just a couple of blocks from both BAM and Park Slope, tucked away on a mixed-income thoroughfare in Prospect Heights. There are only eight tables, and the owner-chef John Policastro cooks in the nouvelle style, while his wife handles the clientele. The food is fresh, cooked and spiced with flair, and the wine list is substantial, so it is no surprise that this is a neighborhood favorite. Figure on spending $20 per entrée. Tuesday through Thursday, you can get a three-course deal—only $25.

GREEN PARADISE. 609 Vanderbilt Ave. near Dean St., 230-5177. Call for hours.

This tiny vegetarian restaurant with an Afro-Carribean theme is dedicated to healthful dishes, such as fresh juices, fried zucchini balls that double as falafel, and seasonal specials. There's often a friendly local scene here.

JOY INDIAN RESTAURANT. 301 Flatbush Ave. bet. Prospect Pl. and St. Marks Ave., 230-1165, daily noon–11 p.m.

You can get a very satisfying traditional Indian meal here—samosas, tandoori dishes, naan and other special breads, and curries. For the hordes of local home-office writers and entrepreneurs in the area, there are affordable "lunch box to go" combos, and special dinners for two. No liquor license as of this writing, BYOB.

MAMA DUKE. 243 Flatbush Ave. at Bergen St., 857-8700, M–Sa noon–6 p.m.

This is mostly a takeout place—with the added spice of celebrity. Mama Duke is run by Janice Combs, the real-life mama of Sean, aka "Puffy," Combs. There's crusty fried chicken, candied yams, collard greens, and mac and cheese.

NEW PROSPECT CAFÉ. 393 Flatbush Ave. bet. 7th and 8th Aves., 638-2148, M–Th 11:30 a.m.–10 p.m., F–Sa 11:30 a.m.–11 p.m., Su 10:30 a.m.–10 p.m.

A very small restaurant with a homey atmosphere and good food, this is a favorite of many locals for dinner and Sunday brunch. The menu tends toward fish, chicken, and vegetarian dishes, with dinners ranging from $12 to $18 per entrée. Reservations recommended for three or more.

TAVERN ON DEAN. 755 Dean St. at Underhill Ave., 638-3326, M 4 p.m.–1 a.m., Tu–F 4 p.m.–4 a.m., Sa 11 a.m.–4 a.m., Su 11 a.m.–1 a.m.

Low-key and vaguely British, this family-friendly restaurant has a good bar and even better vibes. It's a neighborhood place, where you can get the latest news and just hang out comfortably. They serve real food, like salmon and burgers. Young kids will appreciate the crayons on the tables. Average entrée is $15.

TOM'S RESTAURANT. 782 Washington Ave. at Sterling Pl., 636-9738, M–Sa 5 a.m.–5 p.m.

A hop, skip, and jump from the Brooklyn Museum (and three long blocks past Flatbush Avenue) is a former ice cream parlor that harbors one of the best breakfasts around. Since 1936 Tom, and now Tom's son, Gus, have been serving up big, inexpensive, and tasty breakfasts and lunches. Three enormous apple pancakes cost just $6, a big bowl of grits is about $2, and the French toast is made of challah bread. The muffins are huge, and the eggs and home fries are first-rate. Tom's also makes a mean egg cream—and is kid-friendly. People come from afar for the 1950s style and warm, friendly feeling. No, rumors notwithstanding, this is not the "Tom's Diner" of Suzanne Vega's song.

SHOPPING

Clothing

✪ **CASTOR & POLLUX.** 67½ 6th Ave. at Flatbush Ave., 398-4141, Tu–Sa 10 a.m.–8 p.m., Su 1–6 p.m., www.castorandpolluxstore.com

Co-owners Anne-Catherine Luke and Kerrilynn Hunt have successfully put their finger on a certain lifestyle pulse, with their appealing Connecticut wannabe logo (horses) and casual, pricey wear and accessories for in-shape, fashion-conscious women. Although slightly off the beaten track, it has an enthusiastic coterie of customers.

✪ **CHRIS CREATIONS WEARABLE ART.** 645 Vanderbilt Ave. at Park Pl., 783-6420, Tu–Sa 11 a.m.–7:30 p.m., Su 1–6 p.m.

Don't judge this book by its cover; once inside this old pharmacy-turned-boutique, you'll find one-of-a-kind handmade coats, evening wear, jewelry, handbags, and decorative items for the home. You may find a hand-painted cape reminiscent of a Scandinavian winter, done by a Norwegian immigrant, or a unique wool jacket that would be ten times the price at Bergdorf. These are pieces that people will ask you about for years—at realistic prices.

✪ ◉ **HARRIET'S ALTER EGO.** 191 Flatbush Ave. bet. Dean St. and 5th Ave., 783-2074, Tu–Sa 11 a.m.–8 p.m. Su 11 a.m.–5 p.m., www.urbanfacez.com.

Here, there's a collection of one-of-a-kind knit hats, bags, and accessories. And you'll find some deliciously feminine clothes as well, some made from fabrics imported from Africa. It's all at affordable prices. Their Web site aims to "document and promote urban culture from the perspective of African, Latino, and Indigenous peoples."

◉ **HOOTI COUTURE.** 321 Flatbush Ave., at 7th Ave., 857-1977, Tu–Su 11 a.m.–8 p.m.

Hooti's one vintage store that leaves you smiling instead of sneezing from mothballs. Prices go from $1 for a rhinestone hair clip to $500 for a full-length mink coat. In between are affordable alligator, crocodile, and leather handbags, vintage shoes and dresses, and lots of accessories, including cowboy boots. If you insist on buying something you can't wear, there are lamps, old wooden bowls, decorative stuff for the kitchen and bedroom, garden furniture from the 1950s and 1960s and so on. Allison, the statuesque owner (yes, she's modeled), has a great sense of style and will help you out; prices are flexible, too. There's new merchandise weekly. Yes, "hooti" is a pun on "haute" couture.

✪ **PIECES.** 671 Vanderbilt Ave. corner of Park Pl., 857-7211, Tu–Th 11 a.m.–8 p.m., F–Sa 11 a.m.–9 p.m., Su 11 a.m.–6 p.m.

Hip, sexy, fun clothes and accessories for both men and women are sold here, including some one-of-a-kind pieces designed by Brooklyn locals. It's the kind of clothing that celebrates the body; if you aren't already feeling body-confident, you sure will when you step out in one of their imaginative, attractive outfits.

Other Neighborhood Shops

BICYCLE STATION. 560 Vanderbilt Ave. bet. Bergen and Dean Sts., 638-0300, Tu–Sa 10 a.m.–7 p.m., Su 10 a.m.–4 p.m.

This small bike shop is not for bicycling fashionistas, but for those who want high-quality care from professional mechanics for their two-wheelers. Owner

Michael Rodriquez is well-known in Brooklyn racing circles for his excellent wheel-building capabilities, but he's also a top-notch mechanic.

HIBISCUS FLOWERS & CAFÉ. 564 Vanderbilt Ave. bet. Bergen and Dean Sts., 638-8850, M–Sa 9 a.m.–6 p.m., www.hisbiscusflowershop.com.

This is a combo health-food eatery ("shots of wheat grass" advertised on the countertop) and a very affordable, very helpful flower-and-garden shop.

PETITE FLEUR. 71 6th Ave. corner of Flatbush Ave., 623-6443, daily 10 a.m.–8 p.m.

Just when you thought you knew what to expect when you turned a corner in Brooklyn—another pizzeria, Jamaican patty shop, or restaurant, right? *Wrong!*—you stumble on this very Parisian little home-decorating store. Run by two longtime locals, it sells elegant linens and special signed ochres-ware glazed pottery made in Provence, tasteful antiques from Brittany, ranging from a lovely armoire to tiny silver serving implements to a knockout collection of old oyster dishes. In the back there's a custom flower shop where you can get a very French bouquet, called a *torsade*. A gem.

ACCOMMODATIONS

BROWNSTONE BROOKLYN BED & BREAKFAST (see p. 15).
BED & BREAKFAST MARISSA'S (see p. 14).

Windsor Terrace

ABOUT WINDSOR TERRACE

Windsor Terrace—some think of it as the northernmost corner of Park Slope—has one of everything that a neighborhood needs: a subway station, a park, a movie theater, a couple of decent restaurants, a bakery, a meat market, a fresh-food store, a little café to meet friends in, and a great old bar. It's a quiet mini-neighborhood of about ten blocks two- and three-story row houses, sandwiched between two of Brooklyn's most spectacular green areas, Prospect Park and Green-Wood Cemetery.

Windsor Terrace was settled by Irish Catholics, whose imprint is still seen in Farrell's Bar and the local Catholic school, Bishop Ford High School, which has educated generations of Brooklynites. Historically, this is the kind of practical working- and middle-class white neighborhood that has produced the backbone of New York's service corps, including lots of police and firemen (and actually, Rogers Fire Extinguishers is still operating on 10th Avenue). In the past decade, increasing numbers of yuppies have bought homes here, including computer experts, editors, and other professionals. There are still many blocks where the American flag is still regularly flown on many a house. There's a neighborliness here that you can see in the frequent house parties, cooperative babysitting arrangements, street fairs, and kid-friendly Halloween festivities.

History buffs will be interested to learn this little tidbit, compliments of the New York Public Library: Windsor Terrace's library service began in 1922, as a three-thousand-book collection housed in a pharmacy. It later moved to a library created from two abandoned street cars. (The current branch, at 160 East 5th Street, is just that: a library.)

For tourists, Windsor Terrace's main attraction is the sense you get that people can live in New York City yet enjoy such quiet, residential streets. Most homes are owner-occupied and well tended. On their way to the **Pavilion** movie theater or from **Prospect Park**, locals who haven't tried **Elora's** should—but wait until you are famished, the portions are fireman-sized.

HOW IT GOT ITS NAME It's named after Windsor, England.

POINTS OF CULTURAL INTEREST

🎓 PUBLIC SCHOOLS.

Among those considered to be New York City's best public elementary schools are PS 154 (1625 11th Avenue) and PS 295 (330 18th Street). (Source: *New York City's Best Public Elementary Schools,* 2002, by C. Hemphill with P. Wheaton.)

WINDSOR TERRACE RESTAURANTS

ELORA. 272 Prospect Park W. off 17th St. 788-6190, daily 11 a.m.–11 p.m.

Just a stone's throw away from Prospect Park, Elora's is one of those "but keep it a secret" restaurants. An extensive menu of Spanish and Mexican dishes includes a vegetarian platter, brochette with meat, or lamb and shrimp topped with a thick stewy brown sauce, plus lobster and broiled chops. If you haven't eaten for a month, try the tasty, outrageously oversized chicken fajita, brought to the table steaming hot in a skillet. Desserts are recommended— note the plural—especially the melt-in-the-mouth chocolate mousse cake. Café tables outside are the best bet, weather permitting. Entrées are in the $9–12 range.

EVA'S RESTAURANT. 551 4th Ave. corner 16th St., 788-9354, daily 8 a.m.–8 p.m. Cash only.

It's been called the "best Ecuadorian restaurant in New York" by food writers. Eva's is a small café on a four-lane highway that's one of the boundaries of the Park Slope neighborhood. You'll find good seafood at low, low prices, which is why people come to Eva's. There are no menus, lots of noise from a perpetually loud television, and little English is spoken, but the fish stews, fresh daily soups, and, most famously, the shrimp dishes are very good. Also recommended: juices and shakes.

FARRELL'S BAR. 215 Prospect Park W. at 16th St., 788-8779, daily 11–1 a.m.

You can get a really, really cold Bud here. Farrell's is a historic bar, supposedly one of the first bars to open in Brooklyn after Prohibition was repealed, and it has stayed the way it was: an old-fashioned Irish saloon. Its decor is polished wood, mirrors, and brass, and it's strictly standing-room only. We haven't checked the truth of the statement, but writer Joe Flaherty reputedly once said that Farrell's Bar in Brooklyn "had urinals so large they looked like shower stalls for Toulouse-Lautrec." The place echoes with old memories, and is a favorite with cops, firemen, and old-timers.

LAURA'S. 1235 Prospect Ave. at Reeve Pl., 436-3715, M–Sa 5–11:30 p.m., Su 11 a.m.–4 p.m.

Locals return time and again to this intimate restaurant for what some say is "original Italian" food. The quality can vary, but when it is good, it is excellent. Soups and pasta are the best bets. Entrées range from $10 to $15. BYOB.

RHYTHM-N-BOOZE. 1674 10th Ave. at Prospect Ave., 788-9699, M–Th 4–11 p.m., F noon–11 p.m., Sa noon–4 p.m., Su noon–4 p.m.

This sports-style bar and café has good burgers, but despite its name, not much (yet) in the way of music. There's a weekend brunch from noon to three, and it's open for dinner daily, providing one more option for local residents who don't feel like schlepping to Park Slope for a quick informal dinner.

SHOPPING

GREENMARKET. Prospect Park W. and 15th St., April–Nov. W 8 a.m.–3 p.m.

It's small, but it's good. A little greenmarket with fresh fruit, vegetables, healthy baked goods, and so on. (See greenmarket on Saturdays at **Grand Army Plaza**.)

TERRACE BAGELS. 224 Prospect Park W. bet. Windsor Pl. and 16th St., 768-3943, M–F 6 a.m.–10 p.m., Sa–Su 7 a.m.–11 p.m.

Some of the best bagels in Brooklyn are made here. They supply the Park Slope Food Co-op, and other discerning customers.

15

Red Hook
and
Columbia Street

A note to readers: This is officially one neighborhood—but two quite different experiences. So bear with us, and read separately about what we are calling Red Hook Peninsula (the area to the southwest of the Gowanus Expressway) and the Columbia Street area. Apologies to those on whose geographic toes we tread.

☛ **TIP:** Web sites about Red Hook include: www.waterfrontmuseum.org and www.gowanus.org/redhook.htm (covers both neighborhoods). Also you can get on a listserve called "redhookgreenhook," with information about activities and planning issues in Red Hook, via www.treebranch.com/tbnetwork/listservs.htm.

ABOUT RED HOOK PENINSULA

It's gritty. It's a fringe neighborhood. Don't expect many amenities, such as cafés or shops. Look instead for magic and imagination, vision and eccentricity.

Take artists and put them in the industrial, grunge-romantic waterfront setting of old Red Hook: alchemy happens. You will see the magic in the **Hudson Waterfront Museum and Showboat Barge, Sunset Music Series,** and the **Kentler International Drawing Space.** You'll see imagination at the **Spring Festival and Pier Show,** usually held in a Civil War–era warehouse, and the **Open Studio and Garden Tours,** which draw thousands of visitors to the area.

The surprising, wonderful Coffey Street Pier, renovated in the late 1990s, has incredible views of the Statue of Liberty and Governors Island, especially at sunset.

Appreciate this while it lasts, folks. **Fairway,** the giant food store from the Upper West Side of Manhattan, is slated to open up a huge, fifty-thousand-square-foot facility at the end of Van Brunt Street in 2004, bringing in its wake the likelihood of more retail stores and the certainty of more traffic. There's been

Red Hook

A peninsula bounded by Erie Basin, Gowanus Bay, and Buttermilk Channel; some authorities include Columbia St. area north of the Brooklyn-Battery Tunnel as part of Red Hook

BROOKLYN HEIGHTS, DOWNTOWN

PARK SLOPE

SUNSET PARK

COBBLE HILL

CARROLL GARDENS

RED HOOK

GOWANUS

Cobble Hill Historic District

Carroll Gardens Historic District

Cobble Hill Park

Carroll Park

Brooklyn-Battery Tunnel

Brooklyn-Queens Expwy.

Buttermilk Channel

Atlantic Basin

Erie Basin

Gowanus Bay

Gowanus Canal

Henry Street Basin

Henry Street Terminal

Breakwater Terminal

Warehouse Pier

Red Hook Park

Coffey St. Pier & Park

Beard St. Warehouses

Hudson Waterfront Museum/ Showboat Barge

Clearview

Piers: Pier 7, Pier 8, Pier 9A, Pier 9B, Pier 10, Pier 11, Pier 12, Pier 41

Streets: Grace Ct., Willow Pl., Joralemon St., Garden Pl., Sidney Pl., Henry St., Hicks St., Columbia St., Court St., Boerum Pl., Clinton St., Atlantic Ave., Pacific St., Amity St., Congress St., Verandah Pl., Warren St., Baltic St., Kane St., Strong Pl., Tompkins Pl., Cheever Pl., Tiffany Pl., Irving St., Sedgwick St., DeGraw St., Sackett St., Van Brunt St., Union St., President St., Carroll St., Summit St., Woodhull St., Rapelye St., Bowne St., Seabring St., Commerce St., Imlay St., Delavan St., Verona St., Visitation Pl., Pioneer St., King St., Sullivan St., Wolcott St., Dikeman St., Coffey St., Van Dyke St., Beard St., Reed St., Conover St., Ferris St., Richards St., Dwight St., Otsego St., Lorraine St., Creamer St., Bay St., Halleck St., Bryans St., Percival St., Centre St., Bush St., Garnet St., Mill St., W 9th St., 9th St., Huntington St., Nelson St., Luquer St., 4th Pl., 3rd Pl., 2nd Pl., 1st Pl., Smith St., Hoyt St., Bond St., Hamilton Ave., Livingston St., Schermerhorn St., State St., Dean St., Bergen St., Wycoff St., Warren St., Butler St., Douglass Ct., Douglass St., Pacific St., 1st St., 2nd St., Carroll St., Union St., 2nd Ave.

278

Smith St., Court Pl.

talk of **IKEA** moving in, too, but that's a political football that's been met both with stiff resistance and support from the community.

It's not empty here; there are businesses (see p. 397, **Look Who's Here** box) Some 70 percent of the ten thousand residents in Red Hook live in Red Hook public housing, and the area businesses employ many of them for unskilled and semiskilled jobs, according to the local development corporation. The area is one of Brooklyn's remaining industrial zones, bringing jobs to blue-collar workers and immigrants. If you think it's desolate, come at seven a.m. and you'll see a hive of activity.

Brooklynites just looking to discover new crannies in the borough should know that in good weather, there is always a weekend fiesta going on at the vast **Red Hook Recreational Area** on Columbia Street, as crowds of Dominicans, Mexicans, and other Latino immigrants enjoy picnics and, for no price of admission, intense soccer games. At the makeshift taco stands that spring up around the games you can get some of the best, freshest tacos in the city.

HOW IT GOT ITS NAME Red Hook was called Roode Hoek by the Dutch, so the name is straightfoward: "Roode" because the soil was red, "Hoek" because of the peninsula at its south end, which hooks out into New York Bay. You can see the hook on a map.

BY SUBWAY Take the A, C, or F train to Jay Street-Borough Hall, exit at Jay Street and transfer to the B-61 bus at the corner of Smith and Livingston Streets. Get off at Van Dyke Street. Or take the F or G train to Smith-9th Street and transfer to the B77 bus. Be prepared to wait for the bus.

☛ **TIP:** A bike map of Red Hook peninsula is available from the Red Hook Local Development Corporation. However, the office is only open during the week, normal business hours.

☛ **TIP:** B61 Bus: A $2.00 Tour Through Brooklyn. Get a Map
One of the best, cheapest ways to see Brooklyn in all its local glory is just by riding the B61 bus from its starting point here on Van Brunt Street, all the way through to Williamsburg's Bedford Avenue. So grab a map and a window seat, and watch as gruff Red Hook gives way to gentrifying Columbia Street.

☛ **TIP:** Transportation is a challenge. Red Hook is hard to reach, except by B61 or B77 bus. There's no subway connection that doesn't involve a bus, either. It's best to travel by car—or bike here—as the distances can be long. Consult a detailed map.Stick to Van Brunt Street, which enables you to avoid getting lost in the Red-Hook Houses project.

☛ **TIP:** Red Hook is perfectly safe, if you possess average New York City street smarts. But the population density is low, so, for instance, this is not a place to encourage young teenagers to ride their bikes alone.

 ## What's **NEW?**

Whither Red Hook?

What's next in Red Hook? That's still an open question.

Red Hook is the last of Brooklyn's westward-facing waterfront neighborhoods with its fate still in the balance. Williamsburg and Greenpoint have been designated for residential development. It seems certain that the Brooklyn Bridge Park will extend along much of the waterfront in the area around Brooklyn Heights to Piers 1 through 5, and the use of other piers is under review. Sunset Park's waterfront is already an industrial area.

With so much waterfront access, some views of the Statue of Liberty and New York Harbor, and so much raw space, Red Hook is virgin territory. The possibilities are tantalizing. There is some speculation that the huge Imlay building, with unbelievable Manhattan views, has been purchased by private investors for upscale residential development.

The big debate is whether the area should be residential or mixed use, meaning a combination of industrial and residential. Its assets are the following: waterfront on three sides, proximity to major highways and tunnel (to Lower Manhattan), and its stock of interesting old buildings. Its liability is lack of public transportation.

As we go to print, Red Hook continues to quietly hum along with a bustling industrial business community, a small community of residents, some artists, and a great deal of open space. Wide-scale gentrification would raise real estate prices, so these industrial companies, which employ many low-income residents of Red Hook Houses, might leave. Should New York be protecting the unskilled and semiskilled jobs here? Or should the precious waterfront be used for housing, parks, and service businesses? Can "mixed use" work here? Therein lies the challenge. Call it a struggle for the soul of a neighborhood.

Look Who's Here

Most companies don't bother to hang out shingles, so there's no way a casual visitor could know what's here. Here's a smattering: Snapple has a production facility. There are creatives: magazines and set-production companies who work for Blue Man Group and *Sesame Street*. The vast, renovated Beard Street Pier houses a lot of furniture and upholstery companies. Food processing includes an applesauce-processing company, and a kosher dairy, too. TIME, the moving company, and school-bus transport companies park here, as well as a courier service that runs packages for Wall Street clients. There are a handful of small specialty glassworks companies (see below). On the waterfront, Hess barges oil into Red Hook; the Erie Basin Bargeport handles the Macy's fireworks. Cement being used to rebuild the World Trade Center site is mixed here, and barged quickly across to Manhattan. The proximity to the water, the Brooklyn Battery Tunnel, and the BQE makes this a natural site for certain industries and businesses.

Historical Notes

Water and transportation have been defining factors in the development of Red Hook. A marshy area unsuitable for farming, it was transformed by the development of New York Harbor, quickly becoming one of the nation's premier shipping centers. Boats from all over the world docked, loaded, and unloaded here. Typical nineteenth-century industrial harbor life grew up around the port: bars, boisterous eateries with inexpensive, hearty food; shops for ship repair and maintenance; flophouses for the workmen, and expensive homes for the mercantile class (Red Hook was second only to Brooklyn Heights in the development of row houses). Rough, colorful, and often violent, this waterfront was dominated for decades by Italian, Irish, Scandinavian, and German dockworkers and their Longshoremen's Union. An enclave of Lebanese tradesmen, who settled on Atlantic Avenue and whose ancestors still run shops there, also worked in port trades.

After World War II, the once-thriving industrial, residential, and maritime life of Red Hook died under the combined impact of a decline of the New York Harbor and Robert Moses's construction of the highway system to ease middle-class access in and out of New York. Cut off from Carroll Gardens' shops, churches, and social life, and now on the wrong side of the BQE, Red Hook went into rapid, steep decline. Most of the area was gutted to clear way for low-income housing projects, leaving only the extreme eastern blocks of old row houses intact. From the 1960s through the 1980s, "Red Hook" was synonymous with a crime-plagued, inner-city neighborhood. In the mid-1990s, the daytime murder of a dedicated and beloved school principal made headline news, a reminder of the social ills of the area.

However, by the late 1990s Red Hook's dirt-cheap rents and waterfront possi-bilities began to attract some artists and musicians, dreamers and developers. Behind the industrial façades, they now are creating museums, molding archi-tectural glass, making music—and renovating buildings. Substantial properties have been purchased by ex-policeman-turned-developer Greg O'Connell, and warehouses on Van Brunt and Van Dyke have been renovated for use by small businesses. Crime in Red Hook declined in the 1990s (as it did in the rest of New York City). But the majority of Red Hook's estimated fifteen thousand residents are still poor and live in housing projects.

Years of political fights have ensued over various city plans to use Red Hook for sludge waste and waste-transfer stations. The community has successfully fought these off.

Kidstuff

☺ Use your imagination. Picnic at **Coffey Pier**, go to the festivals, have a **CircuSunday** at the **Waterfront Museum**.

POINTS OF CULTURAL INTEREST: ARCHITECTURE, ARTS GROUPS, GALLERIES

SPECIAL EVENTS.

The Red Hook Waterfront Arts Festival (May); Red Hook Earth and Surf Parade (June); CircuSundays, Carroll Gardens/Cobble Hill/Red Hook artists annual open studio tour (May–June), see www.gowanusartists.com; Sunset Music Series (summer).

BEARD STREET WAREHOUSES. Van Brunt St. and the waterfront.

Owned by local resident Greg O'Connell, the historic, renovated Beard Street Pier building has both office space and studio space for artists. Tenants include several magazines, theatrical production companies, designers, and more. It's an extraordinary structure, worth a visit. Eventually, plans call for the building of a public-access promenade alongside the water.

BEARD STREET PIER. Van Brunt Street and the waterfront.

The well-known arts group called Dancing in the Streets has held The Young People's Performance Festival at the Beard Street Pier. It is also home to the entire fleet of six **New York Water Taxis,** which you can take from either DUMBO or Sunset Park.

BROOKLYN WATERFRONT ARTISTS COALITION (BWAC). 499 Van Brunt St. 596-2507, www.bwac.org.

BWAC hosts three major Brooklyn arts exhibits. In spring, the Pier Show at the Van Brunt Street Piers in Red Hook is an uncurated exhibit of over two hundred artists. Nearly ten thousand people attend annually, over a five-week period. In the summer, BWAC hosts the well-known *Between the Bridges* out-

GLASSBLOWING INDUSTRY

Glassblowing was a Brooklyn specialty a hundred years ago. And it is again today. In Red Hook, there are a variety of glassmakers. **Flickinger** specializes in bending glass, Thomas Tisch in glass etching, and **CarveArt Glass,** located in a historic building, texturizes and colors glass.

doors sculpture show, a curated exhibit that started in 1978 and uses the Manhattan skyline as a backdrop. In the fall, returning to the Beard Street Pier, BWAC hosts the uncurated Small Works Show, featuring one hundred "compelling small works."

DANCE THEATRE ETCETERA. 287-2224, www.dancetheatreetcetera.org.

Going on its third decade, DTE is one of those institutions that make Brooklyn Brooklyn. It's iconoclastic and irreverent. DTE produces **Dancin' in the Streets** programs and the **Red Hook Waterfront Arts Festival** in May.

ERIE BASIN BARGE. At water's edge, behind Beard St. Pier.

Bring your kids and show them where those cute red tugboats live. This is where several hundred tugs and barges dock when they're not plowing the Hudson or East River.

FLICKINGER GLASS STUDIO. 204–207 Van Dyke St., Pier 41, 875-1531, www.flickingerglassworks.com.

This art-glass studio makes lamps, bowls, platters, and serving dishes, all out of glass. Most of their work, however, is custom designed for architects and designers. They use over six thousand steel molds, some of them created in the 1800s for antique lighting fixtures and other purposes. Charles Flickinger became involved in the art of bent glass years back, while working on the restoration of the Statue of Liberty's torch.

J. K. BRICK & COMPANY, also known as **BROOKLYN CLAY RETORT AND FIRE BRICK COMPANY.** 76 Van Dyke St.

The first New York City designated landmark in the Red Hook area, this 1859 storehouse "has the distinctive basilica-like form of mid- and late-nineteenth-century industrial workshops," according to the New York City Landmarks Preservation Commission. The company manufactured clay retorts (oblong vessels made of fired clay in which coal was heated to produce gas used in gas lighting) and a full line of refractory bricks, used by the then-growing iron and steel industry. It was made an official landmark in December 2001. It is currently occupied by **CarveArt,** a glassworks company.

JERARD STUDIO. 481 Van Brunt St. at 4th Beard St. Pier, 852-4129, www.jerardstudio.com.

John Jerard and Mary Crede create puppets, mechanical costumes, and stage sets. Their credits include work for such Broadway blockbusters as *The Producers* (they designed those great pigeon puppets and the tank tops worn by the showgirls) and *Beauty and the Beast,* as well as the Chicago Lyric Opera Company. They design furniture, and, in their words, "solve visual problems."

KENTLER INTERNATIONAL DRAWING SPACE. 353 Van Brunt St. off Wolcott St., 875-2098, www.kent lergallery.org. Open for shows or call for an appointment.

The Kentler is a nonprofit gallery that runs monthly and bimonthly exhibitions of local, American, and international artists. Paper is the theme here. That is, the gallery is dedicated to bringing to the public contemporary drawings and works on paper. You'll find the Kentler in the heart of old industrial Red Hook, located in the storefront space of a studio-residence building, one of several in the area that were renovated under New York City's Artist Housing Program begun in 1984. The gallery is named after the building's original nineteenth-century owners, a local men's haberdashers for the dockworkers of Red Hook by the name of "Kentler," which you can see chiseled just below the roof.

STEVE'S KEY LIME PIE.

Yup. Here's where they make it. Red Hook.

ENTERTAINMENT: CONCERTS, PARADES, ART SHOWS, AND MORE

Summer in Red Hook

Why bother with a rental in Fire Island when you could save your money and play in Red Hook near (if not in) the water? If you get there early, the Red Hook Pool is quiet and amazingly large. Other special events for your calender:

♩ ☺ **HUDSON WATERFRONT MUSEUM AND SHOWBOAT BARGE** (also known as Lehigh Valley Railroad Barge # 79). Temporarily docked at Gowanus Industrial Park, 699 Columbia St. Permanent home is Pier 45, Garden Pier, 290 Conover St., 624-4719, www.waterfrontmuseum.org. Call or check Web site for location, directions, event schedule.

What a wonderful adventure! The peace and quiet is overwhelming at this museum boat. It's poetry-in-motion, a character-filled historic wooden barge built in 1914, rescued, restored, and docked on the Brooklyn waterfront. The barge is listed on the National Register of Historic Places. The goal of the project, launched in 1986, is to "create public waterfront access and cultural programs aboard an historic wooden barge."

When you visit its home base in Red Hook at Garden Pier, there are spectacular views of the Statue of Liberty and the New York Harbor. In summer, don't miss the homegrown entertainment here. The **Sunset Music Series** offers six jazz and folk concerts featuring original music, and the June **CircuSundays** are intimate and old-fashioned. The barge is available for school and group tours, weddings, parties, and environmental-education classes.

The Waterfront Museum graced Brooklyn as its permanent home in 1994, after seven years of making ports-of-call, including such places as Liberty State Park and Hoboken, New Jersey, and Piermont and the South Street Seaport in New York. In 1998, the Waterfront Museum's Barge won designation by the UN as the "Regional Craft of the International Year of the Oceans" for opening up waterfronts for the use and enjoyment of the public.

It's all the brainstorm of museum director and barge captain, David Sharps, an iconoclastic man with a romantic vision of the Brooklyn waterfront—not to mention a large dose of tenacity. (See "Captain's Log" on the Web site.) Hats off, Captain!

Free! **OPEN STUDIO AND GARDEN TOURS.** 596-2507.

Artists from Brooklyn Heights to Red Hook open their working studios to visitors for two afternoons on a given weekend. There are lots of opportunities for first-time collectors, with paintings, sculpture, and other works of art ranging in price from $50 to $5,000. This is part of the **Spring Festival and Pier Show**.

☺ **RED HOOK WATERFRONT ARTS FESTIVAL.** Annual event in May.

Bring the kids. It's earthy, fun, silly, community-ish. The festival starts with the "Earth and Surf Parade" with music, giant puppets, and a procession of people in crazy costumes. Or drop in during the day for a hodgepodge of live music, dance, and spoken word performances, free dance workshops, delicious food by local vendors, cultural workshops for all ages, community resource tables, and boating.

☺ **SPRING FESTIVAL AND PIER SHOW.** May–June, Sa–Su, 596-2507. Call or watch listings for time and place.

Ten thousand visitors came to view the work of 250 artists, dancers, and performers in the 1998 show. Organized by the BWAC, the Brooklyn Waterfront Artists Coalition, the Spring Festival and Pier Show has been called the "the world's most democratic art show," and a "wildly eclectic mix of art." There are also performances, films, photography, and outdoor sculpture.

This annual artist-run show began in 1979, and for the past six years has taken place in the dramatic setting of the Red Hook piers, in an 1840s-era stone and wood warehouse, loaned for the occasion by waterfront developer Greg O'Connell.

☺ **SUNSET MUSIC SERIES.** 246-8050, www.geocities.com/BourbonStreet/Quarter/8536/book.html. A weekend event in the summer; call for schedule.

Blues, swing, rock, jazz, and country are all a part of the live music scene along the waterfront. The concerts are usually held at the Hudson Waterfront Museum. But check for information.

☛ **TIP: Shuttle Bus** A free shuttle bus operates to and from the Hudson Waterfront Museum from the neighborhoods of Park Slope, Brooklyn Heights, and Carroll Gardens for all performances. Directions, maps, and show and shuttle information can be obtained by calling 624-4719 or by visiting www.waterfrontmuseum.org, or the Sunset Music Series Web site at www.geocities.com/sunsetmuse.

PARKS AND PLAYGROUNDS

☺ 🌑 **COFFEY STREET PIER AND PARK, AKA LOUIS VALENTINO JR. PARK.** Richards and Kings Sts., daily 7 a.m.–9 p.m.

James Dean would have loved it here. Coffey Street Pier is one of New York City's unknown peaceful destinations, at the end of nowhere in this mostly abandoned industrial section of Brooklyn. The pier was newly renovated in 1998 and, as piers go, it is gorgeously done, providing the average Tom, Dick, and José with access to a billion-dollar view. (In keeping with this democratic sentiment, the pier is dedicated not to a politician but to "hero firefighter Louis Valentino Jr.") You can see Staten Island, the Statue of Liberty, Manhattan's skyline, and the Brooklyn and Manhattan Bridges. You can see where the Hudson and East Rivers meet, Governor's Island, and more.

Bring your kids, your paints, your fishing rod, or come alone for the solace of a beautiful view. You won't be alone, of course; there are picnickers and lots of men fishing. Some local kids swim; it's at your own risk.

You can launch your own kayak (there are no rentals or facilities whatsoever here) from the Coffey Street Pier and paddle to the South Street Seaport or Jamaica Wildlife Refuge.

☺ **GARDEN PIER IN RED HOOK.** Pier 45, 290 Conover St., on the industrial waterfront, 624-4719. Open year round.

A New York gem, this beautiful little waterside garden, isolated at the end of a long, unused dock in Red Hook, is open to the public twenty-four hours a day. Its peaceful views of New York Harbor and the extraordinary quiet here are hard to match. The place is small—there's only one bench. But the idea behind it—that New Yorkers should have public access to the waterfront—has vast implications. Come in the summer and enjoy a country-style patch of garden with thriving black-eyed Susans and other beautiful, tough flowers appropriate to the setting. This is also where the Hudson Waterfront and Showboat Barge is docked. *Note:* the Pier was under repair as of 2003; call ahead.

GOWANUS DREDGERS CANOE CLUB.

This shoestring volunteer group rents canoes from spring to early fall. It's not a "club" with a clubhouse. (See p. 164.)

RED HOOK PIER PROMENADE.

There are six hundred square feet of public-access space along the pier.

☺ **RED HOOK RECREATION AREA/RED HOOK POOL.** Between Clinton, Bay, and Henry Sts., 722-3211.

Come to this vast recreational area to experience a weekend fiesta or see some serious soccer games. It's nothing formal, but huge numbers of Dominicans and other Latino families gather on good-weather weekends to cook, eat, and play. Locals set up small cooking stands to feed the crowd. Everybody's welcome.

The facilities here include many sports fields, an excellent four-hundred-meter composite track, and the larger-than-Olympic-sized Red Hook Pool, with a separate wading pool and an indoor fitness center. It gets crowded on weekends, and used to be somewhat rough, so the wise come early.

Note: Bike or car transportation is recommended. The nearest subway is a hike away, at the corner of Smith and 9th Streets; from there you can pick up the B77 bus and get off at Clinton and Bay Streets.

RED HOOK FOOD AND RESTAURANTS

FAIRWAY. 480 Van Brunt St.

A major store will open in this Civil War–era warehouse, called Van Brunt Stores. As we go to press, it is under construction.

HOPE & ANCHOR. 347 Van Brunt St. at Wolcott St., 237-0276, M–Th 9 a.m.–10 p.m., Sa 9 a.m.–11 p.m., Su 9 a.m.–9 p.m.

Hooray! Finally a good upscale diner has arrived in Red Hook. You can get breakfast all day, enjoy the bar scene and retro-red décor with banquettes, and also bring the family for dinner. If you're pining for the diner of your youth, try the BLT and desserts here.

♫ **LIBERTY HEIGHTS TAP ROOM AND SUMMER BEER GARDEN.** 36 Van Dyke St. at Dwight St., M–F 4–11 p.m., Sa 4 p.m.–1 a.m., Su 4–11 p.m., www.parkslopebrewingco.com.

Stop in for a brick-oven pizza pie and a fresh brew, made by the Park Slope Brewing Company. There's a summer beer garden and roof deck with great views, and the requisite pool table as well. There's a mellow guitar player on Thursdays, and on the weekends, bands play 1960s and 1970s music.

LILLIE'S. 46 Beard St., corner of Dwight St., 858-9822, daily 6 p.m.–4 a.m.

Come and hang out, and, if it's a summer Sunday, stay for a BBQ in the backyard. Lillie's is one of the hubs for local pioneers in Red Hook, so you may find out from Lillie herself and the crowd how Red Hookers view the universe. In its previous incarnations, this bar used to be frequented by longshoremen, and the "Red Hooker" drink is a tropically sweet concoction of rum and fruit juices. Call for information about shows in the new performance space.

360. 360 Van Brunt St. bet. Sullivan and Wolcott Sts., 246-0360, W–Su 5–11 p.m.

Francophiles rejoice! As we go to press, a good French restaurant, open for dinner only, has arrived in Red Hook. Entrées are in the $12 and up range.

SONNY'S OF RED HOOK. 253 Conover St. bet. Reed and Beard Sts., 237-8888, W–F only. Opens late afternoons; call for hours.

This is the quintessential local joint. And it is Sonny Balzano's, despite what the sign outside says. While there are newer, fancier bars and clubs in this gritty neighborhood, you can't beat Sonny's for Red Hook authenticity. Have a drink, and, if there are some Red Hook old-timer residents around, find out how Sonny's got started. Good stories abound.

Columbia Street

ABOUT COLUMBIA STREET

Is this still Red Hook? Or "Carroll Gardens West"? Or simply the "Columbia Street renaissance"? Real estate agents, old-timers, and newcomers may call this little area by different names. But no one disputes that the area is experiencing the biggest change since Robert Moses built the BQE in 1966, slicing Red Hook (including Columbia Street) off from the rest of Carroll Gardens some fifty years ago.

Until the mid-1990s, outsiders shunned Columbia Street as dangerous and isolated. Not that the old area was an altogether lousy place to live. There was unemployment, some crime, some drugs, some low-income housing. But there's more than one ripe tale from old-timers about how great it was to grow up here, where everyone knew everyone's business—and their grandmother's, too.

But in the 1990s Carroll Gardens began to change, and it rippled across the BQE to Columbia Street. Now, after a decade of stop-and-start improvements, the process of gentrification seems to have reached a faster pace. You can almost watch the process happen on a street-by-street basis. Take Tiffany Place. Number 1 Tiffany Place was the first industrial building in this little area to be recast into residential units. Following like falling dominos, numbers 42 and 60 Tiffany Place (an 1860s factory and a 1920s industrial building, respectively) are being turned to condos.

Community gardens have been cleared and planted. Young families are moving in. The three live-poultry plants that used to provide fresh poultry (and the sounds and smells of the country, including the occasional chicken-chase) have burned down, or moved out. Artists who want big space and low rent are moving out, to **Beard Street Pier,** as the Columbia Street area "goes residential."

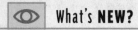 **What's NEW?**

On the Waterfront: Changes the Dockworkers Woulda Never Believed.

Ever seen Elia Kazan's *On the Waterfront*, with Marlon Brando struggling against the bosses? Fifty years ago, there was a rough-and-tumble Longshoremen's Union—run port here. Today, the 1.3-mile area spanning Piers 6 through 12 stretching from Red Hook to Cobble Hill is New York City's last active port area. The question is, what happens *tomorrow*?

With shipping in decline in New York City these days, city planners have decided it's a shame to waste the Columbia Street area's spectacular views of the New York Harbor, the Statue of Liberty, and Lower Manhattan on industrial use. Which explains why the area has been under study for possible development—for a park, housing with views, a museum—or continued industrial use, which preserves blue-collar jobs in Brooklyn. The Port Authority of NY/NJ owns all but one of the twelve piers. The leases for the current businesses occupying Piers 6 through 11, American Warehousing and American Stevedoring, run out in 2004. Carnival Cruise Lines has proposed the construction of two terminal buildings, a large parking garage, and a conference center, at Pier 7, near the foot of Atlantic Avenue. Each cruise ship can carry over a thousand passengers—travelers who would be pouring into Brooklyn on their way to and from vacation. Imagine! And then, of course, there's the **Brooklyn Bridge Park.**

PARKS AND PLAYGROUNDS

BROOKLYN BRIDGE PARK.

It's almost too good to be true: A big, beautiful park is under consideration, which would transform Columbia Street into a place where you could access the waterside views. The park would run all the way from DUMBO, opening up all kinds of recreational opportunities for this otherwise park-deprived section of Brooklyn. See p. 242.

Columbia Street Community Gardens

It's surprisingly green here. There are four community garden spaces within six city blocks of each other. If you just love the idea of local urban activists transforming slummy, garbage-strewn empty lots into works of nature and art, these little gems are worth a springtime pilgrimage. And free movies are shown on some summer weekends in the community gardens. As you walk along Columbia, check out the 🎬 **Amazing Garden** (movies shown in the summer) and **The Backyard Gardens,** as well as these favorites:

🎬 **SUMMIT GARDEN.** Corner of Columbia St. and Summit St.

This great garden space is as richly colored as a Merchant-Ivory film, when it's in full bloom with flowers, fruit trees, potluck dinners, and summer film screenings.

HUMAN COMPASS GARDEN. Corner of Columbia St. and Sackett St.

There's a sculpture tucked into every corner, and a rose garden occupies the sunniest spot. Named after Leonardo's famous "human compass" drawing, this multifunctional green space hosts weekend classes for kids, runs an outdoor movie series called "Reels on Wheels" and has potluck dinners and political meetings. A yearlong cleanup started in 1992.

COLUMBIA STREET RESTAURANTS

ALMA. 187 Columbia St. at Degraw St., 643-5400, Su–Th 5:30–10:30 p.m., F–Sa 5:30–11:30 p.m., Sa–Su 10 a.m.–2:30 p.m. brunch. www.almarestaurant.com.

Food for the soul. Alma, brought to Brooklyn compliments of chef Gary Jacobson, previously of Zarela, created a stir when it opened. Sophisticated Mexican food, Oaxacan-style, and good drinks make Alma worth a trip, but the skyline views from the roof garden on a summer evening make it a must. ("If only I could see Manhattan like this, *from* Manhattan," mused one Manhattan expat.) Alma proved that Columbia Street is no longer a poor culinary cousin to Smith and Court. On the ground floor, there's a bar named **B61**—after the local bus that connects Carroll Gardens West to the rest of the world.

DEFONTE'S SANDWICH SHOP. 379 Columbia St. at Luquer St., 625-8052, M–Sa 6 a.m.–4 p.m.

You could easily miss this unassuming storefront (indeed, we did in our first book), but it has been thriving since 1922 because the sandwiches are so darned good. Try a multilayered hero with fresh vegetables, grilled vegetables, and several kinds of cured meats. Close to the Columbia Street "renaissance."

FERDINANDO'S FOCACCERIA. 151 Union St. bet. Hicks and Columbia Sts., 855-1545, M–Th 10 a.m.– 6 p.m., F–Su 10 a.m.–9 p.m. No credit cards.

Turning a hundred years old in 2006, this tiny Sicilian diner on the waterfront side of the BQE will give you some feel for the working-class Italian Red Hook of yesteryear. There's romance in the old tiled floors and pressed-tin ceiling. But what keeps this focacceria busiest are its lunch specialties—such as rice balls with ricotta, and *panelli*, a stuffed Sicilian bread—as well as the high-voltage Manhattan Special, a Brooklyn-made coffee-flavored soda.

HELEN'S FABULOUS CHEESECAKES. 126 Union St. bet. Columbia and Hicks Sts., 722-7691, M–F 7 a.m.–7 p.m., Sa–Su 9 a.m.–10 p.m. Cash only.

Acclaimed for its outrageously light cheesecakes and half a dozen flavors of scones, Helen's café sells an appealing range of eat-in, takeout, or take-to-a-party foods. On a given day, this cafe might have on display red organic turkey mole, grilled vegetables, *pozole* soup with pork, five different kinds of soups, and a number of quiches. Helen, who lives in Tribeca, not Brooklyn (*gasp!* A reverse commuter!), makes a point of using only organic ingredients. There's a large, wisteria-covered back garden with winding Japanese paths and wrought-iron seats.

⦿ ☺ **SCHNÄCK.** 122 Union St. off Columbia St., 855-2879, daily 11 a.m.–1 a.m. www.schnackdog.com.

Alice-in-Wonderland oversized red banquettes and delicious, gulp-in-one-bite, baby hamburgers are just two of the things that are right about Schnäck. It's invitingly informal, with a retro décor that's a nod to the old neighborhood, including an enormous Dodgers poster. More important, they produce family-friendly, well-cooked meals: breakfast, lunch, and dinner. The home fries aren't the usual greasy mush, but half-inch-thick solid slices, crisply fried on the outside and not overcooked inside.

SHOPPING

FRANK'S DEPARTMENT STORE. 128 Union St. near Columbia St., 875-2043.

Franks displays housedresses in the store window: the flowery kind that go over your slip and that you wear in the kitchen, cleaning the house, or working in the garden. There's an unusually large selection here, along with other necessities of life, like plastic scuffs and hair rollers, from the 1940s. That's about when Frank's opened.

✪ **JKH SPEC.** 83 Summit St. near Columbia St., 875-4554. By appointment only.

You'll find delicate hand-wrought gold-wire jewelry here, crafted downstairs in this Yale-educated artist's studio. Prices range from $20 to $300. You may see some of her work sold at upscale retailers, such as Barneys.

MARGARET PALCA BAKES. 191 Columbia St. bet. Sackett and DeGraw Sts., 802-9711, M–Sa 7 a.m.–6 p.m., Su 7 a.m.–2 p.m. Cash only.

Margaret has been baking in Brooklyn for over twenty years, and turns out great *rugelach*, muffins, brownies, fruit tarts, and chocolate-chip cookies, with all-natural ingredients. Margaret's unpretentious little hipster café, with a handful of little tables and chairs, opened in 2000 and sells her homemade crusty breads, fresh soups, and hearty made-to-order sandwiches to hungry locals for giveaway prices—under $5.

ROSE BUD. 144A Union St. off Hicks St., 935-9918. Call for seasonal hours.

This little flower-and-garden-supply shop sits perkily right atop the roaring traffic of Robert Moses's BQE. The owner, who studied at nearby Pratt, is helping Brooklyn go green by helping new homeowners turn old cemented back-yards into blooming wonders.

REGALAH BAKERY. 155 Columbia St. bet. Kane and Degraw Sts., 625-4672.

Regalah makes gorgeous and tasty cakes, cookies, and cupcakes, and has a special talent for making gaily decorative special-occasion cakes. You'll see her handiwork at some of the better gourmet food markets in Brooklyn. *Note:* You have to order ahead here; there's no retail shop to walk into.

⚙ **UNION MAX.** 110 Union St. bet. Hicks and Columbia Sts., 222-1785, F–Su 1–7 p.m.

Slip into another life. This vintage store is so cram-packed with old stuff that you could reinvent yourself and emerge refurbished from head to toe: new clothing, belts, jewelry, shoes, coats, scarves. You could also reinvent your apartment with some cool old framed pictures, lamps, small odds and ends of furniture, maybe a beat-up trunk, vases, old kitchenware.

16

Sunset Park
and Green-Wood Cemetery

ABOUT SUNSET PARK AND GREEN-WOOD

Green-Wood Cemetery is reason enough to make the trek to Sunset Park. From a culinary angle, hungry visitors may be happily surprised to discover a small Chinatown as well as some remarkably good and inexpensive Polish and Latino restaurants in this unassuming slice of Brooklyn.

Fabulous, historic Green-Wood Cemetery is a peaceful urban retreat set in 478 acres of rolling parklike hills. It is privately owned; you can take your chances on casually wandering in, but it's better to arrange a visit by calling in advance. Your efforts will be rewarded. It is the burial site of the nineteenth- and early-twentieth century's rich and famous—William Colgate of soap fame, Boss Tweed of Tammany Hall, abolitionist Henry Ward Beecher, and entrepreneur-philanthropist Peter Cooper, among others. Its elaborate Victorian mausoleums, obelisks, sculpture, and wonderful inscriptions offer an unmatched look at the history of old New York. Of Brooklyn's many historic sites, Green-Wood Cemetery is the most evocative of the borough's patrician heritage.

Contemporary Sunset Park, on the other hand, is an American melting pot par excellence. Built more than a century ago by working-class immigrants, it is still a first stop for many newcomers to the United States.

About half of Sunset Park's one hundred thousand residents are Hispanic. They include a large number of Dominicans, as well as Ecuadorians, Nicaraguans, and Puerto Ricans, and, most recently, many Mexicans. Mexicans constitute the largest immigrant group in the United States, but they are relatively new to New York City (estimates vary between one hundred thousand and two hundred thousand in all of New York City) and there's a rapidly growing contingent from the province of Puebla now living in Sunset Park. You can see this diversity in a slew of small restaurants between 20th and 40th Streets that read like a map of Central America, with Mexican, Dominican, Salvadoran, and Ecuadorian eateries.

Sunset Park & Greenwood Cemetery

Sunset Park, including Green-Wood Cemetery: bounded by New York Bay, Prospect Expressway, 8th Avenue, and 65th Street

PARK SLOPE

10th St.
11th St.
12th St.
13th St.
14th St.
15th St.
16th St.

Prospect Park W

West Dr.
Prospect Park S
Windsor Pl.
Sherman St.

F M 16th St.

M,N,R

Prospect Ave.

Prospect Expwy

17th St.
18th St.
19th St.
20th St.
21st St.
22nd St.
23rd St.
24th St.

20th St. Pier
21st St. Pier
23rd St. Pier
Pier A

4th Ave.

278

M,N,R 25th St.
26th St.
27th St.
28th St.
29th St.
30th St.
31st St.
32nd St.
33rd St.
34th St.

✝ 9/11 Chapel

Greenwood Cemetery

29th St. Pier
30th St. Pier
31st St. Pier
33rd St. Pier
35th St. Pier

35th St.

M,N,R,W 36th St.
37th St.
38th St.

39th St. Pier

39th St.

M,W

New Utrecht Ave.

18th Police Precinct Station

Sunset Park

41st St.
42nd St.
43rd St.
44th St.
45th St.

M,W

S U N S E T   P A R K

Gowanus Expwy.

M N,R

Latino Shops & Restaurants

Brooklyn Public Library

46th St.
47th St.
48th St.
49th St.
50th St.
51st St.

7th Ave.
8th Ave.
9th Ave.
10th Ave.

M,W

BENSONHURST →

1st Ave.
2nd Ave.
3rd Ave.
4th Ave.
5th Ave.
6th Ave.

52nd St.
53rd St.
54th St.
55th St.
56th St.
57th St.
58th St.
59th St.
60th St.
61st St.
62nd St.

Asian Shops & Restaurants

Fort Hamilton Pkwy.

BOROUGH PARK

57th St. Pier

NY Water Taxi

N,R M

278

Faith Camii Mosque

N

63rd St.
64th St.
65th St.

N M

Gowanus Expwy.

65th St.

Shore Pkwy.
Wakeman Pl.

66th St.
67th St.

66th St.

BAY RIDGE

Asians, including many immigrants from Canton province of China and increasing numbers from Hong Kong, represent over two-fifths of the Sunset Park community. Immigrants from Poland, India, Jordan, Yemen, and other Muslim nations, as well as a contingent of fourth- and fifth-generation Norwegian-Americans—descendants of Sunset Park's earliest nonnative settlers—round out an almost global cast. Since the 1970s, a number of young American-born professionals have also moved into the area, seeking affordable brownstones.

HOW IT GOT ITS NAME The area now known as Sunset Park took its name in the 1960s from a local park, which sits high above surrounding streets and commands a view of New York Bay. This area was previously known as part of Bay Ridge (the southern side) or simply called "South Brooklyn" (the shorefront area).

BY SUBWAY M or R train to any stop between 25th and 59th Streets. Express D, N to 36th Street stop, or the N, R train to 59th Street stop. For Green-Wood, use the 25th Street M or R stop.

HISTORICAL NOTES

Irish Catholics fleeing the potato famines of the mid-nineteenth century were among the earliest European pioneers to settle this part of Brooklyn. Polish immigrants followed in the 1880s, forming a community near the Czestochowa Church on 25th Street—now the site of a new wave of Polish immigration—and laboring in Green-Wood Cemetery and Park Slope's **Ansonia Clock Factory**. Scandinavians found work at the shipyards in the late nineteenth century and created a "Little Norway" from 45th to 60th Streets, where some of their descendants still live. The Finns here were the first in the nation to create cooperative housing, when in 1916 they joined together to build themselves affordable apartments, which are still in use today. Many of the Irish and Scandinavians moved into Bay Ridge by the 1920s. However, the slack was taken up by the huge Italian immigration that populated so much of Brooklyn and first settled in this waterfront area around the turn of the century. Saint Rocco's Chapel on 27th Street was a focal point of Italian life.

The neighborhood went into decline during and after the Depression. Like that of Carroll Gardens and Red Hook, Sunset Park's economic base suffered as construction of the Gowanus Expressway in the 1940s cut a swath through the neighborhood, and again in the 1950s, when a shift to containerized shipping rendered Brooklyn waterfront facilities obsolete. The suburbs lured residents, and housing prices plummeted. Sunset Park's recent revival has been led by immigration, community activists, and the local Lutheran Medical Center. It remains a working-class neighborhood, and the housing stock has largely been repaired and refurbished, the 5th and 8th Avenue commercial strips are vibrant, and even the waterfront industrial area is bustling.

 ## What's **NEW?**

Soon, a Cemetery You Needn't Die to Get Into

True, Green-Wood will soon be all filled up. But there is a growing number of cultural events being held here, giving you a happy reason to visit.

Otherwise, we haven't detected big changes in the area. There aren't any big plans for the Sunset Park waterfront area, unlike in Williamsburg and Greenpoint. There's near-capacity industrial operation at the waterfront Bush Terminal Market, which is filled with garment businesses and other niche manufacturers requiring access to transportation. As for gentrification, there are rumors of yuppies escaping from higher-rent neighborhoods to the brownstones and affordable shopping of Sunset Park. But it's a rumble, not a roar.

For the time being, the most visible changes here are demographic, with increasing prominence of Mexican over other Latino groups on 5th Avenue, and a growing diversification of Asian nationalities along 8th Avenue.

POINTS OF CULTURAL INTEREST

SPECIAL EVENTS.

Chinese New Year (February) is celebrated with a parade, costumes, and firecrackers along 8th Avenue. Chinese restaurants are closed during the celebration. Memorial Day Concert at Green-Wood Cemetery (May). Two historic commorative ceremonies—Irish Patriot and Battle of Brooklyn (August; see **Green-Wood Cemetery**). There are free concerts in August every Wednesday evening. Parade of Flags on 5th Avenue (October).

BOTANICAS (for instance, the Botanica Jerusalem on 23rd St. and 5th Ave.)

Those mysterious stores with plaster statuettes of patron saints, candles, amulets, beads, oils, and pamphlets—you see them all over Brooklyn, but especially in Latino neighborhoods, such as 5th Avenue, from Park Slope through to Bay Ridge. Botanicas sell the accoutrements of folk religious practices, including Santeria, that combine traditional African spiritual rituals with Christian traditions. Spiritual readings called *consultas* and spiritual cleansings are sometimes performed at botanicas.

BROOKLYN CHINESE-AMERICAN ASSOCIATION. 5000 Eighth Ave. at 50th St., 438-0008.

Whether you're an interested tourist or a cultural preservationist, if you want to know what's going on in Brooklyn's Asian community, ask here. It's a community organization that runs tons of programs at over a dozen sites. These are the folks who bring you Brooklyn's Chinese New Year Parade, among other things.

BUSH TERMINAL AND BROOKLYN ARMY TERMINAL. Along the waterfront, bet. 28th and 65th Sts.

Bush Terminal. Use your imagination if you visit this large industrial site. Irving T. Bush first opened this area to industrial development in 1890. It had once been the site of Wild West shows, and later it was the location of Irving's father's oil business. With some foresight, Mr. Bush anticipated the development of the huge shipping industry and related heavy industry and manufacturing jobs that would keep Brooklyn's economy going for decades. The waterfront declined after World War II. Today the area including Bush Terminal and the new Harborside industrial complex is abuzz with small and large businesses.

Brooklyn Army Terminal. The whole story here is in its original name: the New York Port of Embarkation and Army Supply Base. The terminal was built in 1918, after World War I, but in time for World War II. In fact, if you know someone who fought in Europe in World War II, he most likely left from this terminal.

18TH POLICE PRECINCT STATION HOUSE. 4302 Fourth Ave., corner of 43rd St.

Now the Sunset Park School of Music, this landmark was designed by police department architect George Ingram in 1890. It looks like a medieval fortress.

FAITH CAMII MOSQUE. 5911 8th Ave. at 59th St., 438-6919.

This Turkish mosque was constructed in 1980 from an old Irish and Norwegian dance club—adding yet another layer to Brooklyn's archeology of immigration. One of New York's most beautiful mosques, it is dimly, pervasively calm inside. The first thing you will see is the *sadirvan*, a large and decorative tile fountain with several low faucets, a ritual bath in which Muslims wash their feet and hands prior to prayer. The large inner prayer room, used by up to six hundred people on Friday nights for prayers, is plain (according to Muslim custom), with a large wall made of decorative handmade tile imported from Kutahya, Turkey. The mosque is open to the public except at prayer times; ask for a tour. The bookstore on the premises sells prayer rugs and religious texts and objects.

GREEN-WOOD CEMETERY. The main entrance is on 5th Ave., at the end of 25th St., 768-7300, daily 8 a.m.–5 p.m. (Memorial Day to Labor Day 7 a.m.–7 p.m.), www.Green-Wood.com.

World-famous Green-Wood Cemetery is a vast parklike and entirely man-made environment of rolling hills, paths, and lakes. The Victorian Gothic gate at 5th Avenue and 25th Street is just one of the architectural masterpieces here, along with enormous mausoleums and ornate Victorian monuments.

Roam the serene setting or hunt for the tombs of the rich and famous. The roster of Green-Wood's nineteenth-century inhabitants goes on and on: pharmaceutical giants Edward Squibb and Charles Pfizer; *New York Times* founder Henry Raymond; Nathaniel Currier and James Merritt Ives of lithographers Currier and Ives; Henry E. Steinway of piano fame (whose mausoleum has room for more than two hundred bodies); Charles Tiffany, founder of the Tiffany store; Louis Comfort Tiffany, the stained-glass artist; Charles Ebbets, after whom the Dodgers' ballpark was named; Samuel Morse, of the code by the same name; plus the inventors of, respectively, the safety pin, carbonated water, the sewing machine, and the steam locomotive. Also buried here are James Renwick Jr., architect of the Smithsonian Institution; Richard Upjohn, architect of Trinity Church in Manhattan; Peter Cooper, inventor of Jell-O and founder of Cooper Union; Henry Bergh, founder of the American Society for the Prevention of Cruelty to Animals (ASPCA); Lola Montez, companion to composer Franz Liszt, painters Asher Brown Durand, William Merritt Chase, John Kensett, William Holbrook Beard, and others; and William Marcy Tweed, also known as Boss Tweed of Tammany Hall. Plain folk also are buried here, as told by tales like the following on simple, old headstones: "Nelly, age 2, leaving an empty hearth and broken hearts."

Still a lovely place to roam today (and quite safe, due to extensive security), the 478-acre Green-Wood was used as a park in the 1850s by locals and tourists, according to historical accounts. In fact, the popularity of Green-Wood's open spaces was one of the reasons used to justify the creation of Manhattan's Central Park in 1856.

Special Green-Wood events:

Memorial Day concert at Green-Wood. Thousands of people attend a band and chorale concert here. It's a fabulous event, free, fun—and full of puns.

August commemorative ceremonies. Call for information on the Irish-American Parade Committee parade to the grave of Matilda Tone, wife of Irish patriot Theobald Wolf Tone. Also a Battle of Brooklyn commemorative ceremony honoring the patriots who fought here over 225 years ago, during the Revolutionary War.

Performances at Green-Wood's 1911 Chapel. See below, p. 416.

Tours: Call Green-Wood Historic Fund at 788-7850 for tours that benefit restoration projects of the Cemetery, led by Jeff Richman, author of *Brooklyn's*

Green-Wood Cemetery: New York's Hidden Treasure; John Cashman at 469-5277; Big Onion Walking Tours 499-3001; Justin Ferrate of Tours of the City 212-779-0727; or the Brooklyn Center for the Urban Environment 788-8500.

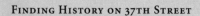

FINDING HISTORY ON 37TH STREET

The Brooklyn Historical Society publishes wonderful educational packages, including a Sunset Park walking tour for schoolchildren. Among the things pointed out are "seashells mixed in with the concrete" at 37th Street and 4th Avenue. The booklet explains that "the shells are left over from the days when oysters were one of the biggest boom trades in this part of Brooklyn." And note several bluish bricks set in the sidewalk in front of 441 37th Street, like the kind used in Spain about five hundred years ago.

GREEN-WOOD CEMETERY CHAPEL, 500 25th St. at 5th Ave., 768-7300, www.Green-Wood.com.

What an interesting venue for a theatrical performance! The intimate 1911 Chapel, seating only about a hundred people, has recently been the venue for some cultural events—effectively returning the cemetery to a nineteenth-century kind of community use. It has been host to performances, for instance, of Danzas Espanolas, the Brooklyn High School of the Arts Band, and improvisatory guitarist David Grubbs.

Occasionally 1911 Chapel is also home to the "Only the Dead" play series, developed by the **Brooklyn Lyceum,** which dramatizes the lives of some of the six hundred thousand "residents of Brooklyn's most beautiful neighborhood," as the theater puts it. Part of the proceeds is donated to Green-Wood's Monument restoration trust. (See **Brooklyn Lyceum,** p. 357.)

FERRY SERVICE TO MANHATTAN. 58th Street Brooklyn Army Terminal to Pier 11 Wall St., NY Water Taxi, 212-742-1969, 6:40–9:40 a.m., Brooklyn to Manhattan; return trip, 4–7 p.m. every 20 minutes from Pier 11, www.nywatertaxi.com.

Why would a ferry be a "point of cultural interest"? Because this ferry route got started right after the 9-11 attacks on the World Trade Center, enabling workers to reach their workplaces in Lower Manhattan. It proved so popular that it was extended in 2003 to permanent service. Look for the yellow catamarans with black-and-white checks. About $5 each way—cheaper than a cab, faster than a subway. What a glorious way to go to work.

LATIN MUSIC SHOPS IN SUNSET PARK

There are really a *lot* of music shops here, for one small neighborhood—more than in Park Slope, or Brooklyn Heights, or Carroll Gardens. What's going on? See below, page 425.

☗ PUBLIC SCHOOLS.

PS 172 (825 Fourth Avenue) is considered by experts to be one of Brooklyn's best public elementary schools. (Source: *New York City's Best Public Elementary Schools*, 2002, by C. Hemphill with P. Wheaton.)

SUNSET PARK COURT HOUSE. 4th Ave.

Located in the heart of Sunset Park, the courthouse was build in 1931, during a period of prolific courthouse construction in New York. The building, designed by Mortimer Metcalfe, who helped in the design of Grand Central Terminal, is in Classic Revival style.

☺ ✪ **YOUNG DANCERS IN REPERTORY.** 231 60th St. bet. 2nd and 3rd Aves., 567-9620, www.young dancersinrep.org.

How nice 'tis when dreams come true. This award-winning youth dance school was founded in 1985 as a professionally oriented teenage touring ensemble, the first and only of its kind in Brooklyn. Under direction of Carol Mezzacappa, who is on the faculty of the Jose Limón Dance Institute in Manhattan, students have performed at the UN, Washington's Kennedy Center, the South Street Seaport, and the Dance Grand Prix Italia (an Italian international dance festival), on television, and at many other venues. Forty performances are presented annually by the Teen Touring Ensemble. Its house on 60th Street was donated by Dial Poultry, Inc.

ENTERTAINMENT
☺ **MELODY LANES.** 461 37th St., off 5th Ave., 832-2695, Su–Th 9 a.m.–11 p.m., F–Sa 9–2 a.m.

A long-standing favorite, if you like bowling. Children three and up can bowl here, to 1970s disco beat–and it's a great place for kids' birthday parties.

PARKS AND PLAYGROUNDS
⏱ ♫ SUNSET PARK

A slightly seedy twenty-four-acre park with unbelievable views of the New York Harbor—especially, you guessed it, at sunset. There are summer concerts here in the park.

SUNSET PARK POOL AND RECREATION CENTER. 7th Ave. bet. 41st and 44th Sts., 965-6578. Call for hours.

This enormous Olympic-size pool run by the New York City Parks Department is located alongside an elegant old building, which also houses a community center that holds arts and crafts and aerobics classes. The quietest time for a swim is early on a weekday; it is extremely busy during weekends. Lockers are available, but bring your own locks. You'll find an urban crowd from the surrounding neighborhoods.

SUNSET PARK RESTAURANTS

5th and 4th Avenues: Latino

Both Mexican and Dominican restaurants abound. They are not upscale, like the ones you might find in Manhattan's tourist areas, nor are they sanitized, like many of the "Tex Mex" chains at suburban malls. Expect small cafés to be noisy, with big-screen televisions blaring Mexican news or Spanish soap operas, and a jukebox playing as well. Not much English is spoken, the meat is served in small pieces on jagged-cut bone, and you can see big, battered old pots on the stove, but the food is authentic—and when it's good, it's delicious.

EL TESORO. 5th Ave. at 40th St., 972-3756, daily 7 a.m.–9 p.m. Cash only.

There are two restaurants side-by-side here; this one has a bright red awning. "The Treasure," as it would be called in English, is a good Ecuadorian restaurant. Come for the ceviche, an Ecuadorian specialty, and black clams. It's clean and friendly, with tables for several dozen people, and a little English is spoken.

INTERNATIONAL. 4405 5th Ave. at 44th St. 438-2009, daily 7 a.m.–9 p.m.

International is a popular, inexpensive American-Spanish restaurant where you can get a reliable meal of beans and rice, steak and roast pork chops, stuffed tortillas, and breakfast anytime. Check out the lobster special for $14.25 and fairly large menu of soupy rice dishes, including paella, chicken in soupy rice, rice and green pigeon peas stew, and Dominican sausage in yellow rice. It has often played host to visiting politicians come election time.

LAS ANTILLAS. 4413 4th Ave. at 44th St., 438-1994, daily 10 a.m.–8 p.m. Cash only.

Note that this is located on 4th, not 5th Avenue. Dominicans have long resided in the area, but Las Antillas still makes food reminiscent of home: *sopa de gallina*, pigeon peas, plaintains, mango with cheese, and rotisserie chicken significantly less expensive than what you'll find in the adjacent neighborhoods of

Park Slope or Bay Ridge. Another good, inexpensive Dominican restaurant nearby is Isabela's, 4412 4th Avenue at 44th Street, 832-6715.

LOS COMPADRES. 5807 5th Ave. at 58th St., 567-2760, daily 8 a.m.–8 p.m. Cash only.

Sporting an awning the colors of the Mexican flag, this combo bakery/takeout is located on a multi-ethnic corner, across from an Italian pizzeria, bagel store, and Mexican grocery. You'll see a modest counter display of cheese, avocados, limes, and green *tomatillos*, but in the kitchen they're cooking up tacos, quesadillas, and homemade soups. There are only three cramped tables here.

RICO'S TACOS. 505 51st St. corner of 5th Ave., 638-4816, daily 10 a.m.–9 p.m. Cash only.

Nose-tingling sauce, fresh tamarind juice ladled out of a vat, a mini-taco filled with meat, and an abundance of freshly diced vegetables are the reasons there are so many people chowing down at this particular joint. There's no menu in English, and, in fact, not much English is spoken at all.

RICO'S TAMALES OAXAQUEÑOS. 5th Ave. at 46th St. No phone.

You might think twice about eating off the street in Oaxaca, Mexico, but you can here—if you manage to get past the bodacious Felliniesque character serving it. The chicken and pork tamales, spiced up with mole poblano, are *auténtico*. Yes, it's that little shanty on the corner. There's another bright yellow shanty serving food across the street.

USULUTECO. 4017 5th Ave. bet. 40th and 41st St., 436-8025, daily 8 a.m.–9 p.m. Cash only.

You can get breakfast, lunch, or dinner in this cheerful Salvadorian restaurant with a bright blue awning. It serves traditional dishes, such as enchiladas, *salpicon* salad, and homemade soups. There's a jukebox with Latin music, and a bilingual menu (if not staff).

8th Avenue: Asian

Dim sum, or a conventional dinner, can be had at more than a dozen Chinese restaurants. You can pick up exotic ingredients at various Chinese shops, or at a great Middle Eastern food market.

☛ **TIP:** Dim sum is served from 8 a.m. until about 2 p.m. at many local restaurants.

CHINA CAFÉ INC. 4924 8th Ave. at 50th St., 686-6602, daily 10 a.m.–10 p.m.

For a twist on traditional Chinese cuisine, try this eatery. Offering up dishes that include lo mein Hong Kong style and congee with frog, China Café is perfect for the foodie seeking new frontiers. Traditionalists can enjoy prime rib over rice, or homemade specials, such as vegetable with garlic sauce. Entrées start at $8.

CHINESE OCEAN RESTAURANT. 5606 8th Ave. corner of 56th St., 587-8686, daily 8–2 a.m.

If you are a twosome or a foursome, come to this family-sized Cantonese restaurant sporting festive pink tablecloths. This place will immediately remind you of Hong Kong—if you've ever been there. Gently cooked tofu, poultry, and especially seafood are nicely turned out, and the portions are more than adequate. Entrées cost $8 and up. If you don't want MSG, say so.

GIA LAM. 4810 8th Ave. bet. 48th and 49th Sts., 633-2272. **Gia Lam II.** 5606 8th Ave. bet. 56th and 57th Sts., 567-0800, daily 10 a.m.–11 p.m.

There's no better dish on a humid summer day than a refreshing bowl of Vietnamese *pho,* with fresh sprigs of mint and sprouts to add into your soup filled with noodles and any type of meat you desire. A bargain: A bowl of *pho* starts at $4; add an appetizer for $3 and up.

JADE PLAZA. 6022 8th Ave. bet. 60th and 61st Sts., 492-6888, daily 8–2 a.m.

A Sunset Park veteran, Jade Plaza has maintained its elegance and reputation as one of the classier eateries on the block. This is a great place for dinner; try the spicy rack of veal with black bean sauce. From $8 to $20 for entrées.

KAKALA CAFÉ. 5302 8th Ave. corner of 53rd St., 437-9688, daily 10 a.m.–3 a.m.

Its slogan is "New Generation on 8th Avenue." Indeed, this pan-Asian café is part of the new breed of businesses opening up in Brooklyn's own Chinatown, attracting the hip, younger Chinese clientele. Stop in for lunch to taste the eel udon or chicken-leg-soup spaghetti, or for a late-night snack of dim sum with a swig of Tsing Tao beer. And it's inexpensive.

LAI'S GARDEN. 4418 8th Ave. at 45th St., 633-6366, daily 9:30–midnight.

It's an old-fashioned kind of place, Lai's Garden, with large tanks of lobster to choose from and standard favorites, such as lo mein with seafood. Pork stew with bitter melon over rice is about as adventurous as you'll find here. The seafood dishes are the highest-priced on the menu, ranging from $10 to $20.

NYONYA MALAYSIAN CUISINE. 5323 54th St. corner of 8th Ave., 633-0808 or 972-2943, daily 11 a.m.–11:30 p.m.

Something unusual: a Malaysian restaurant. Here you will find unique dishes that are artfully presented, extremely tasty, and very fresh. You can try homemade roti in a tangy brown sauce, pearl noodle soup served in a clay pot, steamed sea bass in *teo chow* style—that is, brought to the table in a vegetable-packed fish steamer. The wood-paneled decor is meant to be reminiscent of Malaysian outdoor food stands, adding to the general sense that you are in a foreign outpost. A three-course dinner costs under $20.

Bakeries, Cafés, Ice-Cream Parlors, and Quick Meals

DRAGON BAY BAKERY. 5711 8th Ave. bet. 57th and 58th Sts., 853-8188 daily 6:30 a.m.–8:30 p.m.

With an array of lights flashing at the entrance, you could easily mistake this bakery for a nightclub. But don't let the atmosphere fool you. Inside, the self-serve shelves are stuffed with buns filled with everything from tuna fish to lemon jam to taro and the classic ham & cheese. At the counter you can pick up fresh cakes and cream puffs.

HONG FUNG BAKERY. 5124 8th Ave. at 52nd St., 854-6290, daily 9 a.m.–9 p.m.

HFB Inc., which is what the regulars call it, is the ideal pit stop for a sweet drink or a slice of cake while you're shopping on 8th Avenue. With its lively atmosphere—and the always-crowded counter—try the fresh cream puffs or a piece of white cake with strawberries.

KOLAWSTER BAKERY. 5804 8th Ave. near 58th St., 439-8545, daily 7 a.m.–8 p.m.

Don't let the name "Kolawster" fool you; this is indeed a Chinese bakery, and nobody quite remembers how or why it kept the previous owner's name. The selection is vast, and the prices are low for mixed-nut rolls, mini-mooncakes with lotus-seed paste, yellow egg-bean cakes, and shrimp chips. The prices are right.

SUNDAES AND CONES. 5622 8th Ave. at 57th St., 439-9398, daily 10 a.m.–10: 30 p.m.

For a buck-fifty a scoop, this mom-and-pop ice-cream shop offers homemade ice creams of all different flavors. Try the taro, lychee, Reese's peanut butter, or chocolate chip. They also make homemade ice cream cakes in a variety of shapes for every occasion.

SUNSTONE TORTILLAS EXPRESS. 5411 5th Ave. corner of 54th St., 439-8434, M–Th 11 a.m.–10 p.m., F–Su 11 a.m.–10:30 p.m. Cash only.

Despite the glossy colored photos in the window, which just about scream "fast food!," the menu claims that food here is "fresh, without artificial spices, chemical spices, MSG, lard, or preservatives." Vegetarians say this is the best place in the neighborhood for a fresh, veggie-laden taco.

● **TEA & TEA.** 58-01 8th Ave. at 58th St., 437-6622, M–F 11:30 a.m.–11:30 p.m., Sa–Su noon–11:30 p.m.

Don't let the name fool you: This café also offers real food, as well as other mouthwatering drinks along with their spectacular selection of cold or hot teas. Sample the delicious mung-bean shake, the kumquat-lime juice, or the traditional black tea with milk, with a side of their scrumptious samosa.

VEGA DELI. 5417 5th Ave. near the corner of 54th St., M–Sa 9 a.m.–10 p.m. Cash only.

"It's not really good for you, but oh, it's delicious—and just like in Puerto Rico!" is what the pretty lady in the nearby bakery said about Vega Deli—and she's right. Jose Colon, the deli proprietor, makes a few classic Latino fried foods: *mafongo, pastelillos de guava y yuca*, and *alcapurrias* (meat-filled, elongated savory dumplings). Snag an extra napkin, because these deep-fried treats are greasy.

SHOPPING

This section takes you to two key shopping areas of Sunset Park: Latino 5th Avenue and Chinese 8th Avenue.

5th Avenue

You're still in Brooklyn, but you'll feel like you are in another country.

Stroll up 5th Avenue on a weekend, or late in the afternoon on a weekday, to get the flavor of this bustling, working-class neighborhood. Along a half-mile stretch of shops selling inexpensive merchandise, you can't miss the displays of oversized valises, bikes piled high, backpacks hanging off shop awnings, tin taco warmers for sale, and signs in both English and Spanish for "Reckless Fashion," "Toda Moda," and "Señorita" above racks of skimpy outfits for women, costing under $15. Street vendors on the corners sell peeled oranges in bags, and *churros* (a doughnutlike sweet). If you wander into a food market, you'll discover otherwise hard-to find ingredients for an authentic Latin-American meal.

8th Avenue

The most concentrated Chinese and Asian retail area is along 8th Avenue from about 53rd to 60th Streets, marked, again, by telling store signs: "Oriental and Medical," "Dragon House Gift Shop," "Get Well Pharmacy," and "Sweet Home Furniture." The food stores are overflowing—fresh-fish markets brimming with glassy-eyed fish, and produce stands piled high with exotic vegetables and roots. Peking ducks hang in the restaurant windows. There are Chinese nail salons, Chinese record stores, and ginseng and tea shops. Neatly dressed, well-organized families, with children in tow, purposefully head to the stores, a restaurant, or home.

Specialty Food Shops
5th and 4th Avenues

GREENMARKET. 4th Ave. bet. 59th and 60th Sts., July 12–Oct. 25, 8 a.m.–3 p.m.

It's a seasonal greenmarket, and worth a visit for the fresh, locally produced fruits and veggies.

JUN'S MARKET. 4921 5th Ave. corner of 50th St., 435-9078, 24/7.

Owned by Koreans, this overflowing vegetable market serving a Latino community has an unusual selection of tropical fruits and vegetables. Here you can find special ingredients such as guava, sour oranges, chayote, *mamey,* Dominican eggplant, cactus leaves, and green *guajes.*

LA GRAN VIA BAKERY. 4516 5th Ave. bet. 45th and 46th Sts., 853–8201, daily 8 a.m.–8 p.m.

You can't miss this spot. The display window is chock-a-block with kiddie birthday cakes featuring a photo or cartoon characters; there are also spectacular, three-tiered wedding cakes. For a snack, try one of the traditional Latino specialties, like coconut pudding, pastries, or sweet breads made of corn or coconut.

MAS QUE PAN BAKERY. 5401 5th Ave. at 54th St., 492–0479, M–Sa 7 a.m.–7 p.m., Su 8 a.m.–5 p.m.

The wedding cakes with edible flying buttresses displayed in the window would turn the head of the most dedicated bachelor. Stop inside this airy bakery for *tembleque* (coconut pudding), *pastelillos* with guava and powdered sugar, or pineapple or coconut confections. There are a few seats for coffee, if you have to nibble right then and there. And they deliver.

8th Avenue

BIRLIK ORIENTAL FOOD/HALAL MEAT MARKET. 5919 8th Ave. near 60th St., 436-2785, daily 8 a.m.–10 p.m.

Turkish, Middle Eastern, and Asian foods make for an eclectic mix at Birlik's, which covers almost half a block along 8th Avenue. Feast your eyes and taste buds on the olives, cheeses, more than fifty fresh herbs and spices, and a deli counter with fresh meat and sauces. There is a wonderful fresh fruit and vegetable market here, too.

GOLDEN DRAGON EVERY WARE INC. 4514 8th Ave. bet. 45th and 46th Sts., 436–1930, daily 10 a.m.– 8:30 p.m.

At lunchtime, you might find the shopkeeper surrounded by her friends, eating a hot meal at the counter, but don't let that intimidate you. If you're looking for shoes, clothing, blankets, or Chinese tchotchkes, this modest store may have a treasure awaiting you.

☺ **HONG KONG SUPERMARKET.** 6013 8th Ave. corner 60th St., 438-2288, daily 9 a.m.–10 p.m. Parking lot on the premises.

Busy, crowded, brash, and commercial—like Hong Kong itself—this block-long, suburban-style supermarket carries every conceivable item you might want to make a Chinese meal at home: condiments; utensils; mixes; fresh fruits and vegetables; and canned, salted, pressed, and vinegary ingredients you may never have heard of before. It is educational just to browse, so bring the kids. If you don't find what you want here, check **T & H Supermarket** in, of all places, Bensonhurst.

LIEN HUNG SUPERMARKET, INC. 5705 8th Ave. corner 57th St., 435-3388, daily 9 a.m.–8:30 p.m.

A family-owned Chinese supermarket, Lien Hung serves a Cantonese clientele. Roam the aisles and consider such delectables as shrimp sauce, fermented turnips, pickled ginger, spiced preserved bean curd, fresh fish, twenty-five-pound bags of rice, and more. Counters of fresh fish line this medium-sized market. The smell may remind you of the seashore, but you'll leave with a good, affordable selection of lobster, snapper, crab, and shrimp.

NAIKEI TRADING CORP. U.S.A. 4721 8th Ave. bet. 47th and 48th Sts., 853-6635, daily 10 a.m.–8 p.m.

The smell of Chinese herbs and roots permeates your nostrils as you walk into Naikei. A family-owned establishment, where you may find their preteen son and daughter behind the counter with mom and pop, Naikei sells original Jin Cha Chinese tea, and fresh roots and herbs for mental and physical ailments. First-time shoppers might try the packaged teas, ready-made cures made for everything from bowel relaxing to dieting, conveniently placed at the front of the store.

TEN REN'S TEA AND GINSENG COMPANY. 5817 8th Ave. near 58th St., 853-0660, daily 10 a.m.–8 p.m., www.tenren.com.

Natural herbs have been used in Chinese diets for thousands of years. Decide for yourself if they really improve sexual deficiencies, decrease blood fat and cholesterol, stave off baldness, and cure headaches, depression, and all kinds of diseases.

A tea-and-ginseng international marketing consortium, Ten Ren's Tea and Ginseng Company has locations from Manhattan to Los Angeles, Canada to the Far East. It's as homey as an airport duty-free shop (in contrast to the family businesses surrounding it), but well-trained staff do offer visitors a taste along with an informative lecture about the health benefits of green tea.

WINLEY SUPERMARKET. 5515 8th Ave. at 56th St., 851-1027, daily 8:30 a.m.–8:30 p.m.

You'll find Chips Ahoy cookies across the aisle from Chinese Digestive crackers before you walk up a ramp to an attached store next door that carries just about every kitchen utensil necessary to cut, dice, whip, froth, fry, broil, cook, carve, or bake some fabulous international dish with your newfound ingredients.

Other Shopping

LATIN MUSIC SHOPS IN SUNSET PARK

Ten little music stores, all in a row? That's Sunset Park.

It's easy *not* to notice these little shops, but once you start looking, you can count one, two, sometimes even three music shops per block along the mile-and-a-half strip of 5th Avenue from 44th to 59th Street. The sheer amount of music on sale here is disproportionate, relative to the rest of Brooklyn. Mexican and Latin music CDs and videos are sold not just in proper "music stores," but in unlikely venues, such as behind travel agencies and on the walls of those "everything stores" that sell cheap baby strollers, cardboard suitcases, and umbrellas.

Most of the CDs are imported from northern Mexico and feature traditional folk music, such as *ranchera, nortena, grupera,* and *sondera.* The CD label photos usually show men on horses, in sombreros or cowboy hats. They're so corny it's kitsch, yet so authentic you can almost feel the homesickness of a community that buys this much music from back home.

FERNANDEZ RECORDS. 5011 5th Ave. between 50th and 51st Sts., 871-2120, daily 9 a.m.–8 p.m.

If you loved the smash hit movie *Buena Vista Social Club,* like salsa, or just want to soak up some Latin sound, absolutely take a trip here. With wall-to-wall CDs, Fernandez is the biggest Latino record store in Brooklyn, and probably has one of the best Latin music selections in New York. There's salsa, *merengue, guajiro,* and reggae in this well-organized shop. A huge Mexican selection fills a big space the size of a small *casita.* The only regional Latin music that's underrepresented in Brazilian, which, the owner explains, costs $16 and up per CD; the average CD price here is affordable, in the $12 range.

The staff is friendly and knowledgeable (though their English is limited). If you don't see what you want, ask; the owners have four specialty Latin music shops in the Big Apple, so they can often get it from another store. Their slogan is *"La Más Completa"*—they've got that one right.

Other

Of almost a dozen Latin music shops along 5th Avenue here are a few. Most are open 9 a.m.–7 p.m. Only Gonzalez has a Web site to date. From 5th Avenue at 44th to 59th Streets:

LA PACHANGA. 4424 5th Ave. at 45th St., 972-5261.
GONZALEZ RECORDS. 4612 4th Ave., 439-5762, www.gonzalezrecords.com.
SONIDO LATINO. 511 47th St. at 5th Ave., 972-6590.
LA FERIA DEL DISCO. 5505 5th Ave., bet. 55th and 56th Sts., 492-3840.
ELIZABETH RECORDS. 5814 5th Ave., 930-8645.
MARTINEZ RECORDS. 5914 5th Ave. at 59th St., 765-1322.

COSTCO WHOLESALE CLUB. 37th St. and 3rd Ave., 832-9300, M–F 10 a.m.–8:30 p.m., Sa 9:30 a.m.–7:00 p.m., Su 10 a.m.–6 p.m. For information, call 965-7610.

This national discount store attracts every possible nationality in Brooklyn. You can shop here for the discounted prices, but another reason to come to Costco is the human parade: it's a microcosm of the tremendous ethnic diversity in Brooklyn.

MCGOVERN'S FLORIST. 750 5th Ave. at 25th St. 768-6770, M–F 8 a.m.–6 p.m., Sa–Su 8 a.m.–4 p.m.

This four-generation family business, opened over a century ago, is famous for its beautiful antique glass-encased display area, which is a New York City landmark. They sell indoor and outdoor plants and provide many flowers and arrangements for **Green-Wood Cemetery**, across the street.

TIEN WEI AQUARIUM. 5822 8th Ave. bet. 58th and 59th Sts., 567-7176, daily 11 a.m.–8 p.m.

The kids will love this well-kept aquarium store, open since 1994. There are at least six dozen different sizes of goldfish and other low-maintenance pet alternatives.

ZAPATERIA MEXICO II. 4505 5th Ave. at 45th St., 851-4074, daily 10 a.m.–8 p.m.

Did you know that Mexicans invented the cowboys? They did, and here you'll find an incredible display of imported cowboy boots and related gear from Mexico, priced between $120 and $170. If you get into it, try a cowboy shirt for about $45, or an authentic sombrero.

YALE PICTURE FRAME & MOLDING CORP. 770 Fifth Ave. at 28th St. 788-6200, M–Th 9 a.m.–
5 p.m., F 9 a.m.–2 p.m., Su 11 a.m.–2 p.m., www.yalepf.com.

For those in the know, this is one of the city's best and best-priced custom-
framing shops. They have supplied high-end outlets, including the Museum of
Modern Art, and frequently handle original works of art. Note: Call before setting out on Sundays, and avoid Fridays.

17

Williamsburg

ABOUT WILLIAMSBURG: KIDS AND HIPSTERS

Only the nuttiest novelist could invent a place like Williamsburg.

It's famous as the epicenter of new and emerging art in the United States. Informal estimates peg the number of "kids and hipsters"—artists, performers, musicians, writers, and wanna-bes—living and working in the area at five to ten *thousand,* a sizeable chunk of Williamsburg's population of one hundred thousand. But it's not an "artist's colony" in the quaint sense of a reclusive little village. Williamsburg is a mind-set, a big late-night discussion about the meaning of life. Its culture is octopus-like, extending little tentacles in the form of restaurants, bars, galleries, illegal lofts, quirky shops, and wall murals far into neighboring Greenpoint and Bushwick.

There's art aplenty here. But there's no single "museum" in which to see it. The art is being made, discarded, recycled, rethought. It is diffused among nearly a hundred galleries (we've listed the most prominent, below), theaters, and multipurpose "performance spaces" that host live music, burlesque, dance, and multimedia events. There are galleries everywhere—in cafés, in restaurants, and even in clothing boutiques. Williamsburg is wildly interdisciplinary. Dance becomes performance becomes art becomes music becomes politics. The word "indie" as in "independent of mainstream culture and corporate ownership" is waved around like a national flag.

But back to the nutty novelist. Did we forget to mention? Williamsburg is also a place of great historical interest (see Historical Notes, p. 432). Further, within its ample geographic boundaries you will find four communities that have absolutely no good reason to be proximate, other than by historical whimsy: ethnic Italians; insular Hasidim; a shrinking number of Latinos; and the largely white, middle-class "kids and hipsters," most of whom were raised in places other than New York City. The following focuses on the latter group of new "immigrants."

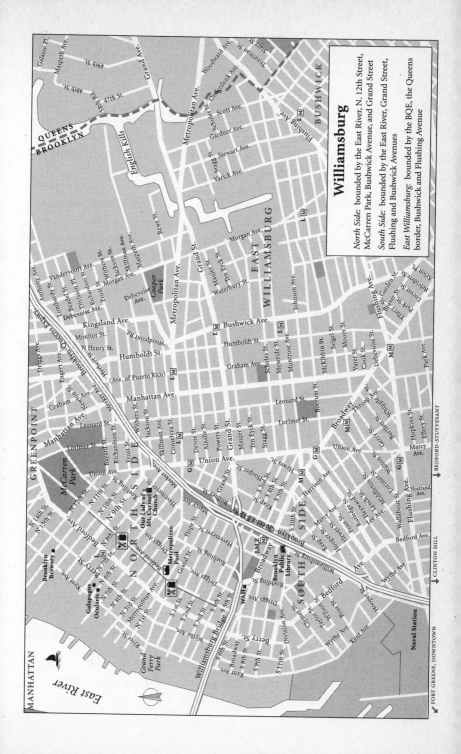

Williamsburg

North Side: bounded by the East River, N. 12th Street, McCarren Park, Bushwick Avenue, and Grand Street

South Side: bounded by the East River, Grand Street, Flushing and Bushwick Avenues

East Williamsburg: bounded by the BQE, the Queens border, Bushwick and Flushing Avenue

☛ **TIP:** For current events For the latest information on Williamsburg, look for the free local papers, such as *Waterfront Week* and *11211*, stacked up at most cafés. Or on the Internet: www.billburg.com. and www.freewilliamsburg.com.

For armchair visitors: Imagine a sprawling area of two-story brick buildings, narrow streets, and a no-nonsense industrial environment. Williamsburg is bounded on one side by a long stretch of East River waterfront with Manhattan views, currently inaccessible, but about to be developed into high-rise apartment buildings and a waterfront park (see What's New, below).

An inexplicable sense of leisure pervades the Bedford Avenue environs. Is this really New York? On an average weekday, at eleven a.m., the cafés are packed with young people leisurely reading the paper and greeting friends. Perhaps some are tourists. Harried middle-aged Park Slopers could save a lot of money if, instead of their weekly therapy sessions, they just drove to Williamsburg, to hang around for an hour. It's that laid-back.

Who *are* these folks? In hipster Williamsburg (as opposed to the Hasidic, Italian, or Latino areas), the residents' age is between postcollege and pre-AARP. Some graying Williamsburg pioneers are now hitting their forties, with families and concerns over schools and baby-sitters. But locals say that the latest influx of newcomers tend to be in their mid-twenties. (That's as we go to press; construction of fancy high-rise housing on the waterfront could attract an older, more moneyed crowd.) Judging from the smattering of British, Italian, French, and German accents you hear, Williamsburg has acquired an international cachet. People learn about it on the Internet. Kids graduating from college, those with a creative bent and alternative-lifestyle ambitions, make a beeline here. Williamsburg's the place to be.

New York City has a vast service economy that employs graphic artists, jingle writers, freelance editors, jewelry, fashion, and interior designers, photographers, actors, set designers, musicians, makeup artists, singers, Web designers, and creative types of all flavors. Some "Billyburgers" make a living doing these jobs. Others find ways to explore their inner artist, while eking out a living by waiting tables or working in local shops. Lots of them have roommates, as you can see from the informal ads posted on bulletin boards and telephone poles. There's an underground barter economy unique to Williamsburg. One freebie magazine that is distributed widely here cheerfully relies on barter. An ad in the magazine is worth a month of coffee here, $100 worth of clothing there, a free paint job for the office, and so on. Perhaps some of the younger crowd get subsidies from home; they are gently jibed as being "trustafarians."

Hipster Williamsburg is infected by a kind of off-the-beaten-track youthful sense of optimism. That's the case even when the "Billyburgers" are whining (not infrequently) about hangovers, heartbreaks, and landlords. It's all part of the

Williamsburg thing, the angst of being an artist, and the related pleasures of trying to carve oneself an unconventional slice of the biggest apple of them all.

HOW IT GOT ITS NAME Williamsburg was named in 1810 after the man who surveyed the area, Colonel John Williams, reputedly a grandnephew of Benjamin Franklin. The original spelling included an "h" at the end; only a few places, such as the Williamsburgh Savings Bank, still use the old spelling. While we are on the subject of names, almost every street from Wythe to Ellery (north of the park) is named after one of the fifty-six American patriots who signed the Declaration of Independence.

BY SUBWAY To Northside Williamsburg (most of our "New Williamsburg"), from 14th Street in Manhattan, take the L train to Bedford Avenue and No. 6th. Or the G train to Metropolitan Avenue and transfer to the Manhattan-bound L train, one stop to Bedford Avenue. Stay on the L train for points deeper into Williamsburg. To Southside Williamsburg (most of our "Old Williamsburg"), take the Z, J, or M train to Marcy Avenue exit at Broadway.

 ## What's **NEW 1**?

Not *IF*, but WHEN: Along the Waterfront, High-rises and Public Parks

The fate of the Williamsburg waterfront has been yo-yoing for years between visions of a residential area and industrial uses, notably a power plant. But in 2003, under Mayor Bloomberg, New York City has finally decided which way the Williamsburg waterfront will go. Here's the plan:

- a mile and a half of development allowing high-rise apartment buildings from ten to twenty stories tall
- a multimillion-dollar waterfront park with recreational facilities stretching between the Pulaski Bridge in Greenpoint and the Williamsburg Bridge
- an esplanade along the river
- an eight-acre riverfront state park at North 12th Street
- playing fields, to be built by New York University and used by students who study at their Greenwich Village campus, at North 7th Street
- rezoning, so that more homes and businesses can be built inland, in a big area that covers 170 blocks
- making loft residences legal
- preservation of the Domino Sugar Factory and other viable local industrial areas

There are, however, still some "ifs:"

If New York City wins the Olympics 2012 bid, the waterside facilities will be used for archery and beach volleyball competition.

If all those NYU students come to Williamsburg to play sports, for certain they will want to live here.

If you can believe it, there's talk of a high-speed ferry connecting Williamsburg to Manhattan.

If all this happens, it can't be long before someone opens a hotel here, too (though we haven't heard any reliable reports of such).

 ## What's NEW 2?

And now, the gentrification of . . . *Bushwick???*

Bushwick has a reputation as a poor, tough, mostly Latino, inner-city neighborhood. Imagine beat-up houses and empty lots, a high rate of unemployment and related ills, a dearth of city services, and a handful of community self-help organizations battling the odds. It's the kind of place that would not please a suburban mother when she arrived to help hang curtains in her daughter or son's first postcollege apartment. Moms notwithstanding, young people who want to live in Williamsburg but can't afford the Bedford Avenue area are moving here, in the area near the Morgan stop.

And there are signs of new life. **Renaissance Estates and Rheingold Gardens**, a suburban-style residential development, is being built off Bushwick Avenue. **Office Ops,** a nonprofit that helps local artists, has opened its doors and shows summer outdoor films on the roof. **Combustive Arts,** a burgeoning offbeat cultural center, is attracting visitors, and there are some galleries, an attempt to start a health-food cooperative, and loft parties. Whether sections of Bushwick will be carried along on the wave of Williamsburg's rejuvenation, and how the new and old residents will get along, remains to be, um, scene.

HISTORICAL NOTES

Question: What do Rabbi Teitelbaum, Henry Miller, Commodore Perry, and Captain Kidd have in common?

Answer: Williamsburg.

The tale is told that Captain Kidd, the famous pirate, frequented a dock belonging to the seventeenth-century farmer Jean Mesurolle, a pioneer in this part of the Brooklyn woods. Whether or not it is true, Williamsburg was settled as early as the 1660s by Northern European farmers and their African slaves. The area began to develop under the influence of David Dunham, the so-called father of Williamsburg, who opened a steam ferry and helped finance the building and incorporation of the Village of Williamsburg in 1827. By the 1850s, there was some industry and a resident population of about thirty thousand people here.

In the mid-nineteenth century, parts of Williamsburg were a suburban retreat popular among rich New Yorkers of German and Irish backgrounds. Commodore Perry and William W. Whitney transversed the East River by Fulton Ferry to come to fancy restaurants and hotels in the area. Peter Luger Steak House, founded in 1887, saw some of this carriage trade. At the same time, heavy industry located here, including businesses whose names later became household words: Astral Oil (which became Standard Oil), Brooklyn Flint Glass (which became Corning Glassware), and the Pfizer Pharmaceutical Company.

The upstairs-downstairs demographics of Williamsburg changed radically with the opening of the Williamsburg Bridge in 1903. Working-class immigrants, mostly Jews escaping overcrowding on the Lower East Side of Manhattan, poured into Williamsburg—indeed, the *New York Tribune* of that era refers to the bridge as "Jews Highway." Italians settled in the area between Union and Bushwick Avenues. Lithuanians, Polish, and Russian Orthodox immigrants established small communities nearby.

The **Metropolitan Pool,** built in 1922, served those immigrants, as did one of New York's earliest and still-finest low-income housing complexes, the Williamsburg Houses, dating from the 1930s. Many famous Brooklynites, Henry Miller among them, got their start here. And, of course, the upper crust fled to more exclusive resorts. In the economic crash of the 1930s, most of the middle class, including Williamsburg's original Jewish families, moved away. Today a different, but highly visible, Jewish presence remains—about fifty-thousand Satmar Hasidim from over a dozen sects, who arrived as Holocaust refugees in 1946.

From the 1950s through the 1980s, Latinos settled here in numbers, first Puerto Ricans, and more recently Dominicans and Mexicans. The destruction of low-income housing and resultant social unrest occasioned by the building of the Brooklyn-Queens Expressway in 1957 was a turning point in the area, which remained stagnant, poor, and overcrowded for decades. Considerable tension built up between the Latino and Hasidic communities, mostly over real estate and housing.

Since the 1990s, young artists fleeing Manhattan's staggeringly high rents have breathed new life into the half-dozen streets approaching the waterfront, again transforming Williamsburg. Latinos, Orthodox Jews, Italian-Americans, and European and American artists reside in Williamsburg today. As the young population increases, the "kids" move into East Williamsburg, Greenpoint, and Bushwick, too. Remarkably, all these layers coexist in a perfectly odd mix.

☛ TIP: Take a Trip on the L Train

The lifeline to Williamsburg is the L subway (you may be surprised to learn that it even exists). Also known as the "Canarsie Local," the L coming from Manhattan dumps you right onto gentrified Bedford Avenue, the hub of Williamsburg's small commercial center. Going toward Manhattan, the L transverses 14th Street. Jam-packed at three a.m. with young people returning from Manhattan clubs and nightlife to Williamsburg, the L is jam-packed again at eight a.m., with workers on their way to Manhattan jobs. (Sometimes it's the same people.) It's gotten so crowded that at peak hour you might have to let several trains go by before jamming yourself in . . . just like, *gasp!*, Manhattan used to be.

The L runs through much of Williamsburg, so, if you have a lot of time, get a one-day MTA Fun Pass and just take the L train from stop to stop, get out, walk around, and go to the next stop. Dress down! The second stop, Lorimer, is a busy commercial street in a residential neighborhood that's a mix of Italian, Latino, and hipster. The third stop is Graham Avenue, a little community shopping street that feels like a small town. The next stop, Grand Avenue, is a bigger, more commercial street with lots of discount shops, some restaurants. There won't be much to see in the way of shops, restaurants, and galleries farther out, at the stops named Montrose, Morgan, Jefferson, DeKalb, and Myrtle, unless you are traveling with a local who knows his or her way around.

NITTY-GRITTY, INDUSTRIAL WILLIAMSBURG

PENICILLIN: Pfizer, the giant pharmaceutical conglomerate, long had a presence in Brooklyn. Penicillin wasn't discovered here, of course, but it was first mass-produced in a Williamsburg area plant.

CHINESE FOOD: "BoBo Poultry" for years supplied the bulk of Chinatown's chickens. And, there's a chance you've munched on a fortune cookie made by East Williamsburg's Wonton Foods.

SUGAR: You don't need to go farther than Kent Avenue to get a sense of what old industrial Williamsburg looked like. The **Domino Sugar Factory** has been in operation for over a century.

WOVEN GOODS: In the mid-twentieth century, Brooklyn was home to many weaving mills, supplying New York's famous rag trade. Most of that business has since moved to the Far East, but Newcastle Fabrics on Wythe Avenue remains, spinning out specialty textiles for uses as diverse as covering stereos and long-range military missiles.

BEER: In the 1840s, beer factories were established in Bushwick by German émigrés fleeing revolution. An area around Scholes and Meserole has so many breweries it became known as Brewers Row. Rheingold Beer was born here. More recently, **Brooklyn Brewery** has stepped into the void, once again producing a Brooklyn beer.

PASSOVER GOODIES: Spilkes and Oberlander's, two local kosher bakery wholesalers, used to whip up tons of kosher Passover macaroons, and several hundred thousand dollars' worth of Passover cakes, cookies, and sweets.

CONVERSIONS, CONDIMENTS, AND CHANGE: Many grubby old manufacturing buildings have emerged from the pressure-cooker of gentrification in ways that make the spaces incredibly cool. A recent residential conversion is the old mustard-manufacturing plant on Metropolitan Avenue between Kent and Wythe. Mayonnaise was churned out of the building now occupied by **Galapagos** and **Ocularis**. And after all that mustard and mayo, it's only fitting that Williamsburg's **RealForm Girdle Building** is now occupied by a minimall of cute little fashion shops clearly designed for the small-of-waist. Sometimes change can be hard to stomach.

Kidstuff

☺ **MCCARREN PARK.** And for teens, **Bedford Avenue.**

POINTS OF CULTURAL INTEREST

SPECIAL EVENTS.

Barc Valentines Festival (February); Graham Avenue street festival (May); Critic's Choice Summer Beer and Food Festival (Brooklyn Brewery, June); Feast of the Giglio, Our Lady of Mount Carmel Church (July); BARC Dog Parade (September); Brooklyn Brewery bashes (check Web site for dates); Simchas Torah, religious festival of Hasidic Jews (Spring). Open Studio tours occur, but not on a scheduled basis.

Free! Art Galleries and Performance Arts Spaces

Don't even *think* about trying to see all of the galleries here in a day. One seasoned local resident swears that it took more than two days straight to go to all the galleries in the area—by bike. Note that the galleries have limited hours, and most are commercial, not nonprofit, spaces.

One good place to start is the listings of the **Williamsburg Gallery Association**, 599-3002, www.williamsburggalleryassociation.com.

Founded in 2002 with twenty-three charter members, the WGA hosts collaborative events from time to time, featuring Williamsburg and Greenpoint artists. Check their Web site for fun events like gallery crawls with brunch foods prepared by local restaurants. A great resource.

BELLWEATHER. 335 Grand St. near Marcy Ave., 387-3701, M–F noon–6 p.m., www.bellweathergallery.com.

Founded in 1999, Bellweather specializes in emerging artists and represents the careers of fifteen up and comers. The director comments, "I exhibit all media but have a penchant for smart, funny, and good-to-look-at style and content."

CH'I: AN ART SPACE. 184 Kent Ave. #511 until 2004; thereafter 293 Grand St., 302-3689, W–Su 11 a.m.–7 p.m. or by appointment, www.qianartspace.com.

Ch'i showcases paintings, photography, monoprints, and sculpture in ten exhibitions per year, featuring emerging and established artists from the United States, Canada, and Asia. The works are tied together "by their basis in examining how the world and its inhabitants interrelate," according to gallery director, Tracy Causey-Jeffery. Prices for the art shown here, which also tends "to emphasize texture and space," range from $300 to $15,000.

FOXY PRODUCTIONS. 129 Bedford Ave. #1, 218-9016, F–Su noon–6:00 p.m. www.foxyproduction.com.

Foxy Productions fosters international and American emerging artists, with a focus on interdisciplinary practices, interactive situations, and collaborative ventures. Prices range from $200 for multiples to $6,000 for unique works.

JESSICA MURRAY PROJECTS. 210 No. 6th St. at Driggs Ave., 384-9606, F–M noon–6 p.m., www.jessica murrayprojects.com.

To give you an idea of what Jessica Murray's gallery shows, here's a random selection from a spring 2003 exhibit. The work of one artist, Scott Teplin, "exposes the humorous discomfort associated with the sexual intellectual and abstinent failure." Meanwhile, Jeff Scher's piece "exploits the iconographic nature of white bread . . . through a short film showing 78 paintings on paper, featuring a single slice of Wonder Bread rotating in limbo." Art!

MCCAIG-WELLES GALLERY (AND CUSTOM FRAMING). 149 Havemeyer St., 384-8729, www.mccaig welles.com.

It's rather a surprise to see this gallery, with its deep-blue tiled entrance and airy gallery space inside, on a largely Latino street. This gallery specializes in graffiti and street art—mostly multimedia painting. The artists range from mid-career to well known.

MOMENTA ART. 72 Berry St. bet. No. 9th and No. 10th Sts., 218-8058, F–M noon–6 p.m., www.momentaart.org.

A pioneer in the Williamsburg gallery scene, this small, stark, nonprofit space shows a range of works, from video installations to pen-and-ink. Momenta has gained a strong reputation since it opened here in 1995, transplanted from Philadelphia. It's artist-run and is dedicated to presenting the work of emerging and underrepresented artists, with an emphasis on socially and/or politically engaged work. It's a collaborative sort of place; this gallery publishes a newsletter for each show that includes not only information about the artists, but suggestions of other galleries. Momenta Art has co-curated exhibitions for the Brooklyn Museum and the Brooklyn Public Library's Lobby Gallery.

PARKER'S BOX. 193 Grand St., 388-2882, F–M 1–7 p.m., www.parkersbox.com.

Parker's Box aims to show experimental contemporary art—including painting, sculpture, installation, performance, video, and other media—by U.S. and international artists. And the unusual name? According to the British-Irish team of owners, "In the twenties and thirties our building was the Billiards Academy, and 'Parker's Box' was a controversial rule of billiards introduced at that time as a way to make the game more exciting. The Billiards Federation justified the introduction of the Parker's Box rule by stating that it was 'to prevent boredom in the gallery' (the gallery being the public). This is part of our intention, too."

PIEROGI 2000. 177 No. 9th St., 599-2144, F–M, noon–6 p.m. and by appointment, www.pierogi2000.com.

Founded in 1994 by California-born artist Joe Amrhein, Pierogi is one of the galleries that's put Williamsburg on the map as a center for emerging American artists. Its shows get reviewed not only by the *New York Times*, but also by French, German, and Japanese publications, and the gallery is appearing with increasing frequency in international art fair venues, such as Art Basel, the New York Armory Show, and ArtForum Berlin.

While it has grown in influence and even space (expanding from a nook to 1,300 square feet of gallery space today), Pierogi sticks to its populist beginnings and still shows affordable cutting-edge work. You can pop in and peruse "flat files" in the entrance area that hold original works by over six hundred artists, which sell from $50 up to $1,500. Prices are higher for works in the gallery shows. *Pierogi Press* is a periodical featuring poetry, prose, and artwork.

SCHROEDER ROMERO. 173A No. 3rd St. near Bedford Ave., 486-8992, F–M noon–6 p.m. and by appointment, www.schroederromero.com.

This top-notch gallery gets its shows reviewed favorably by some of the toughest critics in town. Schroeder Romero's mission, simply, is to promote the work of emerging and midcareer artists in all mediums. They prefer solo shows. In 2003, they hosted a decade retrospective of Williamsburg art, called, appropriately, *Decade*. In general, they show contemporary art in all mediums. And who are "they"? Schroeder started FEED, one of the first Williamsburg galleries; Romero was with Holly Solomon Gallery and participated in the Guggenheim Museum's retrospective show *The Worlds of Nam June Paik*.

SOUTH FIRST. 60 No. 6th St. bet. Wythe and Kent Aves., 599-4884, F–Sa 1–9 p.m., Su 1–7 p.m. www.south first.com.

South First shows contemporary art by emerging artists, with a focus on project-based art. They also create affordable editions of selected work by emerging artists geared to new collectors; a set of ten artist editions costs $1,000.

WAH: WILLIAMSBURG ART & HISTORICAL SOCIETY. 135 Broadway underneath the Williamsburg Bridge, 486-7372, Sa–Su noon–6 p.m. or by appointment, www.wahcenter.org. See also **Kings County Savings Bank**, p. 443.

Located in a beautifully renovated 1868 bank building, WAH is a neighbor to Peter Luger Steak House—but instead of steaks or greenbacks it serves up the latest in Williamsburg art. The nonprofit gallery space, opened in 1997, has showcased everything from wild Coney Island poster art to the work of celebrated photographer Kim Iacono. The driving force behind it is Japanese-born painter Yuko Nii, who is a Pratt graduate and a Williamsburg resident.

It's a busy place. Its mission is to be a "multifaceted, multicultural art center," and there's a calendar of art shows, poetry, and staged readings, fashion shows, symposia, and lectures. Look for listings of annual events, namely: "Bridge" art shows (which have included artists from Cuba, Japan, Palestine, Russia, Slovenia, Turkmenistan, Vietnam, Israel, and Germany and other European nations); "Art & Ability"—shows of work by artists with disabilities; a January "Salon," showcasing local artists; a May dance festival, plus a film festival.

The Williamsburg Arts and Culture Festival features galleries, businesses, open studios, and a historical tour.

WAX—WILLIAMSBURG ART NEXUS. 5 No. 7th St. bet. Driggs Ave. and Roebling St., 599-7997, T–Su 10 a.m.–6 p.m. or by appointment, www.wax205.com. Call or check Web site for current festivals, shows, availability.

Call them facilitators. This is a nonprofit multidisciplinary arts center that offers affordable space for rehearsals and performances, including a fully equipped black-box theater and a visual-arts gallery. Opened in 2000 as a collective of four twenty-something performing artists, WAX is one response to the pocketbook reality of high Manhattan rents that forced many artists into Brooklyn in the late 1990s. WAX helps emerging artists who, simply, need a place to work and show their work.

Other Galleries

Other artist-run galleries that seem to be here to stay are listed below. Most are open only on the weekend, so call ahead or check local listings.

ASTERISK GALLERY. 258 Johnson Ave., 646-334-4019, www.asterisk-nyc.org.

It's a big space—five thousand square feet, on three levels. Watch for upcoming shows. If the trend follows this gallery, then the gallery/art scene is expanding into new territory. Expect a hodgepodge of music, art, and people.

BLACK & WHITE GALLERY. 483 Driggs Ave., 599-8775, Th–M 1–7 p.m., blackandwhiteartgallery.com.

Black & White Gallery is a venue for young American talent exploring contemporary themes and concepts through painting, drawing, photography, and sculpture.

BROOKLYN FIRE PROOF, INC. 101 Richardson St., 302-4702, Su–M 1–6 p.m.

CAVE. 58 Grand St. bet. Wythe and Kent Aves., 388-6780, F–Su 1–6, or by appointment.

DOLLHAUS. 37 Broadway, 384-6139, www.dollhaus.org.

An unusual sensibility defines the shows at this gallery—which is named after dolls but also the first mental institution for women in Germany.

EYEWASH. 387-2714.

Eyewash is a migratory gallery that mounts exhibitions throughout Williamsburg.

FIGUREWORKS. 168 No. 6th St., 486-7021, F–Su 1–6 p.m.

FISH TANK GALLERY. 93 No. 6th St., 387-4320, F–M noon–6 p.m.

FRONT ROOM. 147 Roebling St. at Metropolitan Ave., 782-2556, www.frontroom.org.

GALLERY PLUS. 145 Java St. (1 floor at Kurier Plus-Polish Weekly Magazine), 389-3018, www.freewilliamsburg.com/galleries.

GOOD/BAD ART COLLECTIVE. 383 So. 1st St. at Hooper St., 599-4962, www.goodbad.org.

HOLLAND TUNNEL. 61 So. 3rd St. bet. Berry St. and Wythe Ave., 384-5738, Sa–Su 1–5 p.m.

JACK THE PELICAN PRESENTS. 487 Driggs Ave., 782-0183, F–M noon–6 p.m.

LAZY J. 199 No. 7th St. at Driggs Ave., 302-1634, www.crossingthetsdottingtheis.com.

LUNAR BASE, INC. 197 Grand St. bet. Bedford and Driggs Aves., 599-9205, www.lunarbaseart.com.

MINE METAL/ART. 177 Grand St., 963-1184.

MODERN MEDIUMS. 104 Roebling St. at No. 6th St., 302-9507, www.modernmediums.com.

MONK GALLERY. 301 Bedford Ave. bet. So. 1st and So. 2nd Sts., 782-2458, www.monkgallery.com.

OPEN GROUND GALLERY. 252 Grand St. bet. Driggs and Roebling Sts., 387-8226, www.open-ground.org.

PARLOUR PROJECTS. 214 Devoe St. #1 bet. Bushwick Ave. and Humboldt St., 723-8626, Su noon—4 p.m. and by appointment.

PLUS ULTRA. 235 So. 1st St. past Roebling St., 387-3844, S—Su noon—6 p.m., www.plusultragallery.com.

PRISKA JUSCHKA FINE ART. 97 No. 9th St. bet. Berry St. and Wythe Ave., 782-4100 or 212-987-6177, Th—M noon—6 p.m. or by appointment, www.priskajuschkafineart.net.

ROEBLING HALL. 390 Wythe Ave. at So. 4th St., 599-5352, F—M noon—6 p.m., www.BrooklynArt.com.

SAFE-T-GALLERY. See *Greenpoint.*

SIDESHOW. 319 Bedford Ave., 486-8180, F—M noon—6 p.m., www.sideshowgallery.com.

SPACE 101. 101 No. 3rd St. bet. Berry St. and Wythe Ave., 218-6211, F—M noon—7 p.m.

65 HOPE ST. CERAMICS. 65 Hope St. bet. Marcy and Havemeyer Sts., 963-2028, Th—Su noon—8 p.m.
    More studio than gallery, for over a decade, Hope has created a community of artists working in ceramics. Monthly rentals available.

STAR 67. 67 Metropolitan Ave. 3rd flr. bet. Wythe and Kent Aves., 486-0387, F—Su noon—6 p.m., www.star67.org.

31 GRAND. 31 Grand St. at Kent Ave., 388-2858, Sa—M 1—7 p.m., www.31grand.com.

VELOCITY GALLERY. 281 No. 7th St., 302-1709.

Other Points of Contemporary Interest

BROOKLYN BREWERY. 79 No. 11th St., , free tours Sa noon—5 p.m., www.brooklynbrewery.com. Call for calendar of other special events.
    It's not just beer; it's a beer *culture.* The pride of Brooklyn, this fifteen-year-old brewery pumps out hearty brews, such as Brooklyn Lager, Brooklyn Weisse,

Brooklyn Brown Ale, Brooklyn East India Pale Ale, Blanche de Brooklyn, Black Chocolate Stout, Brooklyn Ale (originally Pennant Pale Ale), and special Monster barley wine. You'll find these and other craft-brews all across New York City. That thirst-quenching fact is due in part to Steve Hindy and Tom Potter (respectively a former foreign correspondent and a former banker), who founded Brooklyn Brewery and also have spurred the New York distribution of "world-class" beers imported from Belgium, Britain, and Germany.

Founded in Park Slope (where the two entrepreneurs were neighbors), Brooklyn Brewery opened the Williamsburg facility in 1996, marking Brooklyn's first commercial brewery in twenty years. Company material notes that pre-Prohibition Williamsburg was home to many breweries; one ten-block area with eleven breweries was known as Brewers Row. The Brooklyn Brewery's very modern brew house and tanks are set in at 1860s-era former iron foundry. (See listing p. 445.)

BROOKLYN INTERNATIONAL FILM FESTIVAL. www.brooklynfilmfestival.org.

Watch out, Sundance, here comes Brooklyn.

Started in 1997 in Williamsburg, the Brooklyn International Film Festival seeks to expose and promote local and international filmmakers—while feeding its audiences the best indie film the world has to offer. In 2003, they received over 1,500 submissions from seventy-three countries—and opened with a screening of the Merchant-Ivory–produced film *Merci Docteur Rey*. BIFF has shown features, documentaries, narrative shorts, and animated and experimental shorts. It's spirited, multicultural, diverse, sophisticated, and tolerant. And, growing too big for its original Williamsburg britches, BIFF has had to relocate to bigger venues at BAM and the Brooklyn Museum.

EL PUENTE COMMUNITY CENTER. 211 So. 4th St., 387-0404.

El Puente started as a community center dedicated to improving living conditions in the poor areas of Williamsburg. And they have had some successes; for instance, in helping to reclaim **Grand Ferry Park,** and in smoothing tensions that arise between different ethnic groups residing here. Success breeds success; they now also run four youth art companies: TEATRO EL PUENTE, EL PUENTE DANCE ENSEMBLE, EL PUENTE MURAL GROUP, and a youth videos production group. They won a 1999 National Endowment for the Arts Coming Up Taller Award for "outstanding arts programs nurturing the creative promise of young people."

☺ FESTIVAL OF THE GIGLIO

The highlight of this July festival honoring San Paolino di Nola is a procession in which several hundred men reenact an early medieval procession, complete with bands and dancing in the streets, by carrying a four-ton, sixty-five-foot painted wooden spire for a mile and a half. There's an accompanying street fair lasting over a week. If you are interested in religious festivals or ethnic celebrations, don't miss this one. (See **Our Lady of Mount Carmel Church.**)

Hasidic Community

Y̶ou can't miss them in the blocks on Bedford below Broadway, the men in long black coats and earlocks and women in modest, long-hemmed, long-sleeved styles. Their lives are built around Torah study, prayer, and adhering to the rigorous disciplines laid out in early and medieval Judaic scholarly writings.

Travel along Rutledge Road to view synagogues and yeshivas of the Satmar Hasidim housed in nineteenth-century mansions, like the one built by the founder of the company that became the Jack Frost sugar empire, or take note of the low-income housing on Kent Avenue, populated mostly by Hasidim. Known for their anti-Zionist views, they have counterparts living in Jerusalem who do not acknowledge the existence of the state of Israel, claiming that nationalism is a false route to the messianic era.

Almost by definition, the inward-looking, closed community of Satmar Hasidim is not interested in becoming a tourist attraction. And it is best not to disturb this pious community on holidays or Sabbath.

To better understand this lifestyle, see the PBS documentary *A Life Apart: Hasidism in America,* filmed primarily in Brooklyn.

OFFICEOPS. 57 Thames St. near Morgan Ave. L stop, 418–2509, www.officeops.org.

Bushwick is becoming East Williamsburg. Witness OfficeOps, described by the Brooklyn Arts Council as a "creative arts and industry community center." They provide facilities for independent promotion, production, and presentation of media, performance, photographic, literary, and educational disciplines. And their **Rooftop Films** shows flicks on the roof in the summer.

PUBLIC SCHOOLS.

Children Charter School (11 Bartlett Street) is considered to be among New York City's best public elementary schools. (Source: *New York City's Best Public Elementary Schools,* 2002, by C. Hemphill.)

RABBI J. TEITELBAUM PLACE. Williamsburg St. East and Marcy Ave.

This picturesque Old World intersection, a retail area peppered with small

Jewish stores located under the BQE, is named after the religious leader of the
Satmar Hasidim, Rabbi Joel Teitelbaum.

SLICK'S MOTORCYCLE REPAIR. Wythe Ave. and No. 1st St.

No, that long row of motorcycles is not a bikers' club, just the shop of an idio-
syncratic longtime resident and entrepreneur, "Slick," who sometimes runs his
TV outside on warm summer nights while fixing motorcycles.

Points of Historical and Architectural Interest

DOMINO SUGAR FACTORY. Kent Ave. from So. 1st to 5th Sts.

The dark, hulking factory that dominates Kent Ave. has been sweetening the
Williamsburg waterfront for more than a hundred years. Until 2003, a meager
staff of several hundred workers ran a twenty-four-hour-a-day automated operation, offloading sacks of sugar from boats that arrived at the refinery's docks.
Real estate developers have been eyeing this prime site, which commands views
of Manhattan's midtown skyline.

KINGS COUNTY SAVINGS BANK. 135 Broadway.

A New York City landmark, the 1860s Kings County Savings Bank is "one of
New York's most magnificent French Second Empire buildings," according
to the *Guide to New York City Landmarks*. Today it houses **WAH Center** (see
listing, p. 438).

NEW ENGLAND CONGREGATIONAL CHURCH. 79 So. 9th St.

Built in the 1850s in New England style by settlers from that region of the
United States, the New England Congregational Church represents an unusual
combination of brownstone materials and Italianate style. It is a New York City
landmark.

OUR LADY OF MOUNT CARMEL CHURCH. 275 No. 8th St., 384-0223, by appointment.

This church organizes The Feast of Our Lady of Mount Carmel and San
Paolino, one of New York City's most famous Italian festivals and street fairs,
held every July.

❷ REALFORM GIRDLE BUILDING. 218 Bedford Ave bet. No. 4th and No. 5th Sts.

This is Williamsburg's quaint concept of a mall: an old factory building with
a central hallway and a bunch of shops for locals and tourists alike. Here you will
find the not-inexpensive **Bedford Cheese Shop**; the Internet Garage, that fabulous alternative to Kinko's, a neighborhood place run by Hasidim where hipsters
can log on; **Spoonbill & Sugartown Books** and **Earwax**, where you can buy indie

music and feed your mind and soul, respectively; a few sexy clothing boutiques, such as **Otte**; a yoga place; and, of course, the **Verb Café**, for that first cup of morning coffee (even if it's almost noon).

RENAISSANCE ESTATES AND RHEINGOLD GARDENS. Area bounded by Forrest St., Stanwix St., Melrose St., and Bushwick Ave. (in Bushwick).

There's a new, attractive, suburban-style development of almost three hundred affordable homes, including condos (the first in the area), rental units, plus amenities like a day-care center and community center here. And lots of green open spaces. It was built on the once fetid, abandoned 6.7-acre site of the old Rheingold Brewery plant. The effort required collaboration by community leaders with urban planners from Columbia University and environmental experts in brownfield cleanup. This is a major development that promises to spark a spruce-up of nearby Bushwick Avenue.

WILLIAMSBURGH BRANCH OF BROOKLYN PUBLIC LIBRARY. 240 Division St. at Marcy Ave., 302-3485. Currently closed for renovation.

Check out this old library, called "the finest of all the branch buildings" by the editor of the *Brooklyn Times* in 1905. This 26,000-square-foot Classical Revival building was built between 1903 and 1905 with funds from a large gift given by Andrew Carnegie to New York City. (Of the $5.2 million given by Carnegie for the construction of new library buildings, $1.6 million was earmarked to build twenty branches in Brooklyn.) This site was chosen because of the huge population in the district and the tremendous need for a library here. The original featured a central-delivery desk, radially arranged stacks, wood wainscoting, and fireplaces. The library was renovated in 1953 and landmarked in 1999.

WILLIAMSBURG BRIDGE. Walkway entrance on Brooklyn side is at Williamsburg Bridge Plaza, Driggs Ave. and Broadway; on the Manhattan side, at Delancey St.

The views of Manhattan are spectacular. And, oh, is there history. Immigrants escaped tenement life to the fresh air of Brooklyn via this bridge. Jazz great Sonny Rollins spent much time playing atop the bridge's footpath and in 1962 released an album called, appropriately, *The Bridge*.

Bikers, strollers, runners, walkers, and the subway J, M, and Z lines also cross regularly. Until 1994, when cracks were discovered in the span, the more secluded sections of the bridge were a favorite site for not-quite-legal birthday parties, rock concerts, Halloween parades, and other rollicking festivities. Today about four hundred people a day cross the Williamsburg Bridge, from Hasidim pushing baby carriages to joggers fresh from art class. The bridge turned one hundred years old in 2003.

WILLIAMSBURG HOUSES. Maujer St. to Scholes St., Leonard St. to Bushwick Ave.

This public-housing project, built in 1937, was the first of many in New York City. Many experts still consider it to be one of the best, with its low, four-story buildings with courtyards, columned entrances, and other visual amenities.

WILLIAMSBURGH SAVINGS BANK. 175 Broadway.

When built, this was a Williamsburgh Savings Bank. Located at the foot of the Williamsburg Bridge, it's an Italian Renaissance–style building from the early twentieth century. It is a landmark.

ENTERTAINMENT

Note: In our 1999 edition, we wrote, "Williamsburg is one short subway stop from Manhattan, many residents take the L train into town for entertainment." Increasingly, the traffic flow now goes the *other* way.

☛ **TIP: 11211**
Named after the zip code for Williamsburg, this advertising-supported magazine, like so much in Williamsburg, is itself a youthful multimedia enterprise. *11211* is at once a business, a community-building campaign, a self-styled editorial platform, and maybe a piece of conceptual art-in-progress. This slick-looking freebie, found stacked in almost any popular Williamsburg venue (and some like-minded East Village joints), is one of several free publications that take the pulse of the neighborhood. www.11211.com

BROOKLYN BREWERY AND TOURS/EVENTS. 79 No. 11th St., 486-7422, free tours Sa noon–5 p.m. "Tasting Panel" F 6 p.m.–10 p.m., www.brooklynbrewery.com.

Brooklyn Brewery events always draw a large crowd of locals and visiting beer lovers. Call or check the company Web site calendar. There's an annual June Critic's Choice Summer Beer and Food Festival featuring dozens of Brooklyn's best restaurants, and **Friday night tastings**.

🐾 *Free!* ☺ ✪ **BARC DOG PARADE.** 486-7489, www.barcshelter.org. September.

This annual pet parade is a Brooklyn Mardi Gras with a doggie theme. A thousand costumed pets and their owners (some dressed like dogs) march through the main streets of Williamsburg to music played, incongruously, by the local Italian marching band associated with the religious Giglio festival, and the local hipster **Hungry Marching Band**. Like Coney Island's Mermaid Parade, a carnival atmosphere takes over as streamers and confetti fly, and one imaginative float after another entertains thousands of onlookers.

For $1, you can enter contests such as the "Patty Duke Pet and Owner

Look-Alike," "J. Lo Best Butt Contest," and "Coco Chanel Best Dressed Dogs." The parade, conceived in 1987, starts at **BQE Pets** and ends at **McCarren Park**. Proceeds go to the dog shelter.

Dancing, Music, Performance, and Night Scenes
(more than just a bar)

♪ **BOOGALOO.** 168 Marcy Ave. bet. Broadway and So. 5th St., 599-8900, T–Su 6 p.m.–4 a.m. Subway: G to Metropolitan Ave.; J, M, Z to Marcy Ave.; L to Lorimer St.

Boogaloo is for people who *wake up* at night. You can count on DJs, local and not-so-local bands, and occasionally mind-bending electronic music—always something different. It's a touch glam, with sensational red sectional seating and a bar that's lit from below.

♪ **BROOKLYN LOFT.** 250 Varet St. bet. Bushwick Ave. and White St., 386-3615, F–Sa 2 a.m.–noon, www.robpromotions.com. Call for program or check the Web site.

If your idea of dancin' the night away is to keep on partying well past sunrise on Sunday mornings, the Brooklyn Loft's "718" parties were, as of 2003, one place to go. Après-party parties here start at about two a.m. and wind down just in time for a late Sunday brunch. Absolutely the only way to arrive is by cab.

CLEM'S. 264 Grand St., 387-9617, M–F 4 p.m.–4 a.m., Sa–Su 2 p.m.–4–a.m.

An austere, clean space, Clem's makes no pretensions to be anything other than a corner saloon, furnished in a timeless style with a handsome dark bar and matching custom shelving behind. Splurge on a $7 specialty cocktail, or save with a bottled or draught beer. Clem is the guy with sandy hair and glasses.

♪ **GALAPAGOS.** 70 No. 6th St. bet. Wythe and Kent Aves., 782-5188, Su–Th 6 p.m.–2 a.m., F–Sa 6 p.m.–4 a.m. Cash only.

Galapagos, a multimedia warehouse space opened back in 1988, is the brain-child of Robert Elms, whose idea for the nondescript building was to mix it up with rock and DJ music, and edgy dance, theater, and various hybrids of performance art. Come for movies, music, beer, and a scene.

IVY SOUTH. 270 So. 5th St. off Berry St., 599-5623, daily 6 p.m.–4 a.m.

The newest place to rock out.

♪ **LEVEL X.** 107 No. 6th St. bet. Berry St. and Wythe Ave., 302-3313, daily 6 p.m.–4 a.m.

The only thing fishy, aside from the fact that the $5–$9 drinks are more expensive than elsewhere in the area, is that this fashionable DJ bar is a renovated fish market. There's nightly music, a large bar, and a well-heeled young clientele. It's slicker than many older, grittier places.

♫ **M. SHANGHAI BISTRO & DEN.** 129 Havemeyer St. bet Grand and So. 1st Sts., 384-9300, restaurant Tu–Su 5 p.m.–midnight, F–Sa 5 p.m.–2 a.m.; dim sum brunch Sa–Su 11 a.m.–4 p.m.; bar Su–W 5 p.m.–2 a.m., Th–Sa 5 p.m.–1 a.m.; Den Tu–Sa 9 p.m.–4 a.m., www.mshanghaiden.com.

Part Chinese restaurant (upstairs) and part music club Den (downstairs), this joint is a hangout spot near the Lorimer stop on the L train. The crowd is quirky, as are the live musical performances, which include bluegrass and jazz (Thursday), electro (Friday), and disco (Saturday). Check out the cozy back booth. A new Japanese market, KOI, is opening soon next door.

♫ **NORTH SIXTH.** 66 No. 6th St. bet. Kent and Wythe Aves., 599-5103, M–Th 4 p.m.–2 a.m., Sa 4 p.m.–4 a.m., Su noon–1 a.m., www.northsix.com.

North Sixth has made a reputation as a hot music club with indie music, live shows, and lots of dancing. It encompasses several spaces, including a large concert hall equipped with a real stage, good sound equipment, an open dance floor, and a bar that's big enough to accommodate a crowd of several hundred. There are shows upstairs and downstairs, with covers between $5 and $10.

PETE'S CANDY STORE. 709 Lorimer St. bet. Frost and Richardson Sts., 302-3770, Su–T 5 p.m.–2 a.m., W 5 p.m.–3 a.m., Th–Sa 5 p.m.–4 a.m.

Pete's Candy Store is a watering hole, music venue, and home-away-from-home for the late-twenties to early-thirties hipster-and-posthipster set. The dim interior is impeccably shabby chic, with a minuscule performance space and the air of an old vaudeville stage—hardly a shocker, given that one of the owners is a set designer. (Yes, Pete's was once a candy store.) All the retro is endearing; the bar sells old cocktail favorites, such as the Sidecar, Grasshopper, and Dark & Stormy, for $6–$8.

Musically, Pete's has mostly a mellow country, folk, and bluegrass arena vibe. On Sunday nights in the summer, the staff fires up the grill outdoors and serves heaping plates of BBQ for the bargain price of $6. There is a Bingo Night (Tuesday) and Quiz Night (Wednesday).

♫ **STINGER CLUB.** 241 Grand St. bet. Driggs Ave. and Roebling St. (just east of Driggs Ave.), 218-6662, daily 6 p.m.–4 a.m., www.thestingerclub.com. Cash only.

Red light suffuses this space, glaring off the red vinyl booths and liquor bottles. It's a dark, sexy vibe with live music seven nights a week, usually rock, bluegrass, or indie rock, with a DJ spinning late nights. Sometimes there's a cover, in the $3–$5 range. That's affordable for both the sideways mobile twenty-somethings and the multi-ethnic, multicultural patrons. Out back in the garden, you can use the *kamado* (sort of a hibachi) for do-it-yourself grilling (hot dogs and Jamaican jerk chicken, for instance).

In the event you're feeling particularly wild and want some free drinks, make sure you check out the "Super Specials" on the menu, unprintable here.

♪ **WILLIAMSBURG MUSIC CENTER.** 367 Bedford Ave. at So. 5th St., 384-1654, Sa 2–6 p.m. Cash only.

You can catch a jazz performance workshop featuring local singers and instrumentalists working out their latest riffs.

Theater and Film

BLACK MOON THEATRE CO. 140 Clay St., 389-2929, www.blackmoontheatrecompany.org.

The edgy, modernist productions of Black Moon Theatre Company, under the direction of René Migliaccio, have received some critical acclaim in recent years. This multiethnic company follows a school called "expressionistic realism." They're eclectic, borrowing from classic and non-Western genres, combining traditional techniques with multimedia effects. Log on to their Web site for a Black Moon dramatic moment.

BRICK THEATER. 575 Metropolitan Ave. bet. Union Ave. and Lorimer Sts., 907-3457, www.bricktheater.com.

Watch listings for music, theater, dance, and mixed media at the performance space here. The first Sunday night of each month, The Brick hosts a regular variety show titled "Sunday Brick-a-Brac." Don't let the cheap tickets ($5) fool you. This new theater is ambitious, and its early productions were intellectually demanding. (During the 2003 Iraq War, they hosted actor/writer Wallace Shawn's *Designated Mourner* and subsequently produced *Habitat*, by downtown theater personality Michael Gardner.)

CHARLIE PINEAPPLE THEATER. 248B No. 8th St. near Driggs Ave., 907-0577.

This small local theater, opened in 2002 by a husband-and-wife team, aims to produce five plays annually, showcasing established and emerging playwrights, dance, and music. In between shows, they rent out the space for dance rehearsals, yoga, and so on. With its de rigueur art gallery (this *is,* after all, Williamsburg), they are a welcome addition to the local cultural fruit salad.

COMBUSTIVE ARTS AKA COMBUSTIVE MOTOR CORP. 250 Varet St. near White St., 390-8825. L train to Morgan Ave. Call for directions.

Combustive Arts is one of the surprises you'll discover that suggest change is afoot in Bushwick. It's a performing arts space with edgy taste, and a center for film, shows, and events for the growing art community in Bushwick. For similar developments, see **OfficeOps.**

OCULARIS FILMS. 70 No. 6th St. bet. Wythe and Kent Aves., 388-8713, www.ocularis.net. Call for schedule and times; only occasional showings. Cash only.

Ocularis is Williamsburg's funky, fabulous local movie theater. Like Siamese twins, Ocularis and the now-famous **Galapagos** are joined at the hip. They share a space in what used to be an old mayonnaise factory (there are still vats overhead). You walk in, and you're in Galapagos, a well-designed bar and performance space, with a little indoor pond that makes the environment feel simultaneously industrial and tropical, like a nice, dark urban jungle. Ocularis is housed in the back room of Galapagos. You literally walk through the bar to get there.

Ocularis has matured into a full-fledged art theater, with programming that pundits call "intelligent."

Ocularis was started by a young Irishman who started showing movies on his roof. It became a kind of homemade movie theater determined to run first-rate independent, cult, and classic films, and for years it did so only on Sunday nights. It's grown from a place where local filmmakers screened their fresh, often experimental material (this still happens) to a media center with glossy brochures, impressive speakers, and day trippers from Manhattan. There's sometimes live music beforehand, and a BYOB policy.

PARKS AND PLAYGROUNDS

GRAND FERRY PARK. Grand and River Sts. on the waterfront bet. the Domino Sugar Factory and the ConEd Factory. About a ten-minute walk to the Williamsburg Bridge and twenty minutes to the L train stop at Bedford Ave.

The views! There's an open cobblestone area, a stone footbridge, and a cute picnic area. Manhattan looms right across the water. Climb up to the viewing mound to get a sweeping look at the East River. The seventy-foot smokestack remains, a relic from the Pfizer Chemical Company that once had big plants here.

Between 1800 and 1918, Grand Ferry Park served as a ferry landing for boats shuttling passengers every five minutes between Brooklyn and Manhattan's Grand Street on the Lower East Side. In 1974, **El Puente** Williamsburg community youth organization created an open public space at the landing, which eventually led to the establishment of this lovely riverside park, opened in 1998. It was a small, sweet victory for locals, who for twenty-five years had been trying to expand public access to the waterfront. (See **What's New,** p. 431.)

☺ ✪ **METROPOLITAN POOL.** 261 Bedford Ave. corner of Metropolitan Ave., 599-5707. Call for times.

This beautiful, copper-ceilinged indoor public pool underwent a multimillion-dollar renovation, reopening in 1997. Originally called Metropolitan Bathhouse, it was built in 1922 when public bathing facilities were high on the priority list for improving the health of poor immigrant communities. The original architect was Henry Bacon, who also designed the Lincoln Memorial. Today it is gleaming new, and one of only ten city-owned indoor pools in the Big Apple.

There's a Ladies Only swim time (M, W, F 10 a.m.–noon) for Orthodox Jewish women and others who prefer privacy. A $75 annual membership buys access to the pool, weight room, and computer rooms upstairs—and to public pools at Asser Levy, Sunset Park, or Red Hook.

WILLIAMSBURG RESTAURANTS AND CAFÉS

New Williamsburg
Sweets and Cafés

✪ **BLISS.** 191 Bedford Ave. bet. No. 6th and 7th Sts., 599-2547, M–F 9 a.m.–11 p.m., Sa–Su 10 a.m.–11 p.m. Cash only.

For organic vegan cuisine, come to this tiny, upbeat café located on the main drag and decorated with the work of local painters. Heaping salads, marinated tofu sandwiches, and various combinations of healthful foods, plus combos of freshly squeezed fruit and vegetable juices, are the draw here.

FABIANES CAFÉ AND PASTRY SHOP. 142 No. 5th bet. 1st and 2nd Sts., 218-9632, M–Sa 7:30 a.m.–11 p.m., Su 7:30 a.m.–8 p.m.

Airy and brightly lit, this large and upscale café offers up a creative selection of desserts and fresh sandwiches. Feast on a *dulce de leche* cupcake ($2) or arguably Brooklyn's best lemon tart topped with fresh raspberries ($4). Try a mozzarella, pesto, and tomato sandwich of the toasted persuasion, served atop a bed of arugula salad ($6).

L CAFÉ. 189 Bedford Ave. near the L train stop, 388-6792, daily 9 a.m.–midnight, Sa–Su 10 a.m.–midnight. Cash only.

The tourist buses haven't started to come to Williamsburg yet, but surely someday the history of arty "Billyburg" will be written—and when it is, the L Café will take its place in the sun. This charmingly shabby little joint, named after the "L" subway stop on the corner, has long been a good place to hang around and find out about impromptu shows, bands, and neighborhood news. A shady outdoor dining area in back is a relaxing place to enjoy bagels, focaccia sandwiches, and endless coffee as you while away an afternoon reading the paper or planning your next move.

MAMA'S ICES. Corner Lorimer and Metropolitan. No phone. Open seasonally.

A local hangout place that sells ices and Italian sausage, you can't miss Mama's. Just look for the bright yellow trailer.

SAL'S PIZZERIA. 544 Lorimer St. corner Metropolitan Ave., 388-6838.

More than a pizzeria, Sal's, opened in 1967, dishes up great big heroes (try the veal and peppers) and pasta specials like penne with grilled chicken, spinach, or broccoli, baked casseroles of stuffed shells and ravioli, and more. This is a hungry workingman/woman's kind of place.

⊘ **SQUEEZE.** 198 Bedford Ave. at No. 6th St., 782-9181, daily 8 a.m.–9 p.m.

Squeezed into a tiny space, this cheery, postage stamp–sized shop is beloved by locals who need a quick, inexpensive health-food fix. You can find spicy soy hot dogs, veggie chili, sprout-stuffed sandwiches, and lots of freshly squeezed (or is it squoozen?) juices. Squish into a corner to munch here, or take out.

THE READ CAFÉ. 158 Bedford Ave. bet. No. 8th and No. 9th Sts., 599-3032, M–Th 8 a.m.–10 p.m., F 10 a.m.–11 p.m., Sa–Su 9 a.m.–10 p.m., www.thereadcafe.com.

A quaint, rustic café, tiny Read Café stands out because of its large purchasable library with an eclectic collection of art, philosophy, and poetry books. Patrons are invited to gorge on homemade soups, chai, pastries, and coffees, along with some good literature. Folk art, bookshelves, and magazine racks holding independent magazines line the walls. It's a good place to pick up fliers about neighborhood happenings.

Restaurants

ACQUA SANTA. 556 Driggs Ave. at No. 7th St. 384-9695, M–Th 5–11 p.m., F 5 p.m.–midnight, Sa 11 a.m.–midnight, Su 11 a.m.–11 p.m.

Acqua Santa is a small trattoria that is known for its big, provocative mural (go see for yourself)—and rustic Italian food. Try the gourmet pizza selections, simple pastas, and the filet mignon. It's quieter than some other "Billyburg" joints. Brunch in the garden is a favorite. Average entrées are $14.

♫ **ALLIOLI.** 291 Grand St. bet. Havemeyer and Roebling Sts. 218-7338, M–W and Su 6 p.m.–midnight, Th–Sa 6 p.m.–1 a.m.

Like garlic? Want to check out the latest hot neighborhood in Williamsburg?

Try chef José Diego Gonzalez's generously portioned tapas, such as grilled sardines, baby squid, tomatoes, basil, and *tostada con anchoas de l'escala*. On Thursdays, you can dine while flamenco dancers spin. In fine weather, relax in the garden where leafy trees, uneven flagstones, and neighborhood noise reassure you that you're not in Galicia, Spain, whence this cuisine originated. Entrées are in the $15 range; tapas are about $5 apiece.

ANYTIME. 93 No. 6th St. bet. Berry St. and Wythe Ave., 218-7272, 24/7.

Open "anytime," you can eat in or take out. This place makes you feel like the Food Fairy: you wave your magic wand and voilà, a meal appears. Creative folks who keep unconventional hours should keep this restaurant front and central in their Blackberrys. Low prices.

BEAN. No. 8th St. off Bedford Ave., 387-8222, daily 5–11 p.m.

This informal restaurant serves up tasty Mexican food. The burritos in particular are *deliciosos*. Try the jicama salad or fried *bacalao* served with chipotle cream and *pico de gallo*, and top it off with a homemade fruit cobbler of the day. Other specials include turkey mole, dairy-free *yucadillas*, and fresh, tasty guacamole. Dinner costs under $10.

BONITA. 338 Bedford Ave. bet. So. 2nd and So. 3rd Sts., 384-9500, Su–Th 11 a.m.–11:30 p.m., F–Sa 11 a.m.–midnight.

Bonita tends to please those who *don't* like it hot. Opened by the owners of the popular **Diner** nearby, Bonita serves up good appetizers and features a diner-style counter. Good sangria, good food, inexpensive.

CARMAYA. 139 No. 6th St. bet. Bedford Ave. and Berry St., 302-4441, M–F 6 p.m.–midnight, Sa–Su noon–midnight.

Some locals complain that it's touristy, because Carmaya is distinguished by an unusually high-tech decorative touch. But the bar is friendly, and there's a good selection of tasty Italian dishes. Cornballs will appreciate touches like "salami" dessert (actually thinly sliced biscotti covered with fudge). There's a garden, too. Average entrées in $15 range.

CHEERS THAI RESTAURANT. 612 Metropolitan Ave. bet. Lorimer and Leonard Sts., 599-4311, M–Th 11:30 a.m.–11 p.m., F–Sa 11:30 a.m.–11 p.m., Su 1–11 p.m.

There's a patio open in the summer, and a full menu of well-prepared Thai dishes, including "bosom friend" (shrimp and calamari in spicy chili sauce), curries, and vegetarian dishes. A local favorite.

CHICKENBONE CAFÉ. 177 So. 4th St. bet. Driggs Ave. and Roebling St., 302-2663, Tu–W and Su 5 p.m.–2 a.m., Th–Sa 5 p.m.–4 a.m.

The South Side, where it's typical to find an abandoned, graffitied building next to an unspeakably hip bar, is the grittier and noisier counterpart to Williamsburg's hipster-laden northern section. Chickenbone Café, located one block from the bridge and the BQE, rides that same line between raw and polished. Cedar paneling, exposed brick wall, and a metal bar impart a textured industrial feel, yet the dim lighting and smell of cedar give the place an air of coziness and warmth. The menu consists of light bites, such as soup, salad, sandwiches, and sweets, with an internationally inspired twist. (Note the Vietnamese sausage, foie gras, coconut curry, and dried beef from former Yugoslavia.) The place is bursting with personality; note little blurbs describing the history of each mixed drink—written by a man whose specialty is ancient mathematic poetry. Entrées under $10.

CHICKEN EMPORIUM. 545 Lorimer St. corner of Devoe St., 302-3000, daily 10 a.m.–11 p.m.

"Indian and soulful American food" is what they advertise here, and indeed, you can get a full menu of Indian foods, from *daal poori* to veggie *jalfrazi* to mulligatawny soup. Or you can stick with a good ol' tuna salad or a "gosht BLT"—a naan bread wrapped around lamb, bacon, lettuce, tomato, and curried mayo. You can eat here at a little table, but it's better to take out. Entrées are under $9.

DINER. 85 Broadway off Berry St., 486-3077, lunch noon–4 p.m., dinner 6 p.m.–midnight.

Like at the Empire Diner in Manhattan, things are jumping at this restored 1922 diner with a retro feel and booth seating for about forty-five people. Even Inspector Clouseau wouldn't miss the French flair here—cassoulet, mussels, French fries, and steak—amid the otherwise down-home Americana: fried or roasted chicken with sides of spinach, mashed potatoes, and other comfort foods. Save room for Kate's killer chocolate cake. The bar serves wine, beer, and hard liquor, and it is busy all day until two a.m. Entrées are under $12.

FADA. 530 Driggs Ave. at No. 8th St., 388-6607, daily 5 p.m.–midnight.

You don't have to hike to Smith Street or Manhattan to find a good French bistro. Fada is located just about a block from the L train stop. It tends toward flavorful Provençal French dishes that have more personality than the very simple décor. Fada appeals to a Euro crowd.

KASIA. 146 Bedford Ave. corner No. 9th St., 387-8780, M–F 6 a.m.–9 p.m. Cash only.

A Polish-American diner, Kasia feeds the neighborhood breakfast, chicken soup, and other steamy, home-cooked meals. It's just like eating at Mom's: homemade, delicious, and almost as cheap.

MOTO. 394 Broadway corner of Hooper St., 599-6895, Su–Th 6 p.m.–2 a.m., F–Sa 6 p.m.–3 a.m., www.cir call938.com.

Little, hip, and cheap, Moto is conveniently located between the two nonhipster populations who also live in Williamsburg: Hasidim and Puerto Ricans. There's panini for lunch and edgy entertainment in the evening, recently by a group called Nervous Cabaret.

OZNOT'S DISH. No. 9th St. at Berry St., 599-6596, M–Th 11 a.m.–11 p.m., F 11 a.m.–midnight, Sa 10 a.m.– midnight, Su 10 a.m.–11 p.m.

From its unusual name to its eclectic menu to its artful Indo-Moroccan décor, Oznot's remains an original. Oznot's takes traditional fare and turns it on its ear by adding Mediterranean, Moroccan, and Indian flavorings, christening brunch dishes with quirky titles like "camel boy eggs" and "*gulabi's* French toast." To be a chef here one needs to be an experimenter who rarely fails. The sunny patio is perfect for those relaxing, bottomless-coffee-cup brunches. Ask about their top-notch wine and beer selection.

PLANET THAILAND. 133 No. 7th St. off Bedford Ave., 599-5758, Su–Th 11:30 a.m.– 1 a.m., F–Sa 11:30–2 a.m.

A neighborhood staple, Planet Thailand remains a hot spot that's often crowded at dinner, and although the service can be frantic, the food is delicious and cheap. If all the seats are taken, eat at the counter and watch the chef whirl, sizzle, and steam as he juggles thirty orders with a beatific smile. Expect local art on the walls, local artists at the tables. The average entrée costs $8.

RELISH. 225 Wythe Ave., at No. 3rd St., 963-4546, M–F 11 a.m.–midnight, Sa–Su 11:30–1:30 a.m.

Nostalgic, romantic, young "Billyburg" supports *three* retro diners. Relish is a popular spot housed in an old silver boxcar. Feast on well-prepared foods from your American childhood (you don't have to bring a dictionary to deconstruct this menu). Locals, um, relish the inviting lounge and, weather permitting, the garden area.

♫ **SEA.** 114 No. 6th St. at Berry St., 384-8850, Su–Th 11:30–1 a.m., F–Sa 11:30–2 a.m. Reservations only for large parties.

SEA is big and modern and Thai, but the prices are strictly Chinatown cheap. The space is made for large parties, with two bars, plus a DJ, lounge chairs, and a waterfall-reflecting pool. There's a huge menu—and not just seafood, either.

♫ **TEDDY'S BAR AND GRILL.** 96 Berry St. at No. 8th St., 384-9787, Su–Th. 11 a.m.–midnight, F–Sa 11– 2 a.m. Cash only.

Teddy's front room has atmosphere up the wazoo (it was established in 1894, before the Williamsburg Bridge was built) with Brooklyn-made stained-glass windows and an old-fashioned ceiling. (But if you want to talk, skip the ambience and head for the boring but quieter back room.) The crowd is a mix of visitors, blue-collar end-of-the-bar types, and local artisans. Depending on the evening, you may catch some jazz, funk, or country music. On Saturday nights Teddy's livens up with a DJ who spins good music for dancing. Festivities gear up around 9:30 p.m. The food's fine, the beer is fresh (Brooklyn Brewery is nearby), and the chips are delicious. Teddy's Bloody Marys are just what the doc ordered for Sunday morning blues.

♫ **VERA CRUZ.** 195 Bedford Ave. bet. No. 6th and 7th Sts., 599-7914, M–Th 4–11:30 p.m., F–Sa 4 p.m.–midnight, Su 2–11 p.m. Reservations are recommended.

Vera Cruz is a hip little Mexican joint (instead of sombreros on the walls, you'll see retro photos of a Mexican Marilyn Monroe look-alike). You come here for the ambience: the sidewalk bar scene and cozy garden dining in the summer, the friendly chat among locals, and sometimes extraordinary live music with, say, leading Afro-Cuban musicians. The stick-roasted corn *con queso* and cactus-salad appetizers are delicious, but many main courses—fajitas, enchiladas, and the like—are standard fare. Good service; costs about $25 per person.

WASABI. 205 Bedford Ave. bet. No. 5th and No. 7th Sts., 302-2035, daily noon–3 p.m., 5–11 p.m.

It's not the most sophisticated sushi in town, but the portions are ample. Wasabi also has branches in Greenpoint (638 Manhattan Avenue) and Carroll Gardens (213 Smith Street).

Old Williamsburg
Restaurants

ANTOJITO'S MEXICANOS. 105 Graham Ave. bet. Boerum and McKibben Sts., 384-9076, daily 8 p.m.– 8 p.m.

Revisit your college-era, backpacking, poor-as-dirt trip to Mexico City here, with a meal of goat tacos, quesadillas, and *pambazos* (that's a fried roll grilled with sausage and potatoes).

BAMONTE'S. 32 Withers St. bet. Union and Lorimer Sts., 384-8831, M and W–Th noon–10 p.m., F–Sa noon–11 p.m., Su noon–10 p.m.

Classic Italian fare is served at this big, popular, old-fashioned family restaurant known for its white-shirted waiters, dim lighting, and big portions. Bamonte's has been in business for over a century, which explains the velvet drapes, linoleum, and gold décor. Meat entrées cost $18 on average, and the pasta, which is excellent, costs somewhat less.

CUCHIFRITOS. 293 Broadway corner of Marcy Ave. No telephone, 24/7.

Unpretentious and clean, little Cuchifritos is tucked underneath the elevated J/M Marcy Avenue subway stop. It specializes in traditional fast food, Puerto Rican–style. Rumor has it that aficionados come from all over the city for the *alcapurrias,* stuffed plantains, sausages, ribs, and soups. If your restaurant Spanish isn't up to snuff, just get up, look in the pots to see what's cooking, and point out what you want.

GRAHAM AVENUE—A SNAPSHOT OF TRANSITION

Williamsburg has changed so much, it's hard, walking down Bedford, to remember that this is a neighborhood in transition. From what? Walk down heterogeneous Graham Avenue, lined with three-story buildings, reminiscent of a small-town main street with new and old intermingled:

CARMINE'S PIZZERIA. 346 Graham Ave. off Metropolitan Ave., 782-9659, daily 11 a.m.–11 p.m.
   Old. An old-fashioned pizzeria, some say it's the best in the neighborhood.

PHOEBE'S. 323 Graham Ave., 599-3218, M–F 8 a.m.–8 p.m., Sa–Su 9:30 a.m.–8 p.m.
   New. A fellow in granny glasses pores over a *New York Times* editorial here midmorning, nursing a third cup of coffee.

THE NINES. 320 Graham Ave., 218-6040, T–Su noon–9 p.m.
   New. Hipster's heaven. A great sense of style informs the collection of vintage and designer clothes and accessories.

S. CONO'S PIZZERIA. 303 Graham Ave., 782-3199, daily 7 a.m.–10 p.m. Cash only.
   Old. Park your ambivalence elsewhere, because you get to choose from fifteen different sauces for your pizza and pasta: from *scungilli* marinara to primavera to seasonal broccoli rabe.

CONO AND SONS O'PESCATORE. 301 Graham Ave. at Ainslie St., 388-0168, M–Th 11 a.m.–10 p.m., Sa 11 a.m.–midnight, Su 11 a.m.–10 p.m.
   Old. Long-established Cono and Sons is a white-tablecloth, family-run neighborhood institution where the waiters are professionals (not actors waiting for their first off-off-Broadway call). The portions are big. Entrées range from $12 to $20.

GIANDO ON THE WATER. 400 Kent Ave. 387-7000, M–Th, noon–9:30 p.m., F noon–10 p.m., Sa 4 p.m.–midnight, Su 3–10 p.m.

Giando's view is extraordinary—you can gawk at New York's famous skyline from midtown to the tip of Manhattan Island. A favorite among Japanese tourists who come by the busload, according to some old-timers, Giando is almost "too nice for the neighborhood." The dress code spans informal to dressy, and the Italian food and service are good. Bring your parents and try the Sunset Dinner—it's a full gourmet meal.

GOTTLEIB'S RESTAURANT. 352 Roebling St. at Division St., 384-9037, M–Th 10 a.m.–9 p.m., F 10 a.m.–2:30 p.m., Su noon–5 p.m. Kosher.

One of Brooklyn's *frummest* kosher delis, Gottleib's is a sit-down restaurant with great corned beef and other traditional Jewish meat dishes, located near the Williamsburg Bridge.

GREEN & ACKERMAN DAIRY RESTAURANT. 216 Ross St. bet. March and Lee Aves., 625-0117, Su–Th 11 a.m.–7:45 p.m., F 8 a.m.–3 p.m. Kosher.

Vhat's on the menu at this large kosher dairy restaurant, you *vant* to know? It changes every day. But always, there are three kinds of soup, blintzes, fish, rice, sandwiches of all kinds. And endless amounts of Eastern European advice dispensed along with it.

LA LACONDA. 32 Graham Ave. bet. Withers and Frost Sts., 349-7800, M–Sa 11 a.m.–11 p.m. Cash only. Weekend reservations recommended.

Slightly off the beaten track, come here for Neapolitan home-style cooking of the Old World school. Portions are hefty, so you can rely on a light meal of soup or pizza, or, if you are starving, go for a full main course of veal, chicken, or pasta.

PETER LUGER STEAK HOUSE. 178 Broadway bet. Bedford and Driggs Aves. (at the Brooklyn base of the Williamsburg Bridge), 387-7400, M–Th noon–10 p.m., F–Sa noon–10:45 p.m., Su 1–10 p.m. Cash, debit cards, and personal checks only. Parking lot and valet. *Reservations absolutely necessary.*

Reserve well in advance—two weeks for lunch and at least a month ahead for dinner! You don't have to step too far into Brooklyn to get to Peter Luger; just pop over the Williamsburg Bridge and you're there. In business since 1887, one of New York's most famous restaurants deserves a visit from everyone who loves steaks. The portions are enormous, the atmosphere is noisy and informal, with oak floors and tabletops, and the waiters can be a classic pain in the neck. Aged porterhouse steaks, grilled on the bone, are considered the absolute best of the genre. Plan to spend $50 to $60 per steak.

PUPA TZELEM MATZA BAKERY. Corner Broadway and Keap St. No phone. Open seasonally, Su–Th 11 a.m.–7:45 p.m., closes early on F.

The grass is always greener, even at a schmurah matzoh factory. Why else would you find that Mendel from Borough Park prefers the matzoh here? (See **Borough Park.**)

SAL'S PIZZA AND HOT PLATES. 544 Lorimer St. bet. Devoe and Anfeli Sts., 388-6838, daily 10 a.m.–11 p.m. Cash only.

One of Williamsburg's several popular pizzerias, Sal's makes a great pie. Try the Sicilian, and, if the weather is right, treat yourself to a homemade ice.

Bars and Cafés

♫ **THE ABBEY.** 536 Driggs Ave. bet. No. 7th and 8th Sts., 599-4400, daily noon–4 a.m.

Long, spacious bar, big pool room, great jukebox: all the makings of an amiable neighborhood watering hole. There's hip-hop and techno DJs on Sunday nights, and occasional rock music scheduled throughout the month.

ART LAND. 609 Grand St. at Leonard St., 599-9706, daily 1 p.m.–4 a.m.

A small space that feels large, Art Land is rough around the edges yet as comfortable as the mismatched parlor furniture resting on its well-trodden wooden floor. The bar has an unassuming air and attracts a racially diverse crowd that makes no claim on the word "hipster," unlike many of the other Grand St. bars. There's tabletop Ms. Pacman game, a pinball machine, and works from local artists. Drinks are cheap, and there's daily entertainment: folk performances on Sunday, open mic on Tuesday, tango classes on Wednesday, jazz on Thursday, and DJs spinning on weekends.

BEMBE. Berry and So. 6th Sts., 387-5389, daily 6 p.m.–2 a.m.

Don't be fooled into thinking you're in South Asia. This pretty bar on Williamsburg's South Side is decorated like a vacation spot—and some of the drinks are on the South Asian side, as well.

♫ **BLACK BETTY.** 366 Metropolitan Ave. corner of Havemeyer Ave., 599-0243, daily kitchen 6:30 p.m.–midnight, bar 6:30 p.m.–4 a.m.

Black Betty is a hip Middle Eastern restaurant and performance space, in an innocuous little storefront across from International Aluminum. You enter through the restaurant and step up under an arch into the subtly lit bar to see a small stage in the corner and a number of tables spread throughout the room. There's often some sort of music going on. The crowd is generally better dressed than what you'll find at some of the nearby dive bars, and is a mix of twenty- and thirty-somethings from diverse backgrounds. Munch away on moussaka, falafel, and Moroccan paella—and enjoy the good drinks.

BLUE LADY LOUNGE. 769 Metropolitan Ave. bet. Humboldt St. and Graham Ave., 218-6997, Su–Th 6 p.m.–2 a.m., F–Sa noon–4 a.m.

Another "Billyburg" scene, a bit farther out into the pioneering district.

BROOKLYN ALEHOUSE. 103 Berry St. corner No. 8th St., 302-9811, daily 3 p.m.–4 a.m.

Brooklyn Alehouse serves a full range of Brooklyn Brewery brews. With chunky wood benches and tables, stained-glass windows, and a beautiful mahogany bar, this is a great place to get revved up or wind down.

BROOKLYN BREWERY FRIDAY NIGHT TASTING. 79 No. 11th St. bet. Berry St. and Wythe Ave., 486-7422, F 6 p.m.–10 p.m.

A must visit. On Friday nights, Brooklyn Brewery's "Tasting Panel" draws a large crowd of locals and visiting beer lovers. You can get small samples, and some grub, too. There's a small-town feel here, as friends meet and people play pool, and, as the evening wears on, dance. (See **Brooklyn Brewery**.)

♫ **CHARLESTON BAR AND GRILL.** 174 Bedford Ave. bet. No. 7th and 8th Sts., 782-8717, daily 3 p.m.–2 a.m.

The Charleston offers live rock music every weekend, featuring no-name bands from Williamsburg and the tristate area. Founded (officially) at the end of Prohibition, Charleston still sports a Depression-era mahogany bar and an old fireplace mantel dating from when it was a malt-and-hops place. No cover, one-drink minimum; the action starts at nine p.m.

D.O.C. 83 No. 7th St. at Wythe Ave., 963-1925, daily 6 p.m.–3 a.m.

Dark, intimate, and stylishly Old World, this Italian wine bar invites you to relax and relate over wine, crusty bread with Italian spreads, or a platter of imported cheeses.

Question: What does "D.O.C." mean, anyway?

Answer: Denominazione di Origine Controllata—That's an official Italian-government seal of confirmation that a bottle of wine was produced within the wine region it claims on the label.

EL SOL. 50 Marcy St. corner of Hope St. 384-8671, daily 2 p.m.–4 a.m.

A vestige of old Williamsburg. This bar's worn wooden floors and scratched wooden bar are as telltale a sign of age as wrinkles on a, well, we won't go there. People come from miles around for the meat, shrimp, lobster, and octopus pasteles, only $2.50 each. It's deliciously in the middle of nowhere, one dark lonesome block from the BQE and across from some industrial buildings.

IONA. 180 Grand St. bet. Bedford and Driggs Aves., 384-5008, daily 2 p.m.–4 a.m. Cash only.

A pub for the serious drinker, named after an island between Britain and Ireland, Iona has twenty beer taps, about half from England, Scotland, and Ireland, served in imperial pint glasses at an eminently reasonable price. Don't be surprised if you hear a Scottish accent coming from behind the bar as you watch a game or play Ms. Pacman. On pleasant nights, head out to the unprissy backyard (Martha Stewart certainly *wouldn't* approve) where you can play ping-pong, sit on some old wooden benches, and chill. There's backyard grilling in the summer and also a coffee-and-tea bar.

LAILA LOUNGE. 113 No. 7th St. bet. Berry St. and Wythe Ave., 486-6791, M–Th 6 p.m.–2 a.m., F–Sa 6 p.m.–"until the end of the party" or 4 a.m., Su 4 p.m.–2 a.m.

Recipe: Mix equal parts party, bar, and gallery, and the concoction you get is the Laila Lounge. There's something different every evening: classic movies on Mondays (one July there was a monthlong Truffaut festival), open mic and live singers on Wednesday, Sunday afternoon parties that start at four p.m. and continue with live jazz at nine. It's in a former garage space, with high ceilings and exposed brick walls, with a back garden.

METROPOLITAN. 559 Lorimer St. near Metropolitan Ave., 599-4444, daily 3 p.m.–4 a.m.

You'll know this divey gay bar by the flamingo-pink brick façade, right across from the subway exit. The inside is big and well-used, with scuffed wood floors, a pool table, arcade games, and a jukebox filled with dance, indie rock, and top-forty tunes. The real gem, however, is the large, smoker-friendly, outdoor patio, with plenty of seating and concealing latticework, perfect in summer for quiet conversations under where the stars would be, if not for the tobacco pollution.

MUGS ALE HOUSE. 125 Bedford Ave. at No. 10th St., 486-8232, daily 2 p.m.–4 a.m.

You can test beers to your heart's content here, chugging through a satisfyingly large variety of on-tap ales and brews. Mugs is a big, airy bar with cozy booths up front and lots of seating in back, plus the usual bar menu.

♫ **POURHOUSE.** 790 Metropolitan Ave. at Humboldt St., 599-0697, M–F, 4 p.m.–4 a.m., Sa–Su 2 p.m.–4 a.m., www.pourhouse.com.

Once upon a time Pourhouse was just a simple sports bar. You can still watch

TV or shoot pool while listening to the jukebox. But there's something going on almost every night. For instance, on Mondays, it's spoken-word performances; Tuesdays, open mic; Wednesdays, classic films in the rear parlor, with an old-fashioned projector. And so on. On Saturday you can listen to live bands, and on Sunday afternoon join a team trivia tournament.

R BAR. 451 Meeker Ave. at Graham Ave., 646-523-1813, daily 6 p.m.–3 a.m.

This bar has a Gay Pajama Party every week along with jukebox, pool, darts, and lots of games.

ROSEMARY'S GREENPOINT TAVERN. 188 Bedford Ave. bet. No. 8th and No. 7th Sts., 384-9539, daily 9–4 a.m.

It ain't pretty, the bartender looks like a grandmother, and three of the four taps are Budweiser—yup, another Williamsburg dive. The décor is nearly ugly enough to be ironic, with a ceiling crowded by fake hanging plants and Christmas lights draped all over the place like glowing electric spiderwebs. The crowd is made up of locals of all ages looking for a cheap beer, and thirty-two ounces of Bud for $3.50 fits the bill perfectly.

SOUTHSIDE LOUNGE. 41 Broadway bet. Wythe and Kent Aves., 387-3182, daily 2 p.m.–4 a.m.

People come here to chat, and there are DJs a few nights a week.

SWEETWATER TAVERN. 105 No. 6th St. off Bedford Ave., 963-0608, daily 3 p.m.–4 a.m.

Sweetwater sports black walls, a warped floor, and an old-fashioned tin ceiling. Listen to punk and heavy metal from the jukebox while playing buck hunter or pool, or watch television up front while sipping a draught beer. The space feels like it should be smoky and looks like the kind of place where one might make a shady rendezvous to strike a dark bargain.

TURKEY'S NEST TAVERN. 94 Bedford Ave. at No. 12th St., 384-9774, daily 11–4 a.m.

Declared by the *New York Press* "Best Place to Get Drunk and Gamble That's Not OTB," the Nest is far from flashy. Pool, pinball, arcade buck-hunting and bowling, Quickdraw video gambling, and drinking will keep you busy. You'll see mullets alongside gristly gray hair, as you listen to the jukebox's country and rock tunes, sipping on a $3.50 thirty-two-ounce beer.

♫ **YABBY.** 265 Bedford Ave. near Metropolitan Ave., 384-1664, daily 11–4 a.m. www.yabbylounge.com.

Pure Williamsburg. Step 1. Take one old auto shop. Step 2. Clean it up some. Step 3. Call your friends and start serving beer and wine. Yabby's may have the neighborhood's longest happy hour: Tuesday through Saturday, drinking at reduced happy-hour rates starts at two p.m. There's a big outdoor area where you can catch some rays while you relax in the midday sun and nurse that drink. Locals dance to live music; call for information.

SHOPPING

Old Williamsburg

Specialty Food Shops

B & B MEAT MARKET. 168 Bedford Ave. bet. No. 7 and No. 8th Sts., 388-2811, M–F 7:30 a.m.–8 p.m., Sa 8 a.m.–6 p.m. Cash only.

You'll find a good selection of meats and prepared foods here, including traditional sausages, smoked bacon, sauerkraut, and other Polish specialties.

BRUNO'S BAKERY. 602 Lorimer St. bet. Conselyea and Skillman Aves., 349-6524, daily 7 a.m.–8 p.m. Cash only.

If you haunt Greenwich Village, surely you know "the other" Bruno's, on LaGuardia Place. The Williamsburg location is where these traditional Italian breads and pastries—sourdough and olive and herb breads and fine chocolate confections—are baked. Bruno's chocolate pear royale and cake of chocolate mousse, hazelnut, and pear mousse won accolades from the retail bakers trade association of New York. Their seasonal specials, like an edible chocolate cornucopia at Thanksgiving, are legends-in-the-making. You can buy these goodies here, cheaper, and get a wake-me-up cuppa coffee to go.

MATAMOROS PUEBLA GROCERY. 193 Bedford Ave. bet. No. 6th and No. 7th Sts., 782-5044, daily 8 a.m.–8 p.m.

Drop in to this humble bodega to get the flavors (literally) of Williamsburg's Mexican community. They sell tourist kitsch from Mexico, such as traditional clothing and knickknacks, and fresh spices for Mexican food. You can also pick up some fresh tacos, soups, and other Mexican *comidas* from the back counter.

TEDONE LATTICINI. 597 Metropolitan Ave. bet. Lorimer and Leonard Sts., 387-5830, M–Sa 8 a.m.–5:30 p.m. Cash only.

For over seventy-five years Tedone has been making excellent homemade cheeses and antipasti here. The sole owner, Georgia Tedone, is now an elderly lady who continues to work her special brand of magic turning out sixty pounds of fresh, warm mozzarella every morning.

New Williamsburg

BEDFORD CHEESE SHOP. 218 Bedford Ave. (RealForm Girdle Bldg.) bet No. 4th and No. 5th Sts., 599-7588, M–Sa 10 a.m.–9 p.m., Su 10 a.m.–7 p.m., www.bedfordcheeseshop.com.

Frank is the cheesemonger here, and he knows his stuff. Lots of sophisti-cated domestic and imported cheeses are sold here, with enough other sides to make a dinner. Pick up a fresh brick-oven bread, some condiments, and you're all set.

GREENMARKETS

There's a big greenmarket on Saturday 8 a.m.–3 p.m. at Lorimer Street and Driggs Avenue, and a smaller seasonal greenmarket from July to October at Havemeyer Street and Broadway, Thursdays 8 a.m.–5 p.m.

JOE'S BUSY CORNER DELI. 552 Driggs Ave. at No. 7th St., 388-6372, M–Sa 6:30 a.m.–6:30 p.m. Cash only.

"Like having your auntie around the corner," is what locals say about Joe's, but the big-hearted guys behind the counter look more like football linebackers. They sell fresh ravioli, stuffed artichoke hearts, string-bean salad, frittata, chicken cutlets, olives, hot peppers, mushroom salads, roasted potatoes, and made-on-the-premises mozzarella. And heroes.

LAURA BAMONTE'S BAKERY. 263 No. 6th St. corner of Havemeyer St., 384-9662, Tu–F 7 a.m.–6 p.m., Sa–Su 8 a.m.–6 p.m. Cash only.

The daughter of the family that owns the famous Bamonte's restaurant opened this delightful new bakery in 1995. In warm weather you can sit outside under an umbrella and soak up the "Billyburg" vibes while enjoying a croissant, a slice of apple pie, or a tiramisu.

NAPOLI BAKERY. 616 Metropolitan Ave. corner of Lorimer St., 384-6945, M–Sa 8:30 a.m.–7 p.m.

Do the walls of a decades-old bakery acquire the delicious smell of freshly baked goods? Maybe. This tiny place used to be a pizzeria, and before that another bakery. Walk in and get a whiff of warm bread, and you'll be sure to walk out with a fresh loaf of semolina bread.

QUALITY MEAT MARKET. 172 Bedford and No. 7th St., 388-3437, daily 8:30 a.m.–8:30 p.m.

A surreal transition from the edgy pulse of Williamsburg to the comfort of Poland. The traditional meat is there, but what makes this store great is the opposite-wall display of imported jams and mustards, homemade pickles, and Polish noodles.

SETTE PANI BAKERY. 602 Lorimer St. bet. Conselyea St. and Skillman Ave., 349-6524, daily 7 a.m.–8 p.m.

Wow. Don't miss this bakery. It turns out marvelous mousse cakes, handmade chocolates, marzipan figurines, and lots of cookies. From the outside, it's the Santa Fe pink building across from Orlando Funeral Home.

Old Williamsburg
Interesting Neighborhood Shops

CREST HARDWARE. 558 Metropolitan Ave., bet. Lorimer and Union St., 388-9521, M–Sa 8 a.m.–6 p.m.

Crest is a great, big, useful hardware store. It also gained some fame in the late 1990s as the host to the zany once-a-year "Crest Hardware Show," conceived and curated by Gene Pool, known as the man who wore a suit made of grass on national television. As you walked through the store, you would suddenly happen upon some gizmo among the saws, or an atomic frog or film reel in the paint section. These days, all you find is . . . paint.

NATHAN BORLAM. 157 Havemeyer St. near So. 2nd St., 782-0108, Su–Th 10 a.m.–5 p.m., F, closes mid-afternoon; closed Sa. Checks accepted. Call to hear a tape for travel and parking directions.

Nathan Borlam is Williamsburg's most famous old store, and you shouldn't miss it if you are looking for boys' and girls' clothing in classic styles—at discount prices. This family-run business is in its sixth decade of operation. Some of the same high-quality merchandise you'll find here is sold at Manhattan's better department stores for 30 percent more.

New Williamsburg
See separate listing for Vintage.

BIG GENIUS. 540 Metropolitan Ave. bet. Lorimer and Union Sts., 302-4002, daily noon–midnight.

There's something for everyone here—you can log on to the Internet, get a buzz from their really strong coffee, rent a video, and also buy a wide range of art supplies. They do custom canvas-stretching, as well.

BQE PET SUPPLY AND GROOMING. 253 Wythe Ave., 486-7489, M–Sa 10:30 a.m.–7 p.m.

Like NPR's radio stars Click and Clack, BQE is run by gregarious locals who effortlessly keep up an informative patter about Williamsburg, both old and new. People who have moved to Williamsburg from elsewhere actually bring their visiting parents and friends here to meet and greet, it's that homey. These are the folks who conceived of the **BARC Dog Parade**.

There seem to be a lot of dog owners (and dogs) in Williamsburg—where else do they hand you a business card for the dog walkers club?—and they congregate at this incredibly cheery, somewhat zany, extraordinarily busy neighborhood pet-supply store. *Don't* trip over the dozen or so dogs and cats underfoot;

the strays from BQE's dog shelter freely hang out in the store. And please *do* notice the animal-motif gate. They say in the past five years a lot more pedigreed dogs have moved into the neighborhood. Canine gentrification.

⊘ ✪ BROOKLYN INDUSTRIES. 162 Bedford Ave. bet. No. 8th and 9th Sts., 486-6464, M—Sa noon—9 p.m., Su noon—8 p.m., Web site under construction.

A spacious and bright clothing store packed with Brooklyn pride. Pick up a soft cotton Brooklyn T-shirt and show your loyalty. Other Brooklyn-based companies sell their goods here, such as beanies, backpacks, and original clothing designs. Constant sales in the back of the store offer choice items that are sometimes marked down by as much as 80 percent. There's another store in Park Slope, at 152 5th Avenue (789-3447).

CLOVIS PRESS. 229 Bedford Ave. off No. 4th St., 302-3751, daily noon—10 p.m.

Clovis Press sells new and used fiction, classics, art books, and contemporary international art magazines. It's been around since 1998, and has a selection of underground comic books among other collectibles. The store's name, by the way, is not in honor of France's Ol' King Clovis, but after a pooch belonging to Amanda, the founder of this lovely bookstore. Occasional readings are scheduled.

⊘ CRYPTO. 241 Bedford Ave. bet. No. 1st and No. 2nd Sts., 486-7092, Tu—F noon—8 p.m., Sa 11 a.m.—9 p.m., Su noon—8 p.m.

The big glass-pane windows suggest staid Madison Avenue, but once you step into the shoes sold at Crypto, you'll know you're in hip Brooklyn.

⊘ EARWAX. 218 Bedford Ave. (RealForm Girdle Bldg.) bet. No. 4th and No. 5th Sts., 486-3771, M—F noon—8 p.m., Sa 11 a.m.—9 p.m., Su noon—8 p.m.

Rows of new and secondhand records and CDs are crammed into this brightly lit music haven. With music genres ranging from jazz to Afro-beat, much of the selection is eclectic. The occasional mainstream artist's label can be found lurking around, but is most likely covered by a used Arlo Guthrie LP or a Bob Dylan cover band. Retro-heaven. Prices for used records and CDs are $4—$10.

⊘ FRED FLARE. 175 No. 10th St., 599-9221, www.fredflare.com.

Fred Flare is a nationally known brand that is popular among teenagers. They don't have a store here, but there are two seasonal sales. Fred Flare's *"spring bling!"* is retail therapy at its finest. Brightly colored guitar-pick earrings ($24 for three pairs) printed with pop-song titles, or a clear blue portable record player ($195), make the perfect gift for anyone from the record-playing music elitist to the quirky pop princess. There's no sign; look for the pink Dumpster.

⭐ **LANDING** 242 Wythe Ave. at No. 3rd St., 218-9449, daily noon—8 p.m., www.landingbrooklyn.com.

Landing is Williamsburg's mothership of locally made clothing—and it also provides wall space for local artists and photographers, and the occasional venue for a party. Half art gallery, half boutique, it tastefully displays clothing that has more aesthetic appeal than pocketbook practicality. Knit underwear hangs on the same rack as one-of-a-kind T-shirts selling for upwards of $40. Jewelry, accessories, ceramics, and the custom-made wooden furniture scattered around the store are for sale. Some Brooklyn designers sold here include H. Fredriksson, Detox, Lona D, Black Angus, and others.

MAIN DRAG MUSIC. 170 No. 5th St., corner of Driggs St., 388-6365, M—Sa 11 a.m.–9 p.m., Su 11 a.m.–9 p.m., www.maindragmusic.com.

A few years ago, two young entrepreneur musicians started a sociable hole-in-the-wall shop selling vintage guitars for working musicians, mostly locals. Their bigger new store reflects the shifts in the neighborhood: there are more guitars, more repair technicians for amps and instruments, and they've opened new music rooms with a piano so that kids (and adults) can take lessons.

METAPHORS. 195 Bedford Ave. bet. No. 6th and No. 7th Sts., 782-0917, M—Sa noon–8 p.m., Su noon–6 p.m.

The arty women's clothing here may look like vintage, but it's not. Appliqué skirts go for about $60, and fifties-style dresses cut to accentuate a cute figure are in the $120 range. There are accessories, as well, like pretty rayon scarves and jewelry. For the young at heart.

⭐ **NYDESIGN ROOM.** 339 Bedford Ave. bet. So. 3rd and So. 4th Sts., 302-4981, Tu—Su noon–7 p.m., www.nydesignroom.com.

Blending commerce, art, and community, nydesignroom is the creation of three local artists. If you're a shopper, you can get nifty T-shirts made out of recycled material in the summer, and clothes of recycled cashmere in the winter. Or you might find interesting, colorful home decorative items such as tables, pillows, or decorative functional cubes. If you're an artist, you're welcome to come in and talk about color, design challenges, and ART.

⭐ **ONE SIXTY GLASS.** 160 Berry St. corner of No. 5th St., 486-9620, www.onesixtyglass.com. Call for hours.

An art gallery/studio/store, one sixty glass is housed in a huge warehouse. Amid twisting pipes and unfinished concrete floors are several roaring glass-blowing ovens; artists of varying ages and skill levels are bent over them in concentration. There's unusual art glass sold here, perfect for the home or a gift. Six-week glass-blowing classes are given for $550. The camouflage building is easy to miss, but keep an eye out for the chalkboard out front that serves as an awning/door marker.

OTTE. 218 Bedford Ave. (RealForm Girdle Bldg.) bet. No. 4th and No. 5th Sts., 302-3007, M–F 1–8 p.m., Sa–Su noon–8 p.m.

Flirts alert. One of the treasures of this Williamsburg-y mall in the old Real-Form Girdle Factory is tiny, tasteful Otte. Like its Greenwich Village counterpart, Otte sells contemporary urban femme fatale clothing brands, such as Mint, Rebecca Taylor, as well as such brands as Free People.

PILGRIM HOME AND BODY. 202 Bedford Ave. bet. No. 5th and No. 6th Sts., 599-0023, M–Sa noon–8 p.m., Su noon–6 p.m.

This shop aims for a homey, relaxing, and earthy feel. The staff is unobtrusive as customers scour the selection of decently priced housewares and toiletries.

☺ **SAM & SEB.** 208 Bedford Ave. bet. No. 5th and No. 6th Sts., 486-8300, M–Sa 11 a.m.–8 p.m., Su 11 a.m.–8 p.m., www.samandseb.com.

A children's store that's screaming with personality, Sam & Seb is perfect for the neighborhood. Legwarmers and T-shirts featuring Bob Marley, KISS, and Che Guevara and other political and cultural icons are available for those as small as six months old. But fashion statements don't come cheap: even the T-shirts sell for around $26 a pop.

✪ **SARKANA CLASSIC ART MATERIALS.** 14 Dunham Pl. bet. So. 6th St. and Broadway, 599-5898, W–Sa noon–6 p.m., http//.store.yahoo.com/sarkana.

Artists who pioneered in "Billyburg" in the 1980s suffered for lack of a traditional art store (though local hardware stores have done their best). Sarkana was started by Elena Grossman, originally from Latvia, in 1995. This tiny, high-end supplier of handmade or hand-ground art supplies used to have a street-level store on Bedford Avenue. It now sells out of the artist/owner's studio underneath the Williamsburg Bridge. And in case you are squirreling away the word "sarkana" for future crossword-puzzle use, it is Latvian for "red."

✪ **SPACIAL ETC.** 199 Bedford Ave. corner of No. 6th St., 599-7962, daily 11 a.m.–9 p.m., www.spacialetc.com/ and www.brooklynhandknit.com.

This little gift shop sells a colorful collection of items such as hand-knit hats, scarves, and summer knits, unusual handmade jewelry, and home decorative items. The appealing knits are produced by their *"Brooklyn Hand Knit"* label, now a full-fledged international business, with knitters in Tibet and markets in London. (You are likely to see the same knitwear in exclusive Manhattan stores at a higher markup.) Other items by Brooklyn artists sold here include photographic lampshades by AE Jennings, and porcelain by Klein-Reid.

SPOONBILL & SUGARTOWN, BOOKSELLERS. 218 Bedford Ave. (RealForm Girdle Bldg.) bet. No. 4th and No. 5th Sts., 387-7322, daily 11 a.m.–9 p.m. www.spoonbillbooks.com.

Reflecting the artistic bent of the neighborhood, Spoonbill boasts a depth of inventory of titles on art and architecture, mostly from the 1960s to the 1990s. The selection has been culled with a connoisseur's eye for certain art and social trends; for instance, a circa 1970 fascination with the concept of shelter. There's an open area with sensible low seating for kids, some toys, and a rug. And there are some new books, and sizeable sections on gardening, philosophy, nonfiction, and fiction. (Predictably, *original* hipster authors, such as William S. Burroughs and Herman Hesse, apparently sell well.)

STINGRAY DIVERS. 762 Grand St. bet. Graham Ave. and Humboldt St. 384-1280, Su–F 9 a.m.–7 p.m., Sa 9 a.m.–6 p.m.

Who'da thunk it? Oddly located in land-locked Williamsburg, Stingray is a family-run, full-service dive shop with instructors on staff and recreational, technical, wreck, and cave gear. They describe themselves as "active local divers" and also make regular trips to dive in places like north central Florida (cave-diving paradise), Cozumel, Mexico, York Beach, Maine, and the Philippines.

Vintage and Collectibles

Vintage and collectible shops are scattered throughout the area. We list just a few.

AMARCORD. 223 Bedford Ave. bet. No. 4th and No. 5th Sts., 963-4001, daily 1–8 p.m., www.amarcordvintagefashion.com.

High-end, fashionable European vintage clothing for both women and men is sold here. Prices for leather handbags, Italian shoes, dresses, and outfits are palatable, between $30 and $150 for most women's garments. The original shop is in the East Village, and fashion designers and filmmakers have been known to scour their warehouse at 242 Wythe Avenue—by appointment only.

⊘ BEACON'S CLOSET. 88 No. 11th St. bet. Berry St. and Wythe Ave. 486-0816, M–F noon–9 p.m., Sa–Su 11 a.m.–8 p.m., www.beaconscloset.com.

Screamingly chic and painted a fluorescent pink, this spacious and funky store is the heart and soul of Williamsburg's renowned vintage shopping scene. With a selective and efficient buy/sell/trade system, Beacon's Closet is able to customize their merchandise by season. Many choice items are available for both sexes. As vintage stores go, this one is easy to maneuver; the merchandise is color-coordinated. They've moved from the original location and now have 5,500 square feet of clothes—rarely priced much over $20. There's another one in Park Slope, at 220 5th Avenue (789-3447).

⚫ **DOMSEY EXPRESS.** 431 Broadway bet. Hooper and Hewes Sts., 384-6000, M–F 9 a.m.–6 p.m., Sa 10 a.m.–7 p.m., Su 11 a.m.–5 p.m. Another location 1609 Palmetto St. bet. Wykoff and Myrtle Aves., 386-7661, M–Sa 10 a.m.–7 p.m., Su 10 a.m.–5:30 p.m., www.domsey.com.

Domsey's, although smaller and tamer since it moved from its rambling Kent Street warehouse, is still a rush. There's a frenzied mass of secondhand clothing (often brand name) here, sold at cheaper-than-Salvation-Army prices. The oldest pieces seem to be from the seventies and eighties, looking quite new, a few with original labels. There's always some designer clothing, too, but it's all mixed up together. Everything is hand-chosen, and clean. And, thankfully, they don't weed out such items as striped vinyl pants or horrifically (yet delightfully) sleazy button-downs that scream seventies retro-tacky.

⚫ **FLUKE VINTAGE CLOTHING.** Bedford Ave. bet. No. 7th and No. 6th Sts., 486-3166, W–Su 1–8 p.m.

A hole-in-the-wall clothing antique store but with a tasteful—if not picky—selection of items from the 1970s and thereafter. The original-model Wonderbras and toys hidden around the store lend a nostalgic aura. Most items are between $10 and $50.

GREEN VILLAGE USED CLOTHING AND FURNITURE, AKA SIDNEY'S. 460 Driggs Ave. near No. 11th St., 599-4017, M–Th 9:30 a.m.–5:30 p.m., F 9:30 a.m.–3 p.m., Su 10 a.m.–5:30 p.m.

This is a great place to buy used props, for theater or for life. The stuff is beat up, but there's lots of it—books, kitchenware, belts, computer monitors, stuffed chairs, kitchen chairs, rocking chairs, crutches, golf clubs, sofas, sewing machines, vintage clothing, coats, shoes, and you-name-it. The Hasidic gentleman who runs the place, Sidney, is a local legend. Don't be surprised to see him or his family trading on eBay in the open office behind all the junk.

ISA. 88 No. 6th St. bet. Berry St. and Wythe Ave., 387-3363, M–F 1–9 p.m., Sa noon–10 p.m., Su 1–7 p.m.

Catering to those with an expansive budget (or willing to compromise a week's worth of food), Isa's spacious store boasts a huge collection of Marc Jacobs clothing and carries vintage couture. The store is light, and there are always records spinning, and a large soft couch beckons you to take a seat and survey the possibilities.

⚫ **LINT.** 318 Bedford Ave. near So. 2nd St., 387-9508, Tu–Su 1–8:30 p.m.

Lint is tiny but bursting with choice vintage items for both sexes. Its four walls are lined with clothing racks. The small dachshund that greets and then attaches itself to every visitor gives a homey feel to the store. T-shirts run about $8; restructured ones can cost you around $20. Dresses, pants, and skirts are around $14, and are slightly worn but good quality.

MOON RIVER CHATTEL. 62 Grand St. bet. Wythe and Kent Aves., 388-1121, W—Sa noon—7 p.m., Su noon—5 p.m., Web site underway.

Think urban country with a large dose of environmental consciousness. You can get recycled glass carafes, new, but also old-fashioned kids' toys, appealing farm tables made out of reclaimed barn siding, old claw-footed bathtubs, funky Art Deco chairs, and so on, in prices ranging from $25 to $3,500.

TWO JAKES. 320 Wythe Ave. bet. Grand and So. 1st Sts., 782-7780, W—Su 11 a.m.—7 p.m., www.usedoffice furniture.com.

Not quaint, but entirely practical, Two Jakes is a perfect place to begin assembling a home office or to start outfitting an upstart business: desks, chairs, filing cabinets, bookcases, lamps, coat trees, and typewriters of varying vintage, from clunky Underwoods to electric Smith-Coronas. In fact, there's ten thousand square feet of the stuff here, so the downsizing of some corporate enterprise across the river can be your gain. Two Jakes also does rentals to the film and TV industries, provides fabrics to upholster your secondhand seating, custom strips any vintage piece in their inventory, and has related design services.

UGLY LUGGAGE. 214 Bedford Ave. bet. No. 5th and No. 6th Sts., 384-0724, daily noon—7 p.m.

A humorous collection of tasteful flea-market 1950s finds, from furniture to knickknacks, is sold here. The collection varies, of course, but the price is right, and the store's owners have an eye for comfy, old-fashioned kitsch. If you like it, you'll *love* it.

Most of the following events are annual events; most (but not all) are free. Check the chapter listings for contact information and details. You can also get up-to-date events listings, week by week, at www.go-brooklyn.com.

BROOKLYN CALENDAR

JANUARY
Chinese New Year (Sunset Park)
First Saturday (Brooklyn Museum)
Polar Bear Swim (Coney Island)

FEBRUARY
Black History Month (boroughwide)
BARC Valentine's Day
    (Williamsburg)
First Saturday (Brooklyn Museum)
Martin Luther King Day
    (boroughwide)

MARCH
First Saturday (Brooklyn Museum)
Irish American Parade (Bay Ridge,
    Park Slope)
Women's History Month
    (boroughwide)

APRIL
Brooklyn International Film Festival
    (BAM)
Brooklyn Jewish Film Festival (BAM)
Brooklyn Jazz Festival (multivenue)
Cherry Blossom Festival (Brooklyn
    Botanic Garden)
Good Friday Procession
    (Bensonhurst)
Earth Day Celebration (Gowanus)
First Saturday (Brooklyn Museum)
Opening day for Carousel, etc.
    (Prospect Park)
Plant Sale (Brooklyn Botanic Garden)
Sidewalk Antique Market, weekends
    (Atlantic Avenue; Greater Carroll
    Gardens)

MAY
Bay Fest (Sheepshead Bay)
Brooklyn Botanic Garden Spring Fest
EcoCruise (Gowanus)

DanceAfrica Bazaar (BAM Cultural District)

Fifth Avenue Street Fair (Park Slope)

First Saturday (Brooklyn Museum)

Fort Greene/Clinton Hill House Tour (Fort Greene/Clinton Hill)

House and Garden Tour (Brooklyn Heights)

House Tour (Prospect Heights; Park Slope area)

Lefferts Gardens Crafts (Prospect Park)

"Local Produce" Arts Festival (Park Slope)

Memorial Day Concert (Green-Wood Cemetery)

Norwegian Constitution Day (Bay Ridge)

Red Hook Waterfront Arts Festival (Red Hook)

Sidewalk Antique Market, weekends (Atlantic Avenue; Greater Carroll Gardens)

SONYA Studio Stroll (Fort Greene/Clinton Hill)

You Gotta Have Park Day (Prospect Park)

Victorian House Tour (Flatbush)

JUNE

Beer and Food Fest at Brooklyn Brewery (Williamsburg)

Caribbean Fair in Prospect Park (Prospect Park)

Celebrate Brooklyn series (Prospect Park)

CIRCUSundays (Red Hook)

Concerts on Promenade (Brooklyn Heights)

Cyclones season starts (Coney Island)

Dance Africa (BAM)

"Earth and Surf" Parade (Red Hook)

EcoCruise (once a month)(Gowanus)

Fifth Avenue Festival (Bay Ridge)

Finnish Celebration (Sunset Park/ Green-Wood)

First Saturday (Brooklyn Museum)

Fulton Art Fair (weekends; Bedford-Stuyvesant)

Gay & Lesbian Pride Parade (Park Slope)

June Balloon @ Children's Museum (Heart of Brooklyn)

Juneteenth Celebration (Fort Greene)

Mardi Gras on Avenue M (Midwood)

Medgar Evers College Tribute (Bedford-Stuyvesant/Crown Heights)

Mermaid Parade (Coney Island)

MetroTech Urban Garden Festival (Downtown)

Outdoor Concerts @ Kingsborough Community College (Sheepshead Bay)

Outdoor Music, noon–2 P.M. MetroTech (Downtown)

Pier Show (weekends) (Red Hook)

7th Heaven Street Fair (Park Slope)

Sidewalk Antique Market, weekends (Atlantic Avenue; Greater Carroll Gardens)

Smith Street Fun Day Fair (Carroll Gardens)

Sunset Music series (Red Hook)

Welcome Back to Brooklyn Festival (Prospect Park)

JULY

Aqua Nights, New York Aquarium (Coney Island)

Art Show in Park (Bedford-Stuyvesant)

Bastille Day Celebration (Carroll Gardens)

Beachside Fireworks on Fridays (Coney Island)

Between the Bridges Sculpture (DUMBO)

Celebrate Brooklyn series (Prospect Park)

CIRCUSundays (Red Hook)

Circus Weekend (Coney Island)

Coney Island Short Film Festival (Coney Island)

Cyclones season (Coney Island)

First Saturday (Brooklyn Museum)

Fulton Art Fair (weekends; Bedford-Stuyvesant)

Gowanus Block Party/Canoe Rides (Gowanus; Carroll Gardens area)

Hot Dog Eating Contest (Coney Island)

Independence Day Celebrations (boroughwide)

International African Arts Fair (July 4) (Bedford-Stuyvesant)

Macy's Fishing Contest (Prospect Park)

Martin Luther King Jr. Concerts (Flatbush)

Outdoor Music at MetroTech (Downtown)

Outdoor Concerts @ Kingsborough Community College (Sheepshead Bay)

Outdoor Film Series, Empire Fulton Ferry Park (DUMBO)

Outdoor Films @ Narrows Botanical Gardens (Bay Ridge)

Procession of Giglio (Bensonhurst)

Sand-sculpting Contest (Coney Island)

Saturday Nite Films @ Coney Island Museum (Coney Island)

Seaside Summer Concerts @ Asser Levy Park (Coney Island)

Sidewalk Antique Market, weekends (Atlantic Avenue; Greater Carroll Gardens)

Sunset Music Series (Red Hook)

Village Voice/Siren Music Festival (1 night) (Coney Island)

AUGUST

Celebrate Brooklyn series (Prospect Park)

Beachside Fireworks on Fridays (Coney Island)

Block Park @ Brooklyn Brewery (Williamsburg)

Brighton Jubilee (Brighton Beach)

CIRCUSundays (Red Hook)

First Saturday (Brooklyn Museum)

Kidflix (Bedford-Stuyvesant)

Outdoor Concerts @ Kingsborough Community College (Sheepshead Bay)

Outdoor Films @ Narrows Botanical Gardens (Bay Ridge)

Pakistani-American Independence Celebration (Coney Is. Ave.)

Rooftop Films, Office Ops (Williamsburg)

Santa Rosalia Feast (Bensonhurst)

Sidewalk Antique Market, weekends
(Atlantic Avenue; Greater Carroll
Gardens)

Sunset Music Series (Red Hook)

Weeksville Family Festival (Bedford-
Stuyvesant)

SEPTEMBER

Atlantic Antic Fair (Atlantic Avenue;
Carroll Gardens area)

Antique Auto Show (Floyd Bennett
Field; Sheepshead Bay)

Art Show on Emmons Avenue;
(Sheepshead Bay)

BARC Dog Parade (Williamsburg)

Caribbean American Labor Day
Parade (Heart of Brooklyn)

Court Street Crawl (Carroll Gardens
area)

First Saturday (Brooklyn Museum)

Flatbush Frolic (Flatbush)

Great Irish Fair (Coney Island)

Greenpoint/YMCA Street Fair
(Greenpoint)

9-11 Memorials (boroughwide)

Renewable Brooklyn @ BCUE
(Prospect Park)

Santa Rosalia Festival (Bensonhurst)

OCTOBER

Brooklyn Eats (Downtown Brooklyn)

DUMBO) Underground Film Festival
(DUMBO)

d.u.m.b.o art center festival
(DUMBO)

First Saturday (Brooklyn
Museum)

Gowanus Studio Art Tours (Carroll
Gardens)

Gowanus Oktober Fest (Gowanus;
Carroll Gardens)

Halloween Parade (Carroll Gardens;
Park Slope)

House Tour (Bedford-Stuyvesant)

Polish Culture Festival
(Greenpoint)

Ragamuffin Parade (Bay Ridge)

Small Works Shows (Red Hook)

Third Avenue Festival (Bay Ridge)

NOVEMBER

First Saturday (Brooklyn Museum)

Thanksgiving Programs
(boroughwide)

DECEMBER

Dyker Heights Christmas Lights
(Bensonhurst)

First Saturday (Brooklyn
Museum)

Lefferts Homestead Winter Festival
(Prospect Park)

Lighting of Hanukah Menorah
(Prospect Park)

Christmas and Kwanzaa Celebrations
(boroughwide)

New Year's Eve Fireworks (Prospect
Park)

TOURS: HISTORICAL, FOOD, MUSIC, AND MORE

All phone numbers are in the 718 area code unless otherwise indicated.

GENERAL TOURS

Big Onion Walking Tours (walking/various neighborhoods). (212) 439-1090. $12 adults, $10 students. www.bigonion.com

BRIC Tours (bus/walking/various itineraries). (866) 462-5596 x29. $38 including three-course meal. www.brooklynx.org/tourism/grouptours

Brooklyn Attitude Tours (coach/walking/can be customized). 398-0939. www.brooklynattitude.com

Brooklyn Center on the Urban Environment (bus/walking/boat/varied neighborhoods & environment). 788-8500. Free. www.bcue.org

Brooklyn Historical Society "Walks & Talks" (varied neighborhoods). 222-4111. $10 for members, $15 for public; $12 seniors/students. www.brooklynhistory.org

Gray Line (double-decker bus, Brownstone Brooklyn). 397-2600 x233. $35 adults; $25 children. www.graylinenewyork.com

Metro Tour Service (various neighborhoods). 789-0430. $25.

92nd St. YWCA (bus/walking/various neighborhoods). (212) 415-5500. $25. www.92y.org

New York Like a Native (walking/short & long options/various neighborhoods). 393-7537. $12–$30. www.nylikeanative.com

INDIVIDUALS WHO GIVE TOURS

Bernie's New York (coach/walking/various neighborhoods). 655-1883. $10.

Dr. Phil Talks and Walks (coach/walking/various neighborhoods). (888) 377-4455. $15.

Justin Ferate Tours of the City (coach/walking/various neighborhoods/to be arranged). (212) 779-0727

THEME TOURS

Brooklyn Brewery (factory tour). 486-7422. Free. www.brooklynbrewery.com

Green-Wood Cemetery (walking). Different rates. www.green-wood.com

Braggin' About Brooklyn (bus/walking/African-American history). 771-0307. www.brooklynx.org/tourism/braggin

Hasidic Crown Heights Tours (walking/Hasidic neighborhoods). 953-5244. Adults $15, students/seniors $10, kids under 12 $8. www.jewishtours.com

NY Transit Museum (walking/New York City subway/transportation). Rates vary.

ART TOURS

Brooklyn Art and Garden Tour (walking/Brooklyn Museum/Botanic Gardens). (866) 462-5596 x29. $38 including three-course meal. www.brooklynx.org/tourism/grouptours

Brooklyn Arts Council (various). 625-0080. www.brooklynartscouncil.org

Brooklyn Waterfront Artists Coalition (open studio/Red Hook). 596-2507. Free. www.bwac.org

d.u.m.b.o art under the bridge (open studio/DUMBO). 694-0831. www.dumboartscenter.org

Municipal Art Society (art and architectural/Williamsburg/Park Slope/others). (212) 439-1049. $15. www.mas.org

Williamsburg Gallery Association (open studio/Williamsburg/Greenpoint/ Bushwick). www.williamsburggalleryassociation.com

BIKE TOURS

Tours by Bike (bike/custom tour only/Brownstone Brooklyn/to be arranged). (877) 865-0078. www.toursbybike.com

Waterfront Bike Tour (bike/irregular schedule/Brooklyn waterfront). 243-0849. www.waterfrontmuseum.org/dredgers

BOAT, CANOE, AND WATER TOURS

Brooklyn Center on the Urban Environment (boat/walking/Gowanus Canal). 788-8500. www.bcue.org

Dorothy B. VIII (three-hour boat ride/Manhattan Skyline/Statue of Liberty). 646-4057. $15, seniors $13, kids $10. www.dorothyb.com

Friends of Gateway (walking/Gateway Park). Free. www.treebranch.com

Gowanus Dredgers (boating/Gowanus Canal). 243-0849.
   www.waterfrontmuseum.org/dredgers
Shorewalkers (walking/ethnic restaurant/Brooklyn shoreline). 428-4558 or
   421-2021. $3 (meal not included). www.shorewalkers.org

DO IT YOURSELF

Jolly Red Trolley (hop on/hop off a trolley/"Heart of Brooklyn"). 965-8999.
   Free. www.heartofbrooklyn.org
B-61 Bus (public bus/many neighborhoods). $2. www.mta.nyc.ny.us
Brooklyn Historical Society Brochures (walking/Bed-Stuy/Bay Ridge/others).
   222-4111 x23. www.brooklynhistory.org

EVENING TOURS

Big Apple Jazz Tours (cab/bus/jazz clubs/you can customize). (212) 304-8186.
   www.bigapplejazz.com
Big Onion Walking Tours (walking/Brooklyn Bridge). (212) 439-1090.
   ww.bigonion.com
Dorothy B. VIII (three-hour boat ride/Manhattan Skyline/Statue of Liberty).
   646-4057. $15, seniors $13, kids $10. www.dorothyb.com

FOOD TOURS

Culinary Walking Tour (New School/ethnic/walking/various neighborhoods).
   (212) 229-5690. $65 includes lunch and expert tour. www.newschool.edu
NoshWalks (ethnic food/walking/various neighborhoods). (212) 222-2243.
   $18. www.noshwalks.com

HOUSE AND GARDEN TOURS

All are self-guided
Brooklyn Heights (walking/late-nineteenth-century homes). 858-9193. $25.
   www.brooklynheightsassociation.org
Brownstoners of Bedford-Stuyvesant (walking/late-nineteenth-century homes).
   953-7328 or 574-1979. $10.
Fort Greene/Clinton Hill House Tour (walking/late-nineteenth-century
   homes). 789-5492/717-1277. $10.
Park Slope House Tour (walking/late-nineteenth-century homes). 832-8227.
   $20. www.parkslopeciviccouncil.org
Victorian Flatbush House Tour (walking/late-nineteenth-century homes). 859-
   4632. $20. www.fdconline.org

MUSIC TOURS

Big Apple Jazz Tours (cab/bus/jazz clubs/you can customize). (212) 304-8186.
   www.bigapplejazz.com

Hush Hip-Hop Sightseeing Tours (luxury bus five-hour tour/South Brooklyn
   area). (212) 714-3527. $85, students $60. www.hushtours.com

OTHER

Prospect Park Ravine Tour (walking/Prospect Park Ravine). 965-8999. Free.
   www.prospectpark.org

Borough Hall (walking/one hour maximum/Borough Hall building). 875-4047.
   Free. www.brooklyn-usa.org

INDEX OF BROOKLYN

Performances

Historic Brooklyn

BRIDGES

CHURCHES AND KEY RELIGIOUS INSTITUTIONS

HISTORIC DISTRICTS

SHOPPING INDEX
Artisanal: Made in Brooklyn

By Nonfood Attributes